Ancient North Americans

Ancient North Americans

Edited by

Jesse D. Jennings

The University of Utah
and The University of Oregon

W. H. Freeman and Company
New York

Project Editor: Larry Olsen
Copy Editor: Joyce Coleman
Production Coordinator: Linda Jupiter
Illustration Coordinator: Richard Quiñones
Artists: Rulon E. "Jay" Nielson, Eric Hieber
Compositor: Allservice Phototypesetting Company
Printer and Binder: The Maple-Vail Book Manufacturing Group
Cover: Eric Jungerman

Library of Congress Cataloging in Publication Data

Main entry under title:

Ancient North Americans.

  Includes some chapters from Ancient native Americans
published in 1978.
  Includes bibliographies and index.
  Contents: Changing direction in archeological
thought / Frank Hole—Origins / Jesse D. Jennings—
Alaska and the Northwest coast / Don E. Dumond—[etc.]
  1. Indians of North America—Antiquities.   2. North
America—Antiquities. I. Jennings, Jesse David,
1909–
E77.9.A53 1983   970.01   82-15897
ISBN 0-7167-1428-0

Printed in the United States of America

2 3 4 5 6 7 8 9 0   MP   1 0 8 9 8 7 6 5 4

Contents

Preface

Ancient North Americans is the first volume of a two-volume series that attempts to give an authoritative summary of the past 30,000 years of New World prehistory. Some of the chapters in this volume were originally part of a single volume entitled *Ancient Native Americans* (W. H. Freeman and Company, 1978). That book was intended for the general reader and archeologist who needed short reviews of current archeological thought about the Western hemisphere and its regional prehistory. The book was used by quite a number of teachers as a textbook for college courses. However, many teachers of North American and South American prehistory asked for a single book with better coverage of their area of study. The present two-volume series is an attempt to fulfill those requests. Because the archeology of North America and South America is usually taught in separate courses, we believe that the publication of two volumes will better fit the curricula at most universities.

Ancient North Americans contains two new chapters and ten chapters that have been extensively modified through the addition of new data and the revision of some sections. The rewriting of the chapters was guided and improved by suggestions from several anonymous reviewers, direct letters to the editor, and reviews in professional journals. Of course, some reviewers demanded changes that were outside the concept of the book, but most comments were heeded and appropriate modifications made. This opportunity is taken to thank all reviewers; if this volume is better than the earlier version, they share the credit.

Chapter One, Changing Directions in Archeological Thought, is a new chapter that introduces the reader to some of the methods and theories of American archeology that are used by the authors of later chapters. Chapter Eight, The Northeastern United States, is another new chapter that provides more extensive coverage of that area than was the case in the previous edition.

The other portion of *Ancient Native Americans* has similarly been given wider coverage and revision and appears in a separate volume entitled *Ancient South Americans*.

It is a pleasant duty to acknowledge the courtesies shown us by several people and institutions. Photographs were made available to us by the National Geographic Society, The Smithsonian Institution, Rene Millon and Stephen Williams of the Peabody Museum, and William Coe of the University of Pennsylvania Museum. Most of the drawings were done by Rulon Nielson of the Utah Museum of Natural History. Ursula Hanly assisted with the correspondence and typing required in assembling these chapters. To John Staples of W. H. Freeman and Company I offer thanks for many years of encouragement and tolerant friendship. To my wife Jane I owe even more for her endless forbearance and support.

September 1982   Jesse D. Jennings

About the Authors

Dr. C. Melvin Aikens is Associate Professor of Anthropology at the University of Oregon. His publications reflect his interest in the archeology of the Southwest, the Great Basin, and the Pacific Northwest and particularly in those relationships of the prehistoric populations that crosscut the arbitrary geographical boundaries that we have assigned to their world. Dr. Aikens, who received his Ph.D. from the University of Chicago in 1966, has served as Field Director of the University of Utah Statewide Archeological Survey, as Assistant Professor of Anthropology at the University of Nevada, and as an NSF Science Faculty Fellow in Japanese Archeology at Kyoto University.

Dr. T. Patrick Culbert is Professor of Anthropology at the University of Arizona. A specialist in the Mayan civilization, especially in its evolution and ultimate collapse, Dr. Culbert has done extensive fieldwork at Tikal and Poptun, Guatemala, and is the author of *City and State in the Maya Lowlands* and *The Origins of Civilization in the Maya Lowlands* (with R. E. W. Adams). Since receiving his Ph.D. at the University of Chicago in 1962, he has taught at the University of Mississippi and Southern Illinois University and served as Visiting Professor at the Universidad de San Carlos in Guatemala. Dr. Culbert has been active in several programs of the Society for American Archaeology and currently serves as cochairman of the Committee on Archaeological Employment.

Dr. Don E. Dumond is Professor of Anthropology at the University of Oregon and received his Ph.D. in 1962 from the same institution. Beginning archeological research in southwestern Alaska in 1960, he completed his tenth field season in that region in 1975. His publications include more than a score of titles devoted to Alaskan and Arctic prehistory, some of which are cited in Chapter Three. He has also written about various aspects of ecology, demography, social organization, archeological method, and the prehistory and ethnohistory of Mexico. During 1976 and 1977, he held a fellowship from the National Endowment for the Humanities to pursue documentary research on the Maya of nineteenth-century Yucatan.

Dr. Robert E. Funk is State Archeologist at the New York State Museum in Albany, New York. He has conducted fieldwork in Yucatan and Indiana but since 1960 has specialized in the prehistory of the Northeastern United States. His particular research interests include the Paleo-Indian and Archaic periods, as reflected in such monographs as *Recent Contributions to Hudson Valley Prehistory, Aboriginal Settlement Patterns in the Northeast* (with W. A. Ritchie), and *Adaptation, Continuity, and Change in Upper Susquehanna Prehistory* (with B. E. Rippeteau). He received his Ph.D. from Columbia University in 1966 and is Visiting Professor of Anthropology at two campuses of the State University of New York.

Dr. James B. Griffin is Professor Emeritus of Anthropology at the University of Michigan, Curator Emeritus of the University of Michigan Museum of Anthropology, where he served as Director for many years, and a member of the National Academy of Sciences. Educated at the Universities of Chicago and Michigan, Dr. Griffin received his Ph.D. in 1936 and since that time has been involved in both fieldwork and teaching in such diverse places as Siberia, Central Mexico, and Copenhagen. Although his archeological interests are cosmopolitan, Dr. Griffin's speciality is the eastern United States, and he is the author of such classic works as *The Fort Ancient Aspect* and *Archeology of the Eastern United States.*

Dr. Elmer Harp, Jr., is Professor of Anthropology at Dartmouth College and was for many years chairman of the Anthropology Department. Educated at Harvard University, where he received his Ph.D. in 1953, Dr. Harp is a veteran of fourteen expeditions to the Arctic and sub-Arctic regions, including work as a consultant for the archeological surveillance of the trans-Alaska oil pipeline. Dr. Harp is the author of numerous papers and monographs concerning Arctic and sub-Arctic archeology and is especially interested in the uses of photography in archeological research.

Dr. Frank Hole is Professor of Anthropology at Yale University. A specialist in the prehistory of Southwest Asia, he has also done archeological research in

Mexico and Texas. Dr. Hole served as editor of *American Antiquity* from 1974 to 1977. After receiving his Ph.D. at the University of Chicago in 1962, he taught at Rice University. He has held several NSF grants for foreign research and was active during the 1970s in many aspects of contract archeology. Among his publications is a textbook, *An Introduction to Prehistoric Archeology,* coauthored with Robert F. Heizer.

Dr. Jesse D. Jennings is Distinguished Professor of Anthropology at the University of Utah and a member of the National Academy of Sciences. He was formerly chairman of his department, Director of the Utah Museum of Natural History, and president of the Society for American Archeology. He received his Ph.D. from the University of Chicago in 1943 and was for many years associated with the National Park Service. Originally interested in cultural or social anthropology, Dr. Jennings soon succumbed to the fascination of cultural history, change, and stability as seen through the archeological record. Although he has done research in the Great Basin, the Southwest, and Polynesia, Dr. Jennings disclaims any area of specialization. His real interest is in the kind of synthesis exemplified by this series.

Dr. Stephen C. Jett is Associate Professor of Geography and acting department chairman at the University of California, Davis. His interests include cultural and historical geography, the Indians of the American Southwest, and, as reflected in this volume, Precolumbian transoceanic contacts. Dr. Jett received his Ph.D. from Johns Hopkins University in 1964 and has also taught at Ohio State University. He is the author of numerous publications on geographical, anthropological, and conservationist topics, including *Navajo Wildlands,* which won awards from the American Institute of Graphic Arts and the Western Book Publishers Association.

Dr. William D. Lipe is Associate Professor of Anthropology at Washington State University. He received his Ph.D. from Yale University in 1966 and has taught at the University of Oklahoma and the State University of New York at Binghamton. In addition, he has served as Research Archaeologist and Assistant to the Director at the Museum of Northern Arizona. His fieldwork has centered around the Colorado Plateau, especially southeastern Utah, and his research focus has been prehistoric settlement patterns and resource use. He is also actively concerned with cultural resource management and public interpretation of archeology and has published several seminal articles on those topics.

Dr. Jon Muller is Associate Professor of Anthropology at Southern Illinois University at Carbondale. Although he was originally interested in the northern and central Great Plains, Dr. Muller's dissertation work with Southern Cult art styles began his specialization in the archeology of the Southeast, particularly the settlement and organization of the Kincaid environs along the lower

Ohio River. Dr. Muller received his Ph.D. in 1967 from Harvard University, where he was a Woodrow Wilson and Dissertation Fellow. In addition to his research and teaching activities, Dr. Muller serves on the Board of Directors of the Illinois Archaeological Survey.

Dr. Waldo R. Wedel is Senior Archeologist of the United States National Museum of Natural History, the Smithsonian Institution, with which he has been associated since 1936. He received his doctorate from the University of California, Berkeley. The archeology and aboriginal human ecology of the Great Plains and the relationships of Plains peoples at all periods with those of neighboring areas comprise his main field of interest. For his pioneer studies in human ecology of the Plains Indians, he received the 1947 award of the Washington Academy of Sciences in the biological sciences. He is a member of the National Academy of Sciences and the author of *Prehistoric Man on the Great Plains* and other works.

Ancient North Americans

Changing Directions in Archeological Thought

Frank Hole

In this introductory chapter, Dr. Hole reviews the different ways archeologists reconstruct the prehistoric past from the sites and artifacts they discover during fieldwork. Through the years, archeologists have added many methods and techniques, drawn in part from ancillary sciences, and have continually refined their interpretations. Hole's review helps the reader understand the changing theoretical positions that affect the way we interpret the past. The beginning student will find it helpful to read this chapter both before and after reading the remainder of the book, because the ideas contained in it are exemplified and illustrated in other chapters.

The study of the human past requires a combination of scientific skill, historical insight, the ability to make use of a miscellany of technical aids, and luck. In some respects archeology is a science, in others an art in which discovery and interpretation rather than experimentation are the norm. There is room in archeology for personal contributions and equal room for controversy among archeologists over interpretations. This is especially true when the topic concerns origins: When did the first humans appear? Who were the first people to reach the Americas? When did the first civilization develop? Such questions spark heated debate, for the answers depend on the latest finds and on hunches about what will be found tomorrow. Debate also arises over how sites should be excavated or how discoveries should be interpreted. What provides a satisfying explanation to one archeologist may not satisfy others. While such debates permeate archeology, they are by no means a sign of weakness. Rather, they reflect our intense interest in the past and our compelling urge to understand it. In this friction between competing ideas we often gain powerful insights and thus advance our discipline.

My review is intended to reflect this condition. It is neither a dispassionate nor inevitable comment upon the field; any other archeologist writing this chapter would have done it differently. I have tried to be critical in the sense of looking beneath the surface, but not in the sense of being negative. My feelings for archeology are entirely positive, and my outlook on its future is hopeful because, year by year, we see new discoveries, new techniques, and new ideas that deepen our appreciation of our human heritage.

* * * * *

The American hemisphere encompasses nearly all of the geographic diversity that one can find on earth, a diversity that gave shape to an equally heterogeneous collection of native cultures. One of the goals of archeology is to recognize and chart the courses taken by these different peoples—to understand their developments, their successes, and their failures. It is an important goal, for most of the native peoples of the Americas had no written language. During the centuries of conquest by Europeans, the native cultures were extinguished, often with scarcely a recorded trace. Archeology remains the sole means by which we can know these lost civilizations and thereby provide a heritage of this hemisphere for all Americans.

Even though America differs from some other parts of the world in having been populated relatively recently and in possessing a relatively uniform native racial composition, the archeological remains throughout the American continents exhibit considerable diversity. This cultural diversity is paralleled by the linguistic diversity of the native peoples, whose languages were as varied as those spoken throughout the remainder of the world. The linguistic diversity was accompanied by a rich oral tradition, symbolic behavior, and conceptions of magic and religion, whose characteristics have been recorded in part by ethnographers. Ethnographers tell us that the tangible remains we find on the continents only dimly illuminate the intellectually profound and esthetically sublime accomplishments of native American peoples. The richness and variety of prehistoric American cultures, like the modern cultural mosaic, defy facile representation.

Wherever they may work, archeologists excavate sites, study artifacts, and piece together clues to human cultures long extinct. But our understanding of these past cultures changes continually as new remains are discovered or new ideas or techniques are invented to help analyze and interpret them. In *A Study of History,* Toynbee (1972:13) writes that history is protean: You have no sooner caught it in one shape than it changes into something almost unrecognizable, for "to change shape is the very nature of history, because it is in the nature of history to go on adding to itself." The same can be said of prehistory.

Just as our knowledge of the past continually changes with the advent of new discoveries, archeologists' interpretations of the past also change with the advent of new ideas and techniques. Since the science of archeology is not static, it is wise to pause periodically to assess its current positions. One way to do this is to review some of the major approaches presently in use and some of the reasons why they came into being. This short essay is not intended to give a comprehensive history of archeology; readers who wish fuller expositions of the history of archeology or different viewpoints on matters discussed here should consult *A History of American Archeology* (2nd ed.) by Willey and Sabloff (1980), Ford's (1977) assessment of the state of the art, Dunnell's excellent reviews of Americanist archeology (1979, 1980), Longacre's article on current thinking (1970), or Renfrew's (1980) view of American archeology from the perspective of European prehistoric and classical archeology.

CHANGES IN ARCHEOLOGY

About two decades ago, two books on American archeology appeared. *Method and Theory in American Archaeology,* by Willey and Phillips (1958), reviewed the entire hemisphere in terms of a series of five cultural stages, of which the last two, Classic and Postclassic, existed only in Mesoamerica and Peru. *Prehistoric Man in the New World,* edited by Jennings and Norbeck (1964), was a collection of articles by regional specialists that provided strictly culture-historical and somewhat encyclopedic reviews packed with detail. Although the two books were based on the same archeological evidence, the contrast could hardly have been more striking. The first volume focused on theoretical concerns, viewing the entire hemisphere within the same frame of reference, whereas the latter almost entirely eschewed theory in favor of the matter-of-fact exposition of dates, places, and artifacts. Since the publication of these two books, much has changed in American archeology.

Apart from the steady increase in knowledge resulting from new field discoveries, the most significant change has been the development and increasing use of radiocarbon dating, which was introduced in 1950. Radiocarbon dating measures the radioactivity of the carbon isotope C14 in pieces of wood, charcoal, or other organic material. Throughout their lives, all organisms continually acquire C14 through normal metabolic processes. After death, the C14 in the organism is no longer replenished and slowly decays, so that, after 5730 years, half of it will have been depleted. By using sensitive instruments, scientists can measure the amount of C14 in an object and thus estimate its age. Before radiocarbon dating, archeologists generally established relative ages by stratigraphy and by comparing artifacts. When artifacts from two separate sites differed greatly, often there was no rational way to tell whether one site was older or younger than the other. Radiocarbon dating was a revolutionary development, for it allowed ages to be assigned to sites separated widely in space and to artifacts manufactured of different types of material.

Accurate dating has made possible regional studies that deal with questions of historical development and the processes underlying change. Precise dates have provided the means for detecting "events" in prehistory, such as the relatively short time during which hunters aided nature in decimating the Pleistocene fauna in North America. A good series of dates for certain areas, such as the arid West, has made clear the impressive stability of some cultures over 10,000 or more years. Moreover, accurate dates have made it possible to distinguish between donors and recipients of inventions, such as agriculture or hieroglyphic writing. Accurate dates have provided key evidence bearing on the question of transoceanic influences (Chapter Twelve). Today, adequate dates are available for the majority of archeological situations in the Americas. Of course, we must remember that the dates are not absolute facts but estimates derived from analytical techniques and subject to the limitations of other laboratory procedures.

If dating has been the enduring change of the last twenty years, it has not been the most visible. The most pervasive changes have been a result of the philosophical debate over whether archeology can or should be a science and, more recently, in the United States, the impact of "public archeology" with its own set of goals and procedures.

During the decade of the 1960s, a new approach to archeology arose that was labeled the *New Archeology*. Many of its proponents claimed that the discipline could advance only through the strict application of one form of scientific method—formal hypothetico-deductive reasoning—using a model of scientific explanation described by philosopher Carl Hempel (1965, 1966). "New archeologists" sought to generate and test general laws that would explain all human behavior (Spaulding, 1973). In pursuit of these goals, they ignored particular historical reconstructions as irrelevant and unscientific. But this faith in a narrow mode of scientific thinking was misplaced, for New Archeology produced few substantive results in spite of the passions it aroused and the print it produced. Preferring theory to practice, the New archeologists did very little digging. Renfrew (1980:296) describes the extent of the situation succinctly: "One fears that as far as fieldwork is concerned, the first decades of the New Americanist archaeology will be seen at our next centennial as a kind of archaeological dark age, accompanied by the partial eclipse of literacy."

More enduring, and paralleling the development of New Archeology, has been a marked acceleration in the use of scientific techniques for analyses of archeological evidence. One manifestation of this trend is the widespread use of interdisciplinary teams to deal with the many types of remains that can be recovered from sites. Specialists in geomorphology, chemistry, paleontology, botany, palynology, and zoology often work alongside archeologists in the field and laboratory, adding their perspectives to the cultural picture (Brill, 1971; Brothwell and Higgs, 1963; Ford, 1979). Many of these interdisciplinary investigations have concerned prehistoric diet and environment (Clason, 1975; Dimbleby, 1967). The routine application of flotation to recover small organic remains, such as seeds, from sites has opened up new interpretations of diet. Complementary analyses of pollen and fecal remains and studies of stable isotopes in bone collagen may reveal the kind of plants that were eaten (Van der Merwe and Vogel, 1978). Most would agree that interdisiplinary collaboration has resulted in impressive accomplishments, yet even today few archeologists make effective use of it, in part because relatively few specialists are available to do the work (Butzer, 1971, 1975, 1980).

Related to this interdisciplinary participation is a revolution in technical aids to archeology, including the use of aerial photos, radar (R. E. W. Adams, 1980), and other forms of remote sensing such as magnetometry and sonar, which are used in locating sites or features buried under water or on land (Lyons and Avery, 1977; Morain and Budge, 1978). Neutron activation analysis, used to detect trace elements, allows the determination of sources of material such as obsidian or clay in pottery. A slowly developing area of scientific applications in archeology is concerned with these matters. At present, a number of journals such as *The Journal of Archaeological Science, Archaeometry,* and *MASCA Journal* provide a forum for these technical studies. This side of archeology will continue to grow because of the proliferation of technical methods in other fields such as geophysics, analytic chemistry, and forensic medicine. It is safe to assume that archeologists will increasingly borrow these techniques and apply them to their own data.

The last twenty years have also seen marked changes in the handling and analysis of data through the use of computers. In the 1960s, archeologists looked forward to the day when computers would enable them to develop systems for nearly instantaneous analysis of objects as they came out of the ground, providing daily feedback into field decisions on how and where to dig (Hymes, 1965). This has not happened. Computers have had relatively little impact on archeological results or theory, but they have provided a valuable means for storing archeological data in the form of site files and inventories of artifacts from sites (Gaines, 1981), and they have made possible complex, multivariate statistical analyses of data (Hodson and Doran, 1975). However, these statistical analyses have proved less useful than many had hoped, chiefly because of the nature of archeological data. Most archeological data do not readily lend themselves to nontrivial statistical analysis, for a number of reasons—particularly the many factors that intervene between the times an artifact is used, discarded, and finally recovered by excavation. It remains to be seen whether the latest computer applications, involving mathematical modeling of cultural processes and simulations of archeological situations, will produce real insights or prove to be just another form of technical virtuosity (Reidhead, 1979; Renfrew and Cooke, 1979).

Whoever looks back at archeology after twenty more years will probably remark on the development of public archeology (McGimsey and Davis, 1977; Schiffer and Gummerman, 1977), or "cultural resource management" as it is sometimes called. In North America, a reported $200 million a year is spent on public archeology. Although a multitude of small projects contribute to this total, the budgets of many projects exceed $1 million, an unprecedented level of support for archeology (King, 1981). The magnitude of the archeological effort in the United States exceeds that in any other region, but the excavation, preservation, and restoration of sites is seen as worthwhile in most countries of the Western hemisphere, and an organization, the New World Conference on Rescue Archeology, has arisen to further this goal.

Public archeology is not new: during the Depression it was practiced as a means of putting unemployed people back to work and thus bolstering a sagging economy. Many important archeological sites were excavated at that time, especially in the southeastern United States. Under the name *salvage archeology,* public archeology continued to be practiced after World War II when dams were constructed in the Plains and western states. Here the goal was to preserve specific traces of native American heritage where these remains would have otherwise been lost. This work produced a wealth of systematic information. The current concept of public archeology, however, is quite different from that which motivated those earlier salvage programs (Wilson, 1978).

Today, after years of political lobbying by a handful of dedicated archeologists, legislation requires archeological intervention in virtually any disturbance of public land or, in some instances, private land (McGimsey, 1972). Laudable as were these lobbying efforts to save a rapidly diminishing number of sites, they set in motion forces that may prove not so praiseworthy—for example, the use of archeology to accomplish nonarcheological objectives by forestalling development of roads, public utilities, or other modifications of the earth's surface. On the positive side, the impact of this legislation has been to increase vastly the number of persons employed as archeologists and, correspondingly, to increase the amount of information available. A favorable result has been the encouragement of systematic, broadscale archeology in hitherto little-explored regions such as along the Alaska pipeline or on vast tracts of government land.

Unhappily, but understandably, much of the information created by public archeology is not assimilated. It comes from scattered plots of land and is reported in obscure places, in largely individualistic and nonstandard formats, and at a rate that defies comprehension. Moreover, many of the reports are effectively lost through being buried in government or corporate files. A new publication, *Abstracts in Contract Archeology,* may help alleviate this problem.

Wherever public archeology may be done, it is a product of the political process and is thus subject to political as well as scientific and historical considerations. It thus comes under a different kind of scrutiny, and its results are measured in terms of many kinds of costs and benefits. This kind of scrutiny has led to a new kind of criticism from both inside and outside the archeological profession—that there is often a disproportionate funding of routine and sometimes mediocre archeology. Unfortunately, the enabling legislation could not deal with the question of site significance; instead, it had to cover all cases uniformly. However, most archeologists and lay observers would agree that archeological sites vary in quality and significance. In particular, it is becoming apparent that not every trace of aboriginal occupation that happens to lie on public property is unique, or interesting, or worthy of preservation. As this fact comes to be measured against costs and benefits, we may expect to see a change in emphasis within public archeology. It will have to take its place along with other national and social priorities in the competition for funds and other limited resources (McGimsey, 1978; Plog, 1978; Rabb et al., 1980). We may expect to see beneficial changes in archeological practices in the coming years as archeologists focus relatively more attention on sites and regions that promise to be particularly informative or that have special educational possibilities.

The last twenty years have also seen a surge of interest in historical archeology. For the first time there is serious academic interest in the archeology of recent European, African, and Asian immigrants to the continent (Noel-Hume, 1969; South, 1977; Schuyler, 1978). Sparked by reconstructions of colonial life at Williamsburg and Plymouth, and fueled by the nostalgia currently manifest in the United States, interest has spread to the study of industries such as fishing, lumbering, manufacturing, and mining as well as to the investigation of various immigrant ethnic groups (Schuyler, 1980). Now American archeologists are studying the remains of the alien or non-Indian cultures that conquered and colonized the New World after 1492. This burgeoning field of historic archeology has been stimulated by cultural-resource management and is closely related to ancillary studies in history, technology, and American civilization (King, 1978).

THE NATURE OF ARCHEOLOGICAL KNOWLEDGE

Our understanding of prehistory results from an interplay between substance and style—that is, from the interaction of the actual evidence recovered from the earth with the manner in which archeologists think and write about that evidence. Whatever happened in the past is done and cannot be changed. Archeologists uncover this past but they do not create it. Archeological evidence consists of things—artifacts and other materials—removed from the earth, and of the association of these things (that is, their contexts) with one another and with the sites in which they occur. Evidence also consists of sites in relation to one another and to the landscapes surrounding them. Yet, while the human past is finite, and events and data derived from these events are constant, human interpretations of them are not. Further, our perceptions of the form of prehistory are subject to the singularly perverse fact that archeological evidence is almost always ambiguous. Interpretations change as facts accumulate and as archeologists develop new methods and theories for interpretation. Style in archeology changes just like styles in clothing, architecture, or art—in response to technological changes and to social and political concerns. As these changes redirect its focus, prehistory grows and changes.

The careful reader of the chapters in this volume will recognize the unevenness of archeological substance, for each of the authors mentions the spotty distribution of information or lack of crucial regional or temporal coverage. In fact, for many of the periods in some of the regions discussed, there have been no excavations whatsoever. In other regions, sites have been excavated in neither logical nor chronological sequence. Understandably, the greatest activity has been in regions with the most spectacular remains and in areas where access to sites has been relatively easy. In other parts of the Americas, such as the vast stretches of lowland South America where the humid forest environment makes investigation difficult, and where archeologists are relatively few, the advances have been and will be slower.

This problem of uneven coverage can be partly corrected, but many archeological sites have been entirely destroyed or buried. Moreover, sites are discovered by a combination of luck and of what archeologists call site survey—the deliberate search for sites. Although we know that the sample of excavated data is very small compared with what is potentially available, we have no accurate way to estimate how much of the archeological record has been destroyed by natural processes such as erosion or by modern construction, nor how much remains undiscovered.

The vast amount of detail presented in archeological reports suggests, erroneously, that a great deal is known about ancient peoples. Actually, we know little about even the most knowable of things, such as tools, diet, and the precise ages of sites. In their reports, most archeologists group artifacts that are similar in material, manufacture, style, and time, and distinguish these collections from other similar regional groupings. In minute detail, they describe the artifacts, count them, and illustrate them. The result is a succession of things, a catalog of goods arranged in roughly chronological sequence. It should not be surprising that the usual archeological unit of discussion in these reports—the period, complex, or phase—has few, if any, implications for understanding cultures, tribes, or specific peoples.

Some authors leave it at this, but others attempt to infer human activities, population movements, trade, or conflict from the temporal and geographic distribution of artifacts. The remains found in a site inform us about that society's adaptation to its environment and its relationship with neighboring peoples. Viewed in their immediate contexts, such as graves, houses, and workshops, artifacts reveal such aspects of social structure as differentiation in rank and status. By analyzing artifacts and sites in time and space, and in relation to their physical and social environments, and by interpreting them with the aid of theories about change, evolution, ecology, and culture, archeologists can reconstruct some of the form of ancient societies.

Along with the ability to reconstruct and interpret more mundane aspects of prehistoric life, such as what people ate, there are also heartening trends toward deeper analyses that try to understand the individual in prehistory (Hill and Gunn, 1977) and ritual and intellectual activities (Redman et al., 1978). Only recently have prehistorians begun to call on historical and anthropological linguists, who are able to reconstruct the vocabulary and concepts of ancient languages, to help flesh out the bare bones of American prehistory as we know it today (Marcus, 1980). Ethnoarcheology (the study of living peoples whose ways of life bear some resemblance to those of prehistory) and ethnohistory (the study of historical sources concerning people who are interesting archeologically) are often used to suggest cultural features that are difficult, if not impossible, to establish archeologically—for example, the uses of artifacts, the links between social organization and environment, and ideologies (Spores, 1980). The behavior that produced the artifacts and the sites that we excavate is very difficult to infer from just the objects and sites themselves. Archeologists thus seek out information from living peoples as well as from historical sources to help them interpret their data (Gould, 1980).

Unfortunately, archeological remains can inform on some matters and not on others. It is problematic whether we will ever be able to discover ways to make what we find in the ground spring to fully rounded life, for we cannot find and interpret what no longer exists. Sounds and smells, languages and beliefs are intangible, and their archeological absence deprives us of much that is distinctly human and interesting. We can recover and interpret things that resist decay, such as projectile points, remains of houses, pottery, figurines, and burials. From these we can infer what people ate, what the environment was like, how big the people were, whether they had short or long lifespans, whether they accorded unusual respect to any individuals, how skillful they were in making implements, what their art styles were, and many other things. But we may never learn whether certain people were matrilineal or believed in one God. And we will certainly never have the complete story on any group of people.

In spite of its limitations, archeology remains our only means for learning about human prehistory—that is, about history before people began to write and, ultimately, to record their own history. As long as we insist on seeing and feeling evidence of human handiwork before we make statements about the course of human prehistory, we will depend on archeology.

CONTRASTING APPROACHES TO PREHISTORY

What we lack in archeological substance, we compensate for in technical virtuosity and in style. The custom in archeology has been to treat the substance according to our technical skill and our concern for the prevailing intellectual, social, and political issues. Dunnell (1979) was correct when he said that American archeology lacks a unifying theoretical base. It comprehends, rather, a variety of different approaches, or styles, some of which are discussed below.

Regional Culture Histories

The regional approach is grounded in the concept of the culture area (see Figure 2.17), derived from ethnographic research, which states that cultures within distinct geographic provinces share many fundamental properties (Steward, 1955:78–97). Regional studies or culture histories have been the prevailing mode of presenting American archeology since it has been possible to arrange prehistoric remains chronologically. Essentially, such studies discuss sites and artifacts from distinct regions as they change in time and as their relationships with other regions can be observed. The chronicle is the most direct form of presentation: it conforms exactly to the basic data, material recovered from the ground which has been placed in a framework of time and space. The differentiation of geographic areas is based on evidence of an underlying similarity among the archeological remains of a region and a correspondence between geography and culture. There is clearly an element of validity in this approach, particularly if the geographic boundaries are drawn carefully and narrowly, but its applicability depends largely on the complexity of the cultures and on the length of time involved. For example, the technologically simple Paleo-Indian remains, which vary little from one place to another, can be described continent-wide. However, as time passes and cultural remains become more diverse, and as humans increase in numbers and adapt to different local environments, one must restrict the geographic boundaries more narrowly to continue dealing with strictly comparable material.

Although the regional approach is simple and direct, it has a number of disadvantages. For one, when archeologists employ a strictly regional perspective, they may fail to recognize similarities between their local material and that from other regions. For example, taking a broad perspective, one can discern a geographic symmetry of development from the simpler cultures at the northern and southern extremes of the hemisphere to the agriculturalists in the temperate latitudes and the high civilizations in the central regions. Regional studies largely ignore the implications of such comparisons.

When authors focus on a single region, moreover, movements of specific groups of people in and out of that region—the type of movements that are indicated in linguistic evidence—are difficult to discover archeologically. To date, in American archeology, we have usually studied in a statistical fashion nameless peoples of only approximate antiquity, rather than known lineages whose peregrinations can be traced over time. The notorious mystery of the Navajo intrusion into the Southwest is a reminder that population movements can be demonstrable linguistically but are hard to track down archeologically. Similarly, the origins of the peoples who would become known as the Toltecs (or, later, Aztecs) have not been traced. Regional syntheses also tend to ignore variability and to emphasize the most advanced, or spectacular, remains at any period. Thus, reviews of the Classic Maya focus on the centers of architecture and art rather than on hamlets or sites that suggest specialized functions. Or, in North America such reviews tend to emphasize sites with burial or temple mounds at the expense of others in the same region that contain no such structures. At best the regional chronicle is a compromise, but for many purposes it is more useful than dealing with the entire hemisphere simultaneously, as Willey and Phillips attempted to do. The regional chronicle's main advantage is that it reduces and arranges the data for ready comprehension.

Diffusion

Diffusionist views, unlike certain other theories on culture change, are currently out of favor among American archeologists. Nonetheless, as Jett indicates in his chapter, some facts are easier to explain by diffusion than by independent invention. Diffusionism is a theory used to explain change in culture; it stems from the beliefs that (1) invention is a relatively rare phenomenon, (2) some people are more creative than others, and (3) inventions or good ideas flow outward from these centers of creativity. For Western civilization, Egypt and, later, Classical Greece and Rome were such centers of creativity. As Jett shows, the peoples of Asia should be credited with equal creativity, although little of that creativity affected Europe. Inasmuch as most native American archeological remains and the cultures from which they derived differ vastly from the cultures of Europe, most American archeologists staunchly defend indigenous development—in some cases so excessively as to prevent legitimate inquiry into the nature of the presumed contacts. Most archeologists emotionally deny that transoceanic contacts had more than fleeting impact, but the idea remains alive. The development of radiocarbon dating has helped to clarify some formerly disputed issues related to diffusion, but, since diffusionism has never had a large following in America, the impact has been minimal.

Despite the fact that transoceanic influences are generally discredited, there is no doubt that widespread interareal contacts did occur through trade of minerals, food products, and exotic goods. Less certain, and a continuing source of debate, is the degree of direct influence from the civilizations of Mexico represented by such specific North American cultural manifestations as the construction of temple mounds or the spread of maize agriculture.

The problem of influences is complicated by the fact that, so far, the data have been mute. Even employing neutron activation analysis to identify the sources of obsidian does not necessarily teach us anything about how the stone moved from its source to where it is finally found by archeologists. Nor does remarking a similarity in the styles of various artifacts necessarily teach us whether they had a common source. For example, when similar projectile points occur in North and South America, we are inclined to doubt, but cannot readily disprove, that they were made by the same hands. But when figurines wearing earspools are found in Mesoamerica and North America, then archeologists must seriously consider whether they are evidence for culture contact, the diffusion of an idea, or independent invention (Griffin, 1980). The way such an issue is settled says something about the style of the decision-maker—that is, about his operating assumptions concerning both the meaning of the evidence and the way cultures operate and interact. Thus the confident assertion of one prehistorian may be dismissed out-of-hand by another, yet it may be impossible on any scientific grounds to prove or disprove either stand.

Evolution

To the extent that it recognized sequential stages of increasing complexity in American prehistory, *Method and Theory in American Archaeology* (Willey and Phillips, 1958) was a protoevolutionary book. But, unsupported by any explicit evolutionary theory explaining the sequence of stages, the book merely related what had happened, using for organization a form of cultural typology called "stages." *Prehistoric Man in the New World* (Jennings and Norbeck, 1964) made no effort to generalize at all.

Some archeologists see the widespread use of ideas of cultural evolution as a natural outgrowth of the scientific approach of the 1960s. In fact, however, the theory grew out of more traditional historical and scientific concerns and only became once more palatable in the 1960s, after decades of disfavor, due to the work of ethnologists who reconstructed historical progressions of culture from observations of living peoples. As it is currently used, evolution as a prehistorical theory traces the slow acquisition, over a long period of time, of political control over a population. Ultimately, it is hypothesized, certain individuals or lineages would form an elite or uppermost class in a stratified, more complex society. Religion, ideology, and noneconomic political motivations are relegated to insignificant roles in most evolutionary archeological thinking.

The evolutionary way had been foreshadowed by the great European prehistorian V. Gordon Childe (1951a, b), who showed how human "progress" could be measured through archeological evidence. However, it was Julian Steward (1955), an American ethnologist, who first attempted to discern the regularities underlying the development of early civilizations. That is, he believed he could discover the factors that gave rise to these civilizations by comparing many instances and observing which elements were common to all. His purpose was explicitly evolutionary, stressing the comparative, generalizing approach that was later taken up in a somewhat different form by Robert Adams (1966) in *The Evolution of Urban Society: Early Mesopotamia and Prehispanic Mexico.* In a series of lectures in honor of the nineteenth-century anthropological evolutionist Lewis Henry Morgan, Adams compared the development of two early civilizations. In each instance, Adams attempted to show multiple lines of causality that converged to produce the characteristic forms of society as the cultures in these two regions achieved the status of urban civilizations. He thus prefigured a systematic approach that would identify changing social organization as the critical element of emerging civilization (Hill, 1977; Renfrew, 1973). Moreover, Adams was concerned with the processes by which these significant changes came about.

Since the writings of Steward and Adams, many archeologists have focused on individual variables, such as population growth, warfare, and trade, that they feel might lead to increasing political complexity (by which they partly mean the growth of social inequality) (Sanders and Marino, 1970; Sanders and Webster, 1978). Again, these theorists devote little attention to possible noneconomic stimuli such as religion and particularly forceful individuals—although there are signs that this policy is changing (see, for example, Adams, 1973).

"New Archeology"

Until the 1960s, style in archeology was shaped more by the limitations of its substance than by overriding theories of either its relevance or potential. Archeologists throughout the world determined the arrangement of their finds in time and space and offered plausible explanations to account for changes. But the powerful message of the 1960s was that this was not enough (Binford and Binford, 1968).

During the late 1950s, in the shadow of Sputnik, the United States turned toward technology to help resolve social and political issues. If the goal was to stay ahead of the Russians and the means was science backed by unlimited enthusiasm and funding, one by-product was a generation of students who excelled in mathematics and science—often at the expense of the humanities. The ability of science and engineering to overcome obstacles and solve problems was proved by the visible success of American scientists in landing humans on the moon, and the lesson was not wasted. The effects reached archeology in the 1960s in the form of "New Archeology" (Binford, 1972). Almost overnight, ideas and questions that had puzzled scholars for centuries turned into "problems," which it was thought could be solved by applying the scientific method. The search for solutions through science alone was not only proper, it was essential and urgent: archeology would be science or it would be nothing (Watson et al., 1971). The effects of this shift to science continue to be felt in archeology throughout the world, particularly where English is the language of theoretical discussion, for many archeologists are no longer content merely to arrange their data descriptively.

Paradoxically, the style of the "New Archeology," as it labeled itself in the United States, was polemical and programmatic rather than objective and substantive. The New archeologists expended far more effort in publicizing their approach and proselytizing new recruits than in applying their ideas. According to the creed, the hypothetico-deductive method was the only proper approach to archeology, because it (supposedly) dissociated the inferential procedure from the individual scientist by making every aspect of that procedure explicit. Mathematics combined with new jargon became the language for expressing and testing these hypotheses. This new language was supposed to reduce complex and confusing ideas to simple, logical, unequivocal formats, using statistics to detect patterns too subtle for the unaided mind to see or express. New archeologists deprecated their predecessors' humanistic thinking by labeling it subjective, unscientific, and irrelevant.

It has been said that the cornerstone of New Archeology is an evolutionary point of view coupled with systems theory (Willey and Sabloff, 1980:186). But this analysis is misleading. As first described in Lewis Binford's classic paper "Archaeology as Anthropology" (1962), New Archeology divides sociocultural systems into three realms, as represented by technomic, sociotechnic, and ideotechnic artifacts. We may think of these as objects pertaining to technology (tools), social relationships (rank and status), and ideology (religion). Binford (1962:217) was concerned with correlations between the various components of systems: "Processual change in one variable [such as environment or size of population] then can be shown to relate in a predictable and quantifiable way to change in other variables [such as tools or social ranks]." This notion of process (as the mechanism underlying cultural evolution) bears little resemblance to the evolution of Tylor and Morgan, based on the comparative method.

Binford's tripartite typology of artifacts is in fact cultural materialism, taken without embellishment from the writings of Karl Marx through the work of Leslie A. White (1959). Binford's paper does not consider the underlying philosophical rationale for Marxism but treats the philosophy as the basis for a research strategy, a way of doing archeology. Marxism provided Binford with both the categories into which artifacts could be placed and the theory to explain their interrelations. His hypothetical research design is simply a detailed protocol for implementing Marx's master research design. Although Binford does not explicitly claim primacy within cultures for the technoeconomic system, much of the New Archeology that followed his article proceeded along manifestly Marxist lines. Such work correlated environmental variables with site types and artifacts and sought to explain social changes in terms of changes in economic systems. Thus New Archeology reinforces the suggestion that social and ideological organization in a culture is an adaptive response to technoeconomic conditions.

The current infatuation with "economic man" indicates that the Marxist model still prevails in spite of a great deal of evidence against it. Ethnographic sources have always made it clear that people in primitive societies are more concerned with social, ritual, and ideological matters than with the more mundane problems of subsistence, technology, and economics. Archeological analyses that stress the primacy of economic motivation in human behavior and offer theories of cultural evolution based largely on economic factors fail to take into account these findings of ethnology, or, for that matter, of history and sociology.

This is not to argue against a materialist approach as one way of looking at some archeological data: it is to refute the suggestion that it is the *only* way. Marxism provides a tool for thinking about cultural systems and, as with any other tool, its use determines what we view as important, what we measure, and how we account for what we observe. The difficulty with New Archeology is not so much that the trite correlations are uninteresting as that they are one of the few products of a research strategy that denies the possibility of alternative approaches to the evidence. Marvin Harris (1968:638) reminds us that we must be careful not to disregard social theories merely because they are politically unpopular. On the other hand, we ought not to be afraid to run counter to the counter-culture when doing so provides insights.

Today the polemical New Archeology described above is no longer practiced, but some of its better aspects continue to be influential. In particular, it has become more common to devote explicit attention to research design and to planning archeological work in relation to one's goals. Another legacy is the extensive development of data banks that researchers can use to test hypotheses about the relation of cultural developments to environmental and other variables. The influence of New Archeology is also seen in the continued interest in systems, whether in simple, local hunting groups or in empires. Finally, today's emphasis on the social dimensions of archeological remains goes straight back to Binford's 1962 paper. Through New Archeology, the broader discipline of archeology changed and grew, building on its successes and learning from its mistakes.

APPROACHES BORROWED FROM OTHER FIELDS

In their desire to wrest a little more information from intractable objects and contexts, archeologists have been remarkably eclectic in picking up ideas from other fields. For example, from biology they have borrowed concepts of ecology and systems analysis that have provided the framework for relating individual sites to one another and to the environments in which they occur. The ecological approach—which stresses the interrelations of components in a natural system—expedites a shift in attention from single sites to whole regions. It focuses on underlying patterns of settlement and, more particularly, on how certain societies interacted with their immediate environments (Steward, 1955:30–42). As Michael Jochim (1979) explains in his review, ecology encourages archeologists to think of human groups as utilizing territories according to seasonal schedules and to conceive of and discover remains of separate but contemporary groups living in the same region. The perspective of systems theory directs archeologists' attention to the dynamic aspects of prehistoric societies—that is, their adaptations as elements within a complex, interacting system composed both of other societies and of the organic and inorganic worlds around them (Plog, 1975).

Although ecology provided the first impetus for archeology to move beyond convenience inventorying of sites to systematic site survey, geography—with its

theories and its empirical findings about the spatial organization of settlements—gave rise to new uses of intensive surveys (Hodder, 1978; Hodder and
Orton, 1976; Johnson, 1977; Parsons, 1972). Geographers have found that
modern human settlements are arranged in space to allow for ease of communication and transportation. Assuming an underlying economic rationale, geographers postulated a model of settlement systems in which large sites, perform-
ing many economic or political functions, were surrounded by smaller sites.
These smaller sites performed fewer functions and were in turn surrounded by
their own smaller satellites of lesser importance.

Reasoning that the hierarchical system could apply equally well to the prehistoric past, archeologists presumed that the correspondence of site survey data
with the geographic model could suggest the probable economic and political
organization of a prehistoric culture. The techniques were originally designed to
work in regions where society has reached an appreciable level of economic and
social complexity, such as that found in the areas of the higher civilizations, but
they have only recently been applied in American archeology (Steponaitis, 1978,
1981). An example of such recent work is Fekri Hassan's (1978, 1979) study of
population change, which uses estimates that could only be made from accurately dated survey data and a special method of inferring the numbers of people
that lived in given sites. The issue is particularly important because many of
the theories about emerging organizational complexity depend on population
pressure, which is a matter of both demography and ecology (Cohen, 1977).
Additional approaches borrowed from other fields and applied to archeological
studies include information theory, econometrics, game theory, and catastrophe
theory (Clarke, 1978; Johnson, 1978; Reidhead, 1979; Renfrew and Cooke,
1979).

THE PERSONALIZATION OF ARCHEOLOGY

Many archeologists have chosen to deal on a more individual or personal level
with artifacts that bear traces of use or that are examples of unique handiwork
by attempting to reconstruct the steps in their manufacture and/or use. Use-
wear analyses of lithic artifacts and stylistic studies of ceramics are examples of
this type of research. In a few cases (Cahen and Keeley, 1980), analysts have
been able to reconstruct such processes as the precise steps in the manufacture of
a flint tool. This work required a tedious and careful fitting-together of the
many pieces chipped from the raw stone that were found distributed over the
site. Microscopic use–wear analysis aims to discover the uses to which tools
were put by analyzing the patterns of wear on their surfaces (Hayden, 1979);
for example, working hides leaves marks on a tool different from those left by
working wood. Similarly, careful studies of pottery designs (Hill and Gunn,
1977) can reveal the hands of individual artisans. These analyses have long been

a tool for classical archeologists, who have identified the work of numerous pot-painters, but they have been applied only recently to the much more difficult wares of America's domestic craft production.

Such studies of American artifacts may sometimes appear more ingenious than important, but motivating all of them is the hope of recovering some of the flavor of the past, of heightening our appreciation of our forebears. These studies personalize archeology in the sense that, through them, we deal explicitly with the activities of individuals in the past rather than just with the collective products of anonymous groups. These studies personalize the process of doing archeology, in another sense, too, for the analysts become intimately involved with the past as they manufacture and use artifacts in the same way as did prehistoric peoples.

Another kind of personalization in archeology comes through ethno-archeology, in which archeologists experience living contexts in which artifacts similar to those they find are used and discarded (Gould, 1980). Such studies have involved the manufacture of pottery, the use of stone tools, and the observation of primitive agricultural practices. In the absence of suitable living subjects, some archeologists have turned to experimental archeology. For example, they chip stone tools and use them on varied materials in order to determine use–wear patterns. By comparing the duplicates with the original, prehistoric objects, the experimenters can correctly deduce the latter's functions (Ingersoll et al., 1977). The purpose of both ethnoarcheology and experimental archeology is to generate a richer array of interpretive possibilities and to gain deeper insight into the nature of archeological remains. In some instances ethnographic and historic sources can be used to move backward from the present into the past (Spores, 1980). The North American Southwest and the Arctic, for instance, are places where native peoples continue to live in communities that their ancestors inhabited before Europeans reached the Americas. In these places contemporary individuals can still inform on matters of archeological interest. Such communities are regrettably few, however, and only belatedly have these native Americans themselves become involved in prehistory as archeologists and as consumers of research findings.

SOME OUTSTANDING QUESTIONS

A series of questions relating to changes in and differences among societies has long occupied the attention of philosophers, historians, archeologists, and the reading public. Epitomizing this interest are the discussions of how nations rise and fall, a theme popularized by the great historian Edward Gibbon in his *The Decline and Fall of the Roman Empire*. Although anthropologists and archeologists in recent years have found the rise of nations more fascinating theoretically (Service, 1962, 1975; Renfrew, 1973; Flannery, 1972), their fall is equally a concern, and one that has dominated the thinking of Mayanists for a long time (Thompson, 1954). The implicit assumption has often been that cultures "rise" over time because knowledge and techniques of living grow cumulatively (Childe, 1951b). Biology and systems theory have shown that, in general, life forms become more complex and hence "higher" with the passage of time. Falls are considered a sign of sickness, a breakdown attributable both to natural and sociological factors. Falls have seldom been investigated in American archeology outside the Mayan area, in part because evolutionary theories do not account for them and in part because attention has been diverted to any subsequent rises. The next decade may bring more efforts to compare such developmental factors as levels of complexity, the pace of change, and changes of state (rises and falls) among different regions. Do cultures, as some historians maintain, go through life cycles, inevitably to be replaced by the next culture on the rise? Archeology clearly has much to contribute to this kind of investigation.

Somewhat related to this research is the question of "core regions" or "nuclear areas"—areas in which the pace of development was quickest and the highest cultures arose. We are well acquainted with this phenomenon through empirical evidence. According to Willey and Phillips (1958), Mesoamerica and the Andes evolved further than any other region of the Americas. Why did the other cultures of North and South America not achieve a similar complexity with equal rapidity and thoroughness? That situation is paralleled in Southwest Asia and the Far East, where the early core regions were narrowly circumscribed. Clearly, powerful environmental factors were operating in these cases, but the precise nature of these factors has yet to be determined. One such factor is no doubt agriculture, which produces the raw materials that can be harnessed by human effort to provide increasing amounts of energy. But is agriculture the complete answer? The issue is not strictly archeological, but the answers may well reside in archeological materials.

Investigation of comparative levels of development is another way of determining the factors that encourage or inhibit the spread of ideas and techniques. Diffusion is not doubted as a general process, although specific instances, such as transoceanic examples, may be disputed. But why do people adopt some things and not others? And why do some people remain conservative while others are innovative? Archeology can contribute to such investigations by providing evidence about the actual course of events, the pace of changes, and specific environmental and social changes.

CONCLUDING REMARKS

Most of us are interested in our past, our roots. Where did we come from? Who were our forebears? How did they gain their livelihood and rear their families? What was their style of life? Our interest is born of the innate awareness that we are, in some measure, products of our past. Many peoples, however, have no concern with their past. For some this disinterest is simply pragmatic; they have trouble enough dealing with the present and preparing for the future. Others simply do not believe that the past could hold anything different from the present. Still others would deny that the past has any relevance to modern concerns, because what is important has either already been revealed in holy writ or will be revealed by living prophets.

As archeologists we may disagree with such views but we cannot ignore them. They bear on our work directly when we wish to investigate remains in areas where the native peoples hold these views. In parts of America such feelings may stop archeological work altogether. In a few places archeological projects are being carried out explicitly to inform on a tribe's history, but it is more usual for native Americans to feel a sense of outrage at the violation of their heritage. They feel that the predominantly Anglo archeologists are guided by the dictates of science or by their peculiar notions of history rather than by any sympathy with tribal identity (Trigger, 1980).

Many people get involved in archeology as a way of learning about the human past before the presence of written records. But interest in archeology may also derive from a kind of antiquarian curiosity about old, or strange, or artful objects made by people long dead. Equally, it may result from a fascination with discovering the unknown, from the enjoyment of piecing together the puzzle of the past, or from the desire to earn an income out-of-doors. Some see the past as a laboratory in which to test theories about human change and achievement. Others find the past a lesson book from which they hope to learn to interpret the present and manipulate the future. Archeology is a means to realize all these goals.

In the end we all have motives for studying the past, whether they derive from an appreciation of the handiwork of the ancients, from broad comparative historical concerns, or from the attempt to derive scientific laws that will hold for all mankind. The aspects of the past that we emphasize as archeologists reflect both our immediate concerns and the tools we have to work with. The study of archeology is a social phenomenon that incorporates current values and preoccupations. Archeologists in our society are educated citizens who, like any others, feel strongly about many issues. And, like other humans, archeologists find it difficult to separate their understandings of the past from their beliefs about the present and the future.

We have seen in these pages that there are various ways to do archeology and to think about the past. We have stressed how archeology itself has changed as a result of new discoveries, new techniques, and new ideas. With this in mind, readers can now turn to the following chapters of this volume, in which individual archeologists tell the prehistories of their regions. I hope that readers would look beyond the matter-of-fact prose to contemplate the ideas contained in these articles and to consider how the authors have organized their data and derived interpretations from them. This volume summarizes the state of American archeology in the early 1980s—but in no sense is it a complete story. One of the exciting features of the study of prehistory is that it grows and changes. In another ten or twenty years, while the facts presented here will not have changed, new data or better ideas will have caused a reappraisal of much that is written here. We build on the past in archeology as in our lives. To know that past gives us a foundation on which to build.

References Cited and Recommended Sources

Adams, Richard E. W. 1980. Swamps, canals, and the locations of ancient Maya cities. *Antiquity* 54:206–214.

Adams, Robert McC. 1966. *The Evolution of Urban Society: Early Mesopotamia and Prehispanic Mexico.* Chicago: Aldine.

———. 1973. Discussion. In *Research and Theory in Current Archeology,* ed. C. L. Redman, pp. 321–327. New York: Wiley.

Binford, Lewis R. 1962. Archaeology as anthropology. *American Antiquity* 28:217–225.

———. 1972. *An Archaeological Perspective.* New York: Seminar Press.

———, and Sally R. Binford (eds.). 1968. *New Perspectives in Archaeology.* Chicago: Aldine.

Brill, Robert H. (ed.). 1971. *Science and Archaeology.* Cambridge: M.I.T. Press.

Brothwell, Don R., and Eric Higgs (eds.). 1963. *Science in Archaeology.* New York: Basic Books.

Butzer, Karl W. 1971. *Environment and Archeology,* 2nd ed. Chicago: Aldine.

———. 1975. The 'ecological' approach to prehistory: are we really trying? *American Antiquity* 40:106–111.

———. 1980. Context in archaeology: an alternative perspective. *Journal of Field Archaeology* 7:417–422.

Cahen, Daniel, and Lawrence H. Keeley. 1980. Not less than two, not more than three. *World Archaeology* 12:166–180.

Childe, V. Gordon. 1951a. *Social Evolution.* New York: Schuman.

———. 1951b. *Man Makes Himself,* rev. ed. New York: Mentor Books.

Clark, Grahame. 1970. *Aspects of Prehistory.* Berkeley: University of California Press.

———. 1979. Archaeology and human diversity. *Annual Review of Anthropology* 8:1–20.

Clarke, David L. 1978. *Analytical Archaeology,* 2nd ed. New York: Columbia University Press.

Clason, A. T. (ed.). 1975. *Archaeozoological Studies.* New York: Elsevier.

Cohen, Mark N. 1977. *The Food Crisis in Prehistory.* New Haven: Yale University Press.

Dimbleby, Geoffrey W. 1967. *Plants and Archaeology.* New York: Humanities Press.

Dunnell, Robert C. 1979. Trends in current Americanist archaeology. *American Journal of Archaeology* 83:437–449.

———. 1980. Americanist archaeology: the 1979 contribution. *American Journal of Archaeology* 84:463–478.

Flannery, Kent V. 1972. The cultural evolution of civilizations. *Annual Review of Ecology and Systematics* 3:399–426.

———. 1973. Archeology with a capital "S." In *Research and Theory in Current Archeology,* ed. Charles L. Redman, pp. 47–53. New York: Wiley.

Ford, Richard I. 1977. The state of the art in archaeology. In *Perspectives on Anthropology 1976*, ed. A. F. C. Wallace et al., pp. 101–115. Special Publication No. 10, American Anthropological Association.

———. 1979. Paleoethnobotany in American archaeology. In *Advances in Archaeological Method and Theory*, vol. 2, ed. Michael B. Schiffer, pp. 286–336. New York: Academic Press.

Gaines, S. W. 1981. *Data Bank Applications in Archeology*. Tucson: University of Arizona Press.

Gould, Richard A. 1980. *Living Archaeology*. Cambridge: Cambridge University Press.

Griffin, James B. 1980. The Mesoamerican–Southeastern U.S. connection. *Early Man* 2:12–18.

Harris, Marvin. 1968. *The Rise of Anthropological Theory*. New York: Crowell.

Hassan, Fekri A. 1978. Demographic archaeology. In *Advances in Archaeological Method and Theory*, vol. 1, ed. Michael B. Schiffer, pp. 49–103. New York: Academic Press.

———. 1979. Demography and archaeology. *Annual Review of Anthropology* 8:137–160.

Hayden, Brian (ed.). 1979. *Lithic Use–Wear Analysis*. New York: Academic Press.

Hempel, Carl G. 1965. *Aspects of Scientific Explanation and Other Essays in the Philosophy of Science*. New York: Free Press.

———. 1966. *Philosophy of Natural Science*. Englewood Cliffs, N.J.: Prentice-Hall.

Hill, James N. (ed.). 1977. *Explanation of Prehistoric Change*. Albuquerque: University of New Mexico Press.

———, and Joel Gunn (eds.). 1977. *The Individual in Prehistory*. New York: Academic Press.

Hodder, Ian (ed.). 1978. *The Spatial Organisation of Culture*. Pittsburgh: University of Pittsburgh Press.

Hodder, Ian, and Clive Orton. 1976. *Spatial Analysis in Archaeology*. Cambridge: Cambridge University Press.

Hodson, J. E., and Frank R. Doran. 1975. *Mathematics and Computers in Archaeology*. Cambridge, Mass.: Harvard University Press.

Hymes, Del (ed.). 1965. *Symposium on the Use of Computers in Anthropology*. The Hague: Mouton.

Ingersoll, Daniel, John E. Yellen, and William Macdonald (eds.). 1977. *Experimental Archeology*. New York: Columbia University Press.

Jennings, Jesse D., and Edward Norbeck (eds.). 1964. *Prehistoric Man in the New World*. Chicago: University of Chicago Press.

Jochim, Michael A. 1979. Breaking down the system: recent ecological approaches in archaeology. In *Advances in Archaeological Method and Theory*, vol. 2, ed. Michael B. Schiffer, pp. 77–117. New York: Academic Press.

Johnson, Gregory A. 1977. Aspects of regional analysis in archaeology. *Annual Review of Anthropology* 6:479–508.

———. 1978. Information sources and the development decision-making organizations. In *Social Archaeology: Beyond Subsistence and Dating*, ed. Charles L. Redman et al., pp. 87–112. New York: Academic Press.

King, T. F. 1978. Archeology and historic preservation: a case for convergence. In *Social Archaeology: Beyond Subsistence and Dating*, ed. Charles L. Redman et al., pp. 431–437. New York: Academic Press.

———. 1981. How effective is the U.S. program to save America's heritage? *Early Man* 3:4–12.

Kramer, Carol (ed.). 1979. *Ethnoarchaeology*. New York: Columbia University Press.

Longacre, William A. 1970. Current thinking in American archaeology. *Bulletin of the American Anthropological Association*, vol. 3, no. 3, part 2, pp. 126–138.

Lyons, Thomas R., and Thomas E. Avery. 1977. *Remote Sensing: A Handbook for Archeologists and Cultural Resource Managers*. Washington, D.C.: U.S. Government Printing Office.

McGimsey, Charles R. 1972. *Public Archeology*. New York: Seminar Press.

———. 1978. Cultural resource management—archeology plus. In *Social Archaeology: Beyond Subsistence and Dating*, ed. Charles L. Redman, pp. 415–419. New York: Academic Press.

———, and Hester A. Davis (eds.). 1977. *The Management of Archaeological Resources: The Airlie House Report*. Washington, D.C.: Society for American Archaeology.

Marcus, Joyce. 1980. Zapotec writing. *Scientific American* 242:50–64.

Morain, S. A., and T. K. Budge. 1978. *Instrumentation for Remote Sensing in Archaeology*. Washington, D.C.: U.S. Government Printing Office.

Noel-Hume, Ivor. 1969. *Historical Archaeology*. New York: Knopf.

Parsons, J. R. 1972. Archaeological settlement patterns. *Annual Review of Anthropology* 1:127–150.

Plog, Fred T. 1975. Systems theory in archaeological research. *Annual Review of Anthropology* 4:207–224.

———. 1978. Cultural resource management and the 'new archeology'. In *Social Archaeology: Beyond Subsistence and Dating,* ed. Charles L. Redman et al., pp. 421–437. New York: Academic Press.

Rabb, L. Mark, et al. 1980. Clients, contracts, and profits: conflicts in public archeology. *American Antiquity* 82:539–551.

Redman, Charles L., et al. (eds.). 1978. *Social Archaeology: Beyond Subsistence and Dating.* New York: Academic Press.

Reidhead, Van A. 1979. Linear programming models in archaeology. *Annual Review of Anthropology* 8:543–578.

Renfrew, Colin (ed.). 1973. *The Explanation of Culture Change: Models in Prehistory.* Pittsburgh: Pittsburgh University Press.

———. 1980. The great tradition versus the great divide: archaeology as anthropology? *American Journal of Archaeology* 84:287–298.

———, and Kenneth L. Cooke (eds.). 1979. *Transformations: Mathematical Approaches to Culture Change.* New York: Academic Press.

Sanders, William T., and Joseph Marino. 1970. *New World Prehistory.* Englewood Cliffs, N.J.: Prentice-Hall.

———, and David Webster. 1978. Unilinealism, multilinealism, and the evolution of complex societies. In *Social Archaeology: Beyond Subsistence and Dating,* ed. Charles L. Redman et al., pp. 249–302. New York: Academic Press.

Schiffer, Michael B. 1976. *Behavioral Archeology.* New York: Academic Press.

———, and George Gummerman (eds.). 1977. *Conservation Archaeology: A Guide for Culture Resource Management Studies.* New York: Academic Press.

Schuyler, Robert L. (ed.). 1978. *Historical Archaeology: A Guide to Substantive and Theoretical Considerations.* Farmingdale, N.Y.: Baywood.

——— (ed.). 1980. *Archaeological Perspectives on Ethnicity in America.* Farmingdale, N.Y.: Baywood.

Service, Elman R. 1962. *Primitive Social Organizations: An Evolutionary Perspective.* 2nd ed., 1971. New York: Random House.

———. 1975. *Origins of the State and Civilization.* New York: Norton.

South, Stanley A. 1977. *Method and Theory in Historical Archeology.* New York: Academic Press.

Spaulding, Albert C. 1973. Archeology in the active voice: the new anthropology. In *Research and Theory in Current Archeology,* ed. Charles L. Redman, pp. 337–354. New York: Wiley.

Spores, Ronald. 1980. New World ethnohistory and archaeology. *Annual Review of Anthropology* 9:575–603.

Steponaitis, V. P. 1978. Location theory and complex chiefdoms: a Mississippian example. In *Mississippian Settlement Patterns,* ed. B. D. Smith, pp. 417–453. New York: Academic Press.

———. 1981. Settlement hierarchies and political complexity in nonmarket societies: the formative period of the Valley of Mexico. *American Anthropologist* 83:320–363.

Steward, Julian H. 1955. *Theory of Culture Change: The Methodology of Multilinear Evolution.* Urbana: University of Illinois Press.

Thompson, John E. S. 1954. *The Rise and Fall of the Maya Civilization.* Norman: University of Oklahoma Press.

Toynbee, Arnold. 1972. *A Study of History,* revised and abridged, with Jane Caplan. New York: Weathervane Books.

Trigger, Bruce G. 1980. Archaeology and the image of the American Indian. *American Antiquity* 45:662–675.

Van der Merwe, N., and J. C. Vogel. 1978. 13C content of human collagen as a measure of prehistoric diet in Woodland North America. *Nature* 276:815–816.

Watson, Patty Jo, Steven A. LeBlanc, and Charles L. Redman. 1971. *Explanation in Archeology: An Explicitly Scientific Approach.* New York: Columbia University Press.

White, Leslie A. 1959. *The Evolution of Culture.* New York: McGraw-Hill.

Willey, Gordon R., and Philip Phillips. 1958. *Method and Theory in American Archaeology.* Chicago: University of Chicago Press.

———, and Jeremy A. Sabloff. 1980. *A History of American Archeology,* 2nd ed. San Francisco: W. H. Freeman and Company.

Wilson, Rex L. 1978. Changing directions in the federal archeology programs. In *Social Archaeology: Beyond Subsistence and Dating,* ed. Charles L. Redman et al., pp. 439–448. New York: Academic Press.

(Courtesy of Donald V. Hague, Director of the Utah Museum of Natural History.)

CHAPTER TWO

Origins

Jesse D. Jennings

Dr. Jennings tells the remarkable story of the slow, inexorable movement of an Asian population into the virgin territory of the two American continents. In a chapter that raises as many questions as it answers, we are introduced to many of the themes that will appear throughout the later chapters—climate, environment, dating, subsistence, technology. Those first people—the Paleo-Indians—began a fascinating chapter in human history; it is appropriate that we should begin this account with them.

At once the most important and the least dramatic event in American history was the passage of the first human from Asia into the New World 30,000 or more years ago. No one knows just when it happened, or exactly where. Nor can one speak with certainty about the physical appearance, weaponry, or clothing of the long-forgotten first American. We do not know what motives led the emigrant eastward. Nor can the conditions that were encountered be readily described except through inference. It is the consideration of such questions, and of others arising out of the search for convincing first answers, that shapes this chapter.

There is no reasonable doubt as to the source of the human population that finally covered the hemisphere; the first American was of Asian stock. Research in biology, language, and archeology demonstrates this; no space need be wasted here in presenting the varied evidence pointing to the one conclusion. It is the timing of the entry that has not yet been determined.

THE FIRST HUMAN ENTRY INTO NORTH AMERICA

Thanks largely to the findings of geologists, we can determine rather closely when human entry *could* have happened and, what is equally important, when it could not. Over the last 40,000 years, conditions would more than once have allowed passage on foot overland where the shallow waters of the Bering and Chukchi seas now separate Asia from North America. A time span so long, of course, goes back deeply into the last major episode of the Pleistocene, or Ice Age. It is widely realized that Ice Age events were never static; they were not merely periods of ice as opposed to periods of no ice. On the contrary, the ice masses, like modern glaciers or ice caps, were dynamic entities. The Greenland ice cap, the interior ice of Iceland, and the enormous Antarctic ice fields today effectively display the dynamic actions—ice currents or rivers, lateral outflow, interior stresses—of the ancient masses. But the short-range studies made possible by modern technology merely report the behavior and internal physical attributes of the ice itself. Our concern here is how the ancient ice mass that covered over half of North America affected that continent and the rest of the world.

To begin, one must note that the Plesitocene, as a major geological epoch, endured for two million years or more—possibly as much as four million. On at least four occasions the high latitudes and high elevations of the world were alternately clear and covered with ice. The formation of the major glaciers and ice caps was evidently rather closely synchronized or simultaneous around the world, including in South America, as were the warmer ice-free periods. As the ice deposits increased in depth or thickness, the ice flowed outward from a center so that the edges advanced and the ice area increased. Similarly, the ice margins retreated as warming conditions melted the ice. The advance–retreat rhythm occurred in response to meteorological and environmental factors not fully understood, but its effects on the world environment are known. One major effect of ice fields around the world, and especially of the ice cap covering all of Canada to a depth of perhaps 3 kilometers, was the locking-up of tens upon tens of thousands of cubic kilometers of water, which lowered the level of the oceans by many meters. Lowering the present sea level by as much as 100 meters would create very different continental outlines, with many now shallowly submerged areas left high above the ocean shores. The Japanese islands, for example, would have been connected to the Asian mainland as the shallow waters of the Yellow and China seas retreated. At the same time, most of the islands of the East Indies (Sumatra, Java, Borneo, and so on) would have been connected to Southeast Asia as the floors of the Jerva Sea and the Gulf of Siam were freed from sea waters.

Of more importance here, however, is the emergence of the floor of today's very shallow Bering and Chukchi seas to form a land bridge over 2000 kilometers in width, at its maximum. This vast area, known as Beringia, provided a wide path into what is now called interior Alaska—a path which was at its widest and *not* ice-covered when the Late Pleistocene ice was at maximum extent. The Beringian avenue was available to East Asians, and to interior Northeast Asian Siberian peoples.

Pleistocene geological history in the Northern hemisphere is thus a history of ice formation and movement and of the climatic, geomorphological, and environmental changes attendant upon the behavior of the ice. The four major ice ages or glacial advances are thought to have lasted for short periods, each measurable probably in thousands of years, whereas the ice-free periods were very lengthy, measurable in tens or hundreds of thousands of years. Of the sequence of ice ages, only the last, or Wisconsin glacial advance, is of interest here.

Thanks to radiocarbon dating, it is possible to fit the events of the Wisconsin stage into a reliable and reasonably tight chronological framework. Because the entire period with its several advance–retreat cycles was short, the last half is well within the range of optimum radiocarbon dating. Although Figure 2.1, derived from Butzer (1971), shows the Wisconsin stage as lasting 60,000 years, some glaciologists would say that the first substage began later than 40,000 BP; the figure shows that there were one major and two minor ice advances between 25,000 and 10,000 years ago. The Bering bridge could have been open for all but about 2000 years of that time. It is even possible that the short retreats climaxing at 14,000 and 10,000 years ago were of lesser magnitude than Figure 2.1 shows and that the land bridge may never entirely have disappeared until after 9,000 or 10,000 BP.

Thus, the time when humans could walk from northeastern Asia into Alaska is set; it was, in fact, almost any time during the Late Pleistocene. Admittedly, the timing is not precise, and an even *earlier* date for the entry is not precluded, though the next oldest emergence of the bridge (an event that occurred dozens of times during the Pleistocene) cannot be bracketed in time with certainty. Such an earlier entry was possible, however, as far back as 65,000 BP. Why are the earlier dates rarely emphasized? The answer is that, as far as archeological knowledge is concerned, human conquest of Northeast Asia occurred *only after* 50,000 to 40,000 BP. If extreme eastern Siberia lacked population until after 40,000 BP, penetration by Asiatic peoples into the New World was clearly impossible. However, farther south the caves of Pekin have yielded specimens of Erectus and Neanderthal variants of *Homo sapiens*. The possibility of immigration from the Pekin area toward Beringia must therefore not be overlooked. For the moment, however, a late Wisconsin date of 30,000 BP comfortably accommodates, by antedating, all persuasive evidence of Paleo-Indian presence in the Americas. Although claims for earlier incidents of entry abound, the supporting data are incomplete or weak in other ways. However, acceptable demonstrations of earlier arrivals can be expected as the search for ever-earlier sites continues.

Total certainty is also not possible about the first human point of entry. Although the route out of Asia into the American continent is generally accepted as being across Beringia, through the Alaskan Refuge, and thence southward between the flanks of the Cordilleran and Laurentide glacial masses, another school of thought also exists. Although we have no extensive information about the nature of the inter-ice terrain where the inland corridor would have lain, opponents of the route often argue that it must have been swampy, studded with lakes in summer, and gripped by permafrost in winter. The game in such surroundings, they suggest, would not have been plentiful, nor the hunting prospects necessarily inviting, nor travel easy except perhaps in winter.

The alternative, of course, is a coastal water route. To such there also are

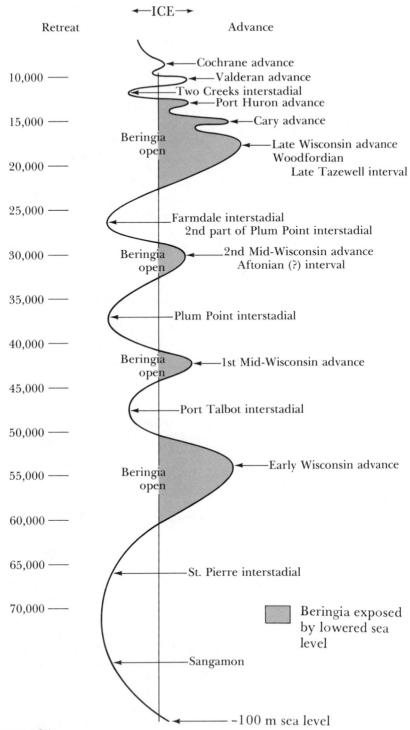

FIGURE 2.1
Ice advance-and-retreat rhythm during the Wisconsin stage of the Pleistocene, in years BP.

objections, the main one being that use of a coastal or open-ocean entry route would require some kind of open-water voyaging capabilities earlier by thousands of years than most archeologists believe they existed. And, since to posit the coastal route requires more unproved but interlocking assumptions than the overland route requires, the coastal alternate has attracted no great following. Knut Fladmark (1978, 1979) has for years been one of the most insistent advocates of a coastal entry. Basing his arguments on some recent geological findings, he identifies a series of West Coast sea-level refugia and assesses the possibility of "refuge hopping" from the Aleutian Islands to Juan de Fuca Strait, Cape Flattery, and Puget Sound as easy and likely. Even if we accept the existence of unglaciated refugia, the requirement of water-transport capability among Paleolithic cultures remains the crucial part of Fladmark's argument. But the sea route need not even be invoked as long as the frequent long-term availability of an overland alternate route is a tenable supposition. Moreover, the patchwork of geological and biological evidence supporting the hypothesized chain of refugia remains unconvincing. Although his ideas will not be utilized here, one cannot deny Fladmark's charge that land-locked American scholars rarely look at either the ocean or the beaches and are, in consequence, highly myopic as to even the possibilities of a sea-borne passage, a long trek along the beaches, or a combination of these approaches in the first settlement of the West Coast.

THE EARLY NORTH AMERICAN ENVIRONMENT

The Pleistocene

Next we will review the environment that the newly arrived immigrants faced. The weather, the vegetation, and the faunal resources of Beringia and the Refuge would have been identical with those of northeastern Siberia. The climate would have been quite cold and therefore dry. The floral community could be described as a desert steppe, composed largely of grasses and sagebrush; most likely it was a mosaic, or a mix of steppe, tundra, and arctic savanna, a reconstruction increasingly supported by pollen analyses (Graham, 1979). Moreover, the paleontological finds show that the major fauna were, as might be expected, steppe species. The dominant animals were the mammoth, bison, horse, and giant antelope, all of which required heavy forage; horse and bison, of course, are herd animals requiring open country. There were tundra-dwelling caribou and musk oxen as well. By sharing the same environment with Siberia, Beringia and the Refuge would impose neither adaptive stresses nor environmental constraints on the vanguard of the migrants. On the contrary, the same cold and dry conditions existed in both areas, and, more important, an obstacle-free route lay open toward the south.

For arrival in Alaska was just a beginning. Although early immigrants would have found the way eastward blocked by Laurentide ice east of the McKenzie River, it lay open to the south after about 25,000 BP. The ice of the Cordilleran and Laurentide glaciers was, after about 40,000 BP, less massive and probably did not overlap east of the Canadian Rocky Mountains. Moreover, the advances of the masses were evidently not synchronous. Palynological evidence indicates that vegetation of generally steppe–tundra type grew in the ice-free passageway for at least 25,000 years. (There is, however, evidence that the passage closed briefly at about 14,000 BP.) As yet fossil faunal data have been found at only two stations. The first is at Medicine Hat, Alberta, where mammoth, horse, camel, dire wolf, and saber-toothed cat remains—estimated to date from 17,000 BP—were recovered from between two deposits of Laurentide tills (glacial drifts of mixed stones, soil, and sand). The other location is at the Old Crow Basin in eastern Alaska, where a similar inventory of fauna has been recovered from numerous localities (see Figure 2.2).

With the gross environment already identified at the point of entry from the corridor, the next question is: What were conditions like to the south of the ice during the Late Pleistocene? West of the Mississippi Valley, the environment was not greatly different from today's, although at the glacier edges there still would have been mixed steppe–tundra or forest (see Figure 2.3). Vegetation is, of course, the clue to animal species and vice versa, as we have seen. As Figure 2.3 shows, today's succession of continental biologic zones prevailed 15,000 to 10,000 years ago; they were, however, much compressed. In the critical millennia between 20,000 and 10,000 years ago when the ice was achieving its final maximum, the plains, much smaller than today, were not a sea of grass but an even richer savanna, a grassland studded with clumps of trees. We have seen, of course, that prairie existed at the mouth of the corridor by 12,500 BP. Between the tundra at the edge of the ice and the steppe or plains vegetation in the Southwest lay a zone of coniferous forest or taiga and steppe.

Moreover, the entire southern third of the continent was well watered. Springs, streams, and lakes were abundant. An example is the high Llano Estacado of west Texas. Convincing if quite controversial studies of this region show that the flora consisted in large part of conifers (spruce and pine) during the Tahoka pluvial, which was a period of markedly cooler and moister climate lasting from about 23,000 to 16,000 BP. Fossil lakes (recognizable today as dry playas) and stream courses (now dry) testify to a formerly well-watered land. In central and east Texas, what is now grassland is described as having been an open woodland deciduous forest with an understory of grasses, herbs, and shrubs until about 16,000 BP. At the same time, between the pine–spruce forests of the Llano Estacado and the mixed woodlands of east Texas, there lay a broad belt of juniper and piñon parkland. Thereafter, many arboreal species disappeared, so that woodlands became parklands. By 6000 BP, the treeless plains of today had come into being over most of Texas.

Nothing has yet been said about the country east of the Mississippi River and south of the Canadian ice. The contrasts between today and 20,000–12,000 BP

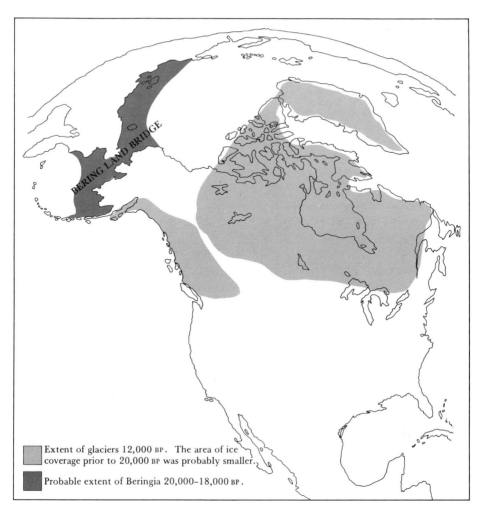

Extent of glaciers 12,000 BP. The area of ice coverage prior to 20,000 BP was probably smaller.

Probable extent of Beringia 20,000–18,000 BP.

FIGURE 2.2
Beringia and the distribution of glacial ice.

are far more extreme than in the western two-thirds of the United States just examined. At the greatest extent of the ice there were no Great Lakes, no New England states, and no New York City. Ice covered all. The Blue Ridge Mountains of Appalachia were covered with tundra, and caribou fed in the Shenandoah Valley. Owl-roost pellets found in the same valley contain bones of such subarctic creatures as the arctic shrew, the pine marten, and the arctic hare. At the Saltville, Virginia, bone bed, dated at 13,400 BP, there were caribou, moose, bison, musk oxen, mammoth, and mastodon; the most numerous bones were of mastodon.

When the last retreat of the ice began, it progressed rapidly. By about 10,500

32

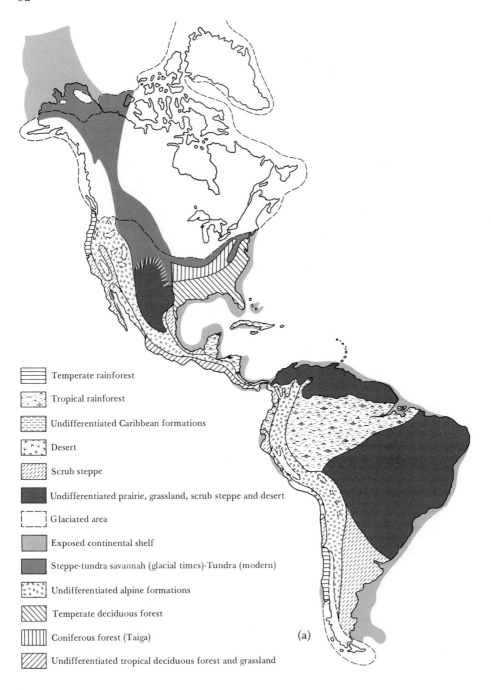

Temperate rainforest

Tropical rainforest

Undifferentiated Caribbean formations

Desert

Scrub steppe

Undifferentiated prairie, grassland, scrub steppe and desert

Glaciated area

Exposed continental shelf

Steppe-tundra savannah (glacial times)-Tundra (modern)

Undifferentiated alpine formations

Temperate deciduous forest

Coniferous forest (Taiga)

Undifferentiated tropical deciduous forest and grassland

(a)

FIGURE 2.3
Glacial (a) and modern (b) environments.

(b)

BP Labrador was free of ice. Spruce trees were gone from the Virginia hills and the forests of modern times were taking shape. Now-extinct mastodon and giant elk still roamed the Middle West and the East, but most of the eastern fauna—especially that sought by humans—belonged to modern species.

The world the newcomers faced south of the ice was therefore familiar, and they could exploit its resources with their imported technology as long as they stayed in the steppe–tundra mosaic. In view of the distribution of early human sites, and of the fact that elephant and bison require coarse grasses and sedges, one must conclude that between 15,000 and 10,000 BP what is today the northern Plains area was not taiga but much more open, with grassy, parklike vegetation between scattered clumps of conifers. The presence of spruce is amply documented by a spate of pollen studies from Texas to Wyoming (see Wright, 1970). The forest fringing the ice was probably not typical of areas where fauna is scarce. More likely the forest was an open woodland offering an easy transition from the steppe–tundra to the grasslands, where long-horned bison and elephants (southern species rather than those found in the Arctic) were available, as they were in the Middle West and Southeast.

In concluding the consideration of the Pleistocene environment, I must emphasize that this description of broad continental conditions is supported by hundreds of detailed studies (in palynology, plant macrofossils, and so on) of small areas or even single locations and can be accepted as correctly presenting the gross facts about climate and food resources. Thus, the environment was arctic in Beringia and Alaska, as well as along all the upper tier of states in the United States, until about 12,000 BP. The situation would favor or even enforce a hunting economy; evidence of the gathering of vegetable foods is minimal until after 9000 or 8000 BP.

The Holocene

EAST OF THE ROCKIES □ After 12,000 BP, environmental changes were rapid, even extreme. The changes in climate were those one would expect to be correlated with withdrawal and final disappearance of the continental ice (except for local mountain glaciers and the Greenland ice sheet). There was a warming trend and a reduction of overall available moisture. The reduction in moisture can be linked to a northward shifting of the west-to-east cyclonic belt–jet stream and to the resultant gradual warming. Vegetation followed the ice edge as ground and air temperatures rose; precipitation, in general, decreased.

One of the most interesting single papers on the paleoclimates of the Holocene is by Bryson, Baerreis, and Wendland (1970). Using data from radiocarbon-dated organic matter associated with geological events and paleosoils, palynology, and modern weather records, they present a dramatic graphic summary of the northward retreat of the ice and the summer–winter frontal zones of storm paths and of the concomitant shift of vegetational zones (Figure 2.4).

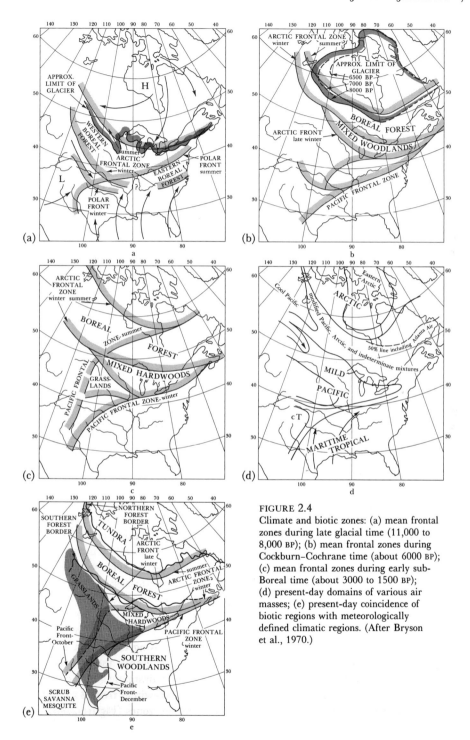

FIGURE 2.4
Climate and biotic zones: (a) mean frontal zones during late glacial time (11,000 to 8,000 BP); (b) mean frontal zones during Cockburn–Cochrane time (about 6000 BP); (c) mean frontal zones during early sub-Boreal time (about 3000 to 1500 BP); (d) present-day domains of various air masses; (e) present-day coincidence of biotic regions with meteorologically defined climatic regions. (After Bryson et al., 1970.)

Moreover, the three men discovered from radiocarbon dates that on several occasions significant environmental change was linked to quick transitions in quasi-steady regional or continental climates. The point is that there was not a gradual or complacent linear progression of climatic change for the Holocene period. Rather, the climatic and biotic changes were swift and abrupt, or step-like. The concepts of steps and quasi-steady states are very useful for archeologists in their attempts to explain apparently sudden cultural changes. We may be sure, for example, that the expansion of the small grassland area of 12,000 BP to more or less its present range, which happened over about 1000 years, accounts for the wide distribution of the long-horned bison.

The climatic episodes listed in Figure 2.1 bespeak fluctuating climates with effective moisture differences. The general trend, however, from the end of the Wisconsin stage until today has been toward less effective moisture for the Plains and western North America (see Jennings, 1978). Many intensive microclimatic studies of small research areas (such as O'Connell, 1975) tend to confirm the broader-based studies (see, for example, Bryson et al., 1970).

All the evidence indicates that the Paleo-Indians were hunters of big animals, some now extinct, such as the caribou, mammoth, musk ox, and long-horned bison. In the limited southern plains or savannas of 12,000 to 10,000 years ago, there were mammoths, camelids, horses, tapirs, dire wolves, and other now-extinct animals such as peccary and a giant armadillo. In the Great Basin there were giant ground sloths, but firm evidence that they were preyed upon by humans is lacking. All the other animals cited above were hunted, however, where they occurred.

DISAPPEARANCE OF THE MEGAFAUNA ☐ Mention of the megafauna always raises the question of their extinction. Why are there none left? This reasonable query remains unanswered, although it has been much thought and speculated upon.

The factual evidence is that elephant extinction was rapid, with long-horned bison (*B. antiquus*) disappearing next. All the other species cited in the preceding paragraphs seem to have disappeared at about the same time or a little later than the *Bison antiquus*. Thus, after about 8000 BP the megafauna consisted of a somewhat smaller bison (*B. occidentalis*) and modern species—pronghorn antelope, elk, deer, mountain sheep, and goats. The latter were animals that thrived in both the vast reaches of the Plains and in the expanding woodlands, necessitating modified or new procurement techniques. The smaller modern bison (*B. bison*) appeared much later.

One favorite and common-sense explanation for the megafauna's disappearance is that the changing climates and rapid changes in vegetation mentioned earlier changed the regional habitat so greatly that it no longer favored several species. Reduction or disappearance of the late Wisconsin water resources would have rapidly reduced the amount of coarse grasses and reeds available for the elephant bands. For such species, adaptation to a plains or desert ecobase is impossible: the elephant population dwindled and disappeared about 11,200 years ago. The big-horned bison held on longer, but they too were gone by about 9500 to 9000 years BP.

Another cause advanced to explain the extinctions is again a biological one. In the face of worsening climate and resultant increased stress, the elephants perhaps dropped below the critical biological mass—that is, the necesary number of individuals—required for herd protection from such nonhuman predators as saber-tooth tigers. Still more important, the rate of reproduction may have fallen below the rate of naturally occurring deaths. A minus birth rate would have assured disappearance of the species at a very rapid rate.

Disease has also been invoked as a cause. But the perennially favorite explanation, most recently espoused by Martin (1973), is that the human hunter, history's most efficient predator, administered the coup-de-grace through a phenomenon called *overkill*. This term means merely that the kill rate exceeded the regenerative capacity of the species. If all or some of the causes advanced above were operative, the overkill toll could well have been the final push to extinction. Grayson (1980) has carefully reviewed the history of the theories of extinction; he finds none convincing. His article is recommended to anyone interested in the history of ideas.

But all these explanations of megafaunal extinctions overlook the well-documented fact that the end of the Pleistocene was marked all over the world by extinctions. Many species simply died out. The disappearance of horses and camels in North America offers an example. One can get caught up in speculation on this matter, but evidence is lacking. What we have documented is drastic climate change; to this event we need only add the presence of human bands and the fact of rapid extinction. Of far greater interest to students of human history is the culture change that followed the climate changes and game losses. To such students, the reasons for the loss of the species are a peripheral matter; what interests archeologists are the human adaptations that were made necessary by the fact of extinction.

WEST OF THE ROCKIES □ The preceding sections, of course, are concerned entirely with the Plains and the eastern woodlands. A series of entirely different events characterized the third of the continent west of the Rocky Mountains. The largest physiographic–climatic–environmental province in the West is the Great Basin. There the evidence of an early moister regime is indisputable and widespread. Prior to 14,000–12,000 BP the entire West was characterized by large lakes and many swampy areas. Evidence about water resources is best defined in the Great Basin because the area lacks external drainage. The overall vegetable resources, however, were the same 12,000 or 14,000 years BP as they are today. The same can be said for the biotic environment, which can be generalized as a dry steppe. The dominant vegetation was sagebrush (*Artemisia*), with juniper-piñon communities on the many short north-south-trending mountain ranges—a topographic feature lacking in the rest of the continent. Above the juniper–piñon forests were stands of spruce, fir, and pine. The entire region, however, was much richer than is usually believed in subsistence resources for humans because of the vast lakes and attendant aquatic vegetation, animal life, and water fowl.

By 12,000 BP the megafauna used by humans was evidently the modern species known today. Although mammoth, horse, and camel fossils have been found, no association with humans has yet been suggested. Thus we have, over most of the West and exemplified in the Great Basin, the anomaly of a semi-desert studded with rich and concentrated subsistence resources uncharacteristic of the entire Plains area to the east. As will be apparent in later chapters, this desert environment had important implications for the cultural history of the area; human adaptation there to a series of specialized econiches was quite different than in the East. The evidence is, however, that the Great Basin was occupied well-nigh simultaneously with the rest of the continent.

PHYSICAL TYPE OF THE EARLY AMERICANS

Assuming that the time of human entry, the climatic control of the passage over Beringia to what is now the United States, and the sequence of changing environments at the conclusion of the Pleistocene have now been documented sufficiently—if not in great detail—we must now consider a new topic, the physical attributes and appearance of the first Americans. Again, probabilities rather than certainties must be invoked. Although today's descendants of the founding population—the American Indians—are recognized as a distinctive and unique population, Indians are believed to have achieved their distinctiveness on the American continent itself. While the Asiatic affiliation of the American Indians is recognized, no one would describe them today as an Asiatic group. Several authorities point out, for example, that the first immigrants must have been an exceedingly hardy and viable small group, or series of small groups, who had survived the rigorous screening of the Arctic environment. Thus there would have been a very small gene pool, and the distinctive American Indian attributes would have developed through normal genetic processes, operating in isolation and without significant genetic increments after about 10,000 BP. As summarized from several sources in Jennings (1974b:56), the modern American Indian can be described as

> being of stocky rather than gracile build, regardless of overall stature which may be either short or tall. The stockiness applies to both sexes. The extent of skin pigmentation is less than seen in the Old World but the ability to tan is exceptionally high. The eyes are dark. The hair is coarse and straight, and body hair is scant in both sexes. Females often have the Mongoloid fold. Incisor teeth are distinct in the frequency of the shovel-shape. Blood types A^2, B, D^u, and r are lacking. The sickle cell anomaly is not found in Indian blood. The Indian male is rarely bald and rarely becomes grey in old age.

Moreover, Indians are extremely susceptible to common Eurasiatic diseases, such as the common cold, measles, and tuberculosis. Their complete lack of immunity to these diseases is regarded as further evidence of their long period of isolation from the Old World.

Archeologists have to date found few skeletons of the ancestors of the American Indians. Persuasive arguments as to their probable appearance, however, have been provided by several authors. From his studies of modern Asian populations, Birdsell proposes that the first Americans can be described as generalized primitive Caucasoids, who were pushed farther and farther into the Arctic by increasing population pressures in Eurasia. It is true that occupancy of the Arctic zone can be demonstrated only for the Middle and Late Wisconsin periods. This early *Homo sapiens* Birdsell (1951) calls *Amurian*. The enclaved Ainu of Japan would be "living fossil" representatives of this strain. The latest fossil *Homo sapiens* at the famous Pekin site would be Amurian in type, as would the first Americans. Birdsell also suggests that the Mongoloid strain had begun to evolve and that the Amurian group entering the New World might have had an infusion of these new Mongoloid genes.

Birdsell's entirely theoretical proposal is fully congruent with the conclusions reached by Neumann, whose interest in the original population was expressed in a more empirical manner. Neumann (1952) studied skeletal collections from early American sites on the assumption that skeletons recovered from a single site representing a short period of occupancy would constitute an essentially homogeneous population. He concluded that there had been eight sequential population types over the last 10,000 years. Only the first two types are of significance here. The oldest Neumann calls *Otamid,* the next oldest *Iswanid.* He, too, sees similarities between the Otamid and the latest skeletal material from Pekin. The Otamid skull is long, of moderate height, with heavy supraorbital ridges that have a slight swelling or bun-shaped occipital morphology. He describes the body build as slender and gracile, the stature as short. Stewart (1973), in another study, also allied the early Americans with the late *Homo sapiens* specimens from the Pekin locality. In connection with physical type, Kennedy (see MacNeish, 1978) views the putatively early California skulls as closely resembling the Cro-Magnon of Europe. Not too different from Birdsell's view is Neel's (see MacNeish, 1978) opinion that the earliest Americans were primitive Caucasoids who later blended with classic Mongoloids.

In a restudy of Neumann's data, Long (1966) does not entirely agree with the Otamid reconstruction but asserts that the Iswanid is a valid physical type and exists as a "basic and widespread group [from] archaic to historical times." In his study Long goes on to emphasize that the American Indian physical type resulted from microevolutionary genetic factors. He hypothesizes that the American Indian developed from a small original population rather than in a series of continuous increments. Of course, none of these authors are concerned with the later, documented entry of the Aleutian, Eskimo, and Deneid populations. In the absence of better data, we will assume here that the founding New

World population consisted of Asiatic *Homo sapiens* of Caucasoid–Mongoloid mixture and that the American Indian physical type evolved in the New World in response to a variety of environments and evolutionary processes.

Despite the scholars' assertions reviewed in the preceding paragraphs, we have but few ancient skeletal sources of information. The first of the early human remains that seems credible is a find, reported by Wendorf et al. (1955), from Midland, Texas. Although the specimen was discovered on the surface of a deep and extensive blowout in a cluster of dunes near Midland, the geological circumstances, carefully researched by the study team, make the find credible. The specimen is 10,000 or more years old and fits the Otamid description convincingly. The skull is that of a young female, described as having a slight and gracile body; the skull itself is long, highly vaulted, and even possesses the specified occipital bun. Many other finds have been described and claims for extreme age made about them, but in all cases there is doubt as to the exact provenience or the geological or cultural association. These other specimens include the Tepexpan find near Mexico City, the Santa Barbara skull from California, and the Minnesota woman, as well as several others. Ages of 40,000 and 50,000 years are being claimed for several skeletons in southern California. These claims, although they have attracted much attention, must be disregarded until the dating technique used—one based on bone-acid racemization (reversal of protein polarity)—is better understood (Von Endt, 1979).

EARLY TECHNOLOGY

Even more vexing than the problem of physical type is the question of the tool kit and of the overall technology possessed by early humans in America. It is obvious that this technology was suitable for an arctic environment and the taking of big game. Very likely, tailored skin clothing was standard. Presumably the stone tool kit would have been Asiatic in all respects, but no definitive statements can yet be made about the nature of the stone tools with which other utensils and tools were fabricated. Krieger (1964) has long contended that there was a well-developed technology, which he characterizes as the preprojectile stage. Certainly this hypothesis is compatible with the Asiatic evidence, particularly that from Siberia and northeastern Asia. Unfortunately, none of the complexes Krieger defines occur in well-controlled circumstances: most are surface finds and cannot be assigned either a geological or chronological age. Hence, Krieger's views have yet to prevail.

A primary reason that nothing definitive can yet be said about the tool kit and technology of the first Americans lies in an assumption made at the beginning of prehistoric studies, that whatever tools the earliest Americans were using would have been Asiatic imports. This assumption comes down to the idea that the fluted-point technology associated with the Folsom and Clovis finds would, of course, have had Asiatic prototypes. The truth is, no such prototypes have been found. The scholars may not even be worrying about the right questions. What we need to know is: What was the tool kit possessed by the Asian emigrants at 25,000, 30,000, or even 35,000 years ago?

A European scholar, Müller-Beck, may have provided a reasonable answer. His views are several years old; they were first published in 1966 and 1967, before any of the several American sites older than 12,000 BP were discovered or reported. In 1967 his scheme ran against popular thought, but today it seems more persuasive in the light of some of the very finds discussed below. In brief, Müller-Beck derives North American tool kits from earlier Eurasiatic Paleolithic tool assemblages: it is as simple as that. He defines American tools as *Mousteroid*—that is, technologically similar to products of the European Mousterian culture (the archeological type associated with the Neanderthal). At no point is he saying that the Mousterian of Europe entered North America, merely that the technological, technical, or typological complex he is discussing resembles the Mousterian complex so well known to European scholars. The Mousteroid flint-working style, or base, is characterized by tools with bifacially chipped blades or points, by a big industry in prismatic flake knives, and by the use of unmodified flat flakes for cutting and scraping. Together these traits comprise a readily recognizable complex.

After examining many collections in Asia and the United States, Müller-Beck estimated that this complex appeared in the New World by 30,000 years ago. His map (Figure 2.5b) shows the Mousteroid tradition through Alaska and down into the northern Plains by 28,000–26,000 BP. The next two maps (Figure 2.5c and 2.5d) show the distribution of the bifacially chipped cultural kit all over North America, south of Canada, by 10,000 BP. However, a later Paleolithic complex had also spread over Siberia and into Beringia by 11,000–12,000 BP. In order to distinguish this later complex from the technologically different Mousteroid, Müller-Beck calls it *Aurignacoid*, because it is reminiscent of the Aurignacian of Central Europe. It is characterized by slotted bone knives, polyhedral (many-sided) cores, arrows, harpoon heads, microflint tools, and narrow burin types.

There is also the matter of Diuktai Cave, and the so-called Diuktai culture of eastern Siberia, found along the Aldan River (35,000 to 12,500 BP) from Ezhantsy to Diuktai. The upper layers of this cave, dating to 12,690 ± 120 BP, have yielded an assortment of flakes, but bifacially chipped, triangular, leaf-shaped, and oval blades are also numerous in the large collections. Mochanov (1978) and others suggest that the terminal Diuktai sequence in the cave may provide the prototypical Aurignacoid artifacts from which the beautifully made, bifacially chipped tools of the American Paleo-Indian evolved. But the terminal Diuktai dates are only a few years older than the fluted American points, so the timing may render this argument futile.

Thus, to date, most authors continue to see well-chipped fluted points as uniquely American forms. That view has been reinforced by Dumond (1980), who combed the Alaskan literature to demonstrate that while the tool traditions

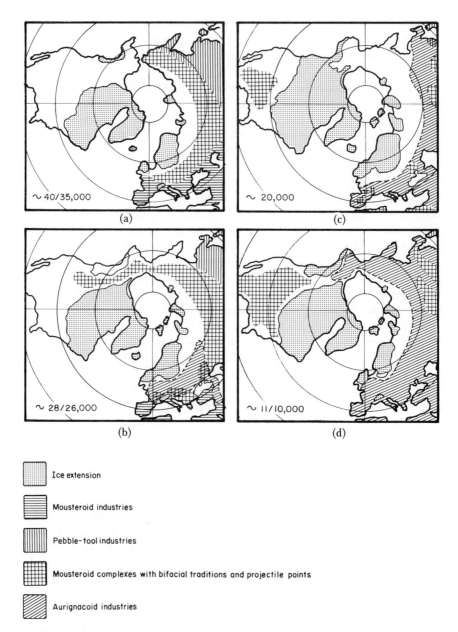

(a)   ~ 40/35,000

(c)   ~ 20,000

(b)   ~ 28/26,000

(d)   ~ 11/10,000

Ice extension

Mousteroid industries

Pebble-tool industries

Mousteroid complexes with bifacial traditions and projectile points

Aurignacoid industries

FIGURE 2.5
Distribution of Moustero–Aurignacoid cultures during late Wisconsin times: (a) at the end of the
Middle Upper Pleistocene; (b) at transition between Middle and Late Neo-Pleistocene; (c) at
maximum ice extension in Late Neo-Pleistocene; (d) at the end of the Late Upper Pleistocene, in
years BP. (After Müller-Beck, 1966.)

of the Alaskan cultures, after 11,000 BP, produced microlithic small cores and flakes, burins, and occasional bifacially chipped blades obviously derived from Asia, these traditions had no link with those of the early hunters to the south.

The Aurignacoid nature of the Alaskan cultures after 11,000 BP is thus made clear by Dumond, although he does not utilize the term *Aurignacoid* suggested by Müller-Beck. However, Chard (1974), in his summary of the prehistory of northeastern Asia, did use *Aurignacoid* as a meaningful term in his analysis of the later Paleolithic cultures of Japan. In a general way Müller-Beck would identify the Paleo-Indians and the later American Indian complexes found south of Canada as both derived from the Mousteroid complex. The modern cultures most closely allied to the succeeding Aurignacoid complex would be the Eskimos and Aleuts of Alaska today.

PERIODS OF EARLY HUMAN PRESENCE

Although Müller-Beck's ideas promise a solution, it is clear that we cannot at this moment determine the origin of the earliest Paleo-Indian tool kit. Thus, we had best move on to consider the evidence we do have for human presence in the New World. The scheme offered by MacNeish (1978) has attracted some attention but should be rejected because its chronological span is extravagantly long and because the validity of many sites he discusses is open to serious challenge. MacNeish has recognized these problems. Instead, we will use here Haynes' (1969) more conservative and simpler scheme. Haynes has devised a three-period scheme to which the chronology outlined in the opening paragraphs of this article is keyed. The early period would fall before 30,000 years BP; the middle one terminates at 12,000 BP; and the late one extends from 12,000 to 7,000 or 8,000 BP. Although there are no archeological sites that can be safely ascribed to the early period, Haynes, along with many students, evidently thinks that acceptable evidence of human occupancy earlier than 30,000 BP will one day develop. For the middle period there are only a few convincing locations, which will be dealt with shortly. About the late period there is no doubt, since abundant evidence exists of human activity on the continent at that time. We will now review some of the key locations where evidence of human occupation at these three periods has been encountered.

Early Period

Haynes' early period is, as indicated, as yet unsupported by reliable evidence. One location where much excavation has been carried on—the Calico Hills near Yerma, California—has been advanced as belonging to this little-known time. Simpson and Leakey recovered much flaked chert from this area, a very small percentage of which they identified subjectively as formed by human workmanship. One can agree that the selected flakes, if found in a site with recognizable, unquestioned chipped-flint artifacts, would pass as debris. However, the scores of professional archeologists and geologists who viewed the specimens and the location of discovery during an invitational site visit in 1970 were highly skeptical that the site gave evidence of human occupation. The most compelling reasons for doubt are that (1) there were no acceptable archeological finds (charcoal, hearths, or recognizable artifacts), and (2) the geological formation containing the specimens is probably of pre-Wisconsin age. Haynes (1973) has dealt with these discrepancies by unequivocally rejecting the evidence, as do I.

A number of other claims have been made for early-period sites, none of which need be taken seriously as yet because of flaws or inadequacies in the evidence or the record. This list includes the Taber child locations in Canada at 40,000 to 60,000 BP, the Yuha Desert and Los Angeles burials ranging from 17,000 to 22,000 BP, the Santa Barbara Island finds ranging from about 25,000 to 35,000 BP, and several South American finds. I would emphasize that the sites are *not* viewed skeptically here because of the ascribed ages. The problems lie in inadequate reporting or vague descriptions of the details of the finding or in other such deficiencies in the controls. When such problems combine with claims of extreme age, most scholars tend to maintain a conservative, "wait and see," position as is done here. The Yuha cairn burial case, for example, is completely obscured by controversy over the accuracy or usefulness of the chemical tests of age and by inadequate excavation procedures. Moreover, the archeological attributes of this burial style led Wilke (1978) to ascribe an age of 4000–5000 BP. He completely rejects the claims of the proponents—who are not archeologists (Bischoff et al., 1978). As a believable find, the Yuha burial simply does not measure up on the evidence presented to date.

Middle Period

For Haynes' middle period, at least five North American locations fit the criteria of archeological control, proper radiocarbon age, *and,* in some cases, the Mousteroid affinities of the few artifacts (such as utilized prismatic flakes). These sites are: Old Crow site in Alaska; the Fort Rock caves, Fort Rock Valley, Oregon; Wilson Butte Cave, Idaho; Shriver site, Missouri; and Meadowcroft Shelter, Pennsylvania. Numerous South American locations also fall late in the middle period or at its terminal boundary. There are also questionable claims for several locations in Mexico, but for one reason or another each of them has been challenged as unproved.

The earliest of the North American locations is Old Crow Flats, located on the Porcupine River at the extreme eastern edge of the Alaskan Refuge area. Irving and Harrington (1973) have issued a preliminary report. The site is a rich Pleistocene fossil bed at a locality labeled 14N. The bones in the bed appear

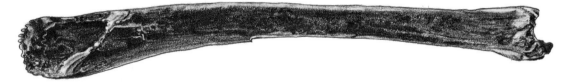

FIGURE 2.6
Fleshing tool from Old Crow Flats.

to have been redeposited on a streamside bar. Transport distance, however, was short; the bones are not battered or water-worn. They are now covered by many feet of alluvial sediment. The excavators recovered from the bone bed a well-made caribou bone flesher and two mammoth bones which apparently were deliberately crushed or flaked when green. The flesher (see Figure 2.6) is remarkably modern in appearance, and there is no doubt that it is a tool created by human hands. Its age is 27,000 ± 3,000 BP. The age is from radiocarbon dating of apatite derived from the tool itself. The mammoth bones are of the same age. Although no stonework was present, one has no hesitancy in accepting this find as authentic.

Equally authentic, but more informative as to stone tools, is Meadowcroft Shelter near Avella in eastern Pennsylvania (Adovasio, 1975). The deposits in the shelter are colluvial in origin. The site lies alongside, and well above, Cross Creek, a tributary of the Ohio River. Although occupancy was more or less continuous, the concern here is only with stratum IIa. One date ascribed to this layer comes from charcoal found in the lowest firepit in the stratum. The other date is from a carbonized fragment of simple plaited basketry made from what appears to be birch bark. The dates are 19,650 ± 2400 and 19,150 ± 800 BP. There is a lower stratum (I), from which only charcoal has been recovered; its dates run from 37,000 to 21,500 BP. No cultural material such as chipped flint has yet been recovered from stratum I. From stratum IIa, however, have come three prismatic flakes, one chipped biface, and one "Mungai" knife, which can be described as a retouched, flat prismatic flake. These artifacts are shown in Figure 2.7. The objects, except for the prismatic flaked knife, resemble other Paleo-Indian finds from the Fort Rock Cave, Shriver, and Wilson Butte sites. However, the prismatic blades and the "Mungai" knife are similar to finds from both Blackwater Draw and the Lindenmeier location. The Meadowcroft evidence lends credence to some of Krieger's attributions of sites to his preprojectile stage. The Meadowcroft site was evidently excavated with extreme care and is the most convincing of the middle-period sites reported to date. It can be taken as establishing beyond reasonable debate the existence of a human population south of the ice toward the close of this period. Although the Meadowcroft evidence is deemed acceptable here, Haynes (1980) has alleged that carbon samples used in the radiocarbon assay were probably contaminated and the

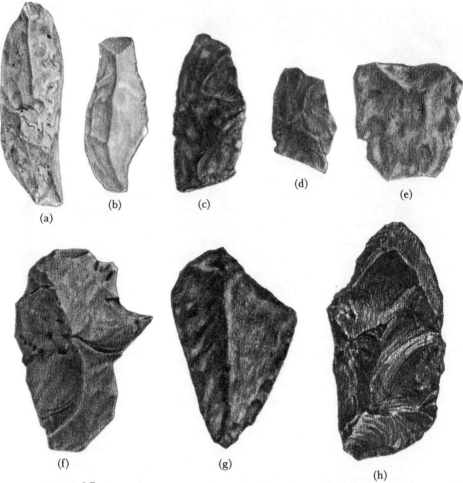

FIGURE 2.7
Representative artifacts from the lowest cultural stratum at Meadowcroft Shelter: (a–c) prismatic blades; (d–f) flaking detritus; (g) "Mungai" knife; (h) biface. (After Adovasio, 1975.)

results therefore erroneous. Adovasio et al. (1980) have offered an adequate response to Haynes' caveat.

Another source of evidence about the middle period are the flint-tool collections and the circumstances at the Shriver site in Missouri. Although reported in only a preliminary way (Reagan et al., 1978) the site, an open location, is important for two reasons. It contains a buried Paleo-Indian occupation that is equated on stylistic grounds with the Folsom Paleo-Indian phase. Beneath this deposit, however, lay an unfamiliar congeries of chert objects characterized as unifacial flake tools, derived from prepared cores of tortoise and tabular forms.

cm

FIGURE 2.8
A sample of stone tools from the Shriver site. (From Reagan et al., 1978.)

The authors describe the tools as not classifiable within the existing topological categories used by American archeologists. Unfortunately, neither the pre-Paleo-Indian nor the possible Folsom-phase collections here were associated with datable organic material. An effort to date the chert by thermoluminescence, a technique not fully refined or controlled and whose limitations are not altogether understood, did yield dates of about 10,700 ± 1000 BP for the Folsom finds, and about 13,000 ± 1500 BP for the lowest layer. These dates must be regarded as no more than reasonable estimates that agree "with the geologic stratigraphic correlation hypothesized for the region." However, the artifacts tend to inspire confidence in the 13,000 BP date ascribed to the lowest or "Shriver" complex, because the Shriver artifacts, like those from other locations yielding pre-12,000 BP dates, are amorphous flakes showing direct use as cutting/scraping tools and possible occasional deliberate retouching (see Figure 2.8).

Without putting undue emphasis on the matter just yet, it is necessary to mention the increasing interest in the possibility of a pre-lithic or pre-Clovis bone tool industry. (The Clovis people were early mammoth hunters.) As more Paleo-Indian kill sites are discovered and excavated, more bones evidently fractured "to a pattern" are being reported. Usually these are the strong, massive leg

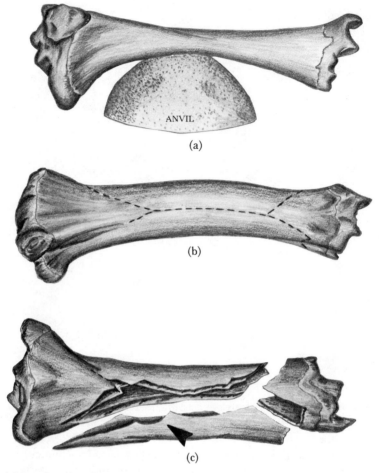

(a)

(b)

(c)

FIGURE 2.9
Bovid tibia before and after spiral fracture: (a) arrow marks impact point;
(b) dotted lines indicate fracture on dorsal side; (c) exploded ventral view of tibia—
note the curved indentation and obtuse angle at impact point (indicated by arrow
pointer). (After Bonnichsen, 1978.)

bones of elephants, horses, or bison. They are considered "expediency" tools for
one-time use in butchering game and are not to be confused with the cylindrical
bone or ivory rods or points widely associated with the Clovis fluted points and
other tools.

The fragments are created by striking one of the long leg bones a heavy blow
at about the middle of the shaft. The blow results in a spiral fracture that
produces two bone pieces that are called "choppers" and are thought to be used
in dismembering a carcass; one piece at least will have a sharp, pointed end (see
Figures 2.9, 2.10). Sharp-edged splinters are also formed; these are called

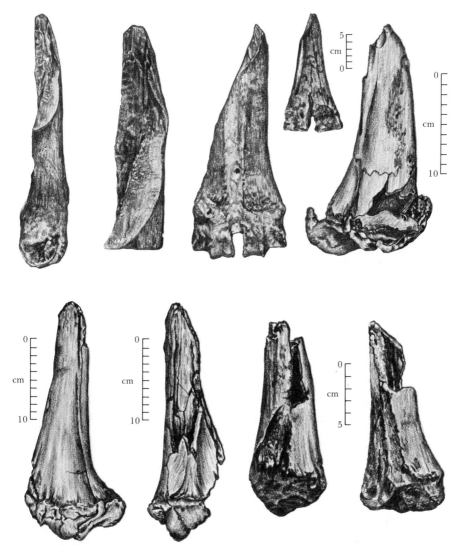

FIGURE 2.10
Distal long bone choppers. (After Stanford, 1979, and Frison, 1978.)

"knives" and can be sharpened by removing flakes just as can be done with flint. Frison (1978) describes some specimens from the Vore and Casper kill sites in Wyoming.

At two other locations—the Selby and Dutton sites in extreme eastern Colorado, said to date as early as 15,000 BP—the presence of a number of these fractured and fragmented bones is reported by Stanford (1979). Wheat (1979) also reports a number from the Jurgens site in Colorado. Bonnichsen (1978) argues that more than a hundred specimens from sites in Old Crow Flats are tools.

Whether these bone-chopper and knife fragments are tools or merely scraps remaining after bone-marrow extraction is a problem, but definitive proof will, one fears, be long delayed. About all that can be done now is to note the increasingly frequent recognition of the forms and the increasing number of locations where they are found. The finds portend an eventual recognition of a bone-tool industry—tools that were quickly created, used, and discarded—that ran alongside, and was associated with, the amorphous-flake industry of pre-Clovis times. While one can be skeptical of this idea, one cannot deny the patterning of the specimens or the occasional use-polishing of the choppers and the sharpening (by removing percussion flakes) of the bone splinters. Both the frequency with which they are being discovered recently and the fact that they are numerous when flint tools are not found (at kill sites)—and not found when flint tools are numerous—argue that these bone fragments are in fact manufactured tools. That they are older than the flint tools has not, however, been proved, although some archeologists make that claim.

Late Period

For the late period the evidence of human population is, of course, overwhelming. The problem is to select which location to describe to exemplify the cultures of that period.

Most authors divide the late period into a more or less logical group of subseries or periods: the Llano or Clovis (11,500–11,000 BP), the Folsom (11,000–10,200 BP), and the Plano (10,000–7,000 BP). Although the three terms will be used here, retention of a brief Folsom period is actually based more on sentiment than logic. The Folsom and Plano lifeways are only variations on a single cultural theme, whereas the first, or Llano, period is to some degree distinctive.

LLANO SITES ☐ In general the Llano culture and its remains are associated with the brief period of time when the mammoth was the preferred prey of the Paleo-Indian. The rudimentary evidence, which is consistent from location to location, associates the remains of one or more mammoths with a tool kit, always characterized by the Clovis Fluted point (see Figures 2.11 and 2.12), prismatic flake knives, edge-chipped flat-flaked knives, smooth bone or ivory cylinders of unknown use, flint debris, and very little else. At one site, Murray Springs, a unique ivory "wrench" was found that has counterparts in objects from the Ukraine.

Hester (1975) has interpreted evidence from a number of Llano Estacado sites as providing a plausible description of the Llano lifeway. He points out, for

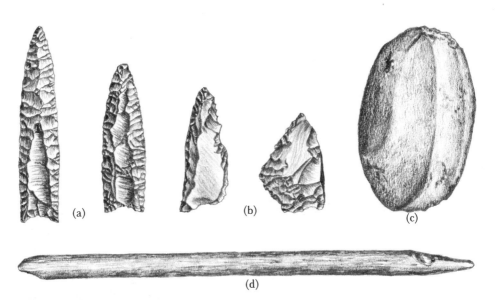

FIGURE 2.11
Artifacts from Blackwater Draw, locality 1: (a) fluted points; (b) scrapers; (c) hammerstone; (d) worked bone.

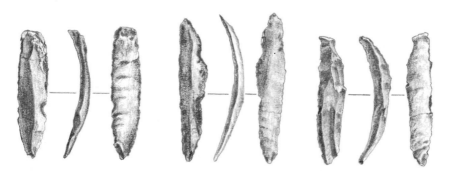

FIGURE 2.12
Clovis blades from Blackwater Draw, locality 1.

example, that the major kill-site locations are at the edges of ponds or stream channels, with the campsites somewhere nearby, usually on a slight eminence or elevation. He thinks the prey were killed by stalking since there is almost always only a single animal. The tool types all point toward big-game hunting as the basic economy. In addition to the mammoth, the other animals represented include camelids, horse, dire wolves, a giant armadillo, four-horned antelope, and sloths. Once killed, the animal was butchered on the spot—its body dismembered and its bones scattered over a small area.

Hester contends that Llano life was a roving one—probably cyclical, with the people returning to the same sites year after year. He bases this assumption, quite reasonably, on the source of the raw materials used in making stone tools. The favorite Llano stone at Blackwater Draw was Alibates chert, with a more refractory material called Edwards chert a poor second choice. These two famous quarries were used by successive cultures from the Llano period to historic times. Hester speculates that the normal socioeconomic unit was very small, consisting of only 10 to 20 individuals. Even so, he reckons that the Llano Estacado contains 10 pure Llano sites, out of a total of some 80 known Paleo-Indian locations in an area 160 by 240 kilometers (38,400 square kilometers). This total works out to one site for every 518 square kilometers. But, of the pure Llano groups, there would be only one band for every 4000 square kilometers. Although we must recognize that these figures are unreliable, being mere estimates based on the number of sites Hester knew when he wrote, they do support the concept of a sparse, mobile population.

There are many known Clovis sites, such as Blackwater Draw, New Mexico; Naco, Lehner, Murray Springs, and Escapule in Arizona; Dent, Nebraska; Domebo in Oklahoma; and Union Pacific in Montana—as well as some known but not yet excavated sites. None is more famous than Blackwater Draw (Hester, 1972), which will be described here briefly. At the time it was used by the Llano hunters, Blackwater Draw was a large lake fed by strong springs. Around the edges were extensive swamp zones supporting large stands of aquatic grasses and other plants. It appears that at this site the Clovis campsites were located close to the western shore of the lake rather than on the customary hillock or ridge. The many kills reported are of individual animals, some of which appear to have been mired in the boggy soil of the lakeshore. This famous site remained in continuous use for several thousand years; there are also Folsom and Plano campsites along the west shore.

The stratigraphy of the long-dry lake sediments at the BW1 location, the Llano–Clovis-type site, is sharp and clear. The basal layer contains Llano materials, with Folsom above the Llano and with the several Plano cultures occurring last or topmost in the stratigraphic column. Since the middle 1930s, this location has provided a yardstick and reference point for the basic Plains chronological sequence of cultures, a sequence that has reappeared time after time at other sites excavated later. Incredible as it seems, this site was worked by nine major expeditions but was never adequately reported until Hester published a synthesis of the finds of these many expeditions. Hester sought to present a coherent picture of the data recovered, the artifacts removed, and the circumstances that made the lake such a desirable hunting spot.

Such neglect does not characterize all the important Llano locations, however. At the Lehner, for example, Haury and his associates (1959) conducted a careful excavation and published their detailed observations of this important find. Here the remains of nine mammoths were uncovered along with specimens of horse, bison, and tapir. The tools included not only Clovis Fluted projectile points but also prismatic knives, uniface chipped scrapers, and flat-flake knives. There was also evidence of fire. Pollen studies conducted later indicated that the environment at the time of the kills was very like today's, as far as vegetation was concerned, but probably somewhat moister than today. The time span for the Llano period is very short. The radiocarbon date of nearly all the kills is between 12,000 and 11,200 BP.

EASTERN PALEO-INDIANS □ The continental distribution and quantity of fluted points presents an interesting anomaly. Although the classic Paleo-Indian sites from after 12,000 BP lie west of the Mississippi and Missouri rivers, fluted points are far more common east of these rivers. Several types quite variant from either Folsom or Clovis have been found in sufficient quantities to have been assigned local, regional names. There are also several well-known eastern locations where many fluted points, many almost classic Clovis in type, have been collected. In eastern New York and in New Jersey, such sites as Port Mobil, Dutchess Quarry, West Athens, Kings Road, Potts, and Plenge are examples. Clovis Fluted points have come from most of these locations. Those from Plenge are particularly good specimens, as are those from Parkhill in Ontario. The excellent Plenge site collections, however, are particularly frustrating, and largely useless, because the only specimens described by Kraft (1973) are surface finds made by local amateurs. (Excavations made in 1973 had not been reported as of 1980.) There are many other sites in the East—such as Shoop in Pennsylvania, Williamson in Virginia, Hardaway in Tennessee, and Reagan in Vermont—where scores of Clovis-style fluted points and much scrap from their manufacture have been known and recovered for years (see Figure 2.13).

Why then were the scantier and rarer western Clovis finds so often emphasized to the exclusion of the eastern ones? There are three parts to the answer: (1) in the East extinct animal bones never occurred in association; (2) rarely was charcoal or other organic material available for use in dating the deposit; and (3) most of the locations were shallow deposits in open fields where the specimens lay on the surface or were turned up by the plow. Thus the simple answer seems to be that because the eastern sites lacked extinct faunal remains, datable organic material, and any geological seal or association, scholars did not take the eastern finds seriously. In short, not even strong typological similarities can by themselves guarantee antiquity.

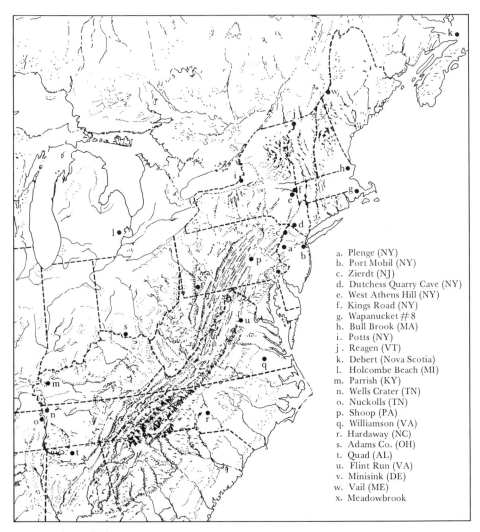

a. Plenge (NY)
b. Port Mobil (NY)
c. Zierdt (NJ)
d. Dutchess Quarry Cave (NY)
e. West Athens Hill (NY)
f. Kings Road (NY)
g. Wapanucket #8
h. Bull Brook (MA)
i. Potts (NY)
j. Reagen (VT)
k. Debert (Nova Scotia)
l. Holcombe Beach (MI)
m. Parrish (KY)
n. Wells Crater (TN)
o. Nuckolls (TN)
p. Shoop (PA)
q. Williamson (VA)
r. Hardaway (NC)
s. Adams Co. (OH)
t. Quad (AL)
u. Flint Run (VA)
v. Minisink (DE)
w. Vail (ME)
x. Meadowbrook

FIGURE 2.13
Eastern Paleo-Indian sites.

This skepticism has had to give way, however, after the discovery of sites that meet the criteria for credibility and acceptance. Some of the sites mentioned above—West Athens Hill and Dutchess Quarry—have been test-excavated to reveal shallow but believable stratigraphy. At Dutchess Cave a radiocarbon date of 12,500 BP was derived from a caribou bone allegedly associated with a fluted point. West Athens Hill was both a living and quarry site, but no hearths were observed. Dozens of point fragments were found, presumably broken during manufacture. Thirteen fluted points are illustrated in the site report (Funk, 1973); none are classic Clovis, although they are described as "conforming" to the Clovis Fluted type. No materials datable by C14 were recovered. The flint scrap tended to be concentrated in what are called clusters. Many scrapers from the clusters show crushed and battered—hence dulled—working edges, leading Funk to conclude that tools of wood, bone, and antler were manufactured at the site as well as basic flint forms. The site, on a hill, is believed to have been a quarry, a living site, and a game-spotting location. There are several tools made of exotic flint from Pennsylvania, western New York, and Ohio, as well as from the distinctive local Normanskill material. The implication, of course, is that here, as in the West, the Paleo-Indians were wide-ranging hunter–foragers.

Despite the early "softness" of the evidence at most of the eastern locations, there are now enough firm data to let us say, without hesitation, that eastern and western Paleo-Indian complexes have similar tool kits and are almost co-eval. It is possible to speak thus positively because of the finds at four sites: Flint Run in Virginia, Shawnee–Minisink in Delaware, Debert in Nova Scotia, and Bull Brook in Massachusetts (see Figure 2.14). Evidently the Vail site in Maine should also be included in this cluster (Gramly and Rutledge, 1981). (The Shoop site in Pennsylvania, the Williamson area in Virginia, and the many other locations all over New England mentioned above, whose provenience and chronology are not as well-controlled, are probably of the same age.) The certainty, however, comes from the four places cited above where extensive search has provided large numbers of artifacts, datable charcoal from fireplaces, and concentrations of artifacts and flint scrap. The concentrations marked the location of family camps or even houses in villages or settlements of several households. The first of the four to be discovered was Bull Brook, dated at about 9000 BP; Debert is somewhat earlier at 10,600 BP. At neither did the bones or other evidence of the preferred prey survive. Both, however, yielded a varied tool kit of retouched prismatic blades, fluted points, burins or engraving–cutting tools, steep-bitted scrapers or woodworking tools, and retouched flakes of irregular shape for use in butchery. This tool kit indicates a broad spectrum of activities, including on-site manufacture of other tools with flint tools. Both sites were buried but lacked clear-cut internal stratification.

The eastern Paleo-Indian has been studied by Gardner (1974) and his associates and by McNett et al. (1975). In a long-range program, Gardner, with a multidisciplinary team, has been studying a complex of sites at Flint Run, Virginia. The site is about 50 miles west of Washington, D.C., on the south fork of the Shenandoah River. At Flint Run there is an extensive stratified village or base camp, the Thunderbird site; a long-exploited jasper quarry; and flint-processing camps, one of which is known as the Fifty site.

Thunderbird has been the scene of the most extensive excavation. It is located on a long ridge a few hundred meters west of and paralleling the river channel. Excavation has revealed hunting camps and processing camps on fans extending out onto the floodplain. Debris occurs at "hot spots" (as at Debert and Bull

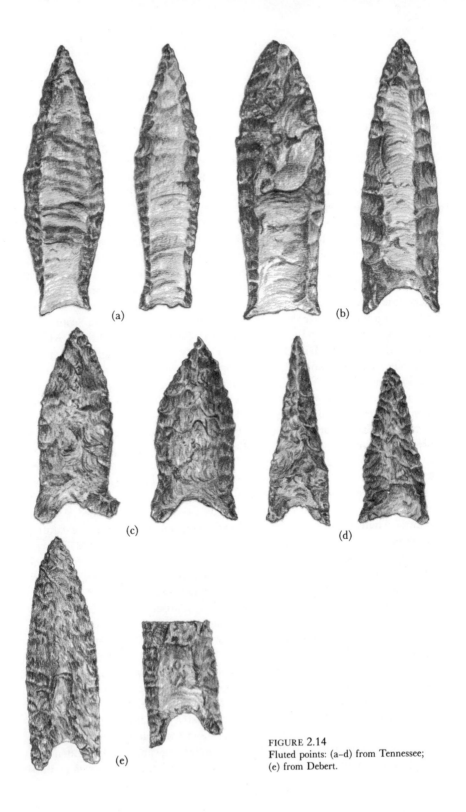

FIGURE 2.14
Fluted points: (a–d) from Tennessee;
(e) from Debert.

Brook) on the terrace, where structures or shelters using vertical posts for framing are associated with use surfaces and fired areas. If these were houses, they are the earliest known (10,900 BP) structures in the Americas. They are not, however, *firmly* associated with the Clovis level of occupancy and may relate to the next or Archaic level; the evidence has been blurred by recent farming activity. From the lowest levels at Thunderbird, a near-classic Clovis point and several other, more variant pieces were recovered. Above the Clovis finds are later Paleo-Indian and Archaic levels. Other hot spots, apart from the structures, appear to be almost exclusively the result of final flint-knapping work; the evidence is the presence of core fragments, of myriads of flakes created by pressure or hammer (baton?) blows, and of broken, not whole tools. The quarry sites, like other such locations, yield largely cores, primary (percussion) flakes, and unfinished pieces labeled *preforms*. These finds imply that tools were only half-finished at the quarries themselves, which are usually located near outcrops of chert or jasper.

The Flint Run investigators have gone rather carefully into the paleoclimate of the region. Using a widespread series of pollen studies, they have reconstructed the floral chronology of the Flint Run district as following a familiar sequence. At 10,000 BP, the mountain zone was covered by tundra while the foothills were dominated by spruce and pine. There were extensive upland-plateau grasslands, with the floodplain showing deciduous species and many extensive bogs. The bogs, except in one or two instances, were long ago sealed off by deep Recent sediments. Fauna, at 11,000 years BP, were the already familiar, now-extinct assemblage associated with tundra and boreal vegetation—mastodon, mammoth, caribou, two species of musk ox, moose, and bison. By 9300 BP the animals were modern species. Note that this timing does not exactly coincide with that of the vegetational data for the Plains, where grass must have been dominant by 10,500 to 11,500 BP.

At the Shawnee–Minisink site in Pennsylvania, McNett has already recovered a near-classic Clovis point and many other tools from what seems to be a rich and as yet barely sampled Clovis site. This project is also a long-range study, so a large corpus of fully controlled new data will be generated in ensuing years. Dragoo (1976) offers his findings at Wells Creek in Tennessee as evidence of strong and early Paleo-Indian use of the area. The site is described as an extensive stone-chipping deposit, where alleged Clovis points in all stages of manufacture have been recovered. The other tools found include pieces that may be preforms or blanks destined originally to be finished elsewhere, prismatic flake knives, and many scrapers, cleavers, spokeshaves, picks, and raclettes. Such tools correspond to specimens from Folsom.

Other locations all over the East, Southeast, and Middle West—more than can be described here—yield abundant early Paleo-Indian debris (see Figure 2.13). The great surge of interest in this period during the 1970s resulted in the mounting of programs such as the Thunderbird and Minisink efforts, which will beyond doubt establish the presence of a heavy Llano–Clovis complex everywhere south of the 11,000 BP ice edge. (In fact, it is believed that Debert was occupied when the glacial ice was fewer than 100 kilometers away, with caribou and other tundra species serving as prey.) Whether complete contemporaneity of the eastern and western complexes is demonstrated soon or is delayed a few years, it remains true that there are several hundred more fluted points reported in the East than in the West. Moreover, the associated tools—broad bifaces, scrapers of all kinds, crescentic flake knives—that attest to varied tasks and extensive manufacturing processes are of kinds fully familiar from western Paleo-Indian sites. The likelihood that occupation in the East was by the same people as in the West is increased by the presence in both areas of the same tools. If the quirks of sampling and search yield more eastern sites that can be dated and thus controlled chronologically, we might see the Dutchess Cave date of 12,500 BP being oft-repeated.

FOLSOM–PLANO SITES □ Returning to a review of the western sites where the data are abundant and in good control, we must first examine the epoch-making Folsom, New Mexico, discovery of 1926–1927. Folsom was the *first* fully authenticated find of bison bones in association with tools of human workmanship. It revealed the beginning of a new gathering or harvesting system, marked by use of the trap or fall technique of harvesting game. At Folsom, 23 *Bison antiquus* were evidently trapped, killed, and butchered. During the butchery, 19 fluted points of a type previously unknown to archeologists were lost, to be found in the 1920s in full association with the bones of the kill. The points were unique in their delicacy and distinctive form (see Figure 2.15). The site demonstrated the existence of a Paleo-Indian population during Late Pleistocene times and opened up the whole field of Paleo-Indian study, which is still being actively pursued today. The Folsom–Plano cultural system—the settlement patterns, the basic tool kit, the areas and pattern of exploitation, and most other basic subsystems in the culture—persisted for several millennia.

But at Lindenmeier, which was probably a base camp, a broader understanding of the Folsom culture is to be gained. Lindenmeier, located near Fort Collins, Colorado, suffered the same neglect as Blackwater Draw—that is, inadequate reporting—from its excavation in the 1930s until after 1970. The all-important difference was that Lindenmeier was excavated by the late F. H. H. Roberts, who kept meticulous notes and records. He simply never published anything other than seasonal preliminary reports. Thanks to Wilmsen (1973), some of the significance of the find has now become apparent. Located on the marshy banks of a Late Pleistocene lake, long since covered by sediment from the low hills surrounding the high valley, the Lindenmeier site was quite extensive. As at Thunderbird, there were many hot spots where debitage, broken tools, fire-darkened hearths, and food scrap were abundant. The location had also been used by Llano peoples, but the heaviest use was by a Folsom group. An occasional mammoth and many bison were killed and butchered there. The tool kit, aside from the delicate fluted points, includes the crescent-bladed spokeshave used in shaping or smoothing spear or dart shafts or other slender cylin-

FIGURE 2.15
Folsom Fluted points from Lindenmeier.

drical objects, fine-pointed graving or cutting tools, scrapers for a variety of tasks, prismatic flake knives, and drills.

Folsom sites generally are merely kills. It is both interesting and regrettable that Lindenmeier is the only large village site to be excavated, and its partial interpretation lagged long after its excavation. However, Frison (1978) reports that the newly discovered Hanson site in the Bighorn Basin, north central Wyoming, is also an extensive village. It has barely been sampled as yet, but several hard floors, blanketed with clean sand 1–2 cm thick, have been identified as a lodge (possibly implying a skin tipi). The dwelling floors and much debitage, including fluting flakes of Folsom type, argue that this location was a permanent settlement; it is not one of the familiar kill sites. The excavation has revealed that the site was probably a special-use camp established largely for collecting and knapping the several good-quality flints common in the area. Excavation at the location will probably continue.

Lindenmeier, Plainview, Midland, Hell Gap, and other stratified sites on the Plains also yield what have been called *Plainview* points. On the basis of its form, this point has been described as an "*Un*fluted" Folsom: it is very similar to the Folsom except that the long, fluted flakes whose scars give the Folsom point its thin, biconcave cross-sectional outline were never removed (see Figure 2.16). Debate continues over the relationship between the classical Folsom and the Plainview points. Which is older? Are they contemporary? Stratigraphy, radiocarbon dating, and typology have all failed to provide a firm answer. My own opinion is that the Plainview is contemporary with the Folsom but persisted to set a model for the many lanceolate unfluted types that follow in rather quick succession over all the Plains, although not in the East.

At the Olsen–Chubbuck site, to be described below, Wheat (1972) found and described a Firstview point, which further confuses the issue; the Firstview and Plainview appear to be the same. The evidence from Bonfire Shelter (Dibble and Lorrain, 1968) tends to support the brief popularity of the Plainview point as marking a transition from the Folsom toward the various later unfluted and elongated projectile types. At Bonfire, deep in the southern Texas plains, three

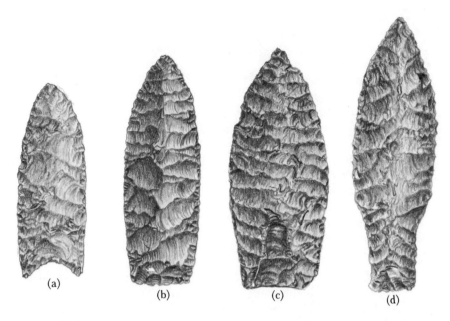

FIGURE 2.16
Plano points: (a) Plainview; (b) Milnesand; (c) Browns Valley; (d) Hell Gap.

separate bison stampede kills were uncovered. In the lowest, dated at 10,200 BP, was a Folsom point. Immediately above, the slightly later second kill yielded only Plainview points. On the other hand, Irwin (1971) places the Plainview type ahead of the Folsom on the strength of the Hell Gap site finds. The truth is that the stratigraphy (which is equivalent to the dating) for all these sites was probably correctly observed and reported. The differing stratigraphic positions may reflect a broad distribution over many hundreds of horizontal miles. The Plainview point may have developed in the northern Plains and later been adopted in South Texas as it gained in popularity. Before the matter can be decided, more and better evidence will be required.

Hell Gap is one more Plano location that assumes importance by its great chronological depth. The cultures represented there cover a 3200-year time span, from 11,200 BP to 8,000 BP—about the full duration of the Paleo-Indian occupancy of the Plains. Lying in eastern Wyoming, the finds consist of several contiguous locations that could be collapsed or combined to form a stratigraphic column-sequence on the strength of radiocarbon dates, geological formations, and internal evidence within the sequent strata. Actually the objects and other evidence found at Hell Gap were scanty; the importance of the site rests with the time depth and culture sequence revealed.

At this juncture a triad of carefully excavated kill sites should be described in order to exemplify the wealth of information such sites contain. First is the Olsen–Chubbuck kill site in east–central Colorado, not far from Kit Carson and near the Kansas line (Wheat, 1972). It is Folsom–Plainview in age at 10,200

BP. The kill occurred where a long, narrow gully (3 meters wide by possibly 2 meters deep) lay across the path of a bison herd (*B. occidentalis*) stampeding down a steep hillside. Approximatley 190 animals of both sexes and all ages were injured or killed in the trap. Butchery began immediately, in the course of which (and during the kill itself) more than 60 tools were lost or discarded— Firstview (Plainview) and San Jon points, cobbles for breaking bones, and flint-flake knives and scrapers. By working slowly and with great care, Wheat exposed many heaps of bone and discovered that the butchery process followed a consistent pattern. It was doubtless efficient and rapid. The bone piles showed that, after skinning and removal of the bison's savory hump meat, the forelegs and shoulder girdle were removed, stripped of meat, and discarded. Next, the hind legs and pelvic girdle were cut free, the meat removed, and the bones discarded on the foreleg bones. Usually in the scrap heap the hind legs lay above the pelvic bones. Next atop the heap were chains of vertebrae, with skulls attached. Animals wedged deeply into the narrow bottom of the arroyo rarely showed any evidence of butchery; their bones were still articulated upon discovery. In addition to providing details about butchering techniques, the site allowed for an analysis of the age distribution of the herd—number of calves, yearlings, and so on. The chipped flint showed that a wide range of raw materials had been collected and utilized (including some Texas Alibates flint pieces), reinforcing the ideas widely held about the cyclical wandering of the Folsom-Plano bands.

In Wyoming, Frison has discovered and excavated a number of bison kill sites since 1965. One, the Casper site near Casper (Frison, 1974), is of interest because it is not a fall but an unusual variation on the trap or cul-de-sac technique. The site, dated 8000 BP, is an extensive bone bed located between the horns of a fossil parabolic dune. The heavy animals could not ascend the shifting sand of the steep dune face. As they milled, their escape was cut off by the hunters, and they were slaughtered one by one. This location also provided information on the herd composition, which suggests that selective killing was practiced, since there are more carcasses in the 0.6- to 2.6-year range than a random herd would normally have. The associated points are almost exclusively of the Hell Gap type.

Frison et al. (1976) report a kill of yet a third type. Here in a fossil arroyo, very deep and ending headward with a steep-walled jumpup or knickpoint forming an unscalable barrier, they found remains of a kill of about 100 bison. The technique involved driving several small herds upstream until the animals were wedged helplessly against each other in the narrow gully. The date of this kill at the Hawken location (in extreme northeastern Wyoming, near Sun Dance) is 6500 BP. Aside from the detailed paleogeomorphological reconstructions made by the authors, the site is important as the type site for a new Plano knife point, here called the Hawken Side-Notched. The form is very similar to a quite distinctive style found farther west in the northern Great Basin, called Northern Side-Notched. They are also similar to, but distinct from, an Idaho series of side-notched points called Bitterroot.

In view of their large number, no Plano sites other than Hell Gap, Olsen–Chubbuck, Hawken, Plainview, Casper, and Bonfire will be described here. However, several other locations have given their names to distinctive and chronologically separate projectile knife types: for example, Eden, Claypool, Scottsbluff, Milnesand, San Jon, Agate Basin, and Angostura. Some of these were kill sites; others may have been frequently used campsites.

During the Plano period, the now-extinct *Bison occidentalis* gave over the historic *Bison bison*. In Chapter Six Wedel deals effectively with the apparent extreme fluctuation of bison herd size, the localization of herds in favorable areas, and the cultural results this fluctuation in numbers produced in the Plains area.

CENTRAL AMERICAN SITES □ Several Central American finds—Tepexpan, Valesquillo, Tlacopaya, and Hueyatlaco—have been ascribed an antiquity of over 10,000 years. Internal stratigraphic evidence, however, and anachronistic archeological associations have caused these sites to be widely disputed. At Iztapan researchers did discover mammoth bones aged about 11,000 BP, with flint tools in good association; this is regarded as an authentic find. Gruhn and Bryan (1977) have reported a site in Guatemala, Los Tapiales, dated at 11,200 BP, whose artifacts are not entirely consistent with other Paleo-Indian locations. The site lies very high, in a mountain meadow at 3200 meters, a few kilometers west and north of Guatemala City. Although bifacially chipped blades and two apparent Clovis Fluted-point bases were recovered, many of the flint specimens are burins and gravers. The remains are scanty; no bones from food animals survived. The site, interpreted as a short-lived hunting camp, is entirely credible, albeit unusual.

SUMMARY

The intent of this chapter has been to provide a succinct survey of the beginnings of human history in the New World. Hence, our attention has been largely confined to North America. The occasional scantiness of the evidence and the areas of outright ignorance that surround the saga of the first Americans have been emphasized. What the evidence says, as I read it, is that the Asians—not very many of them—entered the Americas by way of the Beringian land bridge, which was then a vast plain characterized by arctic steppe–tundra vegetation and megafauna. The first dated evidence of humans comes at about 27,000 BP. By about 19,000 BP, however, small hunting bands were already below the southern edge of the ice in what is now the United States. They were using a Eurasiatic tool kit, typologically reminiscent of the Mousteroid level of technology.

For most of the last 25,000 years, there was a corridor opened from the Refuge to the northern Plains. The corridor was a steppe where the familiar fauna grazed. It opened into the endless grasslands that now characterize the Plains. The Paleo-Indian hunters can be divided on cultural grounds into the earlier Llano and the subsequent Folsom–Plano. The lifeways of the two groups were similar in their apparent concentration on now-extinct big game, their cyclical wanderings from one resource to another, and their frequent returns to favorable hunting locations. Villages, or at least base camps, as well as kill sites have been identified in both the Plains and the eastern United States; the eastern locations are numerous, with more being reported each year. The eastern and western occupancies were no doubt contemporaneous, a fact that bespeaks a very rapid expansion of the hunters over the ice-free portion of the hemisphere.

The Llano peoples' preferred game was the mammoth, usually young, single individuals, and they normally hunted in ambushes or in boggy or marsh locations where the animal's movements would be hampered. The environment was transitional from a well-watered Pleistocene one, characterized by open parkland—savanna and many wet locations where coarse grasses were abundant—to the drier grasslands of the Plains.

The Folsom–Plano groups concentrated on the longhorn bison (*B. antiquus* and *occidentalis*) that dominated the drier grasslands after the extinction of the mammoth. Although ambush killing of single animals may have continued, the bison hunters developed the mass-kill technique. The procedure required a task force larger than the family, as it involved driving a small herd of bison over a cliff or into a box canyon, arroyo, or other kind of blind trap, such as a crescentic sand dune. This mass-kill technique required control over a sizable group of hunters, unlike the Llano single-kill technique. The settlement patterns of the two culture groups appear to have varied, with the Llano tending to camp near water sources (sometimes on knolls) and the Folsom–Plano camps tending to be slightly removed downwind but on elevations from which the watering holes and the animal range could be constantly observed.

The preceding pages offer a sample of the literature and give the beginning reader a glimpse of how the Indian conquest of the New World began. But this chapter can only be an introduction to the reams of data available on the ever-fresh and increasingly (chronologically) deep story of the Paleo-Indian.

Further research should continue to push the evidence of human occupancy on both American continents farther back into time, perhaps into the mid-Wisconsin (40,000 BP) range. This chapter has dealt almost exclusively with North America, with a very brief excursion into Central America, for two reasons. The first reason is that human settlement began in North America. The second is that research on Paleo-Indian matters in North America has been unceasing since the late 1920s. It must exceed by a hundredfold the amount of study devoted to the same time period by Latin American students, perhaps because they have concentrated on the vast ruined cities from a later period. Alas, as indicated, some of the few allegedly early Central American sites cannot even be accepted as fully authenticated examples.

FIGURE 2.17
North American culture areas.

This chapter is an introduction in another sense, too. It introduces the chapters that follow by describing the significant climatic changes between 20,000 and 10,000 years ago. The changes in climate, fauna, and flora since 10,000 BP are also reviewed. The adaptation the native Americans made to the areal expansion of life zones and resources and to the continuous population increase constitute the cultural history unfolded in the following chapters. It is widely believed, even if not constantly reiterated, that the climatic changes following the retreat of the ice set up certain subsistence stresses. These stresses in turn led to the marked shifts in adaptation to different resources that characterize the ubiquitous Archaic cultures of the two continents. Thus, some would argue that all American cultures subsequent to the Paleo-Indian derived directly from the new set of environments.

Anthropologists and geographers have long recognized the inescapable fact that the world's environments, over broad regions, are so different that a variety of lifestyles or patterns would of necessity evolve to "fit" their various resources and characteristics. Examples would be the desert West as opposed to the Plains, where the bison lingered after the Paleo-Indians. Sharply different from either was the Southeast. There the deciduous hardwood forests and the dense canebreaks in the myriad swampy stream valleys supply even today a rich and varied fauna and flora, where the living is "easy" for the hunter and collector. Such broad regional uniformities led to the establishment of distinctive culture areas.

The remaining chapters of this book are organized around the culture areas of the hemisphere and the unique resources of each. (Figure 2.17 shows the major areas.) To some degree, the exchange of culture traits and patterns between regions is also noted. The culture-area treatment employed does *not* imply that regional events transpired in isolation. More correctly, the culture-area idea should be recognized as the convenient, even traditional way in which archeologists have held the diverse and varied data down to a manageable mass. Even so, the bulk of the data to be compressed into the regional sections increases annually, and meaningful summaries become more difficult to prepare because of the growing difficulty of assessing the new data.

The careful reader will note that most of the later chapters treat evidence for Paleo-Indian occupation in their special areas. These discussions serve to provide more detail, and in some cases they offer interpretations different from those in this section.

References Cited and Recommended Sources

Adovasio, James M. 1975. Excavations at Meadowcroft Rockshelter, 1973–1974: a progress report. *Pennsylvania Archaeologist* 45:3:1–30.

———, J. D. Gunn, J. Donahue, R. Stuckenrath, J. E. Guiday, and K. Volman. 1980. Yes Virginia, it really is that old: a reply to Haynes and Mead. *American Antiquity* 45:3:588–595.

Birdsell, Joseph B. 1951. The problem of the early peopling of the Americas as viewed from Asia. *Papers on the Physical Anthropology of the American Indian.* New York: The Viking Fund.

Bischoff, James L., Morlin Childers, and Roy J. Shlemon. 1978. Comments on the Pleistocene age assignment and associations of a human burial from the Yuha Desert, California. *American Antiquity* 43:4:747–749.

Bonnichsen, Robson. 1978. Critical arguments for Pleistocene artifacts from the Old Crow Basin, Yukon: a preliminary statement. In *Early Man in America from a Circum-Pacific Perspective,* ed. Alan Lyle Bryan, pp. 102–118. Occasional Papers no. 1, Department of Anthropology, University of Alberta. Edmonton: Archaeological Researches International.

Borden, C. E. 1975. *Origins and Development of Early Northwest Coast Culture to About 3000 B.C.* Archeological Survey of Canada, Paper no. 45.

Bryan, Alan L. 1969. Early man in America and the Late Pleistocene chronology of western Canada and Alaska. *Current Anthropology* 10:4:339–367.

——— (ed.). 1978. *Early Man in America from a Circum-Pacific Perspective.* Occasional Papers no. 1, Department of Anthropology, University of Alberta. Edmonton: Archaeological Researches International.

Bryson, Reid A., David A. Baerreis, and Wayne M. Wendland. 1970. The character of late glacial and post-glacial climatic changes. In *Pleistocene and Recent Environments of the Central Great Plains,* ed. Wakefield Dort, Jr., and J. Knox Jones, Jr., pp. 53–74. Lawrence: Department of Geology, University of Kansas, Special Publication no. 3.

Butzer, Karl W. 1971. *Environment and Archeology: An Introduction to Pleistocene Geography,* 2nd ed. Chicago: Aldine.

Chard, Chester. 1974. *Northeast Asia in Prehistory.* Madison: University of Wisconsin Press.

Dibble, David S., and Dessamae Lorrain. 1968. *Bonfire Shelter: A Stratified Bison Kill Site, Val Verde County, Texas.* Austin: Texas Memorial Museum. Miscellaneous Papers no. 1.

Dragoo, Don W. 1976. Some aspects of eastern North American prehistory: a review, 1975. *American Antiquity* 41:1:3–27.

Dumond, Don E. 1980. The archaeology of Alaska and the peopling of America. *Science* 209: 4460:984–991.

Fladmark, Knut R. 1978. The feasibility of the Northwest Coast as a migration route for early man. In *Early Man in America from a Circum-Pacific Perspective,* ed. Alan Lyle Bryan, pp. 119–238. Occasional Papers no. 1, Department of Anthropology, University of Alberta. Edmonton: Archaeological Researches International.

————. 1979. Routes: alternate migration corridors for early man in North America. *American Antiquity* 44:1:55–69.

Frison, George C. 1974. *The Casper Site: A Hell Gap Bison Kill on the High Plains.* New York: Academic Press.

————. 1978. *Prehistoric Hunters of the High Plains.* New York: Academic Press.

————, Michael Wilson, and Diane J. Wilson. 1976. Fossil bison and artifacts from an early altithermal period arroyo trap in Wyoming. *American Antiquity* 41:1:28–57.

Funk, Robert E. 1973. The West Athens Hil site (Cox 7). In *Aboriginal Settlement Patterns in the Northwest,* ed. William A. Ritchie and Robert E. Funk. New York State Museum and Science Service, Memoir 20, pp. 9–36. Albany: State Education Department.

Gardner, William M. 1974. *The Flint Run Paleo-Indian Complex: A Preliminary Report, 1971–73 Seasons.* Archeology Laboratory, Department of Anthropology, Occasional Publication no. 1. Washington, D.C.: Catholic University of America.

————. 1975. Paleo-Indian to Early Archaic: continuity and change in eastern North America during the Late Pleistocene and Early Holocene. *Proceedings of the IXth International Congress of Prehistoric and Protohistoric Scientists,* Nice, France.

Graham, Russell V. 1979. Paleoclimate and Late Pleistocene faunal provinces. In *Pre-Llano Cultures of the Americas: Paradoxes and Possibilities,* ed. Robert L. Humphrey and Dennis Stanford. Washington, D.C.: Anthropological Society of Washington.

Gramly, R. M., and Kerry Rutledge. 1981. A new Paleo-Indian site in Maine. *American Antiquity* 46:2:254–261.

Grayson, Donald K. 1980. Vicissitudes and overkill: the development of explanations of Pleistocene extinctions. In *Advances in Archeological Method and Theory,* vol. 3, ed. M. Schiffer. New York: Academic Press.

Gruhn, Ruth, and Alan L. Bryan. 1977. Los Tapiales: A Paleo-Indian campsite in the Guatemalan highlands. *Proceedings of the Philosophical Society* 121:3.

Haury, Emil W., Ernest Antevs, and John F. Lance. 1953. Artifacts with mammoth remains, Naco, Arizona: I, II, III. *American Antiquity* 19:1:1–24.

————, Edwin B. Sayles, and William W. Wasley. 1959. The Lehner Mammoth site, southeastern Arizona. *American Antiquity* 25:1:2–30.

Haynes, C. Vance, Jr. 1969. The earliest Americans. *Science* 166:3906:709–715.

————. 1973. The Calico site: artifacts or geofacts? *Science* 181:4097:305–310.

————. 1980. Paleoindian charcoal from Meadowcroft Rockshelter: is contamination a problem? *American Antiquity* 45:3:582–587.

————, and E. Thomas Hemmings. 1968. Mammoth-bone shaft wrench from Murray Springs, Arizona. *Science* 159:3811:186–187.

Hester, James J. 1972. *Blackwater Locality No. 1: A Stratified, Early Man Site in Eastern New Mexico.* Ranchos de Taos, New Mexico: Fort Burgwin Research Center.

————. 1975. Paleoarchaeology of the Llano Estacado. In *Late Pleistocene Environments of the Southern High Plains,* ed. Fred Wendorf and James J. Hester, pp. 247–256. Ranchos de Taos, New Mexico: Fort Burgwin Research Center.

Hopkins, David M. 1967. The Cenozoic history of Beringia—a synthesis. In *The Bering Land Bridge,* ed. David M. Hopkins, pp. 451–484. Stanford: Stanford University Press.

Humphrey, Robert L., and Dennis Stanford (eds.). 1979. *Pre-Llano Cultures of the Americas: Paradoxes and Possibilities.* Washington, D.C.: Anthropological Society of Washington.

Irving, William N., and C. R. Harrington. 1973. Upper Pleistocene radiocarbon-dated artifacts from the northern Yukon. *Science* 179:4071:335–340.

Irwin, Henry T. 1971. Developments in early man studies in western North America, 1960–1970. *Arctic Anthropology* 8:2:42–67.

Jennings, Jesse D. 1974a. Across an Arctic bridge. In *The World of the American Indian,* ed. Jules B. Billard, pp. 29–70. Washington, D.C.: National Geographic Society.

————. 1974b. *Prehistory of North America,* 2nd ed. New York: McGraw-Hill.

————. 1978. *Prehistory of Utah and the Eastern Great Basin.* Salt Lake City: University of Utah Anthropological Papers no. 97.

Kraft, Herbert C. 1973. The Plenge Site: a Paleo-Indian Occupation Site in New Jersey. South Orange: Seton Hall University.

———. 1977. Paleoindians in New Jersey. In *Amerinds and Their Paleoenvironments in Northeastern North America*, ed. Walter S. Newman and Bert Salwen, pp. 264–281. New York: Annals of the New York Academy of Sciences, vol. 288.

Krieger, Alex D. 1964. Early man in the New World. In *Prehistoric Man in the New World*, ed. J. Jennings and E. Norbeck, pp. 23–81. Chicago: University of Chicago Press.

Lahren, Larry, and Robson Bonnichsen. 1974. Bone foreshafts from a Clovis burial in southwestern Montana. *Science* 186:147–150.

Leakey, Lewis B., Ruth D. Simpson, and Thomas Clements. 1970. Man in America: the Calico Mountain excavations. *Britannica Yearbook of Science and the Future*, pp. 65–79.

Long, Joseph K. 1966. A test of multiple-discriminant analysis as a means of determining evolutionary changes and intergroup relationships in physical anthropology. *American Anthropologist* 68:2:1:444–464.

MacNeish, Richard S. 1978. Late Pleistocene adaptations: a new look at early peopling of the New World. *Journal of Anthropological Research* 34:4:474–496.

McNett, Charles W., Jr., Sydne B. Marshall, and Ellis E. McDowell. 1975. Second season of the upper Delaware Valley early man project. Washington, D.C.: Department of Anthropology, American University.

———, Barbara A. McMillan, and Sydne B. Marshall. 1977. The Shawnee-Minisink site. In *Amerinds and Their Paleoenvironments in Northeastern North America*, ed. Walter S. Newman and Bert Salwen, pp. 282–296. New York: Annals of the New York Academy of Sciences, vol. 288.

Martin, Paul S. 1973. The discovery of America. *Science* 179:969–974.

Mochanov, Juri A. 1978. The Paleolithic of Northeast Asia and the problem of the first peopling of America. In *Early Man in America from a Circum-Pacific Perspective*, ed. Alan Lyle Bryan. Occasional Papers no. 1, Department of Anthropology, University of Alberta. Edmonton: Archaeological Researches International.

Müller-Beck, Hansjürgen. 1966. Paleohunters in America: origins and diffusion. *Science* 152: 3726:1191–1210.

———. 1967. On migrations of hunters across the Bering land bridge in the Upper Pleistocene. In *The Bering Land Bridge*, ed. David M. Hopkins, pp. 373–408. Stanford: Stanford University Press.

Neumann, George K. 1952. Archeology and race in the American Indian. In *Archeology of Eastern United States*, ed. James B. Griffin, pp. 13–34. Chicago: University of Chicago Press.

Newman, Walter S., and Bert Salwen (eds.). 1977. *Amerinds and Their Paleoenvironments in Northeastern North America*. New York: Annals of the New York Academy of Sciences, vol. 288.

O'Connell, James F. 1975. The prehistory of Surprise Valley. *Ballena Press Anthropological Papers* 4.

Reagan, Michael J., Ralph M. Rowlett, Ervin G. Garrison, Wakefield Dort, Vaughn N. Bryan, and Chris J. Johannsen. 1978. Flaked tools stratified below Paleo-Indian artifacts. *Science* 200:4347:1272–1275.

Stanford, Dennis. 1979. The Selby and Dutton sites: evidence for a pre-Clovis occupation of the High Plains. In *Pre-Llano Cultures of the Americas: Paradoxes and Possibilities*, ed. Robert L. Humphrey and Dennis Stanford, pp. 101–123. Washington, D.C.: Anthropological Society of Washington.

Stewart, T. D. 1973. *The People of America*. New York: Scribners.

Von Endt, David W. 1979. Techniques of amino acid dating. In *Pre-Llano Cultures of the Americas: Paradoxes and Possibilities*, ed. Robert L. Humphrey and Dennis Stanford, pp. 71–100. Washington, D.C.: Anthropological Society of Washington.

Wendorf, Fred, Alex D. Krieger, and Claude E. Albritton. 1955. *The Midland Discovery: A Report on the Pleistocene Human Remains from Midland, Texas*. Austin: University of Texas Press.

Wheat, Joe Ben. 1972. The Olsen-Chubbuck site: a Paleo-Indian bison kill. *American Antiquity* 37:1:2. Memoirs of the Society for American Archaeology no. 26.

———. 1979. The Jurgens Site. Memoir 15. *Plains Anthropologist* 24-84:2:1–153.

Wilke, Philip J. 1978. Cairn burials of the California deserts. *American Antiquity* 43:3:444–447.

Wilmsen, Edwin N. 1973. *Lindenmeier: A Pleistocene Hunting Society*. New York: Harper and Row.

Wright, H. E., Jr. 1970. Vegetational history of the central plains. In *Pleistocene and Recent Environments of the Central Great Plains*, ed. Wakefield Dort, Jr., and J. Knox Jones, Jr., pp. 157–172. Lawrence: Department of Geology, University of Kansas, Special Publication no. 3.

The upper Naknek drainage on the Alaska Peninsula, looking southeast. The mile-and-a-half-long Brooks River drains Brooks Lake (*right*) into Naknek Lake (*left*), all part of a complex of lakes and rivers that was formed by Late Pleistocene glaciers and now provides spawning grounds for five species of salmon. The spruce forest visible south of Brooks River has become established only in the past 500 years. In the far distance is the Aleutian Range, beyond which is the Pacific coast. The mountains in the left background are blocked from view by a haze of volcanic ash from the eruption of Mount Trident, an active volcano near the Valley of Ten Thousand Smokes in Katmai National Park and Preserve.

CHAPTER THREE

Alaska and the Northwest Coast

Don E. Dumond

In this chapter and the one that follows, the remarkable adaptive qualities of human beings become immediately clear. Despite the seemingly bleak and barren nature of much of the Alaskan, arctic, and subarctic environments, humans not only lived there but thrived and developed a series of rich and diverse cultures. The inhabitants of the frozen reaches of the Far North and the Indians of the Northwest Coast of North America are known for the great wealth of their material culture and their extremely successful adaptation to a region of bountiful resources.

Today, mainland Alaska is a great plate that juts from North America into the northern seas (Figure 3.1). Its interior flatlands and low uplands are ineffectually separated from the North American interior by low but nearly continuous mountain chains, and its rocky southern coast abuts its still more southerly counterpart in the Northwest Coast of southeastern Alaska, British Columbia, Washington, and Oregon. Ten millennia ago, however, the Alaskan mainland was a part of Asia, from which it became separated at Bering Strait only as waters rose to form the Chukchi Sea on the north and the Bering Sea on the south. Its importance to American prehistory is precisely the result of its unique geographic situation.

During the Pleistocene epoch, central Alaska experienced a lesser amount of glaciation than did much of North America, including the Northwest Coast. At the height of the last glacial event, continuous ice in Alaska was confined to the east–west trending mountain ridges of the south and the north.

East of the Alaskan border, in the Yukon Territory, the mountain glacier systems of North and South Alaska curved toward one another and nearly joined along the northern extension of the Rocky Mountains, so that during the height of the Pleistocene the Alaskan interior formed a relatively ice-free bowl, rimmed on the north, east, and south by almost continuous glaciers and covered by tundra vegetation containing more grass and *Artemisia* than the present shrub

FIGURE 3.1
Map of Alaska and the Northwest Coast.

tundra of the Arctic. Out of this bowl, a narrow ice-free corridor led eastward, passed between the Cordilleran glacier system of the west (formed on the Rocky Mountains, the Coast Mountains, and the St. Elias Range) and the massive continental ice sheet centered around what is now Hudson Bay, and opened southward through Canada into what is now the United States. Recent research suggests that this corridor remained open—whether inviting or not in its windy, proglacial aspect—during all but the climax of glaciation around 16,000 BC, and that the major glaciers had melted almost entirely by 8000 BC (Mathews, 1979; Reeves, 1971).

NATIVE PEOPLES

At the time of earliest European contact, the coast of Alaska north of the Alaska Peninsula was the home of people adapted to life along a winter-frozen coast. They spoke two distinct Eskimoan languages, one of which was also spoken by Pacific coastal people of the region around Kodiak Island and Prince William Sound. West of about 159° west longitude, on the tip of the Alaska Peninsula and throughout the Aleutian Islands, were found the Aleuts, who existed by open-water hunting and fishing and spoke one or more languages classified with Eskimoan in an Eskaleutian stock. The Alaskan interior was peopled by broadly adapted hunters and fishermen of the coniferous forest. These people spoke several distinct languages, all of which are included in the Athapaskan family, the western extreme of a great linguistic block that extended eastward as far as Hudson Bay.

The northern Northwest Coast was the home of the Eyak, Tlingit, and Haida, whose languages are usually included with Athapaskan in the Na-Dene linguistic phylum. Farther south lived the Penutian-speaking Tsimshian of British Columbia, the Wakashan speakers—Bella Bella, Kwakiutl, Nootka, and others—and the coastal segment of the great Salish family, all of whom belonged to classic Northwest Coast culture, with its maritime or littoral subsistence and its emphasis on property and social rank. South of the Athapaskans of the Fraser Plateau, to the east, lived river-fishing interior Salish, who were of standard Columbia Plateau culture type.

Other Penutian speakers, who occupied the lower Columbia River and the central and southern Oregon coast, were more peripherally involved in the Northwest Coast pattern and provided a transition to the cultures of northern California.

The prehistoric background of these people will be described by means of several cultural traditions, each of which represents a distinct lifeway that persisted for a number of human generations and is evidenced archeologically by broadly similar sets of artifact assemblages. This description will also be divided between two areas. The first, termed for simplicity *Arctic Alaska,* includes the Alaskan coast from the Alaska Peninsula northward (the area in which the winter coastline is frozen), the interior of mainland Alaska, and nearby regions of the Yukon Territory of Canada. The second, termed the *Pacific Rim,* takes in all of the Alaskan coastline lying upon the Pacific Ocean proper, including the Aleutian Islands, as well as most of British Columbia and the western portions of Washington and Oregon. Each area description concludes with a brief interpretive summary.

THE ARCHEOLOGY OF ARCTIC ALASKA

By 2000 BC or slightly before, there is evidence for differentiation between the tool assemblages of the Alaskan interior and those of the coast. This differentiation may be presumed to relate to ethnic differentiation among the peoples who used the tools. The archeology will therefore be set out in two parts, the first relating to the time before 2000 BC, the second to all later times. The cultural traditions referred to, and their relationships, are diagrammed in Figure 3.2.

Before 2000 BC

Putative evidence of very early human activity was first discovered about 50 kilometers east of the modern border between Alaska and the Yukon Territory, a region that pertained to the unglaciated heart of Alaska when it formed an extension of Asia during the Pleistocene. As indicated in Chapter Two, eroding sediments at the edge of the Old Crow River have produced a collection of fossil animal bones and some modified bones concluded to be artifacts. Radiocarbon dating has been inconsistent, with some investigators inclined to accept dates between about 24,000 and 27,000 BC and others supposing the actual age to be greater (Morlan, 1978). Similar finds have been reported from some other locations in Alaska proper but have been less thoroughly studied (Bonnichsen, 1979).

Otherwise, the earliest apparent dates that pertain to human activity are about 11,000 BC for stone-chipping debris from a cave on the Bluefish River, a tributary of the Old Crow (Cinq-Mars, 1979), and 11,000 to 14,000 BC for bone thought to have been broken by humans at the Trail Creek caves on Seward Peninsula (Larsen, 1968b). With one exception—from the same Trail Creek caves—all other apparently early tool complexes of Alaska consist of stone rather than bone implements, and bone waste is also rarely preserved. Even among these stone assemblages, some once suggested to be particularly early have been shown to have been improperly defined or erroneously dated. These last include, in particular, the assemblages referred to as Palisades I and the British Mountain complex (Dumond, 1978, with references).

THE PALEOARCTIC TRADITION (9500–6000 BC) □ The stone complexes that are unequivocally early already show considerable diversity, manifest particularly in the presence or absence of bifaces in general, of fluted points

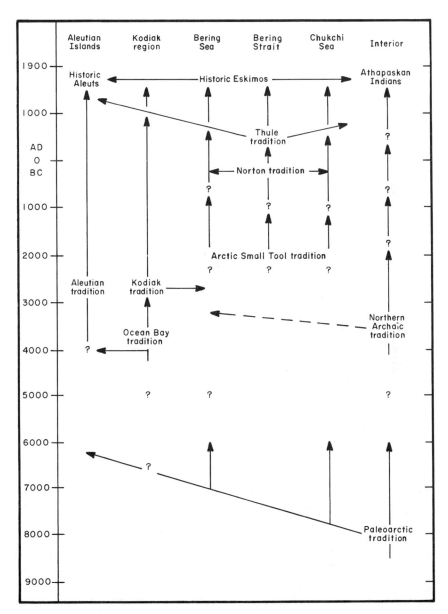

FIGURE 3.2
Major cultural traditions in Alaska.

in particular, and of certain apparently specialized implements such as types of burins (Figure 3.3). What the collections have strikingly in common is that they are dominated by products of a blade technology and include at least some blade cores in which the wedge-shaped form of the core was created before blades were removed. Although notable differences in scale are present, it is most common for these cores to be small, having provided miniature blades termed *microblades*. Examples of wedge-shaped cores from which the blades removed do not exceed five centimeters in length have sometimes been referred to as *campus-type* microcores, after the site on the University of Alaska campus where they were first discovered.

A number of collections also include larger blades struck from a variety of types of cores as well as more or less discoidal and bifacially worked flake cores, some of which reflect what might be called a Levallois technique of shaping the flake before detachment from the core. These collections are taken here to be the basic version of the tradition. More variant collections are of two kinds—those that also include some specialized stone projectile points and those that lack bifacially chipped stone entirely. For present purposes, however, all of these may be designated the *Paleoarctic* tradition (Dumond, 1980b).

Sites are located either in areas that were untouched by the latest major local glacial episodes or in zones that were deglaciated early, suggesting that camps were in close proximity to remnant glacial ice. They are dated by radiocarbon nearly as early as 9500 BC and at least as late as 6000 BC. Only one of them (Dry Creek, in central Alaska) has yielded a significant quantity of clearly associated faunal remains, especially archaic bison that seem dimly to reflect the Late Pleistocene Alaskan megafaunal assemblage of grazing herbivores of the productive tundra—bison, elephant, and horse.

Among specific assemblages of the basic sort are the well-represented Akmak and less well-represented Kobuk complexes from the site of Onion Portage on the Kobuk River in northeastern Alaska (Anderson, 1970); similar, more scanty finds from the north slope of the Brooks Range and the Noatak River drainage; the very similar collection from the Ugashik Narrows phase of the upper Ugashik River on the Alaska Peninsula far to the south (Henn, 1978); and, in addition to materials from Dry Creek, collections from central Alaska of the Denali complex as defined by West (1967, 1975).

Assemblages of the first variant mentioned above are more diverse in total inventory, although they include the same basic blade and core artifacts (Dumond, 1977:41-43, 1980b). At Healy Lake, in the Yukon–Tanana Uplands, the lowest levels of a shallow stratified site yielded a complex designated *Chindadn*, which includes some very thin, teardrop- and triangular-shaped points slightly more than five centimeters in length. A few other collections contain both microblades and projectile points with fluted bases. These latter include a poorly dated site on the Utukok River (Humphrey, 1970), the possibly erroneously dated site (2400 BC) of Girls Hill (Dumond, 1980b), and the Putu site (both Girls Hill and Putu are near the Sagavanirktok River in the Brooks

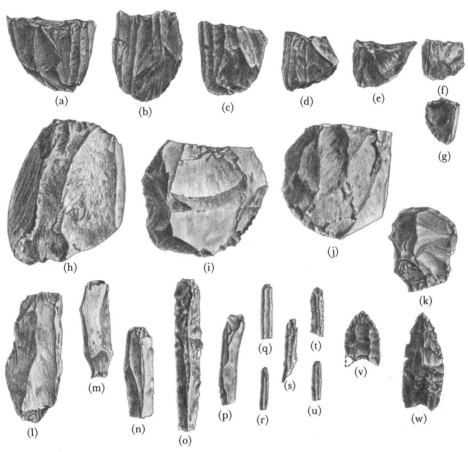

FIGURE 3.3
Artifacts of the Paleoarctic tradition: (a–g) wedge-shaped cores; (h) blade core; (i, j) core bifaces; (k) end scraper; (l–u) blades; (v, w) fluted and incipiently fluted points. (a, p, q) Anangula blade site, Anangula Island; (v, w) Batza Tena, an undated site in central Alaska; all others, Alaska Peninsula.

Range). Putu may be the most accurately dated site: a determination from an apparent hearth yields a date of about 9500 BC (Alexander, 1973, 1979). Although the dating of these fluted points in Alaska is a matter of disagreement, much evidence suggests that they do pertain to the Paleoarctic tradition (Dumond, 1980b).

The second variant is represented by two sites separated in space and time. One is the Anangula blade site, on Anangula Island just off the coast of Umnak Island in the eastern Aleutians. The collection from this site lacks bifacially chipped implements entirely, and the plentiful blades include a majority made from cores that received little advance shaping other than the flattening of a striking platform. The site dates to about 6000 BC (Aigner, 1978), and the latest geological research in the Anangula area indicates that the sea level had risen to about its present height by the time the site was occupied, so that the use of boats must have been known (Black, 1975) and an oceanside economic adaptation can be presumed. Speculation that the lack of bifaces was somehow a feature of littoral or even maritime orientation, however, is negated by the second collection, from what is called the Gallagher Flint station on the Sagavanirktok River near the Putu site, on the north slope of the Brooks Range. Although in many features strikingly similar to the assemblage from Anangula, this one— dated at about 8600 BC (Dixon, 1975)—is well in the interior.

Relationships of the Paleoarctic tradition lie particularly toward the west. Eastward in north–central Canada, no remains of human occupation are known until substantially later than the period under discussion. And although attempts have been made to compare fluted points of Paleoarctic tradition collections to early collections from what is now the continental United States (for example, Alexander, 1973; Humphrey, 1970), the presence in the arctic sites of the extensive and highly characteristic microblade industry is itself enough to set these assemblages apart from those proceeding from, say, the contemporary Clovis levels of the more southerly North American sites. These points may, however, indicate the beginning of communication between the people of Alaska and those already present in the south at the final retreat of the glaciers.

In northeastern Asia, however, the past few years have revealed evidence of obvious relevance to the prehistory of the American Arctic. Oval, bifacially chipped projectile heads and knives, disc-shaped cores, wedge-shaped blade cores, blades, microblades, scrapers, and a variety of burins are characteristic of collections in the Aldan River region that may date earlier than 30,000 BC and that persisted to 8000 BC, by which time similar assemblages had appeared on the Kamchatka and Chukchi peninsulas as well as in Alaska (Dikov, 1968; Mochanov, 1978). It thus seems clear that the Alaskan representatives of the Paleoarctic tradition hark back to a time when Alaska was a peninsula of Asia, thrusting against the continental ice of the New World. It seems likely that these Alaskans were hunters of grass-eating herd animals, roaming a dry but grassy tundra of a type now vanished (Dumond, 1980b; West, 1981, with references). One striking exception may be the Anangula blade site of 6000 BC, at which people of similar artifactual tradition may well have already embraced a life based on resources of the coast.

THE NORTHERN ARCHAIC TRADITION (4000–2000 BC) □ Although some researchers have argued that transitional assemblages linking those of the Paleoarctic tradition to later tool complexes must be present within mainland Alaska, no indisputable evidence for them has yet been produced. Rather, the well-dated sequences now available seem to indicate a hiatus of at least a thousand years between the youngest Paleoarctic sites and the oldest sites of the succeeding tradition.

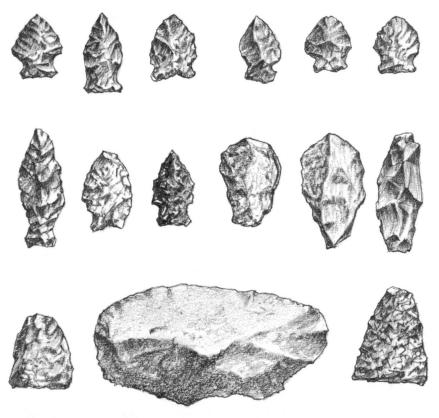

FIGURE 3.4
Artifacts of the Northern Archaic tradition; Palisades site, Cape Krusenstern.

Well-dated deposits from the site at Onion Portage have produced material assigned to two sequential complexes of what has been designated the *Northern Archaic* tradition (Anderson, 1968). The earliest stages, beginning around 4000 BC, include somewhat asymmetrical side-notched points with deep, wide notches and bases that are commonly rather convex; large, unifacially chipped knives; and chipped end scrapers. As time goes on, some of the projectile points become shorter, the scraping implements change somewhat, and notched cobbles, apparently designed to be hafted as axes, appear. Still later, the bases of the side-notched points tend to evolve into stems produced by corner notching; notched water-worn cobbles appear, supposedly used as sinkers; and some slate objects with crudely polished or striated faces are found. All of these are stages of what is termed the *Palisades* complex. By about 2600 BC, lanceolate points are found with the stemmed points, and the way is prepared for the *Portage* complex of about 2500 BC, when all projectile points are of generalized leaf or lanceolate form (Figure 3.4).

A number of other collections characterized by side- or corner-notched points have been reported—the great majority from the Alaskan interior but at least four of them from the coast. Most are not well dated, although those that are support the dating from Onion Portage.

Some other assemblages, of similar date and content, also include microblades. Among these are the complexes designated *Tuktu* (Campbell, 1961) and *Ugashik Knoll* (Henn, 1978) from Alaska, and others from as far east as the Yukon Territory and the southwest portion of the Northwest Territories in Canada, where they may occur equally early (MacNeish, 1964; but see Workman, 1978).

Unlike the case of the Paleoarctic tradition, the most characteristic implement of the Northern Archaic tradition—the side-notched point—finds no clearly widespread analog in Siberia. Rather, these points are reminiscent of artifacts of the Archaic stage of eastern North American prehistory, parallels to which occur in the United States as far west as the Great Basin. For this reason, this tradition has been conceived as marking a major incursion of Indian hunter-collectors moving northward from North America after the end of Pleistocene glaciation, an incursion coinciding fairly closely with the spread of forests during the warming of the Thermal Maximum (Anderson, 1968; Dumond, 1977). In any event, these were people adapted to the use of fully modern terrestrial resources.

After 2200 BC: The Coast

Between 2500 and 2000 BC, there appear clear indications of a new and widespread occupation near the coast, thought by many scholars to be that of ancestral Eskimos. There also appear at least hints of the presence of contemporary but divergent populations farther in the interior.

THE ARCTIC SMALL TOOL TRADITION (2200–1100 BC) □ This tradition was first discovered at Cape Denbigh on Norton Bay, where its representative was called the *Denbigh Flint* complex (Giddings, 1951, 1964). Manifestations of it are now known to occur from the Bering Sea side of the Alaska Peninsula in the southwest, northward along a strip of tundra-covered land adjacent to the Alaskan coast, throughout the Brooks Range, and, beyond Alaska, along the coastal zone of northern Canada and the Arctic Archipelago to Greenland. The origin of the Arctic Small Tool tradition is unclear. Elements of the technology suggest it was derived ultimately from some aspect of the Paleoarctic tradition. However, the apparent presence virtually everywhere in Alaska of the intervening and dissimilar assemblages of the Northern Archaic tradition suggests that, if this was the case, then any such transition must have occurred somewhere outside of Alaska, probably in Asia.

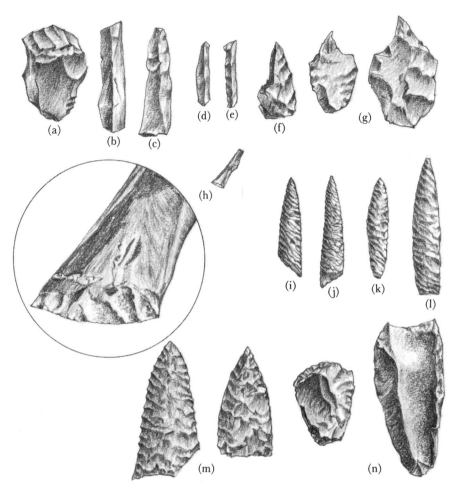

FIGURE 3.5
Artifacts of the Arctic Small Tool tradition, Denbigh Flint complex: (a) microblade core;
(b–d) microblades; (e) burin spall; (f, g) burins; (h) burin spall and much enlarged view of
retouched cutting edge; (i, j) sideblades; (k, l) projectile endblades; (m) large projectile (possibly
harpoon) blades; (n) scrapers.

The various collections are remarkably uniform, including small endblades
and sideblades, often bipointed; burins struck on small bifaces; microblades;
some variety of carefully made scrapers; occasional larger knifelike bifaces;
small adze blades with polished bits; and burinlike implements in which the
struck burin facet is replaced by a polished face (Figure 3.5). Alaskan collections do not include oil lamps, and the finds include no organic artifacts, for
reasons of poor preservation. In the eastern Arctic, however, some small tog-

gling and nontoggling harpoon heads of organic material are attributed to this period, and stone lamps appear sporadically.

Most of the Alaskan sites are the remains of temporary camps; they appear both along the coast proper and farther inland in the adjacent tundra zone, where they are frequently on streams. Constructed houses, apparently intended for winter occupation, are known so far from only four locations, all of them between 55 and 250 kilometers from the coast: Onion Portage on the Kobuk River, Howard Pass between the Noatak and Colville drainages in the Brooks Range, and the upper portion of both the Ugashik and Naknek River drainages on the Alaska Peninsula (Dumond, 1969, 1981; Henn, 1978). In this last area, the houses were square (about four meters on a side), excavated into the contemporary surface as much as half a meter, warmed by a central fire, and entered by an entryway that sloped downward into one side of the house in tunnel fashion.

Subsistence was apparently balanced between hunting and fishing, with the emphasis on caribou and salmon or other anadromous fish, where these fish were available. Interestingly, there is nowhere direct evidence that sealing through the winter ice (a technique that has often been thought indispensable to hunters who reside permanently on the arctic coast) was practiced by carriers of the Arctic Small Tool tradition, or that boats were in use, or that there was any consistent use of dogs. That is, there is no real evidence for the existence at this early time of the key attributes of later Arctic Eskimo culture, despite the fact that the distribution of northern historic Eskimos coincided with that of Arctic Small Tool people almost exactly.

After the widespread Small Tool occupation, there is a hiatus in the Alaskan sequence as it is now understood, although many investigators presume (on technological grounds) that Small Tool people were ancestral to most later coastal residents. Even though the break was apparently not exactly contemporaneous throughout (it occurred after about 1500 BC in the north and after 1100 BC in the south), it is sufficiently consistent to hint that the subsistence base of the people disappeared rather suddenly. The cause of any such occurrence is uncertain, but a period of climatic deterioration has been thought to be involved to some extent. In eastern Canada and Greenland (see Chapter Four), this same general time witnessed the more nearly unbroken transition from Pre-Dorset to Dorset, with Dorset people being somewhat more restricted to the coastline than their Pre-Dorset, Small Tool tradition ancestors.

This interval of transition also witnessed the very brief occupation of the enigmatic Old Whaling culture, known only from a single location on one beach ridge in northern Alaska (Giddings, 1967). That brief presence of apparent strangers had, however, no measurable effect on the development of Alaskan cultures, and it will be glossed over here. The temporal break ended in Alaska with the earliest manifestations of the Norton tradition, some stone implements of which suggest a measure of derivation from those of the Arctic Small Tool tradition.

THE NORTON TRADITION (1000 BC–AD 1000) □ This tradition includes all of the earliest Alaskan collections that contain pottery as well as some without pottery but in which the stone implements are reminiscent of those of the contemporary pottery users. A few of the former cultures, from northern Alaska, have been referred to elsewhere as *Choris* culture, and a number of the latter, as *Ipiutak* culture. Here all are treated as a single great unit.

The earliest known, or Choris form, of the Norton tradition is represented in few sites and by only limited published descriptions (Giddings, 1957, 1967). It apparently dates from the centuries immediately after 1000 BC. Choris pottery, the earliest in Alaska and clearly derived from Asia, is fiber tempered and decorated over the outside with linear stamping. Although some stone-working seems to reflect workmanship of the Arctic Small Tool tradition, the microblade has been abandoned, burins have changed, projectile points are larger, and oil lamps and crudely scraped slate tools are in use. At Cape Krusenstern, one beach ridge of Choris date yielded a cache of lanceolate points similar in many respects to unfluted lanceolate forms of Paleo-Indian assemblages of the North American Plains.

Elsewhere, occupation of the corresponding period displays variation. A site immediately south of Point Barrow has yielded a complex whose characteristic Choris ceramics are associated with stone implements even more strongly reminiscent of those of the Arctic Small Tool tradition. This may be validly dated to the late second millennium BC (Campbell and Cordell, 1975). A putatively similar assemblage proceeds from a site in the vicinity of the Firth River in northwestern Canada (MacNeish, 1956), in which stratigraphic displacements by frost action are extreme, making associations suspect (Mackay et al., 1961). There are no clearly similar assemblages from the Bering Sea coast, where sites of the ordinary Norton aspect of the Norton tradition appear probably no earlier than 500 BC.

The properly Norton form of the Norton tradition is what has been called Norton culture in the Bering Strait vicinity. It appears as far south as the Alaska Peninsula and even somewhat beyond, north to Point Hope and Point Barrow and east as far as the Firth River in extreme northwestern Canada (Ackerman, 1964; Bockstoce, 1979; Dumond, 1981; Giddings, 1964, 1967; Henn, 1978; Larsen and Rainey, 1948; Lutz, 1973; Nowak, 1973). The earliest manifestations appeared by about 500 BC, and the entire zone from the Alaska Peninsula to the Firth River in Canada was involved by the beginning of the Christian Era. The dominant pottery is now check-stamped, although linear-stamped ware identical in all respects to that of Choris collections occasionally appears in some locations. Although most projectile points are more crudely made than those of the Arctic Small Tool tradition, virtually all of the tool kit of that tradition is retained, except for the microblade and burin technology. In addition, the oil lamp is consistently present, and polished slate implements appear, although they are rare in many of the earliest sites (Figure 3.6). In all but the southern Bering Sea region, houses seem to have been confined to the

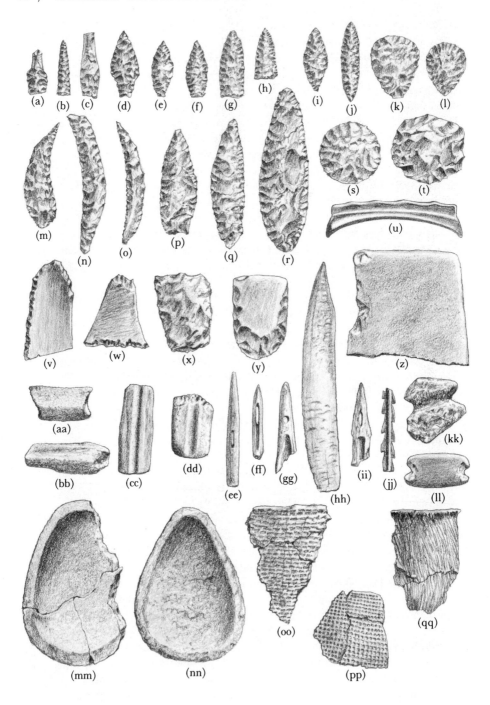

(a) (b) (c) (d) (e) (f) (g) (h) (i) (j) (k) (l)

(m) (n) (o) (p) (q) (r) (s) (t) (u)

(v) (w) (x) (y) (z)

(aa) (bb) (cc) (dd) (ee) (ff) (gg) (hh) (ii) (jj) (kk) (ll)

(mm) (nn) (oo) (pp) (qq)

coast. Permanent habitations are usually at least roughly square and excavated as much as half a meter into the contemporary surface, with sloping entries—scarcely distinguishable from houses of the Arctic Small Tool tradition from the Aläska Peninsula. The *kazigi*, or Eskimo combination ceremonial house and men's house, was probably present (Lutz, 1973). The toggling harpoon was in use; at Point Hope, the deposits (there termed *Near Ipiutak*) include a large toggling harpoon head presumably intended fɔr whaling.

Although people of the specifically Norton form of the Norton tradition appeared on coasts throughout mainland Alaska, it was only in the south, around the Bering Sea, that they endured. There they underwent a steady evolution until as late as AD 1000, their artifacts dividing into as many as three sequential phases (Dumond, 1981). In the north, not long after the beginning of the Christian Era, they were superseded by other people (perhaps their own descendants) of still another form of the Norton tradition, the *Ipiutak* culture—a way of life that was to last to about AD 800. Characteristic Ipiutak assemblages lack some of the important Norton diagnostics, namely, pottery, ground slate, and oil lamps. Yet projectile blades, the side-hafted, asymmetrical knives called sideblades, and other implements are so obviously Norton that, if one were to excavate an ordinary Norton camp in which the sometimes rare pottery was absent because no pot had been broken and in which no tool of the even rarer ground slate had been lost, one would simply classify the site as Ipiutak (Figure 3.7).

Especially striking are the lavish burial goods from the Ipiutak cemetery at Point Hope (Larsen and Rainey, 1948). In addition, permanent habitations—square, excavated into the contemporary surface, with a rudimentary entrance passage—are known from the same site, where they number in the hundreds and are scattered along several beach ridges. Generally similar houses are known from a few other coastal sites, as are temporary campsites.

Although in recent years a few sites and more scattered finds of implements of one or another aspect of the Norton tradition have been reported from the Alaskan interior, by far the greater number are known from the coast—a circumstance that is easily explained by an emphasis on coastal subsistence far exceeding that of the earlier people of Arctic Small Tool tradition. In the south, beginning almost with the Christian Era, this subsistence interest was apparently responsible for a progressive spread of Norton influence across the Alaska Peninsula to the North Pacific. By AD 600, the local tradition that had existed on the Pacific coast of the Alaska Peninsula had been all but overwhelmed

FIGURE 3.6 (*Opposite*)
Artifacts of the Norton stage of the Norton tradition: (a–c) drill bits; (d–h) projectile points; (i, j) sideblades; (k, l) bifacial knives; (m–o) scrapers; (p–r) lance points or knives; (s, t) discoidal knives; (u) labret; (v, w) polished slate fragments; (x, y) adze blades; (z) whetstone; (aa, bb) faceted whetstones; (cc, dd) sandstone abraders; (ee) antler harpoon foreshaft; (ff) antler arrowhead fragment; (gg) antler harpoon head; (hh) ivory harpoon head or possibly harpoon icepick; (ii) antler harpoon head; (jj) leister prong fragment; (kk, ll) stone net sinkers; (mm, nn) stone lamps; (oo, pp) check stamped potsherds; (qq) linear stamped potsherd.

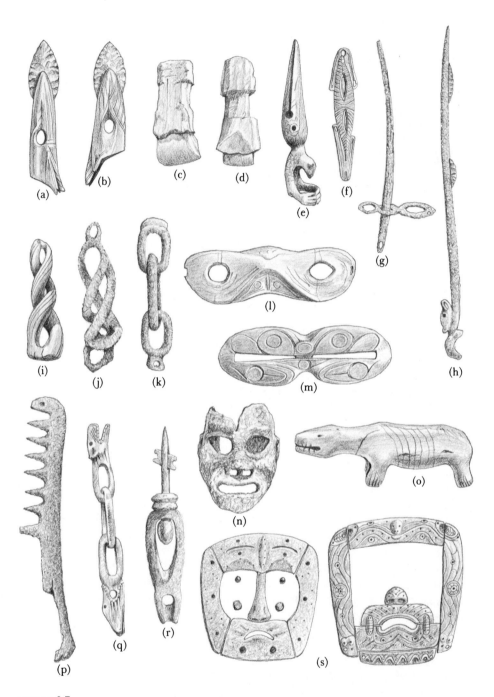

FIGURE 3.7
Artifacts of the Ipiutak variant of the Norton tradition: (a, b) harpoon heads; (c, d) bone adze heads with slate blades; (e) ivory openwork carving; (f) ivory ornament; (g, h) ivory lance heads or daggers; (i) ivory swivel; (j) ivory openwork carving; (k) ornamental linked ivory object; (l, m) ivory snow goggles; (n) human effigy of antler; (o) ivory polar bear effigy; (p) unidentified ivory implement; (q) ornamental linked object; (r) swivel; (s) masklike ivory carvings usually found associated with burials.

(G. H. Clark, 1977), and collections from as far away as Cook Inlet were noticeably affected.

THE THULE TRADITION (AD 100–1800) □ This tradition includes all prehistoric Eskimo remains from St. Lawrence Island and the nearby coast of Siberia, which date from after about AD 100, as well as remains from the northern Alaskan coast after about AD 500 and from the southern coasts after about AD 1000. In Canada and Greenland, it includes all remains after about AD 1000 or 1100. The Alaskan collections are characterized by a consistent, heavy use of polished slate and by dependence on coastal resources, with coast dwellers notably skilled in open-water hunting. This is what has also been called *Neo-Eskimo* or the *Northern Maritime* tradition (see, for example, Larsen and Rainey, 1948; Collins, 1964).

The earliest known manifestations of the Thule tradition are those termed *Okvik* and *Old Bering Sea* from the Siberian coast and from St. Lawrence and other islands around Bering Strait. Although it appears likely that they had their origin in the Norton tradition (Dumond, 1965, 1977; Larsen, 1968a), this hypothesis has not been conclusively demonstrated. They are characterized by an extensive use of polished slate; by pottery, often fiber-tempered and some of it impressed on the exterior with relatively broad corrugations (broader than the linear impressions of Choris and Norton pottery); and by an extensive organic artifact inventory, including numerous toggling harpoons in different sizes designed specifically for seals, walrus, and whales. Okvik–Old Bering Sea art, which was produced in the period from about AD 100 to 500, forms one of the high points of all Eskimo decorative work. It includes numerous elaborate ivory objects—carved human figures, ivory chains, and so on—as well as harpoon heads covered with spectacular patterns of parallel lines, dots, and encircled bosses (Figure 3.8). Houses were about three meters square, with a flagstone floor excavated into the contemporary surface. They were entered by a relatively long (about six meters) entrance tunnel, the floor of which dipped lower than that of the house in order to trap cold air and reduce drafts while still providing ventilation.

The best-known collections are from St. Lawrence Island (Collins, 1937; Geist and Rainey, 1936) and from the site of Okvik on one of the small Punuk Islands immediately to the east (Rainey, 1941). Although the artifact collections display no clearly consistent difference from site to site, the art styles permit discrimination between two major stylistic groups—hence the distinction between Old Bering Sea and Okvik. There are two differing views of the meaning of these stylistic differences. The first, and probably the most common, is that the Okvik style is the older—some proponents of this view have suggested an origin for Okvik several millennia before the Christian Era. The second view, favored here, is that the two were contemporaneous (see Ackerman, 1962); this surmise is supported by radiocarbon evidence. In the latter view, both Okvik and Old Bering Sea developed during the time that the Ipiutak variant of the Norton tradition was to be found on the Alaskan coast north of Bering Strait

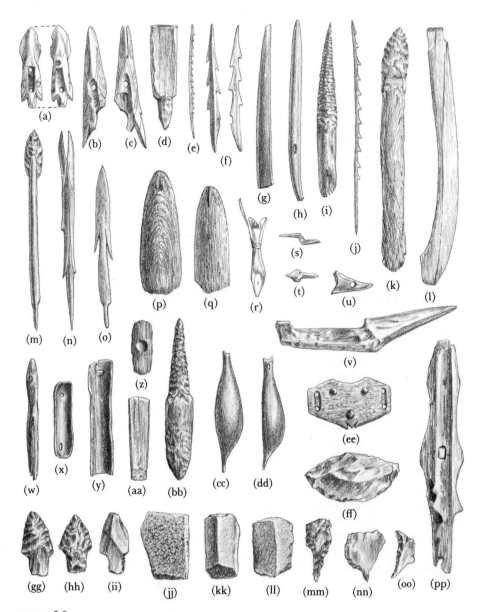

FIGURE 3.8
Artifacts of the early Thule tradition from St. Lawrence Island: (a–c) ivory harpoon heads; (d) ivory harpoon socket piece; (e) ivory fish spear point; (f) ivory sideprongs for bird darts; (g) ivory harpoon foreshaft fragment; (h) ivory harpoon foreshaft; (i) ivory icepick; (j) ivory fish spear point; (k) hafted knife; (l) wooden adze handle; (m–o) arrowheads; (p, q) wooden wound plugs; (r) walrus-tusk knife sharpener; (s, t) ivory pegs for end of throwing board; (u) ivory finger rest for harpoon shaft; (v) ivory meathook; (w) wooden drill shaft; (x, y) ivory fat scrapers; (z) ivory drill mouthpiece; (aa) ivory wedge; (bb) ivory icepick; (cc, dd) ivory fishline sinkers; (ee) bone ice creeper; (ff) *ulu* blade; (gg–ii) knife blades; (jj–ll) whetstones; (mm) hand drill; (nn, oo) gravers; (pp) throwing-board fragment.

and that the late phases of the Norton version of the Norton tradition were to be found in Alaska to the south.

In the second half of the first millennium AD, Okvik–Old Bering Sea was succeeded around St. Lawrence Island by another local development that has been termed *Punuk*. This culture was characterized by an art style that has much in common with its predecessors, particularly Okvik. The evolution of the Punuk style, which also involved the use of lines, dots, and circles on ivory implements, was apparently accompanied by no significant shift in subsistence or other workaday matters. Items such as polished stone implements and pottery scarcely changed from earlier forms, although the pottery was by now plain and tempered with heavy gravel. After AD 1200, implements became still more plain and pottery shapes changed somewhat, resulting in the material culture of the late prehistoric Eskimos of St. Lawrence Island (Figure 3.9).

By AD 500, when the Punuk style was becoming recognizable on St. Lawrence Island, a related but different Thule tradition manifestation known as *Birnirk* (from a site near Point Barrow) was spreading along the northern Alaskan coast from Bering Strait to Point Barrow, replacing Ipiutak. It was also apparently appearing in some places on the corresponding Asian coast, where its implements mingled with those of Punuk style. The most thorough published analysis of specific Birnirk stylistic and artifactual elements (Ford, 1959) concluded that the major source of the material culture lay in Old Bering Sea–Okvik. The lifeways suggested by the collections are closely similar, but the mainland environment of Birnirk is indicated in an increased use of caribou antler rather than ivory for harpoon heads and other implements. Like the Punuk collections, Birnirk assemblages represent people oriented toward the coast; in areas favorable for whaling, the necessary harpoon heads are found as well as numerous remains of buckets and other items made of baleen. Whalebone was used in house construction. The thick, gravel-tempered pottery, almost identical in paste to that of Punuk, was impressed on the outside with circular designs—targets or spirals—apparently applied with a paddle and often overstamped heavily. Birnirk proper disappeared before AD 1000, but from it developed the lifeways of all the later prehistoric coastal people of northern Alaska. The final result was embodied in the northern Eskimos encountered by Europeans—people skilled in winter ice-hunting, some of them settled in large villages at favorable whaling locations, and organized economically and ceremonially into whaling crews, each of which centered around a whaleboat-owning, *kazigi*-dominating entrepreneur known as the *umialiq*.

The most southerly house ruins of probable Birnirk affiliation have been reported around Cape Nome, on the southern coast of the Seward Peninsula, where they are dated to about AD 600 (Bockstoce, 1979). South of this, the introduction of Thule tradition lifeways lagged somewhat. On the Bering Sea coast of the Alaskan mainland, the earliest known representative is a collection termed *Nukleet*, from Norton Bay, of about AD 800. The assemblage is dominated by polished stone. Rectangular houses possessed the deeply sunken en-

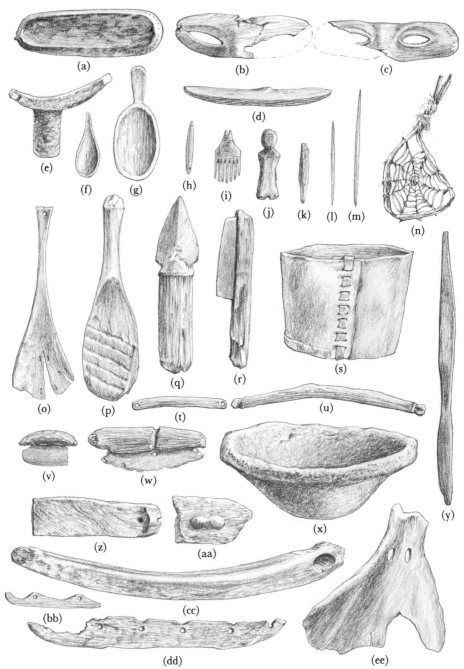

FIGURE 3.9

Artifacts of the Thule tradition from St. Lawrence Island: (a) ivory vessel; (b, c) wooden snow goggles; (d) toy wooden kayak; (e) drum handle and rim fragment; (f) antler spoon; (g) antler ladle; (h) ivory browband; (i) ivory comb; (j) bark doll; (k) bone drill point; (l, m) ivory awls; (n) baleen ice scoop; (o) bone ladle; (p) wooden pottery paddle; (q, r) hafted slate knives; (s) baleen vessel; (t) wooden pail handle; (u) wooden bow drill; (v, w) slate *ulus* with wooden handles; (x) pottery lamp; (y) toy wooden bow; (z, aa) ivory sled shoes; (bb) toy wooden sled runner; (cc, dd) ivory sled runners; (ee) bone snow shovel.

trance tunnel or cold trap. Similar assemblages appear southward along the coast until they occur on the Bering Sea side of the Alaska Peninsula at about AD 1000. Only relatively minor evolutionary changes took place between that time and the arrival of the Russians shortly after AD 1800. By the later phases of the Thule tradition, there existed throughout the Alaskan coast all of the major items of the ethnographically known Eskimo culture: fully equipped kayaks, *umiaks,* dog sleds, sunken houses with deep entrances, and the almost staggering series of specialized tools and weapons. Of these last, artifacts of bone, antler, and ivory included parts for specialized arrows, darts, and spears for birds and fish; toggling harpoon heads and nontoggling harpoon dart heads for various sea mammals; and dart heads for land mammals, often split to take polished slate endblades. Artifacts of stone included varieties of polished projectile heads of slate as well as some chipped ones of harder stone, varieties of double-edged knives, and, of course, the familiar transverse-bladed *ulu.*

THULE EXPANSION □ After about AD 1000, and without any depopulation of the coast, there was a measure of expansion away from it. This expansion included movements by groups onto the treeless north slope of the Brooks Range, where they concentrated particularly on caribou hunting. It apparently also included movements upstream along major rivers into the forested interior, which led to a steady diversification in the use of resources. Land hunting and especially river fishing became more and more important. The lifeway of the Thule people of the forested upper reaches of the rivers of central Alaska has been called the Arctic Woodland culture (Giddings, 1952). Despite the weakening of their dependence on ocean resources, all these new inland people retained the use of certain coastal products—especially sea-mammal oil—which they obtained either by trade or by seasonal hunting trips to the coast. In some cases the expansion must have increased their contacts (not always friendly) with interior and thinly settled Indian groups.

The most notable expansionist adventure was the Thule migration across northern Canada to Greenland that apparently took place around AD 1000 or immediately thereafter (see Chapter Four). An analogous movement, however, occurred in the south of Alaska.

As was indicated earlier, people of the Norton tradition had begun to drift across the Alaska Peninsula to the Pacific coast long before AD 1000, presumably as a reflection of their increased interest in hunting sea mammals in open water. Under the impulse of the Thule tradition that movement increased dramatically. But unlike northern Canada, where Thule people replaced or absorbed their Dorset cousins of a substantially different material culture, on the Pacific coast the importation of Thule stone implements resulted in a renewed emphasis on techniques and implement forms familiar long since in that region. The developing Thule tradition of the north, in its increased use of polished implements devoted especially to sea hunting, had been moving ever closer in material culture to the earlier peoples of Kodiak Island (to be mentioned shortly). The most exotic importation to the Pacific at this time was the thick, gravel-tempered Thule pottery that appeared on southern Kodiak Island around AD 1000. Never used in quantity in the northern portion of the island, it nevertheless was adopted elsewhere on the Pacific coast, in settlements of the Alaska Peninsula and along Cook Inlet (D. W. Clark, 1966; G. H. Clark, 1977; De Laguna, 1934; Dumond and Mace, 1968).

After 2000 BC: The Interior

Despite an increasing amount of work in recent years, the prehistory of the Alaskan interior is still seen only dimly. Some researchers are sure that small wedge-shaped microcores similar to those of the Paleoarctic tradition endured until the Christian Era. Together with key artifacts of the Northern Archaic tradition, these supposedly formed a long-standing interior tradition, presumably of ancestral Indians. Other researchers disagree (Shinkwin, 1979, with references). As mentioned earlier, the first millennium AD apparently did witness the presence of Norton-like assemblages in some interior river drainages. Beyond these two sets (or putative sets) of complexes, there is little evidence of the existence of inhabitants in the interior at this time. Exploration has discovered only a single short-term occupation at the site of Onion Portage, which included well-made lanceolate projectile points of obsidian and has been dated radiometrically at about AD 500. These points have been compared to a few other, undated implements from the Brooks Range (Anderson, 1972) and may be further evidence of a fairly widespread, if sparse, interior population.

Evidence is slightly more satisfactory for the period after AD 1000. Defined first on the basis of a small collection from Anaktuvuk Pass (Campbell, 1962, 1968b), the late *Kavik* complex was said to be characterized by small contracting-stem projectile points. More recently, this information, with collections from the site of Klo-Kut near Old Crow in northwestern Canada and from the upper Tanana River and the Copper River drainages, has permitted the definition of a prehistoric phase of Athapaskan Indian culture. This phase includes Kavik points, various scrapers and bifaces, and a bone technology, and is dated from about AD 1000 to 1800. In areas near sources of copper, to this basic complex is added a hammered copper technology that includes tanged points, awls, and knife blades (Shinkwin, 1979).

Although the various collections referred to above are heterogeneous among themselves, they do not exhaust the variation present in recent cultures of the interior. Farther west, along the lower Yukon River, are sites that vary even more strikingly. Although almost certainly inhabited by late prehistoric Indians, these yield many implements generally thought typical of Eskimo sites—objects such as bone toggling-head harpoons, polished slate transverse knives or *ulus*, bow drills used with a mouthpiece to hold the upper end of the drill, and pottery (De Laguna, 1947). The archeological impression of the acculturation of the recent lower river Indians is confirmed by ethnography (see, for example, Osgood, 1940).

Thus, whatever the degree of ancient homogeneity of ancestral peoples in the interior, the more recent Athapaskan-speaking Indians have displayed regional variety in material culture. This variety is completely in keeping with their impressive ability—known from historic times—to sustain life by use of regionally varied and not always plentiful resources.

Summary: Arctic Alaska

The first widespread and indisputable occupation of Alaska was by microblade-producing hunters of the Paleoarctic tradition, whose affiliations lay in northeastern Asia. Present throughout the area from about 9500 to 6000 BC, they probably focused their attention on remnant herds of the herbivores that had once ranged the dry but relatively grassy tundra of the Late Pleistocene and that were in the process of extinction. By 6000 BC, at least one set of these people may have established a more stable adaptation to the Pacific seacoast in the eastern Aleutian Islands. Elsewhere, however, they were to vanish shortly afterward as the Alaskan landscape achieved its modern aspect—despite the continued presence of such herd animals as the caribou and musk ox.

By 4000 BC, this population's place had been taken by equally widespread people of the notched-point-chipping Northern Archaic tradition, now apparently of American affiliation. These hunters and collectors of the modern forests and tundra margins continued their sway until around 2000 BC and, deep in the interior, possibly later.

By about 2200 BC, the Arctic Small Tool tradition represented a generalized hunting people adapted to life on the tundra strip inside the coast. Their subsistence was based on river fishing, land-mammal hunting, and the seasonal quest for sea mammals. These people spread across all of arctic North America to Greenland; in the east, their descendants of a millennium and a half later would be the bearers of Dorset culture. Although their precise origin is uncertain, the absence of any apparent immediate predecessors within Alaska suggests that they represent a new influx of people from Asia, probably as an Asian outgrowth of a Siberian branch of the Paleoarctic tradition.

By the last centuries before the Christian Era, the presumed descendants of the Arctic Small Tool people in Alaska (those of Norton tradition) occupied the coast from the Alaska peninsula northward. Equipped with new techniques derived in part from Asia, more sedentary, and more completely adjusted to life on the seacoast, they spread as far east along the Arctic coast as it was possible for them to do and still maintain their customary life. At Bering Strait, these same people initiated a cultural florescence based on the heavy use of sea mammals, which resulted in the pattern of living represented in the Thule tradition. Succeeding centuries saw increasing specialization in the use of sea products by some of these people as well as subsidiary developments by others toward specialized dependence on salmon and caribou.

Around AD 1000, possibly as a result of warmer weather that brought a change in the path of sea-mammal migration, North Alaskan coastal hunters moved eastward across northern Canada to Greenland. Meanwhile, the interest in open-water hunting brought on a similar southward expansion to the coast of the Pacific, rich in sea mammals, and pottery and other peculiarly Thule traits appeared on Kodiak Island.

By about this same time—AD 1000—there is clear evidence for the presence in the interior of ancestral Athapaskan Indians. Their earlier history is presently uncertain.

THE ARCHEOLOGY OF THE PACIFIC RIM

South of the Alaska Peninsula, along the coast of the unfreezing North Pacific from the Aleutian Islands to modern Washington and Oregon, there is at least presumptive evidence that some of the earliest cultural traditions were shared and that later times saw some maintenance of communication from the vicinity of Vancouver Island northward (although the two extremes of this very lengthy coastline—some 4000 kilometers—were distinctive in their ultimate developments). The traditions by means of which the discussion here is organized are diagrammed in the appropriate parts of Figure 3.2 and in Figure 3.10. In the Pacific Rim region, a marked adaptation to the coast becomes apparent around 4000 BC, a date that will be taken as the major division in this description.

Before 4000 BC

The character of the earliest tool assemblages bears the stamp either of the Paleoarctic tradition, mentioned earlier, or of a southern counterpart (which is here termed the *Paleoplateau* tradition)—or of some combination of the two.

THE PALEOARCTIC TRADITION (8000–4000 BC) □ Assemblages clearly related to this tradition occur on the southern margin of arctic Alaska, along the Bering Sea slope of the Alaska Peninsula, where they have thus far been dated in the Ugashik drainage, and elsewhere, at 7000 BC and later (Dumond, 1981; Henn, 1978). As mentioned earlier, a variant is also known from Anangula Island in the eastern Aleutians, where it is dated at about 6000 BC and may represent people already adapted to a coastal livelihood. Although no similar collection is yet known from the vicinity of Kodiak Island, immediately across the Alaska Peninsula from Ugashik, at least one assemblage among the earliest known from that area (of about 4000 BC) exhibits evidence of a moribund microblade industry (D. W. Clark, 1979). It and its affiliates are thus suspected to have had a Paleoarctic origin.

Farther southeast, by 6000 BC—possibly even 8000 BC—people deriving microblades from cores (at least some within the formal range of those of the

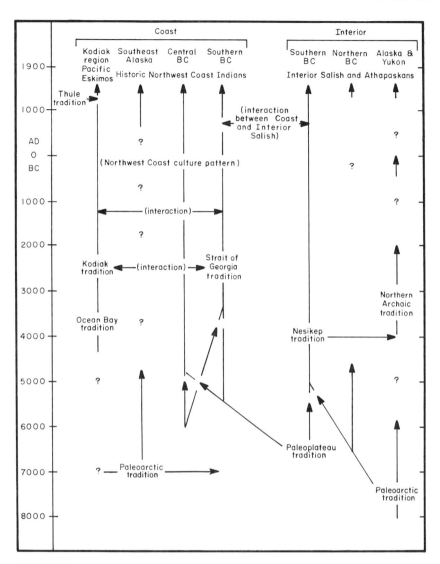

FIGURE 3.10
Major cultural traditions in the northern portion of the Pacific Northwest and adjacent regions.

Paleoarctic tradition) were in the vicinity of modern Juneau, Alaska, at a site on Ground Hog Bay (Ackerman, 1973; Ackerman et al., 1979). These people apparently were also to be found eastward in northern British Columbia in the upper drainage of the Stikine River, whence proceeds an undated microblade assemblage (Smith, 1971). Similar Paleoarctic artifacts, possibly dated as long ago as 8000 BC, have also been discovered at the site of Hidden Falls on Baranof

Island (Davis, 1980). Farther south, at the site of Namu on the central British Columbia coast, Paleoarctic-like microblades appear, in an assemblage that also includes some bifacial implements, dated as early as 7800 BC (Carlson, 1979; Hester and Nelson, 1978). Microblade makers using some cores still within the range of variation of those of the Paleoarctic tradition were present in the Queen Charlotte Islands by 5000 BC (Fladmark, 1970, 1971a, b)—the earliest occupation known on that archipelago. By the same time, they were also present in the interior of southern British Columbia around the confluence of the Thompson and Fraser rivers (Sanger, 1970), where, however, they followed assemblages of the Paleoplateau tradition. Here, too, the technique of micro-blade production was somewhat changed; blades were produced chiefly from cores in which the weathered cortex surface formed the striking platforms. Although corner- and side-notched projectile points are also associated (at a date early enough to have provided a prototype for similar implements of the North-ern Archaic tradition of arctic Alaska), by 4000 BC microblades constituted about 50 percent of the collections, which are assigned to what is termed locally the *Nesikep* tradition.

Still later—after 3000 BC—microblades appeared in assemblages in the Strait of Georgia area, and possibly as early as 4500 BC they occurred as part of an otherwise typical Columbia Plateau assemblage at the site of Ryegrass Coulee in south-central Washington. At about this point, the southward distribution is broken. It must be stressed that, from central British Columbia southward, the earliest appearance of microblade technology is in complexes that also contain bifacial implements of types that were apparently derived from the south, from representatives of the next tradition to be discussed.

THE PALEOPLATEAU TRADITION (8000–3000 BC) □ Toward the south-ern edge of the area covered by Pleistocene glacial ice, the assemblages for which greatest age has been claimed were obtained from the several terraces of the Fraser River in the vicinity of modern Yale. They make up a collection known as the *Pasika* complex. These pebble tools and scrapers have been said to date from the Late Pleistocene and to represent the ancestors of makers of later artifacts represented in the vicinity. However, their validity as an early cultural assemblage has been called into question on various grounds (Borden, 1975: 55–60, with additional references). Because it is not yet clearly possible to relate these tools and scrapers systematically to other remains in the area, they will not be dealt with further here (but compare Carlson, 1979).

Further evidence of the possible presence of hunters in the same general region comes from near the town of Sequim on the northern Olympic Peninsula of Washington, where in 1977 were found the remains of a mastodon (*Mammut americanum*). Into a rib of the animal had been driven—while it was alive—a bone splinter that has been interpreted as a bone projectile point, around which the bone had subsequently partly healed. The find was apparently dated by radiocarbon at about 10,000 BC. The distribution of the bones suggested the carcass had been butchered, although the only apparent stone artifact in the vicinity was a single flaked cobble spall. The actual cause of the animal's death is uncertain, but the remains have been said to demonstrate human presence on the Olympic Peninsula at that date (Gustafson et al., 1979).

The foregoing aside, the earliest concrete evidence of what will here be called the Paleoplateau cultural tradition is from locations in the Columbia–Fraser Plateau and from the canyon of the Fraser River in south–central British Columbia. In the middle Columbia region it includes material from Five Mile Rapids near The Dalles, Oregon (Cressman, 1960), and the Windust and Cascade phases of the lower Snake River (Leonhardy and Rice, 1970; Rice, 1972; see also Figure 5.11, this volume). More fragmentary indications of the existence of the same adaptation proceed from the zone west of the Cascade Range and its northward extension, the Coast Mountains of British Columbia.

Between about 8000 and 6000 BC, the Columbia Plateau collections include projectile points with shoulders, relatively short blades, straight or contracting stems, and straight or slightly concave bases; occasional lanceolate or leaf-shaped points; lanceolate and ovoid knives; some burins, cobble choppers, and discoidal cores; some fairly large blades struck from polyhedral cores; and some projectile heads produced from discoidal cores through the use of a Levallois-like technique. Mullers or grinders also were in use, although not common. Portions of the assemblage—the discoidal cores, the blades, and the blade cores—are reminiscent of portions of some complexes of the Paleoarctic tradition. These southern collections, however, lack all trace of microblades and include a characteristic congeries of projectile points that is unrepresented in the Arctic. The traces of early bison hunters at Lind Coulee (Daugherty, 1956) apparently pertain to this culture type; the bone refuse elsewhere includes modern land mammals, large and small, and shell refuse consists of river mussel.

After about 6000 BC, the bipointed or leaf-shaped Cascade point became typical in an assemblage otherwise little changed. Around 5000 BC, this assemblage was joined by a series of large side-notched projectile points. Game remains now include bones of anadromous fish, which probably indicate the use of a new resource.

For a time following 7000 BC, the basic Paleoplateau assemblage is reflected in the lowest deposits in the canyon of the Fraser River, where they are interpreted as indicating a late summer occupation coinciding with the Fraser River salmon runs (Borden, 1975). To the east, a northward movement of Paleoplateau people reached the Interior Plateau of the upper Fraser, Thompson, and Columbia River systems around 6000 BC (Sanger, 1969). Some lanceolate points of the same date may also reflect the influence of Plano people from the plains to the east, who were apparently moving northward in central Canada at the same time. Similar Paleoplateau-like complexes are reported from the Chilcotin Plateau to the west (Mitchell, 1970).

In general, it seems evident that the Paleoplateau tradition assemblages are related to those of the contemporary northern Great Basin and perhaps to others still farther south, of what has been called a San Dieguito-like horizon (see Chapter Five).

The degree to which the Paleoplateau tradition is present on the coast itself is not yet clear. In the early deposits at Five Mile Rapids (located on the western edge of the Plateau), seal bones appear, indicating acquaintance with sea mammals, if only those taken while pursuing salmon migrating upriver. Paleoplateau tradition artifacts are present on the western slope of the Cascade Range in Oregon (Newman, 1966). Some investigators (for example, Butler, 1965) have suggested that the Paleoplateau tradition was ancestral to later developments of the lower Columbia River, which culminated in the culture of the Penutian-speaking Chinook Indians; the evidence available from the region is enough to indicate that this relationship was likely but not enough to demonstrate it conclusively.

Fragmentary collections are known from both western Washington and British Columbia that probably pertain to the same tradition (Bryan, 1963; Mitchell, 1971:60, Table X). A single point possibly diagnostic of such a complex was also found in a stratum well above the mastodon (mentioned above) near Sequim, in a level dated after 5000 BC (Gustafson et al., 1979). Much better documented is the earliest component from the Glenrose Cannery site on the South Arm of the Fraser River, about 20 kilometers above its mouth. Dated at 5000 BC or earlier, the assemblage is reminiscent of one of the earliest phases of the Fraser Canyon and of the Cascade phase of the Columbia Plateau (Matson, 1976); it includes bone waste of elk, deer, beaver, mink, dog, and seal.

Farther north at Namu, leaf-shaped points appear at about 3500 BC, where they occur with the older microblades. Paleoplateau-like leaf-shaped projectile points, crude bifaces, scrapers, and other implements also appear in undated assemblages, assigned to the Cathedral phase, from several sites now under high tides in an inlet east of Namu (Borden, 1975; Hester and Nelson, 1978). Still farther north at Prince Rupert, in a lowest horizon dated from 3000 or 2500 BC and later, chipped stone implements include heavy leaf-shaped points, chipped points with square bases, large leaf-shaped knifelike bifaces, and scrapers and cutting implements of boulder chips and pebbles. This Paleoplateau-like material does not represent people adapted only to life inland, however, as is made clear by the series of bone harpoons that are barbed and with line guards to hold the line or with gouged line holes (MacDonald, 1969).

After 4000 BC

A maritime emphasis of adaptation is clearly manifest after 4000 BC.

THE OCEAN BAY TRADITION (4000–3000 BC) □ In the Kodiak Island group and on the nearby Alaska Peninsula coast, the earliest known complexes are dated between 4000 and 3000 BC (D. W. Clark, 1966, 1979; G. H. Clark,

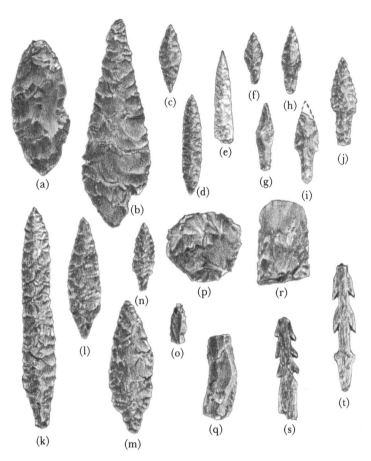

FIGURE 3.11
Artifacts of the Ocean Bay tradition, Alaska Peninsula: (a–n) projectile points and knives;
(o, q) blades; (p) discoidal core; (r) adze blade with polished bit; (s, t) bone harpoon dart heads.

1977) and may be assigned to an Ocean Bay tradition. Collections include large numbers of leaf-shaped, percussion-flaked knives or heavy projectile heads; percussion-flaked knives or projectile blades with rather weakly developed, tapering stems; and a variety of scrapers. One site yielded some better-made projectile blades with relatively long stems, triangular in cross-section, as well as a few gougelike adze blades with polished bits. A single stone vessel apparently used as a lamp for burning sea-mammal oil has been found, and—as indicated earlier—at least one site has yielded some microblades from its basal levels. Little organic material is preserved, but one exceptional site had preserved barbed bone harpoon dart heads designed to hold within the animal by barbs alone rather than by "toggling" or twisting in the wound (Figure 3.11). Also recovered were remains of numerous sea mammals, caribou, bear, water birds, shellfish, and various salt-water and anadromous fishes (Dumond, 1980a). Of these, cod, halibut, sea otter, porpoise, and albatross imply the use of boats for working a substantial distance offshore, which clearly indicates that the people were specialized for coastal life. The location of at least one of the sites suggests that river fishing was also important. Thus, materials of the Ocean Bay tradition constitute a horizon of the Pacific Eskimo region of the fourth millennium BC and can be supposed to have begun in an earlier blade-making tradition.

In the eastern Aleutian Islands, comparable artifacts have been recovered from several locations (Aigner et al., 1976; Turner and Turner, 1974). The most strikingly Ocean Bay-like projectile heads were those discovered on Anangula Island in 1974 near the older blade site (of Paleoarctic tradition), where they have been dated at about 4000 BC (Laughlin, 1975). Thus, although some researchers have rejected the notion, the presence of the Ocean Bay tradition within the Aleutian Islands appears probable.

THE ALEUTIAN TRADITION (AFTER 3000 BC) □ West of about 158° west longitude, there ensued the long development of a tradition of stone implements manufactured by chipping and of bone implements in which the barbed harpoon dart head—rather than the toggling harpoon head—was particularly notable (Figure 3.12). Although there is at present no known early and homogeneous archeological horizon through the region that clearly represents its initial settling by ancestors of recent Aleuts, various investigators have suggested that both the very much earlier blade collection (Paleoarctic tradition) of Anangula Island and the Ocean Bay tradition are related to that development. In any event, it is clear that people ancestral to the modern Aleuts were occupying the Fox Island group at least as early as 3000 BC, the Rat Island group at least as early as 1000 BC, and the Near Island group at least as early as 600 BC. There is no evidence of any kind to suggest that the Aleutian Islands were populated from the west—that is, directly from Asia.

On the Alaska Peninsula, the province assigned to the Aleutian tradition includes the region around Chignik and the major Hot Springs site at Port Moller (Workman, 1966; Okada and Okada, 1974), where occupation apparently spanned the time from before 1000 BC almost until contact. Westward, approaching the tip of the peninsula at Izembek Lagoon, excavations have uncovered a semisubterranean house constructed about AD 1000 using a framework of whale mandibles. Associated artifacts include both chipped stone implements reminiscent of those from Port Moller and polished slate and pottery of the Thule tradition, such as are known around the Bering Sea at AD 1000 and later (McCartney, 1974). From the easternmost Fox Islands have been reported a similar mixture of chipped stone and polished slate from the end of the first millennium AD (Turner and Turner, 1974). At Umnak Island in the western Foxes, early occupation is known to date from about 3000 BC. Houses were

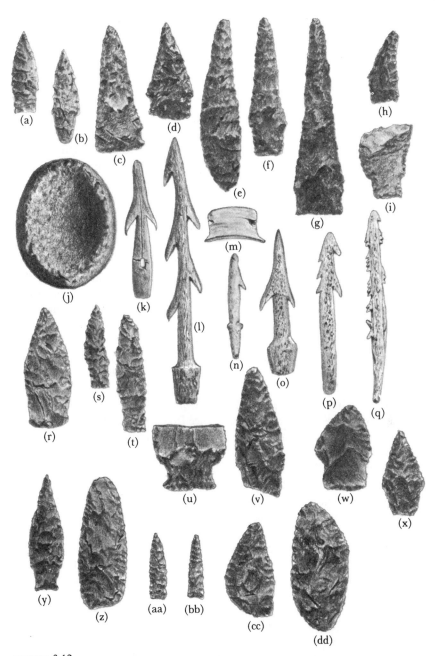

FIGURE 3.12
Artifacts of the Aleutian tradition: (a–i, r–dd) stone projectile points and knives; (j) stone lamp; (k, l, n–q) bone dart heads; (m) ivory labret. (a–q) Umnak Island; (r–dd) Chignik region, Alaska Peninsula.

elliptical and were apparently entered from the roof. The heavily excavated site at Chaluka on the same island was occupied from about 2000 BC. Subsistence orientation was always toward the sea; large numbers of fish, hair and fur seals, sea lions, sea otters, and some whales were taken. Only very late—certainly after AD 1000 and possibly after AD 1500—did polished slate appear among the implements (Aigner, 1966; Aigner et al., 1976; Denniston, 1966; Lippold, 1966).

At Amchitka in the Rat Islands to the west, the stone and bone artifacts (in a sequence beginning around 1000 BC) are similar to those from Chaluka. Faunal food trash included sea mammals, birds, fish, and invertebrates. The fish were ocean varieties but predominantly those of the area close inshore (Desautels et al., 1970). A house from about AD 1500 was subrectangular, about five to six meters in size, and apparently was entered through a hole in the roof. Associated tools included polished *ulus,* which apparently mark the earliest appearance of polished slate on the island (Cook et al., 1972).

Still farther west, collections from the Near Islands are stylistically the most variant of all those in the Aleutian chain. Chipped stone artifacts of about 600 BC include a very high proportion of elliptical to leaf-shaped bifaces reminiscent of some of those from Umnak and, in particular, of those from the much earlier Ocean Bay tradition. The polished slate *ulu* appeared very late, perhaps little earlier than the arrival of the Russians in the eighteenth century (McCartney, 1971; Spaulding, 1962).

In summary, there appears to have been continuous and undisturbed development in Aleutian territory, during which local cultures diverged only gradually from one another. Late in the sequence, a period of more rapid change is marked by the introduction of polished slate *ulus* and other implement styles in what seems to have been a wave of influence from the Bering Sea to the east, a wave that ultimately washed lightly over the entire chain of islands.

THE KODIAK TRADITION (AFTER 3000 BC) □ Whereas the Aleutian tradition of implement manufacture to the westward emphasized stone chipping, in the Kodiak region and the adjacent mainland there developed a robust tradition based on the polishing of slate. This tradition can be traced through three stages.

By 2500 BC, the older assemblages of the Ocean Bay tradition had been transformed. The people of the first or Takli stage of the Kodiak tradition—presumably Ocean Bay descendants—now polished long thrusting implements of slate, which they first sawed to shape. Yet they still relied to varying degrees on chipped stone implements, such as those their ancestors used (D. W. Clark, 1979; G. H. Clark, 1977). There is no evidence of a change in subsistence. Bone artifacts include harpoon dart heads, wedges, awls, and parts of fish spears or leisters (Figure 3.13). In bone waste, sea mammals predominate.

The next or Kachemak stage, dating from about 1500 BC to AD 1000, includes assemblages with a great variety of implements of polished slate that were

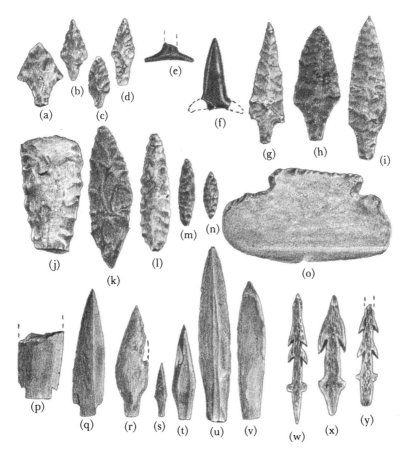

FIGURE 3.13
Artifacts of the Kodiak tradition, Alaska Peninsula: (a–d, g–i, k–n) chipped projectile points and knives; (e, f) labrets; (j) adze blade with polished bit; (o) polished slate *ulu;* (p–v) polished slate projectile blades; (w–y) bone harpoon dart heads.

predominantly chipped to shape before grinding. The transverse knife or *ulu* appeared. Oil lamps of stone were plentiful, and a number of them were decorated with reliefs carved within the bowl. There were labrets of stone or bone and a wide variety of bone implements, most notably harpoon dart heads. The primary orientation remained toward sea-mammal hunting with a strong subsidiary emphasis on fishing, including salt-water fishing for codfish and halibut. The distribution of assemblages of this stage includes the Kodiak Island group and the adjacent mainland coast as well as Kachemak Bay, much of Cook Inlet, and Prince William Sound still farther east (D. W. Clark, 1966; G. H. Clark, 1977; De Laguna, 1934).

In the third or Koniag stage, after AD 1000, the Kodiak people experienced the major impact of pressure from people of the Bering Sea. This pressure reflected the expanding Thule tradition of northern Alaska. The result was a convergence of material culture between peoples of Thule and Kodiak traditions, although with only minor innovations. One noticeable introduction was pottery, which, although taken up on southern Kodiak and on Cook Inlet, was not in consistent use. Ultimately, this amalgam resulted in the historically known Koniag of Kodiak Island and their neighbors—people of Eskimo speech with much in common with their Thule neighbors to the north but whose culture was derived most significantly from that of the earlier, less modified Kodiak tradition (D. W. Clark, 1974).

INTERMEDIATE REGIONS OF THE NORTHWEST COAST (AFTER 3000 BC) □ Although several sites are in the process of excavation between Prince William Sound in Alaska and Vancouver Island in British Columbia, the region is still not yet represented by adequate sequences. What is known is that by about 2500 BC microblades of the Paleoarctic tradition had disappeared and there were developments in the direction of the Northwest Coast culture of later times, with the appearance of polished slate, bone implements, and sea-mammal waste and the beginning of substantial shell middens. Examples include the site of Hidden Falls on Baranof Island (mentioned in connection with the Paleoarctic tradition) and a site on Prince of Wales Island, both in Alaska (G. H. Clark, 1979; Davis, 1980), and sites on the Queen Charlotte Islands and at Prince Rupert in British Columbia. At the last location, stone labrets occur by the early Christian Era in burials. Stone clubs and other implements of pecked stone also appear, together with slender, polished slate points. Still later, stone implements become rare. The projectiles are predominantly of bone, including both harpoons with line holes and composite toggling harpoons. Transverse knives are of shell, and there is much evidence of woodworking (MacDonald, 1969).

The site at Namu may inject a note of variation, however. Although by 2500 BC microblades disappeared, shell middens began to accumulate. Bone projectile points, harpoon dart heads, awls, and wedges began to occur. Significant proportions of sea mammals were apparently taken by boat, but the usual polished and pecked stone implements of Northwest Coast sites are thus far unknown (Hester and Nelson, 1978).

THE STRAIT OF GEORGIA TRADITION (AFTER 3000 BC) □ Still farther to the south, a seaward shift in subsistence emphasis is suggested by the Eayem phase of the Fraser Canyon, dated from about 3500 to 1500 BC. During that time, chipped, stemmed points derived from the earlier Paleoplateau tradition were joined by chipped and partially ground slate points and knives (Borden, 1975). Eayem-like assemblages have been recovered from other sites nearer the mouth of the Fraser, including one only about 20 kilometers from the present seashore (Borden, 1975; Calvert, 1970). An apparently related assemblage comes from the Helen Point site on Mayne Island in the western Strait of Georgia; it dates from 2500 BC or earlier (Borden, 1975:93; Carlson, 1970). This last assemblage, as well as one other, departs from the usual inventory in that it includes some microblades.

It has been proposed that the Eayem phase and all similar and contemporary components of the sites just referred to should be classed together as a regional cultural manifestation to be termed the *Charles* phase (Borden, 1975:97). This phase is presumed to be characteristic of the entire Strait of Georgia and southern coastal mainland of British Columbia of that time and is thought to have formed the base for the development of a tradition leading directly to the culture of the ethnographically known coastal Salish people. In keeping with other terminology used here, this manifestation can be called the *Charles* stage of the Strait of Georgia tradition.

The Mayne Island assemblage just referred to has been compared to contemporary assemblages of the Takli stage of the Kodiak tradition, and together, it has been suggested, they represent a common North Pacific cultural horizon of the third millennium BC (Carlson, 1970). It is equally reasonable to extend the same comparison to all collections of the Charles stage of the Strait of Georgia tradition. With an eye to the nature of most assemblages from the poorly known area north along the coast (G. H. Clark, 1979; Davis, 1980), it is possible to conclude with some confidence that a sphere of communication embraced at that time most of the Northwest Coast from Puget Sound to Kodiak Island. Situations such as that at Namu, however, may bespeak the presence of some enclaves of people who did not participate in the major network of coastal communication. Thus it is reasonable to take the Strait of Georgia tradition to represent in at least a general way the development of Northwest Coast culture as a whole.

The next manifestation of the Strait of Georgia tradition, the Locarno Beach stage (see Mitchell, 1971), includes as distinctive features chipped basalt points, often with contracting stems, nearly identical to those of the preceding stage; microblades and cores; chipped slate knives; polished slate points and knives; small, polished celts or adzes; labrets; earspools; and bone and antler implements that include bilaterally barbed points, wedges, foreshafts, and toggling harpoons of either one piece or composite form (Figure 3.14). Subsistence was based on both land and sea products, with sites predominantly located beside salt water, both in the Strait Islands and the Fraser Delta. The Locarno Beach stage is dated at least as early as 3000 BC and lasts to about 200 BC.

From shortly before the Christian Era until, probably, late in the first millennium AD, the Strait of Georgia archeological materials can be assigned to the Marpole stage of the Strait of Georgia tradition. Distinctive artifacts continue to include microblades and chipped stone points in a variety of forms, but now they

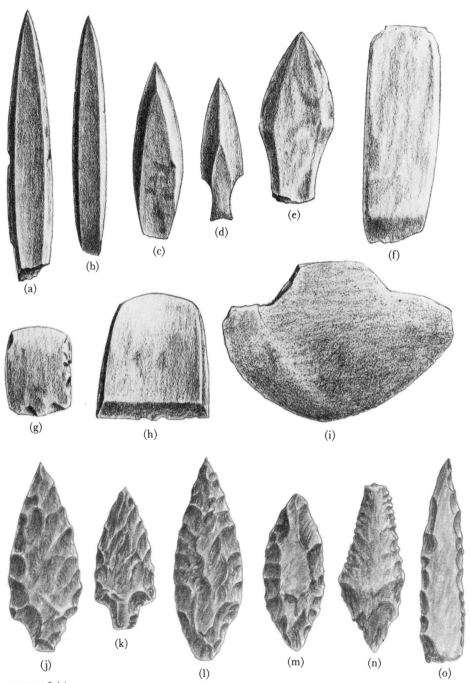

FIGURE 3.14
Artifacts of the Gulf of Georgia tradition, from the Fraser Delta region; (a–e) ground slate points;
(f–h) polished adze blades; (i) ground slate *ulu;* (j–n) chipped stone points; (o) chipped and ground point.
(a–d, g, j–o) Locarno Beach Stage; (e, f, h, i) Marpole Stage; (a–i) after Borden, 1962; (j–o) after
Mitchell, 1971.

also include an increased number of large, polished slate points and the transverse polished slate knife or *ulu*, apparently used to process fish. Barbed, nontoggling harpoon dart heads, tied by a line secured against projecting guards, were used for hunting sea mammals. Subsistence includes fish from the heavy runs of the Fraser River as well as other fish, birds, shellfish, sea mammals, and land animals.

By now settlements were large; habitations were probably the long cedar-plank house known among historic coastal Salish. The presence of numerous woodworking tools suggests the use of the dugout boat. Differences between burials—in the value and amount of grave goods and in the presence or absence of skull deformation—probably reflect status distinctions. Dentalium shells, disk beads, copper, and large and carefully chipped stone points are thought to represent wealth items and to imply the presence of institutions for the manipulation of property analogous to the historic potlatch. Sculpture in antler and stone plainly presages historic Northwest Coast culture. In short, the historical patterns of that spectacular culture appear to have been present by the beginning of the Christian Era.

By AD 1000, in the Late Prehistoric stage of the Strait of Georgia tradition, the ethnographic patterns reported for the Coast Salish at contact were even more certainly present in the Fraser Delta, the Strait of Georgia, and the San Juan Islands. Distinctive artifacts include triangular points of polished stone, with thinned bases for insertion into a harpoon head of antler or bone, polished adzes, and various composite fish hooks and toggling harpoon parts. Although changes are evident in the form of the most favored harpoons and certain other artifacts, the heritage of the Marpole stage is unmistakable. A variant is present in the Fraser Canyon, where during the Esilao phase the long plank houses of the coast were replaced by circular pithouses covered with poles, bark, and sod; this must have been an upriver Salish culture somewhat influenced by Salish relatives still farther to the interior (Borden, 1968; Mitchell, 1971).

Moving south along the coast, archeological materials are consistently late and pertain to developed Northwest Coast culture. Many of the known sites are protohistoric and historic, such as the well-published site at Ozette, Washington. Unpublished excavations near the mouth of the Columbia River indicate that the Northwest Coast lifeway appeared there by the beginning of the Christian Era. On the coast of Oregon south of about 43° north latitude, however, the Northwest Coast pattern yields to the cultures of the subregion of northern California.

A Glance at the Interior

After the climax of microblade production around 4000 to 3000 BC, the making of microblades was gradually abandoned in the area of the confluence of the Thompson and Fraser rivers. After AD 500, collections are characterized by small, side-notched, triangular projectile points, polished nephrite adzes, tubular copper beads, steatite carvings, and objects of ocean shell. Thus the Nesikep tradition moved from its early blade-producing stages to assemblages characteristic of the interior Salish peoples of the time of European contact—an evolution that has been interpreted as representing the development of only a single people (Sanger, 1969, 1970). Portions of the late assemblage were shared with others, however: the small, triangular arrow points were an important feature of the sites of northern British Columbia attributable to historically known Athapaskans, the descendants of whom still reside in the area (Smith, 1971).

Summary: The Pacific Rim

Elements of the Paleoarctic tradition not only established themselves in the eastern Aleutian Islands but also penetrated southward through much of the Northwest and appeared on the central coast of British Columbia shortly after 8000 BC. Meanwhile, hunter–collectors of the Paleoplateau tradition apparently moved northward with the recession of the Cordilleran glaciers between 10,000 and 7,000 BC and spread into the coastal zone and at least as far north as central British Columbia. There they encountered and mingled with carriers of northern ideas, a confluence manifested chiefly in the production and use of microblades in a technology derived from the Paleoarctic tradition. These northern ideas were then transported southward and arrived in the Fraser Plateau as early as 5000 BC. In turn, southern ideas—such as those responsible for the fabrication of side-notched projectile points—were transmitted northward. This vast regional interchange was integral to the peculiar character of the developing coast and interior cultures of British Columbia and Alaska. Thereafter, people derived from carriers of one or both of these great traditions began to show an aptitude for life on the seacoast.

In the north, this predilection apparently resulted in the Ocean Bay tradition, which by 4000 BC was present from Kodiak Island to the eastern Aleutians. From this tradition there probably developed, in the west, the long-lived Aleutian tradition of stone-chipping hunters of the oceanside and, finally, the historic Aleuts. In the east, the Ocean Bay culture engendered the equally long-lived Kodiak tradition of slate-polishing hunters and fishermen. Both of these peoples experienced incursions after AD 1000 from bearers of the Thule tradition of arctic Alaska. The result was, in the Aleutians, a slight influence marked by the spread of slate grinding and, in the Kodiak region, amalgamation with carriers of the Kodiak tradition to produce the historic Pacific Eskimos.

In the south, the Paleoarctic and Paleoplateau traditions merged in a similar coastal lifeway in the Strait of Georgia region—a lifeway so strongly reminiscent of that of the Kodiak area that it suggests that communication, once established, continued along the coastline. This lifeway was ancestral to later cultures not only of the Kodiak region, then, but also to that of virtually all Northwest Coast Indians. These Indians, based in the more southerly extension of the region with its greater marine and intertidal resources and in particular its mountainous hinterland rich in fish and game, surpassed their Kodiak cousins to produce the spectacular culture of abundance that is famous in the ethnographic literature.

From the evidence available, it is not clear whether the transmission of ideas both northward and southward between the Northwest and Alaska was initiated by a relatively massive movement of people from the north who arrived as far south as present Washington and Oregon or simply by sustained communication once occupation of the formerly glaciated zones opened to the slowly expanding populations of both north and south. If the first supposition is correct, then one might tentatively suggest that the ancestors of most people of true Northwest Coast culture entered the New World as part of a post-Pleistocene migration. This would include the forebears of the recent peoples who speak Salishan, Wakashan, and Na-Dene (among whom all the Athapaskans would of necessity be included) but not of the Penutian-speaking Tsimshian. The Tsimshians' linguistic relatives all lie to the south in a distribution more suggestive of derivation from people of the Paleoplateau tradition. They must represent a part of the population already present in America before the latest glacial advances of the Pleistocene.

If the intermingling of northern and southern influences resulted almost solely from diffusion, it is possible as an extreme case to argue that only the Eskimo–Aleuts—reputedly the most Asian of all American natives in physique and language—were derived from the Old World by migration in post-Pleistocene times. In such a case, all others of the Northwest (and all other American Indians) must have been present in the New World since well before the time of the Paleoarctic and Paleoplateau traditions as they have been described here.

Unfortunately, although both constructions assume the presence of people in southerly portions of North America before the recession of the major glaciers of the Late Pleistocene, neither Alaska nor the Northwest provides any clear and unambiguous trace of these supposed earlier immigrants to the Western Hemisphere.

CONCLUDING NOTE

It should not be surprising that in a composite region such as that dealt with here—a region stretching more than 3000 kilometers directly north–south (across 28 degrees of latitude) and nearly 5000 kilometers east–west (across 50 degrees of longitude), with coasts strung more than 10,000 kilometers through various seas—the attention of archeologists has been, and remains, focused primarily upon questions of time and space. The questions "who?" and "where?"

and "when?" are rendered enormous simply by the extent of the land, and until they are answered in at least a rudimentary way it is impossible to answer many questions like "what were they doing?" and "why?" That many of the elementary time–space questions have not been answered at all should be evidenced by the gaps in this presentation.

Nevertheless, the particular characters of both separate regions dealt with here—Alaska and the Northwest Coast—are such that, even from the beginning of active archeological research (eighty years ago in the south, scarcely sixty in the north), the questions have addressed aspects that seem particularly modern. These aspects are two—behavior and ecology.

The almost universal attention paid to the first aspect, specific behavior, is accounted for by the circumstance that archeology on both the Northwest Coast and in Alaska has been undertaken not only in places inhabited by descendants of the peoples whose history is being sought, but in the midst of people whose traditional culture is so strong that questions of artifact function can usually be answered definitively by any shovel hand. That is, all archeology is to a very significant extent ethnoarcheology: the immediate answers from local people are adequate to settle most behavioral concerns regarding late periods of prehistory. It was to be expected, then, that modern attempts to systematically project behavioral data with confidence *beyond* the immediate past would lead to some more formal and self-conscious ethnoarcheological research in the north—and so they did, resulting in projects of various sorts (for example, Ackerman, 1970; Binford, 1978; Campbell, 1968a; Hall, 1971; Oswalt, and VanStone, 1967; VanStone, 1972, with additional references).

As to the second aspect, ecology, the environment exerts pressure in such a forcible way in arctic Alaska that it cannot be ignored, and the question has been inescapable: "How and when (and why) did people learn to live here?" On the Northwest Coast, the accounts of early travelers and ethnographers raised questions of similar cogency about the development of the striking (if often misunderstood) wealth, extravagance, and waste of historic Northwest Coast Indian culture. "How has it been possible," it is asked, "for such wealth to be accumulated regularly by a hunting people, and for how long has this abundance existed?" The efforts of recent years, with the increasing maturity and improving methodology of archeology, have been inevitably to improve the answers to the primary questions rather than to change the questions themselves. So, for instance, the discovery that the Late Pleistocene tundra of the Bering Platform contained relatively high proportions of grass and *Artemisia* led some paleoecologists to hypothesize the presence at that time of a particularly productive tundra–steppe biome (West, 1981, with references). Although the more extreme positions in this regard are vigorously disputed (for example, Colinvaux, 1980), the arguments must nonetheless lead ultimately to an improved conception of the environmental context of very early archeological remains. Meanwhile, within the strictly archeological endeavor, extended collection methods and analytical tools are being employed to secure ever-better environmental evidence (see, for example, Morlan, 1977, 1978).

Both of these emphases must lead to the improvement of all such treatments as the present one and to better understanding of the peoples they concern.

References Cited and Recommended Sources

Ackerman, Robert E. 1962. Culture contact in the Bering Sea: Birnirk–Punuk period. In *Prehistoric Cultural Relations Between the Arctic and Temperate Zones of North America*, ed. J. M. Campbell, pp. 27–34. Arctic Institute of North America, Technical Paper 11.

———. 1964. *Prehistory in the Kuskokwim–Bristol Bay Region, Southwestern Alaska*. Washington State University, Laboratory of Anthropology, Report of Investigations 26.

———. 1970. Archaeoethnology, ethnoarchaeology, and the problems of past cultural patterning. In *Ethnohistory in Southwestern Alaska and the Southern Yukon*, ed. Margaret Lantis, pp. 11–48. Lexington: University Press of Kentucky.

———. 1973. Post Pleistocene cultural adaptations on the northern Northwest Coast. In *International Conference on the Prehistory and Paleoecology of Western Arctic and Sub-Arctic*, ed. S. Raymond and P. Schledermann, pp. 1–20. Calgary: University of Calgary Archaeological Association.

———, T. D. Hamilton, and R. Stuckenrath. 1979. Early cultural complexes on the northern Northwest Coast. *Canadian Journal of Archaeology* 3:195–210.

Aigner, Jean S. 1966. Bone tools and decorative motifs from Chaluka, Umnak Island. *Arctic Anthropology* 3:2:57–83.

———. 1978. *The Lithic Remains from Anangula, an 8500 Year Old Aleut Coastal Village*. Universität Tübingen, Institut für Urgeschichte, Urgeschichtliche Materialhefte 3.

———, B. Fullem, D. Veltre, and M. Veltre. 1976. Preliminary reports on remains from Sandy Beach Bay, a 4300–5600 BP Aleut village. *Arctic Anthropology* 13:2:83–90.

Alexander, Herbert L. 1973. The association of Aurignacoid elements with fluted point complexes in North America. In *International Conference on the Prehistory and Paleoecology of Western Arctic and Sub-Arctic*, ed. S. Raymond and P. Schledermann, pp. 21–32. Calgary: University of Calgary Archaeological Association.

———. 1979. The Putu complex. Unpublished paper read at the 43rd International Congress of Americanists, Vancouver, B.C.

Anderson, Douglas D. 1968. A Stone Age campsite at the gateway to America. *Scientific American* 218:6:24–33.

———. 1970. Akmak. *Acta Arctica* 16.

———. 1972. An archaeological survey of Noatak Drainage, Alaska. *Arctic Anthropology* 9:1: 66–117.

Binford, Lewis R. 1978. *Nunamiut Ethnoarchaeology*. New York: Academic Press.

Black, Robert F. 1975. Late-Quaternary geomorphic processes: effects on the ancient Aleuts of Umnak Island in the Aleutians. *Arctic* 28:3:160–169.

Bockstoce, John. 1979. *The Archaeology of Cape Nome, Alaska*. University of Pennsylvania, University Museum Monograph 38.

Bonnichsen, Robson. 1979. *Pleistocene Bone Technology in the Beringian Refugium*. Archaeological Survey of Canada Paper 89.

Borden, Charles E. 1968. Prehistory of the lower mainland. In *Lower Fraser Valley: Evolution of a Cultural Landscape*, ed. A. H. Siemens, pp. 9–26. Vancouver: B.C. Geographical Series 9.

———. 1975. *Origins and Development of Early Northwest Coast Culture to About 3000 BC*. Archaeological Survey of Canada Paper 45.

Bryan, Alan Lyle. 1963. *An Archaeological Survey of Northern Puget Sound.* Occasional Papers of the Idaho State University Museum 11.

Butler, B. Robert. 1965. Perspectives on the prehistory of the lower Columbia River. *Tebiwa* 8:1:1–16.

Calvert, Gay. 1970. The St. Mungo Cannery site: a preliminary report. *B.C. Studies* 6–7:54–76.

Campbell, John M. 1961. The Tuktu complex of Anaktuvuk Pass. *Anthropological Papers of the University of Alaska* 9:2:61–80.

———. 1962. Cultural succession at Anaktuvuk Pass, arctic Alaska. In *Prehistoric Cultural Relations Between the Arctic and Temperate Zones of North America,* ed. J. M. Campbell, pp. 39–54. Arctic Institute of North America, Technical Paper 11.

———. 1968a. Territoriality among ancient hunters: interpretations from ethnography and nature. In *Anthropological Archeology in the Americas,* ed. B. J. Meggers, pp. 1–21. Washington, D.C.: Anthropological Society of Washington.

———. 1968b. The Kavik site of Anaktuvuk Pass, central Brooks Range, Alaska. *Anthropological Papers of the University of Alaska* 14:1:33–42.

———, and Linda Seinfeld Cordell. 1975. The Arctic and Subarctic. In *North America,* ed. S. Gorenstein. New York: St. Martins Press.

Carlson, Roy L. 1970. Excavations at Helen Point on Mayne Island. *B.C. Studies* 6–7:113–135.

———. 1979. The early period on the central coast of British Columbia. *Canadian Journal of Archaeology* 3:211–228.

Cinq-Mars, J. 1979. Bluefish Cave I: a Late Pleistocene eastern Beringian cave deposit in the northern Yukon. *Canadian Journal of Archaeology* 3:1–32.

Clark, Donald W. 1966. Perspectives in the prehistory of Kodiak Island, Alaska. *American Antiquity* 31:3:356–371.

———. 1974. *Koniag Prehistory.* Universität Tübingen, Institut für Urgeschichte, Tübinger Monographien zur Urgeschichte 1.

———. 1979. *Ocean Bay: An Early North Pacific Maritime Culture.* Archaeological Survey of Canada Paper 86.

Clark, Gerald H. 1977. *Archaeology on the Alaska Peninsula: The Coast of Shelikof Strait, 1963–1965.* University of Oregon Anthropological Papers 13.

———. 1979. Archeological testing at the Coffman Cove site, southeastern Alaska. Unpublished paper read at the annual meeting of the Northwest Anthropological Conference.

Colinvaux, Paul A. 1980. Review of Cwyner and Ritchie, Arctic steppe–tundra. *Quarterly Review of Archaeology* 1:1:2–15.

Collins, Henry B., Jr. 1937. *Archeology of St. Lawrence Island, Alaska.* Smithsonian Miscellaneous Collections 96:1.

———. 1964. The Arctic and Subarctic. In *Prehistoric Man in the New World,* ed. J. D. Jennings and E. Norbeck, pp. 85–114. Chicago: University of Chicago Press.

Cook, John P., E. J. Dixon, and C. E. Holmes. 1972. *Archaeological Report, Site 49 RAT 32, Amchitka Island, Alaska.* Las Vegas: Holmes and Narver.

Cressman, L. S. 1960. Cultural sequences at The Dalles, Oregon. *Transactions of the American Philosophical Society* (n.s.) 50:10.

Daugherty, Richard D. 1956. Archaeology of the Lind Coulee site, Washington. *Proceedings of the American Philosophical Society* 100:3:223–278.

Davis, Stanley D. 1980. Hidden Falls: a multicomponent site in the Alexander Archipelago of the Northwest Coast. Unpublished paper read at the annual meeting of the Society for American Archaeology.

De Laguna, Frederica. 1934. *The Archaeology of Cook Inlet, Alaska.* Philadelphia: University of Pennsylvania Press.

———. 1947. *The Prehistory of Northern North America as Seen from the Yukon.* Memoirs of the Society for American Archaeology, no. 3.

Denniston, Glenda B. 1966. Cultural change at Chaluka, Umnak Island: stone artifacts and features. *Arctic Anthropology* 3:2:84–124.

Desautels, R. J., A. J. McCurdy, J. D. Flynn, and R. R. Ellis. 1970. *Archaeological Report, Amchitka Island, Alaska 1969–70.* Costa Mesa, Calif.: Archaeological Research, Inc.

Dikov, N. N. 1968. The discovery of the Paleolithic in Kamchatka and the problem of the initial occupation of America. *Arctic Anthropology* 5:1:191–203.

Dixon, E. James, Jr. 1975. The Gallagher Flint Station, an early man site on the North Slope, arctic Alaska, and its role in relation to the Bering Land Bridge. *Arctic Anthropology* 12:1:68–75.

Dumond, Don E. 1965. On Eskaleutian linguistics, archaeology, and prehistory. *American Anthropologist* 67:5:1231–1257.

———. 1969. Prehistoric cultural contacts in southwestern Alaska. *Science* 166:1108–1115.

———. 1977. *The Eskimos and Aleuts.* London: Thames and Hudson.

———. 1978. Alaska and the Northwest Coast. In *Ancient Native Americans,* 1st ed., ed. J. D. Jennings, pp. 43–94. San Francisco: W. H. Freeman and Company.

———. 1980a. A chronology of native Alaskan subsistence systems. In *Alaska Native Culture and History,* ed. Y. Kotani and W. B. Workman, pp. 23–47. Osaka: Senri Ethnological Studies 4.

———. 1980b. The archeology of Alaska and the peopling of America. *Science* 209:984–991.

———. 1981. *Archaeology on the Alaska Peninsula: The Naknek Region, 1960–1975.* University of Oregon Anthropological Papers 21.

———, and Robert L. A. Mace. 1968. An archaeological survey along Knik Arm. *Anthropological Papers of the University of Alaska* 14:1:1–21.

Fladmark, K. R. 1970. A preliminary report on lithic assemblages from the Queen Charlotte Islands, British Columbia. In *Early Man and Environments in Northwest North America,* ed. R. C. Smith and J. W. Smith, pp. 117–136. Calgary: University of Calgary Archaeological Association.

———. 1971a. Early microblade industries of the Queen Charlotte Islands, British Columbia. Paper read at the annual meeting of the Canadian Archaeological Association.

———. 1971b. Radiocarbon dates from the Queen Charlotte Islands. *The Midden* 3:5:11–12.

Ford, James A. 1959. Eskimo prehistory in the vicinity of Point Barrow, Alaska. *Anthropological Papers of the American Museum of Natural History* 47:1:1–272.

Geist, Otto W., and Froelich G. Rainey. 1936. *Archaeological Excavations at Kukulik, St. Lawrence Island, Alaska.* Miscellaneous Publications of the University of Alaska 2.

Giddings, J. L. 1951. The Denbigh Flint complex. *American Antiquity* 16:193–203.

———. 1952. *The Arctic Woodland Culture of the Kobuk River.* University of Pennsylvania, Museum Monographs.

———. 1957. Round houses in the western Arctic. *American Antiquity* 23:2:121–135.

———. 1964. *The Archeology of Cape Denbigh.* Providence: Brown University Press.

———. 1967. *Ancient Men of the Arctic.* New York: Knopf.

Gustafson, Carl E., R. D. Daugherty, and D. W. Gilbow. 1979. The Manis mastodon site: early man on the Olympic Peninsula. *Canadian Journal of Archaeology* 3:157–164.

Hall, Edwin S., Jr. 1971. Kangiguksuk: a cultural reconstruction of a sixteenth century Eskimo site in northern Alaska. *Arctic Anthropology* 8:1:1–101.

Henn, Winfield. 1978. *Archaeology on the Alaska Peninsula: The Ugashik Drainage, 1973–1975.* University of Oregon Anthropological Papers 14.

Hester, James J., and Sarah M. Nelson. 1978. *Studies in Bella Bella Prehistory.* Simon Fraser University, Department of Archaeology, Publication 5.

Humphrey, Robert L., Jr. 1970. The prehistory of the arctic slope of Alaska: Pleistocene cultural relations between Eurasia and North America. Ph.D. thesis, University of New Mexico. University Microfilms 71-9277.

Larsen, Helge. 1968a. Near Ipiutak and Uwelen–Okvik. *Folk* 10:81–90.

———. 1968b. Trail Creek. *Acta Arctica* 15.

———, and Froelich G. Rainey. 1948. *Ipiutak and the Arctic Whale Hunting Culture.* Anthropological Papers of the American Museum of Natural History 42.

Laughlin, William S. 1975. Aleuts: ecosystem, Holocene history, and Siberian origin. *Science* 189:507–515.

Leonhardy, Frank C., and David G. Rice. 1970. A proposed culture typology for the lower Snake River region, southeastern Washington. *Northwest Anthropological Research Notes* 4:1:1–29.

Lippold, Lois. 1966. Chaluka: the economic base. *Arctic Anthropology* 3:2:125–131.

Lutz, Bruce J. 1973. An archaeological *karigi* at the site of UngaLaqLiq, western Alaska. *Arctic Anthropology* 10:1:111–118.

McCartney, A. P. 1971. A proposed western Aleutian phase in the Near Islands, Alaska. *Arctic Anthropology* 8:2:92–142.

———. 1974. Prehistoric cultural integration along the Alaska Peninsula. *Anthropological Papers of the University of Alaska* 16:1:59–84.

MacDonald, George F. 1969. Preliminary culture sequence from the Coast Tsimshian area, British Columbia. *Northwest Anthropological Research Notes* 3:2:240–254.

Mackay, J. R., W. H. Mathews, and R. S. MacNeish. 1961. Geology of the Engigstciak archaeological site, Yukon Territory. *Arctic* 14:25–52.

MacNeish, Richard S. 1956. The Engigstciak site on the Yukon arctic coast. *Anthropological Papers of the University of Alaska* 4:2:91–112.

———. 1964. Investigations in southwest Yukon: archaeological excavation, comparisons and speculations. *Papers of the Robert S. Peabody Foundation for Archaeology* 6:2:201–471.

Mathews, William. 1979. Late Quaternary environmental history affecting human history of the Pacific Northwest. *Canadian Journal of Archaeology* 3:145–156.

Matson, R. G. 1976. *The Glenrose Cannery Site*. Archaeological Survey of Canada Paper 52.

Mitchell, Donald H. 1970. Excavations on the Chilcotin Plateau: three sites, three phases. *Northwest Anthropological Research Notes* 4:1:99–116.

———. 1971. Archaeology of the Gulf of Georgia area, a natural region and its culture types. *Syesis* 4, Supplement 1.

Mochanov, Iuri A. 1978. Stratigraphy and absolute chronology of the Paleolithic of northeast Asia. In *Early Man in America*, ed. A. L. Bryan, pp. 54–66. Department of Anthropology, University of Alberta, Occasional Papers 1.

Morlan, Richard E. 1977. Fluted point makers and the extinction of the arctic-steppe biome in eastern Beringia. *Canadian Journal of Archaeology* 1:95–108.

———. 1978. Early man in northern Yukon Territory: perspectives as of 1977. In *Early Man in America*, ed. A. L. Bryan, pp. 78–95. Department of Anthropology, University of Alberta, Occasional Papers 1.

Newman, Thomas M. 1966. *Cascadia Cave*. Occasional Papers of the Idaho State University Museum 18.

Nowak, Michael. 1973. A preliminary report on the archaeology of Nunivak Island, Alaska. *Anthropological Papers of the University of Alaska* 15:1:18–31.

Okada, Hiroaki, and Atsuko Okada. 1974. Preliminary report on the 1972 excavations at Port Moller, Alaska. *Arctic Anthropology* 11 (supplement):112–124.

Osgood, Cornelius. 1940. *Ingalik Material Culture*. Yale University Publications in Anthropology 22.

Oswalt, W. H., and J. W. VanStone. 1967. *Ethnoarchaeology of Crow Village, Alaska*. Bureau of American Ethnology Bulletin 199.

Rainey, Froelich G. 1941. Eskimo prehistory: the Okvik site on the Punuk Islands. *Anthropological Papers of the American Museum of Natural History* 37:4:443–569.

Reeves, Brian O. K. 1971. On the coalescence of the Laurentide and Cordilleran ice sheets in the western interior of North America with particular reference to the southern Alberta area. In *Aboriginal Man and Environments on the Plateau of Northwest America*, ed. A. H. Stryd and R. A. Smith, pp. 205–228. Calgary: University of Calgary Archaeological Association.

Rice, David G. 1972. *The Windust Phase in Lower Snake River Region Prehistory*. Washington State University, Laboratory of Anthropology, Report of Investigations 50.

Sanger, David. 1969. Cultural traditions in the interior of British Columbia. *Syesis* 2:1–2:189–200.

———. 1970. The archaeology of the Lochnore–Nesikep Locality, British Columbia. *Syesis* 3, Supplement 1.

Shinkwin, Anne D. 1979. *Dakah De'nin's Village and the Dixthada Site: A Contribution to Northern Athapaskan Prehistory*. Archaeological Survey of Canada Paper 91.

Smith, Jason W. 1971. The Ice Mountain microblade and core industry, Cassiar District, northern British Columbia, Canada. *Arctic and Alpine Research* 3:3:199–213.

Spaulding, A. C. 1962. *Archaeological Investigation on Agattu, Aleutian Islands*. University of Michigan, Museum of Anthropology, Anthropological Papers 18.

Turner, Christy G., II, and Jacqueline A. Turner. 1974. Progress report on evolutionary anthropological study of Akun Strait district, eastern Aleutians Alaska. *Anthropological Papers of the University of Alaska* 16:1:27–57.

VanStone, James W. 1972. Nushagak, an historic trading center in southwestern Alaska. *Fieldiana: Anthropology*, vol. 62.

West, Frederick Hadleigh. 1967. The Donnelly Ridge site and the definition of an early core and blade complex in central Alaska. *American Antiquity* 32:3:360–382.

———. 1975. Dating the Denali complex. *Arctic Anthropology* 12:1:76–81.

———. 1981. *The Archaeology of Beringia*. New York: Columbia University Press.

Workman, William B. 1966. Prehistory at Port Moller, Alaska Peninsula, in light of fieldwork in 1960. *Arctic Anthropology* 3:2:132–153.

———. 1978. *Prehistory of the Aishihik–Kluane Area, Southwest Yukon Territory*. Archaeological Survey of Canada Paper 74.

The treeline at Nastapoka River, east coast of Hudson Bay. The small spruce tree in the foreground is about 100 years old. It is surrounded by a thicket of dwarf birch.

CHAPTER FOUR

Pioneer Cultures of the Sub-Arctic and the Arctic

Elmer Harp, Jr.

Dr. Harp describes the history of archeology in what must surely be one of the least hospitable areas on earth for carrying out fieldwork. Through his description we see the slow process through which knowledge about the prehistoric inhabitants of this little-known frozen world has come to light. The diversity and richness of their culture are reflected in the variety of their tool assemblages and the often esthetically appealing quality of their workmanship.

THE REGIONAL ENVIRONMENTS

The northeastern quadrant of North America, here divided into the sub-Arctic and Arctic, consists of three major geographic provinces: the large eastern portion of the Canadian mainland that surrounds Hudson Bay; the Canadian Arctic Archipelago; and Greenland, the largest island in the world (Figure 4.1). The continental part of this vast region is transected from northwest to southeast by the treeline, which marks the northern limit of forest growth and serves as the nominal boundary between the subarctic and arctic environmental zones.

The first of these geographic provinces is essentially a shallow basin, with Hudson Bay in the center. Several large rivers drain into this depression, including the Thelon–Dubawnt system; the Kazan, Churchill, Nelson, and Albany from the west and south; and the Great Whale and Eastmain rivers from the east. The terrain west of Hudson Bay is a plain with low to moderate relief, extensively covered by marine deposits and glacial till; the Quebec–Ungava country to the east is a rocky, glaciated plateau with an average elevation of about 300 meters. As a whole, this province coincides approximately with the Canadian Shield, which is basically composed of ancient pre-Cambrian rocks, among the oldest on earth. In many areas the Shield has been stripped bare of all soil cover by past glaciation, leaving the rock surfaces striated or scoured to a high polish.

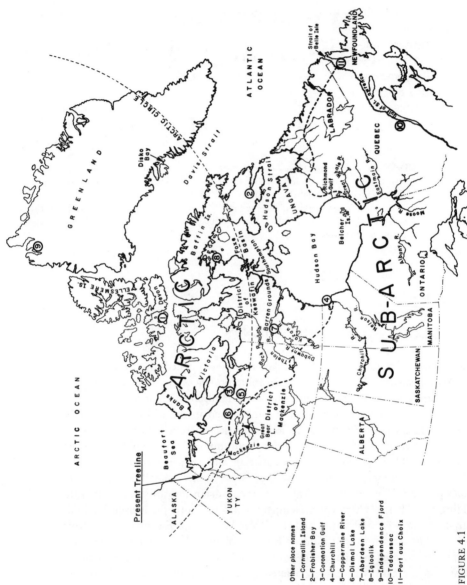

ARCTIC OCEAN

ARCTIC CIRCLE

GREENLAND

Disko Bay

Davis Strait

Present Treeline

ALASKA

Beaufort Sea

Banks

Victoria

YUKON TY

Mackenzie R.

Great Bear L.

District of Mackenzie

Coppermine

Back R.

Thelon R.

Dubawnt R.

Barren Grounds

District of Keewatin

Foxe Basin

Baffin Is.

Hudson Strait

UNGAVA

Hudson Bay

Richmond Gulf

Belcher Is.

Eastmain R.

QUEBEC

LABRADOR

Strait of Belle Isle

NEWFOUNDLAND

ATLANTIC OCEAN

SUB-ARCTIC

ALBERTA

SASKATCHEWAN

MANITOBA

ONTARIO

Churchill R.

Nelson R.

Albany R.

Moose R.

Nottaway R.

ARCTIC

ELLESMERE IS.

Devon

Other place names
1—Cornwallis Island
2—Frobisher Bay
3—Coronation Gulf
4—Churchill
5—Coppermine River
6—Dismal Lake
7—Aberdeen Lake
8—Igloolik
9—Independence Fjord
10—Tadoussac
11—Port aux Choix

FIGURE 4.1
The Arctic and the sub-Arctic.

The Canadian Archipelago, with a combined land mass of about 1,300,000 square kilometers, is completely arctic in character, and one-tenth of it is covered with permanent ice and alpine glaciers. Along the eastern margin rises a mountain chain with elevations up to 3000 meters, and the coastlines are deeply dissected by fjords. Otherwise, the physiography of the islands is extremely varied, including plains, plateaus, rolling terrain, and rift valleys; the interior consists largely of rock-strewn barrens.

Greenland is notable as the northernmost land in the world, reaching to within 700 kilometers of the North Pole. Its massive inland ice cap, which covers about 1,800,000 square kilometers, extends down in some places to meet the sea, but elsewhere there are coastal fringes of ice-free land. The topography of this border country is predominantly mountainous and pierced by deep fjords, and it does not provide lavish life support for large animal populations.

Before the coming of the Europeans, each of these geographic provinces was successfully occupied by aboriginal peoples. These native hunters were precisely adapted to specific environments, and their culture areas correlated closely with the two major ecological zones that make up the region as a whole. This unity of cultural adaptation and environment was particularly the case in the Arctic, which was occupied solely by the Eskimos, or Inuit. [Editor's note: The term *Inuit* is used here as a preferred substitute for *Eskimo*.] The subarctic adaptation was more varied, and this region was occupied by several different Indian tribes and bands belonging to the Athapaskan and Algonquian linguistic families. The adaptations were also affected, of course, by the special character of the biomes that were inhabited.

The Arctic

The Arctic is commonly defined as the circumpolar zone that lies north of the treeline, a border that coincides roughly with the 10°C (50°F) isotherm for the month of July. Substantial forests cannot develop where the average temperature of the warmest month of the year is below 10°C. Note also that the treeline has no immediate geographic relationship with the Arctic Circle, the imaginary line that circumscribes the earth at about 66°67′ north latitude. That is a purely astronomical convention, which relates to seasonal changes and the alternation of night and day. However, despite the lack of linear correspondence between the treeline and the Arctic Circle, the polar pattern of diurnal variation, in association with the shifting seasons, exerts profound influence on all plant and animal life in the Arctic as well as on the psychological states of the human beings who dwell there.

The Arctic is generally characterized by long, dark, severely cold winters and brief summers. In Keewatin District, for example, west of Hudson Bay, mid-winter temperatures average below −32°C (−25°F) for two months at a time, and during the frequent northwest storms such temperatures may be depressed by a wind-chill factor to −73°C (−100°F). Winter snowfall averages from 1 to 2 meters in Keewatin, while in eastern Ungava–Labrador it may amount to over 3 meters. Summer is cool and short, with no more than 50 frost-free days in the southern Arctic, but it is a time of intense growth and flowering. There are several hundred species of mosses, lichens, and other ground-hugging flora, and they mature rapidly in the long hours of sunlight. Toward the south, dwarf willows, alders, and birch may flourish in protected microenvironments, but all species gradually fade out toward the north, until in the high latitudes of the Archipelago one comes finally to virtually lifeless landscapes of dry, rocky barrens.

The relatively few species of land animals in the Arctic include lemmings, ground squirrels, weasels, wolverines, foxes, the arctic wolf and arctic hare, polar bears, and occasional barren-ground grizzly bears, but the most important food animal is the barren-ground caribou. Several major herds of this species, totaling now less than a million head, roam the barrens west of Hudson Bay, and smaller aggregations are scattered in the Archipelago, the Quebec–Labrador peninsula, and Greenland. Another large land mammal, the musk ox, exists in small residual herds in the barren grounds of central Keewatin, the northern islands of the Archipelago, and Greenland.

Bird life is abundant throughout the Arctic, especially numerous species of shore birds and migratory waterfowl that breed and nest there in the summer. Insect life includes bees, spiders, and several species of flies, and in early summer hordes of mosquitoes parasitize man and beast alike. The surrounding marine waters afford rich food resources of sea mammals, although some species have suffered from excessive commercial hunting in the last century. The most common seals, including the Bearded, Jar, and Ringed varieties, are fundamental to the Inuit subsistence economy, and small herds of walrus still exist in some areas. Arctic char, salmon, and lake trout are the principal food fishes.

One peculiar feature of the Arctic, the widespread occurrence of permafrost, is noteworthy. Because the summers are chilly and brief, Arctic surface soils thaw only to shallow depths, and much of the land is therefore underlain by permanently frozen subsoil. This eliminates the possibility of seepage, and low-lying places consequently develop into waterlogged bogs or ponds that evaporate very slowly in the cool air. Hence, some areas become complex mazes of lakes and meandering waterways, and overland travel through them is extremely difficult.

The Sub-Arctic

The so-called treeline, which separates the Arctic from the sub-Arctic, is not, in fact, a line but rather a broad transitional zone that includes both the tundra and the boreal forest. Approaching it from the north, one first encounters outlying isolated clumps of stunted conifers in sheltered valleys; these increase in size and density toward the south, until at last the closed boreal forest appears. This forest is almost impenetrable for humans, who must travel through it along the natural drainage systems. The boreal coniferous forest is frequently called the *taiga,* a term originally adopted by Russians from the Tungus reindeer herders of eastern Siberia; like the arctic tundra, it has a circumpolar distribution across both hemispheres. Black and white spruce dominate the northern portions of the taiga, while hemlock, tamarack, and pine occur toward the south; along its southern edges the taiga is gradually supplanted by deciduous hardwood forests, or it disappears at the border of the high plains.

The winter climate of the taiga is as severe as that of the tundra, but summers are warmer and longer, having up to 100 frost-free days. Annual precipitation generally exceeds that of the Arctic, and winter snowfall tends to be deep and softly packed within the wind-sheltered depths of the forest.

Animal species are more numerous in the taiga than in the tundra. Woodland caribou are plentiful in the lichen meadows of the transitional zone, while moose is the chief game animal in the deeper forest. Migratory waterfowl constitute another important food resource. Various species of small fur-bearing animals, such as marten, lynx, beaver, fox, and mink, assumed primary economic significance with the advent of the Europeans.

In concluding this brief survey of regional environments, I must emphasize that the culture areas of the present and recent past do not coincide precisely in a geographic sense with those of prehistoric time. Although arctic and subarctic biomes have existed throughout humanity's presence in the New World, cyclical changes of climate in the post-Pleistocene era caused northward or southward shifts in the boundaries of these zones. Such alterations in the distribution of flora and fauna, in turn, stimulated a corresponding ebb or flow of peoples and cultures, all of which will be explained more fully in later sections of this chapter.

ARCHEOLOGICAL RESEARCH
IN THE EASTERN NORTHLANDS

The earliest archeological activity in the eastern Arctic was completely unscientific and amounted to little more than surface collecting or random digging, usually as a subsidiary game during exploratory or whaling expeditions. Finally, from 1921 to 1924, Knud Rasmussen, the noted Danish explorer, staged his famous Fifth Thule Expedition, which included ethnologist Kaj Birket-Smith and archeologist Therkel Mathiassen. Their fieldwork marked the beginning of scientific archeology in this quadrant of North America. Mathiassen explored widely on Baffin Island and around northern Hudson Bay, discovering an early whale-hunting stage of Inuit culture that he named *Thule.* He concluded that the Thule culture had originated in Alaska and was ancestral to the modern Inuit of the central and eastern Arctic. Then, in 1925, a second major archeological landmark was established when Diamond Jenness described another hitherto-unknown Arctic culture. This has since come to be known as the Dorset Eskimo culture, but it was not immediately accepted as such by all authorities. Nevertheless, Jenness made the interesting suggestion that Dorset was older than Thule and proposed that a still earlier, pre-Dorset phase might yet be found in the eastern Arctic. Within the next several years Jenness and his colleague, W. J. Wintemberg, discovered other sites in Newfoundland that contained unmistakable Dorset materials, and most professional doubts about the authenticity of the Dorset culture evaporated.

In the 1930s, the status of Thule culture in Greenland was thoroughly investigated by Mathiassen, Helge Larsen, and Erik Holtved, who found no evidence of earlier occupations. However, W. D. Strong discovered traces of Dorset culture in northeastern Labrador, and other Dorset sites were excavated in northern Labrador by Douglas Leechman and at Igloolik, Foxe Basin, by Graham Rowley. It was now perfectly evident that Dorset culture was distinct from Thule, although its origins and degree of affiliation with the Inuit continuum remained obscure.

The years following World War II witnessed a dramatic extension of the Dorset spectrum—culturally, geographically, and chronologically. Eigil Knuth discovered the pre-Dorset Independence I occupation in northeastern Greenland, and escavations by Helge Larsen and Jorgen Meldgaard in Disko Bay, southwestern Greenland, delineated a longer sequence of Sarqaq (pre-Dorset), Dorset, and Thule. In the Canadian Arctic, Henry Collins obtained stratified separation of Dorset and Thule levels at Resolute, Cornwallis Island, and Frobisher, Baffin Island, while his T-1 site on Southampton Island yielded a new, early phase of Dorset culture dating from the seventh century BC. Other projects in this period included my investigations of Dorset and Archaic Indian sites in western Newfoundland and southern Labrador and Jorgen Meldgaard's research on seriated pre-Dorset, Dorset, and Thule occupations in the Igloolik area. Meldgaard proposed an Alaskan origin for the pre-Dorset phase and suggested that the later Dorset culture had derived from, or otherwise had been strongly influenced by, boreal-forest adaptations to the south.

That view was not accepted by most Canadian and American scholars, who professed to see a linear continuum of Inuit cultures in the central and eastern Arctic, stemming primarily from ancestral impulses out of Alaska. This latter interpretation received support in the mid-1950s when Louis Giddings explored along the treeline west of Hudson Bay and found an assemblage of microblade materials that resembled his Denbigh Flint complex core and blade culture in western Alaska. I found similar evidence at Dismal and Kamut lakes, south of Coronation Gulf, and suggested that this was a link between the Dorset continuum and Alaskan forebears. In the 1960s, I also excavated the large Dorset site at Port aux Choix, in northwestern Newfoundland, and confirmed its essential arctic relationships. The *coup de grâce* for the concept of southern origins for Dorset culture was ultimately delivered when Moreau Maxwell described a

3000-year span of pre-Dorset to Dorset evolution in southern Baffin Island, while William Taylor traced similar events in northern Ungava and Hudson Strait.

Within the past few years, the geographic borders of the Dorset realm have been opened still farther to the west and south. Taylor found more pre-Dorset and Dorset sites on Banks and Victoria islands, Ronald Nash excavated in sites of both stages in the vicinity of Churchill on the west coast of Hudson Bay, and Patrick Plumet examined a pre-Dorset occupation at Great Whale River in southeastern Hudson Bay. In that same area, I discovered a complex of surprisingly late Dorset sites in the entrance to Richmond Gulf, the most recent of which dated about AD 1400. From 1974 to 1975 I surveyed further in the Belcher Islands, finding a long range of Dorset occupations dating approximately from 1000 BC to AD 1000.

Thus, after slightly more than half a century of scientific archeological research in the central and eastern Arctic, it appears that the outlines of Inuit prehistory in that region have been established. In contrast to that level of achievement, the sub-Arctic has received relatively little attention from archeologists, and that mostly since World War II. This inequity has generally been due to the differing patterns of European exploration in the two zones and, more particularly, to the delayed expansion of modern commercial enterprise and settlement into the forested interior.

In sub-Arctic Quebec–Labrador the earliest aboriginal occupations are related to the Archaic tradition, a term that denotes a major stage of Indian prehistory in which various semisedentary bands subsisted by means of hunting, fishing, and some gathering of wild foods. The first significant archeological find there was made in 1915, when Frank Speck reported a large Archaic concentration at Tadoussac on the north shore of the St. Lawrence River; this important site was later investigated more fully by W. J. Wintemberg and Gordon Lowther. From 1927 to 1928, W. D. Strong found Archaic materials in northeastern Labrador, and Edward Rogers, who explored the interior of south–central Quebec from 1947 to 1950, recorded a large number of sites that ranged from the Archaic into the protohistoric period. Somewhat later, I obtained a date of about 4300 BC for the earliest Archaic horizon in southern Labrador. Finally, William Fitzhugh, Robert McGhee, and James Tuck have since added to our understanding of the northeastern Archaic by defining a subtradition called the Maritime Archaic, which emphasized a seasonal specialization for sea-mammal hunting along the Atlantic littoral.

The archeology of the taiga and barren lands west of Hudson Bay has been tapped only during the last 25 years. During the 1950s Richard MacNeish traveled the Mackenzie River country, finding sporadic evidence of an early Paleo-Indian occupation that dated prior to about 5000 BC. My own survey, farther east along the middle Thelon River in 1958, indicated that the first people to exploit the barren lands were Indian hunters with lanceolate projectile points of a southern Plano type. Robert McGhee found similar, but considerably later, indications of Plano influence at Bloody Falls on the Coppermine River.

In the southwest Yukon Territory, MacNeish later identified a post-Plano stage of culture, which he named the *Northwest Microblade* tradition, and William Noble's surveys around Great Slave Lake and in the central Macken-zie District have begun to trace the evolution of these early forest-hunting groups into the historic Athapaskan-speaking tribes of that area.

James Wright, after years of fieldwork in Manitoba and Keewatin District, has hypothesized the existence of a specific Shield Archaic subtradition whose bearers may have been the first Algonquian speakers. Most recently, Bryan Gordon has excavated stratified sites on the upper Thelon River and proposed that discrete bands of early tundra hunters were ecologically associated with particular herds of caribou in regular migration territories.

Such, in brief retrospect, is the history of archeological research in northeast-ern North America. It has been clearly determined that human exploitation of the austere subarctic and arctic environments has undergone a long and complex evolution. Given the still-fragmented nature of our knowledge, we can perceive some ancient cultural phases more vividly than others, and it is only fair to add that the transition from prehistory into modern times is the least well known of all. We see that, throughout the 6000 or 7000 years of cultural development in this region, some increments of change must be attributed to migrations and the influx of new people. Equally significant, however, were the constant internal adaptations to the constraints imposed on the indigenes by fluctuating postgla-cial climate. It remains for us now to examine these ancient cultural responses in greater detail.

PREHISTORIC CULTURE SEQUENCES IN THE SUB-ARCTIC

Northeastern North America consists of the newest land surfaces to be found anywhere on the continent, for that region was last to emerge from the glaci-ation of the Wisconsin period. That part of the continent had been blanketed by the vast Laurentide sheet, which originated from a set of highland growth centers in Greenland, Ellesmere Island, Baffin Island, Labrador, and Quebec. From the evidence of terminal moraines we know that the sheet once extended as far as western Alberta and south of the Great Lakes–St. Lawrence River system. When deglaciation began, around 12,000 BC, there was a radial shrink-age of this ice cap back toward its centers of origin, albeit the process was not uniform either geographically or chronologically. The area southeast of Great Bear Lake was freed of ice by about 8000 BC, as was central Keewatin District by 5000 BC. To the south, the Great Lakes had emerged by 9000 BC and the James Bay area by 5500 BC. South–central Quebec was in the clear by 5000 BC, and the ultimate disappearance of the ice cap in mainland Canada occurred about 3800 BC in the mountains of northeastern Labrador. Around 3000 BC the Laurentide sheet had dwindled to its present-day remnants on Baffin, Devon, and Ellesmere islands and in Greenland.

Thus, the spread of early humans into this region became, in effect, a series of centripetal movements, mostly along the radii of deglaciation. As newly liberated landscapes surfaced in the periglacial zone around the periphery of the ice cap, the tundra flora migrated rapidly into the consequent biological vacuum, and various faunal species were then drawn forward by their shifting ecosystems. The human response came last, and in some areas it was delayed for several centuries by residual postglacial features that physically barred movement, such as ice-dammed lakes or marine submergence in the Hudson Bay lowlands. In this period of climatic amelioration we can discern two major thrusts of human influence into the northern frontier lands: the earliest came from the country to the west of Hudson Bay, and soon afterward the second developed east of the Great Lakes and diffused along the St. Lawrence corridor into the Quebec–Labrador peninsula (Figure 4.2).

The first active hunting cultures in present-day subarctic latitudes west of Hudson Bay have been identified with the Paleo-Indian stage. As the forest environment encroached toward the north, however, forming an ever-thickening barrier between the temperate grasslands and the periglacial tundra, new cultural orientations became necessary. The northern Archaic stage emerged in this period of flux, and it was a primary response to forest conditions. In general, this Archaic culture was founded on the ancient big-game-hunting patterns of the preceding Paleo-Indian stage, but as the centuries passed, a variety of regional modifications developed. Caribou hunting remained the chief economic activity in the northern fringes of the forest, but to the south and west other large species, such as elk, moose, and deer, became mainstays. In addition, there was a new emphasis on riverine adaptation and fishing in some areas, on shellfish gathering, and on wild-plant collecting. Far to the east, on the Atlantic littoral, Archaic people developed an important seasonal exploitation of sea mammals.

Furthermore, the Archaic stage was a time of slowly expanding human population. The regional density of hunting camps and larger settlements increased; deeper midden deposits in some Archaic sites attest to prolonged or recurrent occupations; and even the clusters of dwelling units within specific sites are frequently more numerous. All such observations suggest a reduction of migratory habits and an enhancement of sedentary ways. So, as technological capabilities improved and exploitation of local food resources was intensified, the hunting–gathering life of the Archaic people gradually evolved toward greater economic and social stability, and probably also toward firmer territorial relationships.

West of Hudson Bay, the archeological evidence shows that caribou were the most important game animals throughout the entire Archaic stage and into the historic era. The most significant part of this country was the transitional belt

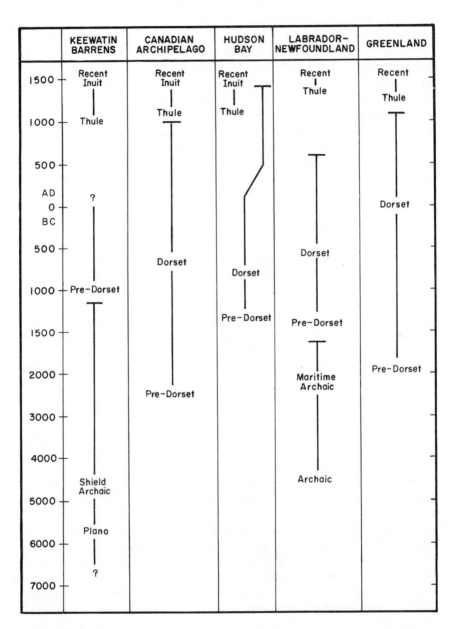

FIGURE 4.2
Prehistoric occupations in the eastern sub-Arctic and the Arctic.

that stretched along the northern edges of the boreal forest. As an ecotone, this zone of mixed environments combined certain advantageous features of both the tundra and the taiga, including plentiful game, supplies of wood for fuel and artifacts, a degree of shelter within the limited forest, and ease of movement through semiopen country. Thus, it afforded a safe operating base for the forest-oriented hunters, from which they could sally forth in summertime, following the migrating caribou herds northward onto the barrens, and into which they could retreat as winter approached.

In this seasonal manner, Archaic hunters became the earliest occupants of the Barren Grounds during the first postglacial warm phase, prior to 1500 BC, when the forest reached approximately 240 kilometers north of the present treeline. Their caribou-hunting sites in central Keewatin were situated along the rivers and lakes that lay athwart the migration paths of the herds, and their northernmost penetration seems to have been along the Thelon River. There, at various narrows or other fording points, the caribou were most vulnerable to interception and ambush as they funneled along habitual paths into the water crossings; correspondingly, the camps, lookouts, and workshop sites of the Archaic hunters were located in these critical places.

One of the most extensive Archaic caribou-hunting sites on the Thelon lay at the west end of Aberdeen Lake, and investigations have shown that the site was occupied on a seasonal basis beginning about 5000 BC. The final Archaic occupation there left a semisubterranean house that has been dated about 1000 BC, a period when the weather was cooler and more unstable than it is today. As this site was most productive in later summer, when the caribou were returning southward toward the forest edges, the substantial lodge, in contrast to a simple summer tent ring, is probably a reflection of the deteriorating weather conditions. In any case, the Archaic hunters abandoned the site after that occupation, never to return.

The cold trend that began around 1500 BC caused the treeline to shift back southward, and we may assume that as of about 1000 BC the forest was so far distant from the Aberdeen site that journeying between the two had become impractical and even dangerous in the face of approaching winter. Thus, as the Archaic people were unable to cope with winter conditions in the Barren Grounds, they had no choice but to retreat southward in order to stay within reach of their customary habitat. The vacuum left by their withdrawal was short-lived, however, because the same cold period stimulated an expansion of pre-Dorset Inuit hunters into the interior barrens. Thenceforward, as the climate oscillated in quickening cycles of several centuries' duration, the northern limits of Archaic summer occupation shifted conformably. In the early years of the Christian era the immediate ancestors of the historic Chipewyan came again to the Thelon country on their summer forays.

Recent studies of the Canadian caribou have shown that four separate herds are distributed from west to east across the Barren Grounds, and each of these herds forages in a discrete geographic area. Furthermore, ethnographic analysis of Chipewyan hunting practices has demonstrated that a direct relationship exists between specific Indian bands and one or another of these herds. Thus, the migratory lifeways of subarctic hunters in the historic period have been governed essentially by the north–south seasonal movements of a single herd, in accordance with an ecological human–animal attachment that has obvious survival value, at least for the humans. This same relationship has also been convincingly proved for the pre-Dorset Inuit who infiltrated the Barren Grounds after 1500 BC, and, although proof is lacking, it is plausible to suggest that the Archaic Indian hunters might have operated according to a similar economic pattern.

In any event, the caribou was the staff of life in this central region, and we see further testimony of its importance in the artifact assemblages found in Archaic sites. The fundamental kit of stone tools is much the same throughout the entire area; aside from frequency shifts in certain types of artifacts, its general character altered only slightly during the long Archaic stage. All of the surviving tool and weapon types were flaked from local varieties of quartzite. They include the following dominant forms: several kinds of large, lanceolate spear or lance points; crude burins and gravers; leaf-shaped side blades for knives; discoidal biface knives; asymmetric and semilunar biface knives; triangular end scrapers; turtleback core scrapers; flat spall scrapers; denticulate or saw scrapers; wedge-shaped cores and coarse prismatic blades; rectangular adze blades; wedges; pebble hammerstones; and numerous amorphous scrap flakes showing edge wear (Figure 4.3). Artifacts made of organic materials, such as bone, antler, or wood, are seldom recovered, except in late period sites.

It is impossible to identify specific functions for all of these implements, but they clearly represent a considerable spectrum of job specialization. Here are all the basic tools for hunting and killing, skinning and butchering, cutting and splitting bone, scraping and softening hides, and cutting, scraping, or adzing wood, antler, and bone for the fabrication of other artifacts. Given the minimal inventories of perishable materials, it is difficult to make further inferences about cultural content or pattern. We must assume, however, that the Archaic hunters possessed, at the very least, sufficient skills and experience for successful winter survival in the boreal forest, particularly with respect to the manufacture of adequate clothing and shelter.

As for cultural evolution among the Archaic peoples of this region, there are several artifact types that serve as dependable, if rather slight, indicators of both continuity and change. The fundamental relationship between Paleo-Indian and Archaic is best established through the medium of the Keewatin lanceolate point with ground basal edges. This type derived from the Agate Basin style of the north–central plains and developed, in turn, by slow stages into several variants with contracting stems. Other such trait linkages are the denticulate or saw scrapers; wedges made from fragments of other kinds of bifacial tools; and the use of broken projectile points for the manufacture of burins. Otherwise, throughout the Archaic stage west of Hudson Bay there was an increase in the

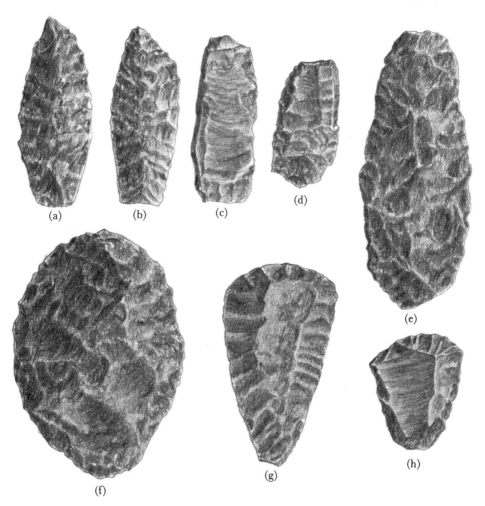

FIGURE 4.3
Type specimens from the Shield Archaic, chipped from coarse-grained quartzite and found at several interior Barren Grounds sites northwest of Hudson Bay: (a, b) Keewatin lanceolate points; (c, d) burinated points; (e) biface knife; (f) skin scraper; (g, h) snub-nosed end scrapers.

frequency of projectile points and scrapers, a gradual shift from large lanceolate points to smaller side-notched types, and a general decrease in the occurrence of large biface tools.

James Wright has suggested that this basic forest culture should be called the Shield Archaic, for its distribution around Hudson Bay conforms closely to the spread of the Canadian Shield itself. He has further postulated that the people of the Shield Archaic spoke an Algonquian language and thus were directly ancestral to the central and eastern Algonquian tribes of the historic period.

There is considerable merit to both these hypotheses, inasmuch as they account for the strong cultural continuities that existed in the subarctic forest zone from the origin of the taiga economy into historic time. Also, this terminology permits us to differentiate other localized specializations that developed elsewhere in the boreal forest, some of them resulting from external diffusion and others arising from internal change and adaptation.

We have seen, for example, that western caribou hunters with Paleo-Indian affiliations were probably the first occupants of the Canadian Shield region west of Hudson Bay. The archeological evidence from interior Quebec is still too scarce to trace these same influences there, but the few facts that we do have indicate the presence of the ancient taiga complex. However, in this region another significant impulse is detectable, one that derived from the northeastern woodlands south of the St. Lawrence (see Chapter Seven) and gave rise to the early cultures of the Quebec–Labrador peninsula. In this area there was a distinctive sub-tradition that has been aptly named the Boreal Archaic.

So far, all evidence relating to the northeastern Boreal Archaic comes from a few sites around the coastal periphery of Quebec–Labrador. Typical of these are one small kill site on the east coast of Hudson Bay a few miles north of Great Whale River; seven workshop sites on raised marine beach lines at Tadoussac on the St. Lawrence River; a number of small locales scattered through the forest in south–central Quebec north of Lake St. John; a series of workshops and settlements in southern Labrador at the Strait of Belle Isle; an Archaic burial ground at Port aux Choix on the northwest coast of Newfoundland; the Old Stone culture along the central coast of Labrador; and a few other recent discoveries in central and northern Labrador. Of all these sites, only one, at Northwest Corners, Labrador, can be identified with any certainty as an interior caribou hunters' camp; all the others were oriented to inland waterways and lakes or toward the sea.

This distribution may not adequately reflect the overall importance of the caribou in Boreal Archaic economy, but it does indicate that there may have been a standard settlement pattern of seasonal migration, with periodic nodes of concentration at certain productive fishing camps. As I shall explain presently, the faunal resources of the sea played a key role in Archaic culture along the littoral of the St. Lawrence and the Atlantic, but the inland aspect of life probably depended heavily on fish and the small fur-bearing animal species, such as hare, muskrat, beaver, wolf, otter, and so on, that inhabit the taiga. The only large game available in the interior plateau country was the caribou, for moose and deer are known to have been quite recent arrivals in the area.

The highest of the sites at Tadoussac, and therefore presumably the oldest of the series, was found on an ancient raised beach that is believed to correlate with the postglacial Champlain Sea stage, dating to about 4000 BC. This site yielded a collection with a high frequency of crudely shaped, percussion-flaked core tools, similar to assemblages from several sites in the interior around Lakes Mistassini and Albanel. It has been conjectured that these finds may represent a pre-Archaic level of culture, perhaps related to a theoretical stage that has been noted elsewhere in North America and that is tentatively called the *Unspecialized Lithic,* or *pre-Projectile Point* stage. The general concept of such a stage is not accepted by all authorities, and it certainly has not been satisfactorily confirmed in the Quebec–Labrador area. On the other hand, it is fully possible that the anomalous inventories from these sites may be a simple reflection of their nature as workshops, where preliminary manufacturing was done either at a crucial lookout point, while hunters waited for the appearance of game, or else in the immediate vicinity of a quarry area. Otherwise, it can be stated positively that the oldest dates presently known for the Boreal Archaic in southern Labrador also reach back to around 4000 BC.

There are no analogs of Paleo-Indian projectile points in Boreal Archaic assemblages, but there are lanceolate forms, ranging from small to large, usually with tapered stems or corner-notched bases. Other point variants are leaf-shaped, triangular, or lozenge forms. In settlement areas with a customarily broad spectrum of artifact types, the points are usually mixed with a great variety of chipped stone biface tools, including large leaf-shaped blades or knives, semilunar knives, percussion-flaked choppers and adzes, side and end scrapers, occasional gravers, and hammerstones and anvils (Figure 4.4).

In the middle and late phases of the Boreal Archaic most of these implements were retained. There was, however, a marked shift in the frequencies of projectile point styles, notably a reduction of the stemmed, lanceolate type in the face of increasing dependence on side-notched points and finally on triangular points. Also, the manufacturing technique of pecking, grinding, and polishing came into fashion as the Boreal Archaic matured. Silicified slate was the favored material for grinding and polishing, and the predominant types made in this manner included long, bayonetlike projectile points with ovoid or faceted cross-sections and what are presumed to be heavy woodworking tools, such as chisels, adzes, and gouges.

Aside from this use of slate, several local varieties of colored quartzite, cherts, and chalcedony were chosen for manufacturing flaked tools. One preferred kind of translucent gray quartzite, which has been found in numerous northeastern Archaic sites, has been traced to a unique quarry near Ramah Bay in northern Labrador. This occurrence, in conjunction with an array of chipped and ground and polished tool types that are commonly found together in the same sites, serves to emphasize the highly uniform character of Boreal Archaic culture from Maine to Labrador. In fact, the combinations of traits are often so precisely alike in many sites throughout the area that one may plausibly regard this as an integrated diffusion sphere.

For years, the concentration of Archaic sites along the shores of the St. Lawrence and in the Strait of Belle Isle area has engendered speculation concerning the economic orientation of these particular locales. Their basic culture, of course, was Archaic, and their elaborate adaptation to the subarctic forest fully justifies the term *Boreal Archaic.* However, these littoral sites confront deep

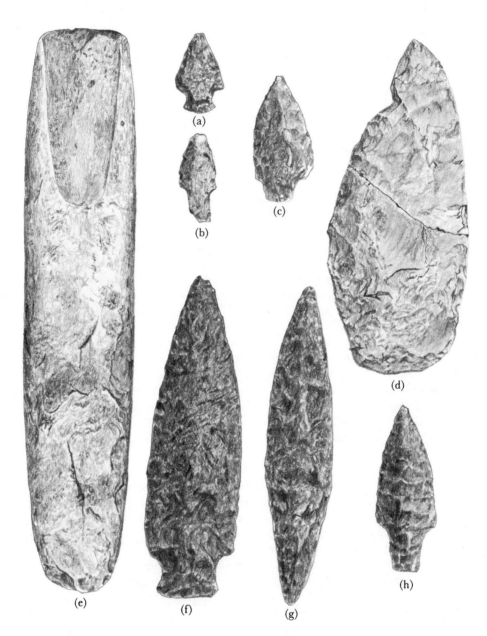

FIGURE 4.4
Northeastern Boreal Archaic artifacts from coastal sites in southern Labrador: (a–c) small projectile points; (d) biface knife; (e) gouge; (f–h) large projectile points.

waters that are exceedingly rich in marine species, especially seals and small whales, and it has been noted that similar ground slate bayonet points were successfully used for prehistoric whale hunting in southern Alaska. Therefore, it was suggested, this coastal expression of the Archaic might well have had a seasonal maritime specialization. Unfortunately, the evidence for such an inference was limited to stone artifacts, and the proposition could never be proved because these littoral sites were all stationed on acidic sands, from which all organic deposits had long since disappeared.

Then, in the late 1960s, a large Archaic cemetery was accidentally uncovered in the village of Port aux Choix on the northwestern coast of Newfoundland. Extensive investigations there produced a rich and unprecedented inventory of coastal Archaic culture as it existed for a period of about 1000 years, between the late third and the late second millennia BC. The preparation of the more than 100 individual burials and the inclusion of red ochre and elaborate grave furnishings testified to a corpus of beliefs regarding the world of the supernatural and life in the hereafter. In addition, the grave goods afforded a comprehensive view of primary food-getting activities, showing strong emphasis on sea-mammal hunting. The complement of stone artifacts included all the ground and polished slate tools and weapons mentioned above, but flaked stone tools were surprisingly few, possibly because they related to mundane, less significant work. But, most interesting of all, there was a well-developed harpoon complex consisting of barbed bone points, open-socketed toggling harpoon heads of bone, and whalebone foreshafts (Figure 4.5). Associated with these were daggers of walrus ivory, antler, and caribou leg bone, as well as eyed needles of bone, caribou scapula skin scrapers, bone beaming tools, and decorated bone combs. Alkaline soils accounted for the preservation of these materials, although wood artifacts did not survive. Finally, the cultural inventory included many shell beads, undoubtedly for the decoration of clothing, and numerous parts of animals and birds (such as seal claws, bird beaks, and so on), together with two conventionalized stone sculptures of killer whales. The latter strongly suggest the practice of wearing amulets and a belief in sympathetic, imitative magic.

Given its level of intricate specialization for marine hunting, this aspect of Archaic culture has been named the *Maritime Archaic,* a term that seems appropriate for all of the closely related bands that coevally inhabited the Atlantic shores from Labrador to Maine. Naturally, the emphasis on marine hunting was purely seasonal, and at other times of the year the Maritime Archaic people continued to exploit the land resources that were of fundamental importance everywhere in the subarctic zone. Although there is no direct archeological evidence, we must infer that these people possessed considerable skill in boat building and seamanship, if only for inshore hunting. The woodland cultures of later periods are known to have had dugout and bark-covered canoes, and in the Boreal and Maritime Archaic we recognize the presence of specific tools, such as ground slate chisels, adzes, and gouges, that were potentially useful for the construction of similar craft.

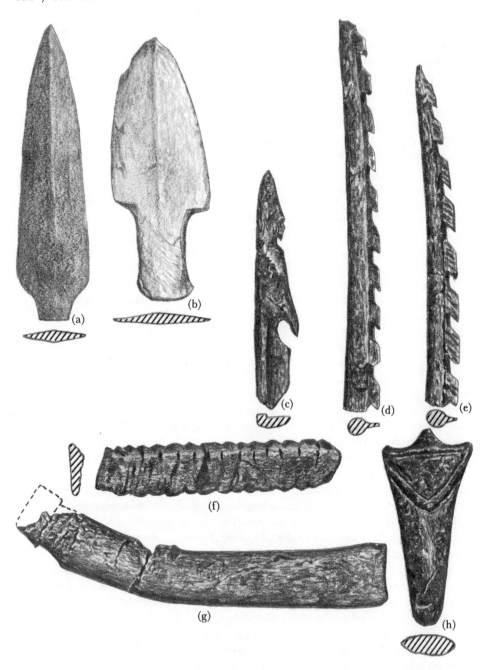

FIGURE 4.5
Northeastern Maritime Archaic artifacts, recovered from burial sites in western Newfoundland:
(a, b) beveled slate projectile points; (c) bone harpoon point with open socket; (d, e) barbed bone fish spear
fragments; (f) serrated stone scraper or saw; (g) bone knife handle with scarfed tip; (h) soapstone
(steatite) amulet.

According to the Port aux Choix cemetery dates, the Maritime Archaic flourished during the first postglacial warm period, and thereafter its influence may have waned as competitive pre-Dorset Inuit moved south along the Labrador coast. Later, in the early centuries of the Christian era, Dorset Inuit culture appears to have dominated these shores. The last Indian practitioners of sea-mammal hunting may have been the Beothucks of Newfoundland, before their ultimate obliteration by European settlers.

In the final analysis, we do not know precisely what became of Archaic culture in the subarctic zone, although it seems eminently logical to assume that it evolved into the various Indian cultures that occupied the region at the time of European discovery. There is sufficient documentary evidence to show that such groups as the Beothucks of Newfoundland, the Montagnais–Naskapi of Quebec–Labrador, the Cree and Ojibwa of the Hudson Bay lowlands, the Chipewyan west of Hudson Bay, and other Athapaskan-speaking tribes living farther northwest all practiced a basic taiga economy, many elements of which are traceable back into archeological horizons.

Except for the Beothucks, all of these people have survived to the present day, although they lost most of their ancient heritage in exchange for metal knives, guns, blankets, beads, and rum. The dictates of the fur trade imposed on them the strange concepts of territoriality and property, an unbalanced stress on trapping and overkill, and artificial migration cycles keyed to isolated trading posts, while their universe of spirits was superseded by a Christian god. To these last representatives of the primeval boreal-forest way of life, the Europeans brought decimating disease, social inferiority, and cataclysm.

THE INUIT: PIONEERS OF THE EASTERN ARCTIC

Even as the occupation of the eastern sub-Arctic by early Indian hunters was initially governed by deglaciation, the phenomena of the Laurentide retreat and subsequent postglacial climatic changes affected the spread of the Inuit across the Arctic. However, the Inuits' adaptation to this circumpolar biome represents a special peak in the long epic of human evolution, for, barring only Antarctica, it was the last terrestrial niche to be conquered. From present archeological evidence, we know that humans had reached into the eastern Arctic by approximately 2500 BC.

Before recapitulating this story, we must consider two related matters. The first concerns the name of the arctic people conventionally referred to as Eskimos. Although it has been otherwise explained, this term is probably a French rendition (*Esquimaux*) of an Algonquian word that means "eaters of raw flesh." Eastern boreal-forest Indians named the arctic hunters in this manner, and the pejorative overtones suggest that early contacts between the two peoples at various places along the treeline were not always congenial. Now, in our time, there is a trend toward use of the alternate term *Inuit* because this is the Eskimos' own word for themselves. It means simply "the people."

The second matter relates to the Inuit as an ethnic group: How are they identified and differentiated from other peoples and cultures? More specifically, how do they differ from the Indians of North America? These questions deserve detailed and complex answers, but here I can offer only a brief characterization of the Inuit and their culture, as known from the period of European contact. At that time they exhibited a remarkable degree of linguistic, cultural, and racial uniformity throughout their entire geographic range, from Alaska to Greenland, despite many regional adaptations to local differences in the environment. Further back in prehistoric time, such adaptational differences were even more pronounced.

Linguistically, the Inuit constitute a unique speech family that has no discernible relationship to any New World Indian language; some scholars believe that it may be akin to the Uralic stock of Eurasia. The Inuit language had an ancestral unity with Aleut, from which it diverged about 6000 years ago. Thereafter it evolved into two distinctive subfamily units; the *Yupik* of southwestern Alaska and the *Inupik,* which includes all dialects between western Alaska and Greenland. The dialects are mutually comprehensible within each of the subfamilies.

From a cultural point of view, the Inuit were the only people who achieved a successful year-round adaptation to the Arctic by means of hunting and fishing, without the benefit of any domesticated food resources. The primary food quest was the hunting of sea mammals, including seal, walrus, and whale, although some groups practiced a dual subsistence economy with seasonal dependence on caribou. The ultimate secret of their success is explained by their specialized weapons for hunting sea mammals, particularly the toggle-headed harpoon, and their elaborate methods for locating, stalking, and retrieving this game, whether in open water, at the ice edge, or through breathing holes in the sea ice in the depth of winter. Aside from the harpoon, they had other more common weapons, such as lances, knives, fish and bird spears, and the bow and arrow. In the characteristically barren arctic environment they capitalized on scarce raw materials with great ingenuity, using all animal parts in the fabrication of their material effects, including skin, gut, bones, claws, horn, ivory, sinew, and baleen. Their cutting implements were generally chipped from stone. Containers were made of skin or, in the case of cooking pots and lamps, of soapstone. The primary fuel was seal blubber, or sometimes caribou fat. The Inuit traveled and hunted at sea in skin-covered boats such as the kayak or the *umiak* and had sledges for winter use, pulled at first by human beings and later by dogs. Naturally, they also had efficient protection against winter cold, including tailored, double-layered skin garments, and a variety of house types adapted to particular seasons and available raw materials, of which the most ingenious was the snow house of the central regions.

Finally, the Inuit also stand somewhat apart from the New World Indian peoples in terms of biological anthropology. They represent a specialized branch of the Mongoloid stock of East Asia, and, together with the Chukchi, Koryak, Yukaghir, and Itelmen of northeastern Siberia, are sometimes referred to as Arctic Mongoloids. Aside from its general resemblance to other Mongoloid peoples, this variant group exhibits certain physiological and structural characteristics that are apparently advantageous for survival in arctic environments. For example, the flat facial morphology, with the depressed nasal profile and accompanying narrow inner aperture, is effective in reducing the loss of body heat. It has also been suggested that slight differences in metabolic rate and the vascular system may function toward the same end. Moreover, the average physical proportions of these people also enhance heat retention and maintenance of the body's core temperature; their typical body build is compact and arms and legs are relatively short in respect to trunk length. This means that there is less skin surface per unit of body mass and consequently a relative decrease in the amount of internal heat lost by radiation. Not all authorities accept this interpretation of the biological evidence. If these are adaptive traits, however, then the Inuit and other Arctic Mongoloids are genetically better equipped than others to withstand some of the stresses of natural selection in polar environments.

The earliest known occupation of the central and eastern Arctic, beginning early in the third millennium BC, is called pre-Dorset. This culture is recognized as the ancestral stock of the Inuit in that region because it forms an unbroken continuity with the succeeding Dorset Eskimo culture. Unfortunately, no linguistic or skeletal evidence is available from this pioneering stage, but its derivation from known Alaskan forebears has been archeologically established. It was part of the wave of the Arctic Small Tool tradition that spread eastward along the North Slope of Alaska into Canada; that tradition, in turn, originated in the Denbigh Flint complex in the Bering Strait area. The direct relationship between the Denbigh complex and pre-Dorset is unmistakable, as the basic tool kit of each contains carefully prepared cores and microblades, burins, retouched burin spalls, incipient side-notched knives, and several other types of artifacts.

The eastward spread of the pre-Dorset hunters occurred toward the end of the first warm period that wasted the Laurentide ice sheet to its present extent by about 3000 BC, and the evidence indicates that they were firmly established around northern Hudson Bay by 2000 BC. Their movement out of the west appears to have developed rapidly, within a span of several centuries, and it passed through the islands of the Canadian Archipelago into northern Greenland. So far, the oldest known sites, dating to about 2400 BC, are on the south coast of Baffin Island, and the pre-Dorset Independence I complex of northeastern Greenland has been dated close to 2000 BC.

The initial postglacial warm period lasted until 1500 BC, by which time the treeline west of Hudson Bay had advanced more than 240 kilometers north of its present position and pre-Dorset had begun to expand southward. During a cold-weather trend in the next four centuries this movement continued; the pre-

Dorset hunters shifted back westward into Victoria and Banks islands, south-ward onto the Canadian mainland, into the Barren Grounds of central Kee-watin, and down along the east and west coasts of Hudson Bay. The pre-Dorset Sarqaq occupation also appeared in southern Greenland at this time.

Pre-Dorset settlement patterns are not yet fully known, but their sites were coastal and based on seal and walrus hunting, with occasional emphasis in some areas on musk ox and caribou. Seasonal orientation is indicated by differing house types, including presumed summer tent locations in residual boulder rings and ovoid winter houses with central slab-rock hearth areas. As these latter dwellings lack well-defined perimeters, it has been inferred that the win-ter houses may have been constructed of snow blocks. In food-rich areas, a few deeper midden deposits suggest recurrent occupation of these preferred sites over long periods of time.

Tool assemblages were made of chipped stone, seal and walrus bone, and ivory. Major types used in hunting include toggle harpoon heads with open sockets, single line holes, and slotted ends for the insertion of triangular stone points (Figure 4.6). The throwing board was apparently unknown, although the possibility of a hooked spear thrower of antler has been reported from northern Foxe Basin. Spears and lances were used against caribou and musk ox, and their open-socketed antler heads frequently had inset side blades of chipped stone. The presence of a short, recurved, composite bow is proved by finds of bow segments and braces. Arrows had foreshafts of wood or bone with blunt tips for birds and small game; for larger game the arrows were fitted with triangular or tapering-stemmed chert points. In the Igloolik area, dogs were present throughout the pre-Dorset occupations and may have been used as hunting aids.

The most important manufacturing tools were burins, used for engraving and sectioning bone and ivory; burin spalls, many of them minutely retouched, for engraving, sinew cutting, and other delicate jobs; numerous small end scrapers of chert, probably for shaping wood, antler, or ivory, and larger, more roughly flaked stone scrapers for hide dressing; a considerable variety of stemmed and side-notched knife blades for hafting in wood or bone handles; fine-grained, granitic abrading stones; adzes of silicified slate for woodworking or shaping soapstone pots and lamps; numerous random flakes of stone, sometimes re-touched, for odd jobs of many kinds; and the ever-present microblades, which were useful for many cutting functions. Generally, these implements were chipped from local varieties of chert, but quartz crystals were also a favored material for microblades. Ground and polished slate knives were used infre-quently for butchering.

We cannot in all instances define specific functions for these tools, but it is clear that many of them were carefully specialized for particular tasks. Hence, the major game animals of land and sea were successfully hunted in all seasons, and suitable tools were at hand for butchering, food preparation, and the ma-nipulation of all raw materials, such as hides, bone, ivory, antler, wood, and stone. Needles of bone and ivory attest to the making of tailored clothing, and

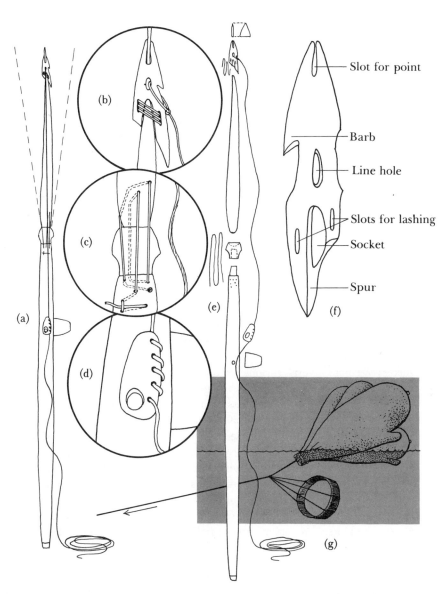

Slot for point

Barb

Line hole

Slots for lashing

Socket

Spur

FIGURE 4.6
Harpoon assembly: (a) assembled harpoon (dashed lines indicate flexibility of foreshaft); (b) harpoon head; (c) flexible joint showing shaft, shaft head, and foreshaft lashed together; (d) line retainer secured to shaft by knob; (e) component parts of harpoon; (f) idealized harpoon head; (g) sealskin floats and drag attached to end of line.

small, ovoid soapstone lamps, as well as natural rock spalls, served as vessels for the life-sustaining fire of burning seal blubber. In some of the later pre-Dorset winter houses, the central hearth boxes made of vertical stone slabs were probably lined with green skins to serve as cooking pots, the contents being raised to boiling temperature by the addition of heated stones.

There is still much to be learned about these pre-Dorset pioneers of the central and eastern Arctic, but we know that they met the progressive challenges of the environment and endured for some 1500 years. Ultimately, in the period from 1100 to 950 BC, their culture evolved toward the patterns that we identify as Dorset, and thenceforward the archeological record becomes more comprehensive. The emergence of the Dorset phase occurred in another warm-weather trend, as the Inuit were spreading back once more into the high Arctic. It was a time of heightened culture change, especially in the core area around northern Foxe Basin and southern Baffin Island, where the genesis of Dorset culture is placed. Although stylistic variation was rapid in the Igloolik area, the overall transition out of pre-Dorset was a notably smooth process, marked by continuity rather than drastic upheaval. By about 700 BC Dorset had achieved its own distinctive character, and in the succeeding centuries it left an imprint of remarkable cultural homogeneity across the eastern Arctic. In addition, we know from skeletal evidence found in Ungava and Newfoundland that the Dorset people were physically related to the specialized Arctic Mongoloids, and thus were true representatives of the Inuit.

In general, Dorset subsistence and domestic activity patterns were much the same as in the pre-Dorset phase, yet even in the face of their obvious adaptive success we note several curious anomalies in their cultural mechanisms. For example, Dorset harpoon gear was lightweight and small, and it lacked the throwing board. It was nevertheless used effectively against the larger species of seal, walrus, and possibly some of the smaller whales, such as beluga. Their sea-mammal hunting techniques seem to have been focused more on winter and spring efforts, judging from the presence of ice creepers made of bone or ivory, small hand-drawn sledges with whalebone-shod runners, and the snow knife, which was presumably used for building snow houses (Figure 4.7). Also, there is no evidence of float and drag equipment for kayak hunting, and no indication of the *maupok* method of hunting seals at their breathing holes through the ice. Hence, the Dorset hunters must have stalked their marine prey along the edges of the shore ice or out on floes. They used fish harpoons and compound leisters in the salmon streams and for char, but the inventory does not include any specific weapons for bird hunting (Figure 4.8). They also seem to have lacked the bow and arrow, a fact which may indicate their greater reliance on summer and fall hunting of caribou with spears at the water-fording places by means of organized drives and ambush techniques. It was formerly believed that the Dorset Inuit did not have domesticated dogs, but the recent discovery of dog bones in two sites on the Belcher Islands proves their limited presence in that phase. They may have been used as hunting aids, or sometimes as food, but they were not employed as traction animals for hauling sledges.

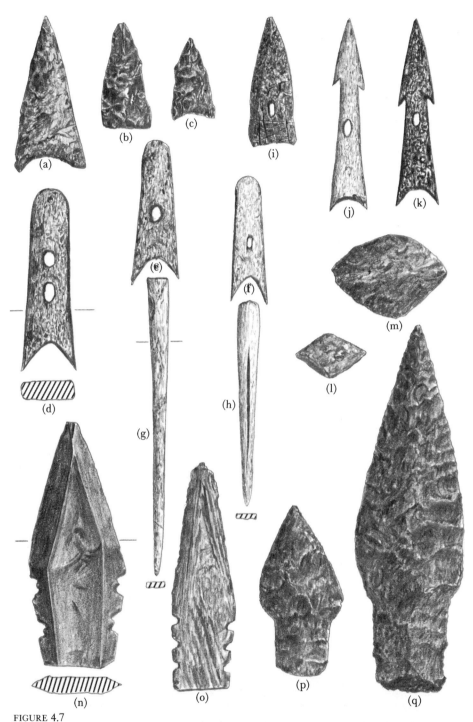

FIGURE 4.7
Dorset Inuit hunting weapons: (a–c) flaked chert harpoon points; (d–f) slotted bone harpoon heads;
(g, h) bone foreshafts; (i) bone harpoon point; (j, k) self-pointed bone harpoon heads; (l, m) chert
sideblades; (n, o) beveled slate lance points; (p, q) flaked chert spear points.

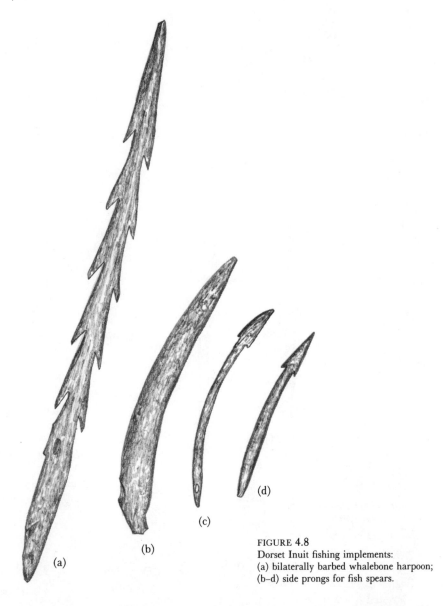

FIGURE 4.8
Dorset Inuit fishing implements:
(a) bilaterally barbed whalebone harpoon;
(b–d) side prongs for fish spears.

In many Dorset sites we have observed an increased frequency of blubber lamps, either simple rock spalls or soapstone vessels, and this too suggests a greater use of snow houses and more emphasis on winter ice hunting. However, the Dorset people built several kinds of houses and shelters, including simple, round summer tents and winter dwellings that were round or sometimes rectangular with floors excavated as much as 60 centimeters below the surrounding ground surface. This latter type did not have a cold-trap entrance, but there was usually a central hearth structure and occasionally side benches or a raised sleeping platform in the rear. Superstructures were framed with driftwood or spruce poles, when available, covered with hides, and banked with sod.

Dorset artisans were expert stone flakers, and their basic core and blade technology was clearly related to the Arctic Small Tool tradition and to the Denbigh Flint complex in the western Arctic. They introduced a new emphasis on grinding and polishing, however, especially for adzes, knives, skin scrapers, flensing tools, and burinlike gravers. They also favored the practice of side notching as an aid to hafting their knives, scrapers, and burins. Another Dorset innovation was the use of caribou tibia and scapulae as skin scrapers. Curiously, the bow drill was missing in this culture, and all holes in bone or ivory artifacts were laboriously incised with delicate cutting tools, such as microblades of chert or quartz crystal (Figure 4.9).

While some art objects of a magico-religious nature have been found in a few pre-Dorset sites, in the Dorset phase this form of expression was elaborate and highly evolved. The Dorset people conceived and executed a fascinating array of realistic and conventionalized carvings in wood, bone, and ivory, depicting human beings, spirit monsters, and the primary animals of their economy. We interpret these through ethnographic analogy with recent Inuit culture, concluding that Dorset hunters were well aware of a powerful supernatural universe around them. There is a substantial possibility that some of their groups maintained an institutionalized form of shamanism.

The Dorset phase attained its maximum distribution in the period from 200 BC to about AD 400, and for some centuries thereafter it persisted strongly in the core area. Viable outlying colonies were scattered through the Arctic Archipelago as far west as Banks Island, along the shores of Hudson Bay, in Greenland and Labrador, and in Newfoundland, where the Dorset occupation existed farther south than any group of Inuit has ever gone. Then, around AD 1000, their ambient world was disrupted by a totally new immigrant force from the west—the Thule people. Confronted with the superior Thule technology and arctic adaptation, Dorset culture suddenly was at a competitive disadvantage. Unable to meet this challenge, it gradually slipped into decline and ultimately disappeared. The last known representatives of the Dorset phase survived in Richmond Gulf, southeastern Hudson Bay, until AD 1400.

The Thule stage was destined to be ancestral to the present-day Inuit of the central and eastern Arctic. Originating from the Birnirk phase in northern Alaska around AD 900 (see Chapter Three), the Thule culture moved rapidly eastward during a period of warming climate when the distribution of permanent pack ice probably shifted northward in the Archipelago. Thule subsistence activities consisted mainly of the hunting of seals, walrus, and large whales. The last were at first taken in open water leads during the spring, but later probably in open summer waters. The sealskin-covered kayak and the more substantial *umiak* were used for this maritime hunting and also afforded means of rapid transportation in the summer. In winter the Thule people used sleds drawn by

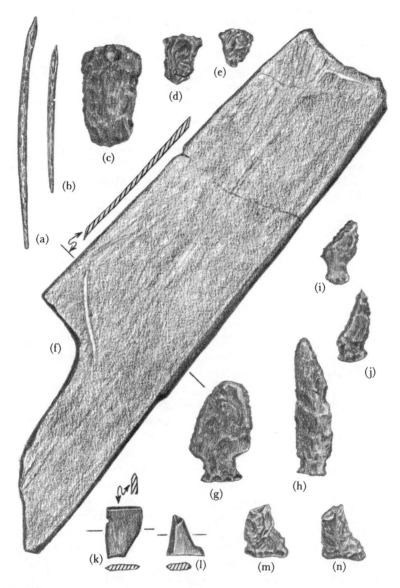

FIGURE 4.9

Manufacturing tools of the Dorset Inuit: (a, b) bone needles; (c–e) flaked chert snub-nosed end scrapers; (f) beveled slate flensing knife; (g–j) asymmetrical flaked chert biface knives; (k, l) ground and polished grooving tools with beveled edges; (m, n) flaked chert burins.

dogs. The bow and arrow was the chief weapon for hunting caribou and musk ox; birds and fish were taken with bolas, bird darts, nets, and leisters; and a wide variety of specialized harpoons were used, often propelled by a throwing board. In the west, the Thule people made a crude, grit-tempered pottery, but this was later supplanted by soapstone vessels in the central region. Thule settlement patterns generally were coastally oriented, and housing consisted of conical, skin-covered tents, temporary snow houses on winter hunting sorties, and permanent winter houses. The last were often semisubterranean, with frames constructed of driftwood or whale ribs and jawbones. They had sod coverings and sloping entrance passages with a cold trap. The size of these settlements proves that the Thule population was larger than the preceding Dorset continuum. Their cultural inventory contains all of the tools, weapons, and other equipment that we customarily see in the Inuits' superb adaptation to the Arctic.

In view of this superiority of numbers and technology, it is not surprising that Dorset culture was forced into a secondary status. The precise reasons for its extinction are still somewhat obscure, but in all probability it did not suffer complete obliteration. We know, in fact, that the two peoples lived more or less side by side in some areas for a period of 200 years, and yet there is no evidence of aggressive conflict between them. Thus, it seems likely that a genetic and cultural blending occurred, a prehistoric example of the overpowering and assimilation of relatively weak indigenous people by relatively powerful invaders. As proof of this acculturation, it has been suggested that several Dorset traits can be seen in later Thule culture: the snow knife and knowledge of snow house construction, the transverse line hole harpoon head, whalebone sled shoes (Figure 4.10), and the use of soapstone for lamps and cooking pots. Also, some authorities claim that vestiges of Dorset culture were perpetuated among the recently extinct Sadlermiut of Southampton Island and the Angmagssalik of East Greenland.

Sometime after AD 1300 there was a reverse movement of Thule culture back toward the west, and for several generations the coastal areas of the central Arctic were abandoned. This development seems in part to have been a response to another cyclical deterioration of the climate; in addition, postglacial isostatic rebound caused a shoaling of the central arctic seas and a consequent retreat of the larger whales to deeper and more distant waters. From that time forward, the various bands of Thule people scattered across the Arctic experienced a generally benign evolution and descent into the local regional components of the historic Inuit. This process has been firmly documented for the Greenlanders, the central Netsilik, and the Caribou Eskimos of the Barren Grounds, all of whose recent origins in the Thule stage can be traced through archeological evidence.

In stark contrast to the contact history of the Indians in the sub-Arctic, most of the Inuit escaped early cataclysmic confrontations with explorers and merchants from the Old World. The Norse episode in Greenland can be dubiously honored as the true beginning of the Europeanization of the New World, and the "skraelings" encountered there by Norsemen, not long after their arrival in AD 985, were Thule people. However, the trauma caused by those foreign colonies, even during a life span of several centuries, was relatively slight; it exerted a mostly ephemeral influence on native life in Greenland. In any case, the first Norse occupation there died of undernourishment, probably by the mid-fifteenth century, and it was the Inuit who survived.

The European whaling industry in North American waters grew constantly through the eighteenth and nineteenth centuries. After the whalers set up win-

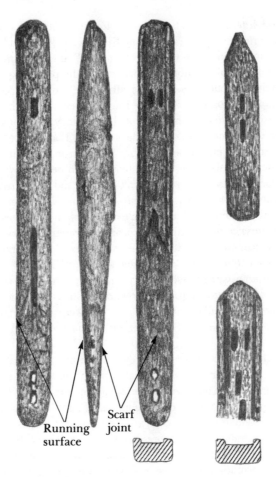

FIGURE 4.10
Whalebone sledge runners of the Dorset Inuit. These sleds were pulled by people, not dogs; the runners were fastened to the sled with rawhide lashings.

tering stations on Baffin Island and elsewhere, however, the exploitation became so severe that the most prized whale species were hunted nearly to extinction by 1910. During this period a few of the Inuit worked aboard ships or in the seasonal shore stations, and some of the eastern groups suffered painfully from new epidemic diseases introduced from abroad. Most of the people, however, remained inadvertently shielded behind central arctic bastions, which the Europeans did not fully penetrate until the early decades of the twentieth century.

Now, in a time of modern enlightenment and raised consciousness, the politicized Inuit Brotherhoods are striving for fraternity and equality in the outer world of humanity. As a consequence, their ancient lifeways will soon be no more.

CONCLUSION

Prehistoric research in the northeastern quadrant of North America has passed through its childhood of antiquarian curiosity and through an adolescence of ethnographic reconstruction and historiography, and it is now in a more mature phase of true anthropological inquiry. It seems safe to claim that we have managed so far to block in the essential outlines of northern prehistory and to establish a crude chronological framework for its development. However, there are still huge areas in both the sub-Arctic and the Arctic that are physically unknown to archeologists, and until they have been adequately explored our publications must remain spotted with approximations and uncertainties. A tantalizing future of problem solving lies ahead as we face up to such matters as the ethnic identity of our archeological assemblages, the movement of people versus the transference of ideas, cultural exchange in the ecotone of the transitional forest, environmental determinism and cultural adaptation, human biological response to cold, the social dynamics of northern hunting peoples, and perhaps myriad other questions that we do not yet perceive. Thus, the perspectives of northern prehistory are still deep and partially shrouded in mystery. The ultimate telling of humanity's early story in these cold regions remains a worthy cause.

References Cited and Recommended Sources

Baird, Patrick D. 1964. *Polar World.* New York: Wiley.

Byers, Douglas S. 1959. The eastern Archaic: some problems and hypotheses. *American Antiquity* 24:233–256.

Collins, Henry B. 1950. Excavations at Frobisher Bay, Baffin Island, N.W.T. *Annual Report of the National Museum of Canada,* Bulletin 118:18–43.

———. 1955. Excavations of the Thule and Dorset culture sites at Resolute, Cornwallis Island, N.W.T. *National Museum of Canada,* Bulletin 136:22–35.

———. 1956a. Archaeological investigations on Southampton and Coats islands, N.W.T. *Annual Report of the National Museum of Canada for 1954–1955,* Bulletin 142:82–113.

———. 1956b. The T-1 site at Native Point, Southampton Island, N.W.T. *Anthropological Papers of the University of Alaska* 4:2:63–89.

———. 1957. Archaeological investigations on Southampton and Walrus islands, N.W.T. *Annual Report of the National Museum of Canada,* Bulletin 147:22–61.

———. 1958. Present status of the Dorset problem. *Proceedings of the 32nd International Congress of Americanists,* 1956, Copenhagen.

Dekin, Albert A., Jr. 1972. Climatic change and culture change: a correlative study from eastern arctic prehistory. Baker Library, Dartmouth College, *Polar Notes* 12:11–31.

Fitzhugh, William W. 1972. *Environmental Archaeology and Cultural Systems in Hamilton Inlet, Labrador.* Smithsonian Contributions to Anthropology, no. 16. Smithsonian Institution Press.

Giddings, J. Louis. 1956. A flint site in northernmost Manitoba. *American Antiquity* 21:3.

———. 1964. *The Archaeology of Cape Denbigh.* Providence: Brown University Press.

Gordon, Bryan H. C. 1975. *Of Men and Herds in Barrenland Prehistory.* Archaeological Survey of Canada Mercury Series, Paper no. 28. National Museums of Canada.

Harp, Elmer, Jr. 1951. An archaeological survey in the Strait of Belle Isle area. *American Antiquity* 16:203–220.

———. 1958. Prehistory in the Dismal Lake area, N.W.T., Canada. *Arctic* 11:4:218–249.

———. 1959. The Moffatt archaeological collection from the Dubawnt country, Canada. *American Antiquity* 24:4:412–422.

———. 1961. *The Archaeology of the Lower and Middle Thelon, Northwest Territories.* Arctic Institute of North America, Technical Paper no. 8.

———. 1962. The culture history of the central Barren Grounds. In *Prehistoric Cultural Relations Between the Arctic and Temperate Zones of North America*, ed. J. M. Campbell, pp. 69–75. Arctic Institute of North America, Technical Paper no. 11.

———. 1964. *The Cultural Affinities of the Newfoundland Dorset Eskimos.* National Museum of Canada, Bulletin 200.

———. 1970a. The prehistoric Indian and Eskimo cultures of Labrador and Newfoundland. *Proceedings of the VIIth International Congress of Anthropological and Ethnological Sciences* 10:295–299.

———. 1970b. Late Dorset Eskimo art from Newfoundland. *Folk* 11–12:109–124.

———. 1975. A late Dorset copper amulet from southeastern Hudson Bay. *Folk* 17:33–44.

———. 1976. Dorset settlement patterns in Newfoundland and southeastern Hudson Bay. In *Eastern Arctic Prehistory: Paleoeskimo Problems*, ed. Moreau S. Maxwell. Memoirs of the Society for American Archaeology no. 31, pp. 119–138.

———, and D. R. Hughes. 1968. Five prehistoric burials from Port aux Choix, Newfoundland. Baker Library, Dartmouth College, *Polar Notes* 8:1–47.

Holtved, Erik. 1944. Archaeological investigations in the Thule district. *Meddelelser om Grønland* 141:1.

Jenness, Diamond. 1925. A new Eskimo culture in Hudson Bay. *Geographical Review* 15:428–437.

Johnson, Frederick. 1948. The Rogers' collection from Lakes Mistassini and Albanel, Province of Quebec. *American Antiquity* 14:2:91–98.

Kimble, George H. T., and Dorothy Good (eds.). 1955. *Geography of the Northlands.* American Geographic Society, Special Publication no. 32. New York: Wiley.

Knuth, Eigil. 1952. An outline of the archaeology of Pearyland. *Arctic* 5:1:17–33.

———. 1954. The Paleo-Eskimo culture of northern Greenland elucidated by three new sites. *American Antiquity* 19:4:367–381.

———. 1958. Archaeology of the farthest north. *Proceedings of the 32nd International Congress of Americanists, 1956*, Copenhagen.

Larsen, Helge. 1938. Archaeological investigations in Knud Rasmussen land. *Meddelelser om Grønland* 119:8.

———, and Jørgen Meldgaard. 1958. Paleo-Eskimo cultures in Disko Bugt, West Greenland. *Meddelelser om Grønland* 161:2.

Leechman, Douglas. 1943. Two new Cape Dorset culture sites. *American Antiquity* 8:4:363–375.

Lethbridge, T. C. 1939. Archaeology data from the Canadian Arctic. *Journal of the Royal Anthropological Institute* 69:187–233.

Lloyd, T. G. B. 1874. On the "Beothucs," a tribe of Red Indians supposed to be extinct, which formerly inhabited Newfoundland. *Journal of the Royal Anthropological Institute* 4:21–39.

Lowther, Gordon R. n.d. The archaeology of the Tadoussac area. Unpublished manuscript, National Museum of Canada.

McGhee, Robert. 1970. Excavations at Bloody Falls, N.W.T., Canada. *Arctic Anthropology* 6:2:52–72.

MacNeish, Richard S. 1951. An archaeological reconnaissance in the northwest territories. *National Museum of Canada*, Bulletin 123:24–41.

———. 1953. Archaeological reconnaissance in the Mackenzie River drainage. *National Museum of Canada*, Bulletin 128.

———. 1954. The Pointed Mountain site near Fort Liard, N.W.T., Canada. *American Antiquity* 19:3:234–253.

———. 1955. Two archaeological sites on Great Bear Lake, Northwest Territories, Canada. *National Museum of Canada*, Bulletin 136:55–84.

———. 1956. The Engigstciak site on the Yukon Arctic coast. *Anthropological Papers of the University of Alaska* 4:2:91–111.

Mathiassen, Therkel. 1927. Archaeology of the central Eskimos, the Thule culture and its position within the Estimo culture. *Report of the Fifth Thule Expedition, 1921–24* 4:1 and 2.

———. 1930a. Inugsuk, a medieval Eskimo settlement in Upernavik District, West Greenland. *Meddelelser om Grønland* 77:145–340.

———. 1930b. An old Eskimo culture in West Greenland: report of an archaeological expedition to Upernavik. *Geographical Review* 20:605–614.

———. 1931a. The present stage of Eskimo archaeology. *Acta Archaeologica* 2:2.

———. 1931b. Ancient Eskimo settlements in the Kangamiut Area. *Meddelelser om Grønland* 91:1.

———. 1934. Contributions to the archaeology of Disko Bay. *Meddelelser om Grønland* 92:4.

———. 1958. The Sermermiut Excavations, 1955. *Meddelelser om Grønland* 161:3.

Maxwell, Moreau S. 1960. The movement of cultures in the Canadian high Arctic. *Anthropologica,* n.s. 11:2:1–13.

———. 1972. *Archaeology of the Lake Harbour District, Baffin Island.* Archaeological Survey of Canada, Paper no. 6, Mercury Series, National Museums of Canada.

Meldgaard, Jørgen. 1952. A Paleo-Eskimo culture in West Greenland. *American Antiquity* 17:3:222–230.

———. 1960. Prehistoric culture sequences in the eastern Arctic as elucidated by stratified sites at Igloolik. *Selected Papers, 5th International Congress of Anthropological and Ethnological Sciences, 1956,* pp. 588–595.

———. 1962. On the formative period of Dorset culture. In *Prehistoric Cultural Relations Between the Arctic and Temperate Zones of North America,* ed. J. M. Campbell, pp. 92–95. Arctic Institute of North America, Technical Paper no. 11.

Morris, Margaret W. 1973. Great Bear Lake Indians: a historical demography and human ecology. Part I: The situation prior to European contact. Institute for Northern Studies, *The Muskox* 11:3–27.

Nash, Ronald J. 1969. *The Arctic Small Tool Tradition in Manitoba.* Department of Anthropology, University of Manitoba, Occasional Paper no. 2.

Noble, William C. 1971. Archaeological surveys and sequences in the central district of Mackenzie, N.W.T. *Arctic Anthropology* 8:1:102–135.

O'Bryan, Deric. 1953. Excavation of a Cape Dorset Eskimo culture Eskimo site, Mill Island, West Hudson Strait. *National Museum of Canada, Bulletin* 128:40–57.

Rogers, Edward S., and R. A. Bradley. 1953. An archaeological reconnaissance in south-central Quebec, 1950. *American Antiquity* 19:2:138–144.

———, and M. H. Rogers. 1948. Archaeological reconnaissance of Lakes Mistassini and Albanel, Province of Quebec, 1947. *American Antiquity* 14:2:81–90.

Rowley, Graham. 1940. The Dorset culture of the eastern Arctic. *American Anthropologist,* n.s. 42:490–499.

Smith, J. G. E. n.d. The ecological basis of Chipewyan socio-territorial organization. Unpublished manuscript, University of Waterloo, Ontario.

Speck, Frank G. 1916. An ancient archaeological site on the lower St. Lawrence. Washington, D.C.: *Holmes Anniversary Volume,* pp. 427–433.

Strong, W. D. 1930. A stone culture from northern Labrador and its relation to the Eskimo-like cultures of the northeast. *American Anthropologist,* n.s. 32:126–143.

Taylor, William E., Jr. 1964. Interim report of an archaeological survey in the central Arctic, 1963. *Anthropological Papers of the University of Alaska* 12:1:46–55.

———. 1967. Summary of archaeological field work on Banks and Victoria Islands, Arctic Canada, 1965. *Arctic Anthropology* 4:1:221–243.

———. 1968. *The Arnapik and Tyara Sites, an Archaeological Study of Dorset Culture Origins.* Memoirs of the Society for American Archaeology, no. 22.

Terasmae, J. 1961. Notes on Late Quaternary climatic changes in Canada. *Annals of the New York Academy of Sciences* 96:1:658–675.

Tuck, James A. 1970. An Archaic Indian cemetery in Newfoundland. *Scientific American* 222:6:112–121.

Wintemberg, W. J. 1939–1940. Eskimo sites of the Dorset culture in Newfoundland. *American Antiquity* 5:2:83–102; 5:4:309–333.

———. 1943. Artifacts from ancient workshop sites near Tadoussac, Saguenay County, Quebec. *American Antiquity* 8:4:313–340.

Wright, J. V. 1972a. *The Shield Archaic.* Publications in Archaeology, National Museums of Canada.

———. 1972b. *The Aberdeen Site, Keewatin District, N.W.T.* Archaeological Survey of Canada, Paper no. 2, Mercury Series, National Museums of Canada.

Alternating mountain and valley topography is characteristic of the Great Basin. Native peoples systematically exploited the resources of different altitudinal zones in the course of their annual round.

During the earlier periods of occupation at Hogup Cave, Utah, the occupants looked out over a shallow lake with fringing marshland. This setting is typical of many Great Basin sites.

CHAPTER FIVE

The Far West

C. Melvin Aikens

Despite the physical diversity of the large region covered in this chapter and the concomitant differences in the adaptations of the prehistoric inhabitants to their environments, there were some remarkable cultural continuities through time and similarities over distance. Dr. Aikens describes some of these similarities and discusses the great variety of successful adaptations among the aboriginal populations in California, the Great Basin, and the Columbia-Fraser Plateau.

The evolution of culture in the Far West may be broadly divided into three general stages. Prior to about 8000 BC, glaciers existed in the Sierra–Cascades and Rocky Mountains and on isolated peaks elsewhere. Great lakes filled the valleys of the Great Basin and the southern California deserts. Mammoth, horse, camel, giant ground sloth, and other species occupied a cooler, more verdant landscape than exists now. The people of this time, who were adapted to climatic and vegetational conditions greatly different from those to follow, appear to have been primarily hunters. By about 5000 BC, postglacial warming and drying had eliminated most of the glaciers and pluvial lakes. The mammoth had become extinct, and over most of the Far West (except in the higher mountains and to a lesser extent in California) arid or semiarid desert vegetation dominated the landscape. Everywhere human foragers depended for their subsistence on the eclectic hunting and gathering of a broad spectrum of plants and animals. The final point of transition is less uniform in time, but by about 1000 BC in California, 500 BC in the Plateau and western Great Basin, and AD 500 in the eastern Great Basin, there had developed trends toward increasing population, intensified subsistence activity, and growing societal complexity and interaction. These stages, as expressed in regional and local culture histories, comprise the main thread of the present account.

The area covered by this chapter includes California, the Great Basin, and the Columbia–Fraser Plateau (Figure 5.1). It is a vast and varied country, unified to some extent by cultural and environmental factors. Early ethnologists saw in the simple, unelaborated lifeway of the Great Basin a relic of an ancient cultural substratum that they believed to be very close to that of the earliest

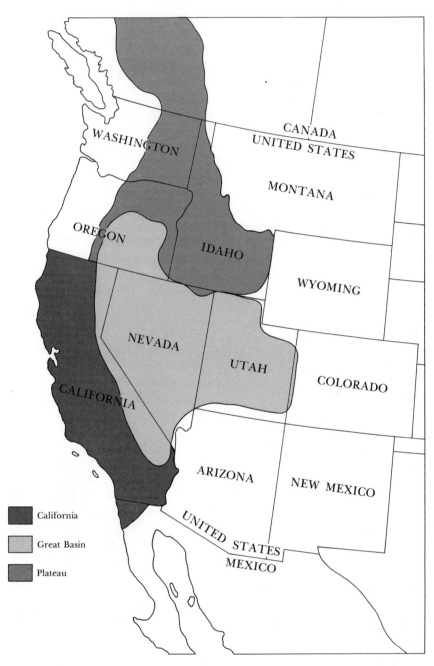

FIGURE 5.1
The Far West.

occupants of the New World. Similarities in basketry, architectural techniques, puberty rites, folktale motifs, and other traits shared among ethnographic cultures of California, the Great Basin, and the Plateau suggested that a common ancient tradition, from which Basin culture had departed the least, must once have characterized all three areas and provided the ground from which distinctive yet ultimately related regional traditions later sprang. In broadest outline, this conception has been borne out by prehistorians' researches, and it can provide the reader with a general frame of reference for the archeological detail to follow.

Of the three provinces, California is the most diverse. In the south and east it is desert; on the west it is seacoast; the great central valley is summer-dry grassland and parkland; and the Coast Range and Sierra Nevada are heavily wooded. Natural foods are abundant, and from quite early times there is evidence of substantial populations living in stable local communities. The Great Basin is a desert by any popular definition, though not to qualify the term would give the impression of a land far less hospitable to human occupation than in fact it was. The topography is one of alternating mountain ranges and valley basins, with altitudinal and topographic variation in the occurrence of effective moisture, giving rise to a series of biotically varied microenvironments that the native peoples exploited by ranging among them in a regular annual cycle. The Plateau is dry and open in the south and wooded to greater or lesser degree in the north. These characteristics are secondary, however, to the overriding fact of the two major river systems, the Columbia and the Fraser, which dominate the southern and northern portions of the Plateau, respectively. The woods and sagebrush–grasslands were exploited for game and edible roots and plants, but the rivers, with their dependable annual runs of millions of salmon, were the central focus of Plateau settlement and economic life.

The importance of environmental factors to hunting and gathering peoples is great, and California, the Great Basin, and the Plateau give perspectives on hunting–gathering adaptations to three distinctive geographic provinces. The comparison of the three is made the more interesting by the likelihood that their cultures stemmed from a common historical source far back in time.

CALIFORNIA

The developmental history of Californian cultures is still far from completely understood, but the broad pattern is evident. Although claims for extremely early occupation remain dubious, clear evidence of Paleo-Indian bearers of the Clovis fluted-point tradition, which probably dates before 8000 BC, has been discovered over much of the state. Clovis points have been found from southern California to the coast ranges north of San Francisco. Though these people may have been even more widespread, finds made so far suggest that they favored lower-lying, more open country, where large Pleistocene game such as the mammoth would have been most common. Closely following this cultural horizon in time—and most probably an outgrowth of it—is the San Dieguito complex, which has about the same pattern of distribution. After approximately 6000 BC, a series of local traditions began to appear, apparently as adaptations to different environmental zones. These then persisted, with some internal development over time, to the historic period.

Broadly speaking, the several local traditions developed along similar lines. They seem to have begun by exploiting a broad spectrum of plant and animal resources, with special emphasis on acorns, wild seeds, fish, and small game. These resources occurred, of course, in varying abundance in the different natural zones of California, and the local traditions reflect this fact. Over time, most of the local societies grew more complex, though the rate of development, and the level of complexity attained, varied from area to area. The cultural patterns of ethnographic (historical) times are the end products of this long evolution. A brief sketch of the historical situation will provide a background for discussion of the archeological record.

Aboriginal California was biotically rich, densely populated, and culturally diverse, more so than any comparable area of North America. Its ethnographic population has been estimated at 300,000 to 350,000 people, and within the modern boundaries of the state about 500 separate ethnic groups or independent communities were counted. Kroeber (1925) grouped the hundreds of small California societies into four broad culture provinces, which coincided with broadly defined environmental zones. Northwest California cultures resembled those of the northern Pacific coast of Oregon, Washington, and British Columbia in their maritime–riverine economy, woodworking industry, and wealth emphasis. Central California societies shared similarities in social customs, basketry, houses, and technical processes with cultures of the trans-Sierran Great Basin. Cultures of the southern California coast and the southern deserts were distinctive in society and architecture, but traits such as pottery-making, maize agriculture (on the Colorado River), and sand painting are evidence of contact with cultures of the Pueblo Southwest.

These similarities suggest the historical origins and contacts of the native Californians. The fact that northwestern California was dominated by speakers of Athabascan and Algonquian tongues, central California by Penutian speakers, and southern California by Shoshonean and Yuman speakers suggests a general historical stability within each of the major provinces for hundreds, and probably thousands, of years past. The scattered, broken distribution of Hokan speakers throughout the state suggests that they might be remnants of a more ancient people, perhaps the original Californians, who were intruded upon and displaced by later arrivals.

Early Peopling

Paleo-Indian period (? to 6000 BC) finds are so far not adequately dated. Those attributed to this period are believed to be old primarily because of their typological similarity to cultural manifestations dated elsewhere. A number of sites in California have yielded coarsely flaked stone specimens that resemble, sometimes strikingly, the Paleolithic handaxes or pebble tools of Europe, Africa, and Asia. It has been suggested that such sites represent a western lithic cotradition ancestral to all later developments in California and the desert West (Davis et al., 1969:76–77), but a widely supported opposing view is that none of these sites demonstrates truly ancient human activity. Manix Lake and Coyote Gulch in southern California, for example, yielded indisputably man-made artifacts, but all are from the surface and are not reliably dated. Though the artifacts do resemble handaxes known to be ancient in Europe and Africa, a restudy of the Manix Lake industry (Glennan, 1976) showed it was probably a relatively recent quarry–workshop complex, where large stone pieces were flaked and shaped into finished artifacts. Although objections to this study have been raised (Simpson, 1976), it remains likely that the coarse Paleolithic-like specimens are simply objects broken or abandoned as unpromising early in the process of reducing large lumps of raw material to finished forms. Similar specimens have been found at many sites of no great age, including some so recent as to contain pottery (Wallace, 1962).

Specimens from other sites, such as Calico Hills and Texas Street, again in southern California, are demonstrably of Pleistocene age, but their identification as true artifacts is in doubt; they do not exhibit the consistent forms and flaking techniques that have characterized human artifacts since earliest times in the Old World. Moreover, in each case it is clear that a small number of specimens fortuitously resembling artifacts were carefully selected from deposits containing hundreds or thousands of pieces of stone or bone broken or abraded by geological forces (Johnson and Miller, 1958; Haynes, 1973). Buried features in Pleistocene deposits at Texas Street and on Santa Rosa Island that have been claimed as fire hearths can equally be attributed to natural causes (Cruxent, 1962; Riddell, 1969).

Human skulls from Laguna Beach and Los Angeles have been dated to 15,000 and greater than 21,000 BC by carbon-14 determinations on the human bone itself (Berger et al., 1971; Berger, 1975), and ages of up to 50,000 BC have been calculated for other California skeletal remains by the aspartic acid racemization technique (Bada et al., 1974; Bada and Helfman, 1975). But the aspartic acid racemization dates are calculated from a rate based on the carbon-14 date for the Laguna Beach skull, and carbon-14 dates for the probable context of the skull are in the range of 6000 to 7000 BC, casting doubt on the 15,000 BC date for the skull itself. Independent confirmation of such ages for human presence in California will be required to dispel the skepticism surrounding these dates.

Paleo-Indian sites with distinctive Clovis Fluted points at Borax Lake, north of San Francisco, and at a number of localities in southern California (Figure 5.2) represent more reliable evidence of early occupation. Lake Mohave, Tulare Lake, and China Lake have each yielded a number of specimens, and many more isolated finds are known (Riddell and Olsen, 1969). All are undated

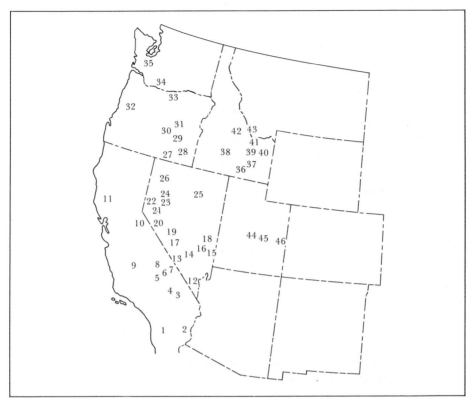

FIGURE 5.2
Fluted-point surface finds in the Far West (see key).

Key to Figure 5.2

Figure 5.2 Location No.	Site	Reference
	California	
1	Cuyamaca Park Pass	Davis and Shutler, 1969
2	Pinto Basin	Warren, 1967
3	Lake Mohave	Campbell and Campbell, 1937; Warren, 1967
4	Tiefort Basin	Davis and Shutler, 1969
5	China Lake	Davis and Shutler, 1969
6	Panamint Basin	Davis and Shutler, 1969; Warren, 1967
7	Death Valley	Hunt, 1960; Warren, 1967
8	Owens Lake	Davis, 1963; Warren, 1967
9	Tulare Lake	Riddell and Olsen, 1969
10	Ebbetts Pass	Davis and Shutler, 1969
11	Borax Lake	Harrington, 1948; Meighan and Haynes, 1970

Figure 5.2

Location No.	Site	Reference
	Nevada	
12	Clark County	Perkins, 1967, 1968
13	Beatty	Shutler and Shutler, 1959
14	Groom Dry Lake	Davis and Shutler, 1969
15	Caliente	Davis and Shutler, 1969
16	Dry Lakes Valley	Davis and Shutler, 1969
17	Lowengruhn Beach Ridge, Mud Lake	Tuohy, 1968
18	Long Valley Lake	Tadlock, 1966
19	Lake Tonopah	Tuohy, 1969; Warren, 1967
20	Huntoon Valley	Davis and Shutler, 1969
21	Fallon Area	Davis and Shutler, 1969; Warren and Ranere, 1968
22	Reno Area	Davis and Shutler, 1969
23	Carson Sink	Warren, 1967; Tuohy, 1968
24	Lovelock Area	Davis and Shutler, 1969
25	Carlin	Davis and Shutler, 1969
26	Black Rock Desert	Clewlow, 1968; Richards, 1968
	Oregon	
27	Guano Valley (Big Springs)	Cressman, 1936; Oregon State Museum of Anthropology files
28	Coyote Flat	Butler, 1970
29	Malheur Lake	Strong, 1969
30	Glass Buttes	Oregon State Museum of Anthropology files; Mack, 1975
31	Eastern Oregon Area	Osborne, 1956
32	Eugene Area	Strong, 1969; Allely, 1975
33	Blalock	Strong, 1969
34	The Dalles	Osborne, 1956
35	Olympia Area	Osborne, 1956
	Idaho	
36	Lake Channel Locality	Butler, 1965
37	Bannock Creek	Butler, 1965
38	Big Camas Prairie	Butler, 1963
39	Pioneer Basin	Butler, 1970
40	Roberts Site	Butler, 1965
41	Birch Creek Sinks	Butler, 1965
42	Upper Salmon River Area	Butler, 1972
43	Birch Creek Area	Swanson and Sneed, 1966; Butler, 1965
	Utah	
44	Acord Lake	Tripp, 1966
45	San Rafael Swell, Silverhorn Wash	Anonymous, 1968; Gunnerson, 1956
46	Moab Area	Hunt and Tanner, 1960

surface finds, but such points have been securely dated by multiple carbon-14 determinations at several sites in the Great Plains and the Southwest to a period between 9500 and 9000 BC. Obsidian hydration measurements on the Borax Lake specimens, as well as their apparent geological context, are also congruent with these dates (Meighan and Haynes, 1970). In the Plains and the Southwest, Clovis points occur in kill sites with the bones of mammoth, giant bison, and other now-extinct big-game animals. At China Lake, the bones of mammoth, bison, camel, horse, and other mammals and birds have been found, eroding out of the lake bed, near Clovis points, though the all-important association of bones and artifacts is not clearly established (Davis, 1975).

At many of the lake-bed sites where Clovis points have been found, there is also evidence of leaf-shaped biface points or knives, crescent-shaped knives, and a variety of heavy scrapers, choppers, and hammerstones. This assemblage, termed the *San Dieguito complex* (Figure 5.3), has been found in buried context at the C. W. Harris site in San Diego, and was dated there by carbon-14 to approximately 7000 BC (Warren, 1967). It thus follows Clovis in time, and appears to be the last manifestation of the Paleo-Indian period in California. The complex has not been formally recognized in more northerly parts of California, but undated artifacts from Borax Lake resemble San Dieguito types very closely, suggesting its presence there.

Southern California

On the south coast, complexes such as Topanga, Malaga Cove, La Jolla, Oak Grove, and Little Sycamore follow the San Dieguito complex and probably derived from it. Warren (1968) has grouped these into the Encinitas tradition, the beginning of which he places about 5500 BC. Manos and metates are abundant; hammerstones and large, crude chopping, scraping, and cutting tools are common; and large, crude projectile points, often leaf-shaped are present but relatively rare. Bone awls, flakers, beads, atlatl hooks, and shell beads and pendants are also characteristic, though of relatively low frequency. A well-developed collecting economy is indicated by abundant remains of shellfish and by the characteristic milling stones. Mammal bones, fish remains, and projectile points are, by contrast, relatively rare, suggesting that hunting and fishing were less emphasized. The Encinitas tradition is superseded after about 3000 BC on the Santa Barbara coast, but apparently lasted until AD 1000 or later in the San Diego area.

The Campbell tradition follows the Encinitas, appearing first on the Santa Barbara coast and only considerably later as a few site-unit intrusions on the San Diego coast. Diagnostic artifacts include side-notched, stemmed, and lanceolate or leaf-shaped points, large knives, and a variety of flake scrapers and drills. The hopper mortar and stone bowl mortar and pestle appear for the first time, and shell, bone, and stone ornaments of styles different from those of the Encinitas tradition are present. The economic base of the Campbell tradition

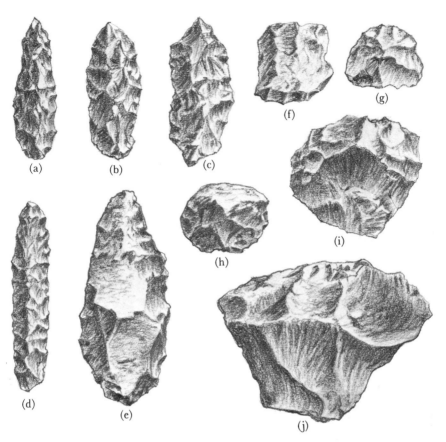

FIGURE 5.3
San Dieguito artifacts: (a–e) knives; (f–i) scrapers; (j) chopper.

was heavily oriented toward hunting, as attested by a relative abundance of points, knives, and scrapers and by abundant bones of deer, elk, bear, seal, small land mammals, and fish, as well as shellfish, in the middens at Little Harbor and the Aerophysics site. Warren suggests that the Campbell tradition stemmed from a migration of inland hunters to the coast, where they became amalgamated with the coastally adapted Encinitas people and developed a productive broad-spectrum maritime hunting and gathering economic base. This cultural tradition was always richest in the Santa Barbara region, where the environment was most favorable to maritime developments, and was less developed where it later penetrated the less favorable San Diego coast.

The ethnographic Chumash represent the historical conclusion of this continuum in the Santa Barbara Channel region, where the protohistoric culture has been given the archeological name Canaliño. This was a rich maritime adaptation that emphasized fishing and sea-mammal hunting, but broad-spectrum hunting and gathering, both along the coastline and in the interior, were also of major significance. The list of Canaliño artifacts is long and includes small projectile points, drills, scrapers, bone awls, bone and shell fishhooks, abalone shell dishes, stone bowls, mortars, pestles, and an abundance of animal effigies, shell beads, and ornaments. The Canaliño is the climax development of southern California and apparently represents a society of considerable wealth and complexity.

Archeological antecedents for the Shoshonean- and Yuman-speaking peoples who lived south of the Chumash in ethnographic times consist of the Cuyamaca phase, representing the Yuman-speaking Diegueño, and the San Luis Rey I and II phases, representing the Shoshonean-speaking Luiseño. Both phases seem to date within the last 1000 years, although their chronology is not very well established. The Cuyamaca phase may be an outgrowth of the local Encinitas tradition, but the San Luis Rey phases are believed to represent a late Shoshonean migration to the coast from the interior deserts (Meighan, 1954; True et al., 1974).

Central California

For central California, a cultural tradition defined principally from excavations in the great central valley around Sacramento includes the Windmiller (3000–1000 BC), Cosumnes (1000 BC–AD 500), and Hotchkiss (AD 500–historic) cultures. All are known almost exclusively from artifacts found with human burials. The nature of the actual settlements is unknown, but the abundance and concentration of human interments in cemeteries suggests that villages were sedentary and occupied over long periods of time.

Windmiller culture sites occur on natural mounds or levees near permanent water. Large, heavy lanceolate, bipointed, and stemmed dart points, along with manos, metates, and mortars, suggest a subsistence economy based on hunting and on the gathering of seeds and acorns (Figure 5.4). Burial finds include distinctive *Olivella* and *Haliotis* marine shell beads, rectangular stone palettes, charmstones in a variety of shapes, and tubular pipes. Burial was by interment; cremation occurred rarely (Ragir, 1972).

The subsequent Cosumnes culture is known from many sites, suggesting a relatively dense population. Large, heavy, chipped stone projectile points, bone bipoints and fish spear barbs, and mortars and pestles give evidence of a hunting–fishing–gathering complex; an increased frequency of mortars possibly suggests a growing importance of acorns as a food source. *Olivella* and *Haliotis* beads and ornaments are numerous, and some are of types different from those of the preceding horizon. Perforated coyote teeth and bear claws, fishtail charmstones, and short bird bone tubes appear as burial offerings. A small but significant percentage of burials have embedded projectile points, indicating

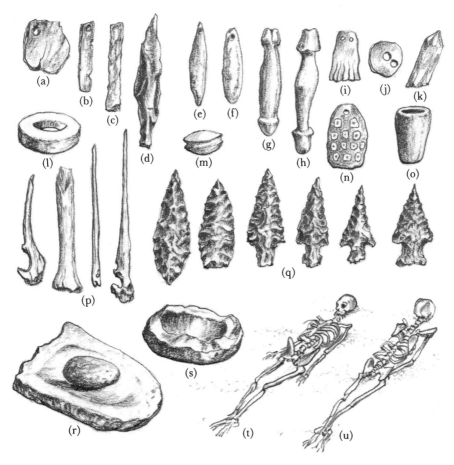

FIGURE 5.4
Artifacts of the central California Windmiller culture: (a) biotite ornament; (b, c) slate ornaments; (d) "bangle"; (e–h) charmstones; (i) shell ornament; (j) shell disk; (k) worked quartz crystal; (l) steatite bead; (m) clay object; (n) shell-inlaid turtle-carapace ornament; (o) stone pipe; (p) bone tools; (q) projectile points; (r) metate and mano; (s) mortar; (t, u) extended supine and prone burials.

violent death. Cremation burials were more common than earlier but were still relatively rare.

The late period Hotchkiss culture is also well represented by numerous sites distributed throughout central California. The relative abundance of portable mortars and cylindrical pestles indicates an economy focused on acorn gathering; small side-notched projectile points and barbed bone fish spears suggest the prominence of fishing, hunting, and fowling. Charred remnants of basketry have been found in some graves. There was at this period a great proliferation of ornaments and beads of *Haliotis* shell, clamshell, magnetite, and steatite.

Both interment and cremation burial were practiced, with cremations becoming increasingly common. This period culminates in the rich ethnographic cultures of the Wintun, Miwok, and Yokuts (Beardsley, 1954).

Earlier formulations treated central coast sites around San Francisco Bay as peripheral to the central valley cultures, but reinterpretation of the Bay Area evidence suggests the existence of a separate coastal cotradition with an integrity of its own and a time depth equal to that of the central valley tradition. The principal site on which this thesis rests is University Village, at the south end of San Francisco Bay. Here many Windmiller-like traits were present, but differences in burial orientation, relative frequencies of shell bead types, flaked stone tools, seed-grinding implements, and quartz crystals, as well as in anthropometric characteristics of the human skeletal remains, are evidence of the site's distinctiveness. Differences between the central coast and central valley traditions are said to be greatest between 2000 and 1000 BC, and to have lessened sufficiently by about 500 BC for a convergence of the originally separate traditions to be postulated (Gerow and Force, 1968; Gerow, 1974).

Northern California

For the north coast ranges, a series of "patterns," or phases, has recently been defined. The Post pattern, provisionally dated between 6,000 and 10,000 BC, represents the Clovis Paleo-Indian evidence already referred to. A period not yet formally defined for the area follows (San Dieguito horizon?). Then comes the Borax Lake pattern, estimated to date between 5000 and 500 BC, which is characterized by broad-stemmed Borax Lake projectile points, burins, manos, metates, and occasional mortars. The remaining time down to the historic horizon is occupied by the Houx aspect, considered to represent a coalescence of the local Borax Lake pattern with a culture stemming from the San Francisco Bay area. Replacement of the mano and metate by the mortar and pestle and a proliferation of projectile points are the principal artifactual changes described. Burins, present in the Borax Lake pattern, continue into the Houx aspect, suggesting a degree of cultural continuity from the older local pattern (Fredrickson, 1974a).

The northwest coast of California gives evidence of a distinctive cultural tradition. Excavations at Gunther Island, Patrick's Point, Tsurai, and Point St. George reveal a people living on shell mounds and practicing a lifeway based on fishing, hunting, and collecting. Bone and shell fishhooks, barbed bone harpoons, small barbed arrowpoints, zoomorphic stone clubs, grooved stone and clay sinkers, pestles, and stone bowl mortars, along with actual shell and bone remains, give evidence of economic pursuits and a technology similar in detail to that of the ethnographic Wiyot, Yurok, Karok, and Tolowa inhabitants of the region. The historic lifeway and adaptation to local conditions, which nevertheless shows many similarities to cultures farther north along the Pacific coast, clearly has existed in this region for the past 1000 years. Two millennia or more of occupation are suggested by a carbon-14 date of 300 BC for the Point St. George site, and there are hints of a different cultural complex at that time. Additional older sites are to be expected at locations back from the present shores, but until their potential is exploited and a longer cultural sequence developed, the antecedents and developmental history of the northwestern California cultures will remain obscure (Elsasser and Heizer, 1966; Gould, 1966).

The Sierra

From the Oroville region of the northern Sierra foothills, Ritter (1970) describes a sequence of four cultural phases spanning the past 3000 years, which suggests a progression from band-level societies focused on the hunting of large game and exploitation of hard seeds to more sedentary tribelets with an economy based on hunting, fishing, and acorn gathering. The Mesilla phase (1000 BC–AD 0) is represented by atlatls and heavy stemmed and side-notched dart points, the mano and metate, and, less common, the bowl mortar and cylindrical pestle. Ornaments are *Olivella* and *Haliotis* shell beads. The Bidwell phase (AD 0–800) saw the introduction of small arrowpoints, which occur with larger dart points. The mano–metate combination continued to predominate over the mortar and pestle as a food-grinding system, implying continued predominance of seed gathering over acorn collecting. Because burials are more abundant and their accompaniments richer than in the Mesilla phase, a more sedentary pattern of occupation is inferred. By the Sweetwater phase (AD 800–1500), cobble pestles and slab mortars dominate the food-processing complex, suggesting a shift of economic focus to the gathering and processing of acorns. New artifacts and types of grave goods suggest an intrusion of peoples from the central valley, and evidence of traumatic deaths may attest to a certain amount of friction accompanying this process. The Oroville phase (AD 1500–historic) represents the ethnographically known Maidu culture, with a well-developed acorn complex, diversified hunting, sedentary villages, and large ceremonial houses. One large archeological site of this period with apparent ceremonial structures seems to have served as a center for a number of nearby smaller villages.

In the southern Sierra foothills, Moratto (1972) has described an occupation beginning with the Chowchilla phase (300 BC–AD 300), during which large, heavy, stemmed and side-notched dart points, bone fish spears, slab metates, manos, cobble mortars, and cylindrical pestles were in use. An economy that emphasized hunting, fishing, and seed gathering, with acorn processing less important, is implied. Settlements were small and have been found only along major streams. During the Raymond phase (AD 300–1500), small corner- and side-notched arrowpoints and bedrock mortars appear, while slab metates and manos continue. A shift to an acorn-processing emphasis is implied, though hunting appears to have still been important. Settlements are more numerous and more diverse. A pattern of centrally based wandering, with seasonal transhumance into the higher Sierra, can be hypothesized. The Madera phase (AD 1500–historic) is marked by small side-notched and unnotched triangular arrowpoints and a proliferation of steatite cylinders, pipes, pendants, earplugs, and the like. The food-processing complex of the Raymond phase continues. An expansion of the local population is indicated by increased numbers of sites. Large settlements with "community houses" appear at key locations on the main streams, and smaller satellite villages or hamlets appear on lesser tributaries. The Madera phase culminates in the historic culture of the Southern Miwok.

Occupation of the high Sierra was apparently always seasonal, controlled by the severe winter cold and snow. There is, however, clear evidence of aboriginal travel into and across the area from a very early period. Obsidian from Sierran or trans-Sierran sources is found in central valley sites as early as 3000 to 2000 BC; Californian shell beads appear in the Great Basin Karlo and Lovelock Cave sites at the same time; and unmodified Pacific coast *Olivella* shells occur at Leonard Rockshelter near Lovelock, Nevada, in a stratum carbon-14 dated to between 6700 and 5100 BC. Evidence of *Olivella* shells at comparably early dates elsewhere in the Great Basin further supports the inference of trans-Sierran travel (Ragir, 1972).

Social Complexity

California's prehistory and ethnology are of great importance for the perspective they offer on the cultural development of hunting–gathering peoples in a rich environment. Whereas such societies are commonly considered to fall low on the scale of sociocultural complexity, the native Californians provide evidence of an impressively high level of cultural elaboration, involving dense population, sedentary village life, and political–economic arrangements of some scale and sophistication. This perspective is a relatively new one, however. Traditional ethnological treatises have pictured Californian society as simple and highly fragmented, divided into hundreds of small, autonomous polities with no significant supralocal political integration (Kroeber, 1962). But models arguing the existence of more complex sociopolitical structures are now being tested against ethnographic and archeological data, with intriguing results. Ceremonial observances, trade fairs, and confederations or alliances linking a number of local communities are known from ethnographic data, and their importance as aboriginal political and economic institutions is now being emphasized. The culling out and focusing of available ethnographic information on the political functions of high-status individuals have made it appear that California societies were regulated to a significant degree by elite persons whose influence was more than local and who regularly participated in affairs transcending the boundaries of local tribelets. And archeological studies of burial practices are giving evidence that elite groups or lineages may be an old phenomenon in California society, going back perhaps several thousand years in some localities. Widespread trade, especially in marine shells, has long been recognized archeologically, and attempts are being made to comprehend this trade within a model of intersocietal political–economic relationships (Bean and King, 1974; Bean and Blackburn, 1976).

Excavations at Tiburon Hills, on the northwestern edge of San Francisco Bay, revealed a cemetery carbon-14 dated at approximately the beginning of the Christian Era. The site, a small earth and shell midden, yielded 44 burials complete enough for detailed study. In the center of the burial cluster was a concentration of cremation and inhumation burials representing seven males, five females, and six children. These 18 individuals were accompanied by 62 percent of all the grave goods from the site. Partly encircling the central concentration was a series of male inhumations with no grave goods. Beyond were scattered males and females with few or no associations and two females and an infant with relatively abundant grave goods. Artifacts of symbolic or ornamental value were predominant, including *Olivella* shell beads, abalone and carved bone pendants, and whistles made of mammal and bird bones. On the basis of the observed patterns, a hierarchical social structure was postulated (T. King, 1974:38):

> The nature of the artifact assemblage, in which non-utilitarian, "sociotechnic-ideotechnic" artifacts predominate, and the distinctly non-random association of elements of this assemblage with the cremated and disarticulated remains of men, women, and children buried in the center of the cemetery, lead me to believe that this cemetery reflects in its structure a form of social organization characterized by ascribed ranking. In other words, I infer that the central cremation zone represents the interment of high-ranking individuals, while persons of lower rank are interred farther and farther from the center. The presence of children and infants in the central area, the slight evidence of sex-based role distinctions, the evidence of social distinctions cross-cutting age/sex divisions, and the "ideotechnic-sociotechnic" weighting of the artifact assemblage all suggest that rank in the society here represented was not achieved on the basis of personal attributes but ascribed on the basis of kin-group membership. Such rank ascription is typical of a "Rank" society in Morton Fried's (1967) terms, or a "Chiefdom" in the words of Elman Service (1962).

Other excavations in the San Francisco Bay region have not exhibited burial patterning of this sort, and King speculates that high-status lineages may have lived somewhat apart from lower-ranking families. A much larger midden about 200 meters from the Tiburon Hills site may have been a commoners' settlement, but it had been badly disturbed and was not examined adequately to provide a test of this hypothesis.

King attempts to explain the appearance of a nonegalitarian, ranked society in this area by a model of population growth and subsequent competition-cooperation. Associating population growth with sedentary residence, he proposes that hunter–gatherer populations would be able, even impelled, to achieve sedentariness where their immediate surroundings contain sufficient natural food resources within one or two hours of travel to see them through an annual round with few periods of food scarcity. Compilation of a map showing potential food resources available within the San Francisco Bay area allowed him to suggest that at localities such as Tiburon Hills sedentariness would be quite possible, while in other places it would be unlikely. As population expanded from more favorable into less favorable localities, competition for resources would grow, and would have to be resolved either through warfare or through cooperative sharing of resources through trade. Either form of interaction would be facilitated by formal organization of elite leadership cadres of the sort apparently represented at the Tiburon Hills cemetery.

From an analysis of burials at three central California sites near Walnut Creek, Fredrickson (1974b) infers a growth in societal complexity over time there, and other studies suggest comparable developments in southern California (Stickel, 1968; L. King, 1969; Decker, 1969). Additional evidence of growing social complexity might be seen in the increase throughout central and southern California over the past several thousand years of both violent deaths and trade goods. Both trends might be expected as part of the process postulated by King.

Blackburn (1974) has shown from ethnographic information that intervillage trade and political integration in native California were fostered by a system of fiestas and ceremonials that were convened frequently by local chiefs. A fiesta was the occasion for travel and exchange among large numbers of people, while the attendant ceremonies provided an affirmation of social solidarity. Such gatherings enhanced the prestige and wealth of the local leadership cadre; among the Chumash at least, guests were expected to make donations toward the fiesta, and the local chief would save some of the offerings for distribution among his own people in times of stress. Trade was thus fostered and regulated within a system that preserved and enhanced the political power of managerial elites. Moreover, ties between the local elites were evidently far-reaching. When a local chief declared a fiesta, attendance by other local chiefs was considered obligatory. The alliance networks thus maintained, functioning in both trade and conflict, seem to have existed all over California and, interestingly enough, were everywhere laid out in such a fashion that they linked together different environmental zones, making their economic logic perfectly clear (Bean, 1974).

Rigorous archeological tests of the proposition that such economic–political integration has great time depth in California have not yet been achieved. But evidence from burials and trade objects suggests its antiquity, and attempts are being made to formulate models in which the trade goods (especially shell beads) increasingly abundant in California sites after about 2000 BC may provide some of the needed tests (C. King, 1974). A well-argued ethnographic hypothesis relating food-resource management through controlled firing of the landscape to the rich and complex growth of Californian cultures upon a hunting–gathering subsistence base also has archeological implications now being explored (Lewis, 1973; Bean and Lawton, 1973). California archeology has entered an exciting period.

THE GREAT BASIN

The evidence currently available suggests that the Great Basin was first widely populated by people of the Clovis Fluted-point horizon between about 9500 and 9000 BC, although there are hints of slightly earlier occupation. Clovis points are found along the low shorelines of now-dry Pleistocene lakes, as are artifacts of San Dieguito-like complexes. The conspicuous lack of milling stones in these sites suggests that the earlier Paleo-Indian culture was less closely adapted to the harvesting of plant foods, especially wild seeds, than was the Desert culture of Archaic type that succeeded it by 7000 BC or so. Most of the earlier Archaic sites that have so far been explored in detail occur in caves along the ancient lakeshores. Their location, as well as their dry and well-preserved contents, indicate that exploitation of lacustrine plants and animals was a major economic emphasis. Lakeshore caves continued to be occupied throughout the prehistory of the Great Basin.

Increasing evidence of upland sites, however, indicates that the wide-ranging cyclical pattern of foraging characteristic of the historical inhabitants was fully established by 3500 BC at the latest. In some favored parts of the region, semisedentary village life was established; in other areas, where food resources were sparser and more scattered, a more mobile, broader-ranging nomadic pattern of existence was apparently maintained. Differences in artifact typology from north to south, and from east to west, indicate the existence of subregional traditions from about 7000 BC onward. For a time, between about AD 500 and 1400, horticultural villagers with affinities to the cultures of the Southwest were established in the eastern Great Basin, but these were replaced well before the beginning of the historical period by practitioners of the more ancient Archaic way of life.

The Great Basin was, in ethnographic times, a desert land sparsely populated by small, far-ranging groups of hunters and gatherers. Most of the historic peoples spoke closely related Numic languages belonging to the great Utaztekan phylum, but in east–central and southeastern California, tongues belonging to the Hokan phylum were spoken. The linguistic evidence suggests that several populations may have moved through the area over the long span of prehistoric time, the Numic speakers being the most recent occupants and the peripheral Hokan-speakers perhaps remnants of an earlier population. The principal importance of Great Basin archeology lies in the glimpses it affords of cultural adaptation to a demanding environment, surely one of the most rigorous in native North America. The adjustments made to nuances of environmental variation, both across space and down through time, have long been and continue to be a major focus of interest in Great Basin studies.

Early Peopling

In the Great Basin, as in California, great age has been claimed for a preprojectile-point or early lithic tradition considered ancestral to all later manifestations. Artifacts found on high strand lines of a now-dry pluvial lake near Fallon, Nevada, were attributed a Pleistocene age (Carter, 1958), and putatively culture-bearing deposits at Tule Springs, near modern Las Vegas, were carbon-14 dated at greater than 26,000 BC (Harrington and Simpson, 1961). Atlatl parts found with the bones and feces of now-extinct giant ground sloth in Gypsum Cave, Nevada, were once claimed as evidence of Pleistocene human occupation there (Harrington, 1933). But more recent work has placed the Fallon finds well within postglacial times (Tuohy, 1970) and has shown that the maximum demonstrable age for human activity at Tule Springs does not exceed 9000 to 8000 BC (Shutler et al., 1967). The atlatl parts from Gypsum Cave have been carbon-14 dated at 900 and 400 BC, removing them from consideration as evidence for early human occupation (Heizer and Berger, 1970). In short, no well-supported evidence of occupation earlier than terminal Pleistocene times has yet been established for the Great Basin.

The earliest carbon-14 date for a Paleo-Indian-period assemblage now known from the Great Basin comes from Fort Rock Cave in south–central Oregon, where a concentration of charcoal lying on Pleistocene lake gravels gave a date of 11,200 BC (Bedwell, 1973). Near the charcoal concentration, also resting on lake gravels, were found a milling stone and a mano fragment, two projectile points, several scrapers and gravers, and a handful of flakes. Lack of detailed documentation of the find-spot has prompted questions about the reported association of artifacts and the carbon-14 date (Haynes, 1969), but the excavator has stated clearly his belief in the association (Bedwell, 1970:53–58). Only additional finds of comparable age from other sites will effectively remove all reasonable doubt, though a considerable antiquity for the artifacts is guaranteed by a carbon-14 date of 8200 BC for an overlying level.

It long was thought that fluted projectile points of the Clovis type, common in the Southwest, Plains, and eastern woodlands, were not significantly represented in the West. But sufficient evidence has now accumulated to make it clear that Clovis folk were widespread in the Great Basin and throughout the West as a whole (Figure 5.2). As noted in the preceding discussion of California prehistory, the age of Clovis points in the West remains to be directly established, since all so far reported have been surface finds. Nevertheless, a date of between 9500 and 9000 BC seems likely.

From a time range subsequent to Clovis comes a series of intergrading complexes, also mostly surface finds, which contain large shouldered and stemmed lanceolate projectile points, along with large leaf-shaped knives or points, crescents, flake scrapers, and domed scraper–planes. In southern California and Nevada this horizon is represented by the San Dieguito complex, dated by carbon-14 determinations to 7000 and 6500 BC at the C. W. Harris site in San

Diego, and believed by Warren (1967) to date to 8000 BC. In the northern Great Basin comparable types occur in the Fort Rock Valley, carbon-14 dated to between 9000 and 6000 BC (Bedwell, 1973). In the eastern Great Basin the earliest level of Danger Cave dates around 9000 BC and contains a small and nondescript assemblage that might conceivably be attributable to the same complex (Jennings, 1957). The Sadmat complex of the Fallon area also exhibits San Dieguito-like artifacts, and presumably belongs to the same period.

Warren and Ranere (1968) point out that the Haskett locality in Idaho and the Olcott site in western Washington extend the web of similarity into the Columbia Plateau as well. Hester (1973:65–68) provides a detailed list of the many local complexes or sites representing this unity, which he terms the *Western Pluvial Lakes* tradition, following Bedwell (1973).

The artifacts of this tradition, like the Clovis Fluted points, occur commonly on the lower strand lines of pluvial lakes. This suggests that their makers were exploiting comparable environments and probably practicing similar lifeways, oriented toward the lakes and marshes common throughout the Great Basin in early postglacial times (Tuohy, 1968; Heizer and Baumhoff, 1970). It is likely indeed that the San Dieguito-like complexes are derived from Clovis antecedents and represent transitional cultures between the Paleo-Indian period and the early Archaic. This relationship is suggested by general similarities in size, form, and flaking technique shared among some of the western post-Clovis projectile points and such Great Plains types of comparable age as Alberta, Scottsbluff, Hell Gap, and Agate Basin. These latter types are recognized as derivatives of the fluted-point tradition on the Plains, and the western points that resemble them may be interpreted as derivatives of the fluted-point tradition in the West.

The Southern Deserts

In the southern California deserts and the southern Great Basin, the San Dieguito complex gave way to the Pinto Basin complex, characterized by stemmed, indented-base and leaf-shaped dart points, knives, drills, choppers, scrapers, scraper–planes, and the mano and metate (Wallace, 1962). Most Pinto Basin sites are known from surface observations and are undated, but at the stratified Rose Spring site near Inyo, California, carbon-14 dates of 1900, 1600, and 1500 BC from the bottom of the sequence may be applicable to the terminal Pinto phase (Hester, 1973:71). Estimates for the beginning of the period range between 5000 and 3000 BC, but these dates are not founded on carbon-14 evidence. The lifeway indicated by the artifact assemblage is that of roving hunters and gatherers. However, a series of postmolds, indicative of light pole-and-thatch houses, discovered near the marshy edge of Little Lake in the Owens Valley suggests a degree of sedentariness, or at least a centralized focus within the nomadic wandering pattern (Harrington, 1957). Two apparent "house rings," found with a Pinto assemblage at the Cocanour site on the south side of the Humboldt Sink near Fallon, reinforce the impression of a certain degree of sedentariness (Stanley et al., 1970).

The Pinto Basin complex is succeeded by the Amargosa complex in the Mohave Desert and by the Rose Spring phase in Owens Valley. Both basically represent a continuation of the older lifeway. The Amargosa complex is known from surface finds of triangular stemmed and notched dart points, drills, flake scrapers, manos, and metates. Small, triangular, stemmed and notched arrowpoints are attributed to the final phase of Amargosa, dated perhaps as late as AD 1000 by Anasazi Pueblo pottery found at the same sites. The Rose Spring phase, known from a stratified open site, contained a similar lithic assemblage, now dated with some carbon-14 support between 1500 BC and AD 500 (Hester, 1973:72).

The latest occupation in Owens, Panamint, and Death valleys is identified with the ethnographically known Paiute and related speakers of Numic languages, who are recognized archeologically by their heavy brownware pottery. The beginning date for these cultures is not firmly established, but the pottery is generally assumed to date to approximately AD 1000. Desert side-notched and small, triangular, side- and corner-notched arrowpoints, flake scrapers, manos, metates, mortars, and pestles are also characteristic of the assemblage. Sites are common on dunes, near streams and springs, and in rockshelters. An economy centered around plant-food collecting and the hunting of small game is indicated.

By AD 1000, Paiute brownware pottery appears in several southern Nevada Puebloan sites, and by approximately AD 1400, the bearers of related ceramics had apparently replaced sedentary farming peoples as far north as the Great Salt Lake region and had moved out onto the Snake River Plain beyond (Madsen, 1975). By historical times, the Numic speakers—Ute, southern Paiute, Shoshoni, Mono–Paviotso, Tubatalabal, and Luiseño—occupied most of the southern California deserts, the northern parts of the Southwest, all of the Great Basin, and much of the northwestern Plains. The remarkable expansiveness of the Numic peoples is one of the striking facts of Great Basin prehistory and has yet to be satisfactorily accounted for.

Along the lower Colorado River in historical times, Yuman-speaking peoples grew maize, beans, and squash on the seasonally inundated floodplains, manufactured a distinctive plainware pottery, and apparently served as a trade conduit between coastal California and the Pueblo Southwest. Their brownware pottery, of Southwestern derivation, is dated to approximately AD 900, and their use of agriculture possibly occurred as early. Although Wallace (1962) emphasizes the gathering aspect of their economy, Rogers (1945) believed that the Yuman-speaking peoples were agricultural, at least in part. Populations occupying the deserts back from the rivers were entirely dependent on hunting and gathering, and a flourishing lacustrine economy was established at Lake Cahuilla, in the Salton Basin (Wilke, 1978). Some historical descendants of this tradition were the Walapai, Yavapai, Yuma, Cahuilla, Mohave, and Maricopa.

Their ultimate prehistorical origins may plausibly be the older Amargosa complex of the region, though southwestern influences were obviously important in shaping the tradition.

The Eastern Great Basin

In the eastern Great Basin, a cluster of dry caves in the Great Salt Lake region contain remains spanning most of postglacial time. The earliest level at Danger Cave, carbon-14 dated to 9000 BC, gives only scant evidence of human presence, but after 7000 BC both Danger and Hogup caves offer rich records of human activity (Jennings, 1957; Aikens, 1970). The Deadman, Black Rock, and Promontory caves appear to have been comparably ancient and long occupied, and exhibit similar if not identical cultural remains (Steward, 1937; Smith, 1941).

Lanceolate and triangular stemmed and notched projectile points, milling stones, coiled and twined basketry, net fragments, bone awls, and the bones of small and large animals are common to all the Great Salt Lake caves (Figures 5.5, 5.6). At Hogup, detailed analysis of the biota brought into the cave by its human occupants between 6400 and 1200 BC showed that seeds of the pickleweed (*Allenrolfea occidentalis*) were apparently of major importance. Not only were the seeds common in human coprolites, but the early deposits were literally golden with the chaff threshed from them. Bison, antelope, sheep, and deer were well represented in the faunal assemblage, but rabbits, hares, and rodents were extremely abundant, indicating that catching and gathering small animals was an activity far more common than the bringing down of an occasional large ungulate. Waterfowl and shore birds dominated the avifauna during this period, implying that open water and marshland then covered the now-dry flats below the cave. The other sites of the region undoubtedly looked out on comparable scenes, and the same general pattern of hunting and gathering in a lakeshore environment was common to them all.

After 1200 BC, evidence of marshland exploitation vanishes at Hogup Cave, and lacustrine deposits in a sediment core from the flats below the site indicate that an abrupt rise in lake level completely drowned the marsh at that time (Mundorff, 1971). Waterfowl disappear from the later record, and occurrences of pickleweed and of the milling stones used to process it decline radically. Only the mammal-hunting system apparently held up, and it shows a shift to relatively greater emphasis on large animals. Intensity of occupation declined markedly, suggesting that the cave was visited primarily by hunting parties that came infrequently and did not remain long. It is not known whether a comparable episode is represented at the other Great Salt Lake caves, because they were not analyzed in a fashion that might reveal such a change.

It has been suggested (Madsen and Berry, 1975; Simms, 1977) that by about 3500 BC a new and significant upland occupation had been established in the northeastern Great Basin and that, by the time marshland plants and animals disappeared from the record at Hogup Cave, the shores of the Great Salt Lake

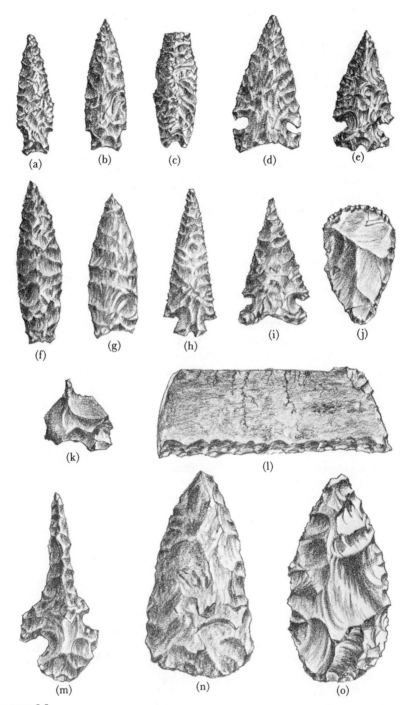

FIGURE 5.5
Lithic artifacts from Danger Cave: (a–i) projectile points; (j) scraper; (k) graver; (l) knife; (m) drill; (n) basalt knife; (o) obsidian knife.

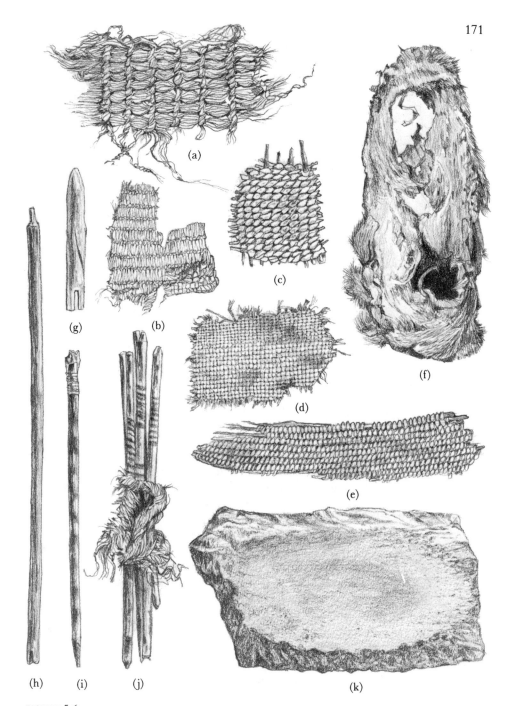

FIGURE 5.6
Artifacts from Danger Cave: (a, b) twined matting; (c) twined basketry; (d) coarse cloth;
(e) coiled basketry; (f) hide moccasin; (g) wooden knife handle; (h) dart shaft; (i) arrow shaft
with broken projectile point in place; (j) bundle of gaming sticks; (k) milling stone.

had been wholly abandoned in favor of the uplands. Proponents of this idea believe that a widespread drowning of lakeshore marshlands by a sudden rise in the level of the Great Salt Lake, as seen at Hogup Cave, lay behind this postulated population shift. It is probably not justified, however, to generalize the drowning of the marsh and subsequent reduction in the intensity of occupation at Hogup Cave to the whole of the northeastern Great Basin (Aikens, 1976). Although upland occupation about this time does seem to have intensified, it is unlikely that there was such massive destruction of marshland resources throughout the Great Salt Lake area as to cause a total human abandonment. Local variations in lake-basin microtopography and underlying geology, as well as stable conditions for the continued survival of marshland zones around major springs and along rivers (D. Weide, 1976), undoubtedly preserved such resources for exploitation at many lowland sites. Upland zones may have become more important in the subsistence cycle, fostering some shifts in the ranges traversed by individual bands of people. Undoubtedly, however, the same species and the same hunting and gathering techniques continued to be relied upon.

In eastern Utah and western Colorado, part of the Great Basin culture area during the Archaic period, sites such as Hells Midden, Deluge Shelter, Thorne Cave, Clydes Cavern, Sudden Shelter, and the Cowboy Caves give evidence of a long occupation by people with lithic traditions related to those of the Great Salt Lake region. Sudden Shelter (Jennings et al., 1980) provides an Archaic sequence carbon-14 dated to the period 5800–1300 BC. Within this sequence, change over time in projectile point styles is particularly crisp and well defined. The widespread Pinto Basin, Elko, Humboldt, and Gypsum Cave projectile-point types are under closer temporal control here than at any other site yet reported, which will make Sudden Shelter a valuable reference point for regional chronologies. The sequence is essentially duplicated at the Cowboy Caves (Jennings, 1980), and an occupation that overlaps it and extends somewhat later in time is present at Clydes Cavern (Winter and Wylie, 1974). The occupation of Thorne Cave is carbon-14 dated to 2200 BC (Day, 1964), and the Archaic levels of Deluge Shelter are dated between 1600 BC and AD 500 (Leach, 1967). Lister (1951) estimates the age of the earliest Hells Midden occupation at about 1500 BC. It is probably much older, however, since it contained some Pinto-like points, dated at Sudden Shelter from sometime before 5800 BC up to about 4400 BC. Hells Midden is one location where the Archaic gives way to the Fremont culture, next to be discussed.

Between AD 500 and 1400, a horticulturally based lifeway with Puebloan affinities occurred throughout the eastern Great Basin. This is the Fremont culture. Fremont ceramics and other artifacts appear during this time in most of the Archaic sites already mentioned, which continued to be used as hunting-gathering stations by Fremont people, but small horticultural settlements dominate the period. Fremont culture apparently developed out of related local Archaic traditions as they adopted new elements from different sources at different times (Aikens, 1972a). It has recently been suggested that a long period of nonoccupancy—at least 1000 and perhaps 2000 years—intervened between the Archaic and Fremont cultures, but this idea is not well supported and seems unlikely to gain acceptance (Madsen and Berry, 1975; Aikens, 1976). Corner-notched and side-notched projectile point styles and the distinctive Fremont one-rod-and-bundle coiled basketry type show clear continuity with the later Archaic of the Great Basin, suggesting a direct genetic connection. Maize appears in preceramic Archaic context on the southern fringe of the Fremont area at Cowboy Caves (Jennings, 1980). Farther north, at Clydes Cavern, maize occurs just below levels bearing Fremont ceramics. The corn is carbon-14 dated at approximately AD 400 (Winter and Wylie, 1974).

Five regional variants of the Fremont culture have been identified north of the Colorado River in Utah, western Colorado, and eastern Nevada (Figures 5.7, 5.8). All were horticulturally based, but the degree of dependence on farming appears to have varied from area to area, and hunting and gathering evidently remained important in all regions. The regional traditions share pithouse and above-ground masonry or adobe architecture, a grayware pottery complex, a distinctive variety of maize, a highly characteristic moccasin type, and the distinctive one-rod-and-bundle Fremont basketry type. An anthropomorphic figurine cult and broad-shouldered anthropomorphic pictographs are also widely shared, but there are distinctive regional differences in style and degree of elaboration of these elements. These shared features indicate a basic cultural unity; at the same time, other evidence shows that the regional traditions were affected by contacts with adjacent non-Fremont areas. The Parowan and San Rafael variants in the south and east, nearest the Anasazi Pueblo area, most closely resemble the Anasazi in painted pottery and architecture. The Sevier, Great Salt Lake, and Uinta Basin variants, farther to the north and west, are less Pueblo-like and more closely resemble the cultures of the western and northwestern Plains (Marwitt, 1970; Aikens, 1972a).

Between AD 1300 and 1400 the Fremont culture vanished. Decreased effective moisture in a broad region across New Mexico, Arizona, and Utah is indicated at this time by tree-ring evidence, pollen sequences, and other paleoclimatic indicators. Inadequate precipitation may have weakened the horticultural economy and, correlatively, the ability of the people to maintain sedentary villages. The culture that replaced Fremont has been identified with the ethnographic Shoshoni, Ute, and southern Paiute, all of whom were nomadic and nonhorticultural, possessed a pottery tradition clearly distinct from that of the Fremont, and spoke closely related Numic languages. In late prehistoric times, they apparently expanded their range from Death Valley, California, north and east to the High Plains east of the Rockies.

The fate of the Fremont people is uncertain. One idea is that they were ancestral Numic-speaking peoples who reverted to a hunting–gathering lifeway, lost their distinctive Fremont traits, and emerged into recent times as the ethnographic Shoshoni, Ute, and southern Paiute (Gunnerson, 1962). This idea is appealingly straightforward, but has been cogently challenged on the grounds

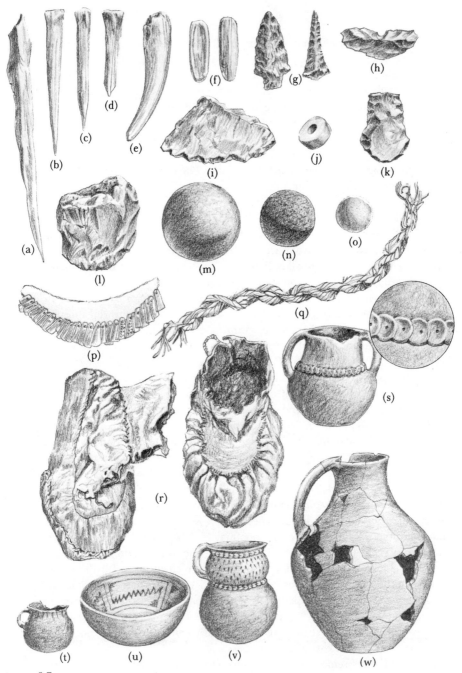

FIGURE 5.7
Fremont culture artifacts: (a) bone splinter awl; (b–d) bone awls; (e) antler flaking tool; (f) bone gaming pieces; (g) points; (h) shaft scraper; (i, k) scrapers; (j) perforated clay disk; (l) rough hammerstone; (m–o) stone balls—(n) is coated half with red ocher and half with black pigment; (p) bone necklace; (q) twisted bark rope; (r) leather moccasins; (s) pot and enlarged view of appliqué treatment; (t) small pot; (u) Ivie Creek black-on-white bowl; (v) pot with appliqué at rim and restricted waist; (w) pottery jar.

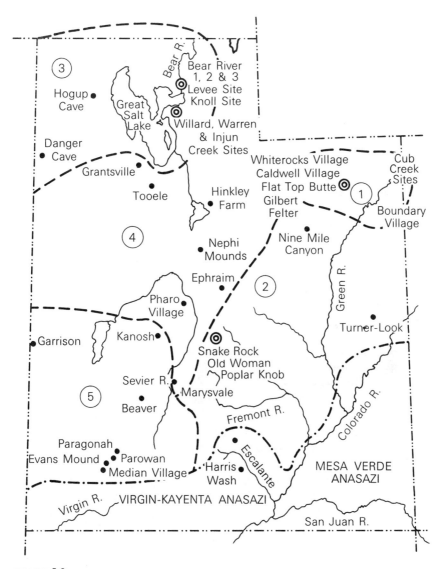

FIGURE 5.8
Fremont culture subareas: (1) Uinta; (2) San Rafael; (3) Great Salt Lake; (4) Sevier;
(5) Parowan.

that no specific continuities in material culture can be traced between the Fremont and the ethnographic groups (Schroeder, 1963; Euler, 1964). If ethnic continuity was maintained, it is argued, some recognizable cultural continuity ought to have been maintained as well, but there is no evidence of it. Alternatively it has been suggested that, weakened by the collapse of their horticultural economy and driven by Numic-speaking invaders, the Fremont folk straggled south into the Pueblo country or eastward onto the High Plains (Wormington, 1955; Aikens, 1967). Neither of these theories has gained general acceptance, because unequivocally Fremont artifacts have never been identified in significant numbers outside the original Fremont range of time and place. It is clear that Fremont cultural identity was completely lost; a generally acceptable explanation of what happened to the people themselves is yet to be developed.

The Central Great Basin

For the south–central part of the Great Basin, carbon-14-dated strata from O'Malley Shelter in southern Nevada suggest that Archaic occupation began there as early as 5000 BC. Occupation at the site was intermittent, with a long hiatus between 4500 and 2600 BC, followed by another occupation similar in character to the first that lasted until 1000 BC. Projectile points of the Elko, Pinto, and Gypsum series dominated these levels. Occupation resumed at about AD 1100, with projectile points of the Rose Spring, Cottonwood, Desert Side-notched, and Eastgate series, along with Fremont, Anasazi, and Shoshonean ceramics. The pottery types were intermingled, suggesting that the site lay in a boundary zone between three cultural areas and saw use by parties from all three. Conaway Shelter, in the same area, shows evidence of two brief occupations around the beginning of the Christian Era and AD 1000, which were similar to those certified for O'Malley Shelter at the same times. Use of these sites as temporary camps for seed collecting and the hunting of mule deer, bighorn sheep, jackrabbits, cottontails, and a variety of smaller mammals is indicated throughout the period of record (Fowler et al., 1973).

Several carbon-14 dates from Deer Creek Cave in northeastern Nevada indicate human occupation there between 8000 BC and AD 1300, but meaningful stratigraphy was lacking at the site, so little more than the fact of human presence is known (Shutler and Shutler, 1963). South Fork Shelter near Elko and two sites near Eastgate, in central Nevada, give good records of Archaic occupation after 2500 BC (Heizer and Baumhoff, 1961; Heizer et al., 1968). Newark Cave, in the Newark Valley, provides an assemblage for the period between 3000 BC and AD 1200 (Fowler, 1968). The lifeway indicated by all these sites is one of hunting–gathering nomadism, with reliance on small game and seed gathering and with the occasional taking of antelope, deer, and mountain sheep. Associated projectile points were predominantly of the Elko series, with small Rose Spring, Cottonwood, Eastgate, and Desert Side-notched arrowpoints representing the latest occupation.

In the Reese River valley, also in central Nevada, systematic archeological survey has disclosed a pattern of archeological site distribution interpreted as indicating seasonal transhumance between the streamside environments of the valley floor and the piñon groves on the mountain slopes. This distribution duplicates the historic Shoshoni pattern in the area and supports an extension of the historic occupation pattern at least as far back as 2500 BC (Thomas, 1973). Work in progress at the extremely deep Gatecliff Shelter not far away has reached a depth of over 7.5 meters, with cultural deposits carbon-14 dated at 6000 BC. Many discrete living floors are represented, and Gatecliff will unquestionably be of major importance to Great Basin prehistory when fully reported (Thomas, n.d.).

The Western Great Basin

In the western Great Basin, early Archaic sites are known from the vicinity of Lovelock, Nevada. Leonard Rockshelter, overlooking the vast Humboldt Sink, contains an early stratum of occupational debris carbon-14 dated at 5100 and 6700 BC. The scanty remains demonstrate the presence of the atlatl and dart, and *Olivella* shell beads give evidence of trans-Sierran contacts at an early date (Heizer, 1951). Hidden Cave, not far away, contains dart points and other artifacts in sediments that have been assigned an age of over 7000 years, based on geological correlations.

A long period for which no firm dates on cultural remains are available is followed by the Lovelock culture, dated between 2600 BC and AD 500 (Loud and Harrington, 1929; Heizer and Napton, 1970). This culture extends from the vicinity of Lovelock in west–central Nevada to the Honey Lake area of northeastern California. It was oriented toward life along the shores of lakes and marshes, as shown by very striking tule decoys covered by the feathered skins of real ducks, by the bones of fish, and by the seeds of marsh plants found in human feces at Lovelock Cave (Figure 5.9). A well-developed twined basketry complex and an abundance of milling stones attest to the importance of wild vegetal foods. Semisubterranean houses are said to be present at the Humboldt Lake bed site and are known from another site near the town of Lovelock, indicating a significant degree of occupational sedentariness, based on the rich waterside economy (Cowan and Clewlow, 1968). A number of carved effigies of fish, frogs, and monstrous zoomorphs have been found in the Lovelock culture area, and occasional burials containing such goods have been interpreted as the graves of shamans (Tuohy and Stein, 1969). Modified and unmodified *Olivella* marine shell beads in some Lovelock culture assemblages indicate trade contacts across the Sierra with California, which further suggests the relative richness of Lovelock culture.

Whether there is historical continuity between the Lovelock culture and the northern Paiute or Washo who occupied the same general area in historical times is disputed. Grosscup (1960) concluded that there was probably a histori-

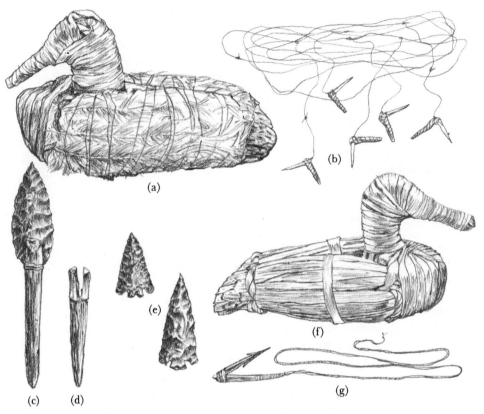

FIGURE 5.9
Lovelock culture artifacts: (a) duck decoy of tule and duck feathers; (b) fishhooks on setline; (c) hafted knife; (d) knife handle; (e) projectile points; (f) tule duck decoy; (g) bone fishhook with wooden shank and twined line.

cal discontinuity between the Lovelock and northern Paiute cultures. Heizer and Napton (1970), on the other hand, assert a clear continuity from Lovelock to historical cultures in the area, pointing out that projectile point and basketry types are similar enough to imply a direct historical connection.

Seasonal occupation of the eastern Sierra Nevada is well indicated by a series of lithic complexes found at the higher altitudes, where snow and cold would effectively prevent any year-round occupation. Best known is the Martis complex, with projectile points of distinctly Great Basin cast, which occurs in the Washo country. It is probably ancestral, through the later Kings Beach complex, to the ethnographic Washo (Elsasser, 1960). A series of complexes both north and south of the Martis area resemble it and Kings Beach and show widespread occupation throughout the Sierra at approximately the same time levels. A maximum age of 1000 BC has been estimated for the Martis complex

(Elston, 1971), but a carbon-14 date of 5100 BC from Spooner Lake in the Sierra suggests that it may be older, as does the similarity of some Martis projectile point types to Great Basin types significantly earlier than 1000 BC (Aikens, 1972b).

The Northern Great Basin

In Surprise Valley, northeastern California, a program of survey and excavation led by O'Connell (1975) discovered five phases of occupation spanning the last 6000 years. The Menlo phase, carbon-14 dated between 4000 and 3000 BC, gives evidence at two sites of substantial semisubterranean earthlodges (Figure 5.10) on the valley floor; it is believed that people ranged out from these to occupy the temporary camps found in several different microenvironmental zones from lakeshore to mountain slope. Many such small sites are located within several hours of foot travel from larger villages. Northern Side-notched and other projectile point types, lanceolate knives, T-shaped drills, tanged knives, and the mortar and pestle constitute the hunting and gathering tool complex. Bones of bison, deer, antelope, and mountain sheep are well represented, with jackrabbits, cottontails, and other small mammals being much less important. Waterfowl and such hibernating rodents as marmots and ground squirrels are conspicuously absent. It is believed likely that the pithouse villages were essentially sedentary settlements occupied the year round. The lack of hibernating animals in the food-bone debris of the house floors, which suggests that the houses were not occupied in the summer months, may reflect living habits like those of the historic Klamath. These people partially dismantled their earth lodges during the summer to dry them out, while living nearby in flimsy structures of brush.

The Bare Creek phase, dated from 2500 to 1000 BC, gives evidence of similar hunting–gathering practices, but the substantial earth lodges were apparently replaced by flimsy saucer-floored structures resembling the brush wickiups of the historic Paiutes of the region. Pinto-series dart points (locally called the *Bare Creek* series) are characteristic of the period, along with ovoid and triangular knives and drills with teardrop-shaped handles. The mortar and pestle persist, and the mano and metate are added to the food-processing inventory. Ungulate bones decline significantly, and jackrabbits, cottontails, marmots, ground squirrels, and waterfowl increase, suggesting a possible environmental change. Increasing aridity might have lessened the local concentration of large ungulates and other resources, and this in turn, it is suggested, could account for the shift to smaller, lighter, and apparently more temporary dwelling structures, reflecting a more extensive, less sedentary pattern of occupation.

The succeeding Emerson, Alkali, and Bidwell phases, which bring Surprise Valley occupation up to historical times, represent essentially a continuation of the Bare Creek pattern, with some stylistic changes in artifact types and the ap-

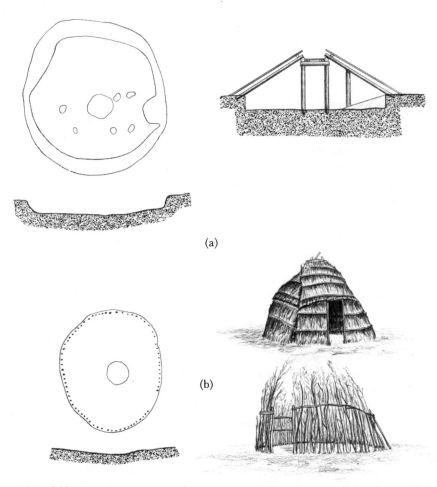

FIGURE 5.10
Surprise Valley dwellings: (a) Menlo phase earth lodge plan and reconstruction; (b) Bare Creek phase wickiup plan and possible ethnographic analogs. (After O'Connell, 1975).

pearance of the bow and arrow during the Alkali phase, dated between AD 500 and 1400.

The change in house and artifact types that took place between the Menlo and Bare Creek phases raises the possibility of a population replacement at this juncture. Sedentary villages with earth lodges are old in the Klamath–Modoc area northwest of Surprise Valley, while brush wickiups and less sedentary habitation patterns are characteristic of Great Basin Numic-speaking peoples as a whole. It may be that the cultural change noted around 2500 BC in Surprise Valley reflects a shift in the ranges of ancestral Klamath–Modoc and Surprise Valley Paiute, as the local environment changed from conditions suitable for the Klamath culture to more arid conditions to which Great Basin Numic culture was better adapted. Such a perspective would see the cultural change as a response to environmental change, a response in which migration rather than local readaptation was the solution. Whatever the conclusion to be drawn about this, the Surprise Valley sequence gives the impression of societies a good deal more localized and sedentary than is commonly envisioned for the Great Basin. Recent discoveries of sedentary occupations to the south of Surprise Valley, near Hallelujah Junction, California, and to the north, at Lake Abert, Oregon, suggest that such sedentariness may have been relatively common at certain periods in favored locations (Elston, 1979; Pettigrew, 1980).

In the Klamath Basin, the historic people occupied villages of large semisubterranean earth lodges not unlike those of the Menlo phase. A carbon-14 date from a pithouse at Nightfire Island on Lower Klamath Lake shows that such structures were in use about 2100 BC. The bottom of the Nightfire Island midden is carbon-14 dated to 4100 BC, and the site was apparently occupied almost to historic times. Projectile point types changed from leaf-shaped and large sidenotched dart points in earlier times to small, stemmed, notched, and barbed arrowpoints in later times, but in other respects the contents of the site showed remarkable continuity from the earliest through the latest occupation. Throughout time, the Nightfire Islanders emphasized fowling, fishing, and the gathering of plant foods to be ground with the mortar and pestle (Grayson, 1973). Nightfire Island thus supports the concept of Klamath culture as old and stable, with the essentially ethnographic way of life extending deep into the past, as argued by Cressman (1956) on the basis of his excavations at Kawumkan Springs Midden on the Sprague River. Obsidian hydration dates recently determined on projectile points from Kawumkan Springs suggest a date of at least 3000 BC for the earliest level of occupation there (Aikens and Minor, 1978).

Caves of the Fort Rock Valley of south–central Oregon revealed a complex having leaf-shaped and stemmed projectile points, crescents, scrapers, scraperplanes, manos and metates, and sandals made of sagebrush bark. Dated between 9000 and 6000 BC, this complex represents the San Dieguito-like Western Pluvial Lakes tradition discussed earlier. Thereafter, occupational intensity begins to decline. The period from 6000 to 5000 BC is characterized by leaf-shaped, corner-notched, and side-notched projectile points, knives, scrapers, manos, and twined basketry. Evidence of occupation all but disappears after the eruption of Mount Mazama around 5000 BC blanketed the landscape with a layer of volcanic ash; not until about 3000 BC was there significant reoccupation. The complex that then appears is dominated by small, slender, corner-notched points, knives, and scrapers. Manos and metates, mortars and pestles, and twined basketry increase markedly in frequency, suggesting intensified concentration on plant food resources. The available archeological record terminates at approximately 1000 BC. Occupation of the region surely continued to historic times, as suggested by numerous surface finds of late projectile point types, but digging by relic collectors destroyed the upper cave layers that might have spanned this period, before they could be studied archeologically (Bedwell, 1973).

Dirty Shame Rockshelter, on a small creek in the rolling Owyhee Plateau region of extreme southeastern Oregon, has given evidence of occupation as early as 7500 BC. Projectile points include rare Windust and Lake Mohave forms and more abundant Northern Side-notched, Humboldt Basal-notched, and Pinto series types. These, along with milling stones, twined basketry, and sandals very similar to those known for the Fort Rock Valley, come from three sequent cultural zones carbon-14 dated between 7500 and 3900 BC. After a 3200-year period for which there is no record of human presence, occupation resumed about 700 BC and continued until AD 1600 or later. Characteristic projectile points of the later period include types of the Pinto, Elko, and Rose Spring series. Of considerable interest are the remains of five or six circular pole-and-thatch houses or windbreaks built under the rockshelter between 700 BC and AD 900, which show close resemblance to ethnographic northern Paiute houses in technique of construction (Wheat, 1967). Coiled basketry and Desert Side-notched arrowpoints appear only in the uppermost levels of the site, postdating AD 900.

In most functionally defined artifact classes, and in biota recovered from the deposits, the later occupation closely resembles the preabandonment occupation. An increase in variety within the functional classes, however, suggests a broader range of domestic activities at the shelter, perhaps signifying longer seasonal residence there, lasting into or through the winter. For both early and late periods, the vertebrate, invertebrate, and plant remains demonstrate extensive exploitation of the moist canyon-bottom environment and little reliance on the resources of the sagebrush grassland of the plateau top. Stone alignments elsewhere on the plateau suggest that drive hunting may have been practiced in the uplands, but these sites remain to be investigated (Aikens et al., 1977).

Hundreds of unexcavated surface sites from the Catlow Valley, Warner Valley, Malheur Lake, Glass Buttes, and Alvord Lake areas have yielded artifacts of all periods from 9000 BC to historical times and give promise of much yet to be learned from them about the prehistory of the northern Great Basin (Cressman et al., 1940; Cressman, 1942; Weide, 1968; Fagan, 1974; Mack, 1975; Pettigrew, 1975).

Continuity and Change

The series of postglacial fluctuations in temperature and moisture that Antevs (1948) termed the *Anathermal* (cool, moist conditions: 7000–5000 BC), *Altithermal* (warm, dry conditions: 5000–2500 BC), and *Medithermal* (modern conditions: after 2500 BC) have been a major focus of interest among Great Basin prehistorians. Their conviction is that, in a desert land of sparse food resources, changes in the environment might require significant changes in the culturally conditioned behavior of the human occupants. Extreme earlier views that a hot, dry Altithermal period rendered the Great Basin largely unfit for human occupation have been tempered by increased knowledge of the archeological and paleoclimatic records. It is now clear that the Ana-Alti-Medi-thermal sequence describes only the broadest outlines of paleoclimatic change in the West. Prehistorians have to reckon with more complex and local paleoclimatic sequences if they are to meaningfully relate changes in environment to changes in cultural–ecological systems.

The issue now being addressed is not whether there was in fact a period of environmental stress severe enough to drive humanity from the Great Basin (it is clear that there was not) but, rather, how demonstrable changes in local environments might have affected the structured system of interrelated economic activities by which a group maintained itself within a region. O'Connell's (1975) discussion of the possible relationship between climatic and cultural change in Surprise Valley and my summary (Aikens, 1970) of the effect that change in the local environment of Hogup Cave had on human use of that site are examples of the current orientation. Work elsewhere by others and work now in progress could extend the list of examples.

Great Basin peoples have long been thought of as extremely mobile, with no fixed residences but only a series of temporary stopping places in an annual round of marches between the sparse and scattered food sources of their country. Archeological evidence of fairly substantial house structures at different periods in Surprise Valley, the Humboldt–Carson Sink area, Little Lake, and other places in the Great Basin is beginning to suggest that there were times in the past when occupation in some locales was quite sedentary, especially around the shores of some of the remnant Pleistocene lakes. (The Fremont culture phenomenon is of course in a different class altogether, since it was founded on agriculture.) Great Basin archeology has long focused on the excavation of caves and rockshelters, but the emphasis is now changing. As it continues to shift toward the study of open sites, other such discoveries are probably to be expected.

The Numic-speaking peoples who occupied the Basin in historic times are believed, on both linguistic and archeological grounds, to have spread over the area only recently, perhaps within the last 1000 years, from a homeland in the southern Great Basin and southern California deserts. The impetus behind this spread has never been satisfactorily accounted for, and the Numic expansion remains one of the intriguing problems of Great Basin archeology. It may be that as we learn more about the waxing and waning of local and regional economic systems over time—perhaps with relative sedentariness possible at some times and more atomistic patterns necessary at others—we can offer an explanation for the Numic expansion in terms of cultural ecology. As O'Connell's Surprise Valley example shows, cultural adaptation to environmental change in a region can be accounted for by the notion of the in-migration of a people already adapted to similar environmental conditions elsewhere, as well as by the assumption of local *in situ* readaptation by the people living there prior to the environmental change. The Numic people, coming from an arid southern homeland, may have been in a sense preadapted to occupy a country on which the earlier inhabitants' hold had been weakened by unaccustomed economic stress in a deteriorating environment. Such an explanation for the Numic expansion is purely conjectural at present, and surely too simple as stated here, but given the current trend of Great Basin studies, it seems a likely direction for further attempts at explaining this phenomenon.

THE PLATEAU

As elsewhere in the Far West, the earliest occupants of the Plateau were probably Paleo-Indians of the Clovis tradition. By 8500 BC, stone-tool industries resembling those of the San Dieguito complex farther south are known in the Plateau, and an Archaic way of life based on broad-spectrum hunting and gathering had been established. Riverside villages of large, substantial semisubterranean earth lodges were well established by at least 500 BC. The classical Plateau way of life, based primarily on salmon fishing and root gathering, was evidently fully established by this time. One of the major questions of Plateau prehistory is just how far back in time one may trace the emergence of the fully mature Plateau culture pattern. Thousands of salmon bones came from an archeological site at The Dalles of the Columbia River, where they were dated between about 7800 and 5800 BC. The earliest earth lodge so far from the site of Alpowa on the Lower Snake River dates to 3000 BC or slightly before. In general, it is not yet clear whether the scantiness of the evidence of riverside occupation before about 500 BC actually reflects a scanty human occupation along the rivers during that time or is merely due to erosion or to deep burial of the archeological deposits of that age by a cycle of heavy flooding in the Columbia River drainage. The several local sequences so far developed for the Plateau show a broadly parallel cultural development across the region. Within this broader picture, some degree of local differentiation is also evident between the northern Plateau, the southern Plateau, and the Snake River Plain to the east.

Ethnographic Plateau culture was dominated by an orientation to salmon fishing, which concentrated populations along the Columbia River and its tributaries in the south and along the Fraser River and its tributaries in the north. Villages of five to ten earth lodges were situated on the floodplains of major streams, where salmon could be taken during the summer spawning runs and stored for winter consumption. During spring and fall, the villages were largely depopulated as people ranged across the uplands back from the rivers, gathering camas lily and kous roots and hunting.

Salish-speaking people occupied the northern Plateau, reaching as far south as the Columbia at one point, and Penutian speakers were concentrated along the middle and upper Columbia. The concentration of Penutian languages along the Columbia and on the western coast of North America south of the river suggests that Penutian speakers have dominated the southern Plateau for a very long time, while linguistic and archeological evidence suggests that the Salishan peoples spread down from the northern Plateau much later (see Chapter Three).

Early Peopling

What is probably the earliest current evidence of human occupation in the Northwest is represented by a few scattered Clovis Fluted points found at The Dalles, at several places in the Puget–Willamette lowland, and on the Snake River plain (Figure 5.2). None of these artifacts has been found in datable context. If, however, they are assigned an age of 9500 to 9000 BC, based on their dating on the Plains and in the Southwest, they immediately precede the earliest carbon-14-dated occupations at The Dalles and Wildcat Canyon on the middle Columbia; at Marmes Rockshelter and the Windust Caves on the lower Snake; at Lind Coulee in east-central Washington; and at the Milliken site on the lower Fraser River of British Columbia. These related assemblages may be grouped with the loosely defined San Dieguito horizon already referred to for California and the Great Basin. Like the complexes known futher south, they are characterized by large leaf-shaped and stemmed lanceolate projectile points, lanceolate and ovate knives, large scrapers, scraping planes and choppers, and a near if not complete absence of milling stones.

The Lower Snake–Upper Columbia Region

The lower Snake River furnishes the most nearly continuous and best-described cultural sequence currently available for the Plateau (Leonhardy and Rice, 1970). It begins with the Windust phase, assigned by ten carbon-14 determinations from Marmes Rockshelter to the period from 8500 to 5500 BC (Figure 5.11). Diagnostic artifacts are of the types just mentioned. Other items found include large prismatic blades struck from polyhedral cores, single- and multiple-faceted burins, and bone awls, needles, and atlatl spurs. Split and broken food-bone refuse represents deer, elk, pronghorn antelope, jackrabbit, cottontail rabbit, and beaver. Shell of the river mussel also occurs. A cremation pit and charred human bones are evidence of burial practices, and *Olivella* shell beads indicate contact with the Pacific coast.

The Cascade phase follows, dated to approximately 5500–3000 BC, although these dates are subject to possible revision. Diagnostic artifacts are medium-sized, finely flaked leaf-shaped Cascade points and edge-ground cobbles. Large side-notched points appear as part of the assemblage after about 5000 BC, but no other changes are noted at that time. Other items are large lanceolate and triangular knives, prismatic blades, tabular and keeled end scrapers, large flake scrapers, polished stone atlatl weights, and bone awls, needles, and atlatl spurs. Manos and small grinding stones of questionable identification also occur. Food remains include the bones of deer, elk, pronghorn antelope, salmon, and steelhead trout. Shell of river mussel also identifies that species as a food source. Burials were both flexed and extended, and in one case capped by a cairn of stones. *Olivella* shell beads were present as burial goods. Recently published

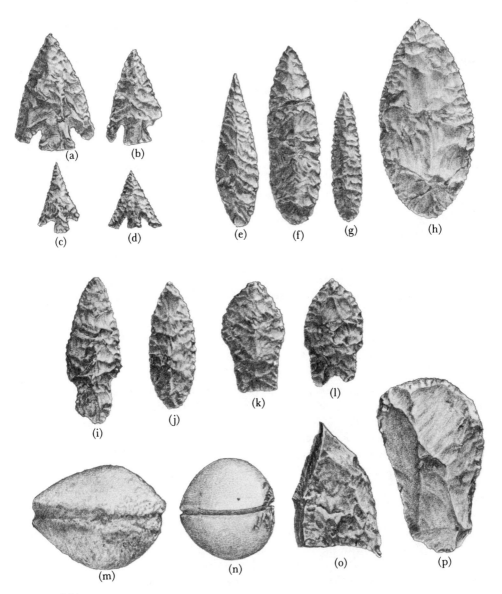

FIGURE 5.11
Diagnostic artifacts of the lower Snake River sequence: (a–d) Harder phase; (e–h) Cascade phase; (i–p) Windust phase.

evidence shows that semisubterranean pithouses were also a characteristic of the phase (Brauner, 1976).

There is clear historical continuity between the Windust and Cascade phases, as shown by their sharing of many artifact types. Significant new elements also appear in the Cascade phase, however. Manos and grinding stones, providing for the first time substantial evidence of vegetal food processing, and the appearance of pithouse architecture and salmon bones indicate that the subsistence-settlement pattern that dominated ethnographic Plateau culture had its beginnings at least as far back as the Cascade phase.

The following Tucannon phase is dated between 3000 and 500 BC. Triangular contracting-stemmed and corner-notched points, small side and end scrapers, sinker stones, hopper mortar bases, and pestles are characteristic items. Bone and antler awls and wedges and a bone net shuttle have also been found, along with the bones of deer, elk, pronghorn antelope, mountain sheep, small mammals, and a relative abundance of salmonid fishes and river mussels. *Olivella* shell beads occurred with a flexed burial of this phase at Marmes Rockshelter.

A break in cultural continuity between the Tucannon phase and the preceding Cascade phase has been hypothesized, but recent work has identified a possible transitional complex characterized by stemmed, indented-base points (Leonhardy, 1975). At Alpowai, a winter village on the lower Snake River that was occupied throughout the past 6000 years, a substantial Tucannon phase component with pithouses and an artifact assemblage linking it to both preceding and succeeding phases evokes a further dimension of cultural continuity (Brauner, 1976).

The beginning date for the Harder phase is fixed by several carbon-14 determinations at about 500 BC, and the terminal date is estimated at approximately AD 1300. During this period, villages of substantial semisubterranean earth lodges are common, notably at the Harder site (Figure 5.12). Diagnostic artifacts include both large basal- and corner-notched projectile points and smaller, more finely made points of similar form, indicating that both the atlatl and dart and the bow and arrow were in use. Small end scrapers, lanceolate and pentagonal knives, pestles, hopper mortar bases, sinkers, and bone awls, needles, beads, and gaming pieces are also common. Faunal remains are as in the preceding phase, with continuing importance of salmonids and the first evidence of the domestic dog.

The Piqunin and Numipu phases together span the final 700 years to historic times. Small, finely made corner-notched and stemmed arrowpoints, matting needles, and composite harpoons are added to an inventory that otherwise is essentially identical to that of the Harder phase. The sites of the earth-lodge villages Wexpusnime and Alpowai give evidence of cultural continuity between the Harder phase and the historic Nez Perce peoples of the area. The Numipu phase is named to account for the historic end of the cultural continuum. There is abundant evidence of contact with whites, the adoption of the horse, and cultural influence from the Great Plains (Leonhardy and Rice, 1970; Rice, 1972).

The Middle Columbia

The Dalles of the Columbia River, a long narrows filled with rapids, was in ethnographic times the most productive salmon fishery on the Plateau and is the locus of a number of archeological sites. The two Five-Mile Rapids sites (Roadcut site, WS-4, and Big Eddy, WS-1) on the Oregon side of the river

FIGURE 5.12
Artist's reconstruction of a Harder phase pithouse from the lower Snake River region.

contain a sequence representing most of the past since 8000 BC (Cressman, 1960). The Initial Early period at the Roadcut site, dated by a carbon-14 determination to 7800 BC, contained a few large prismatic blades, scrapers, and bone artifacts. The Full Early, dated before about 5800 BC, yielded large leaf-shaped and shouldered and stemmed projectile points, ovate blades, and heavy flake choppers comparable to those of the Windust phase on the lower Snake. Also found were burins, bolas or sinker stones, a rich bone and antler industry, an enormous number of salmon vertebrae (125,000 were counted, representing about half the amount observed), and the bones of raptorial birds, badger, marmot, fox, rabbit, beaver, otter, muskrat, and small rodents. In the Final Early levels, bone refuse and bone and antler artifacts are no longer found. The Transitional period is represented at the Roadcut site by a hardpan layer from which only a few artifacts—mostly choppers, scrapers, and peripherally flaked cobbles—were recovered.

The Late period, known from deposits in and overlying a level carbon-14 dated at 4100 BC, extends to historical times. Projectile points assigned to this period belong to a wide range of types, including leaf-shaped points like those of the Cascade phase on the lower Snake, triangular basal-notched forms like those of the Harder phase, and small, delicately made basal-notched and barbed points like those of the Piqunin phase. Edge-ground cobbles, milling stones, choppers, scrapers, and pestles are also characteristic of the Late period. The

Full Historic period shows white trade goods in addition to aboriginal artifacts.

From sites on the Washington side of the Columbia, Butler (1959) has related the Congdon, Indian Well, Big Leap, Maybe, and Wakemap Mound sites to infer a continuum of occupation comparable to that known from the Five-Mile Rapids sites. The Wildcat Canyon site, a few miles upriver from The Dalles on the Oregon side, has an important lower component with carbon-14 dates of 7900, 6100, and 5400 BC that contains projectile point forms like those from the Full Early period at Five-Mile Rapids and the Windust phase on the lower Snake. Pithouse villages are known at Wildcat Canyon, Mack Canyon, and other locations near the mouth of the John Day River, with carbon-14 dates spanning the last 3000 years (Cole, 1967, 1968a, b).

Cultural developments on the upper Columbia closely parallel those noted for the lower Snake region, except that a microblade complex that appears during the Indian Dan phase (4000–1500 BC) is apparently not represented farther south.

The Fraser River

The most northerly Plateau archeological sequence to be mentioned here comes from the Lochnore-Nesikep locality on the Fraser River in British Columbia (Sanger, 1967). The Early period there is dated between 5500 and 3000 BC by two carbon-14 determinations. Leaf-shaped and large side-notched points are earliest, with triangular corner- and base-notched points appearing by 4000 BC. Microblades are present though not abundant; antler wedges and rodent incisor chisels also occur. At the nearby Drynoch Slide site, salmon bones dated to 5100 BC give the earliest evidence of fishing, which continues to be important throughout the rest of the Lochnore–Nesikep sequence. The Middle period, 3000 BC to the beginning of the Christian Era, exhibits stemmed, indented-base as well as side-notched and basal-notched points. Antler wedges, rodent incisor chisels, ground stone celts, and ground stone mauls indicate a well-developed woodworking complex. Deep semisubterranean houses first appear shortly after 1500 BC at the Lochnore Creek site, and pithouses may be two centuries older at the Pine Mountain site. Microblades and tongue-shaped microcores were of great importance during the Middle period, being perhaps the dominant artifact class at that time. The Late period, from the beginning of the Christian Era to historical times, contains corner- and basal-notched points, with small side-notched arrowheads making their appearance about AD 1000. Other artifacts continue from the Middle period, with housepits becoming shallower and microblades being gradually phased out.

Farther down the Fraser and not in the Plateau proper, but occupying a site at a juncture between coast and interior analogous to that occupied by The Dalles of the Columbia River, is the Milliken site (Borden, 1960). The lowest levels there have been assigned to the Milliken phase, which is carbon-14 dated between approximately 7500 and 6000 BC. Large leaf-shaped points, ovate knives, pebble choppers and scrapers, flake scrapers, and burins constitute an assemblage quite similar to the early ones from The Dalles and the lower Snake River. The Milliken site, like those at The Dalles, overlooks a long rapids that was in historic times one of the best salmon fisheries on the Fraser River and a focal point of aboriginal activity. No faunal materials survive in the site deposits, but the location suggests that the site must have been occupied primarily as a fishing station. Subsequent phases continue the local tradition, with evidence of significant influence and elaboration stemming from cultural developments on the Pacific coast appearing after about 1000 BC.

The Snake River Plain

The Snake River plain and the northern Rocky Mountains of Idaho belong to the Columbia–Snake drainage system. Both regions provided the salmon and root crops that were the basis of ethnographic Plateau subsistence. Evidence from the Weis Rockshelter and other nearby sites suggests a cultural continuum in the mountains of northern Idaho running from approximately 5500 BC to the historic Nez Perce culture (Butler, 1962, 1978). The Craig Mountain phase (5500–1500 BC) is a local equivalent of the Cascade phase on the lower Snake but is believed to have persisted significantly later in the mountains. The Grave Creek phase (1500–100 BC) continues the sequence, with only minor and gradual change. The Rocky Canyon phase (100 BC–AD 1700) is characterized by pithouse villages, hunting of deer, elk, and mountain sheep, and collecting of vegetal foods for processing with edge-ground cobble crushers and with manos and metates. The Camas Prairie phase is represented by Double House Village, a late prehistoric site with evidence of a circular mat lodge and a parallel-sided community structure like those of the historic Nez Perce.

The cultural sequence for southern Idaho begins with a handful of artifacts carbon-14 dated to approximately 12,500 BC from the bottom levels of Wilson Butte Cave on the Snake River plain (Gruhn, 1961, 1965). These early dates are controversial (Haynes, 1971), and the assemblage is too small to allow meaningful assessment of its relationship to other early manifestations. This site may, however, figure importantly in the regional prehistory when other finds of this period are made. Elsewhere on the Snake River plain, surface finds of both Clovis and Folsom Fluted points suggest a Paleo-Indian occupation in the 9000 BC time range, and a sequence developed by Swanson (1972) at Birch Creek, near the northeastern extremity of the plain, carries the evidence of human occupation up to historic times.

The Birch Creek phase, dated between 7000 and 5000 BC, is characterized chiefly by large lanceolate points and otherwise is little known. Large shouldered and stemmed lanceolate points found elsewhere in Idaho (Butler, 1967) are apparently of comparable age and are probably associated with the Birch

Creek phase. These points, termed the Haskett type, are similar to those found in the San Dieguito-like complexes of the Great Basin and Columbia Plateau and suggest that the Birch Creek phase may have been affiliated with this early western cultural horizon. The Bitterroot phase, spanning the period from 5000 to 1000 BC, is dominated by large side-notched and unnotched points, end scrapers, and coarsely flaked fleshers. During the Beaverhead phase, dated from 1000 BC to AD 400, large side-notched, corner-notched, and stemmed, indented-base points all occur, along with end scrapers and coarse fleshers, as in the preceding phase. The Blue Dome phase, AD 500 to 1200, continues the tradition, with corner-notched points becoming numerically dominant but little other change indicated. The Lemhi phase, dated between AD 1200 and historic times, is characterized by small side-notched and corner-notched arrowpoints. These artifacts are identified with the Lemhi Shoshoni, ethnographic inhabitants of the area. According to Swanson (1972), this archeological continuum carries ancestral Northern Shoshoni culture back over 9000 years, showing these people to have been collectors of plant foods and hunters of mountain sheep, deer, bison, and smaller game. Their way of life was essentially identical to that of historic times throughout this whole period.

The Emergence of Plateau Culture

As a conclusion to this discussion of Plateau prehistory, several areas of uncertainty may be mentioned. Many believe that the early occupants of the Columbia drainage were broad-spectrum hunters and gatherers who made little use of riverine resources, especially the salmon, until 1000 BC or even into the Christian Era. Semisedentary villages of substantial earth lodges dated to this period and later are abundantly attested to in the archeological record. This has led to the inference that the pattern of ethnographically known Plateau culture—involving the catching, drying, and storing of salmon as a food reserve to make possible stable wintertime settlement—first emerged at about this time. It has been suggested that this characteristic Plateau pattern is earliest in the north, in the Fraser drainage, and that it expanded southward in relatively recent times, perhaps as a function of the southward spread of Salish-speaking peoples. However, despite the undeniable evidence of cultural influence from the north provided by the appearance of microblades on the Columbia, it has not been established that salmon fishing and pithouse architecture spread southward at the same time, or indeed that they had earlier origins along the Fraser than on the Columbia.

On the contrary, current evidence shows that salmon fishing flourished at The Dalles well before 6000 BC and was present on the middle Columbia and lower Snake by the Cascade phase, only slightly later. At the Drynoch Slide site on the Fraser, salmon bones have been dated to 5100 BC. It has also been cogently argued that the Milliken site, lower down the Fraser, was occupied as early as 7000 BC for the express purpose of salmon fishing. In short, the evidence suggests that salmon fishing is as ancient as the first well-established human occupation of the region, which is, after all, what might be expected. It is hardly to be imagined that the most abundant, obvious, and easily taken food resource of an entire geographical province would be neglected by its human inhabitants for some 7000 years before they began to develop a pattern of subsistence and settlement geared to exploiting it.

Surely the ethnographic pattern—of summertime fishing along the major streams, spring and fall hunting and gathering in the tributary canyons and uplands, and winter settlement in the sheltered major canyons—is older than the Christian Era or even 1000 BC. It is true that pithouse villages do not characterize our current archeological record of early times, but this is hardly surprising, considering that the Columbia and Fraser are subject to truly awesome floods. Hammatt (1976) has summarized geological evidence indicating active alluvial cutting and deposition on the Columbia–Snake system between 3000 and 500 BC. The stratigraphic record at the Sunset Creek site also shows that culture-bearing deposits preceding the late pithouse village there were disturbed by fluvial erosion. There were no early pithouses found at Sunset Creek; there is, however, evidence of occupation, consisting of scattered artifacts eroded from their original context and redeposited in sand and gravel lenses, as early as the Vantage phase (Nelson, 1969). And evidence that pithouses were in use by this time has recently been demonstrated by findings at Alpowai, Hatwai, and Givens Hot Springs in the region of the Columbia–Snake River confluence (Brauner, 1976; Ames and Marshall, 1981; Ames, Green, and Pfoertner, 1981; Green, 1982). These sites establish the presence of substantial earthlodge villages on the Plateau from 3000 BC onward; future archeological work will undoubtedly establish a much greater age for the basic ethnographically known Plateau pattern of subsistence and settlement than is currently accepted, though Ames and colleagues caution against interpreting the appearance of earthlodges alone as proving the existence of a fully constituted Plateau cultural pattern at an early date.

Almost all discussions of Plateau prehistory comment on the cultural influences received from the Great Basin between approximately 5000 and 3000 BC. Triangular side-notched, corner-notched, and stemmed, indented-base projectile points, along with manos and metates, are believed to reflect Great Basin influence. Some have suggested that these traits represent a northward displacement of population from an increasingly arid Basin into the more favorable Plateau, but in fact no convincing evidence has been marshalled that these point types are earlier in the Great Basin than in the Plateau. This evidence is necessary if a direction of movement is to be spoken of. In fact, these general types are known from a vast area, including the Columbia drainage, the northern Great Basin, the Snake River plain, the northern Rocky Mountains, and the northern High Plains. Their appearance in the Plateau area, then, is less likely to be a sign of migrations from the Great Basin than an indication of far-flung contacts, geographical awareness, and sharing of ideas among aboriginal peoples throughout the West as a whole.

Southern Idaho, in certain aspects of both environment and culture an exception to much that might be said of the Plateau, is an exception to the preceding pronouncement about Basin–Plateau relationships as well. Linguistic and other traits of the ethnographic Shoshoni there unequivocally show a close relationship to Great Basin cultures. Swanson (1972), emphasizing ecological similarities between southern Idaho and the Great Basin, saw the region as basically akin to the Basin from very early times. In his perspective, southern Idaho was always a subarea of the Great Basin rather than of the Plateau. Salmon runs far upstream on the Snake were comparatively meager; without a major abundant resource to depend upon, people were obliged to use sparser resources, as was characteristic of the Great Basin way of life. The historical occupation by clearly Great Basin peoples might be said to bear out Swanson's assessment, but substantial linguistic and archeological evidence (Goss, 1968; Gruhn, 1961; Madsen, 1975) indicates that the northern Shoshoni probably entered the area within the last 1000 years, contrary to what Swanson believed. Accumulating evidence of pottery and other remains identifiable with the horticulturally based Fremont culture of northern Utah is also beginning to suggest a fairly substantial Fremont presence in the region at about the same time. Ongoing research may offer a new perception of Great Basin influence in this region (Butler, 1982).

CONCLUSION

The first people in the Far West occupied a late Pleistocene landscape, which they shared with herds of elephant, horse, camel, and other ice-age mammals now extinct. The glaciated highlands of the Rockies and the Sierra–Cascades bounded the Plateau on the north, east, and west; in the Great Basin and California deserts to the south were great pluvial lakes. Between 8000 and 5000 BC, the descendants of the Paleo-Indian hunters became broad-spectrum Archaic foragers adapted to the warmer and drier countryside of postglacial times. Within each major region—California, the Great Basin, and the Plateau—a number of local traditions had begun to develop by about 7000 BC (see Figure 5.13).

The divergent economic adaptations and varying levels of societal complexity that developed within the three major regions can be closely related to environmental factors. In California, a general biotic abundance and closely juxtaposed environmental zones made a wide variety of resources available within a narrow compass. This prosperous situation in turn fostered the development of a sedentary lifeway, dense population, and flourishing economic–political intercourse among groups. By historical times, California societies were significantly wealthier and more complex than those of either the Great Basin or Plateau. Great Basin population, by contrast, was far less dense, and the societies were simpler and more nomadic—as they had to be to make a living from the sparse and scattered resources of their desert land. In a few favored places, a more sedentary village lifeway was achieved, and a relatively rich cultural inventory

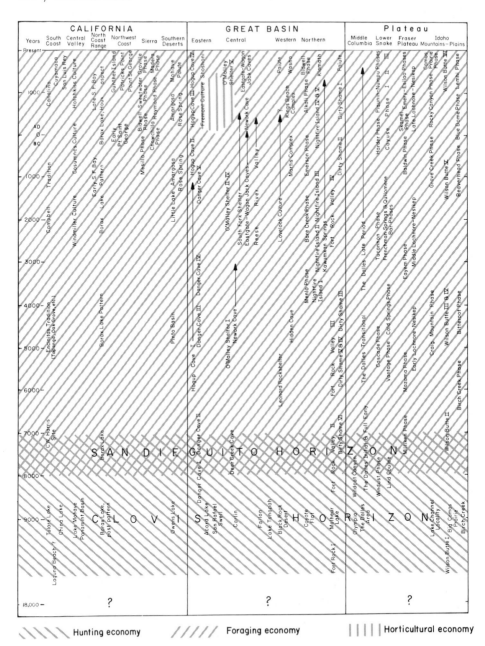

FIGURE 5.13
Regional traditions and local phases or complexes.

developed, but in general the Great Basin lifeway was spartan in comparison to those of California and the Plateau. Plateau societies, much more than those of the other two areas, were shaped by the abundance of a single major food resource. From an early period—how early is yet to be established with certainty—salmon fishing made possible a semisedentary existence, and human groups organized their yearly economic cycle around the seasonal spawning runs.

Systems of resource procurement seem to have varied across the three regions, and these variations also have environmental correlates. Historical records show that, in the Plateau and Great Basin, local abundances of salmon, root crops, or piñon pine seeds seasonally attracted groups of harvesters from hundreds of square miles around. People traveled to where the desired resource was and carried it away themselves. In California, on the other hand, more formalized intergroup exchange was the dominant mechanism for distributing natural resources among the human population. Such interactions are difficult to document archeologically inasmuch as most of the goods involved were probably perishable. But it is striking that archeological finds in California demonstrate a thriving exchange in beads manufactured from marine shells (which may have served as a standard of value) while no comparable specialized trade item has been identified archeologically in the Plateau and Great Basin. This pattern suggests that, in California, where population was much denser than in the Great Basin or Plateau, the local societies tended to husband their own territory's resources and to capitalize on them through systematic exchange relationships that used concretely measurable standards of value. In the other regions, with their lower population density, such control of natural resources may have been neither possible nor profitable, and special tokens of exchange would have served no useful purpose.

ACKNOWLEDGMENTS

I thank the late Robert F. Heizer, Michael J. Moratto, Thomas F. King, and David A. Fredrickson for their comments on the California section of this chapter.

References Cited and Recommended Sources

Aikens, C. Melvin. 1967. Plains relationships of the Fremont culture: a hypothesis. *American Antiquity* 32:2:198–209.
———. 1970. *Hogup Cave.* University of Utah Anthropological Papers, no. 93.
———. 1972a. Fremont culture: restatement of some problems. *American Antiquity* 37:1:61–66.

————. 1972b. *Surface Archaeology of Southwestern Washoe County, Nevada.* Desert Research Institute Publications in the Social Sciences 9.

————. 1976. Cultural hiatus in the eastern Great Basin? *American Antiquity* 41:4:543–550.

————, David L. Cole, and Robert Stuckenrath. 1977. Excavations at Dirty Shame Rockshelter, southeastern Oregon. *Tebiwa Miscellaneous Papers* 4.

————, and Rick Minor. 1978. Obsidian hydration dates for Klamath prehistory. *Tebiwa Miscellaneous Papers* 11.

Allely, Steven. 1975. A Clovis point from the Mohawk River valley, western Oregon. In *Archaeological Studies in the Willamette Valley, Oregon,* ed. C. Melvin Aikens. University of Oregon Anthropological Papers 8:549–552.

Ames, Kenneth M., and Alan G. Marshall. 1981. Villages, demography and subsistence intensification on the southern Columbia Plateau. *North American Archaeologist* 2:1:25–52.

————, James P. Green, and Margaret Pfoertner. 1981. Hatwai (10NP143): interim report. *Boise State University Archaeological Reports* 9.

Anonymous. 1968. Bill Mobley does it again. *Utah Archaeology* 13:1:13.

Antevs, Ernst. 1948. Climatic changes and pre-white man. In *The Great Basin, with Emphasis on Glacial and Post-Glacial Times.* Bulletin of the University of Utah 38:20, Biological Series 10:7:168–191.

Bada, Jeffrey L., and Patricia Masters Helfman. 1975. Amino acid racemization dating of fossil bones. *World Archaeology* 7:2:160–173.

————, Roy A. Schroeder, and George F. Carter. 1974. New evidence for the antiquity of man in America deduced from aspartic acid racemization. *Science* 184:791–793.

Bean, Lowell John. 1974. Social organization in native California. In *'Antap: California Indian Political and Economic Organization,* ed. Lowell John Bean and Thomas F. King. Ballena Press Anthropological Papers 2:11–34.

————, and Thomas C. Blackburn (eds.). 1976. *Native Californians: A Theoretical Retrospective.* Ramona, Calif.: Ballena Press.

————, and Thomas F. King (eds.). 1974. *'Antap: California Indian Political and Economic Organization.* Ballena Press Anthropological Papers 2.

————, and Harry W. Lawton. 1973. Some explanations for the rise of cultural complexity in native California, with comments on proto-agriculture and agriculture. In *Patterns of Indian Burning in California: Ecology and Ethnohistory,* ed. Henry T. Lewis. Ballena Press Anthropological Papers 1:V–XI.

Beardsley, Richard K. 1954. *Temporal and Areal Relationships in Central California Archaeology.* Parts I, II. University of California Archaeological Survey Reports 24, 25.

Bedwell, S. F. 1970. Prehistory and environment of the Pluvial Fort Rock Lake area of south-central Oregon. Ph.D. dissertation, University of Oregon Department of Anthropology.

————. 1973. *Fort Rock Basin Prehistory and Environment.* Eugene: University of Oregon Books.

Berger, Rainer. 1975. Advances and results in radiocarbon dating: early man in America. *World Archaeology* 7:2:174–184.

————, Reiner Protsch, Richard Reynolds, Charles Rozaire, and James R. Sackett. 1971. New radiocarbon dates based on bone collagen of California Paleoindians. *Contributions of the University of California Research Facility* 12:43–49.

Blackburn, Thomas. 1974. Ceremonial integration and social interaction in aboriginal California. In *'Antap: California Indian Political and Economic Organization,* ed. Lowell John Bean and Thomas F. King. Ballena Press Anthropological Papers 2:93–110.

Borden, Charles E. 1960. Djri 3, an early site in the Fraser canyon, British Columbia. *National Museum of Canada Bulletin* 162:101–118.

————. 1968. Prehistory of the lower mainland. In *Lower Fraser Valley: Evolution of a Cultural Landscape,* ed. Alfred H. Siemens. University of British Columbia, British Columbia Geographical Series 9:9–26.

Brauner, David Ray. 1976. Alpowai: the culture history of the Alpowa locality. Ph.D. dissertation, Department of Anthropology, Washington State University.

Butler, B. Robert. 1959. Lower Columbia Valley archaeology: a survey and appraisal of some major archaeological resources. *Tebiwa* 2:2:6–24.

————. 1962. *Contributions to the Prehistory of the Columbia Plateau.* Occasional Papers of the Idaho State College Museum 9.

————. 1963. An early man site at Big Camas Prairie, south-central Idaho. *Tebiwa* 6:1:22–33.

————. 1965. Contributions to the archaeology of southeastern Idaho. *Tebiwa* 8:1:41–48.

————. 1967. More Haskett points from the type locality. *Tebiwa* 10:1:25.

————. 1970. A surface collection from Coyote Flat, southeastern Oregon. *Tebiwa* 13:1:34–57.

————. 1972. Folsom points from the Upper Salmon River valley. *Tebiwa* 15:1:72.

————. 1978. *A Guide to Understanding Idaho Archaeology.* Special Publication of the Idaho State University Museum.

————. 1982. Numic expansion and the demise of the Fremont in southern Idaho. Paper presented at the 18th biennial meeting of the Great Basin Anthropological Conference, Reno, Nevada.

Campbell, Elizabeth W., and William H. Campbell. 1937. The Lake Mohave site. In *The Archaeology of Pleistocene Lake Mohave: A Symposium,* ed. Elizabeth W. Campbell et al. Southwest Museum Papers 11:9–24.

Carter, George F. 1958. Archaeology in the Reno area in relation to the age of man and the culture sequence in America. *Proceedings of the American Philosophical Society* 102:2:174–192.

Clewlow, C. W., Jr. 1968. Surface archaeology of the Black Rock Desert, Nevada. *University of California Archaeological Survey Reports* 73:1–94.

Cole, David L. 1967. *Archaeological Research of Site 35 SH 23, the Mack Canyon Site.* Report of the Museum of Natural History, University of Oregon, to the Bureau of Land Management.

————. 1968a. *Archaeological Excavations in Area 6 of Site 35 GM9, the Wildcat Canyon Site.* Report of the Museum of Natural History, University of Oregon, to the National Park Service.

————. 1968b. *Report on Archaeological Research in the John Day Dam Reservoir Area, 1967.* Report of the Museum of Natural History, University of Oregon, to the National Park Service.

Cowan, Richard A., and C. W. Clewlow, Jr. 1968. The archaeology of site NV-PE-67. *University of California Archaeological Survey Report* 73:195–236.

Cressman, Luther S. 1936. Archaeological survey of the Guano Valley region in southeastern Oregon. *University of Oregon Monographs, Studies in Anthropology* 1:1–48.

————. 1942. *Archaeological Researches in the Northern Great Basin.* Carnegie Institution of Washington, Publication 538.

————. 1956. Klamath prehistory: the prehistory of the culture of the Klamath Lake area. *Transactions of the American Philosophical Society* 46:4:375–515.

————. 1960. Cultural sequences at The Dalles, Oregon: a contribution to Pacific Northwest prehistory. *Transactions of the American Philosophical Society* 50:10.

————, Howel Williams, and Alex D. Krieger. 1940. Early man in Oregon. *University of Oregon Monographs, Studies in Anthropology* 3:1–78.

Cruxent, Jose M. 1962. Phosphorus content of the Texas Street "hearths." *American Antiquity* 28:1:90–91.

Davis, E. L. 1963. The desert culture of the western Great Basin: a lifeway of seasonal transhumance. *American Antiquity* 29:2:202–212.

————. 1975. The "exposed archaeology" of China Lake, California. *American Antiquity* 40:1:39–53.

————, Clark W. Brott, and David L. Weide. 1969. *The Western Lithic Co-tradition.* San Diego Museum Papers 6.

————, and Richard Shutler, Jr. 1969. Recent discoveries of fluted points in California and Nevada. *Nevada State Museum Anthropological Papers* 14:154–178.

Day, Kent C. 1964. Thorne Cave, northeastern Utah: archaeology. *American Antiquity* 30:1:50–59.

Decker, D. A. 1969. Early archaeology on Catalina Island: problems and potential. *University of California, Los Angeles, Archaeological Survey Annual Report* 11:69–84.

Elsasser, Albert B. 1960. The archaeology of the Sierra Nevada in California and Nevada. *University of California Archaeological Survey Reports* 51:1–93.

————, and Robert F. Heizer. 1966. Excavation of two northwestern California coastal sites. *University of California Archaeological Survey Reports* 67:1–150.

Elston, Robert. 1971. *A Contribution to Washo Archaeology.* Nevada Archaeological Survey Research Paper 2.

————. 1979. *The Archaeology of U.S. 395 Right-of-Way Between Stead, Nevada and Hallelujah Junction, California.* Archaeological Survey, University of Nevada, Reno.

Euler, Robert C. 1964. Southern Paiute archaeology. *American Antiquity* 29:3:379–381.

Fagan, John L. 1974. *Altithermal Occupation of Spring Sites in the Northern Great Basin.* University of Oregon Anthropological Papers 6.

Fowler, Don D. 1968. *The Archaeology of Newark Cave, White Pine County, Nevada.* Desert Research Institute Social Sciences and Humanities Publications 3.

————, David B. Madsen, and Eugene M. Hattori. 1973. *Prehistory of Southeastern Nevada.* Desert Research Institute Publications in the Social Sciences 6.

Fredrickson, David A. 1974a. Cultural diversity in early central California: a view from the North Coast ranges. *Journal of California Anthropology* 1:1:41–53.

———. 1974b. Social change in prehistory: a central California example. In *'Antap: California Indian Political and Economic Organization*, ed. Lowell John Bean and Thomas F. King. Ballena Press Anthropological Papers 2:55–74.

Fried, Morton. 1967. *The Evolution of Political Society*. New York: Random House.

Gerow, Bert A. 1974. *Co-traditions and Convergent Trends in Prehistoric California*. San Luis Obispo County Archaeological Society Occasional Paper 8.

———, and Roland W. Force. 1968. *An Analysis of the University Village Complex, with a Reappraisal of Central California Archaeology*. Stanford: Stanford University Press.

Glennan, William S. 1976. The Manix Lake lithic industry: early lithic tradition or workshop refuse? *Journal of New World Archaeology* 1:7:43–61.

Goss, James A. 1968. Culture-historical inference from Utaztekan linguistic evidence. In *Utaztekan Prehistory*, ed. Earl H. Swanson, Jr. Occasional Papers of the Idaho State University Museum 22:1–42.

Gould, Richard A. 1966. *Archaeology of the Point St. George Site and Tolowa Prehistory*. University of California Publications in Anthropology 4.

Grabert, G. F. 1968. *North–Central Washington Prehistory*. University of Washington Department of Anthropology, Reports in Archaeology 1.

Grayson, Donald K. 1973. The avian and mammalian remains from Nightfire Island. Ph.D. dissertation, University of Oregon Department of Anthropology.

Green, Thomas J. 1982. Pit house variability and associations at Givens Hot Springs, southwestern Idaho. Abstracts of Papers, 35th Northwest Anthropological Conference, Burnaby, British Columbia, pp. 15–16.

Grosscup, Gordon L. 1960. *The Culture History of Lovelock Cave, Nevada*. University of California Archaeological Survey Reports 52.

Gruhn, Ruth. 1961. *The Archaeology of Wilson Butte Cave, South–Central Idaho*. Occasional Papers of the Idaho State College Museum 6.

———. 1965. Two early radiocarbon dates from the lower levels of Wilson Butte Cave, south–central Idaho. *Tebiwa* 8:2:57.

Gunnerson, James H. 1956. A fluted point site in Utah. *American Antiquity* 21:4:412–414.

———. 1962. Plateau Shoshonean prehistory: a suggested reconstruction. *American Antiquity* 28:1:41–45.

Hammatt, Hallett H. 1976. Geological processes and apparent settlement densities along the lower Snake River: a geo-centric view. Paper presented at the 29th Annual Meeting of the Northwest Anthropological Conference, Ellensburg, Washington.

Harrington, Mark R. 1933. *Gypsum Cave, Nevada*. Southwest Museum Papers 8.

———. 1948. *An Ancient Site at Borax Lake, California*. Southwest Museum Papers 16.

———. 1957. *A Pinto Site at Little Lake, California*. Southwest Museum Papers 17.

———, and Ruth D. Simpson. 1961. *Tule Springs, Nevada, with Other Evidence of Pleistocene Man in North America*. Southwest Museum Papers 18.

Haynes, C. Vance, Jr. 1969. The earliest Americans. *Science* 166:709–715.

———. 1971. Time, environment, and early man. *Arctic Anthropology* 8:2:3–14.

———. 1973. The Calico site: artifacts or geofacts? *Science* 181:305–310.

Heizer, Robert F. 1951. Preliminary report on the Leonard Rockshelter site, Pershing County, Nevada. *American Antiquity* 17:2:89–98.

———, and Martin A. Baumhoff. 1961. The archaeology of two sites at Eastgate, Churchill County, Nevada. I. Wagon Jack Shelter. *University of California Anthropological Records* 20:4.

———, and ———. 1970. Big game hunters in the Great Basin: a critical review of the evidence. *Contributions of the University of California Archaeological Research Facility* 7:1–12.

———, and ———, and C. W. Clewlow, Jr. 1968. Archaeology of South Fork Rockshelter (NV El 11), Elko County, Nevada. *University of California Archaeological Survey Reports* 71:1–58.

———, and Rainer Berger. 1970. Radiocarbon age of the Gypsum culture. *Contributions of the University of California Archaeological Research Facility* 7:13–18.

———, and Alex D. Krieger. 1956. The archaeology of Humboldt Cave, Churchill County, Nevada. *University of California Publications in American Archaeology and Ethnology* 47:1.

———, and Lewis K. Napton. 1970. Archaeology and the prehistoric Great Basin lacustrine subsistence regime as seen from Lovelock Cave, Nevada. *Contributions of the University of California Archaeological Research Facility* 10.

Hester, Thomas Roy. 1973. Chronological ordering of Great Basin prehistory. *Contributions of the University of California Archaeological Research Facility* 17.

Hunt, Alice P. 1960. *Archaeology of the Death Valley Salt Pan, California.* University of Utah Anthropological Papers 47.

——, and Dallas Tanner. 1960. Early man sites near Moab, Utah. *American Antiquity* 26:1:110–117.

Jennings, Jesse D. 1957. *Danger Cave.* University of Utah Anthropological Papers 27. (Also released as Society for American Archaeology Memoir 14.)

——. 1974. *Prehistory of North America,* 2d ed. New York: McGraw-Hill.

——. 1980. *Cowboy Caves.* University of Utah Anthropological Papers 104.

——, Alan R. Schroedl, and Richard N. Holmer. 1980. *Sudden Shelter.* University of Utah Anthropological Papers 103.

Johnson, Fredrick, and John P. Miller. 1958. Review of "Pleistocene Man at San Diego," by George F. Carter. *American Antiquity* 24:2:206–210.

King, Chester D. 1974. The explanation of differences and similarities among beads used in prehistoric and early historic California. In *'Antap: California Indian Political and Economic Organization,* ed. Lowell John Bean and Thomas F. King. Ballena Press Anthropological Papers 2:75–92.

——. 1976. Chumash inter-village economic exchange. In *Native Californians: A Theoretical Retrospective,* ed. Lowell J. Bean and Thomas C. Blackburn, pp. 289–318. Ramona, Calif.: Ballena Press.

King, Linda B. 1969. The Medea Creek cemetery: an investigation of social organization from mortuary practices. *University of California, Los Angeles, Archaeological Survey Annual Report* 11:23–68.

King, Thomas F. 1974. The evolution of status ascription around San Francisco Bay. In *'Antap: California Indian Political and Economic Organization,* ed. Lowell John Bean and Thomas F. King. Ballena Press Anthropological Papers 2:35–54.

Kroeber, A. L. 1925. *Handbook of the Indians of California.* Bureau of American Ethnology Bulletin 78.

——. 1962. The nature of land-holding groups in aboriginal California. *University of California Archaeological Survey Reports* 56:19–58.

Leach, Larry L. 1967. *Archaeological Investigations of Deluge Shelter, Dinosaur National Monument.* PB 176 960, Clearinghouse for Federal and Technical Information, Springfield, Virginia.

Leonhardy, Frank C. 1975. The lower Snake River culture typology—1975: Leonhardy and Rice revisited. Paper presented at the 28th Annual Meeting of the Northwest Anthropological Conference, Seattle, Washington.

——, and David G. Rice. 1970. A proposed culture typology for the lower Snake River region, southeastern Washington. *Northwest Anthropological Research Notes* 4:1:1–29.

Lewis, Henry T. 1973. *Patterns of Indian Burning in California.* Ballena Press Anthropological Papers 1.

Lilliard, J. B., Robert F. Heizer, and Franklin Fenenga. 1939. *An Introduction to the Archaeology of Central California.* Sacramento Junior College Department of Anthropology, Bulletin 2.

Lister, Robert H. 1951. *Excavations at Hells Midden, Dinosaur National Monument.* University of Colorado Studies, Series in Anthropology 3.

Loud, Llewellyn L., and Mark R. Harrington. 1929. Lovelock Cave. *University of California Publications in American Archaeology and Ethnology* 25:1.

Mack, Joanne M. 1975. *Cultural Resources Inventory of the Potential Glass Buttes Geothermal Lease Area, Lake, Harney, and Deschutes Counties, Oregon.* Final report to the United States Bureau of Land Management. Copy on file, University of Oregon Department of Anthropology.

Madsen, David B. 1975. Dating Paiute-Shoshoni expansion in the Great Basin. *American Antiquity* 40:1:82–86.

——, and Michael S. Berry. 1975. A reassessment of northeastern Great Basin prehistory. *American Antiquity* 40:4:391–405.

Marwitt, J. P. 1970. *Median Village and Fremont Culture Regional Variation.* University of Utah Anthropological Papers 95.

Meighan, Clement W. 1954. A late complex in southern California prehistory. *Southwestern Journal of Anthropology* 10:215–227.

————. 1959. California cultures and the concept of an Archaic stage. *American Antiquity* 24:3:289–305.

————, and C. Vance Haynes, Jr. 1970. The Borax Lake site revisited. *Science* 167:1213–1221.

Moratto, Michael J. 1972. A study of prehistory in the southern Sierra Nevada foothills, California. Ph.D. dissertation, University of Oregon Department of Anthropology.

Mundorff, J. C. 1971. *Nonthermal Springs of Utah.* Utah Geological and Mineralogical Survey, Water Resources Bulletin 16.

Nelson, Charles M. 1969. *The Sunset Creek Site (45-KT-28) and Its Place in Plateau Prehistory.* Washington State University Laboratory of Anthropology Reports of Investigations 47.

O'Connell, James F. 1975. *The Prehistory of Surprise Valley.* Ballena Press Anthropological Papers 4.

Osborne, Douglas. 1956. Evidence of the early lithic in the Pacific Northwest. *Research Studies of the State College of Washington* 24:1:38–44.

Perkins, R. F. 1967. Clovis-like points in southern Nevada. *Nevada Archaeological Survey Reporter* 9:9–11.

————. 1968. Folsom and Sandia points from Clark County. *Nevada Archaeological Survey Reporter* 2:4:4–5.

Pettigrew, Richard M. 1975. *Cultural Resources Survey in the Alvord Basin, Southeastern Oregon.* Final report to United States Bureau of Land Management. Copy on file, University of Oregon Department of Anthropology.

————. 1980. The ancient Chewaucanians: more on the prehistoric lake dwellers of Lake Abert, southeastern Oregon. *Proceedings of the First Annual Symposium of the Association of Oregon Archaeologists,* ed. Martin Rosenson. Association of Oregon Archaeologists, Inc., Occasional Papers 1:49–67.

Ragir, Sonia. 1972. The Early Horizon in central California prehistory. *Contributions of the University of California Archaeological Research Facility* 15.

Rice, David G. 1972. *The Windust Phase in Lower Snake River Region Prehistory.* Washington State University Laboratory of Anthropology Reports of Investigations 50.

Richards, Brian. 1968. A Clovis point from northwestern Nevada. *Nevada Archaeological Survey Reporter* 2:3:12–13.

Riddell, Francis A. 1969. Pleistocene faunal remains associated with carbonaceous material. *American Antiquity* 34:2:177–180.

————, and W. H. Olsen. 1969. An early man site in the San Joaquin Valley, California. *American Antiquity* 34:2:121–130.

Ritter, E. W. 1970. Northern Sierra Foothill archaeology: culture history and culture process. *Center for Archaeological Research at Davis (University of California), Publications* 2:171–184.

Rogers, Malcolm J. 1945. An outline of Yuman prehistory. *Southwestern Journal of Anthropology* 1:167–198.

Sanger, David. 1967. Prehistory of the Pacific Northwest Plateau as seen from the interior of British Columbia. *American Antiquity* 32:2:186–197.

Schroeder, Albert H. 1963. Comments on Gunnerson's "Plateau Shoshonean Prehistory." *American Antiquity* 28:4:559–560.

Service, Elman R. 1962. *Primitive Social Organization: An Evolutionary Perspective.* New York: Random House.

Shutler, Mary Elizabeth, and Richard Shutler, Jr. 1959. Clovis-like points from Nevada. *Masterkey* 33:1:30–32.

————, and ————. 1963. *Deer Creek Cave, Elko County, Nevada.* Nevada State Museum Anthropological Papers 11.

Shutler, Richard, Jr.; C. Vance Haynes, Jr.; John E. Mawby; Peter J. Mehringer, Jr.; W. Glen Bradley; and James E. Deacon. 1967. *Pleistocene Studies in Southern Nevada.* Nevada State Museum Anthropological Papers 13.

Simms, Steven R. 1977. A Mid-Archaic subsistence and settlement shift in the northeastern Great Basin. In *Models and Great Basin Prehistory: A Symposium,* ed. Don D. Fowler. Reno: Desert Research Institute Publications in the Social Sciences 12:195–207.

Simpson, Ruth D. 1976. A commentary on W. Glennan's article. *Journal of New World Archaeology* 1:7:63–66.

Smith, Elmer R. 1941. The archaeology of Deadman Cave, Utah. *Bulletin of the University of Utah* 32:4. (Revised and reprinted in 1952 as University of Utah Anthropological Papers 10.)

Stanley, Dwight A., Gary M. Page, and Richard Shutler, Jr. 1970. The Cocanour site: a western Nevada Pinto phase site with two excavated "house rings." *Nevada State Museum Anthropological Papers* 15:1–46.

Steward, Julian H. 1937. *Ancient Caves of the Great Salt Lake Region.* Bureau of American Ethnology Bulletin 116.

Stickel, E. G. 1968. Status differentiation at the Rincon site. *University of California, Los Angeles, Archaeological Survey Annual Report* 10:209–261.

Strong, Emory. 1969. *Stone Age in the Great Basin.* Portland: Binfords and Mort.

Swanson, Earl H., Jr. 1972. *Birch Creek: Human Ecology in the Cool Desert of the Northern Rocky Mountains, 900 BC–AD 1850.* Pocatello: University of Idaho Press.

——, and Paul G. Sneed. 1966. *Birch Creek Papers No. 3: The Archaeology of the Shoup Rockshelters in East-Central Idaho.* Occasional Papers of the Idaho State University Museum 17.

Tadlock, W. Louis. 1966. Certain crescentic stone objects as a time marker in the western United States. *American Antiquity* 31:5:662–675.

Thomas, David Hurst. 1973. An empirical test for Steward's model of Great Basin settlement patterns. *American Antiquity* 38:2:155–176.

——. n.d. Preliminary progress report: Gatecliff Shelter, Nye County, Nevada. 1975 Excavations. Unpublished manuscript, Department of Anthropology, American Museum of Natural History, New York.

Tripp, George W. 1966. A Clovis point from central Utah. *American Antiquity* 31:3:435–436.

True, D. L., C. W. Meighan, and Harvey Crew. 1974. *Archaeological Investigations at Molpa, San Diego County, California.* Berkeley: University of California Publications in Anthropology 11.

Tuohy, Donald R. 1968. Some early lithic sites in central Nevada. In *Early Man in Western North America,* ed. Cynthia Irwin-Williams. Eastern New Mexico University Contributions in Anthropology 1:4:27–38.

——. 1969. Breakage, burin facets, and the probable linkage among Lake Mohave, Silver Lake, and other varieties of Paleo-Indian projectile points in the desert west. *Nevada State Museum Anthropological Papers* 14:132–152.

——. 1970. The Coleman locality: a basalt quarry and workshop near Falcon Hill, Nevada. *Nevada State Museum Anthropological Papers* 15:143–206.

——, and Mercedes C. Stein. 1969. A late Lovelock shaman and his grave goods. *Nevada State Museum Anthropological Papers* 14:96–130.

Wallace, William J. 1962. Prehistoric cultural development in the southern California deserts. *American Antiquity* 28:2:172–180.

Warren, Claude N. 1967. The San Dieguito complex: a review and hypothesis. *American Antiquity* 32:2:168–185.

——. 1968. Cultural tradition and ecological adaptation on the Southern California coast. In *Archaic Prehistory in the Western United States,* ed. Cynthia Irwin-Williams. Eastern New Mexico University Contributions in Anthropology 1:3:1–14.

——, and Anthony J. Ranere. 1968. Outside Danger Cave: a view of early man in the Great Basin. In *Early Man in Western North America,* ed. Cynthia Irwin-Williams. Eastern New Mexico Contributions in Anthropology 1:4:6–18.

——, and D. L. True. 1961. The San Dieguito complex and its place in California prehistory. *University of California, Los Angeles, Archaeological Survey Annual Report for 1960–61:*246–337.

Weide, David L. 1976. The altithermal as an archaeological "non-problem" in the Great Basin. In *Holocene Environmental Change in the Great Basin,* ed. Robert Elston. Reno: Nevada Archaeological Survey Research Papers 6:174–184.

Weide, Margaret L. 1968. Cultural ecology of lakeside adaptation in the western Great Basin. Ph.D. dissertation, Department of Anthropology, University of California, Los Angeles.

Wheat, Margaret. 1967. *Survival Arts of the Primitive Paiutes.* Reno: University of Nevada Press.

Wilke, Philip J. 1978. Late prehistoric human ecology at Lake Cahuilla, Coachella Valley, California. *Contributions of the University of California Archaeological Research Facility* 38.

Winter, Joseph C., and Henry G. Wylie. 1974. Paleoecology and diet at Clyde's Cavern. *American Antiquity* 39:2:303–315.

Wormington, H. M. 1955. *A Reappraisal of the Fremont Culture.* Proceedings of the Denver Museum of Natural History 1.

Above: Bison herds near Lake Jessie (North Dakota), sketched by John Mix Stanley, Pacific Railroad surveys, July 10, 1853. (Photograph by Smithsonian Institution.)

Below: Bones of 300 butchered bison from Hell Gap period mass kill, about 8000 BC, Jones–Miller site, Colorado. (Copyright © National Geographic Society.)

CHAPTER SIX

The Prehistoric Plains

Waldo R. Wedel

In the nineteenth century, the Plains were called the Great American Desert. It was the considered opinion of informed thinkers that the Great Plains constituted a largely uninhabitable region, that even the Indians had been unable to live there before the introduction of horses and rifles. Actually, as Dr. Wedel demonstrates, the Plains were the home of strong, long-lasting lifeways and fairly complex social organizations for many millennia before the invention of firearms or the introduction of the horse.

The Great Plains are visualized here as that portion of the northern temperate grassland lying east of the Rocky Mountains between 32° and 52° north latitude (Wedel, 1961). North to south, the region measures nearly 2400 kilometers; eastward, it extends 800 to 1100 kilometers from the mountain front to, or slightly beyond, the 95th meridian west. As thus arbitrarily defined for archeological purposes, it covers approximately two million square kilometers of land whose salient characteristics are low to moderate surface relief; a continental climate featuring cold, dry winters, hot, dry summers, and a scanty and uncertain precipitation regimen; and an original or potential native vegetation of perennial grasses with trees limited to stream valleys, scarp lands, and hilly or mountainous localities (Figure 6.1).

The region has been known to whites since the earliest days of Euro-American exploration of the continental interior (Wedel, 1975a). Beginning in the mid-sixteenth century, Spanish adventurers who traversed the dry scrub and desert grasslands of Mexico and the Pueblo Southwest spoke well of the verdant pasturage they encountered when they reached the Llano Estacado, of its prodigious numbers of "wild cows," and of the picturesque dog-nomads who followed the herds as they roamed the land. Later and far to the north, British fur traders from the forested lands of eastern Canada had, by the last quarter of the eighteenth century, begun to apply to the treeless grasslands the designation Great Plains (Lewis, 1975:32). In contrast, the first American explorers in the early 1800s called the central portions the Great American Desert, and considered it unfit for human occupation west of the 98th or 99th meridian; most nineteenth-

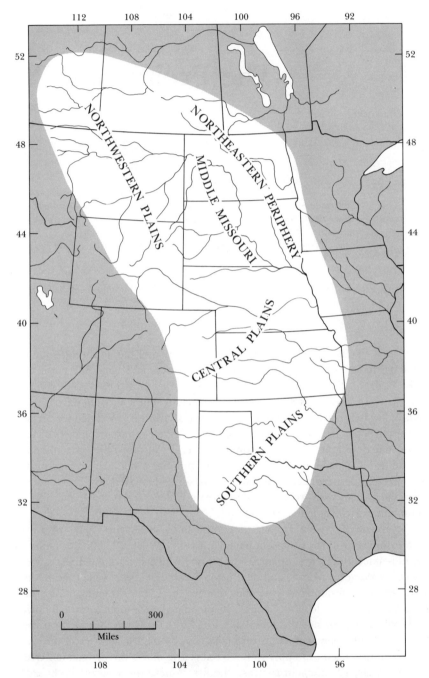

FIGURE 6.1
Map of the North American Great Plains area and its subareas. Subareas recognize the archeological diversity and specializations that took place in Archaic and later periods. (After Wedel, 1961.)

century observers of the native peoples seem to have tacitly accepted the mid-nineteenth-century dictum of Morgan (White, 1959:41) that the prairies (read "plains") were only made tolerable to the Indians by their possession of the horse and the rifle. Many years later, Hough (1930:315) saw matters differently and voiced the opinion that "what would appear to have been the most important event in the life of Asiatic tribes assimilating themselves to American environments was getting in touch with the buffalo." At about this same time, expanding archeological fieldwork was providing new perspectives on native American culture history and indicating that the ethnographically conditioned views of recent human arrival on the Great Plains were out of joint with reality.

Despite the uniformity implied by their usual designation, the Great Plains exhibit much geographical diversity. Topographically, they include flatlands, tablelands, badlands, dunes, hills, stream valleys, and detached mountain masses. They lie in the rain shadow of the Rockies, and their climate is produced largely by the interaction of three principal air masses, whose movements, though varying from time to time, are essentially west to east (Borchert, 1950). Mild air from the Pacific moving eastward has lost most of its moisture content by the time it crosses the Great Basin and the Rockies, where it meets moist, warm, subtropical air pushing north from the Gulf of Mexico and cold dry arctic air flowing south from Canada. A strong flow of westerlies results in an expanding aridity in the Great Plains, which is most pronounced in the west. Changes in circulation patterns that weaken the westerlies and permit the intrusion of moisture-laden tropical air may significantly increase the regional precipitation (see weather system maps in Figure 2.4). Such changes in climatic behavior—varying greatly in frequency, intensity, and duration—and the resulting variations in abundance and distribution of plants and animals in the region are a familiar feature of the environmental setting today; there is accumulating evidence that such changes have been going on for a long period of time as measured in terms of human occupation. For great portions of the Plains region, the moisture available is very often marginal, whether for crop growing in the eastern sections or for grass and pasturage in the western range lands; the vagaries of nature are also reflected increasingly in the archeological record.

The "sea of grass" that greeted the first white explorers was not always thus, but its origins and its evolution through time are still very imperfectly known. Molluscan evidence (Frye and Leonard, 1952:180) suggests a progressive drying of the Kansas–Nebraska region since mid-Pleistocene times, culminating in a biologically severe climate of hot, dry summers and cold, dry winters as far back as 12,000 years ago. There is botanical and pollen evidence that until perhaps 14,000 years ago, when the Des Moines lobe of the continental ice sheet reached its maximum southward extent in present central Iowa, a spruce forest extended from Iowa across northeastern Kansas, Nebraska, and the Dakotas, to merge with the western coniferous forest running eastward from the Rocky Mountains (Wright, 1970). The nature of the contemporary vegetation in the present steppe country of western Kansas and eastern Colorado is still unclear.

The boreal forest was replaced by deciduous forest and this, in turn, by grassland around 8,000 or 10,000 years ago. Thus, by 10,000 years ago, considerable portions of the Great Plains were suited for occupation by large, gregarious herbivores (Bryson and Wendland, 1967), and the archeological evidence indicates that such occupation was indeed taking place. Open forests and parklands, varying from time to time in composition and extent, apparently persisted along the southwestern margins (Wendorf and Hester, 1975).

Historically, the grasses and other vegetation of the region varied from east to west in accord with the observed precipitation and other climatic factors. In the west, beyond the 100th meridian, existed a north–south belt of short grasses (chiefly *Bouteloua* and *Buchloe*) peculiarly adapted to dry soils and to a short, uncertain growing season, with 37.5 centimeters or less of annual precipitation. Eastward, where precipitation rises to 62.5 and finally to 100 centimeters annually, the steppe gave way to mixed grasses and then to tall-grass bluestem prairie. All of this region is included in the needlegrass–pronghorn–grama grass biome of Shelford (1963:328). It is also the heart of the former range of the bison, ecologically a dominant in the short-grass and mixed-grass areas and a resource of prime importance to the human inhabitants throughout most of their residence in the region.

Other food resources, both plant and animal, could supplement the bison or serve as substitutes when that animal was unavailable or in short supply. Animals included pronghorn, mule and white-tailed deer, elk, black and grizzly bears, and numerous smaller fur bearers. Birds were of minor importance as food, but feathers and skins were used for ritual paraphernalia (Ubelaker and Wedel, 1975) and bones in toolmaking. Fish and shellfish were utilized in varying degrees at some periods and in some sections. Important wild food plants included the prairie turnip (*Psoralea*), groundnut (*Apios*), ground bean (*Amphicarpa*), sunflower and Jerusalem artichoke (*Helianthus*), bush morning glory (*Ipomoea*), and prickly pear (*Opuntia*). In prehorse days, pigweed (*Amaranthus*), ragweed (*Ambrosia*), and various grasses may have supplied seeds, young shoots, and the like. Wild plums and chokecherries (*Prunus*), buffalo berries (*Shepherdia*), serviceberries (*Amelanchier*), and other fruits were gathered; in the south, mesquite (*Prosopis*) beans were available. Excepting the pits of the berries and fruits and occasional charred grass seeds, little of the vegetal material is known from the archeological record; its importance in prehistoric times must be inferred primarily from the ethnographic record for tribes in and adjoining the Plains region.

The vegetational and climatic differences between the western and eastern Plains subregions were reflected in the general distribution of native peoples in historic times. The semiarid western steppe has always been primarily an area of hunting and gathering subsistence economies in which human settlement and activities were concentrated along the stream valleys and around the springs and waterholes where the game herds also tended to congregate (Wendorf and Hester, 1962; Wedel, 1963). The domain of Apachean dog-nomads in the six-

teenth century (D. Gunnerson, 1956), these lands were taken over, after introduction of the horse in the seventeenth century, by other tribes drawn from
surrounding areas by the abundance of bison. The customs of these linguistically and culturally diverse newcomers were reshaped by environmental factors
(Oliver, 1962) into the more or less uniform lifeway of mobile, horse-using
bison hunters. They included the Dakota, Cheyenne, Arapaho, Comanche,
Kiowa, and others—the "typical" Plains tribes of Wissler (1922:22).

In the mixed and tall-grass prairies of the eastern Plains, where climate and
soils were suited to maize horticulture, there were settled communities of village
Indians. Fertile, easily worked valley bottom soils made possible an increasingly
productive subsistence economy, often with sufficient crop surpluses to support
trade with the nonhorticultural bison hunters to the west. The villagers were
mainly Siouan and Caddoan speakers. Unlike the horse-nomads, they seem to
have had deep roots in the same region where they lived when the whites met
them; their way of life, divided between seasonal bison hunting and maize-
bean–squash–sunflower cultivation, is now known to have a historical depth of
perhaps a half-millennium before the earliest whites arrived. Their way of
life—in its horticultural practices and crops, its houses and settlement patterns,
its ceramic and other industries—reveals strong relationships with the eastern
Woodland cultures of the Mississippi–Ohio valley—whence the culture, and
probably most of the people as well, were apparently derived. By contrast, the
nonhorticultural, equestrian bison hunters of the short-grass steppe were only
the last variants in a long succession of people following a "true" Plains lifeway based on mobility, portability of possessions, and prime reliance on bison
hunting.

Among all the natural food resources of the Plains, the bison has been most
appropriately termed "the material and spiritual focus of plains life and culture
for thousands of years" (McHugh, 1972:11). The archeological record indicates
that this has been true for at least 10,000 years. To the extent that the animal-
bone refuse from ancient living sites can be regarded as reflecting the associated
environmental setting, it appears likely also that over these millennia there were
wide fluctuations in the number of bison available to their human predators.
Especially suggestive is the work of Dillehay (1974), based on the recorded
presence of bison bones at archeological sites in the Southern Plains of Texas,
Oklahoma, and New Mexico. On the basis of the presence or absence of bison
in the faunal lists (which admittedly are more often suggestive or vague than
they are definitive) he has proposed the following chart of changing long-term
bison populations for the region:

Presence Period I:	10,000 to 6,000–5,000 BC
Absence Period I:	6000–5000 to 2500 BC
Presence Period II:	2500 BC to AD 500
Absence Period II:	AD 500 to AD 1200–1300
Presence Period III:	AD 1200–1300 to AD 1550

Since the data here are drawn from the archeological record, it could be argued that "absence periods" reflect the incompleteness or inadequacy of that record, rather than actual absence of bison. Equally plausible is the view that the data indicate substantially diminished herds rather than their total disappearance. The periodicity, extent, and intensity of human utilization of the Plains—at least prior to adoption of cultigens where feasible—more or less directly reflect the abundance and availability of the number-one food resource, the bison. It can be further suggested that a study similar to Dillehay's on long-term bison population fluctuations in the northern Plains would be desirable.

This chapter is aimed at updating a summary review of Plains archeology and culture history that was prepared some 18 years ago (Wedel, 1964). The same basic outline is followed here. The years since 1962 have witnessed an impressive burgeoning of archeological activity in nearly all parts of the region and the accumulation of much new information. The number of trained workers active today has increased substantially, as has their financial support. Radiocarbon dates in ever-growing numbers have sharply improved our chronological controls. The greater involvement of geologists, palynologists, climatologists, and trained specialists from other disciplines has been highly productive at all time levels from early occupation to the historic period. Ecological studies utilizing midden leavings once routinely discarded are helping to convert the accumulating knowledge into a better understanding of the significance of our findings. All of this means, of course, that the interpretations of a decade or two ago are now in need of revision, as the updated views of today soon will be. It means also that space limitations here will force the slighting of much of the recently acquired information and its significance (Figure 6.2).

THE EARLY BIG-GAME HUNTERS (10,000–5,000 BC)

Nowhere in the Great Plains have the archeological investigations of the past 20 years produced more exciting results than among the remains of the early hunting cultures of the western steppe lands. These investigations have involved primarily game kills and butchering sites, but attention has increasingly been devoted to campsites and habitation levels. The sites date fairly consistently between 12,000 and 7,000 years ago and include both complexes that have elsewhere been termed *fluted-point cultures* and materials of the later makers of unfluted, lanceolate points. In recent years, meticulously detailed interdisciplinary recovery and analysis techniques have increasingly been brought to bear on these materials. Often the major focus of interest has been less on the artifacts that once titillated amateurs and professionals alike and more on the refuse animal bone and what critical study of it can tell the qualified observer about contemporary animal behavior and biology, ancient hunting and butchering methods, and other possible cultural practices of the early hunters. The inferences and understanding thus generated, when cautiously used, can provide

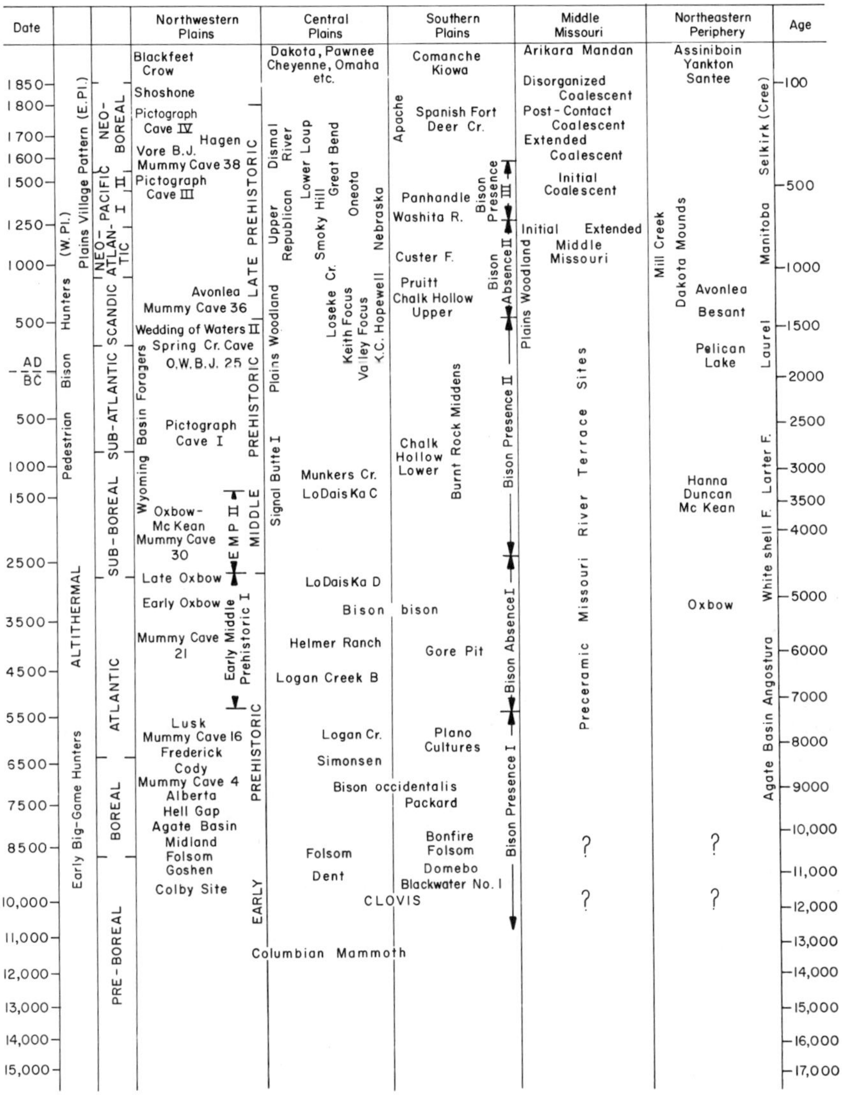

Date				Northwestern Plains	Central Plains	Southern Plains	Middle Missouri	Northeastern Periphery	Age	
1850	Pedestrian Bison Hunters	Plains Village Pattern (E.PI.) (W.PI.)	NEO-BOREAL	NEO-PACIFIC II I	Blackfeet Crow	Dakota, Pawnee Cheyenne, Omaha etc.	Comanche Kiowa	Arikara Mandan	Assiniboin Yankton Santee	Selkirk (Cree)	100
1800					Shoshone			Disorganized Coalescent			
1700					Pictograph Cave IV	Dismal River	Spanish Fort Deer Cr.	Post-Contact Coalescent			
1600					Vore B.J. Hagen		Apache	Extended Coalescent			
1500					Mummy Cave 38	Upper Republican Lower Loup Great Bend Oneota		Initial Coalescent		Manitoba	500
1250			SUB-ATLANTIC SCANDIC		Pictograph Cave III	Loseke Cr. Smoky Hill	Panhandle Washita R.		Mill Creek Dakota Mounds		
1000						Keith Focus Valley Focus	Custer F.	Initial Extended Middle Missouri			1000
500	Bison Hunters				Avonlea Mummy Cave 36	K.C. Hopewell	Pruitt Chalk Hollow Upper	Plains Woodland		Avonlea Besant	
					Wedding of Waters II	Plains Woodland					1500
AD/BC					Spring Cr. Cave O.W.B.J. 25					Pelican Lake	
500			SUB-BOREAL		Pictograph Cave I	Signal Butte I	Chalk Hollow Lower	Bison Presence II		Laurel	2000
							Burnt Rock Middens				2500
1000		ALTITHERMAL				Munkers Cr. LoDaisKa C				Hanna Duncan McKean	3000
1500				MIDDLE PREHISTORIC EMP II	Oxbow-McKean Mummy Cave 30						3500
											4000
2500					Late Oxbow	LoDaisKa D		Bison Absence I			5000
3500			ATLANTIC	Early Middle Prehistoric I	Early Oxbow	Bison bison				Oxbow	
					Mummy Cave 21	Helmer Ranch	Gore Pit				6000
4500						Logan Creek B		Preceramic Missouri River Terrace Sites			7000
5500		Early Big-Game Hunters	BOREAL	PREHISTORIC	Lusk Mummy Cave 16 Frederick	Logan Cr. Simonsen	Plano Cultures	Bison Presence I			8000
6500					Cody Mummy Cave 4 Alberta	Bison occidentalis	Packard				9000
7500					Hell Gap Agate Basin						10,000
8500					Midland Folsom Goshen	Folsom	Bonfire Folsom	?	?		11,000
				EARLY	Colby Site	Dent	Domebo Blackwater No. I	?	?		12,000
10,000			PRE-BOREAL			CLOVIS					13,000
11,000					Columbian Mammoth						14,000
12,000											15,000
13,000											16,000
14,000											17,000
15,000											

FIGURE 6.2
General time relationships of certain archeological complexes and sites in the Plains area.

stimulating new insights into the evolving lifeways of human societies operating over thousands of years.

My designation of these groups as early big-game hunters indicates continuing acceptance of Sauer's (1944) observation that this term adequately reflects what we think we know about one of the principal activities of the early Plains people—the food quest. No implication is intended that their subsistence economy did not also include the seasonal or opportunistic use of vegetal products, small game, and perhaps other comestibles that may have been available from time to time but of which neither direct nor indirect evidence has yet been recognized in the material-culture inventory as now known. The qualifier "early" distinguishes these ancient Americans from the later bison hunters of post-Altithermal times. In time span they correlate approximately with the Early Prehistoric period of Mulloy (1958:219) and the Late Early Prehistoric of Reeves (1973:1222) in the northern Plains.

The Mammoth Hunters

The oldest dated materials with clearly established association of humans and animals in the Great Plains are still those assigned to the Clovis or Llano complex (Sellards, 1952; Wormington, 1957). These finds occur mainly in the western and southern sections. They consist of mammoth kills, which may include as well the bones of camel, horse, and giant bison of species now extinct. They cluster between 11,000 and 11,500 radiocarbon years before present (Haynes, 1964) and are still without known cultural antecedents (Humphrey and Stanford, 1979). When diagnostic artifacts are associated, they usually involve Clovis or "Clovis-like" Fluted spear points, along with choppers, cutting tools, rare millingstones, and several kinds of bone tools. At the better-known Plains sites, such as Miami (Texas), Dent (Colorado), Domebo (Oklahoma: Leonhardy, 1966), and Blackwater No. 1 (New Mexico: Hester, 1972), the number of animals killed ranges from one to perhaps a dozen; but where more than one is indicated, it is possible, and sometimes demonstrable, that several killings are involved. The kills are generally associated with waterholes, springs, or streamside situations, to which a need for water or the presence of better browse or grazing probably drew the animals. Here they were apparently slain by men armed with thrusting or throwing spears, very likely working in groups and perhaps from ambush, and who showed some preference for immature animals and females. Butchering was evidently carried out where the animals fell. There is no evidence of dug pits or other constructed traps.

No campsites, dwelling remains, or burials of the mammoth hunters have yet been described from the Plains; but a sparse, scattered, and transient population, probably camping in the neighborhood of springs and waterholes, may be inferred. Little is known of their tool inventory beyond items found in the kills. At Blackwater No. 1, debris believed to have washed from a Clovis campsite included quantities of Alibates chert from quarries approximately 160 kilometers distant. At the same site a grinding stone is regarded as possible indication of use of plant foods to supplement the meat diet, though it could doubtless have served as well for the grinding of dried meat.

Recently discovered but still incompletely reported finds at the Clovis time level include three or more immature mammoths associated with projectile points and butchering tools near Worland, Wyoming (Frison and Wilson, 1975), which have been dated at 11,200 years before present, and one or more young animals at former spring sites near Wray, Colorado (Stanford, personal communication), with evidence of human involvement in the killing or processing. The UP mammoth kill near Rawlins, Wyoming, which had cutting, scraping, and piercing tools in association but no diagnostic projectile points (Irwin, 1970), also dates to approximately 11,000 years ago. Somewhat beyond the usual time range of the dated human–mammoth associations noted above is the lower level of the Lamb Spring site near Littleton, Colorado. There disarticulated mammoth bones underlay a bed of similarly disarticulated bison bones and yielded a radiocarbon bone date of 11,150 ± 1,000 BC (M-1464). Some of the mammoth bones and fragments from this site are now believed to carry butchering marks; others are regarded as possible bone-skinning tools; and a *Camelops* phalanx from beneath a pile of mammoth bones was clearly worked by humans (Wedel, n.d.a.; Stanford, Wedel, and Scott, 1981).

The Bison Hunters

More abundant and much better known than the sites of the mammoth hunters are the later sites left by people to whom the mammoth was apparently no longer available and who therefore turned their attention to the smaller but more plentiful herd animals that remained. Chief among these were large bison of species now extinct, which seem to have figured to a much lesser extent in the subsistence economy of the preceding elephant hunters. One supposes that these animals, like the mammoth before them, were taken singly or in small groups by stalking, ambush, or other methods available to individual hunters or to small parties, working near waterholes, along game trails, from blinds, with grass fires, or in deep snow where conditions were suitable. Waterholes and the green flats around them, particularly on the drier to semiarid uplands, doubtless attracted bison 10 millennia ago as they did in the nineteenth century. The hazards of hunting bison in such ways may have been reduced somewhat by the seeming tameness of the animals unless they were frightened or aroused (Hammond and Rey, 1953:749), a characteristic remarked upon also by Lewis and Clark on the upper Missouri in the spring of 1805 (Thwaites, 1904:I, 335; II, 17, 27). Such small-scale efforts, witnessed and reported by the sixteenth- and seventeenth-century Spaniards among the Southern Plains dog-nomads (Hammond and Rey, 1953:404; Ayer, 1916:55), would have provided a subsistence livelihood, so long as contact was not lost with the herds. The development of effective meat-preserving methods (such as drying) presumably provided stores of food for use in winter or at other times when the bison were not readily available.

The archeological evidence, as was first hinted at Folsom in 1927, has since shown clearly that long before the coming of the Spanish the prehorse Indians had devised highly successful techniques for procuring adequate meat supplies. These methods exploited the gregarious behavior of the bison and their readiness for headlong flight en masse when they considered themselves threatened, and they featured the mass killing of dozens to hundreds of animals by cooperative efforts. Awareness of the historical depth and widespread use of communal drives, brought about particularly by the archeological work of the past 20 years, has injected new perspectives into western Plains prehistory by dramatizing the multimillennial antiquity of the prime requirement for native peoples' occupation of the Great Plains—primary subsistence from the bison and its products.

Neither historical, ethnographic, nor archeological evidence tells us how often attempted communal bison drives were only partially successful or failed entirely. But the early and apparently spectacularly unsuccessful attempts of Mendoza's Spanish cavalry to corral large numbers of bison in the Southern Plains in October of 1598, though they "tried in a thousand ways to drive them inside the corral" (Hammond and Rey, 1953:401), as well as Hind's observation nearly three centuries later (Hind, 1859:55) among the Saskatchewan Cree that a portion of the stampeding herd broke out of the trap and escaped, remind us that successful mass kills required careful planning, good organization, coordinated execution, and doubtless a measure of good luck insured by ritual sanction—in short, much more than merely chasing a herd of skittish beasts over a bluff or into a pen to its wholesale destruction.

Mass bison kills by such methods as pounding and jumping have been the subject of a voluminous and growing literature, with no end in sight; useful discussions of a general nature are readily available (for example, Forbis, 1962; Malouf and Conner, 1962; Kehoe, 1967; Frison, 1971, 1972, 1974). In historic times, many northern Plains tribes still regularly obtained their winter meat supply by cooperative drives (see Arthur, 1975, for an excellent review). Such a drive usually involved the construction of a corral or "pound" from logs and brush, into which up to 200 or more animals were driven through converging lines formed by piles of brush, sod, stones, or buffalo chips that began wide apart far out on the flats where the herd was gathered. Appropriate rituals to propitiate the animals and help lure them into the trap were celebrated beforehand. In earlier days, before the horse was available to extend the range of gathering operations, the animals were often driven over a cliff or "jump," with or without a corral below, where animals not done in by the fall could be dispatched with lance, dart, or arrow. No jump operation was ever recorded by eyewitnesses, but there are vivid accounts of the scenes at the pound (for example, Hind, 1959:55). For the older prehorse period, we have only the archeological record from which to reconstruct the operation. In broken country, the terrain sometimes provided natural lanes along which the bison could be urged into an artificial enclosure, over a fall, or into a box canyon or escape-proof ravine. With all of these methods, of course, the hunters had to assure themselves that the wind was right, the bison correctly dispersed over the gathering basin, and all participants properly positioned for the drive. If the herd was large enough to stampede blindly and to be unable to turn back before entrapment, and if each hunter did his part well, the chances for success were reasonably good.

The great antiquity of multiple bison kills in the Plains region is indicated by several sites that have been dated either by radiocarbon or by projectile-point typology. At least three of these have yielded fluted Folsom points, but only one has also produced carbon-14 dates. At Blackwater No. 1, several pondside kills of fewer than seven animals each are identified with the Folsom occupation at about 8000 years BC (Hester, 1972:167). At the original Folsom site, where 19 points were found with 23 large bison in proximity to an ancient bog, no dates are available. There are also no dates for Lipscomb, Texas, where 18 points, plus scrapers, flake knives, and chips, were associated with 23 or more large bison (Schultz, 1943), many of whose skeletons were still in articulation.

Much larger numbers of animals, and different projectile point styles, were involved in several other kills that have also yielded dates in the vicinity of 10,000 years ago. At Olsen–Chubbuck (Wheat, 1972) in the Big Sandy drainage of eastern Colorado, the systematically butchered remains of nearly 200 bison (*B. occidentalis*) of all ages and both sexes were uncovered in an ancient arroyo. The beasts had been stampeded and slain by hunters, who left among the debris unfluted points and other artifacts assigned to the Firstview complex. Less than 160 kilometers to the north, on the west bluff line of the Arickaree River, and more than 240 kilometers east of the mountain front, the Jones–Miller site (Stanford, 1974) has yielded the remains of some 300 *Bison antiquus*. The several fall-through-winter kills are associated with Hell Gap projectile points, cutting and scraping tools of stone, and bone implements. Near Casper, Wyoming, no fewer than 75 *B. antiquus* were trapped in a parabolic sand dune and processed by Hell Gap hunters (Frison, 1974). At the extreme southern end of the Great Plains, in the breaks along the Rio Grande 24 kilometers above the Pecos River, lies Bone Bed 2 at Bonfire Shelter, with three radiocarbon dates at about 8000 BC (Dibble and Lorrain, 1968:51; Dibble, 1970). The site has yielded Plainview-like and Folsom points, together with other stone artifacts and the bones of an estimated 120 animals representing a large, now-extinct species within the range of both *B. antiquus* and *B. occidentalis*. Olsen–Chubbuck was a single kill; the others listed involve several events over periods of undetermined length.

The kills just listed are of particular significance not only for their high yield to the hunters and as evidence of the antiquity of human history in this region, but also because the meticulous recovery and analytical techniques employed throughout their archeological examination have made possible meaningful reconstructions of the methods followed by the early hunters; of the number, age, and composition of the quarry herd; and of the procedures by which the animals were processed for final human consumption. The details are readily available in the excellent studies cited and in others still to come, and need not detain us here. To those who still hold that hunting bison on foot was an unproductive business (Farb, 1968:113) and that the prehorse Indians lived perpetually on the verge of starvation, it may be instructive to reflect on Wheat's (1972:114) calculations that the Olsen–Chubbuck herd probably made available to its destroyers approximately 60,000 pounds of meat, tallow, and other products, most of which seems to have been actually butchered out for use. How this amount was divided between fresh meat for immediate use and meat to dry for future consumption is not known, but interesting problems that must have confronted the Indians, and possible solutions, are ably discussed. By implication, periods of feasting, even gorging, undoubtedly occurred after the prehorse hunts, as they did following those of historic times.

In addition to the kill sites and bone beds, Folsom and later Paleo-Indian materials also occur at a growing number of sites where domestic and other activities seem to have been carried on. At Blackwater No. 1, for example, hunting and skin-working tools used in processing game from nearby lakeside kills predominate, including fluted points, plano-convex end scrapers, cutting tools, and a few bone artifacts. A much larger range of materials came from the Lindenmeier site, regarded by Roberts (1936; Wilmsen and Roberts, 1978) as probably seasonally occupied for periods of several weeks at a time by fairly large groups. The people were perhaps drawn to the spot by water, firewood, and game concentrations near waterholes, which provided opportunities for getting a winter's supply of meat and skins for clothing. Other than the points, few of the tools are of distinctive types. No traces of habitations were found. Some indications of Paleo-Indian settlement patterns are emerging from such studies as Wendorf and Hester (1962) on the Llano Estacado and, somewhat outside the Plains, by Judge and Dawson (1972) in the middle Rio Grande.

Hell Gap, an important series of campsites rather than kills, provides the longest and most complete stratigraphic record in the region for the early bison hunters. Here Plainview-like points were found beneath a Folsom occupation, from which circumstance it has been suggested (Irwin, 1971) that this complex—since renamed (Irwin-Williams et al., 1973:46) the *Goshen* complex—is technologically and chronologically transitional from Clovis to Folsom culture. Viewing the post-Clovis manifestations here as "one culture with variations over time and changes in tool kits, but with basic typological unity," Irwin (1971:48) further proposes the term *Itama* culture for a succession of complexes designated *Plainview* or *Goshen* (9000–8800 BC), *Folsom* (8800–8550 BC), *Midland* (8650–8350 BC), *Agate Basin* (8450–7950 BC), *Hell Gap* (7950–7450 BC), *Alberta* (7450–6950 BC), and *Cody* (6750–6350 BC). Throughout this sequence at Hell Gap, the major faunal element in the sites is bison. Subcircular post-mold patterns from the Midland level, and again in the following Agate Basin level, are identified as possible house remains. In a later level identified as the Frederick complex, a circle of rocks is noted as suggestive of the stone tipi rings of later times; with this complex (6350–5950 BC) are included the bones of deer, small animals, and shellfish, as well as bison. The overlying Lusk complex (5950–5450 BC) has a varied tool kit, including Angostura-like points, and also a varied faunal assemblage that perhaps reflects local cultural adjustments to a changing climatic setting.

In the Southern Plains, environmental fluctuations appear to have been associated with cultural changes during the earlier millennia of human occupation. From molluscan and other evidence, it appears that a drying trend began at least 20,000 years ago and then changed to cooler and moister conditions between about 12,000 and 8,500 BC. With the latter climate came also an expansion of boreal forest onto the Llano Estacado. As drier conditions returned, trees again disappeared and lakes and ponds dried up. Concurrently, Folsom peoples appeared on the scene, to be replaced by carriers of the Agate Basin complex, the first in this locality "of [a] series of related projectile point styles attributed to the Plano horizon (Scottsbluff, Milnesand, Portales, Eden, etc.)" (Wendorf and Hester, 1975:275). By about 6000–5000 BC, the region was again mostly treeless except along ravines, and the uplands were essentially without surface water.

THE PLAINS ARCHAIC (5000 BC to AD 1)

The Northwestern Plains

In the Northwestern Plains, archeological thinking has been organized for some years around the temporal sequence set up in the early 1950s by Mulloy (1952, 1954a, b, 1958). This included the Early Prehistoric period, prior to 6000 years ago, characterized by small nomadic groups specializing in bison hunting, and involving Folsom and "Yuma" complexes. Following a time span of uncertain length for which there was then no available archeological evidence but that presumably ended more than 3500 years ago, other peoples appeared whose economy featured plant gathering and small-animal hunting, with little or no emphasis on bison hunting. Two similar but sequent complexes evolved, which were designated the *Early Middle* and *Late Middle Prehistoric* periods. Both were represented at the stratified McKean site in northeastern Wyoming. About AD 500, the Late Prehistoric period began, involving various groups, some of them from the ceramic–horticultural village people of the eastern Plains, who may have been drawn to a western Plains hunting life by an increasing abundance of bison. Some of these groups were directly ancestral to historic hunting tribes of the region.

This basic chronological outline is still being followed, though with important modifications in light of greatly increased data and more adequate time controls. The thesis that the economies of the Middle Prehistoric period comprised small-game hunting and generalized gathering, with little use of bison, is now regarded as applicable primarily to the Big Horn and Wyoming basins. Ecologically, these areas are more like the Great Basin than the Great Plains, and such a setting would have fostered a forager type of subsistence economy. Elsewhere in the Northwestern Plains, including the prairie provinces of Canada, the story throughout seems actually to have been one of relatively simple subsistence groups relying heavily on the bison, "of wandering foot nomads almost wholly dependent on buffalo for food, clothing, and shelter" (Forbis, 1968:40). A period of putative nonoccupation of the region noted by Mulloy, the Altithermal interval, will be discussed later.

Before the last of the early big-game hunters, as represented by the "Plano" complexes, had left the Plains, cultural complexes based on a differently oriented subsistence economy had established themselves in mountainous and hilly sectors of the region, as well as in the broken country that borders much of the flatlands. Unlike the early hunter sites, with their finely fashioned, fluted and nonfluted lanceolate points and indications of specialization in the types of big game taken, the later manifestations are visualized as those of hunters and gatherers with a wide spectrum of interests in food acquisition. They made extensive use of a large variety of small animals, seeds and other vegetal products, and occasionally fish, reptiles, amphibians, and the like. Some of these people made use of caves and rockshelters; others utilized streamside terraces for open campsites. Other than occasional firepits, perhaps used for roasting and baking as well as warmth, there are no indications of habitations, storage pits, or other structural features.

There is seldom much evidence of intensive or prolonged residence; but at some sites, such as Mummy Cave (Wedel et al., 1968; McCracken, 1971, 1977) and Medicine Lodge Creek (Frison, 1975) in northwestern Wyoming, there are very considerable accumulations of domestic refuse, some of which precede the time of some early big-game-hunter sites in the region. Intermittent residence over long periods of time, perhaps on a seasonal basis, rather than continuous uninterrupted occupation, is inferred. This pattern would result from the sort of lifeway described by Mulloy (1954a) as cyclical nomadism and by Flannery (1968) as scheduling.

At Mummy Cave, the fill consists of 38 distinct cultural levels contained in 8.5 meters of detrital material (Figure 6.3). The lower and middle cultural layers yielded relatively few artifacts. Deposition began before 7300 BC, with only medium-sized lanceolate points of mediocre workmanship up to 6000 BC. From 5700 BC, side-notched points reminiscent of eastern Archaic forms were dominant. Other side-notched, stemmed, and shouldered types follow, with cultural layers continuing thin. Thicker and more productive layers appear at around 3300 BC. By about the 2500 BC level, McKean and other indented-base

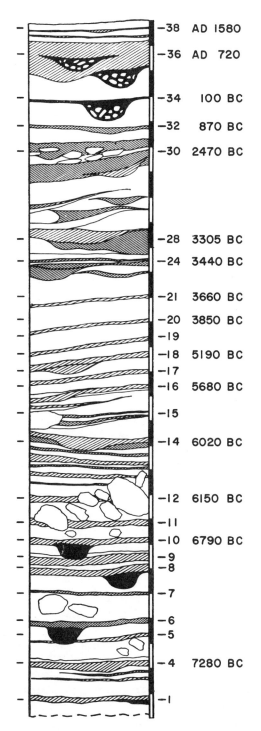

- -38   AD 1580
- -36   AD 720
- -34   100 BC
- -32   870 BC
- -30   2470 BC
- -28   3305 BC
- -24   3440 BC
- -21   3660 BC
- -20   3850 BC
- -19
- -18   5190 BC
- -17
- -16   5680 BC
- -15
- -14   6020 BC
- -12   6150 BC
- -11
- -10   6790 BC
- -9
- -8
- -7
- -6
- -5
- -4   7280 BC
- -1

FIGURE 6.3

Stratigraphic section through floor deposits
at Mummy Cave, Wyoming. Culture levels
numbered 1 to 38. Radiocarbon dates at right.
Right-hand margin of column is in 30-
centimeter intervals. (After Wedel et al., 1968.)

points are plentiful, millingstones are present, and there is a considerable inventory of other materials, including both perishables and nonperishables. Cultural layer 30 revealed tubular bone pipes, coiled basketry fragments, vegetable-fiber cordage and netting, wood trimmings, leather scraps, and many flint chips. Animal-bone refuse includes mountain sheep at all levels; rabbit, marmot, porcupine, wood rat, deer, grouse, and waterfowl are also present, but there is virtually no trace of bison. Pollen was too poorly preserved for climatic studies, and wood-rat nests, from which promising climatic inferences have been made elsewhere in the Wyoming region (Wells, 1970), were apparently not investigated or collected. The general impression here is of a mountain-oriented hunting-gathering lifeway rather than a Plains big-game-hunter tradition.

Another important deeply stratified site is on Medicine Lodge Creek in the Big Horn Mountains, 160 kilometers or so east of Mummy Cave and across the Big Horn Basin (Frison and Wilson, 1975). Investigations are still in progress there, and only brief preliminary statements are available. Cultural evidence begins at just under 10,000 years ago and ends with the historic period. Lower levels contain various forms of lanceolate points to about 6500 BC, roughly the same as Mummy Cave. Just above this level, at 6300 BC, Pryor Stemmed points appear. A midden level dated about 7500 BC yielded bones of gopher, wood rat, rabbit, and other small mammals, with deer, sheep, and bison very scarce. Another, at about 6500 BC, contained large numbers of small fish, and in some levels simple food-grinding tools appeared. Throughout the entire occupation here, intensive use of plants and small animals was indicated; deer and mountain sheep were of some importance at times, whereas bison were consistently rare (Frison, 1978).

As these data indicate, local cultural complexes, in which bison and other large Plains animals seem not to have been the primary meat source, evidently existed along the mountain front zone simultaneously with the bison hunters who were responsible for the kill and butchering at the Horner site, with its complement of Scottsbluff and Eden points, cutting and scraping tools, and other early big-game-hunter characteristics. There is no evidence of direct contact or exchange of points or other artifacts between the Horner-site hunters and the inhabitants of Mummy Cave, a scant 64 kilometers distant.

In the Northwestern Plains, north of the Yellowstone River and east of the Big Horn and Wyoming basins, archeological sites are very unevenly distributed through the 5000-year period that began about 7000 years ago and ended with the beginning of the Christian Era. The same apparently holds for the Central and Southern Plains, except on their eastern and western margins. The first half, roughly from 5000 to 2500 BC, coincides with the Altithermal interval of higher temperatures and increased aridity; from this period there appear to be significantly fewer sites than in later times. At Mummy Cave, cultural levels 18 to 24 or 28 fall within the Altithermal interval, with short-lived occupations suggested before McKean times. Additional investigated sites from this period have been considered by Reeves (1973: Fig. 5 and *pass.*) under the rubric *Early*

Middle Prehistoric I (about 5500–3000 BC). Included are 38 sites, mostly in Alberta, Montana, and Wyoming. There are at least 3 bison kills, 5 rock-shelters, and 21 open stratified campsites. With reference to the Great Plains, most appear to be peripheral, centering in and around the Big Horn Basin and in the broken country to the north and northwest. The impression persists of a largely blank space in the upper Missouri–Saskatchewan region during EMP-I times, where essentially no sites have been reported except in peripheral sectors.

In post-Altithermal times, apparently beginning as early as 3000 BC and multiplying after about 2500 BC, the number of known and investigated sites increases dramatically. Reeves' study of 68 components assigned to the *Early Middle Prehistoric II* (3000–1500 BC) includes bison kills, rockshelters, and fishing stations, 31 of which have been dated. On the basis of stone tool technology, "most easily observed in projectile point styles," he distinguishes several complexes: Early Oxbow (3000–2500 BC) and Late Oxbow (2500–2000 BC), Late Mummy Cave (3000–1500 BC), Oxbow–McKean (2500–2000 BC), McKean (2000–1500 BC), and Powers–Yonkee (2500–1500 BC) (Reeves, 1973:1237ff., Fig. 6). Early Oxbow, with eared Oxbow and Bitterroot Side-notched points, was putatively derived from the Mummy Cave complex and basically mountain oriented. Other key point types in this model are Oxbow Eared for Late Oxbow; Oxbow, McKean, and Bitterroot Side-notched for Late Mummy Cave; Oxbow and McKean for the Oxbow–McKean complex; and McKean points only for the McKean complex. This model raises many provocative questions and requires thorough testing.

The Central and Southern Plains

Plains Archaic materials in the Central and Southern Plains are not well known. Along the eastern margin, Simonsen, Lungren, and Hill in Iowa and Logan Creek in Nebraska carry radiocarbon dates from about 6600 to 4300 BC, in or preceding the early Altithermal range. Simonsen (Frankforter and Agogino, 1960) was a bison kill, and bison bone was plentiful also at Lungren and Logan Creek. Somewhat later are Lansing Man, several Flint Hills sites, and the Munkers Creek complex in eastern Kansas. In Oklahoma, Archaic materials are widely scattered as surface finds. Their time span is suggested by such radiocarbon dates (Bell, 1968) at 7450 BC for a level at Packard site that yielded lanceolate and side-notched points, 4100 BC for Gore Pit near Lawton, and several levels at Duncan–Wilson Rockshelter (Lawton, 1968), where Archaic hunters and gatherers lingered until the third or fourth century AD but left no bison bones in their middens.

Radiocarbon dates from two stratified sites in the Texas panhandle relate to the late Archaic occupancy there. At Chalk Hollow, a small headwater tributary of Palo Duro Canyon about 19 kilometers southeast of Amarillo, 4.7 meters of colluvial terrace fill containing cultural materials included a late midden (about AD 440–840) with small Scallorn-like and other side-notched arrow points, potsherds, and so on. A lower series of relatively thin midden layers contained medium to large stemmed dart points (Castroville-like, Marcos-like, and so on), end scrapers, cutting tools, bone awls and dice (?), and well-built slab hearths. Millingstones and fragments were found at all levels. The associated animal bone suggests a relatively abundant meat diet in some levels, with bison bone especially conspicuous at about 850–950 BC. Freshwater snail shells indicate former live water in the now-dry creek nearby, but they are identical with forms found in roadside ponds in the general locality today and do not suggest any marked climatic shifts during the Archaic occupancy, which here spanned the period of about 1650 to 425 BC. A culturally sterile stratum averaging 30 centimeters or more in thickness separates the lower Archaic midden layers from the upper ceramic–small-point midden (Wedel, 1975b).

The Canyon City Country Club Rockshelter, a few miles upstream from Chalk Hollow, included two levels. Dated at 880 BC and 150 BC, they lacked diagnostic artifacts but "faunal and geological evidence suggested drought conditions" (Hughes, personal communication). Such conditions may help to account for the occupation-free zone at Chalk Hollow between 400 BC and 400 AD. There are no known bison kills in the immediate vicinity of these two sites, but several small bone beds at the eastern edge of the Llano Estacado (Hughes, personal communication; Tunnell and Hughes, 1955; Dibble and Lorrain, 1968:73) east of Palo Duro Canyon have produced stemmed and side- or corner-notched dart points comparable to those from the Archaic levels at Chalk Hollow. The bones are being exposed in the sides and near the heads of rapidly eroding arroyos, suggesting small-group hunts wherein a few animals were corralled at the upper end of a former arroyo that was subsequently filled and is now being reexcavated by erosion. One is reminded here of the apparently similar and approximately contemporaneous Early Middle Prehistoric and post-Altithermal bison traps reported by Frison (1972) in the Powder River Basin of Wyoming.

Texas Archaic sites are generally regarded as representing a hunting–gathering subsistence complex in which bison bone may be present, but only as a relatively minor element in the faunal debris (Dibble and Lorrain, 1968:73), rather than as the product of large-scale jumps or other mass kills. A notable exception is Bone Bed 3 at Bonfire Shelter, where an estimated 800 cows and calves of *Bison bison* cascaded over a canyon rim in one gigantic slaughter at around 650 BC. Between the late Archaic bison bone beds in the northern Texas panhandle and the much earlier occurrences of bison at the Bonfire and Arenosa shelters, nearly 640 kilometers to the south, lies a time gap of 6000 or more years. This gap corresponds roughly to Dillehay's (1974) Absence Period I (6000–5000 to 2500 BC) of bison from the Southern Plains.

Archaic manifestations in eastern Colorado (Breternitz, 1969) probably include the Gordon Creek burial dated at 7700 BC, but without diagnostic artifacts; LoDaisKa complexes C and D, at 1450 and 2890 BC (Irwin and Irwin,

1959); and a number of small sites scattered around the Denver area. Near Kassler, millingstones, points, scrapers, and other tools dated 3500–3800 BC occur in the pre-Piney-Creek alluvium, which also contains molluscs suggesting a warmer and drier climate (G. Scott, 1962, 1963).

The Effects of the Altithermal

The Archaic time span, here considered roughly the period from about 5000 BC to the beginning of the Christian Era for the Plains as a whole, presents a number of intriguing problems for the archeologist and his or her coworkers concerned with Plains prehistory. For one thing, the first half of the period includes the Altithermal, whose higher temperatures and lower precipitation were of still undetermined importance in human affairs at the time. The apparent scarcity of archeological sites datable to the Altithermal, as compared with earlier and later periods, has long been regarded by some as evidence that much of the region—at any rate, its western portion—may have been abandoned by humans, or nearly so, during this interval (see, for example, Krieger, 1950:121; Mulloy, 1958:208; Davis, 1962:11; Wedel, 1961:282). Hurt (1966) cites several radiocarbon-dated sites in Wyoming, Montana, and Canada that fall within this period. He notes, however, that they occur mostly in mountainous or foothill locations where moisture deficiencies would probably have been less acute than on the lower-lying plains. Accepting the thesis that the climate was warmer and drier, he then suggests that the Plains region as a whole was probably never completely abandoned. There may still have been favored areas of greater moisture that could have served as natural refuges for humans and animals. Any human populations that remained may have had to expand and diversify the food basis of their economy to include plants and smaller animals in larger proportions than formerly. More recently, in a comprehensive and wide-ranging review, Reeves (1973) has argued that, even though the regional climate may have been somewhat drier, resulting in an expanded short-grass area, the survival of a "viable but smaller bison population" would have permitted the "same basic strategy as characterized by subsequent and antecedent prehistoric populations, i.e., communal bison hunting."

Still more recently, reasoning from firsthand ranching experience and from analogy with the recent drought of the 1930s, Frison (1975) has observed that the prolonged moisture deficiencies of the Altithermal would be expected to have materially depleted the amount and quality of the short-grass cover. Such an event would reduce significantly the carrying capacity and adversely affect winter survival, spring condition, and general welfare of the herd animals, young and old. In this light, "the main bulk of the bison herds probably abandoned much of the Northwestern Plains during the Altithermal Period, except for some oasis-like areas and followed the expanding shortgrasses as they intruded into the now tall grass areas." Frison points out further that communal bison hunting, always chancy in terms of escaped animals, was most successful with herds of perhaps several score animals or more and less successful with smaller herds, such as would be expectable under Altithermal stresses. In sum, there was "a definite reduction of human occupations on the Northwestern Plains during the Altithermal and the ones that remained were centered in areas peripheral to the Plains" (Frison, 1975:296).

The nature of the Altithermal climate in the short- and mid-grass Plains is becoming better understood, thanks to increasingly intensive analytical studies by paleoclimatologists, geomorphologists, paleobiologists, and others. Given the length of time and the great extent of territory involved, conditions undoubtedly varied widely in detail from section to section and from time to time. Any generalized characterization is thus likely to be grossly oversimplified. Regionwide generalizations tend to mask local details that would have directly affected surface-water supplies, plant and animal life, and human use of specific localities. It remains likely that the apparent scarcity of archeological sites during Atlantic time reflects a significantly smaller human population in much of the Plains region (Wendland, 1978) as compared to later periods. However, arguments have been advanced, first, that appropriate locations have been insufficiently searched and, second, that surface instability and destruction of stream terraces have obliterated or obscured the evidence (Reeves, 1973).

Paleobotanists and paleoclimatologists working on this problem seem to be in substantial agreement that "Atlantic time was warmest of all the Holocene" and that severe desiccation, particularly on the Plains, was a notable feature of the climate (Wendland, 1978:279). By this time, the flora and fauna of the Great Plains grasslands had become essentially like those of recent times. One wonders what would have been the effects on the regional Plains biota of 1500-2000 years of generally dry, hot weather—or of weather presumably at least warmer and drier than the present. There is no obvious analog in recorded history. The record-breaking drought of 1933-1939—as well as the longer but less severe drought postulated for the western United States from about 1729 to the 1740s (Stockton and Meko, 1975)—both constitute little more than fleeting blips on the screen of Holocene time.

Still, there may be some relevance in the systematic and practical observations made during and since the relatively short drought of the 1930s—the most serious on record for the region since it became the seat of a major livestock industry (Ellison and Woolfolk, 1937; Weaver and Albertson, 1956; Albertson and Weaver, 1945; Albertson et al., 1957; Coupland, 1958). When drought struck, the native grasses responded with reduced size and scantier foliage; where it persisted, root damage and finally death resulted. The depleted grass cover produced substantial decreases in forage production, amounting in some instances to 90 percent or even more; the amount of rangeland required for continued maintenance of grazing cattle rose from 4 or 5 to 20, 25, or 30 hectares per animal. At the end of the drought, even with the return of adequate moisture, several years were usually needed to bring forage production and carrying capacity back to normal. In some instances, however, two years of heavy rainfall increased the forage tenfold or more over that available at the height of the drought.

Warming and desiccation, in Altithermal times as in the historically observed droughts, would presumably have affected the uplands first, resulting in significantly reduced grass cover on the interstream areas and the disappearance of ponds and waterholes as the water table dropped. The short-grass steppe may have expanded—but what would have been the effect on the heartland of the steppe as it existed in pre-Altithermal times? In the stream valleys, the effects may have been less disastrous. The major through-flowing streams (such as the Arkansas, Platte, and Missouri) derive much of their water from mountain snow melt and rains outside the region. Shorter rivers (such as the Republican and Loup in the Central Plains) have their sources in high-yielding aquifers whose stored waters have accumulated over countless millennia from widespread precipitation. We do not know exactly how these streams behaved during the Altithermal, but there is no evidence that their flow was suspended or interrupted during any significant part of Holocene time. Depending upon the distribution of headwater and valley-margin springs and seeps, sufficient water may well have been available in portions of the rivers and on some of their major tributaries to support plant and animal life.

Yet, despite the probability of marked subregional variations in climatic conditions, the generally heightened temperatures and reduced precipitation of the Altithermal period may well have adversely affected the native vegetation and faunal resources of upland areas. Such an effect was probably sufficient to reduce substantially or to redistribute the bison and other game available and thus to minimize the utilization of these areas and the consequent evidences of former human presence during this period. But if, at the same time, the perennial streams continued to provide pasturage and browse for large game animals and support for plants with edible parts, seasonal or otherwise intermittent human residence in the valley bottoms might still have been feasible, as Hurt (1966) suggested. That stream-valley vegetation also suffers severely in times of intense drought is clear from the 1930s, when even such drought-resistant native trees as hackberry and juniper—along with much of the underbrush—perished where the water table fell beyond the reach of their root systems. But damage in the stream valleys was probably less extensive and far-reaching than on the interstream uplands. Localized and possibly recurrent droughts might thus have brought about not a general reduction but rather a redistribution of population, with a shift of hunting and gathering groups to the vicinity of surface-water supplies.

The temporary and short-lived Archaic campsites in the valleys—where seasonal or otherwise intermittent hunting and gathering operations and supporting activities were carried on—may indeed have been destroyed or obscured by the unstable fluvial conditions envisaged by Reeves (1973) during Atlantic time. Alternatively, some sites, deeply covered by centuries of flood deposits, could still be awaiting discovery and recognition through erosion, large-scale construction activities, or other ways. Spring Creek (25FT31) in Nebraska and the Coffey site (14PO1) in the Blue River bottoms in Kansas (Grange, 1980; Schmits, 1978) may indicate the shape of things to come when, by design or accident, archeologists look in the right places at the right time. Those two sites, among others, suggest that local settings in Altithermal times may often have differed less than we once thought from the environments of the last two or three centuries and that an austere lifeway would have been feasible.

Interesting, too, is the question of what was happening physiologically to the Plains bison during the Altithermal period. Prior to about 6000–5000 BC, the early big-game hunters from Texas to Montana were in pursuit of bison of larger size than the animals encountered by the whites; after about 3000–2500 BC, it appears to be invariably the smaller *Bison bison* with which humans were associated. In the Wyoming region, the reduction in size from *Bison occidentalis* to *B. bison* may be even more precisely datable, having occurred possibly between about 6500 and 4500 years ago (Wilson, 1974:96; Frison, 1975). The details of this change and its causes—which may include severe biological stresses associated with worsening environmental conditions and excessive hunting pressures—are among the intriguing questions whose solutions may be measurably nearer as a result of ongoing studies of the growing numbers of animal bones being recovered from large kills in the Northwestern Plains.

THE PLAINS WOODLAND (250 BC–AD 950)

In the eastern Plains, the Archaic lifeway—the cyclical or scheduled hunting of small game, the gathering of seeds, tubers, nuts, berries, and other vegetal foods in season, and, when and where the opportunity existed, the hunting of bison—continued into the final centuries of the pre-Christian Era and eventually gave rise to a number of locally and temporally distinct complexes, basically of eastern origin or else strongly influenced by eastern cultures. Archeologically, these complexes are represented by many small sites, often deeply buried, scattered throughout the region from Oklahoma and Texas to North Dakota and the prairie provinces and, apparently in diminishing numbers, westward to the Rockies. During this period pottery making was introduced into the Plains, as was mound burial; neither practice had been associated with Plains Archaic complexes. The basically eastern orientation of these materials is recognized in their usual designation as the *Plains Woodland* tradition.

At most sites a simple creek-valley hunting and gathering subsistence economy is inferred. In the Central Plains the bone refuse suggests that, contrary to the situation in later times, deer and small mammals were a more important source of protein than the bison; but bison hunting seems to have attained greater prominence farther north and west in the region. Maize horticulture is indicated for Hopewellian communities near Kansas City and, more scantily, at a few other sites; only squash remains hint feebly at food-production activities at Sterns Creek in eastern Nebraska (Strong, 1935). Several Woodland variants have been identified and characterized (for example, Wedel, 1959:542–557), including the relatively advanced and perhaps more sedentary Kansas City Hopewellian and, mostly farther west and northwest, the Keith, Valley, Sterns Creek, and Loseke Creek complexes in Nebraska and Kansas, and the Parker variant in eastern Colorado. In the Canadian grassland, the linear, conical, and other mounds of southern Manitoba are regarded as Middle Woodland; the Pelican Lake, Besant, and Avonlea complexes are roughly contemporaneous with Plains Woodland. Less well-known manifestations occur southward into Oklahoma and Texas.

The Kansas City Hopewellian communities (Wedel, 1943, 1959; Johnson and Johnson, 1975) include both larger sites of up to 3 or 4 hectares and smaller ones that could scarcely have accommodated more than two or three houses. The larger sites have fairly heavy concentrations of refuse, numerous storage pits, and a varied assemblage of artifacts in pottery, stone, bone, and other materials. The pottery includes plain, rocker-marked, and zone-decorated wares, along with small amounts of cord-roughened ware, and clearly derives from eastern materials, probably in the Illinois River valley. Imitation bear teeth of bone, conical or mammiform objects of stone and clay, native copper, and obsidian reflect both cultural affinities and trade contacts. Locally distinguishing items include large, corner-notched projectile points, three-quarter-grooved axes, stemmed plano-convex scrapers, conical flint disks, beaming tools of deer innominates and metapodials, and tanged antler-tip projectile points. The house type is unknown. Stone-chambered earth-covered mounds with cremated and secondary skeletal materials on the nearby bluff tops were probably associated with these villages. A long-headed population is inferred. Maize and beans were grown, but the nature of the cultivating tools used has not been determined. Radiocarbon dates tend to cluster in the first five centuries of the Christian Era, with median readings in the third and fourth centuries AD. At least two chambered mound complexes have been radiocarbon dated to the same period.

The Kansas City locale, centering around the junction of the Kansas River and the Missouri, appears to have been a major focus of Hopewellian activity in the region, and a semipermanent residence pattern may be inferred. Related sites about which very little is known occur westward up the Kansas River, north up the Missouri, and south and southwestward into the Arkansas River drainage. In northeastern Oklahoma, the Delaware County locale and the Cooper site (Bell and Baerreis, 1951:27) appear to have been another center of some importance, but the scatter of seven radiocarbon dates at Cooper from 1460 BC to AD 1270 is unacceptably early and late. Oblong posthole patterns attributed to the Cooper variant in southeastern Kansas have been identified as house structures (Marshall, 1972).

Other Woodland complexes in the Central Plains usually have a simpler material-culture inventory (Hill and Kivett, 1941; Kivett, 1952, 1953, 1970).

The Keith-focus and Valley-focus variants are characterized by small sites with small basins identified as possible habitations; by stemmed and corner-notched points that include a somewhat varied assortment of medium to large corner-notched and smaller well-made stemmed "Scallorn-like" forms; and by thick, cord-roughened pottery in large, vertically elongate jars, with calcite tempering usually distinguishing Harlan cord-roughened Keith pottery from Valley ware. Loseke Creek ware often has a rim decoration of single-cord impressions. Charred maize has been found in at least one site. Burials are of various kinds. Keith-focus connections have been assigned to ossuary pits with secondary burials, unmarked by surface mounds and accompanied by shell disk beads and blanks, shell pendants, and chipped stone artifacts (Kivett, 1953). In eastern Nebraska and northeastern Kansas, massed, bundle, and disarticulated burials beneath low, inconspicuous earth mounds that commonly contain evidence of fire are thought to be Woodland affiliated (Hill and Kivett, 1941; Kivett, 1952). The disarticulated bones of multiple burials, some burned, in submound pits in northeastern Nebraska have been attributed to Loseke Creek (Price, n.d.). The Taylor mound, with its ritual interment of seven skulls in a slab cist, is identified as Valley-focus affiliated and is dated to the first century AD. The possibility that these wide variations in burial methods may reflect class distinctions has been suggested (O'Brien, 1971).

The westerly manifestations of Plains Woodland culture in eastern Colorado are becoming better known from several studies. Burial practices and their relationships to Plains complexes elsewhere have been discussed by Breternitz and Wood (1965) and by Scott and Birkedal (1972). Settlement patterns, including rockshelters, mountaintop sites, and open camps, have been analyzed by D. Scott (1973). Hunting and gathering subsistence systems seem generally indicated, with bison procurement in evidence. Charred corncob from Culture complex B at LoDaisKa (Irwin and Irwin, 1959) is assigned to Woodland, but the nature of the cultivation and processing tools used is unclear. Woodland pottery, millingstones, weapon points, and other materials associated with bison and deer bones have been located in post-Piney-Creek alluvium near Kassler, Colorado, and dated at AD 460 (G. Scott, 1962, 1963).

In the Southern Plains of Oklahoma and Texas, Woodland materials or their local contemporary complexes have been found in several stratigraphic contexts. At Duncan–Wilson Rockshelter (Lawton, 1968) in Caddo County, Oklahoma, some 4 meters of fill included a succession of human occupations dated back to approximately AD 430 by radiocarbon and to about AD 220 by extrapolation. Cord-roughened Woodland sherds appear in Levels 15-23 (Level 1 being the top) at about AD 520-870, along with the first appearance of antelope bone. Various nondiagnostic materials occur sparsely at lower levels, including mostly small animal bones and stemmed projectile points identified as Ellis, Gary, and Bulverde. Immediately above, in Levels 10-12 at about AD 827-1070, along with the first indications of bison hunting were found plain potsherds, shaft smoothers, and arrowpoints of Fresno, Washito, Scallorn, and Gary types.

These materials impress one as being closer to the Washita-focus materials from the later levels of about AD 1070–1612.

In the Texas panhandle, rockshelter and campsite locations include complexes dated in the first 10 centuries of the Christian Era. Associated with these complexes are small stemmed or corner-notched "Scallorn-like" points, brown plainware pottery apparently related to New Mexico wares, and limited inventories, generally. At Chalk Hollow the upper midden to about 120 centimeters below ground surface, which was radiocarbon dated between AD 370 and 785, yielded plano-convex scrapers; bifacial chipped knives; milling slabs and mullers of various sizes; split mammal bone awls; bone gaming pieces; obsidian; unformalized hearths with much burned stone; debitage including Alibates agatized dolomite, Tecovas flint, Edwards Plateau chert, and so on; and animal bone in highly variable amounts that included bison, an occasional cervid or pronghorn, coyote or wolf, and unidentified small rodents. A sort of transhumance is perhaps to be inferred here, with regular and repeated winter residence in the protected canyon alternating with spring, summer, and fall residence on the nearby wind-swept uplands, including the shores of the many waterholes now represented by mostly dry playas. The Woodland period materials here follow an 800-year break marked by sterile colluvial deposits, beneath which is a series of short-lived Archaic levels. There are other small sites nearby (Hughes, personal communication), recently dated but still unreported. The changes at these sites in projectile point forms and sizes, from the Archaic to Woodland times, are thought to reflect the transition from the Late Archaic dart weapons system to a Middle or Late Woodland bow and arrow system.

The Woodland influences in the eastern Plains, as reflected in the pottery, burial mounds, and incipient horticulture, did not overspread the Northwestern Plains. Hunting, gathering, and communal bison driving continued in the latter area through the final stages of the Late Middle Prehistoric and into the Early Late Prehistoric period. Local variants at this stage are represented in rockshelters at Mummy Cave level 36 (AD 720), Wedding of the Waters Cave (Frison, 1962), Pictograph Cave II (Mulloy, 1958), Birdshead Cave II and III (Bliss, 1950), Daugherty and Spring Creek caves near Ten Sleep, Wyoming (Frison, 1965, 1968), and in open stratified campsites at McKean Upper and Signal Butte II. A shift in weapons seems to be indicated at this period, with medium-sized stemmed or corner-notched points giving way to smaller types. Definite evidence of the atlatl has been reported from Spring Creek Cave in the Big Horn Mountains by Frison (1965) at about AD 225. Here, in a single-component deposit, associated materials include dart shafts and foreshafts, coiled basketry, bits of sinew, worked bark, tanned skin, porcupine quill work, and several obliquely worn pole butts with wear patterns suggesting use as dog travois frames. The widespread practice of communal bison hunting at this period is indicated by Kobold III and Wardell bison kills in Wyoming (Frison, 1970, 1973), at Old Women's Buffalo Jump in Alberta (Forbis, 1962), and by a number of sites in Saskatchewan (Kehoe, 1973). In and around the Big Horn

Basin, bone refuse includes much bison, as well as elk, pronghorn, mountain sheep, rabbit, and vegetal foods. From surface finds, it appears that many sites show strong similarities to the Spring Creek Cave complex, but with significant variations in proportions of tool types. Mountain sites tend to have more weapon points and more cutting, scraping, and skin-dressing tools. Badlands and open flatland sites have more millingstones and roasting pits, inferentially for the processing of vegetal foods and small game, both of which were utilized when the larger game in the mountains was not readily available or was seasonally absent.

Widely scattered throughout the eastern Dakotas and southern Manitoba, mostly east and northeast of the Coteau du Missouri but occurring in lesser numbers westward to the Missouri River trench, are mounds and earthworks that differ from those farther south. They vary greatly in size, construction, and contents, with radiocarbon dates ranging from about 500 BC to about AD 1000. They include linears and conicals, with burials found in both. Log-covered submound pits are common. Particularly noteworthy is the frequent occurrence of bison skeletons or skulls, seldom found in burial mounds farther south. This occurrence suggests that the bison held an extremely important position in the lifeways of the people involved—perhaps more so than among the Woodland people farther south. One wonders whether bison were perhaps more abundant in the northern, northwestern, and western Plains at this time period than they were farther south, where other foods were drawn upon to a greater degree and the bison may never have achieved comparable ritual or economic importance.

The mounds of this subarea are generally related to complexes better known in the Minnesota region, with Blackduck and Arvilla affiliations variously suggested. In a penetrating analysis of southern Manitoba mound materials and data collected by Nickerson in the early 1900s, Capes (1963) has concluded that the Manitoba mounds were the work of closely related peoples operating under influences dating back to Middle Woodland times. Ossenberg (1974:37), using discrete traits in human cranial samples from Minnesota and the adjacent Plains, concludes that they represent "a cluster of closely related populations ancestral to the Dakota, Assiniboin, Cheyenne, and possibly Blackfoot," and that their affinity to Illinois Hopewell, sometimes postulated from the log-covered submound burial pits, is weak.

The Besant and Avonlea complexes (Joyes, 1970; Kehoe and McCorquodale, 1961) are coeval southern Canadian equivalents of the Plains Woodland complexes farther south. Cord-roughened pottery in Besant levels at about AD 350 has been noted as similar in some respects to Keith-focus pottery in the Central Plains (Kehoe, 1964). Avonlea sites have been broadly characterized (Kehoe and Kehoe, 1968:23) as the earliest evidence for the "complex, ritualized, planned bison drives" in the Late Prehistoric Plains. The same observers regard the Athabascans as probably responsible for introducing into the northern Plains the bow and arrow, complex ritualized bison drives, and the small-point weapons system.

THE PLAINS VILLAGE INDIANS (AD 900–1850)

From at least the tenth century of the Christian Era, and possibly as early as the eighth or ninth, the Woodland complexes of the eastern Plains were giving way to, or perhaps developing into, others of more sedentary character. These later complexes involved settlements of substantial structures scattered along the permanent streams throughout much of the tall- and mid-grass prairies from the Dakotas to Texas, and westward into the short-grass plains of eastern Colorado. Throughout, a dual subsistence strategy was followed, involving in varying proportions the horticultural potential of the arable stream bottoms and the game and wild vegetal resources of the wooded bottomlands and the nearby grassy uplands. To these complexes the term *Plains Village Indians* has been applied (Lehmer, 1954a, b). The Plains Village Indians' way of life, with many modifications in time and space, dominated the eastern Plains for nearly a thousand years. Their contemporaries in the western and northwestern Plains were an assortment of foraging and hunting groups, living in transient or portable dwellings, most or all lacking maize, a few with pottery, and many continuing the pursuit of bison by jumps, pounds, and in other ways—in effect continuing the relatively unspectacular, austere, but presumably effective subsistence economies that had been followed since Altithermal times.

Shared by practically all of the Plains Village complexes were (1) the construction of fixed multifamily lodges, generally larger and more substantially built than the inferred habitations of the Woodland peoples; (2) residence for most of the year in permanent settlements, sometimes fortified with dry moats and stockades and usually containing numbers of underground storage pits; (3) pottery of varied character; and (4) a wide range of artifacts in stone, bone, horn, shell, and other materials. The bone hoe, varying in details of manufacture but usually made from a bison scapula, was a particularly characteristic tool, lingering on into the historic period to compete with the iron hoe introduced by the whites. Throughout the Plains generally, the small, triangular arrowpoints of this period, with or without side notches, are easily differentiated from the weapons of earlier times; also, the plano-convex end scraper became a common item in this period, judging by the artifact inventory. In the fifteenth or sixteenth century, there seem to have been widespread changes in house form, settlement pattern, and perhaps other aspects of the visible record, dating both before and after arrival of the whites.

The Middle Missouri

The early Village Indian period lacks any evidence of white contact and is everywhere marked by square or rectangular house floors and grit-tempered pottery. On the Middle Missouri, complexes represented by such taxonomic units as the Monroe, Anderson, Thomas Riggs, and Huff foci have been organized by Lehmer (1971) into a Middle Missouri tradition. This tradition consists in turn of two major subdivisions—the Initial Middle Missouri (hereafter cited as *IMM*) and the Extended Middle Missouri (EMM). Most IMM sites—including the Over, Anderson, and Monroe foci and the Grand Detour phase—are in South Dakota, either on the mainstem or along the James and Big Sioux rivers; EMM variants—including Archaic Mandan, Thomas Riggs, and Fort Yates foci—are in North Dakota. Long, rectangular semisubterranean houses, with floor area not uncommonly exceeding 90 square meters, are characteristic of both; settlement patterns differ mainly in details. Burial methods for both are unknown, and artifact types are basically very similar except for minutiae of interest mainly to specialists. Largely on the basis of radiocarbon dates, a time span for IMM of about AD 950–1300 was initially proposed (Lehmer, 1971:95); for EMM, sites seemed to be bimodally distributed between about AD 1100–1250 and again at AD 1450–1550. Tree-ring dates from South Dakota sites have been interpreted as indicating markedly different and shorter time spans (Weakly, 1971).

With additional dates, it now appears that while IMM may have been present as early as the ninth or tenth century, both major variants of the Middle Missouri tradition coexisted for most of their respective life spans. The IMM people, represented by no fewer than 35 known sites, are thought to have reached the Missouri valley from southwestern Minnesota and northwestern Iowa and may have been "the only village complex in the Middle Missouri for perhaps two centuries" (Lehmer, 1971:98). From the same general homeland came the EMM immigrants, who settled farther up the main stem in North Dakota. As both groups expanded, they eventually came into confrontation in the Bad–Cheyenne district, where fortified settlements are seen as reflecting a conflict situation.

In the fifteenth century, people abandoning the Central Plains because of drought moved into the Middle Missouri region, introducing new house forms such as the four-post earth lodge and other culture elements. The merging of new ideas and people with local groups gave rise to the Coalescent tradition. This, in turn, spread northward up the Missouri, passing through a series of temporal variants between about AD 1450 and 1680. Its later stages, termed the *Post-Contact Coalescent* and involving the Arikara of history, represent the heyday of Village Indian culture on the Middle Missouri. Farther north, the Mandan and Hidatsa can be traced back into the Terminal Middle Missouri, an outgrowth of IMM and EMM that coexisted in part with the later stages of the Coalescent tradition.

The archeological record—greatly amplified and enriched since 1946 by the Interagency Salvage Program (Wedel, 1967) on the Missouri River—has made clear the lengthy and complex history of the Village Indians in the subregion. Heavily dependent on maize growing and on bison hunting, and living near the northern limits of successful agriculture, these groups would have been particularly susceptible to the well-known vagaries of the Plains climate. They had moved from the woodlands onto the Plains during the Neo-Atlantic climatic episode, when abundant rains would have encouraged corn-growing. Their varied responses to subsequent fluctuations in terms of the climatic model proposed by Bryson and his coworkers (Bryson and Wendland, 1967) have been noted by Lehmer (1970) and others. A thoughtful evaluation of these northern Plains Village cultures is Wood's recent (1974) study.

The Central Plains

In the Central Plains, early Village Indian manifestations include the Upper Republican and Nebraska aspects or phases, the Smoky Hill aspect, and a more recently defined Pomona phase in eastern Kansas. Collectively, these comprise the Central Plains tradition, with most radiocarbon dates in the AD 1000–1400 span (Wedel, 1961, n.d.b; Brown, 1967; Gradwohl, 1969). The first three named units are characterized by square or rectangular houses with rounded corners, quite unlike the long rectangular dwellings of the Middle Missouri people. Villages are generally smaller, unfortified, and less compactly built; houses, especially in the Upper Republican phase, are smaller, commonly from 36 to 67.5 square meters in area. Cord-roughened or plain-surfaced pottery is characteristic, but contacts with a Middle Mississippi complex in northwestern Missouri (Wedel, 1943) introduced shell tempering and other exotic traits to nearby contemporary Nebraska-aspect and Smoky Hill cultures.

Dating of these complexes is still inadequate, as is knowledge of their taxonomic interrelationships. Most Upper Republican mean dates fall between AD 1100 and 1250; but these pertain mainly to a small cluster of sites at Medicine Creek reservoir, Nebraska. Whether these sites truly indicate the life span of Upper Republican throughout their area of occurrence remains to be tested. Time perspective has been injected into the picture by operations at Glen Elder reservoir, Kansas, where Krause (1970) recognizes a Solomon River phase at between the ninth and thirteenth centuries AD and a Classic Republican phase between the eleventh and fifteenth centuries. Seven radiocarbon dates precede AD 900, six follow AD 1250; if validated by further evidence, they would suggest a split occupancy of the Solomon River district, one preceding and the other following the dated Upper Republican occupancy at Medicine Creek. They suggest, also, that Village Indian occupancy began about as early in the Central Plains as on the Middle Missouri, and raise again the possibility of Late Woodland–Upper Republican contacts or transitional stages. The wide distribution of Upper Republican remains, with most sites showing relatively small quantities of refuse, suggests short occupancies and frequent moves to new localities. Their apparent abundance in Nebraska, northern Kansas, and eastern Colorado may actually reflect a relatively small and scattered population. Living mostly in hamlets and single lodges, these people may have moved frequently from one site or district to another, leaving previous habitats essentially unoccupied and unmarked except by decaying earth lodges and trash. Additional radiocarbon dates from other Upper Republican localities, with multiple assays to reduce error, are urgently needed to test this thesis. It has been also suggested (Wood, 1969) that the Upper Republican sites were seasonally inhabited by semihorticultural groups who were compelled by limited local food resources to engage in communal bison hunts at more western locales. At such times the earth lodge villages may have been abandoned in accord with a pattern well established for such historic village tribes as the Pawnee, Omaha, and Kansa. This thesis still lacks acceptable supporting evidence, however (Wedel, 1970).

Despite some later dates, it seems likely that the western Upper Republican communities were largely abandoned in the thirteenth century, perhaps because of drought (Wedel, 1941, 1953). That these drought conditions were real and probably widespread now seems increasingly likely (Bryson et al., 1970). Whether the victims migrated to the Middle Missouri, to the Texas–Oklahoma panhandle, or elsewhere, as has been variously postulated, still remains unclear and will continue to be unclear until a great deal more fieldwork is undertaken in the still little-known intervening regions.

The Southern Plains

In the Southern Plains, there are greatly improved perspectives on the early Village cultures and their interrelationships (Bell and Baerreis, 1951; Buck, 1959; Pillaert, 1963; Bell, 1962, 1973; Schneider, 1969). The Washita River and Custer focuses and the Panhandle aspect all share the rectangular house forms, cord-roughened and plain pottery, and various other material culture traits of the contemporary Village complexes of the Central Plains and Middle Missouri subregions. There are significant differences in detail, however, which assume greater significance as more radiocarbon dates provide better chronological controls. Bell (1962), noting that bison bones are much more plentiful in archeological sites after about AD 1000–1200, has suggested that the Village Indians may have been attracted to the western grasslands from eastern Oklahoma by the increased bison populations and the consequent better hunting that could supplement their already well-developed semisedentary prairie economy. Population pressures in the East may have been a contributing factor. This movement would have been approximately coincident with the apparent abandonment of the Middle Pecos valley by farming Indians and a shift in subsistence economy to bison hunting on the Plains (Jelinek, 1966).

Far too few radiocarbon dates are available for the Oklahoma Village cultures, but it seems likely that the Washita River and Custer focuses were sequent rather than contemporary. The few available Washita dates fall between AD 1100 and 1375; Custer dates between AD 800 and 950. From these figures, Hofman (1975) suggests that out of a Woodland (for example, Pruitt-like) culture base of pottery use and incipient horticulture, with a continued heavy reliance on hunting and gathering and seasonal change of camps, developed the Custer complex with increased emphasis on horticulture, a shift from cord-roughened to smoothed pottery of more varied kinds, and the appearance of bison scapula hoes and bone digging stick tips. In the later Washita River focus sites, there is a marked increase in the number of bone hoes and digging stick tips as well as the first appearance of bison horn core hoes, perhaps implying intensified crop growing. The disappearance from the Oklahoma region of the Washita-River-focus peoples during the fourteenth century, about the time the Spiro ceremonial center climaxed (AD 1350–1400), has been tentatively attributed to drought conditions (Wedel, 1961; Lorrain, 1967) and, more recently, to arrival in western Oklahoma of alien peoples who may have been ancestral Apache or Kiowa (Bell, 1973).

In the Panhandle culture an exotic non-Plains or pseudo-Puebloan architectural style has been associated with an otherwise more or less typical Plains Village material culture complex. The Panhandle culture has been placed in more meaningful perspective largely through an extensive series of radiocarbon dates (Bender et al., 1966, 1967; Pearson et al., 1966). Mean dates range from AD 1120 to 1620; site averages and most individual means run from AD 1250 to 1450. The close correspondence between the beginning date here and the terminal dates of (Medicine Creek) Upper Republican in Nebraska has been noted by Bryson et al. (1970:69), who argue on statistical grounds for a climatic shift after about AD 1160–1200 whereby dry conditions unfavorable to maize growing in Nebraska were offset by wetter climate in the panhandle. They also argue that the drought-stricken Upper Republican peoples migrated to the latter area to continue their semihorticultural economy. Despite some attractive features, this thesis has yet to be supported by convincing archeological evidence.

In the late Village Indian complexes of the eastern Plains (those postdating the sixteenth century) can be recognized the archeological manifestations of the major historic tribal entities of the region. In the north, the Mandan, Hidatsa, and Arikara were the final development from the Middle Missouri tradition (Lehmer, 1971). Farther south, the Pawnees were rooted in the Central Plains tradition through the Lower Loup phase (Wedel, 1938; Grange, 1968), the relationships of which to the earlier Upper Republican and contemporary Middle Missouri complexes still await clarification. In the Kansas-Oklahoma–Texas area, the Wichita tribes who dominated the western Arkansas River drainage can be traced back to the Great Bend (Wedel, 1959, 1968) and Norteño (Jelks et al., 1967) phases and, on an earlier time level, to the Washita River–Custer–Panhandle and perhaps Henrietta complexes. In the western Plains, the Dismal River culture is widely, but not unanimously, regarded as Plains Apache (J. Gunnerson, 1968; Schlesier, 1972; Opler, 1975). Along the eastern margin, the Oneota materials have been tentatively identified with various Siouan tribes— the Fanning site with the Kansa, the Leary site with Oto, and the Stanton site with Omaha. The historical legacy of the easternmost expression of the Central Plains tradition—the Nebraska phase—is still unclear, as are its relationships to the later, or longer-lasting, Oneota remains in the same region.

In the western Plains, beyond the erstwhile Village Indian territory, the Late Prehistoric and Historic periods are manifested in the often scantily represented remains of the nomadic bison hunters. Late arrivals in the region, of diverse linguistic and cultural origins, these people found it most advantageous to operate in accord with bison-hunting systems that were already old in the buffalo country. It is not yet clear who among these groups or their late prehistoric forerunners may have been responsible for the innumerable stone tipi rings, boulder alignments, medicine wheels, and pictographs that add a measure of distinctiveness to the Northwestern Plains. The likelihood that some of these features have astronomical implications is of interest (Eddy, 1974). The numerous and widespread bison jumps and pounds, with their attendant ritual embellishments, for which archeological evidence is beginning to accumulate at earlier time levels, were quite possibly the response to an accelerated influx of human groups. The influx could have been furthered by introduction of the horse or by a sharply expanding bison population that may have peaked throughout the Plains during the historic period (D. Gunnerson, 1972). It is very possible that climatically favored localities in the northern Plains produced an abundance of animals unmatched at any other period of human occupation in the Great Plains (Reher, 1978).

SUMMARY

Despite enormous spatial and temporal lacunae in our information, archeology is confirming an ever more impressive depth of time for prehistoric peoples' occupation of the Great Plains. It is clear, too, that this occupation was subject to constant cultural change, reflecting in part adaptations to climatic and other fluctuations in the natural environment. Occupation was certainly underway more than 11,000 years ago by hunters of the last of the mammoths (Martin and Wright, 1967) and, later, of giant bison in the western Plains. That bison were utilized in quantity on the eastern margin of the Plains by 7000 or 8000 years ago is clear, too, and a regional pattern may be inferred even for the intervening localities from which evidence is still lacking. In the western short-grass plains, hunting economies centering on bison procurement by individual and communal systems alike seem to have been the mainstay of human existence throughout. There was, however, an Altithermal interlude when bison and human populations both seem to have declined. Few archeological sites of this period are known, except in the fringing mountain areas.

Farther east, bison were supplemented by other game animals and relatively abundant vegetal foods that were not generally available except in limited quantities in the short-grass country. Here, eventually, under appropriate environmental conditions, food-producing subsistence economies based on a maize-bean–squash triad were developed or introduced, and greater population aggregates and densities resulted. Trade relations between these communities and the western nomads, whereby horticultural products were exchanged for those from the chase, became increasingly important; introduction of the horse greatly accelerated these interactions. The wealth of solid information pertaining to the Village Indians that has accumulated through nearly four decades of salvage archeology in the northern Plains can be expected to develop new meaning from the belated recognition of the nature and quality of the archeological record now being pieced together in the bison plains from the Rio Grande to Canada. From the ever-changing perspectives of archeology (Wedel, 1982), the bison rather than the horse was responsible for native peoples' successful occupancy of the Great Plains.

References Cited and Recommended Sources

Albertson, F. W., G. W. Tomanek, and Andrew Riegel. 1957. Ecology of drought cycles and grazing intensity on grasslands of central Great Plains. *Ecological Monographs* 27:27–44.

———, and J. E. Weaver. 1945. Injury and death or recovery of trees in prairie climate. *Ecological Monographs* 15:394–433.

Arthur, George W. 1975. An introduction to the ecology of early historic communal bison hunting among the northern Plains Indians. Archaeological Survey of Canada, Paper No. 37. National Museums of Canada, Ottawa.

Ayer, Mrs. Edward E. (transl.). 1916. *The Memorial of Fray Alonso de Benavides, 1630.* Chicago: privately printed.

Baerreis, D. A., and R. A. Bryson. 1965. Historical climatology and the Southern Plains: a preliminary statement. *Bulletin, Oklahoma Anthropological Society* 13:69–75.

———, and ———. 1966. Dating the Panhandle Aspect cultures. *Bulletin, Oklahoma Anthropological Society* 14:105–116.

Bell, Robert E. 1962. Precolumbian prairie settlements in the Great Plains. *Great Plains Journal* 2:1:22–28.

———. 1968. Dating the prehistory of Oklahoma. *Great Plains Journal* 7:2:1–11.

———. 1973. The Washita River focus of the Southern Plains. In *Variation in Anthropology*, ed. Lathrap and Douglas, pp. 171–187. Illinois Archeological Survey.

———, and David A. Baerreis. 1951. A survey of Oklahoma archeology. *Bulletin, Texas Archeological and Paleontological Society* 22:7–100.

Bender, Margaret M., Reid A. Bryson, and David A. Baerreis. 1966. University of Wisconsin radiocarbon dates II. *Radiocarbon* 8:522–533.

———, ———, and ———. 1967. University of Wisconsin radiocarbon dates III. *Radiocarbon* 9:530–544.

Bliss, Wesley L. 1950. Birdshead Cave, a stratified site in Wind River Basin, Wyoming. *American Antiquity* 15:3:187–196.

Borchert, J. R. 1950. The climate of the central North American grassland. *Annals of the Association of American Geographers* 40:1:1–39.

Breternitz, David A. 1969. Radiocarbon dates: eastern Colorado. *Plains Anthropologist* 14:44:1:113–124.

———, and John J. Wood. 1965. Comments on the Bisterfeldt potato cellar site and flexed burials in the western Plains. *Southwestern Lore* 31:3:62–66.

Brown, Lionel. 1967. *Pony Creek Archeology.* Publications in Salvage Archeology no. 5. River Basin Surveys. Washington, D.C.: The Smithsonian Institution.

Bryson, Reid A., D. A. Baerreis, and W. M. Wendland. 1970. The character of late-glacial and post-glacial climatic changes. In *Pleistocene and Recent Environments of the Central Great Plains,* ed. W. Dort, Jr., and J. K. Jones, Jr., pp. 53–74. Special Publication no. 3, Department of Geology, University of Kansas.

———, and W. M. Wendland. 1967. Tentative climatic patterns for some late glacial and post-glacial episodes in central North America. In *Life, Land, and Water,* ed. W. J. Mayer-Oakes, pp. 271–298. Winnipeg: University of Manitoba Press.

Buck, Arthur Dewey, Jr. 1959. The Custer focus of the Southern Plains. *Bulletin, Oklahoma Anthropological Society* 7:1–31.

Capes, Katherine H. 1963. *The W. B. Nickerson Survey and Excavations, 1912–1915, of Southern Manitoba Mounds Region.* National Museum of Canada, Anthropology Papers no. 4.

Coupland, Robert T. 1958. The effects of fluctuations in weather upon the grasslands of the Great Plains. *Botanical Review* 24:5:273–317.

Davis, E. Mott. 1962. *Archeology of the Lime Creek Site in Southwestern Nebraska.* Special Publication no. 3, University of Nebraska State Museum.

Dibble, David S. 1970. On the significance of additional radiocarbon dates from Bonfire Shelter, Texas. *Plains Anthropologist* 15:50:251–254.

———, and D. Lorrain. 1968. *Bonfire Shelter: A Stratified Bison Kill Site, Val Verde County, Texas.* Miscellaneous Papers no. 1. Austin: Texas Memorial Museum.

Dillehay, Tom D. 1974. Late Quaternary bison population changes on the Southern Plains. *Plains Anthropologist* 19:65:180–196.

Eddy, John A. 1974. Astronomical alignment of the Big Horn medicine wheel. *Science* 184: 4141:1035–1043.

Ellison, L., and E. J. Woolfolk. 1937. Effects of drought on vegetation near Miles City, Montana. *Ecology* 18:3:329–336.

Farb, Peter. 1968. *Man's Rise to Civilization as Shown by the Indians of North America from Primeval Times to the Coming of the Industrial State.* New York: Dutton.

Flannery, K. V. 1968. Archeological systems theory and early Mesoamerica. In *Anthropological Archeology in the Americas,* ed B. J. Meggers, pp. 67–87. Anthropological Society of Washington.

Forbis, Richard G. 1962. The Old Women's Buffalo Jump, Alberta. National Museum of Canada, Bulletin 180, *Contributions to Anthropology, 1960,* part I, pp. 55–123. Ottawa: Canada Department of Northern Affairs and National Resources.

———. 1968. Alberta. In *The Northwestern Plains: A Symposium,* ed. W. W. Caldwell, pp. 37–44. Occasional Papers no. 1, Center for Indian Studies. Billings, Mont.: Rocky Mountain College.

Frankforter, W. D., and G. A. Agogino. 1960. The Simonsen site: report for the summer of 1959. *Plains Anthropologist* 5:10:65–70.

Frison, George C. 1962. Wedding of the Waters Cave, 48HO301, a stratified site in the Big Horn Basin of northern Wyoming. *Plains Anthropologist* 7:18:246–265.

———. 1965. Spring Creek Cave, Wyoming. *American Antiquity* 31:1:81–94.

———. 1968. Daughterty Cave, Wyoming. *Plains Anthropologist* 13:42:1:253–295.

———. 1970. The Kobold site, 24BH406: a post-Altithermal record of buffalo jumping for the Northwestern Plains. *Plains Anthropologist* 15:47:1–35.

———. 1971. The bison pound in Northwestern Plains prehistory. *American Antiquity* 36:1:77–91.

———. 1972. The role of buffalo procurement in post-Altithermal populations on the Northwestern Plains. In *Social Exchange and Interaction,* ed. E. N. Wilmsen, pp. 11–19. University of Michigan Museum of Anthropology, Anthropological Papers no. 46.

———. 1973. *The Wardell Buffalo Trap 48SU301: Communal Procurement in the Upper Green River Basin, Wyoming.* University of Michigan Museum of Anthropology, Anthropological Papers no. 48.

———. 1974. *The Casper Site: A Hell Gap Bison Kill on the High Plains.* New York: Academic Press.

———. 1975. Man's interaction with Holocene environments on the Plains. *Quaternary Research* 5:2:289–300.

———. 1978. *Prehistoric Hunters of the High Plains.* New York: Academic Press.

———, and Michael Wilson. 1975. An introduction to Bighorn Basin archeology. *Wyoming Geological Association Guidebook,* 27th Annual Field Conference—1975, pp. 19–35.

Frye, John C., and A. Byron Leonard. 1952. *Pleistocene Geology of Kansas.* Bulletin 99, University of Kansas State Geological Survey.

Gradwohl, David M. 1969. *Prehistoric Villages in Eastern Nebraska.* Publications in Anthropology no. 4, Nebraska State Historical Society.

Grange, Roger T., Jr. 1968. *Pawnee and Lower Loup Pottery.* Publications in Anthropology no. 3. Nebraska State Historical Society.

———. 1980. *Archeological Investigations in the Red Willow Reservoir, Nebraska.* Publications in Anthropology no. 9. Lincoln: Nebraska State Historical Society.

Gunnerson, Dolores A. 1956. The southern Athabascans: their arrival in the Southwest. *El Palacio* 63:11–12:346–365.

———. 1972. Man and bison on the Plains in the prehistoric period. *Plains Anthropologist* 17:55:1–10.

Gunnerson, James H. 1968. Plains Apache archaeology: a review. *Plains Anthropologist* 13:41:167–189.

Hammond, George P., and Agapito Rey. 1953. *Don Juan de Oñate, Colonizer of New Mexico 1598–1628.* Albuquerque: Coronado Cuarto Centennial Publications, 1540–1940, vols. V and VI.

Haynes, C. Vance, Jr. 1964. Fluted projectile points: their age and dispersion. *Science* 145: 3639:1408–1413.

Hester, James J. 1972. *Blackwater Locality No. 1, a Stratified Early Man Site in Eastern New Mexico.* Dallas: Fort Burgwin Research Center, Southern Methodist University.

Hill, A. T., and Marvin F. Kivett. 1941. Woodland-like manifestations in Nebraska. *Nebraska History Magazine* 21:3:146–243.

Hind, Henry Youle. 1859. *Northwest Territory.* Reports of progress; together with a preliminary and general report on the Assiniboine and Saskatchewan exploring expedition, made under instructions from the Provincial Secretary, Canada.

Hofman, Jack L. 1975. A study of Custer–Washita River foci relationships. *Plains Anthropologist* 20:67:41–51.

Hough, Walter. 1930. The bison as a factor in ancient American cultural history. *Scientific Monthly* 30:315–319.

Humphrey, Robert L., and Dennis Stanford. 1979. *Pre-Llano Cultures of the Americas: Paradoxes and Possibilities.* Washington, D.C.: Anthropological Society of Washington.

Hurt, Wesley R. 1966. The Altithermal and the prehistory of the northern Plains. *Quaternaria* 8:101–113.

Irwin, Henry T. 1970. Archeological investigations at the Union Pacific mammoth kill site, Wyoming, 1961. *National Geographic Society Research Reports 1961–1962:*123–125.

———. 1971. Developments in early man studies in western North America, 1960–1970. *Arctic Anthropology* 8:2:42–67.

———, and C. C. Irwin. 1959. *Excavations at the LoDaisKa Site in the Denver, Colorado, Area.* Denver Museum of Natural History, Proceedings no. 8.

Irwin-Williams, C., H. T. Irwin, G. Agogino, and C. V. Haynes. 1973. Hell Gap: Paleo-Indian occupation on the High Plains. *Plains Anthropologist* 18:59:40–53.

Jelinek, Arthur J. 1966. Correlation of archeological and palynological data. *Science* 152: 3728:1507–1509.

Jelks, E. B. (ed.). 1967. *The Gilbert Site, a Norteño Focus Site in Northeastern Texas.* Bulletin, Texas Archeological Society, vol. 37.

Johnson, A. E., and A. S. Johnson. 1975. K-Means and temporal variability in Kansas City Hopewell ceramics. *American Antiquity* 40:3:283–295.

Joyes, Dennis C. 1970. The culture sequence at the Avery site at Rock Lake. In *Ten Thousand Years, Archaeology in Manitoba,* ed. W. M. Hlady, pp. 209–222. Manitoba Archaeological Society.

Judge, W. J., and J. Dawson. 1972. Paleo-Indian settlement technology in New Mexico. *Science* 176:1210–1216.

Kehoe, Thomas F. 1964. Middle Woodland pottery from Saskatchewan. *Plains Anthropologist* 9:23:51–53.

———. 1967. *The Boarding School Bison Drive Site.* Memoir 4, Plains Anthropologist.

———. 1973. *The Gull Lake Site: A Prehistoric Bison Drive Site in Southwestern Saskatchewan.* Publications in Anthropology and History no. 1, Milwaukee Public Museum.

————, and Alice B. Kehoe. 1968. Saskatchewan. In *The Northwestern Plains: A Symposium,* ed. W. W. Caldwell, pp. 21–35. Occasional Papers no. 1, Center for Indian Studies. Billings, Mont.: Rocky Mountain College.

————, and Bruce A. McCorquodale. 1961. The Avonlea Point, horizon marker for the Northwestern Plains. *Plains Anthropologist* 6:13:179–188.

Kivett, Marvin F. 1952. *Woodland Sites in Nebraska.* Publications in Anthropology no. 1. Nebraska State Historical Society.

————. 1953. *The Woodruff Ossuary, a Prehistoric Burial Site in Phillips County, Kansas.* No. 3, Bureau of American Ethnology Bulletin 154, River Basin Surveys Papers.

————. 1970. Early ceramic environmental adaptations. In *Pleistocene and Recent Environments of the Central Great Plains,* ed. W. Dort, Jr. and J. K. Jones, Jr., pp. 93–102. Special Publication no. 3, Department of Geology, University of Kansas.

Krause, Richard A. 1970. Aspects of adaptation among Upper Republican subsistence cultivators. In *Pleistocene and Recent Environments of the Central Great Plains,* ed. W. Dort, Jr., and J. K. Jones, Jr., pp. 103–115. Lawrence: University Press of Kansas.

Krieger, Alex D. 1950. A suggested general sequence in North American projectile points. In *Proceedings, 6th Plains Archaeological Conference, 1948,* ed. J. D. Jennings, pp. 117–124. University of Utah Anthropological Papers no. 11.

Lawton, Sherman P. 1968. The Duncan–Wilson bluff shelter: a stratified site of the Southern Plains. *Bulletin, Oklahoma Anthropological Society* 16:1–94.

Lehmer, Donald J. 1954a. *Archeological Investigations in the Oahe Dam Area, South Dakota, 1950–1951.* Bureau of American Ethnology, Bulletin 158, River Basin Surveys Papers no. 7.

————. 1954b. The sedentary horizon of the northern Plains. *Southwestern Journal of Anthropology* 10:2:139–159.

————. 1963. The Plains bison hunt—prehistoric and historic. *Plains Anthropologist* 8:22:211–217.

————. 1970. Climate and culture history in the Middle Missouri valley. In *Pleistocene and Recent Environments of the Central Great Plains,* ed. W. Dort, Jr., and J. K. Jones, Jr., pp. 117–129. Special Publication no. 3, Department of Geology, University of Kansas.

————. 1971. *Introduction to Middle Missouri Archeology.* Anthropology Papers 1, National Park Service, U.S. Department of the Interior.

Leonhardy, Frank C. (ed.). 1966. *Domebo: A Paleo-Indian Mammoth Kill in the Prairie–Plains.* Lawton, Okla: Contributions of the Museum of the Great Plains, no. 1.

Lewis, G. Malcolm. 1975. The recognition and delimitation of the northern interior grasslands during the 18th century. In *Images of the Plains,* ed. B. W. Blouet and M. P. Lawson, pp. 23–44. Lincoln: University of Nebraska Press.

Lorrain, Dessamae. 1967. The Glass site. In *A Pilot Study of Wichita Indian Archeology and Ethnohistory,* assembled by R. E. Bell, E. B. Jelks, and W. W. Newcomb, Jr., pp. 24–44. Dallas: final report to the National Science Foundation.

McCracken, Harold. 1971. Mummy Cave (Wyoming) archeological project. *National Geographic Society Research Reports, 1965 Projects,* pp. 155–160.

————. 1977. *Mummy Cave Project in Northwestern Wyoming.* Cody, Wyoming: Buffalo Bill Historical Center.

McHugh, Tom. 1972. *Time of the Buffalo.* New York: Knopf.

Malouf, Carling, and Stuart Conner. 1962. *Symposium on Buffalo Jumps.* Montana Archaeological Society, Memoir no. 1.

Marshall, James O. 1972. *The Archeology of the Elk City Reservoir: A Local Archeological Sequence in Southeast Kansas.* Anthropological Series no. 6, Kansas State Historical Society.

Martin, P. S., and H. E. Wright, Jr. (eds.). 1967. *Pleistocene Extinctions: The Search for a Cause.* New Haven: Proceedings, VII Congress of International Association for Quaternary Research, vol. 6.

Mulloy, William. 1952. The northern Plains. In *Archeology of Eastern United States,* ed. J. B. Griffin, pp. 124–128. Chicago: University of Chicago Press.

————. 1954a. Archeological investigations in the Shoshone Basin of Wyoming. *University of Wyoming Publications* 18:1:1–70.

————. 1954b. The McKean site in northeastern Wyoming. *Southwestern Journal of Anthropology* 10:4:432–460.

————. 1958. A preliminary historical outline for the Northwestern Plains. *University of Wyoming Publications* 22:1, 2.

O'Brien, Patricia J. 1971. Valley focus mortuary practices. *Plains Anthropologist* 16:53:165–182.

Oliver, Symmes C. 1962. *Ecology and Cultural Continuity as Contributing Factors in the Social Organization of the Plains Indians*. University of California Publications in American Archaeology and Ethnology, vol. 48.

Opler, Morris E. 1975. Problems in Apachean cultural history, with special reference to the Lipan Apache. *Anthropological Quarterly* 48:3:182–192.

Ossenberg, N. S. 1974. Origins and relationships of Woodland peoples: the evidence of cranial morphology. In *Aspects of Upper Great Lakes Anthropology*, ed. Elden Johnson, pp. 15–39. Minnesota Prehistoric Archaeology Series no. 11.

Pearson, F. J., Jr., E. Mott Davis, and M. A. Tamers. 1966. University of Texas radiocarbon dates IV. *Radiocarbon* 8:453–466.

Pillaert, E. Elizabeth. 1963. The McLemore site of the Washita River focus. *Bulletin, Oklahoma Anthropological Society* 11:1–113.

Price, Raymond S. n.d. Early ceramic period sites in northeastern Nebraska. M.A. thesis, Department of Anthropology, University of Nebraska.

Reeves, Bryan. 1973. The concept of an altithermal cultural hiatus in northern Plains prehistory. *American Anthropologist* 75:5:1221–1253.

Reher, Charles A. 1978. Buffalo population and other deterministic factors in a model of adaptive process on the shortgrass plains. In *Bison Procurement and Utilization: A Symposium*, ed. L. B. Davis and Michael Wilson, pp. 23–39. Plains Anthropologist, 23, no. 82 (Memoir 14).

Roberts, F. H. H., Jr., 1936. *Additional Information on the Folsom Complex: Report on the Second Season's Investigations at the Lindenmeier Site in Northern Colorado*. Smithsonian Miscellaneous Collections 95:10.

Sauer, Carl O. 1944. A geographic sketch of early man in America. *Geographical Review* 34:4:529–573.

Schleiser, Karl H. 1972. Rethinking the Dismal River aspect and the Plains Athabascans, AD 1692–1768. *Plains Anthropologist* 17:56:101–133.

Schmits, Larry J. 1978. The Coffey site: environment and cultural adaptation at a prairie plains Archaic site. MJCA Special Paper no. 1, *Mid-Continental Journal of Archaeology* 3:1:69–185. Kent, Ohio: Kent State University Press.

Schneider, Fred E. 1969. The Roy Smith site, Bv-14, Beaver County, Okla. *Bulletin, Oklahoma Anthropological Society* 18:119–179.

Schultz, C. B. 1943. Some artifact sites of early man in the Great Plains and adjacent areas. *American Antiquity* 8:3:242–249.

Scott, Douglas D. 1973. Preliminary analysis of location strategies of Plains Woodland sites in northern Colorado. *Southwestern Lore* 39:3:1–11.

———, and Terje G. Birkedal. 1972. The archaeology and physical anthropology of the Gahagan–Lipe site with comments on Colorado Woodland mortuary practices. *Southwestern Lore* 38:3:1–18.

Scott, Glenn R. 1962. *Geology of the Littleton Quadrangle, Jefferson, Douglas, and Arapahoe Counties, Colorado*. U.S. Geological Survey Bulletin 1121-L:L-1 to L-53.

———. 1963. *Quaternary Geology and Geomorphic History of the Kassler Quadrangle, Colorado*. U.S. Geological Survey Professional Paper 421-A.

Sellards, E. H. 1952. *Early Man in America*. Austin: University of Texas Press.

Shelford, V. E. 1963. *The Ecology of North America*. Urbana: University of Illinois Press.

Stanford, Dennis J. 1974. Preliminary report of the excavation of the Jones–Miller Hell Gap site, Yuma County, Colorado. *Southwestern Lore* 40:3–4:29–36.

———, Waldo R. Wedel, and Glenn R. Scott. 1981. Archeological investigations of the Lamb Spring site. *Southwestern Lore*, 47:1:14–27.

Stockton, Charles W., and David M. Meko. 1975. A long-term history of drought occurrence in western United States as inferred from tree rings. *Weatherwise* 28:6:244–249.

Strong, William Duncan. 1935. *An Introduction to Nebraska Archeology*. Smithsonian Miscellaneous Collections 93:10.

Thwaites, R. G. (ed.). 1904–1905. *Original Journals of the Lewis and Clark Expedition, 1804–1806*. 8 vols. New York: Dodd, Mead.

Tunnell, C. D., and Jack T. Hughes. 1955. An Archaic bison kill in the Texas panhandle. *Panhandle–Plains Historical Review* 28:63–70.

Ubelaker, Douglas H., and Waldo R. Wedel. 1975. Bird bones, burials, and bundles in Plains archeology. *American Antiquity* 40:4:444–452.

Weakly, Ward F. 1971. Tree-ring dating and archaeology in South Dakota. *Plains Anthropologist* 16:54:2 (Memoir 8).

Weaver, J. E., and F. W. Albertson. 1956. *Grasslands of the Great Plains: Their Nature and Use.* Lincoln, Neb.: Johnsen.

Wedel, Waldo R. 1938. *The Direct-Historical Approach in Pawnee Archeology.* Smithsonian Miscellaneous Collections 97:7.

———. 1941. *Environment and Native Subsistence Economies in the Central Great Plains.* Smithsonian Miscellaneous Collections 101:3.

———. 1943. *Archeological Investigations in Platte and Clay Counties, Missouri.* Bulletin 183, U.S. National Museum.

———. 1953. Some aspects of human ecology in the Central Plains. *American Anthropologist* 55:4:499-514.

———. 1959. *An Introduction to Kansas Archeology.* Bulletin 174, Bureau of American Ethnology.

———. 1961. *Prehistoric Man on the Great Plains.* Norman: University of Oklahoma Press.

———. 1963. The High Plains and their utilization by the Indian. *American Antiquity* 29:1:1-16.

———. 1964. The Great Plains. In *Prehistoric Man in the New World,* ed. J. D. Jennings and E. Norbeck, pp. 193-220. Chicago: University of Chicago Press.

———. 1967. Salvage archeology in the Missouri River Basin. *Science* 156:589-597.

———. 1968. Some thoughts on Central Plains–Southern Plains archaeological relationships. *Great Plains Journal* 7:2:1-10.

———. 1970. Some observations on Two House Sites in the Central Plains: an experiment in archaeology. *Nebraska History* 51:2:225-252.

———. 1975a. Some early Euro-American percepts of the Great Plains and their influence on anthropological thinking. In *Images of the Plains,* ed. B. W. Blouet and M. P. Lawson, pp. 13-20. Lincoln: University of Nebraska Press.

———. 1975b. Chalk Hollow: cultural sequence and chronology in the Texas Panhandle. In *Proceedings of the 41st International Congress of Americanists, I,* pp. 270-278. Mexico City.

———. 1982. *Essays in the History of Plains Archeology.* Reprints in Anthropology, vol. 24. Lincoln: J & L Reprint Co.

———. n.d.a. Investigations at the Lamb Spring site, Colorado. Unpublished manuscript. Final report to National Science Foundation on Project NSF-G17609.

———. n.d.b. The Central Plains Village tradition. Unpublished manuscript. Handbook of North American Indians, vol. 3: Plains.

———, W. M. Husted, and J. H. Moss. 1968. Mummy Cave: prehistoric record from Rocky Mountains of Wyoming. *Science* 160:184-185.

Wells, Philip V. 1970. Vegetational history of the Great Plains: a post-glacial record of coniferous woodland in southeastern Wyoming. In *Pleistocene and Recent Environments of the Central Great Plains,* ed. W. A. Dort, Jr., and J. K. Jones, Jr., pp. 185-202. Special Publication no. 3, Department of Geology, University of Kansas.

Wendland, Wayne M. 1978. Holocene man in North America: the ecological setting and climatic background. *Plains Anthropologist* 23:82 (part 1):273-287.

Wendorf, Fred, and James J. Hester. 1962. Early man's utilization of the Great Plains environment. *American Antiquity* 28:2:159-171.

———, and ——— (eds.). 1971. *Late Pleistocene Environments of the Southern High Plains.* Ranchos de Taos, N.M.: Fort Burgwin Research Center, Publication no. 9.

Wheat, Joe Ben. 1972. The Olsen-Chubbuck site, a Paleo-Indian bison kill. *American Antiquity* 37:1:2:1-180. (Memoir 26).

White, Leslie A. (ed.). 1959. *Lewis Henry Morgan: The Indian Journals, 1859–62.* Ann Arbor: University of Michigan Press.

Wilmsen, Edwin N., and Frank H. H. Roberts, Jr. 1978. *Lindenmeier, 1934–1974, Concluding Report on Investigations.* Smithsonian Contributions to Anthropology, no. 24. Washington, D.C.: Smithsonian Institution.

Wilson, Michael. 1974. History of the bison in Wyoming, with particular reference to Early Holocene forms. *Geological Survey of Wyoming, Report of Investigations* 10:91-99.

Wissler, Clark. 1922. *The American Indian: An Introduction to the Anthropology of the New World,* 2d ed. New York: Oxford University Press.

Wood, W. Raymond (ed.). 1969. Two houses sites in the Central Plains: an experiment in archaeology. *Plains Anthropologist* 14:44:2 (Memoir 6).

———. 1974. Northern Village cultures: internal stability and external relationships. *Journal of Anthropological Research* 30:1:1–16.

Wormington, H. M. 1957. *Ancient Man in North America.* Denver Museum of Natural History, Popular Series no. 4, 4th ed.

Wright, H. E., Jr. 1970. Vegetational history of the Central Plains. In *Pleistocene and Recent Environments of the Central Great Plains,* ed. W. Dort, Jr., and J. K. Jones, Jr., pp. 157–172. Special Publication no. 3, Department of Geology, University of Kansas.

Low aerial view of Serpent Mound, showing nearby structures. (Photograph by D. M. Reeves, Smithsonian Institution.)

CHAPTER SEVEN

The Midlands

James B. Griffin

Outside of the southwestern United States and Mesoamerica, the Middle West has been the scene of the most intensive archeological study in the New World. Dr. Griffin has compressed the rich history of that region, including some recent finds, into a chapter that reflects his mastery of the details and the significance of the archeological data.

PALEO-INDIAN

The earliest reported evidence of early populations in the Midwest comes from the Meadowcroft Shelter, some 50 miles southwest of Pittsburgh (Adovasio et al., 1975). Here there are flint knives, flakes, a scraper, and other tools of flint in the lowest stratum, with radiocarbon dates in the 17,000 BC range. If these results are supported by future work, and if a more adequate assemblage is obtained, this will be by far the oldest acceptable occupation in the area.

The oldest widespread prehistoric complex is best identified by fluted projectile points and knives. This early industry is found over the entire area covered by this chapter except on the extreme northern fringe. It is part of a country-wide occupation, and its general similarity over the entire area is a remarkable phenomenon. There is a great deal we do not know about this complex. We do not know with any certainty when the populations came into the New World or what paths they might have followed to reach the Midwest. Many believe that their technological skills were developed in the Old World and adapted to an arctic environment in northeastern Siberia, allowing them to move into northwestern North America and southward along the eastern flank of the Rocky Mountains sometime shortly before or after the climax of the Wisconsin glaciation (see Chapter Two). The distinctive fluting that removed longitudinal flakes from both faces of the projectile points and knives was apparently developed in the United States, but no one knows where or exactly when.

In Ontario, scattered finds of fluted points reported by Kidd (1951) suggest that the fluted-point sites and activities were above the old Lake Algonquin terrace and that the fluting technique had disappeared before the level of Lake Huron had fallen below the 605 Algonquin level (Griffin, 1965a). Northwest of London, recent work by Roosa (1977) has produced a series of fluted-point sites related to the Barnes complex in central Michigan and to Shoop, Bull Brook, and Debert.

Surveys of fluted-point distributions in Ohio by Prufer and Baby (1963) and in Indiana by Dorwin (1966) have pointed out the heavier concentrations of these forms in the southern parts of both states and a considerable formal variability in artifact shape. The Ohio survey identified almost 500 fluted points in various collections, while the Indiana survey produced nearly 200 with a less intensive review. An even less systematic survey of Illinois identified some 252 specimens from the St. Louis area (Smail, 1951), and locations reported by a number of other archeologists from the state add some 130 to the total (Griffin, 1968). The Wisconsin distribution (Stoltman and Workman, 1969) is primarily in the southern half of the state for a number of reasons; that is probably where most of the population was. The fact that a few fluted points have been found on top of Valders till means that they were deposited after about 9500 BC, which is as early as they are known anywhere else.

In Michigan, studies on a correlation of fluted points and geochronology were begun over 25 years ago (Griffin, 1956; Mason, 1958; Quimby, 1958). Unfortunately, no sites have been located with the amount of occupational evidence desired for an extensive investigation; the best-known of the sites discovered so far is the Barnes site (H. Wright and Roosa, 1966). In general, the observation made in 1956 that the fluted-point occupation was limited to locations higher than the main Lake Algonquin beach is still valid. The drop in lake levels began between 9500 and 9200 BC because of the opening of the drainage from the Georgian Bay area into the Champlain Sea. One fluted point has also been found on the Valders till south of Grand Traverse Bay (Dekin, 1966).

A survey of the distribution of fluted points in Missouri (Chapman, 1975) documents that the largest number of these finds occurred along the lower Missouri and along the Mississippi. Where location is known, it has usually been along the bluffs or terraces along major streams. A few promising potential campsites with scrapers and gravers have not been excavated. Neither Iowa nor Minnesota has had a systematic survey or study of the fluted points. There have been scattered finds in Iowa along the Missouri and Mississippi valleys, but the most important find was a plow-zone cache of 11 complete and fragmentary Clovis points in Cedar County. Iowa has also yielded surface finds of projectile forms associated with hunting sites on the Plains from about 8500–6500 BC.

The interpretation adopted in this chapter is that the fluted-point hunters moved into the Northeast primarily from the south. By 10,000 BC floral and faunal resources in the Ohio valley and far north in Wisconsin, Michigan, and Ontario were adequate for the support of scattered bands of hunters. Each band probably comprised from 15 to 20 closely related individuals. The Ontario population probably entered from southeastern Michigan; the New York, New

England, and Nova Scotia populations may well have moved up the Susquehanna and Delaware and the coastal area from Virginia and the Southeast.

The considerable homogeneity of tool forms over the entire Northeast, and indeed over much of the United States, allows one to characterize the entire area as possessing essentially one technological complex. Many of the locations known from the literature, such as the Kouba site in southern Wisconsin, were probably base camps, though one cannot be sure of this.

The technology of this earliest prehistoric population was adaptable to a wide variety of environments—from coastal plain to upland areas, from river valleys to northern lake environments, from regions in the south with a strong deciduous element in the forest cover to the spruce–pine-dominated areas in the north. Tools included cobblestone choppers; large stone scraping planes; hammerstones and abraders for processing vegetal products for food, shelter, and heat; and the diagnostic fluted or unfluted points and knives for killing and butchering game. Large numbers of end scrapers were made from blades, and some of these have a distinctive spur on each end of the working edge that is almost a diagnostic trait for the period. End scrapers were used in the preparation of leather and perhaps as woodworking or bone-scraping tools. Side scrapers, spokeshaves (used to smooth cylindrical surfaces such as dart or spear shafts), and drills (flakes with a very fine point or multiple points for use as perforators) are characteristic. Flint wedges were employed to split bone, antler, and wood or as grooving tools. Because of unfavorable environmental conditions, no bone tools or ornaments have been found, but we may reasonably suppose that bone awls, needles, knives, flakers, and perhaps shaft straighteners were made.

Poor preservation also affects the faunal assemblages from these early sites. There is no question that these populations had a heavy emphasis upon hunting and were capable of dealing with anything from caribou and elk to rodents. There are many mastodon and mammoth finds in the Midwest, but there is no sound, published evidence that humans slew or butchered these beasts. This holds true for the Southeast and for the whole wooded area east of the Plains. We must also recognize that other foods, such as nuts, seeds, berries, fish, and fowl, were available and not beyond the procurement capabilities of these populations.

EARLY ARCHAIC

A purely arbitrary division is made between the earlier fluted-point hunters and their direct descendants, who are assigned to the time period of about 8000 to 6000 BC. For many years the Early Archaic was not recognized for a variety of reasons, but closer attention to comparisons with Southeastern and Plains assemblages and the opportunity for many more excavations have been productive.

Between 8000 and 6000 BC much of the area acquired a vegetational pattern and an accompanying animal life very like that at the time of European arrival.

Although there are not extensive site excavations and none that have well-preserved bone or vegetable material components that can help us directly study the animal and vegetal food supply, certain inferences about subsistence can be made. A continuing strong emphasis on hide working and on animal hunting and processing is indicated by a continuation of the gravers, scrapers, knives, and projectile points. The last, particularly, have a much greater variation in form than during the earlier period. Continuity of the basic form used earlier is shown at such sites as Holcombe in southeastern Michigan (Fitting et al., 1966), which produced points similar to the Milnesand and other basally thinned points of the Plains. Similar points can be recognized elsewhere, but they are not satisfactorily isolated as part of a recognizable cultural complex.

From other excavations in the Midwest we know of the presence of sandstone abraders, of cobbles for grinding vegetable foods or pounding meat, and of mortars. A chipped flint adze makes its appearance and is the first of the heavy woodworking tools. These tools were important in producing wood for shelter construction, dugout canoes, and wooden containers, and apparently were the prototype for the grooved ax, the gouge, and the celt of later periods.

In southern Illinois and southwestern Indiana there is a sizable proportion of Dalton projectile points, a strong element in Early Archaic levels in the mid-South from about 7500 to 6500 BC. Other lithic forms in this area are the St. Charles, Agate Basin, Quad, and Kirk. In the Miami to Marietta area of Ohio there are indications of points such as Kirk, Kanawha, and LeCroy that have been dated in the lower Kanawha valley and were found in stratigraphic context first in the piedmont of North Carolina.

One of the best-known sites in the western Great Lakes is the Holcombe site, which is neither located on a beach of glacial Lake Algonquin nor identified as a fluted point occupation. While earlier dates have been given for the draining of Lake Algonquin, the best estimate is now 8600 BC, approximately the time when the shift from spruce parkland to pine and mixed hardwoods (Karow et al., 1975) took place. A toe bone at Holcombe identified as barren ground caribou is hardly enough to formulate either a hunting pattern or an environment. The probabilities are that the site and its artifacts were in existence as one of a series of camps from about 8000 to 7000 BC. There are clear indications in the gravers, scrapers, and projectile forms that the complex was in existence within a few hundred years after the time of the fluted-point people.

In Wisconsin the only named phase for this period is the Flambeau, recognized in the north–central part of the state (Salzer, 1974:43–44). It is followed in the same area by the Minoqua phase. In form, both are analogous to the Agate Basin to Scottsbluff sequence in the Plains. A burial at the Renier site (Mason and Irwin, 1960), originally reported as being in an Algonquin deposit, is probably Early Archaic in age. The fossil beach, which was formed by at least 9000 BC, was probably selected as a burial site because of its favorable elevated position. The burial here is interpreted as dating to about 7000 to 6000 BC.

Mason (1963) illustrates a variety of Early Archaic or late Paleo-Indian forms, largely from the Neville Museum in Green Bay. Other museums and collections in Wisconsin also contain specimens that show the range from basally thinned lanceolate forms to Scottsbluff. One such collection is from the Kouba site in Dane County (Ritzenthaler, 1966); another is from excavations of Unit B at the Markee site in southwestern Wisconsin (Halsey, 1974).

On the northwestern side of Lake Superior, the Brohm complex (MacNeish, 1952), which has been duplicated by J. Wright (1972a: Plates 1 and 3) at the Cummins quarry and campsite, is considered Early Archaic. The Cummins finds are on the land side of a fossil Lake Minong beach that was formed about 8000 BC. The points and scrapers are probably somewhat later, however, because they resemble the western Plainview forms. Most of the specimens from this industry were made from taconite.

Typologically later are the complexes at George Lake, Chickinising, and Sheguiandah in the Manitoulin district of Lake Huron. Here Scottsbluff and Eden-like forms are found with early side-notched points (Greenman, 1966; T. Lee, 1954, 1955, 1957). A reasonable estimate of the age of these sites would be from about 7000 to 6000 BC, a time when there is a high pine pollen count from a nearby bog at Sheguiandah. These sites are almost certainly not earlier than the period of the lowest level of Lake Algonquin. George Lake is at an elevation of 97.5 to 90.5 meters above Lake Huron; Sheguiandah is at approximately 65.5 meters; and the Chickinising I site is midway between the two. The artifacts at these sites are primarily fabricated from quartzite from the local deposits. A fine, narrow, lanceolate form, also made of quartzite but found near Flesherton, Ontario, southeast of Owen Sound, has been described by Storck (1972). Different forms, closely similar to those from the Holcombe site but somewhere in the 8000 to 7000 BC range, are illustrated by Storck from his survey of the Bronte Gap just to the north of Hamilton, Ontario (Storck, 1973).

In Ohio the largest number of sites with projectile forms equivalent to the Plains types from the period 8000 to 6000 BC are in the north (Prufer and Baby, 1963: Figure 20; Prufer, 1963, 1966). Such types are also present south of the Ohio River, but are not well dated in that area.

The interpretation adopted here is that the appearance of the Plano forms is the result not of a movement of people abandoning the western Plains but rather of gradual changes taking place in conjunction with changes on the Plains by means of the same social mechanisms or group interactions that allow new ideas and technical developments to move with fair speed over considerable areas. The strength of the Plano forms in the northern part of the Midwest may have been aided by the prairie extension into Minnesota, Iowa, and Illinois; but there are large areas where the eastern Plano forms are found which were not and have never been prairies. The prairie development was later than the presence of these points. The major hypothesis that the relative absence of sites is due to the closed pine forest is rejected partly on the ground that from 8000 to 6000 BC in most of the Lake Forest area there was not a closed pine forest (Brown and Cleland, 1968). Moreover, the scarcity of sites in some states may be due to a failure to devote adequate time and resources to the search for them.

MIDDLE ARCHAIC

During the next 2000 years of adaptation to the environment in the Midwest, 6000 to 4000 BC, not only did the vegetational pattern acquire a completely modern appearance over most of the area, but Indian expansion reached about as far north as it would ever go in the interior. A number of new technological developments appeared during this period, including the grinding and polishing of stone implements. Bone tools appear in a few locations, and there are some early indications of increasing status differentiation among the band members.

From the Cherokee (Iowa) Sewer excavations, a group of archeologists and geologists from the University of Iowa, with contributors from ancillary disciplines, have presented a comprehensive study of the environment (Anderson and Semken, 1980). The study helps us to understand the late-winter bison hunters of that locality from 6400 to about 4000 BC. The several occupations were by small bands of communal hunters who butchered their kill at this locality. The earliest kills are identified from the lanceolate projectile points as late Paleo-Indian, while the side-notched forms found from about 6000 to 2600 BC belong to Archaic projectiles and knives. Bifacial knives occurred in all horizons. Hide-dressing tools, while showing some variability, were essentially similar throughout the sequence; they were probably used in the initial stages of hide preparation. Choppers, hammerstones, a few burin-like tools, and clinker fragments with U-shaped grooves (perhaps shaft abraders) were found in a deposit at 5200 BC, along with a well-shaped, flat millingstone. Domesticated dog was identified in the Middle Archaic horizon of about 4300 BC. Evidence that family units participated in the butchering activities is provided by the identification in two of the Archaic levels of three deciduous teeth, from one or more children about five or six years old.

There are not many data from the period between 6000 and 4000 BC in the Midwest. There may well have been some occupation at Modoc Rockshelter in Illinois, but it is difficult to determine just what the occupation was. Perhaps the winged bannerstone and the Hidden Valley and side-notched forms belong here. A dog burial at the Koster site probably belongs to the same general level.

In north–central Wisconsin, a primarily hunting-tool complex of end and side scrapers, large and small biface points and knives, and bifacially flaked flake knives, wedges, and bipolar cores is identified as the Menocqua phase by Salzer (1974). His estimated age for the assemblage is between 6000 and 5000 BC. Unit B at the Markee site in southwestern Wisconsin might be slightly later (Halsey, 1974).

LATE ARCHAIC

While there were relatively few sites for the preceding periods for which a cohesive complex could be recognized, the situation is vastly different for the final 3000 years of the Archaic. In many areas successive units can be distinguished; in some areas contemporary groups in different types of locations had significantly different behaviorial patterns. The arbitrary time period of 4000 to 1000 BC dates the most complex and diversely developed pre-Woodland societies. Specialized adaptations to broad regional and even local environments are recognized. Plants were important for their food, medicinal, and magical properties. The manufacture of many tools and implements from forest and plant materials was probably common. In favorable localities a rich bone industry has been preserved, and this too must actually have been widespread. The wide variety of faunal remains is testimony to skill in hunting, fishing, fowling, and trapping. Transportation by dugout and birchbark or elmbark canoe was almost certainly in existence from the mouth of the St. Lawrence to the Ohio and Mississippi valleys. The path of distribution of copper and copper implements into the eastern Great Lakes follows the water routes. The best evidence for early houses appears at this time. The ground and polished stone industry reached a high development.

There is considerable evidence for the long-distance movement of goods, some as raw materials but some apparently already in final form. Much of this transported material was eventually placed with burials, a practice interpreted as evidence of belief in both personal and magical power. The importance of burial offerings and their association with red ocher, which was seen at Renier during the Early Archaic, is accentuated in this period. Relatively few of the burials have such grave goods, and the total amount per year per individual in the society is probably quite small. Toward the close of the period, the first pottery makes its appearance, as do the first tropical agricultural plants—squash and gourds.

Sites are of larger size and represent recurrent habitation, sometimes over long periods of time. Many more areas were occupied than in earlier times. Closely related complexes can be identified in rather restricted geographical areas; they represent band or tribal hunting areas. All the evidence during this period points to a population expansion.

James V. Wright (1972a) developed the concept of the Shield Archaic to encompass occupations in the boreal forest between Great Bear and Great Slave lakes southeastward to an interfingering with the Lake Forest formation of the Great Lakes, and eastward as far as Labrador. This area forms a great arc, or "infertile crescent." The very large territory and the considerable time span (from before 4500 BC almost to the historic period) means that it can hardly be a homogeneous assemblage. The economy was based on hunting and fishing, with caribou used as a major animal-protein source and presumably also for bone tools, although the forest soils are not favorable to preservation. The projectile points have seven different hafting or base treatments, and within each category, such as side-notched points, there is great variation. Scrapers are the most common class of stone tools, exhibiting considerable range in size and form. The complex includes end and side scrapers, with a few small "random" scrapers, and two types of scrapers with graver spurs at Keewatin sites in Manitoba and Ontario. Biface blades were general utility tools. There are uniface blades, large wedges, and a few flake knives. Some of the sites on the southern and southeastern borders of the Laurentian shield also include items of copper—spears and ornaments—and slate forms (J. Wright, 1972b). It is debatable whether these are correctly included within the Shield Archaic. One reasonable postulation included in Wright's model is that the hunting–fishing groups who occupied this territory were descendants of Paleo-Indian groups and eventually became the northern Algonquian speakers—from the Montagnais–Naskapi on the east to the central and western Cree.

In the lower Illinois valley, the Helton phase of Cook (1974) at the Koster site Horizon 6 ends just before 2000 BC. The people of this phase were engaged in the hunting and gathering of the rich natural resources and participated in some long-distance trade and exchange. Besides the usual debris indicating chert and ground stone tool manufacture, there are also worked shell fragments. Many of the tools indicate hide and leather working, bone and antler tool fabrication, and probably mat and cloth manufacture. There are large roasting areas, baking pits or earth ovens, and a rectangular house pattern. Some mound burials have been attributed to this period, but the evidence is questionable or at least not fully published.

At the Godar site, north of Hardin in the Illinois valley, over 400 projectile point forms are said to have been recovered, including biface preforms for the Godar Side-notched and the larger Hemphill forms. There were 40 well-made T-shaped drills, 35 full-grooved and three-quarter-grooved axes, 6 drills, hematite plummets, and 3 rhyolite beads. The 24 bannerstones came in tubular, rectangular, bar, and geniculate forms (Titterington, 1950). This complex has analogies to the burials beneath the Hemphill Mound in Brown County up the Illinois River (Griffin, 1941; Knoblock, 1939; Titterington, 1950), and there is strong cultural continuity into the Early Woodland levels in the Illinois area.

The Titterington phase as it is now interpreted by Cook (1974) belongs in the 1500 to 2000 BC range. It has a distinctive burial complex and evidence of a well-adjusted economy. The Titterington phase is found in Horizon 4 at the Koster site, where there is evidence from tools and debris of the manufacture of chert and ground-stone tools and wood items, of hide preparation and leather working, and of bone and antler tool manufacture. The inhabitants of this area utilized resources in about equal proportion from the Illinois floodplain, the upland area, the base of the bluffs, and from the secondary valleys.

While the excavator of groups of extended burials covered with red ocher and limestone slabs at the Etley site claimed these were in two low mounds on a high bluff overlooking the Illinois River north of Hardin, I am skeptical that they were artificial mounds; more likely, they were low natural rises into which the burials were intruded. At this location the 27 to 64 burials (or whatever the exact number was) were accompanied by 75 Sedalia points, 13 Etley Barbed points, 25 full-grooved and three-quarter-grooved axes, 3 saddleback bannerstones, 3 small copper celts, and a long copper awl, square in cross-section. Another burial area, in Marquette State Park, is also on a bluff and was covered with limestone slabs. It contained a compound burial of two individuals extended on their backs. Grave goods consisted of two Sedalia knives, one Etley Barbed point, two grooved axes, two unique engraved shell ornaments, and a brown diorite awl. Near the south end of the park, the Hartford Church location had "several" burials with six three-quarter and one full-grooved ax, four Sedalia points, five Hardin Stemmed points, one Etley Barbed point, three Hemphill spears, and three Godar points.

The Labras Lake site in the southeastern American Bottom opposite St. Louis has Late Archaic occupations, which were uncovered in the recent I-270 excavations (J. Phillips et al., 1980). The excavators identified two areas, each having four domestic dwellings or shelters—one large and three smaller in each group. The internal features represent cooking and storage debris. The sites were apparently occupied for a number of months in the late summer and early fall. The dwelling areas were separated by a central activity area, where tool repair and manufacture took place outside the dwellings. Some shallow pits are interpreted as hearths for processing nuts, among other uses. There were almost 40 small, shallow pits that contained waste materials of lithic specimens, nut fragments, and so on. The storage or refuse pits are deeper and contain more debris and other food remains. Several clusters of refuse pits were near the dwelling areas and roasting pits. The roasting pits are roughly $80 \times 70 \times 40$ cm, and contained backwash organic earth, charcoal, nut fragments, and lithic debris and tools. Processing tools include hammerstones, pitted anvils, and sandstone abraders. Rather crudely made ovoid, unperforated plummets were found. Projectile points similar to the Trimble form of the lower Wabash are present, as are some that resemble both the Godar side-notched type of the lower Illinois valley and the forms called *Helton* in Horizon 6 at Koster. Woodworking, hide-scraping, and meat-cutting flint tools were identified by a use-wear analysis of the tool edges, using stereoscopic examination and comparison with known wear patterns. A cache of 15 biface preforms of nonlocal flint, which had been heat-treated to make it flake more easily, was recovered from the central activity area. Three other bifaces had been made from Spring Hill chert, probably from northeastern Missouri.

Most of the nut remains were hickory, with some acorn, black walnut, and hazelnut. There were few seed remains; most of these were *Polyganum erectuna* (knotweed). Identifiable animal bone was also rather scarce, but deer, elk, turtle, and fish were represented. The occupations took place about 1000 BC, and there were at least two separate periods of use of the location.

West of the Mississippi, in the northern half of Missouri, a number of sites have projectile points and other tools which suggest that the Helton–Tittering-ton complexes are represented some distance into Missouri. Some of these sites are interpreted as summer activity areas for collecting and processing vegetal materials; others are cemeteries, campsites, and hunting stations. Chapman (1975) has called the several sites and their materials the *Sedalia* phase, which he places between 3000 to 1000 BC. Although these open sites do not contain evidence of a textile industry, slightly earlier levels in caves and rockshelters have yielded twined-grass fabric bags, woven-grass sandals, mats, and cloth. Students of the history of this industry have rather forcefully taken the position that it formed part of the technology of the early fluted-point-phase occupants of the East and that there is increasing evidence of its presence and impor-tance into the Woodland and Mississippi periods (Adovasio and Andrews, 1980:60–67).

In Indiana the best-known Late Archaic site is the McCain site in Dubois County (Miller, 1941), although more recent work along the Ohio near Louis-ville by Donald Jansen and east of Cincinnati by Kent Vickery will add another variant of the Late Archaic comparable to Indian Knoll. The McCain site has engraved bone pins or needles that are similar to those from Koster, Indian Knoll, and other sites on this time horizon in the Southeast as far as the Georgia coast.

In south–central Indiana, recent investigations have documented Early through Late Archaic occupations. Indiana University archeologists are defining a French Lick phase of the Late Archaic; they include the McCain site within that cultural grouping. While French Lick shares some features with other, adjoining areas during the 3000-to-1500 BC period, there is enough distinctive-ness at a series of sites around French Lick to justify establishing such a unit. The various functional artifact forms parallel those found in Indian Knoll sites south of the Ohio and in Helton-phase sites of the lower Illinois valley. The French Lick subsistence base is somewhat dependent on hunting, fishing, nut-gathering, and other seasonal occupations. No evidence has yet been found for consumption of seedy plants, berries, tubers, or the early cultigens of the East-ern Agricultural complex, but such evidence will probably turn up eventually. Nor is there yet adequate evidence for a description of the seasonal activities or of such important activities as mortuary practices and trade (Munson et al., 1980).

The populations in the upper Great Lakes area obtained a considerable amount of copper by extensive mining in the Lake Superior area (Griffin, 1961). During the Late Archaic the copper was shaped into various utilitarian forms—spears, knives, *ulus,* adzes, celts, gouges, awls, and fishhooks—which are similar to their bone and stone counterparts (Figure 7.1). These have a wide distribution but are concentrated in Wisconsin and Michigan. Worked and un-worked copper moved over considerable distances, following water routes where possible. Both in eastern Ontario and in the "heartland" of the distribution, the copper is found in the village sites and occasionally in burials as the personal

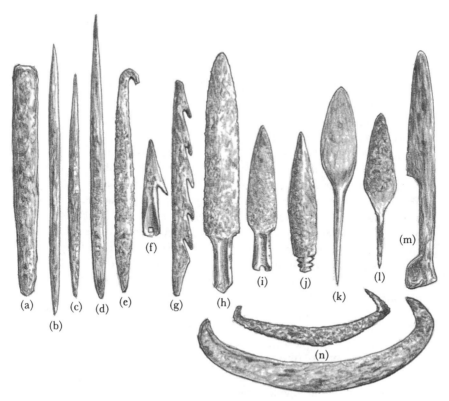

FIGURE 7.1
Utilitarian copper artifacts of Late Archaic, primarily from upper Great Lakes area: (a) chisel; (b, c) awls; (d, e) punches; (f, g) harpoons; (h–l) spear points; (m) knife; (n) "women's" knives, similar to Eskimo ulu.

possessions of the deceased. The copper forms are present in burials associated with the so-called Glacial Kame, Laurentian, Shield Archaic, and other such constructs. It is best to discontinue thinking of the Old Copper culture as a distinct ethnic entity.

The Glacial Kame complex of Ohio, Indiana, Michigan, and adjacent areas is known from a series of burials in gravel knolls. These feature ornaments made from marine shell, circular or rectangular gorget forms, beads, and the sandal-sole gorget. The complex is interconnected with "Old Copper" and is a forerunner of the so-called Red Ocher local complex (Cunningham, 1948; Ritzenthaler and Quimby, 1962). From the latter half of the second millennium BC, Winters (1969) has identified a Riverton complex. These people in the lower Wabash valley followed a seasonal round of activities with some attention to mussel collection. Band size of around 50 people is a reasonable figure. Winters sees strong connections to the western Tennessee Big Sandy complex, but there are also strong ties throughout the Ohio valley and Great Lakes area.

The report is an excellent analysis of Late Archaic activity patterns and of such new features as the presence of tubular pipes of the "Cloud-blower" shape.

THE EARLY WOODLAND COMPLEXES

In the Middle Atlantic area near the beginning of the Early Woodland period, the people began to fashion pottery, perhaps following the lead of Late Archaic groups in the south. The earliest form is a simple, flat-bottomed, flaring-sided container, which often has lug handles. This form is similar to the earlier steatite bowls of the same area; indeed, the first pottery is actually tempered with crushed steatite. Apparently this concept of vessel manufacture, but without the steatite temper, spread rapidly, and local names such as Fayette, Marion, and Vinette I are given to this earliest pottery of the Northeast and Midwest. I do not consider hypotheses of Asiatic and European origin for pottery or for any other features of Woodland culture viable (Griffin, 1966).

Squash is known in Early Woodland sites in Michigan (H. Wright, 1964) and northeastern Ohio by 500 BC; considering its presence in Kentucky and Missouri before 2000 BC, one can assume that it was probably widely spread in the Midwest by 2000 to 1500 BC. Ethnobotanists believe that such native plants as sunflowers and sumpweed were cultivated, a practice perhaps suggested by squash growing (Ford, 1974; Yarnell, 1972). If corn was truly a part of the Late Adena (200 BC) food supply, as suggested by Murphy (1971), it would probably have been more widespread than it evidently was.

The burial ceremonialism that has been noted in Late Archaic reached a high point in Early Woodland times. During this period, construction of mounds for the dead became an important part of mortuary activities from west of the Appalachians to west of the Mississippi and north into Wisconsin and Michigan. While mounds may occur sporadically before 500 BC, they become common after that date. The most notable culture practicing this burial ceremonialism was the Adena complex of the central Ohio valley. There are no major cultural intrusions into the area. The common gift exchange, the movement of valued exotic materials or, more rarely, finished items, and the inevitable cultural diffusion accompanying such activities is, along with local developments, sufficient to account for the observed changes.

The western and central parts of the Northeast exhibit a number of distinctive features in the production and utilization of large leaf-shaped spears or knives of a variety of forms; some of them are "turkey tails," while others are bipointed, ovoid, or have a squared haft. They are often made of a bluish grey hornstone from southern Indiana or from similar formations in Illinois (Didier, 1967). These spears or knives are found in mound-burial associations from Illinois to Ohio or, sometimes, in caches without burials. They may have moved as gifts and must have been of considerable value. They were at least initially roughed out at quarries. We do not know whether secondary shaping took place at villages or camps near the quarries, but closer examination should be made of their find areas, since relatively few village sites have been studied.

Another common burial accompaniment with an even wider distribution is the cache of small triangular points or preforms. These are made of local materials and occur with burials in cemeteries and, rarely, in mounds. Occasionally they appear in a cache not associated with mounds or burials. While a wide variety of chert sources were used, some caches were apparently exchanged over considerable distances. Both the large and small points are found from Illinois and Wisconsin to New England (Willoughby, 1935:126) in association with copper beads and awls, marine shell ornaments, and stemmed points such as the Kramer type in Illinois.

Some artifact types show marked changes in this period. The pipe form became strongly cylindrical, often with a blocked end or a cigar-holder end. Many of these were made from Ohio pipestone from the lower Scioto valley. Such pipes were exchanged into Indiana, Michigan, Killarney Bay, Ontario, New York, New England, and Maryland. The bannerstone disappeared, to be replaced by birdstones and boatstones during the Late Archaic and Early Woodland (Figure 7.2). The three-quarter grooved axe and the celt are the most widely found woodworking tools. The slate gorget of the Late Archaic is also found in this period, exhibiting a variety of forms and made of different materials in different areas.

The intensive study of the Early Woodland occupations at the Schultz site near the mouth of the Tittabawassee River in Saginaw County, Michigan by Doreen Ozker (1977) has revised and expanded the interpretations of that period. The differences in the distribution of food remains in the northern and southern ends of the site indicate that the former was most probably used in the spring and the latter in the fall. The charred nut hulls of hickory, black walnut, and butternut were perhaps processed for their oil, as they do not seem to have been stored. Very few acorns were processed. The nut fragments found in association with the Schultz Thick pottery and specialized activity areas may mean that nut-oil processing was one of the uses of this earliest Woodland pottery. There were also food-processing areas with mussel shells on the floors and features; these also seem to indicate a late spring to early summer occupation. This season is further indicated by the turtle and anadromous fish remains. A high deer count, along with the nut remains and a few squash seeds, are the primary evidence for a fall occupation. Both the egg-gourd and warty squash were present at about 500 BC in the area. Squash was also identified at the downstream Green Point site. One of the egg-gourd seeds was recognized from a clear mold along a coil break of one of the pottery vessels. Deer, beaver, and muskrat were also found in the several excavation units but were most common in the areas associated with fall occupation.

The Schultz Thick pottery is a regional variant of the earliest Midwestern

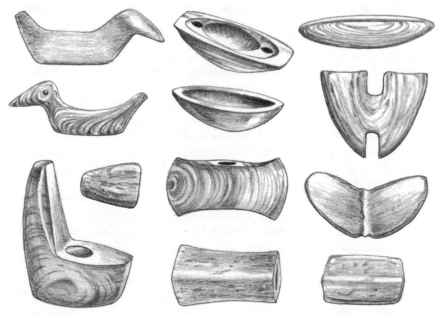

FIGURE 7.2
Polished stone atlatl weights. The birdstones (*upper left*) are Late Archaic and Early Woodland, the boatstones (*upper center*) are Early and Middle Woodland, and the bannerstones are Middle to Late Archaic.

pottery. It is thick, has large temper fragments, is cord-marked on the interior and exterior, and was built above the flattened base by coiling. The walls slant outward with lug handles on the rim similar to those on the steatite vessels found east of the Appalachians. As in other areas with such pottery, it did not function as burial goods but is associated with village activities. Most of the flint tools and debitage at Schultz is of Bayport chert from local limestone deposits; some specimens had been heat-treated. Cores and debitage indicate local flaking activities. The Kramer stemmed projectile point is the most common; some of them were reworked into drills. This point form was first described by P. Munson (1966), who recognized its association with Marion Thick pottery. A few stemmed points resemble the Adena type and a reworked turkey-tail knife is probably of chert from the Dongola quarries in southwestern Illinois. There were also a few side-notched points of a relatively small triangular form. Other flint tools include ovate bifaces, drills, utilized flakes, blades, and biface strike-a-lights.

Only one gorget fragment and a number of other pieces of slate were obtained. The ground stone finds include fragments of three-quarter grooved axes; there were also hammerstones, abraders, and a possible anvil stone. Six copper items were recovered but a copper bead and a small awl with square cross-sections were the only identifiable artifacts. Decomposed pyrite originally formed part of a strike-a-light fire-making kit. Little use was made of shell for scoops or spoons. Antler tips were sometimes made into flaking tools; deer bone was shaped into splinter awls and beaver incisors into cutting tools. The pits of various shapes were associated with activities involving the use of fire; none of them were storage pits. Some were clearly shallow hearths; they were associated with fire-cracked rock, nut remains, and good-sized sections of Schultz Thick. Most of the 13 scattered post molds seemed too large to have been house wall supports.

Other contemporary occupations in the lower peninsula of Michigan have been identified in the Saginaw Bay area; at the Croton Dam mounds near Newaygo by Prahl (1970); below one of the Norton Mounds near Grand Rapids excavated by Flanders (Griffin et al., 1970); and at Moccasin Bluff in southwestern Michigan. These scattered examples are connected across northwestern Indiana into northern Illinois, and down the Illinois valley to the American Bottom (Linder, 1974). Similar small, temporary occupations have been recognized in central Indiana, eastern Iowa, and southern Wisconsin. The burial complex called Red Ocher in the Illinois Valley is probably, I believe, associated with village occupations with Marion Thick pottery—or else there is some temporal overlapping from an early, nonceramic Red Ocher to a later period when the early pottery arrives. The sites in both the Illinois valley and the St. Louis area have burial mounds on the bluffs and camps in the flood plains. Some sites are buried under loess or alluvial deposits. At one site in the American Bottom that had been deeply buried, a large oval post-hole structure 7 by 6 m was found associated with a Dickson contracting stem knife and a local variant of Black Sand pottery. Also discovered were shallow, rock-filled hearths or processing pits around which were found most of the pottery and lithic debris.

The Black Sand complex, first identified in Fulton County, Illinois (Cole and Deuel, 1937), dates from about 500–300 BC. The sites occur both in the flood plain and close to the bluffs in the Illinois valley, probably in relation to former river channels or higher levees in the flood plain. There are small sites of an acre or less, admirably located to take advantage of the wide range of valley-bottom and adjacent upland resources—as their Late Archaic predecessors had done before and as their Havana-complex descendants were to do after them. Black Sand complex pottery has exterior cord-marking on vertical to slightly flaring rims on the body, and subconoidal to rounded bases. There are small rim bosses and either incised decoration in simple linear patterns or pinching on the upper rim. There are at least seven such sites along the Missouri River between St. Louis and Kansas City (Chapman, 1980:12). The only whole vessels come from the lower level of the Peisker site (Perino, 1966) in Calhoun County, Illinois. There should be more evidence of this Early Woodland complex in eastern Iowa, southeastern Minnesota, and Wisconsin than has been reported. In the post-Middle Woodland period, Spring Hollow Incised in Iowa and Dane

Incised at most Wisconsin sites have been misidentified as being on a comparable level with Black Sand. Not much is known of Black Sand trade or exchange patterns, village settlement, or activities because of the small size of the sites and the inadequate excavation techniques and reporting.

The most widely known, if poorly understood, Early Woodland expression is the Adena complex in the Ohio valley, discussed earlier in terms of burial ceremonialism. This complex is found from the Whitewater River valley of Indiana on the west to the upper Ohio valley as far as Pittsburgh on the east, and from the Blue Grass region of the Licking and the Big Sandy and Kanawha Rivers on the south and east to the upper reaches of the Scioto and Muskingum of Ohio on the north. Adena as a mound-building complex may well have not begun until about 500 BC, but many of the artifacts and behavior patterns common after that date originated in the area with Early Woodland complexes. There were once at least 300 to 500 sites in this area that were Adena. Most of the known sites are mounds and represent considerable variation, with area and time, in burial practices and grave goods (Greenman, 1932; Webb and Snow, 1974; Webb and Baby, 1957; Dragoo, 1963). When village sites are excavated and connected to the burial complexes, local river valley groupings will almost certainly be recognized. Serpent Mound, the burial mound near it, and the lower levels of the village site are Adena. A village site from Perry County, Ohio, has recently been reported and assigned to this complex (Bush, 1975). The site produced Montgomery Incised pottery, but one radiocarbon date of 235 BC seems a bit early for this pottery style.

The Adena burial complex was an accentuation of earlier and contemporary burial patterns. The Adenans developed circular earth enclosures that were certainly socioreligious and that sometimes encircle burial mounds. Many of the mounds covered circular dwellings with or without burials on the floor of the dwelling. Burials were made in a number of forms. Many in village sites were cremated, and some cremations were in mounds. Most of the mound burials were extended in a central area, and in late Adena this was often in a carefully prepared log tomb. There were also flexed burials, bundle burials, mutilated or decapitated burials, and burials of separate skulls or other skeletal parts. Cranial deformation by purposeful modification was common. There was no marked preference in orientation of burials. While an adult male often received preferential treatment in terms of grave location and high-status objects, children more often had grave goods.

Grave items were both useful and ornamental. Mica from North Carolina appears shaped into crescents or sheet fragments. Bracelets, beads, gorgets (Figure 7.3), crescents, celts, and adzes were made from Lake Superior copper. There are tubular pipes, including some late effigy forms in Ohio and West Virginia. Highly distinctive of late Adena are engraved stone tablets, probably used during ceremonies for preparation of paints. There is some marine shell, but it is not extensive. The pottery in the first half-millennium or so before the

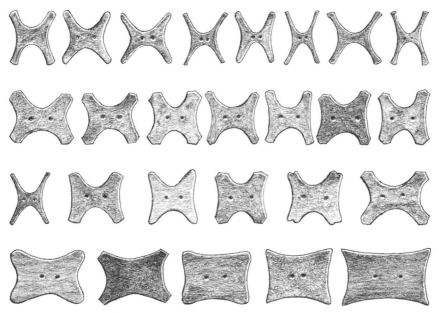

FIGURE 7.3
Adena and Middle Woodland reel-shaped gorgets. Seriation: oldest forms are at lower right, the most recent are top row.

Christian era was Fayette Thick; during the major Adena expression it was Adena Plain, with regional variants of Montgomery Incised now known from Indiana, Kentucky, Ohio, and West Virginia. A number of the projectile point styles, such as Adena and Robbins, are local expressions of similar eastern forms of this period.

House size varies from small, single-family units to larger structures capable of holding 40 people. There are groups of 10 or more structures at some sites; others (possibly transient camps) have from 2 to 4. A central communal hearth and interior storage pits are usually found (Figure 7.4). The Adena people almost certainly did not occupy any one village all year long. Population density would have been less than 0.39 per square kilometer. There was some occupation of shelters in Ohio, but it is doubtful that Adena populations lived in caves or shelters to any degree, although their contemporaries elsewhere did.

The diversity within what has been called Adena is considerable; the term is probably a grouping by archeologists of local complexes in the central Ohio valley that were contemporaneous, contiguous, and that participated in both widespread and highly localized developments. The blend is unique and occurs nowhere else, either as a functioning, interacting macrosociety or as a series of local societies.

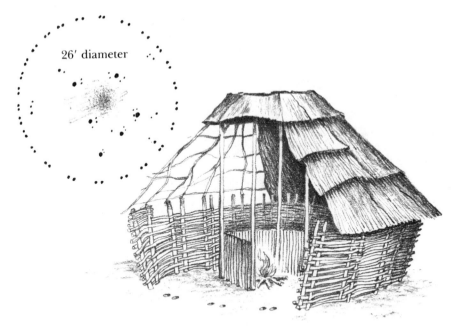

FIGURE 7.4
Postmold plan and cutaway view of restored Adena house, showing probable construction.

MIDDLE WOODLAND: HOPEWELL AND RELATED CULTURES

During a period of time from approximately 100 BC to AD 300, the Middle West was occupied by local regional complexes that can be recognized as participating in a wide range of behavioral patterns inherited from preceding groups and augmented by local progress and by exchange and diffusion from group to group over short or long distances. These Middle Woodland complexes had two dominant areas: one, known as the Hopewell culture, in southern Ohio from Marietta to the Miami River, and the other comprising the Havana societies of the Illinois valley and adjacent areas. Of these, the Ohio area was by far the more dramatic, marking a culmination of many cultural trends of the Archaic and Early Woodland periods. Both the Ohio and the Illinois variants are regarded as Hopewellian societies.

Ohio Hopewell

SUBSISTENCE BASIS □ There have been very few reports on the fauna that furnished the protein and fats for the Ohio Hopewell populations. Parmalee's

(1975) study of the fauna from the McGraw village site is the most adequate. It reports an emphasis on mammals, particularly deer, with much smaller numbers of small mammals, bear, bobcat, and puma. Various turtles, fish, and a few amphibians were also identified. Turkey bones were by far the most common bird remains of the 11 species represented, while river mollusca of some 25 species were used as food and for hoes and knives. The bone artifacts from the mound excavations reveal that bear, deer, elk, turkey, and other fauna were hunted. The identified floral remains from sites in Ohio are also not very numerous because of past excavation practices. They have been summarized recently by Ford (1979), who believes that, while the several Ohio societies did have some gardening activities along with seed- and nut-gathering, both food sources were likely to be unreliable from year to year.

The economic base was probably not adequate to support a social structure more complex than kin-based units with headmen or outstanding hunters, raiders, traders, or religious leaders. The Hopewell populations lived in the river valleys of southeastern Ohio's hill country, in the south–central glaciated plateau, and in the southwestern till plains. These dominantly forested areas of the temperate zone differed from one another but not enough to preclude their human occupants from following basically similar patterns of food procurement in the river valleys, the immediately adjacent uplands, and some prairie openings in south–central and southwestern Ohio. Many of the plants collected by historic Indians in the East for food, medicine, and other purposes are found in the Ohio Hopewell areas and were probably utilized by Hopewell people (Yarnell, 1964).

EARTHWORKS AND BURIAL MOUNDS □ Six major Hopewell sites have been excavated in Ohio, and there are probably well over a hundred little-known or unreported sites. Many other complex earthworks and mound groups have not yet been excavated or have been destroyed. Although there have been other presentations of the cultural material from the six major sites, the careful summary by Morgan (1952) is still one of the best. Some of the other, lesser mounds and sites that have been excavated and reported (Magrath, 1945; Starr, 1960:23–24, 97; A. Lee and Vickery, 1972) are often ignored. The major excavated earthwork sites range from some 5.25 hectares with 21 mounds at Mound City northeast of Chillicothe (Mills, 1922) to the Hopewell site of 45 hectares and 38 mounds (Moorehead, 1922; Shetrone, 1926).

At the six major sites there were over 1150 burials; the exact number will never be known. At Tremper, all of the burials were cremated, and the estimate there is 375 individuals (Mills, 1916). Other burial sites, such as those at Hopewell, also yielded extended, bundle, flexed, and partial skeletal remains (Figure 7.5). The mound, depending on size, often covered single- or multiple-mortuary structures or charnel houses. There were also specially prepared basins or "altars" of puddled clay that contained cremated burial offerings, with or without evidence of cremated human bone. The burial groupings found in mortuary

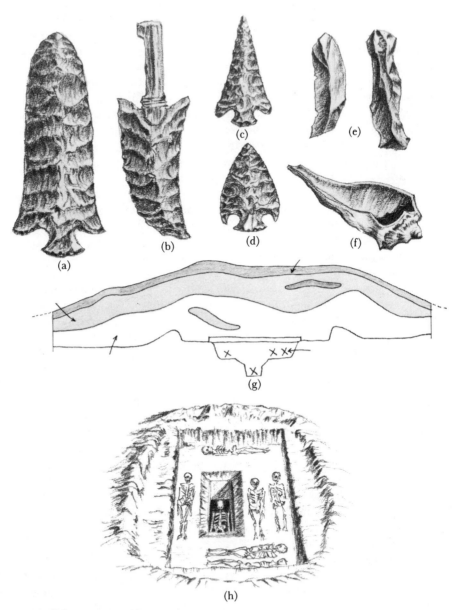

FIGURE 7.5
Hopewell artifacts and diagram of burial mound: (a) obsidian knife or spearhead; (b) obsidian knife, wooden handle (restored); (c, d) spearheads; (e) flake knives; (f) conch-shell dipper; (g) cross-section of Wh6 burial mound; (h) view of central tomb in Wh6 mound. (Parts a–c, e, f from Ohio; parts d, g, and h from Illinois.)

structures probably represent kin groups. Some of the most significant burials were in small mounds, such as that of the cremated male in Mound 11 at Hopewell. In addition to two mica sheets, a few pearl beads, and a polished piece of green chlorite, the grave goods included some 136 kilograms of worked obsidian fragments. This burial I regard as being that of the individual who produced the magnificent Hopewell obsidian spears of which there were between 250 and 500 in altar 2 in Mound 25 at Hopewell. These vary in shape and size, but an estimated 95 percent of all the Hopewell-period obsidian in the Middle West was in these two caches; the source of this obsidian is in what is now Yellowstone National Park (Griffin, 1965b; Griffin et al., 1969).

Another instance of a concentration of items made from an exotic raw material is the presence of 30 to 40 chlorite disks in Mound 1 at Hopewell, found by Squier and Davis (Stevens, 1870:438). The same author mentions that the only other object of this material in the Squier and Davis collection was a gorget from Mound 8 at Mound City, but a few chlorite objects subsequently were discovered in other mounds. It appears that some of the exotic raw materials gathered and brought to Ohio were the property of an individual, to utilize as he wished or to have buried with him—the 3000 sheets of mica and the 90.5 kilograms of galena from Mound 17 of the Hopewell site, for example. From a small mound in the northeastern part of the Newark group, one-half to three-quarters of a cubic meter of mica plates were removed, along with 14 human skeletons, when a lock was constructed on the canal in 1828 (Squier and Davis, 1848:72n). Each of the many items in these long-distance exchanges will have to be studied and interpreted as an individual case. No single model will handle the entire remarkable activity.

Archeologists have long recognized that the many burial items of dress and ornamentation associated with some individuals represented their distinctive roles while they were alive, as did mortuary behavior and accoutrements. In a study of the excavation records for the largest mound at Seip, Greber (1976, 1979) recognized three reasonably distinct burial areas on the floor of the mound. The types of artifacts and burial practices accorded the 123 burials indicate that some 10 percent of the burials represented individuals of "high" social status. She suggests that there were three large social divisions, with smaller social units clustering around a high-ranking individual. The Seip burials are viewed as essentially contemporary but the exact span cannot be given and may represent sequential burial episodes. Further, the rank or role represented by the "high-ranking" burials cannot be identified with certainty. Greber's excavations of the Edwin Harness mound floor revealed a similar pattern of distinctive areas of burial disposition with some adult males distinguished by more elaborate burial goods (Greber, 1979). In these two major burial mounds, the three burial areas perhaps represented separate social groups that can also be ranked by the same type of analysis accorded individuals within each group. Mound 25 at the Hopewell site had three primary mounds which were later covered to form the largest burial mound in the country. If the tripartite division represents clans, these clans would be analogous to those of the southern–central Algonquians. This group was patrilineal in the historic period (Callender, 1979). Not all of the "status" burials in the Harness area or at Hopewell were in the large mounds, but the burial furniture indicates their contemporaneity with some of those in the large mounds.

The large, complex geometric earthworks are unique to Ohio Hopewell and vary from site to site. They were probably constructed over a period of time at any of the large sites, and the large mounds were probably built over a period of several generations. The fill of the mound and of the earthworks contained considerable quantities of village debris, and the areas within the earthworks or near them were village sites. Recent excavations at Mound City and at the Seip group are uncovering the house sites and village debris. At Seip the houses vary somewhat in shape, but they are basically rectanguloid with rounded corners and vary in size. Typical houses are 10.5 to 12 meters long by 9 to 10.5 meters wide. While it might be possible to house an extended family of perhaps 30 to 40 people in such a structure, the interior activities and furnishings would take up much of the space. Large refuse and storage pits occur in the floors; there is evidence of various craft activities involving mica, leather, and wood; and cord-marked, plain, and Hopewell-style pottery appear (Baby, 1976). When these earthwork areas are intensively excavated, we will learn more of the local settlement system. In addition to the major village areas, there probably were other, smaller loci not only for smaller, related groups but also for use in the procurement of food and other supplies during the year.

We cannot now recognize the temporal differences between the major sites. There was certainly temporal overlap between them, but the exact time spans of the sites are not very well known, in spite of valiant attempts by several interpreters to place the sites in time. Nor are accurate estimates of population available. The best estimate of the number of burials at the six major sites is about 1150+. This is certainly not the total number of the people who participated in the life of these sites. Somewhat more accurate demographic figures for the lower Illinois valley Hopewellian occupation give a figure of a bit less than 0.39 per square kilometer. The figure probably could not have been much more than that.

We have evidence of more foreign materials in Ohio than of Ohio materials or artifacts exported to other areas. At least six species of marine shells from the Atlantic and Florida coasts appear; other Florida items are barracuda jaws, ocean turtle shells, and shark and alligator teeth. Large quantities of mica were obtained, probably from southwestern North Carolina and eastern Tennessee. Chlorite was apparently also obtained in the southern Appalachians, meteoric iron came from a number of sources, and cobble-size chunks of galena came from the upper Mississippi valley and the southeastern Missouri Ozark area. Hundreds of pounds of copper were obtained from mines in the Lake Superior district or from copper carried south by glacial action and picked up in northern Michigan, Wisconsin, or Illinois. A small amount of southeastern copper has been identified from the Hopewell site. Silver was obtained from mines in the Cobalt, Ontario area and around Lake Superior or from the glacially transported copper picked up in northern Michigan, Wisconsin, or Illinois. Nodular, bluish flint, probably from Harrison County, Indiana, occurs in great quantities—over 8000 pieces were found in one small mound. In addition to the obsidian mentioned before, Knife River chalcedony from North Dakota has been recovered. It could well have been obtained on the same postulated expeditions that brought obsidian to the Midwest—at least, when chalcedony is found at Middle Woodland sites, obsidian is also found. It is reasonable to postulate that certain items, such as the copper earspools and breastplates, were made primarily in Ohio. The recent identification of southeastern copper sources and the discovery of earspools and panpipes in the Southeast made from these sources has somewhat changed previous interpretations that all Ohio copper came from deposits around Lake Superior. The major distribution of Ohio pipestone platform pipes, outside of Ohio, was into the Illinois valley. This area perhaps received about 100 pipes. Some Illinois pipes were probably made locally. A few Ohio pipestone pipes reached the Davenport, Iowa, area and southwestern Wisconsin, but practically no Ohio pipestone platform pipes occur in southern Michigan, New York, or in the Southeast. A small number of flint lamellar blades, made of stone from Flint Ridge, Ohio, moved into western New York and down the trade routes through eastern Tennessee to Florida.

This trade reflects the wide geographical knowledge of much of the eastern United States that some of its aboriginal inhabitants possessed. Trade helps to explain the apparent speed with which new ideas and techniques moved across long distances. Some of the trade or acquisition was probably done by long-distance travel, but other materials or finished goods may have been exchanged locally and moved from group to group. Each type of good or produce will have to be studied to determine its exchange pattern.

Caldwell's (1964) formulation of the interaction sphere was that it was primarily associated with the religious activities known to archeologists from mortuary locations. He suggested that there was more similarity in these practices throughout the Midwest and Southeast than other archeologists have been able to accept. Struever's (1964) interpretation placed more emphasis on the economic activities of the societies. Population growth resulted from increments to the food supply obtained by manipulating plant resources. These changes resulted in changes in social organization. The interaction sphere was viewed as acting mainly in acquisition and exchange of raw materials and finished goods. This concept was later elaborated into a model postulating trade and exchange on a highly organized, structured, and regulated basis that in most instances goes beyond any available data (Struever and Houart, 1972). The most recent publication on Hopewell exchange patterns by Seeman (1975) presents a more thorough discussion of the problem.

Ohio Hopewell art expression was highly developed in both naturalistic and geometric styles. Animal and human effigies were skillfully sculptured in

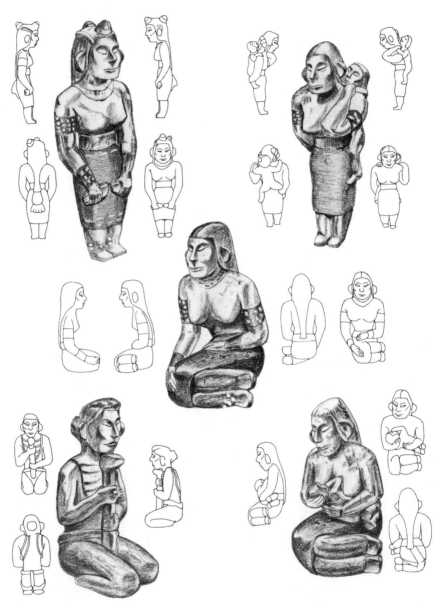

FIGURE 7.6
Hopewell ceramic figurines from the Knight site, Illinois.

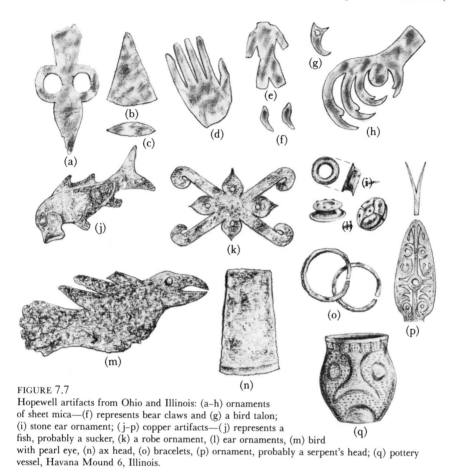

FIGURE 7.7
Hopewell artifacts from Ohio and Illinois: (a–h) ornaments
of sheet mica—(f) represents bear claws and (g) a bird talon;
(i) stone ear ornament; (j–p) copper artifacts—(j) represents a
fish, probably a sucker, (k) a robe ornament, (l) ear ornaments, (m) bird
with pearl eye, (n) ax head, (o) bracelets, (p) ornament, probably a serpent's head; (q) pottery
vessel, Havana Mound 6, Illinois.

Ohio pipestone, and human figurines were made from baked clay (Figure 7.6).
Copper and mica sheets were cut into geometric and effigy forms. Some of the
copper plates have embossed designs of eagles, turkeys, buzzards, and parrots
(Figure 7.7). Cut-out designs may have been stencils for painting designs on
finely woven cloth of native bast fibers. The Ohio Hopewell people also made
fine engravings on animal and human bone, with representations of shamans in
ceremonial dress and many other designs.

Illinois Havana–Hopewell

While exchange activities were being carried on in different ways by the Ohio
Hopewell people, they were neither colonialists nor expansionists. In the Illi-
nois area the development from late Early Woodland into early local Havana–
Hopewellian patterns that occurred around 200 BC seems to have taken place

somewhat earlier than did the Adena to Hopewell shift in Ohio. The use of log tombs and pits below the mound floor is a practice related more to the late Adena than to Hopewell. There is an almost total absence of cremation in the Illinois area burial practices. In Illinois there are no really comparable geometric earthworks, no mounds comparable to the major tumuli in Ohio, and few striking caches of goods. Only in the great deposits of flint-disk preforms at a number of sites in the Illinois valley, totaling some 20,000 specimens, does this area outdo the spectacular Ohio area.

TRADE AND INTERACTION ☐ The trade items in the Illinois–Mississippi valley were few and not very varied. Platform pipes of Ohio claystone are one of the most important exchange items and some of the finest effigy forms were probably made in the Scioto Valley. The Illinois area obsidian specimens are found at more sites but very few specimens come from any one site. They are shaped from obsidian cores in the local projectile point and blade styles. They do not seem to be traded from Ohio to the Illinois area (Griffin, 1965b; Griffin et al., 1969). Knife River flint is known in smaller quantities in Illinois and the upper Mississippi valley. One example from the Snyders Mound Group is a superb instance of knapping skill that could possibly derive from Ross County, Ohio. The flint disk preforms mentioned above probably derive from the Dongola quarries of southwestern Illinois.

The number and variety of copper specimens in Illinois is far less than in Ohio. The beads, celts or gouges, and the few other copper forms were probably made in Illinois, Wisconsin, or Michigan of either mined or drift copper. The celts or gouges placed with adult males, when carefully excavated, are often found to have been wrapped with matting, cloth, or hide. They do not show signs of use as chopping tools, and their precise role in the living societies or as burial furniture is uncertain. Earspools or panpipes with silver are rare, with the silver having been obtained from the Lake Superior basin or from Cobalt, Ontario. Marine shell containers from the Gulf area may well have reached the upper Mississippi valley without going through the Ohio district, perhaps by way of the Chattahoochee to Tennessee–Ohio and upper Mississippi valleys, or up the Mississippi valley. Certainly the major mortuary and village sites in the Havana area had more of the materials called Interaction Sphere goods, but many of the items are likely to have been locally produced, either following ancient techniques and forms or copying imported, manufactured specimens. No sound evidence for redistribution activity along classic lines in Middle Woodland times has been produced, either in the Midwest or throughout the eastern United States.

Although the two regions (Ohio and the Illinois valley) vary in the details of such items as projectile and knife point forms, lamellar blades, the variants of the celt, the use of mollusk shell spoons, marine-shell containers, bone awls, the use of beaver and other incisors, and basic ceramic vessel forms, the overall manufacturing and decorative techniques of these items indicate their contemporaneity and participation in a widespread lifestyle adaptation. These techniques are at the core of the interrelationships of these northern Hopewellian groups; specific examples of exchange and trade are a reflection of the basic similarities. Such examples are a result not a cause; they did not initiate but rather helped to maintain connections within and between societies.

From Illinois there were either strong interaction and exchange at all levels of behavior with resident groups in southern Wisconsin, northern and eastern Iowa, northeastern Illinois, northwestern Indiana, southwestern Michigan, and the Saginaw Valley of Michigan, or there were population movements into these areas, or both. This expansion took place around the time the Havana pottery style had developed and the Hopewell pottery style had recently appeared. Somewhere around AD 1 to 100 would be a reasonably close estimate of the time (Griffin, 1967). There was also cultural expansion west into central and western Missouri, eastern Kansas, and northeastern Oklahoma. Mound burial practices similar to those of the Illinois area appear in southeastern Missouri, eastern Arkansas, and northwestern Mississippi. A little locally made pottery of the Havana Zone-stamped style is known from west–central Mississippi. The Illinois area seems, naturally, to have had closer relations with the lower Mississippi valley than did Ohio Hopewell, while the lower Wabash populations had connections up the Tennessee. Because of its geographic and physiographic difference from the northern glaciated area, southern Illinois, as usual, had a much different series of Middle Woodland societies. Those with the closest affinities to the Illinois valley area lived along the Mississippi valley or in the lower reaches of its tributaries.

BURIAL PATTERNS □ Burials among the western groups were primarily in mounds, although some village burials are known. Mound size varies from only a meter or so high and 6 to 9 meters in diameter to the two or three structures, found at Ogden–Fettie in Fulton County, that were 61 by 53 by 4 meters and 30 by 24 by 2 meters. The other 32 mounds of the latter group were much smaller (Cole and Deuel, 1937).

Brown (1979) has characterized the most common Havana burial pattern as the use of mortuary crypts dug into the earth, usually in rectangular shapes; size and the details of construction vary. Usually the principal burial or burials are placed in the center and have the most grave goods. Burials were wrapped with organic material in some instances, and often remains are preserved of a mat or perhaps of skin coverings that were pinned to the earth by bone skewers. In some of the mounds where the central crypt was apparently kept open for some time, earlier burials in which the flesh and ligaments had decomposed were placed as bundle burials around the periphery of the crypt, while in the central area individuals more recently deceased were placed. It is rare to have grave goods indicating status placed with bundle burials. If, then, mound construction was primarily a status recognition of the crypt burials, were the mounds built for the earlier interments, or were the builders anticipating the inevitable demise of the persons represented by the later extended burials, with their accompanying grave goods?

Analysis of Havana burials in the lower Illinois valley have indicated to some archeologists that the highest-ranked individuals represent hereditary positions or ascribed ranks (Tainter, 1975). The conclusion is based essentially on the amount of energy probably expended in the burial program. This view has been questioned by other analysts, who view the indications of preferential burial treatment as being primarily associated with adult males whose associated materials—personal medicine bundles, personal tools and weapons—probably represent their differing roles in the society (Griffin et al., 1970; Braun, 1979). This view is more compatible with the concept that such burials represented achieved status, but does not deny that some achievers may also have had higher social status than others (Braun, 1979).

SETTLEMENT PATTERN □ There are many more Middle Woodland sites than Early Woodland sites. They are closer together and have deeper village site deposits, and many more burial areas can be attributed to them. The villages, though averaging from 0.4 to 1.2 hectares, may be as small as a 0.1 hectare or as large as 6 or more hectares. At one site in southwestern Wisconsin there were 14 circular to rectangular houses (Freeman, 1969) on about 0.1 hectare of land, and, like the Illinois sites, it had many refuse pits. At some of the larger sites, however, we are not certain that the entire area was occupied contemporaneously. There probably would not have been more than a few hundred people in the largest villages.

Intensive surveys of the lower Illinois valley Hopewellian have pinpointed the location of the larger mortuary and village sites; at the foot of the bluff when the river was close by or near where secondary streams enter the river, farther out in the flood plain. Some sites are located on natural levees of the river and on other locations providing access to the river. A number of sites have also been identified on tributary streams some miles from the river into the prairie upland. Small campsites of Middle Woodland populations are also located along quite small streams. They were perhaps specialized extractive locations used by small task groups. Certainly the settlement pattern is quite different from that portrayed by writers before the 1960s. The larger sites, situated with some regularity about 20 km apart, were occupied continuously by the same social group (as indicated by skeletal studies) (Buikstra, 1979). It has been proposed that new developments in food procurement helped differentiate the Middle Woodland Havana societies from their predecessors, allowing population to grow and society to become more complex. But it is now known that the Middle Woodland people had essentially the same floral and animal subsistence base as the Late Archaic populations of the area. As in Ohio, while there are indications of a small amount of maize, in Illinois sites cucurbits and gourds are more often found. The most important preserved remains are of starchy seeds in some number, and there are indications that a species of *Chenopodium*, a *Polygonum*, and maygrass may have been cultivated, probably not primarily as "mud flat horticulture" (Asch et al., 1979).

Other Traditions

To the north in Minnesota, northern Wisconsin, Michigan, southeastern Manitoba, and western Ontario, a ceramic, mound-building complex is identified as Laurel (Stoltman, 1973, 1974; J. Wright, 1967). This complex has some similarities to Hopewell in pottery and projectile point styles, but the total complex is distinctive from those of other areas. The time range is about 50 BC to AD 800–900. In northern Wisconsin, Salzer (1974) has briefly described a Nokomis phase with some ceramic traits close to Illinois Hopewellian, but his sites and their complex are noticeably different from those of the Trempealeau populations in the southwestern part of the state and the contemporary groups in the southeastern part of Wisconsin. Some eastern expressions of Laurel can be found at Naomikong Point (Jansen, 1968) on the south shore of Lake Superior west of Sault Ste. Marie, at Summer Island (Brose, 1970), and around the north shore of Lake Superior as far as the mouth of the Michipicoten.

Another northern stamped-pottery tradition stands between Laurel and Point Peninsula on the east. This is the Saugeen complex of southwestern Ontario discussed by J. Wright (1967, 1972b). He suggests a beginning date of 500 BC for Saugeen, which is difficult to accept on a comparative basis. The Saugeen burials are in small cemeteries. Villages are on the lower reaches of tributaries of southeastern Lake Huron and northwestern Lake Erie. Fishing was a common activity. House post molds outline structures about 5.2 meters by 7 meters, containing hearths and pits. They are single-family units. Artifacts include celts and adzes, stemmed and corner-notched points and scrapers, slate gorgets, copper awls, axes, and at least one panpipe. I would estimate the time span of Saugeen from about the beginning of the Christian era to AD 800 or 900.

Thus, both Laurel and Saugeen as well as Point Peninsula culture ceramics with dentate-stamped decoration last until AD 800–1000. Since stamping of this type was the hallmark of the Middle Woodland cultures in the Middle West, the archeologists in New York and adjoining areas have referred to all of their stamped pottery complexes as Middle Woodland. This terminology was applied even though the northeastern Middle Woodland lasted 600 years or so after Hopewellian had disappeared in the area where the terminology was instituted. The Middle West was in the Late Woodland and Early Mississippi time periods at the time that Point Peninsula is still being called Middle Woodland.

Many of the sites called by some Western Basin Middle Woodland actually date from 300 to 500 years later than Middle Woodland and should be identified as Late Woodland in the Toledo area. These small bands had a seasonal settlement system exploiting the lakes, marshlands, and upland areas (Stothers et al., 1979).

LATE OR TERMINAL WOODLAND COMPLEXES

No one knows what factors resulted in the gradual disappearance of the broad spectrum of activity that characterized Ohio Hopewell and Havana societies in the Midwest. The process clearly began in late Middle Woodland from about AD 200–400 and cannot be attributed to the introduction of the bow and arrow or to greater emphasis on maize agriculture. These traits do not appear until about AD 700–900 and may have contributed to the development of stockaded villages, which are known in the upper Monongahela and northeastern Lake Erie area by this time. In spite of the gradual disappearance of interregional exchange of raw materials and finished artifacts, many similarities in material culture (such as ceramics, projectile styles, housetypes, and settlement patterns) have been identified from the Appalachians to the Missouri River valley. Attempts to "explain" local cultural shifts by reference to the environmental characteristics of the region are of questionable validity.

Representative of the local complexes immediately following the Middle Woodlands period are the Weaver, Whitehall, and Fox Creek complexes in west–central Illinois; the Raymond phase in southwestern Illinois (see Figure 7.12); early Lewis in southern Illinois; and much of the Allison complex, along with LaMotte and Duffy of the lower Wabash valley. The last three developed from the Middle Woodland societies in the lower Wabash; their ceramic characteristics indicate interaction with groups up the Tennessee valley. In southern Ohio the early Newtown sites fall in this time period, as do the early Cole complex sites of the Scioto region.

The Newtown complex was first identified on the basis of material from the lower levels of the Turpin site near Cincinnati (Oehler, 1950; Griffin, 1952b) and burials in a "stone mound." There are a number of village sites and mounds of this early Late Woodland complex in the area such as the Burkham stone mounds (Black, 1934) overlooking the Miami valley in southeast Indiana; the Chilton site in Henry County, Kentucky (Funkhouser and Webb, 1937); the multicomponent Haag site on a low terrace of the Great Miami in Dearborn County, Indiana (Reidhead and Limp, 1974); and the Lichliter site near Dayton (Allman, 1957). At Lichliter nine houses have been excavated and an additional three or four remain unexcavated. The houses were circular and about 40 feet in diameter; House 1 was formed of some 92 posts 5–7 inches in diameter sunk about 30 inches into the subsoil. So far no stockade has been identified as surrounding this 4-acre village. Projectile points resemble the Lowe type of the lower Wabash and the Chesser-stemmed of southeastern Ohio, and there are also antler-tip points. There were many flint scrapers of various shapes, roughly flaked discs of slate, shale, and schist, chipped stone celts, hoes and picks, nar-

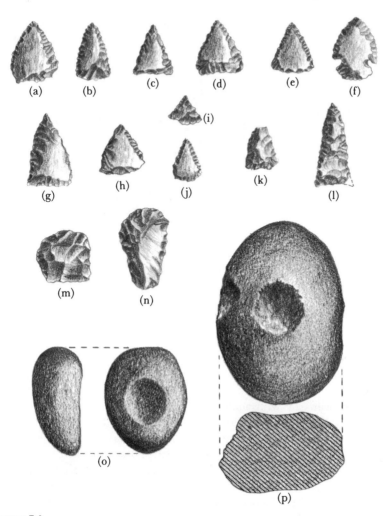

FIGURE 7.8
Late Woodland Effigy Mound artifacts: (a, c–e) Sanders Triangular quartzite points;
(b) Triangular (A) point; (f) corner-notched quartzite point; (g, i–l) Triangular (B) quartzite
points; (m, n) quartzite end scrapers; (o) pecked stone; (p) pecked hammerstone.

row rectangular to ovoid stone gorgets, and hammerstones. No domesticated
plants were identified. The pottery is cord-marked up to a flat or rounded,
undecorated lip. The ware has a granular temper and is fairly large; a few of
the shoulders have a marked angle. I know of one radiocarbon date from the site
of about AD 350 (Crane and Griffin, 1959:182), but the Newtown complex
probably existed from about AD 400 to 800.

Newtown burial practices differ a great deal, from extended burials at
Chilton to compact groups of bundle burials at Burkham and flexed primary,

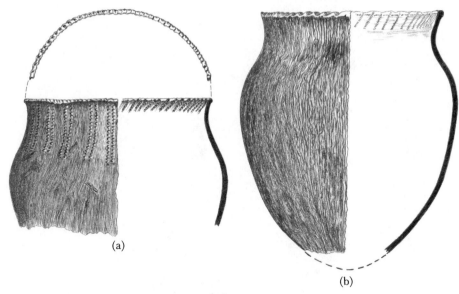

FIGURE 7.9
Madison ceramics: (a) Madison Punctated jar; (b) Madison Plain (cord-marked) jar.

partial bundles and pulverized bones at Turpin. Burial goods are not often found, but elbow stone pipes, a rabbit effigy pipe of stone, bone gorgets, large beads of conch columella, and the cut and ground lower jaws of small mammals are associated primarily with adult males. Several burials were discovered at Fire House site in Newtown, Hamilton County, Ohio. They yielded a mica plate; small stemmed points like the Lowe–Chesser forms; narrow, rectangular bone gorgets like those of Burkham, Turpin, and Chilton; a broken stone elbow pipe; and two circular marine shell gorgets—one engraved with a puma and the other with an opossum. Gorgets of this Fairfield style (Phillips and Brown, 1975:158–161) have been known for at least 75 years but have been difficult to tie down to a cultural context; the context now seems to have been established for at least two of them (T. Cinadr, 1981: personal communication).

Just as the Middle Woodland occupations in the Scioto valley differ from those in the Miami valley, so do those of the Late Woodland. The materials recovered from this period have been called the Cole complex. Certainly some of the sites such as Voss are probably early Fort Ancient, while sites such as Zencor are similar to the Lichliter complex and should be in a comparable time period. It is difficult to tell just where the material called the Intrusive Mound Complex belongs because it has some characteristics of both early and later Late Woodland societies. A number of archeologists working in the Ohio valley east of Marietta have produced evidence for increasing permanence of valley settlements, camps, and special activity areas and of seasonal occupation of shelters in

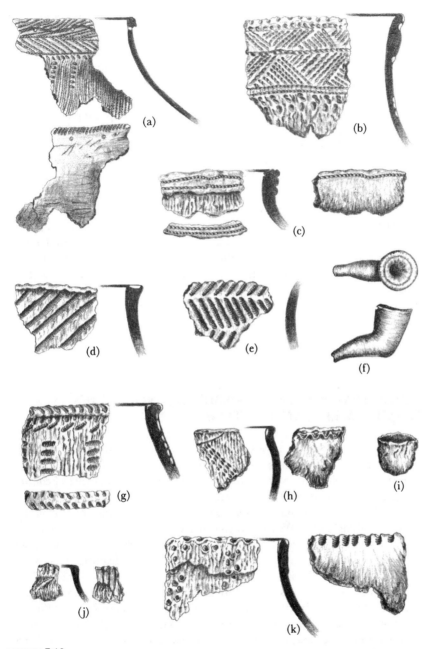

FIGURE 7.10
Late Woodland pottery from Wisconsin: (a, b) Point Sauble Collared; (c, k) Aztalan Collared; (d, e, g, h) Heins Creek Corded Stamped; (f) clay pipe; (i) child's pot; (j) Leland Cord-marked. (After Hurley, 1975.)

Late Woodland times. From central Kentucky shelters there is evidence of squash, gourd, sunflower, maygrass, goosefoot, and sumpweed, suggesting occupation from August to November in a Newtown context. In north–central Kentucky unpublished excavations have uncovered villages with open central courtyards surrounded by occupational and activity areas.

In eastern Missouri some of the early Ralls phase sites, such as the Ross site (Chapman, 1980:130), and the early part of the Meramec Spring phase are representative of Late Woodland. The upper levels of some of the rockshelters in central Missouri have yielded pottery and projectile points that belong in this horizon. Overall, central Missouri shows a gradual transition from Middle Woodland into early Late Woodland (Chapman, 1980:46, 110, 278). In northwestern Illinois, northeastern Iowa, and southwestern Wisconsin the transition from Late Middle Woodland is reflected both in the material culture and in population studies (Jamison, 1971). The cord-impressed rim decoration on late Havana pottery at sites such as Lane Farm (Keyes, 1934; Logan, 1976) has certified this continuity. The potters in this area developed a number of distinctive ceramic decorative styles that reflect their interaction and the continuity of regional development (Figures 7.8–7.10). The linear and effigy mounds constructed by about AD 500 are another distinctive feature that persisted for centuries. Not all of the societies of this interaction area, however, participated in the production of such mounds.

THE TRANSITION TOWARD AND DEVELOPMENT OF MISSISSIPPIAN SOCIETIES IN THE AMERICAN BOTTOM

Excavations conducted as a result of I-270 highway construction along the eastern and southeastern parts of the American Bottom and at adjacent borrow-pit areas on the bluffs have uncovered an almost unbroken sequence of cultural change from about AD 400 to late transient Oneota occupation. Some of the small early Late Woodland settlements revealed ceramics and other material-culture materials on the Weaver–Raymond level. The several small villages of about AD 400–700 represent relatively short-term occupations and exhibit gradual changes in house forms, artifact forms, and ceramic features. One of the early Late Woodland locations has three small, circular, depressed house floors with extended entranceways. So far little or no maize has been found for sites of this time span either in the I-270 excavations or elsewhere in the Midwest. Thus the interpretation that the transition from Middle to early Late Woodland was caused by an increasing dependence on maize is not substantiated. It has also been proposed that the villages became larger, but this also is unsupported by excavated data. The subsistence evidence indicates a continued dependence on hunting and gathering of nuts, seeds, fish, fowl, and mammals from the flood plain and the immediately contiguous upland woods. Variations in the vegetal foods at some of the sites probably reflect the season when the sites were occupied or when the pits were filled.

One of the completely excavated small villages, dated at about AD 700–800, had twelve 2-meter square houses grouped around a central courtyard. In the center of the courtyard was a post pit. There were four large, deep, rectangular pits placed in a rough square around the post pit. The house floors were between 5 and 25 cm deep with wall posts along the walls of the basin. Internal features are rare in these structures and it is probable that much of the food preparation and other activities were conducted outside the single-family structures. Maize is associated with communities of this period but does not seem to have been a primary food source. Tobacco seeds of *Nicotiana rusticum* have been identified from refuse pits.

Somewhat later, in what has been called *Early Fairmount,* the same village plan persists but some villages are larger and maize is more common. Mill Creek flint hoes are present, as are early chunky-stones. The ceramics become increasingly limestone-tempered in the southern part of the flood plain, with smoothed rim areas. Early Monks Mound Red bowls are present and the projectile points are clearly arrowheads. None of these villages are fortified. The amount of village debris and the overlapping of features suggest that the sites were occupied on a yearly basis and had larger populations. This Early Fairmount phase would probably correspond to Griffin and Jones' (1977:487) postulated Pulcher occupations 2 and 3 which were called pre-Fairmount.

Following the above occupations are small communities with wall trench rectangular structures and with a mixture of limestone-tempered and early Powell–Ramey vessels representing a Late Fairmount and early Stirling phase. While maize and Mill Creek hoes testify to the importance of farming, a substantial part of the vegetal material recovered is still of local plants; the seed density is high, with emphasis on *Chenopodium,* maygrass, and *Polygonum.* The woods used in framing the house structures include hickory and oak but the preferred wood was willow. Still later in time are communities with developed Cahokian Stirling to Moorehead phases, but most are still relatively small. One site, Julian, has 28 houses. These were probably all not constructed and occupied at the same time. Sand Prairie phase occupations at about AD 1300–1500 are also present in the I-270 corridor in the American Bottom. One of the features is an emphasis on effigy vessels of turtle, beaver, and conch and on duck-head bowls and long-necked water bottles—which indicate Sand Prairie's participation in forms of this type with many Mississippian complexes of the same time period.

Recognition of the gradual development of these several short-lived communities was made possible by adequate funding, the availability of mechanical equipment to remove large areas of topsoil, and the many skilled excavators. The results have contributed a great deal to our understanding of the growth and changes of Mississippian societies in the American Bottom. Very few mounds of any type were built on these sites, so that the area of the I-270 corridor was functionally quite different from the central area where so many mounds were located and where there were considerably more superimposed house patterns and village debris. Such heavy use and the resultant concentrations have made it quite difficult to determine the size of contemporary communities or population groups and the settlement pattern for any short period of time. This difficulty has in turn made population estimates an interesting, but unreliable, pastime. While it is quite evident that cultural growth in all parts of the American Bottom had a marked similarity, including a number of distinctive cultural products, there are still many questions that cannot be answered with any assurance. There are those who think that the Mississippi valley populations of southeastern Missouri and northeastern Arkansas brought in Early Mississippi products and stimulated the local societies, while others would look to the Caddoan area for the major culture bearers. There is no strong evidence for either position. My own view is that in the American Bottom the shift from Late Woodland into the more complex local Mississippian phases occurred during essentially the same general period of time as the similar shifts that took place to the south and southeast. There were many regional centers of development and impetus from Mesoamerica cannot be identified.

It is also difficult to assess the social, political, and religious organization of the various "suburban" communities and their relationship to the central population concentration. The small villages and hamlets of I-270 seem to have been largely self-sufficient units with a wide variety of food stuffs being consumed. There does not seem to be adequate evidence that they were growing maize or producing other food for postulated specialized craftspeople or for markets. There is little certainty of the degree of political control that was exerted on these smaller enclaves or even on the second-line sites with platform mounds and plazas. One would expect that, at times of major ceremonial events during the year, the large mound centers would have had an influx of participants— but whether they were compelled to attend or did so for other reasons is not known. The only known palisade in the central area, while clearly designed as a defensive structure, does not include much of that area and was constructed and rebuilt over a period of years around AD 1100–1200. Smaller towns such as Mitchell, the Kunneman group, or the Powell area are not known to have had palisades either for defense or as a screen for the central area of their civic-ceremonial activities.

Cahokia

Certainly the "downtown" Cahokia center represents the major focus of the St. Louis–American Bottom area for at least 300 years and acted as a strong catalyst in the restructuring of societies from about AD 950 to 1300 both in the upper Mississippi valley area and a short distance to the south along the Father of Waters. This influence is best known from the presence in these areas of

Stirling-period pottery styles that could have been made at Cahokia. Trade items, including foreign pottery, nonlocal flint objects, and other such indications of interarea exchange are present at Cahokia, primarily in the core area. Some of the trade pottery, which first appears about AD 1100, probably comes from northern Caddoan sites but the precise source has not been identified by Caddoan specialists who have examined the examples. Caddoan projectile points were found on the surface as well as deposited in quiver groups, long since decayed, in Mound 72 and within Mound 34. There was also shell-tempered negative-painted pottery in both of those mounds.

The most interesting indications of interarea exchange with Caddoan societies are the human and other effigy pipes apparently made of bauxite. At least some of them are highly reminiscent of Spiro forms. In marked contrast to the concentration of such pipes in the Craig Mound at Spiro, those in the Cahokia area were found scattered at a number of locations, from small mounds and small settlements to outlying communities, on the bluffs near Collinsville, at a small mound near Piasa Creek north of Cahokia, and in the lower Illinois valley Schild site (Perino, 1971). Trade, as well as the importance of agriculture, is indicated by the large number of various hoe and spade forms made primarily of Mill Creek flint from Union County, Illinois (Titterington, 1938; Rau, 1872). Whether these forms were produced by artisans from Mississippian sites at "factories" in southwestern Illinois or fashioned locally in the Cahokia area is still moot. These examples are a few of many that could be developed to indicate the importance of trade and exchange in the growth of the Cahokian societies. They represent the resumption of widespread interaction among the contemporary groups, during which not only these known material items were exchanged but probably also concepts and practices, engendering new activities difficult to identify archeologically.

The excavations of the last five years have confirmed the gradual shift from the small, rectangular to the square, single-post structures of Late Woodland or Bluff, and on to the wall-trench rectangular forms of emergent and full Mississippian societies. The trend toward increased community size was clearly recognized in the central Cahokia area some years ago. Although population increase is associated with an increase of maize production, the American Bottom people continued to eat an astonishingly varied diet derived from the area's multiple environments (Parmalee, 1975). While deer formed a high proportion of the meat consumed, other mammals, many bird and fish species, and small numbers of reptiles, amphibians, and mussels were also consumed. Fish from the Mississippi River, the Oxbow lakes, and small tributary streams, and the waterfowl made available by the area's location along the bird migration path provided ample protein. The American Bottom people did not display the concentration on a few mammals or birds predicated for food-producing societies in the East. Similarly, while maize was the predominant vegetal food, it was supplemented by other cultivars of the Eastern Agricultural complex (Ford, 1980) and by native nuts, seeds, berries, and tubers. Most of the corn so far identified from

Cahokia is a mixture of the Hohokam–Basketmaker and Eastern races, with the former predominant in early Mississippian sites. The Eastern type resulted from a gradual shift to an eight-rowed cob with larger kernels that is also predominant in many Eastern United States sites after AD 1200. The Eastern type is not an introduction of a new strain of corn from Mexico but a regional development: the number of beans found so far would not fill one Cahokia bean-pot vessel.

Population estimates or the societal structure are difficult to present with any degree of assurance. Many attempts have been and will be made, but adequate evidence to justify confidence in them is not at hand. As Hall (1975:30) has observed: "considering the size of the Cahokia site proper, approaching six square miles, and considering the length of the Mississippian occupation, at least six centuries, let's say 25 generations, and considering the small area explored archaeologically, less than a quarter of one percent," we are a long way from understanding most of the activities that took place, particularly the social and political systems. Certainly this area was more advanced and more complex or structured than many other Mississippian societies, but how much more than such centers as Moundville, Angel, and Kincaid is not clear. From about AD 1100–1400 Cahokia was probably, to adopt contemporary terminology, the most complex chiefdom in the East, but had not reached the level of a highly structured elite with an organized bureaucracy and the other features required for statehood.

Much attention has been and should be given to the Cahokia area, for it was the scene of important developments from about AD 700 to 1700 that produced a major center of Mississippian culture and probably the largest number of mounds of the platform type. These mounds, located on both sides of the Mississippi River, were never accurately counted. This was probably one of the most densely populated areas in the eastern United States from about AD 900 to 1600, which leaves some 700 years for mound and house construction.

There are scattered indications in the flood plain and the immediately adjacent area of complexes comparable to other post-Hopewell Woodland groups in the Middle West, such as Weaver and Fox Creek and White Hall to the north, and Raymond (Figure 7.11), early Lewis, and most of the La Motte complex to the south in Illinois. By AD 700 one can recognize that significant changes have taken place in Cahokia; the ceramic complex, house forms, and early platform (?) mounds of the Fairmount phase represent the earliest expressions of Mississippian culture. The available evidence strongly suggests that this is a local development from the Patrick phase through an unnamed phase that lasted about 300 years (Griffin and Spaulding, 1951). Fairmount is followed by the Stirling and Moorehead phases of AD 900 to 1050 and 1050 to 1250, respectively (Fowler and Hall, 1972; Fowler, 1969, 1974). Toward the end of this period, the Cahokia area reached a climax in known cultural growth, complexity of products, and indications of far-flung direct contact, the last ranging as far

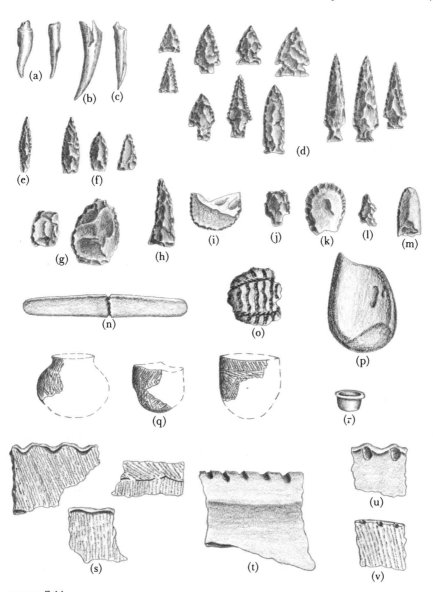

FIGURE 7.11
Raymond complex of Late Woodland: (a) cut antler tips; (b) antler awl; (c) split bird bone awl; (d) projectile points of various types; (e) drill or reamer; (f) ovoid knives; (g) side scrapers; (h) trianguloid knife; (i) flake knife; (j) hafted scraper; (k) thumbnail scraper; (l) graver; (m) chisel; (n) grooved bar—possibly an atlatl weight; (o) clay disk ornamented with impressed cords; (p) pebble celt of basalt; (q) shapes of Raymond Cord-marked jar; (r) miniature bowl of plain ware; (s) exterior views of rim and lip treatment of Raymond Cord-marked; (t) interior view of notched inner lip edge on Raymond Cord-marked; (u) inner rim notching with cord-wrapped-stick impressions; (v) exterior lip edge notching or nicking.

north as the mouth of the Minnesota River, the Strait of Mackinac (by way of Aztalan and the Fox River valley); northwest to Iowa and southeastern South Dakota; northeast to around Danville, Illinois; southeast to the Kincaid site; and south to the Memphis area and near Vicksburg. (Similar exchange between the lower Mississippi valley Coles Creek and Caddoan area to the west has been recognized for some time.) I would suggest, however, that recent estimates of population size for Cahokia are overly generous and that the complexity of social and economic organization that has been postulated may also be exaggerated.

The Illinois Valley

The several Late Woodland societies in the Illinois valley increased in population and showed other indications of changes leading up to about AD 1000, when there is evidence of a gradual shift toward a Cahokia-influenced form of Mississippian. Vessels of Ramey and Powell types were transferred along with other items from the American Bottom. In the Spoon River area there subsequently appears by AD 1100 a series of seven fortified towns on the bluffs, strategically located near a major tributary stream on the west side of the Illinois that gave easy access to the varied environmental zones (Harn, 1978). Only the Larson site was a fortified settlement, with the palisade enclosing an area of about 8 hectares. The Larson-type towns had one or two platform mounds, a plaza, and semisubterranean rectangular houses in planned rows. The houses ranged from fewer than a hundred to well over two hundred and showed continuing occupation for some period of time.

The Larson towns were associated with hamlets, camps, and smaller, specialized activity areas. Population size would have ranged from about 250 to 400 for the smaller towns and 600 to 700 for the larger ones. The cemeteries were located near the bluff and outside of the central town area. The best-known cemetery, Dickson Mound, is the burial area for a nearby hamlet, and was in existence for some 300 years. About 250 burials have been preserved after excavation but an unknown number were either removed or have not yet been excavated. Neither at Dickson nor at other Larson community cemeteries have any of the adult burials had the types of burial goods usually associated with community leaders; so social stratification does not seem to have been well developed. These societies apparently occupied the town sequentially and were still present around AD 1400-1500, when there appears an interesting merger: Oneota pottery decoration placed on local vessel forms at the Crable site and a few other locations. Their earlier associations and material-culture items had been primarily with Cahokia. This association should not be interpreted as one of political or economic domination by Cahokia but as local populations which gradually adopted over many years their own settlement pattern attuned to the specific Spoon River area. Subsistence extractive patterns that had developed over thousands of years continued to be important and supplemented the increased food supply resulting from maize agriculture (Harn, 1980).

The Ohio Valley

The two best-known centers of the lower Ohio River valley are the Kincaid site in southern Illinois (Cole et al., 1951; Muller, 1978) and the Angel site a short distance east of Evansville, Indiana. In neither area does anything occur resembling the gradual, continuous change from Late Woodland to Mississippi that is seen in the American Bottom. Both have their closest cultural relationships with the Tennessee–Cumberland valleys in Kentucky and Tennessee. The Kincaid site in its earlier period received trade materials from the early Cahokia in the form of Ramey and related pottery and flint from Mill Creek in southwestern Illinois. Later, relations with the Tennessee are dominant, as evident particularly in a large amount of Dover flint. Muller believes that the total area known to have been occupied in the town center and the immediate neighborhood is about 36 hectares. There were some 250 structures. The population, assuming five persons a structure, would have been 1250 people, with only about 400 in the central area. Muller's intensive survey in the Black Bottom indicates that the aboriginal horticultural productivity on the 621 hectares of land in the settlement system supporting Kincaid would have been sufficient for about 1500 people. He also feels that such a work force was adequate to have built the platform mounds bordering the plaza and the bastioned palisade of the town. Kincaid was occupied from about AD 1150 to about AD 1500 (Figures 7.12– 7.15). The populations here left little evidence of their participation in the Southeastern Ceremonial complex, but perhaps this is because no burial area for administrative, war, or religious leaders has yet been identified.

Supporting settlements of small hamlets, camps, or limited activities are primarily located in the flood-plane environmental zone. The bottom lands were also a fine location in which to capitalize on the rich native food sources that, coupled with the tropical cultigens, made a more than adequate diet in most years.

In southwestern Indiana the Angel site (Black, 1967; Green and Munson, 1978) and contemporary small villages, hamlets, farmsteads, and camps are distributed along the Ohio River for about 100 km and also along the lower Wabash. The Angel site is the only town and its 40 hectares are enclosed on three sides by a bastioned palisade. It lies on a low terrace adjacent to the Ohio River. There were five platform mounds; Mound A is a split-level construction overlooking the plaza area to the west that was surrounded by individual houses (Figure 7.16). Population estimates for Angel range from 1000 to 3000. It was a functioning civic–ceremonial center from about AD 1200–1400 and most of the population of the total Angel society occupied it. Most of the satellite hamlets and smaller transient settlements were also on the low terraces bordering the

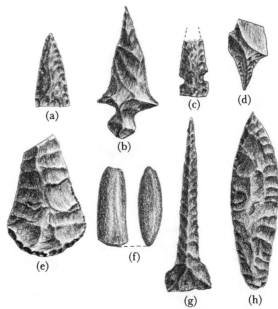

FIGURE 7.12
Flint implements from the Kincaid complex: (a) Madison Triangular point; (b) stemmed point, (c) Cahokia Side-notched; (d) flake drill, (e) flint hoe, (f) polished stone celt; (g) flint drill; (h) flint knife. (After Cole, 1951.)

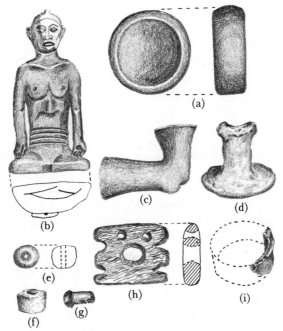

FIGURE 7.13
Miscellaneous ornaments and implements from the Kincaid complex: (a) stone discoidal; (b) small stone figure; (c) baked clay elbow pipe; (d) pottery trowel; (e, f) shell beads; (g) clay labret; (h) cannel coal gorget; (i) cannel coal ring (about 4 centimeters). (After Cole, 1951.)

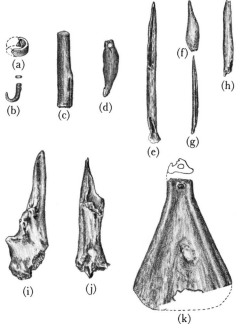

FIGURE 7.14
Miscellaneous bone implements of the Kincaid complex: (a) bone ring; (b) broken fishhook segment; (c) antler punch; (d) perforated bear canine; (e) turkey bone awl; (f, g) bone splinter awls; (h) broken bone needle; (i) deer ulna awl; (j) deer radius awl; (k) deer scapula hoe. (After Cole, 1951.)

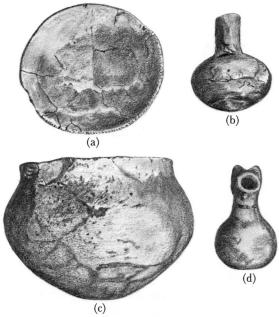

FIGURE 7.15
Representative pottery vessels of the Kincaid complex: (a) flaring-sided bowl; (b) cylindrical neck bottle; (c) large cooking jar; (d) small hooded bottle. (After Cole, 1951.)

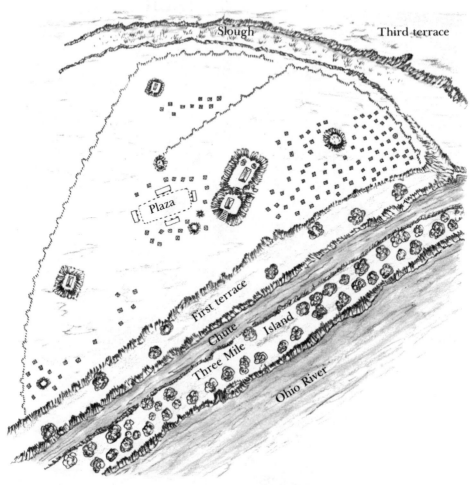

FIGURE 7.16
Sketch of Angel stockaded town with civil and religious buildings on large mounds, the town plaza, and houses of the inhabitants. (After Black, 1967, vol. 2.)

major streams, but a few have been identified on high terraces and upland locations. The major exploitation zone was along the rivers, with their easily tilled soils and many varieties of native foods, game, and fish, but other ecological zones also contributed.

The most intensively occupied area was in the eastern part, where there were many superimposed house structures with square to rectangular floors. The houses were of the usual wattle-and-daub type and the artifacts recovered include the well-developed Mississippian assemblage of pottery bowls, fabric-impressed salt pans, bottles, plates, and jars (Figure 7.17). Perhaps the most

FIGURE 7.17
Representative pottery vessels from the Angel site: (a) jar with rim nodes; (b) large Mississippi jar with loop handles; (c) low rim bowl with notched lip; (d) negative painted carafe neck bottle; (e) short neck, wide mouth bottle; (f) short neck; constricted mouth storage bottle. (After Black, 1967, vol. 2.)

distinctive feature of this assemblage is Angel negative-painted decoration placed most often on interior plate rims. There are a few examples of female effigy and narrow neck bottles with that same decorative technique. A few of the designs are those associated with the Southeastern Ceremonial complex. The small amount of trade pottery includes examples of Ramey Incised from the earlier occupation as well as a few examples from the lower Mississippi valley and the Caddoan area. Three of the arrowpoints closely resemble the Alba form of the Caddoan area. Most of the materials used to manufacture artifacts come from the local area but some of the hoes were made from Mill Creek chert. A well-made kneeling male effigy figure was recovered from Mound F on the western part of the site (Black, 1967: frontispiece). The figure is made of fluorite and was recovered from an intrusive burial in the upper level of the mound. A highly similar form was excavated in Union County, Illinois, in the latter part of the nineteenth century and has been illustrated (Vaillant, 1939: Pl. 13). Such stone effigies are most common in the mid-South, are often found in male-female pairs, and in some instances are associated with charnel house remains, as in the case at Angel.

Following the Angel occupation is a distinctly different Mississippian complex called the *Caborn–Welborn* phase. It had a more dispersed pattern of settlement without fortified towns but with large and small villages, hamlets, farmsteads, and camps. The large villages have not had extensive excavation but may have had populations of 350 or so. They are also located either on or close to the Ohio–Wabash flood plain. This complex dates from about AD 1450–1650 with ceramic connections to the Mississippi valley near the confluence of the Ohio. Decorative designs and techniques with some similarities to those of Oneota also occur. Disk pipes at these sites are also indicative of a Late Prehistoric time period.

The Wabash Valley

Further north in the Wabash valley the Mississippian communities are identified as the Vincennes complex. In central Indiana around Indianapolis an Oliver Phase is concentrated in Marion and Hamilton counties along the White River but extends over a somewhat more extensive area. The phase existed from about AD 1000 to around AD 1200–1300. The sites have a central courtyard with some indications of structures surrounding it, a common pattern for Late Woodland sites. Some maize was grown and at least one cob fragment from the Bowen site was of the Eastern eight-row type. A variety of animal remains was identified, with deer, elk, bear, turkey, and raccoon providing most of the meat. Excavation at the Bowen site did not recover nut fragments or seeds. The Oliver-phase ceramics have similarities to the collared Albee phase in western Indiana, to the Fisher phase in northern Illinois, to cord-impressed decorative styles from central Illinois to southern Wisconsin, and to Fort Ancient products in the central Ohio valley (Dorwin, 1971).

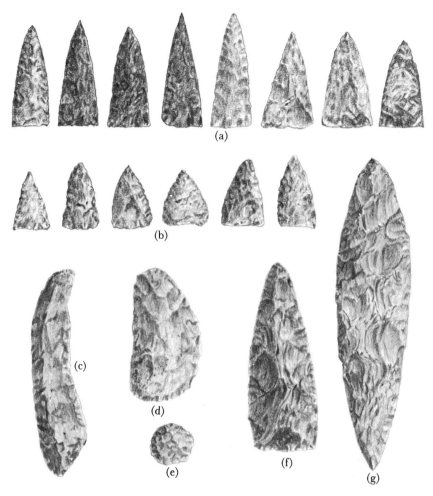

FIGURE 7.18
Lithic implements from northeastern Iowa Oneota: (a, b) triangular arrowpoints; (c–e) scrapers; (f, g) knives. (After M. Wedel, Oneota sites on the upper Iowa River, *Missouri Archaeologist* 2, 1959.)

Oneota and Related Complexes

In the upper Mississippi valley, following the Effigy Mound and other early Late Woodland societies, there was a strong shift toward adoption of some of the behavioral patterns associated with Mississippian societies to the south. There is evidence for population spread from Cahokia to northwestern Illinois and southern Wisconsin sometime between AD 1000 and 1100. One theory is that these groups and others from Cahokia became the Oneota societies (Figures 7.18–7.23). It has also been suggested that Oneota developed from the Effigy

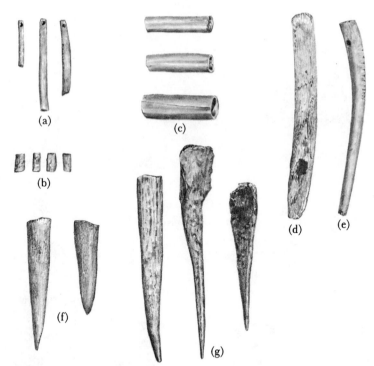

FIGURE 7.19
Bone implements and ornaments from northeastern Iowa Oneota: (a) needle fragments; (b) beads; (c) cylinders or beads; (d) arrowshaft straightener; (e) unidentified perforated and notched bone; (f) worked antler tips; (g) scapula spatulate awls. (After M. Wedel, 1959.)

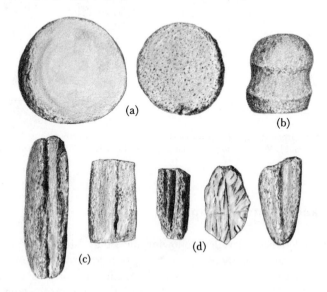

FIGURE 7.20
Stone implements from northeastern Iowa Oneota: (a) mullers; (b) grooved maul; (c) shaft smoothers; (d) abraders. (After M. Wedel, 1959.)

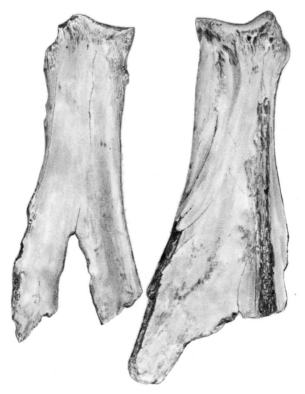

FIGURE 7.21
Bison scapula hoes from northeastern Iowa Oneota sites. (After M. Wedel, 1959.)

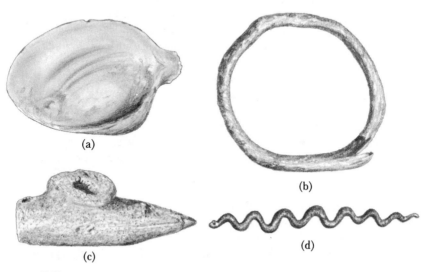

(a)

(b)

(c)

(d)

FIGURE 7.22
Miscellaneous artifacts from northeastern Iowa Oneota sites: (a) shell spoon; (b) metal (brass?) bracelet; (c) Oneota pipe with narrow disk; (d) metal (brass?) serpent. (After M. Wedel, 1959.)

(a)   (b)

FIGURE 7.23
Representative burial vessels from northeastern Iowa Oneota sites: (a) Allamakee Plain;
(b) Allamakee Trailed. (After M. Wedel, 1959.)

Mound complex or that Oneota was a blend of Woodland and Mississippian.
Some ceramic features in northeastern Wisconsin show signs of such influences,
but that location is on the northeastern periphery of both Oneota and Effigy
Mound.

Oneota sites vary in size from little more than 0.5 hectare to 14 to 16 hectares;
in the latter cases, the whole site was probably not occupied contemporaneously.
Many of the sites were fortified. Houses were wigwam types, either oval or, in
northern Illinois and northeastern Iowa, subrectangular with rounded ends.
Houses vary from about 7.5 to 21 meters in length and may well have been
multifamily dwellings. There were also smaller, single-family, oval-house patterns. The pottery is primarily shell tempered, with plain surfaces, rounded
body and base, and a straight rim sloping outward from the neck. The normal
weapon was the bow with a small triangular arrowpoint. At some sites, many
end scrapers, perforators, knives, and other lithic tools, such as abrading stones,
were found. At sites with good preservation, many bone and shell tools for
processing and manufacturing activities have been recovered.

Oneota was less dependent on maize than were the populations to the south,
and their settlements were not as permanent. So far the corn recovered from
northern Oneota sites is primarily of the Eastern race that is a relatively late development. The Oneota peoples were able to occupy several environmental
zones in the upper Mississippi valley, employing techniques of long standing to
obtain their subsistence from native plant and animal resources. It is believed
that these groups were patrilocal and probably patrilineal, particularly in the
early part of the Oneota cultural development. None of the Oneota complexes
participated very much in the belief systems of the Southeastern Ceremonial
complex, nor did they acquire the symbols and forms associated with the extraordinary social and religious practices and beliefs of the strongly agricultural
Southeastern societies.

For many years, Oneota in Wisconsin, Iowa, Minnesota, and Missouri has
been divided into a number of subgroups, one of which perhaps reached the

historic period as the Winnebago and another, presumably, as the Ioway Indians, who were also residents of the adjacent northeastern Iowa–southeastern Minnesota area.

In northern Illinois, northwestern Indiana, and southwestern Michigan, there are occupations of Late and Terminal Woodland that seem to represent groups ancestral to such Central Algonquian-speaking people as the Pottawattomie, Kickapoo, northern Miami, and Illinois. In their material culture products, some of these are very close to the Oneota Chiwere groups, although they belong, of course, to a different language family.

Lower Michigan Late Woodland

The Late Woodland occupations in Michigan began with complexes similar to that of the Fort Wayne Mound, with a strong infusion of concepts and items also found in the post-Hopewell Mound Intrusive culture of Ohio. This similarity is most evident in the southeastern half of the lower peninsula. This area also participated in the developments that produced the Glen Meyer in Ontario, in a series of steps represented at such sites as Riviere aux Vase and the Younge site. There are even suggestions that this area of Michigan was occupied by Iroquoian speakers, and there are maps by linguists and ethnologists that show this. I suspect the situation here was much like that of the northern, eastern, and southern borders of the Five Nations and the Hurons, where Algonquian-speaking groups shared ceramic and utilitarian tool developments with their neighbors.

The western and northern sections of the lower peninsula were interacting with developments in Wisconsin; from about AD 700 to 1100 the ceramic treatment reflects connections with the Late Woodland, Mississippi, and Oneota styles. There are other similarities as well, for this area is part of the Lake Forest environment, which has produced a strong east–west cultural belt for at least 4500 years. The Juntunen site (McPherron, 1967) is perhaps the best known of the typical sites, and probably reflects the developments in adjoining areas not yet delimited in any detail. The populations in these sections were primarily hunters and gatherers who engaged in some agriculture. Their descendants appear on the historic horizon as the Ottawa and Chippewa (Fitting, 1970).

The Fort Ancient Societies

Fort Ancient covers an area nearly equivalent to that occupied by the Adena–Hopewell occupations before it. The several Fort Ancient societies date from somewhere before AD 900 to close to AD 1600. They represent regional groupings in the valleys of the tributaries of the Ohio and along the Ohio River, and over time they became increasingly dependent upon agriculture and increasingly close to Middle Mississippi cultural configurations (Griffin, 1943). In the Miami and Scioto valleys, the earlier Fort Ancient sites clearly derive both culturally and genetically from Late Woodland societies. Early houses are circular; later ones are rectangular. Some sites have evidence of a central courtyard, and a platform mound was excavated at the Baum site. These sites range from 1.2 to 4 hectares and probably had populations of a few hundred people at a time. A wide variety of burial positions were practiced, but single, extended burials are most common. The late, large Fort Ancient sites along the Ohio often had palisades and large rectangular house patterns 15 by 21 meters as well as the more normal 5.5 by 7.5 meter houses. The houses had circular fire basins and two center posts. The later pottery is all shell-tempered Mississippi jar forms, bowls, pans, and a few rare plates (Figure 7.24). By at least AD 1400 shell gorgets of styles normally associated with central and eastern Tennessee make their appearance in Fort Ancient sites—the result of trade and exchange along the old paths of the past, indicating new religious integrating devices between these two areas. The trade goods are of a period that coincides with suggestive but hardly precise references to Shawnee groups in the Ohio valley (Hanson, 1966:171–175, 197).

Monongahela Woodland

In the contiguous area of eastern Ohio, northern West Virginia, and western Pennsylvania, from shortly before AD 1000 to the protohistoric period, a partially agricultural complex emerged with significant areal and temporal variations. In marked contrast to most Fort Ancient sites, the Monongahela locations are usually on saddles between hills. Many of the sites are known to have oval to circular stockades and circular house patterns. The houses are arranged around an open central courtyard. Village size is from about 0.5 to 2 hectares; stockade diameters range from nearly 61 meters to 137 meters. The circular houses are about 6 meters in diameter. The refuse pits had originally been used for food storage. At some sites there is a "Big House," which was probably the council house. A few Monongahela sites are reported to have rectangular, single-family units. Population was from somewhat less than 100 to about 150. Many of the utilitarian tools and weapons are similar to those of Fort Ancient or Owasco–Iroquois groups. The vessel forms and treatment are simpler than in Fort Ancient; the simple wide-mouth jar is almost the only form, although it shows variation in lip and rim shape and decoration. It is estimated that there are well over 500 Monongahela sites, but it is clear that they were not comparable to Fort Ancient in population density. A number of attempts have been made to identify a historic people whose ancestors were responsible for this culture, but none of them are convincing.

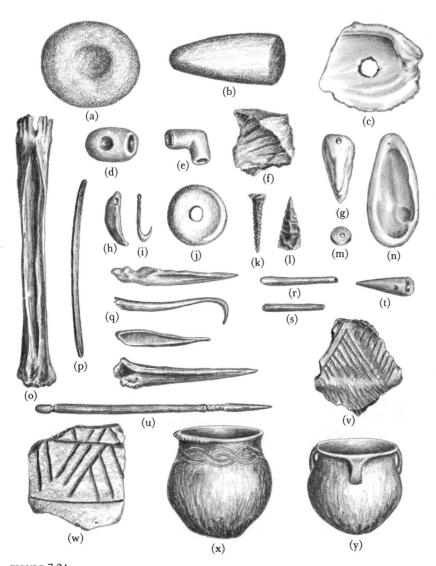

FIGURE 7.24
Artifacts of the Fort Ancient aspect: (a) pitted hammerstone; (b) ungrooved ax; (c) mussel-shell hoe; (d) conoidal tobacco pipe; (e) elbow tobacco pipe; (f) grooved abrading stone; (g) shell pendant; (h) perforated wolf tooth; (i) bone fishhook; (j) discoidal stone; (k) drill; (l) triangular projectile point; (m) disk-shaped shell bead; (n) mussel-shell spoon; (o) beamer (deer metapoidal bone); (p) bone needle; (q) bone awls—ulna (*top*), raccoon penis, splinter, turkey metatarsal; (r) bone (bird) bead; (s) flaking tool (antler); (t) projectile point (antler); (u) hairpin; (v) pottery rim sherd, Feurt focus; (w) rim sherd, Anderson focus; (x) pottery vessel, Baum focus; (y) pottery vessel, Madisonville focus.

References Cited and
Recommended Sources

Adovasio, J. M., and R. L. Andrews. 1980. Basketry, cordage and bark impressions from the Northern Thorn Mound (46 mg 78), Monongalia County, West Virginia. *West Virginia Archaeologist* 30:33–72.

———, J. D. Gunn, J. Donahue, and R. Stuckenrath. 1975. Excavations at Meadowcroft Rockshelter, 1973–74: a progress report. *Pennsylvania Archaeologist* 45:1–30.

Allman, J. C. 1957. A new Late Woodland culture for Ohio—Lichliter village site near Dayton, Ohio. *Ohio Archaeologist* 7:2.

Anderson, D. C., and H. A. Semken, Jr. (eds.). 1980. *The Cherokee Excavations: Holocene Ecology and Human Adaptations in Northwestern Iowa.* New York: Academic Press.

Asch, D. L., K. B. Farnsworth, and N. B. Asch. 1979. Woodland subsistence and settlement in west central Illinois. In *Hopewell Archaeology: The Chillicothe Conference,* ed. D. S. Brose and N. Greber, pp. 80–85. Kent, Ohio: Kent State University Press.

Baby, R. S. 1976. Research continues at Seip Mound Memorial. *Echoes Ohio Historical Society* 15:1–3.

———, and M. A. Potter. 1965. *The Cole Complex.* Papers in Archaeology of the Ohio Historical Society no. 2.

———, ———, and A. Mays, Jr. 1966. *Exploration of the O. C. Voss Mound, Big Darby Reservoir Area, Franklin County, Ohio.* Papers in Archaeology of the Ohio Historical Society no. 3.

Black, G. A. 1934. Archaeological survey of Dearborn and Ohio counties. *Indiana History Bulletin* 11:7.

———. 1967. *Angel Site: An Archaeological, Historical, and Ethnological Study.* Indiana Historical Society.

Braun, D. P. 1979. Illinois Hopewell burial practices and social organization: a reexamination of the Klunk–Gibson mound group. In *Hopewell Archaeology: The Chillicothe Conference,* ed. D. S. Brose and N. Greber, pp. 66–79. Kent, Ohio: Kent State University Press.

Brose, D. S. 1970. *The Archaeology of Summer Island.* University of Michigan Museum of Anthropology, Anthropological Paper no. 41.

Brown, J. A. 1979. Charnel houses and mortuary crypts: disposal of the dead in the Middle Woodland period. In *Hopewell Archaeology: The Chillicothe Conference,* ed. D. S. Brose and N. Greber, pp. 211–219. Kent, Ohio: Kent State University Press.

———, and C. Cleland. 1968. The late glacial and early postglacial faunal resources in Midwestern biomes newly opened to human habitation. In *The Quaternary of Illinois.* University of Illinois, Urbana, College of Agriculture Special Publication no. 14.

Buikstra, J. 1979. *Hopewell in the Lower Illinois Valley: A Regional Approach to the Study of Human Biological Variability and Prehistoric Behavior.* Northwestern University Archeological Program Scientific Papers no. 2.

Bush, D. E. 1975. A ceramic analysis of the Late Adena Buckmeyer site, Perry County, Ohio. *Michigan Archaeologist* 21:9–23.

Caldwell, J. R. 1964. Interaction spheres in prehistory. In *Hopewellian Studies,* ed. J. R. Caldwell and R. L. Hall, pp. 133–143. Springfield: Illinois State Museum Scientific Papers no. 12.

Callender, C. 1979. Hopewell archaeology and American ethnology. In *Hopewell Archaeology: The Chillicothe Conference,* ed. D. S. Brose and N. Greber, pp. 254–257. Kent, Ohio: Kent State University Press.

Chapman, C. H. 1975. *The Archaeology of Missouri,* vol. 1. Columbia: University of Missouri Press.

———. 1980. *The Archaeology of Missouri,* vol. 2. Columbia: University of Missouri Press.

Cole, F.-C., et al. 1951. *Kincaid: A Prehistoric Metropolis.* Chicago: University of Chicago Press.

———, and T. Deuel. 1937. *Rediscovering Illinois.* Chicago: University of Chicago Press.

Cook, T. G. 1974. Koster: an artifact analysis of two Archaic phases in west–central Illinois. Ph.D. dissertation, University of Chicago.

Crane, H. R., and J. B. Griffin. 1959. University of Michigan Radiocarbon Dates IV. *Radiocarbon Supplement* 1:173–198. *American Journal of Science.*

Cunningham, W. M. 1948. *A Study of the Glacial Kame Culture in Michigan, Ohio, and Indiana.* Occasional Contributions from the Museum of Anthropology of the University of Michigan no. 12.

Dekin, A. A., Jr. 1966. A fluted point from Grand Traverse County. *Michigan Archaeologist* 12:37-79.

Didier, M. E. 1967. A distributional study of the turkey-tail point. *Wisconsin Archaeologist* 48:3-73.

Dorwin, J. T. 1966. Fluted points and Late Pleistocene geochronology in Indiana. Indiana Historical Society, *Prehistory Research Series* 6:3:141-188.

———. 1971. The Bowen site: an archaeological study of cultural process in the late prehistory of central Indiana. Indiana Historical Society, *Prehistory Research Series* 4:4.

Dragoo, D. W. 1963. Mounds for the dead: an analysis of the Adena culture. *Annals of the Carnegie Museum,* vol. 37.

Fitting, J. E. 1970. *The Archaeology of Michigan.* New York: Natural History Press.

———, J. DeVischer, and E. J. Wahla. 1966. *The Paleo-Indian Occupation of the Holcombe Beach.* University of Michigan Museum of Anthropology, Anthropological Paper no. 27.

Ford, R. I. 1974. Northeastern archaeology: past and future directions. *Annual Review of Anthropology* 3:384-413.

———. 1979. Gathering and gardening: trends and consequences of Hopewell subsistence strategies. In *Hopewell Archaeology: The Chillicothe Conference,* ed. D. S. Brose and N. Greber, pp. 234-238. Kent, Ohio: Kent State University Press.

———. 1980. "Artifacts" that grew: their roots in Mexico. *Early Man* 2:3:19-23.

Fowler, M. L. 1969. *Explorations into Cahokia Archaeology.* Illinois Archaeological Survey Bulletin no. 7.

———. 1974. *Cahokia: Ancient Capital of the Midwest.* Menlo Park, Calif.: Addison-Wesley.

———, and R. L. Hall. 1972. *Archaeological Phases at Cahokia.* Illinois State Museum Papers in Anthropology no. 1.

Freeman, J. 1969. The Millville site, a Middle Woodland village in Grant County, Wisconsin. *Wisconsin Archeologist* 50:37-67.

Funkhouser, W. D., and W. S. Webb. 1937. The Chilton site in Henry County, Kentucky. *University of Kentucky Reports in Archaeology and Anthropology,* 3:5.

Greber, N. 1976. Within Ohio Hopewell: analyses of burial patterns from several classic sites. Ph.D. dissertation, Case Western Reserve University.

———. 1979. A comparative study of site morphology and burial patterns at Edwin Harness Mound and Seip Mound 1 and 2. In *Hopewell Archaeology: The Chillicothe Conference,* ed. D. S. Brose and N. Greber, pp. 27-38. Kent, Ohio: Kent State University Press.

Green, T. J., and C. A. Munson. 1978. Mississippian settlement pattern in southwestern Indiana. In *Mississippian Settlement Patterns,* ed. B. Smith, pp. 293-330. New York: Academic Press.

Greenman, E. F. 1932. Excavation of the Coon Mound and an analysis of the Adena culture. *Ohio Archaeological and Historical Quarterly* 41:369-523.

———. 1966. Chronology of sites at Killarney, Ontario. *American Antiquity* 31:540-551.

Griffin, J. B. 1941. Additional Hopewell materials from Illinois. Indiana Historical Society, *Prehistory Research Series* 2:165-223.

———. 1943. *The Fort Ancient Aspect: Its Cultural and Chronological Position in Mississippi Valley Archaeology.* Ann Arbor: University of Michigan Press. Reissued 1966 as Anthropological Paper no. 28, University of Michigan Museum of Anthropology.

——— (ed.). 1952a. *Archeology of Eastern United States.* Chicago: University of Chicago Press.

———. 1952b. The late prehistoric cultures of the Ohio Valley. *Ohio State Archaeological and Historical Quarterly* 61:186-195.

———. 1956. The reliability of radiocarbon dates for Late Glacial and Recent times in central and eastern North America. *University of Utah Anthropological Papers.* 26:10-34.

———. 1960. Climatic change: a contributory cause of the growth and decline of northern Hopewellian culture. *Wisconsin Archeologist* 41:21-33.

———. 1961. *Lake Superior Copper and the Indians: Miscellaneous Studies of Great Lakes Prehistory.* University of Michigan Museum of Anthropology, Anthropological Paper no. 17.

———. 1965a. Late Quaternary prehistory in the northeastern Woodlands. In *The Quaternary of the United States,* ed. H. E. Wright, Jr. and D. G. Frey, pp. 655-667. Princeton: Princeton University Press.

——. 1965b. Hopewell and the dark black glass. *Michigan Archaeologist* 11:115–155.

——. 1966. The origins of prehistoric North American pottery. *Atti del VI Congresso Internationale della Scienze Preistoriche e Protostoriche,* Sezioni V–VII:267–271.

——. 1967. Eastern North American archaeology: a summary. *Science* 156:3772:175–191.

——. 1968. Observation on Illinois prehistory in Late Pleistocene and Early Recent times. In *The Quaternary of Illinois.* University of Illinois, Urbana, College of Agriculture Special Publication 14:123–135.

——, R. E. Flanders, and P. F. Titterington. 1970. *The Burial Complexes of the Knight and Norton Mounds in Illinois and Michigan.* Memoir 2, Museum of Anthropology, University of Michigan.

——, A. A. Gordus, and G. A. Wright. 1969. Identification of the sources of Hopewellian obsidian in the Middle West. *American Antiquity* 34:1–14.

——, and V. H. Jones. 1977. The University of Michigan excavations at the Pulcher site in 1950. In *Essays on Archaeological Problems,* ed. B. Fagan and B. Voorhies, pp. 462–490. *American Antiquity* 42:3.

——, and A. C. Spaulding. 1951. The central Mississippi valley archaeological survey, season 1950: a preliminary report. *Journal of the Illinois State Archaeological Society* (New Series) 1:74–81.

Hall, R. L. 1975. *Chronology and Phases at Cahokia.* Urbana: Illinois Archaeology Survey Bulletin no. 10.

Halsey, J. R. 1974. The Markee site (47-VE-195): an Early Middle Archaic campsite in the Kickapoo River valley. *Wisconsin Archeologist* 55:42–75.

Hanson, L. H. 1966. *The Hardin Village Site.* University of Kentucky Studies in Anthropology no. 4.

——. 1975. *The Buffalo Site: A Late 17th Century Indian Village Site (46 Pu 31) in Putnam County, West Virginia.* Report of Archeological Investigations no. 5, West Virginia Geological and Economic Survey.

Harn, A. D. 1978. Mississippian settlement patterns in the central Illinois River valley. In *Mississippian Settlement Patterns,* ed. B. Smith, pp. 233–268. New York: Academic Press.

——. 1980. *The Prehistory of Dickson Mounds: The Dickson Excavation.* Springfield: Illinois State Museum Reports of Investigations, no. 35.

Hurley, W. M. 1965. Archaeological research in the projected Kickapoo Reservoir, Vernon County, Wisconsin. *Wisconsin Archeologist* 46:1–114.

——. 1974. *Silver Creek Woodland Sites, Southwestern Wisconsin.* Report 6, Office of State Archaeologist, University of Iowa.

——. 1975. *An Analysis of Effigy Mound Complexes in Wisconsin.* University of Michigan Museum of Anthropology, Anthropological Paper no. 59.

Jamison, P. L. 1971. A demographic and comparative analysis of the Albany Mounds (Illinois) Hopewell skeletons. Appendix 1. In *The Indian Mounds at Albany, Illinois,* ed. E. B. Herold, pp. 107–145. Davenport Museum Anthropological Papers no. 1.

Jansen, D. E. 1968. *The Naomikong Point Site and the Dimensions of Laurel in the Lake Superior Region.* University of Michigan Museum of Anthropology, Anthropological Paper no. 36.

Karow, P. F., T. W. Anderson, A. H. Clarke, L. D. Delorme, and M. R. Sreenivasa. 1975. Stratigraphy, paleontology and age of Lake Algonquin sediments in southwestern Ontario, Canada. *Quaternary Research* 5:49–87.

Kellar, J. H. 1973. *An Introduction to the Prehistory of Indiana.* Indiana Historical Society.

Keyes, C. R. 1934. Antiquities of the Upper Iowa [River]. *The Palimpsest* 15.

Kidd, K. E. 1951. Fluted points in Ontario. *American Antiquity* 16:260.

Knoblock, B. W. 1939. *Bannerstones of the North American Indians.* La Grange, Ill.: privately printed.

Kuttruff, L. C. 1972. *The Marty Coolidge Site, Monroe County, Illinois.* Southern Illinois University Museum Research Records. Southern Illinois Studies no. 10.

Lee, A. M., and K. D. Vickery. 1972. Salvage excavations at the Headquarters site, a Middle Woodland village burial area in Hamilton County, Ohio. *Ohio Archaeologist* 22.

Lee, T. E. 1954. The first Sheguiandah expedition, Manitoulin Island, Ontario. *American Antiquity* 20:101–111.

——. 1955. The second Sheguiandah expedition, Manitoulin Island, Ontario. *American Antiquity* 21:63–71.

——. 1957. The antiquity of the Sheguiandah site. *Canadian Field Naturalist* 71:117–137.

Linder, J. 1974. The Jean Rita site: An Early Woodland occupation in Monroe County, Illinois. *Wisconsin Archeologist* 55:99–162.

Logan, W. D. 1976. *Woodland Complexes in Northeastern Iowa.* National Park Service Publications in Archeology 15.

MacNeish, R. S. 1952. A possible early site in the Thunder Bay District, Ontario. *National Museums of Canada Bulletin* 136:23–47.

McPherron, A. 1967. *The Juntenen Site and the Lake Woodland Prehistory of the Upper Great Lakes Area.* University of Michigan Museum of Anthropology, Anthropological Paper no. 30.

Magrath, W. H. 1945. The North Benton Mound: a Hopewell site in Ohio. *American Antiquity* 40–47.

Mason, R. J. 1958. *Late Pleistocene Geochronology and the Paleo-Indian Penetration into the Lower Michigan Peninsula.* University of Michigan Museum of Anthropology, Anthropological Paper no. 11.

———. 1959. Indications of Paleo-Indian occupations in the Delaware valley. *Pennsylvania Archaeologist* 29:1–17.

———. 1962. The Paleo-Indian tradition in eastern North America. *Current Anthropology* 3:227–278.

———. 1963. Two late Paleo-Indian complexes in Wisconsin. *Wisconsin Archeologist* 44:4:199–211.

———. 1969. Laurel and North Bay: diffusional networks in the upper Great Lakes. *American Antiquity* 26:43–57.

———, and C. Irwin. 1960. An Eden Scottsbluff burial in northern Wisconsin. *American Antiquity* 26:43–57.

Maxwell, M. S. 1951. *Woodland Cultures of Southern Illinois.* Excavations in the Carbondale Area, Logan Museum Publications in Anthropology, Bulletin no. 7.

Miller, R. K. 1941. McCain site, Dubois County, Indiana. Indiana Historical Society, *Prehistory Research Series* 2.

Mills, W. C. 1916. Exploration of the Tremper Mound. *Ohio Archaeological and Historical Quarterly* 25:262–398.

———. 1922. Exploration of the Mound City group. *Ohio Archaeological and Historical Quarterly* 31:423–584.

Moorehead, W. K. 1922. *The Hopewell Mound Group of Ohio.* Field Museum of Natural History Publication 211. Anthropologial Series vol. 6.

Morgan, R. G. 1952. Outline of cultures in the Ohio region. In *Archeology of Eastern United States,* ed. J. B. Griffin. Chicago: University of Chicago Press.

Muller, J. 1978. The Kincaid system: Mississippian settlement in the environs of a large site. In *Mississippian Settlement Patterns,* ed. B. Smith, pp. 269–292. New York: Academic Press.

Munson, C. A. (ed.). 1980. *Archaeological Salvage Excavations at Patoka Lake, Indiana.* Indiana University Glenn A. Black Laboratory of Archaeology Research Reports no. 6.

Munson, P. J. 1966. The Sheets site: a Late Archaic–Early Woodland occupation in west central Illinois. *Michigan Archaeologist* 12:111–120.

Murphy, J. L. 1971. Maize from an Adena mound in Athens County, Ohio. *Science* 171:897–898.

Oehler, C. M. 1950. *Turpin Indians.* Cincinnati Museum of Natural History, Popular Publication Series no. 1.

Ozker, D. B. V. 1977. An Early Woodland community at the Schultz site 2OSA2 in the Saginaw Valley and the nature of the Early Woodland adaptation in the Great Lakes region. Ph.D. dissertation, University of Michigan.

Parmalee, P. W. 1975. *A General Summary of the Vertebrate Fauna from Cahokia.* Urbana: Illinois Archaeological Survey Bulletin no. 10.

Perino, G. 1966. A preliminary report on the Peisker site, parts 1 and 2. *Central States Archaeological Journal* 13:47–51, 84–89.

———. 1971. *The Mississippian Component at the Schild Site (No. 4), Greene County, Illinois.* Urbana: Illinois Archaeological Survey Bulletin no. 8.

Phillips, J. L., R. L. Hall, and R. W. Yerkes. 1980. *Investigations at the Labras Lake Site,* vol. 1, parts 1 and 2. University of Illinois at Chicago Circle, Department of Anthropology, Report of Investigations no. 1.

Phillips, P., and J. A. Brown. 1975. *Pre-Columbian Shell Engravings from the Craig Mound at Spiro, Oklahoma,* vol. 1. Cambridge: Peabody Museum–Harvard University.

Potzger, J. E. 1946. Phytosociology of the primeval forest in central–northern Wisconsin and upper Michigan, and a brief post-glacial history of the Lake Forest formation. *Ecology Monographs* 16:211–250.

Prest, V. K. 1970. *Quaternary Geology of Canada*. Geological Survey of Canada Economy Geology Report Series no. 1.

Prahl, E. J. 1970. The Middle Woodland period of the lower Muskegon valley and the northern Hopewellian frontier. Ph.D. dissertation, University of Michigan.

Prufer, O. 1963. The McConnell site: a late Palaeo-Indian workshop in Coshocton County, Ohio. *Scientific Publications of the Cleveland Museum of Natural History* (New Series) 2:1–51.

——. 1966. The Mud Valley site: a late Paleo-Indian locality in Holmes County, Ohio. *Ohio Journal of Science* 66:1:68–75.

——, and R. S. Baby. 1963. *Paleo-Indians of Ohio*. Columbus: Ohio Historical Society.

——, and O. C. Shane. 1970. *Blain Village and the Fort Ancient Tradition in Ohio*. Kent, Ohio: Kent State University Press.

Quimby, G. I. 1958. Fluted points and geochronology in the Lake Michigan basin. *American Antiquity* 23:247–254.

Rau, C. 1872. A deposit of agricultural flint implements in southern Illinois. *Annual Report of the Smithsonian Institution for 1868*, pp. 401–407.

Reidhead, V. A., and W. F. Limp. 1974. The Haag site (12 D 19): a preliminary report. *Indiana Archaeological Bulletin* 1:1. Indiana Historical Society.

Ritzenthaler, R. E. 1966. The Kouba site: Paleo-Indians in Wisconsin. *Wisconsin Archeologist* 47:171–187.

——, and G. I. Quimby. 1962. The Red Ochre culture of the upper Great Lakes and adjacent areas. *Chicago Natural History Museum* 36:243–275.

Roosa, W. B. 1977. Fluted points from the Parkhill site. In *For the Director: Research Essays in Honor of James B. Griffin*, ed. C. C. Cleland. Ann Arbor: Anthropological Papers, Museum of Anthropology, University of Michigan no. 61, pp. 87–121.

Rowe, C. W. 1956. *The Effigy Mound Culture of Wisconsin*. Milwaukee Public Museum, Publications in Anthropology no. 3.

Salzer, R. J. 1974. The Wisconsin north lakes project. In *Aspects of Upper Great Lakes Anthropology*, ed. E. B. Johnson, pp. 40–54. St. Paul: Minnesota Historical Society.

Seeman, M. F. 1979. The Hopewell interaction sphere: the evidence for interregional trade and structural complexity. Indiana Historical Society, *Prehistory Research Series* 5:2.

Shetrone, H. C. 1926. Explorations of the Hopewell group of Prehistoric earthworks. *Ohio Archaeological and Historical Quarterly* 35:1–227.

Smail, W. 1951. Some early projectile points from the St. Louis area. *Journal of the Illinois Archaeological Society* (New Series) 2:1:11–16.

Squier, E. F., and E. H. Davis. 1848. Ancient monuments of the Mississippi valley. *Smithsonian Contributions to Knowledge*, vol. 1.

Starr, F. 1960. The archaeology of Hamilton County, Ohio. *Journal of the Cincinnati Museum of Natural History* 23.

Stevens, E. T. 1870. *Flint Chips*. London: Bell and Daldy.

Stoltman, J. B. 1973. *The Laurel Culture in Minnesota*. Minnesota Prehistory Archaeology Series no. 8. Minnesota Historical Society.

——. 1974. An examination of within-Laurel cultural variability. In *Aspects of Upper Great Lakes Anthropology: Papers in Honor of Lloyd A. Wilford*, ed. E. Johnson. St. Paul: Minnesota Historical Society.

——, and K. Workman. 1969. A preliminary study of Wisconsin fluted points. *Wisconsin Archeologist* 50:189–214.

Storck, P. L. 1972. An unusual late Paleo-Indian projectile point from Grey County, Southern Ontario. *Ontario Archaeology* 18:27–45.

——. 1973. *Two Paleo-Indian Projectile Points from the Bronte Creek Gap, Halton County, Ontario*. Archaeology Paper 1, Royal Ontario Museum 1–4.

Stothers, D. M., G. M. Pratt, and O. C. Shane, III. 1979. The western Basin Middle Woodland: non-Hopewellian in a Hopewellian world. In *Hopewell Archaeology: The Chillicothe Conference*, ed. D. S. Brose and N. Greber, pp. 47–58. Kent, Ohio: Kent State University Press.

Struever, S. 1964. The Hopewell interaction sphere in Riverine–Western Great Lakes culture history. In *Hopewellian Studies*, ed. J. Caldwell and R. L. Hall. Scientific Papers 12:3, Illinois State Museum.

————. 1968. Woodland subsistence systems in the lower Illinois valley. In *New Perspectives in Archeology*, ed. S. R. Binford and L. R. Binford, pp. 285–312. Chicago: Aldine Press.

————, and G. L. Houart. 1972. An analysis of the Hopewell interaction sphere. In *Social Change and Interaction*, ed. E. N. Wilmsen, pp. 47–79. Anthropological Papers no. 46, Museum of Anthropology, University of Michigan.

————, and K. D. Vickery. 1973. The beginnings of cultivation in the Midwest–Riverine area of the United States. *American Anthropologist* 75:5:1197–1220.

Tainter, J. A. 1975. The archaeological study of social change: Woodland systems in west central Illinois. Ph.D. dissertation, Northwestern University.

Titterington, P. F. 1938. *The Cahokia Mound Group and Its Village Site Materials*. St. Louis: P. F. Titterington.

————. 1950. Some non-pottery sites in the St. Louis area. *Illinois State Archaeological Society* (New Series) 1:19–30.

Vaillant, G. C. 1939. *Indian Arts in North America*. New York: Harper and Brothers.

Webb, W. S., and R. S. Baby. 1957. *The Adena People No. 2*. Columbus: Ohio Historical Society.

————, and C. E. Snow. 1974. *The Adena People*. Knoxville: University of Tennessee Press.

Willoughby, C. C. 1935. *Antiquities of the New England Indians*. Cambridge: Peabody Museum of American Archaeology and Ethnology.

Winters, H. E. 1963. *An Archaeological Survey of the Wabash Valley in Illinois*. Illinois State Museum, Report of Investigations no. 10.

————. 1969. *The Riverton Culture*. Illinois State Museum, Report of Investigations no. 13, Illinois Archaeological Survey Monograph no. 1.

Wittry, W. L. 1959a. The Raddatz Rockshelter, Sk 5, Wisconsin. *Wisconsin Archeologist* 40:33–69.

————. 1959b. Archaeological studies of four Wisconsin rockshelters. *Wisconsin Archeologist* 40:137–267.

Wright, H. T. 1964. A transitional Archaic campsite at Green Point (2OSA1). *Michigan Archaeologist* 10:17–22.

————, and W. B. Roosa. 1966. The Barnes site: a fluted point assemblage from the Great Lakes region. *American Antiquity* 31:850–860.

Wright, J. V. 1967. *The Laurel Tradition and the Middle Woodland Period*. Bulletin 217, National Museum of Canada.

————. 1972a. *The Shield Archaic*. Publications in Archaeology no. 3, National Museum of Man. Ottawa: National Museum of Canada.

————. 1972b. *Ontario Prehistory*. Archaeological Survey, National Museum of Man. Ottawa: National Museum of Canada.

Yarnell, R. A. 1964. *Aboriginal Relationships Between Culture and Plant Life in the Upper Great Lakes Region*. University of Michigan Museum of Anthropology, Anthropological Paper no. 23.

————. 1972. *Iva Annua* var. *Macrocarpa*: extinct American cultigen? *American Anthropologist* 74:335–341.

View of excavations by New York State Museum at the Cunningham site, a stratified shell midden overlooking Lagoon Pond, Martha's Vineyard, Massachusetts.

CHAPTER EIGHT

The Northeastern United States

Robert E. Funk

Dr. Funk has succeeded in reducing the welter of detail to provide the best extant synthesis of the archeology of the Northeastern United States. The area contains the earliest and best-documented evidence of the Paleo-Indian in the East. Human use of the area continued; about 4000 years ago, the occupancy reached a peak exceeded only in the Late Woodland period.

THE ENVIRONMENTAL SETTING

For the purposes of this chapter, the Northeastern area is confined to the present-day political boundaries of southern Ontario, southern Quebec, New York, Pennsylvania, New Jersey, and all the New England states. This large area is diversified in physiography, topography, drainage patterns, climatic conditions, floral and faunal assemblages, and in the resources useful to prehistoric native Americans.

Within these arbitrary boundaries are seven major physiographic provinces; in a roughly west-to-east order, these are the Great Lakes lowland, the Appalachian plateau, the Adirondack highland, the Hudson–Champlain lowland (part of the Ridge and Valley province), the Piedmont, the New England upland, and the Coastal Plain (Fenneman, 1938). Major drainage basins include the St. Lawrence valley, the upper Ohio valley, the Genesee valley, the Susquehanna valley, the Hudson valley, the Connecticut valley, the Androscoggin valley, and the Penobscot valley.

Several forest types, with associated plant and animal communities, are found within the area. Classificatory schemes differ according to the authority. In the most popular classification, the major forest type is the Lake Forest bordering the eastern Great Lakes and extending eastward into southern Ontario, northern and central New York, and western New England, including the upper St. Lawrence valley (Braun, 1950). This taxon corresponds roughly to the birch–beech–maple–hemlock forest concept. At lower elevations and latitudes, it grades into the oak–hickory forest, which in turn is bordered on the south by the southern hardwoods (Goode and Espenshade, 1950). A series of mixed deciduous and coniferous forests prevails along the northern coast and interior of New England. North of the St. Lawrence valley, the lake forest is bordered by the Canadian boreal forest.

Although many animal species are found throughout the entire area, some have a more limited distribution. For example, the range of the woodland caribou overlaps from the boreal forest into the northern margins of the study area, where the dominant cervid is the white-tailed deer.

Animal and plant associations of the present-day Northeast have been grouped into three biotic provinces by Dice (1943): the Hudsonian (north of the upper St. Lawrence, reaching south of the lower St. Lawrence); the Canadian (most of upstate New York and northern New England); and the Carolinian (southwestern Ontario, southern and eastern New York, Pennsylvania, New Jersey, Staten Island, southern New England). However, these very generalized and intuitively defined zones are an imprecise tool for defining the cultural-ecological potential of the Northeast, and in any case they would be valid only for the modern era. Detailed characterizations of local environments are needed, although the requisite biological data are not often available.

It is important to keep in mind that physiography, climate, flora, and fauna have all changed in the last 15,000 years, since the time when northern parts of the Northeast were first open to human occupancy. Before that time, most of New York, northern parts of Pennsylvania and New Jersey, and all of New England, Ontario, and Quebec were covered by the Wisconsin glacial ice sheet, which had spread from a center in Keewatin (Flint, 1971). The climatic effects of the glaciation were felt by animal and plant species as far south as the Gulf Coast. The lowered sea level—caused by the accumulation of enormous quantities of water in the ice—had exposed large areas of the continental shelf, including Beringia, the Siberian–Alaskan land bridge used by the first human immigrants to the New World (Hopkins, 1979).

When the Wisconsin ice began to melt back from the end moraines, climatic and vegetation zones followed its retreating margins northward. When the front had reached the position of the Valders stadial just north of the St. Lawrence valley, in about 9500 BC, it was fringed by a narrow tundra or spruce-park zone, south of which was a spruce woodland grading into the mixed deciduous forests farther south. A variety of terrestrial animals occupied this environment, as witnessed by their bones found in late-glacial sediments. These animals included Proboscidea (elephants) such as mammoths and mastodons, musk oxen, caribou, dire wolves, ground sloths, and many others. By 8000 BC, the mammoth and mastodon, along with other species, became extinct, for still undetermined reasons, but other cold-adapted fauna, such as musk oxen and caribou, moved north as the ice receded to its present limited extent in Greenland and parts of northern Canada.

As the ice melted, sea level began to rise—at first rapidly, later more slowly—until by 3000 years ago it had approximated its present position. The oceans once again encroached on the continental shelf, a process which drowned some early Indian sites off the New England coast and covered the remains of mammoths and mastodons that had roamed there (Edwards and Emery, 1977).

By 8500 BC, the open spruce woodland in the Northeast had been replaced by a denser spruce–fir forest. Throughout most of the area this changed to a pine–oak forest by 7500 BC, to a deciduous oak–hemlock assemblage by 5500 BC, and to an essentially modern oak–hickory forest by 2200 BC (Davis, 1969; Sirkin, 1977; Bernabo and Webb, 1977). In these forests lived familiar animals: white-tailed deer, elk, black bear, raccoon, woodchuck, gray fox, turkey, grouse, and others. This scenario glosses over many details, since there was considerable local variation in plant and animal associations due to differences in topography, elevation, drainage patterns, and so on.

The changing postglacial environment posed many challenges to the native Americans who inhabited it. Some groups met those challenges successfully, and some probably perished, but in each period most groups adapted well enough to bequeath their social heritage to later generations.

In the following pages, the archeological data are organized into the "historical–developmental" scheme currently favored by most Northeastern archeologists (Figure 8.1). It is historical because it deals with time in radiocarbon years and the sequence of cultures in particular regions, and developmental because it views cultures as passing through successive stages that are defined by certain general criteria. The stages are: Paleo-Indian; Archaic (Early, Middle, Late); and Woodland (Early, Middle, Late). Also used by many archeologists is a "Transitional" stage between Archaic and Woodland. Individual cultures, phases, or traditions are placed within the stages.

Here the terms *culture* and *phase* are used interchangeably to represent once-living societies as inferred from their material remains. Cultures and phases are restricted in time and space, but *traditions* refers to sequences of related phases persisting over relatively long time periods. Also, *horizons* are basically similar cultural units distributed over large areas within relatively short periods, and *horizon styles* are artifact traits spread over similar areas within similar periods. In addition, a *component* is a single occupation of a site by people of one particular culture, and an *assemblage* is a group of artifact traits believed to represent such a component.

Archeologists grow less contented with the historical–developmental framework as research progresses. One reason is that it is not universally applicable everywhere in the northeastern area; some regional sequences were marginal to the main course of events. Certain traits, such as pottery, made their appearance at very different times in different parts of the area. Also, the use of stages creates an artificial sense of discontinuity, when in truth development proceeded without interruption in most areas. Nevertheless, the historical–developmental scheme is used here in the absence of a workable alternative. The presentation as summarized in Figure 8.1 reflects a general consensus among Northeastern prehistorians, albeit tinged by the writer's biases. Of necessity, many complex issues are simply touched on or bypassed; only the broadest outlines of culture

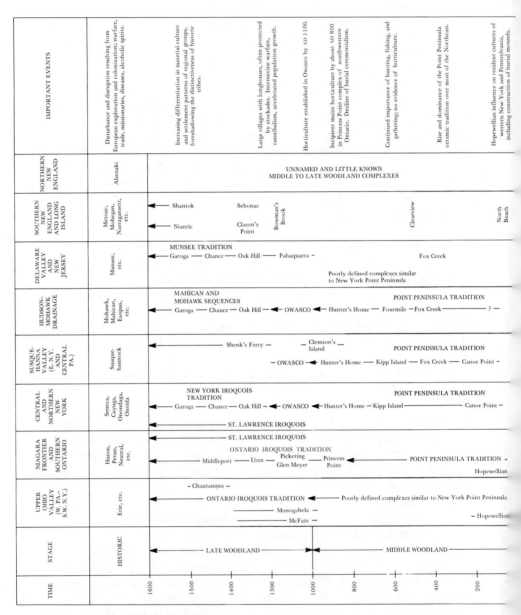

FIGURE 8.1
Cultural sequence and chronology in the Northeast. Principal traditions, phases, and complexes are shown, but some details are omitted.

	EARLY WOOD-LAND			Adena	Middlesex	Middlesex	Adena-Middlesex	Bushkill Adena-Middlesex	Lagoon	Adena-Middlesex	Considerable elaboration of burial ritualism; burial mounds constructed by Adena-related groups in southwestern Pennsylvania, northern New York, and New Brunswick.
1000	"TRANSITIONAL"	LATE		Meadowood Inverhuron	Meadowood Frost Island	Meadowood Frost Island	Meadowood Orient	Meadowood Orient Frost Island	Orient, Coburn		True ceramics introduced about 1200 BC in New York, 600 BC in southwestern Ontario.
				Satchell		Snook Kill Batten Kill Vestal	Snook Kill Batten Kill River	Koens-Crispin	Atlantic	Atlantic	Steatite vessels appeared about 1500 BC.
2000			Panhandle	Lamoka	Batten Kill Frontenac Lamoka	Lamoka	Sylvan Lake	Lackawaxen	Squibnocket	Moorehead	Much evidence of burial ceremonialism by 2000 BC.
				↕ ?	↕ ?						
3000				Brewerton	Brewerton	Brewerton	Vosburg	Vosburg ?			
						Vergennes ?	Vergennes ?			Vergennes	
4000	ARCHAIC	MIDDLE							Merrimac		Exploitation of the diversified and seasonally variable plant and animal resources of the deciduous forests that followed the early postglacial spruce, fir, and pine forests (white-tailed deer, black bear, fish, acorns, mollusks, and so on). Increasing variation of artifact styles in time and space, reflecting adaptation to local environments.
									Stark	Stark	
5000						Neville?	Neville?		Neville	Neville	
6000		EARLY	POORLY KNOWN COMPLEXES WITH BIFURCATED-BASE POINTS								Ground and polished stone woodworking tools first appear about 6000 BC.
			TRACES OF KIRK, PALMER, EVA, AND OTHER EARLY ARCHAIC STYLES								
8000	PALEO-INDIAN		TRACES OF LATE PALEO-INDIAN GROUPS								Broad geographic uniformity in artifact styles. Focal adaptation to late glacial–early postglacial resources including caribou. Some reliance on fish and plant foods.
			EASTERN FLUTED-POINT HUNTERS								
10,000											
	?		?	?	?	?	?	?	?	?	

history are sketched for the Northeast or its subareas. An effort has been made to be as even-handed as possible in coverage of all these subareas, given the limitations on space and the writer's knowledge.

THE EARLIEST INHABITANTS

At this stage in our knowledge of Northeastern prehistory, the earliest clearly identified cultural remains are those of the fluted-point hunters, or Paleo-Indians, dated from about 10,000 to 12,000 years ago. Reasonably convincing evidence of older occupations was obtained at the Meadowcroft Rockshelter in western Pennsylvania by James Adovasio and his associates (1975, 1977). This large and well-stratified site was excavated under carefully controlled conditions. The deepest levels produced a relatively undistinguished series of artifacts dated between 14,000 and 9,000 BC (see Chapter Two). These include a retouched flake knife, a lanceolate projectile point, and many chert flakes, including small bladelike forms. The early C14 dates have touched off considerable controversy because the site is located in the vicinity of coal deposits, believed by some specialists to have contaminated the dated charcoal samples, and the associated faunal and floral remains differ from those generally believed to characterize the late-glacial period of 16,000 years ago (Haynes, 1977, 1980; Stuckenrath, 1977; Mead, 1980; Adovasio et al., 1980).

The site is located well south of the Wisconsin ice margin, a fact compatible with the apparent coevality of early occupations and full glaciation. This correlation is not valid for the Timlin site near Cobleskill, New York, asserted by the original investigators to be of Early Wisconsin age, or about 70,000 years old (Timlin and Raemsch, 1971; Raemsch and Vernon, 1977). Their interpretation is not accepted by Northeastern specialists (Cole and Godfrey, 1977). The most recent work on the site in 1979 and 1980 by Alan L. Bryan and Ruth Gruhn (personal communications, 1980) did not produce convincing evidence for a 16,000 year-old flake industry, in the writer's opinion. Only the fluted point occupations are firmly established for the Northeastern area.

THE EARLY PALEO-INDIAN STAGE

Sites producing assemblages characterized by fluted, bifacial projectile points have been discovered at an accelerating pace since 1960, chiefly because archeological activity has itself been increasing. Major sites now number over 20 in the Northeast. They occur in varied topographic situations, chiefly on terraces and knolls near water sources; both the frequency and variety of artifact types differ from site to site.

Most of the recorded sites have been disturbed by cultivation or by construction activities, with the result that artifacts and lithic debris do not occur in their original underground contexts. Components represented entirely by surface finds include the Shoop site, Pennsylvania (Witthoft, 1952; Cox, 1972); the Plenge site, New Jersey (Kraft, 1973); the Reagen site in Vermont (Ritchie, 1953); Kings Road in upstate New York (Funk, Weinman, and Weinman, 1969); and Port Mobil on Staten Island (Kraft, 1977). Other sites contain partially or wholly intact deposits. These include Bull Brook, in Massachusetts (Figure 8.2) (Byers, 1954, 1955); Debert in Nova Scotia (Figure 8.3) (MacDonald, 1968); Shawnee–Minisink in eastern Pennsylvania (McNett and McMillan, 1974, 1977); 6LF21 in Connecticut (Moeller, 1980); West Athens Hill in New York (Ritchie and Funk, 1973); and Dutchess Quarry Cave nos. 1 and 8 in New York (Funk, Walters et al., 1969; Kopper et al., 1980). A number of additional Paleo-Indian sites in New York, New England, and southern Canada are shown on the location map, Figure 8.4.

Despite the formal and functional diversity among assemblages, there are unmistakable general similarities across the Northeast. Indeed, these regularities are shared with a nearly continent-wide tradition, represented in the Great Plains by the Clovis and Folsom cultures. Diagnostic of these assemblages is the bifacially flaked, lanceolate projectile point bearing the longitudinal grooves or "flutes" produced by the removal of channel flakes from basal striking platforms. Usually predominant are unifacially flaked end scrapers and side scrapers, and there are lesser quantities of biface knives and specialized tools such as gravers, denticulates, drills, and so on. Sporadically represented are "rough stone" tools, including hammerstones and abrading stones. From their inferred functions these various items probably reflect the on-site activities of butchering, the working of animal hides, bones, and wood (that is, manufacturing), and the production of chipped stone tools.

Relatively few radiocarbon dates are available for Northeastern Paleo-Indians. A large number of dates for the Debert site suggest occupation between 10,000 and 11,000 years ago. The 6LF21 site has one date of 8240 BC. Several dates from Bull Brook, averaging around 7000 BC, are considered by most archeologists to be too young in comparison with dates for similar complexes in other regions. An age reading of 10,580 BC ± 370 years on caribou bones from Dutchess Quarry Cave no. 1 is about 1000 years older than even the western U.S. Clovis tradition, and questions have been raised about the association of the bones with the single fluted point in stratum 2. Two dates on the same hearth at the Vail site in Maine are 8350 BC and 9170 BC (Gramly and Rutledge, 1981).

Geochronological evidence helps to set maximum limits on the age of sites located within glaciated parts of the Northeast. Early Man was unable to penetrate most of New York and all of New England and eastern Canada prior to the retreat of the Wisconsin ice. New York and New England were free of ice by 11,000 years ago. Thus Paleo-Indians probably entered the formerly glaciated Northeast from the south and west, following the plant and animal species necessary to their survival as these species moved into the deglaciating zones.

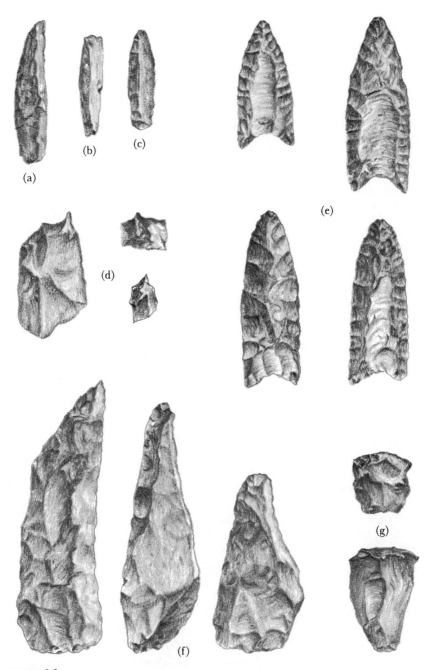

FIGURE 8.2
Flint implements from the Bull Brook site, Massachusetts: (a, b) retouched blades; (c) "twist" drill; (d) uniface gravers; (e) fluted projectile points; (f) side scrapers; (g) end scrapers with graver spurs at front corners.

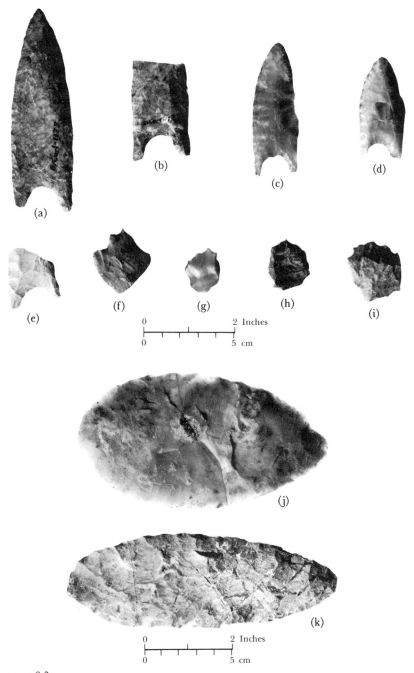

FIGURE 8.3
Early Paleo-Indian artifacts from the Debert site, Nova Scotia: (a–e) characteristic indented-base fluted points; (f–i) perforators; (j, k) large bifaces. (Courtesy of National Museum of Canada.)

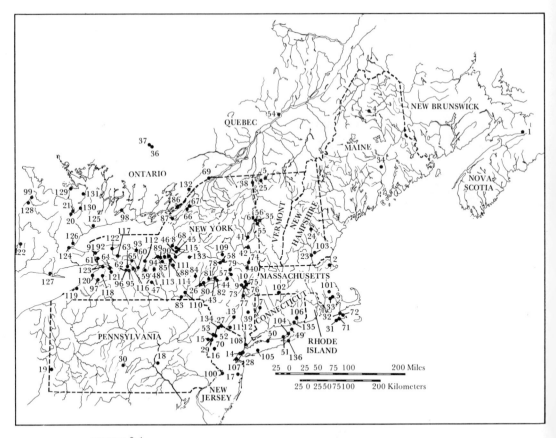

FIGURE 8.4
Map of the major sites and locations referred to in the text.

Paleo-Indian

1. Debert
2. Bull Brook
3. Wapanucket no. 8
4. Munsungan Lake
5. Reagen
6. Davis
7. 6LF21
8. Potts

9. West Athens Hill
10. Kings Road
11. Dutchess Quarry Cave no. 1
12. Dutchess Quarry Cave no. 8
13. Twin Fields
14. Port Mobil

15. Shawnee–Minisink
16. Plenge
17. Turkey Swamp
18. Shoop
19. Meadowcroft
20. Banting
21. Hussey
22. Parkhill

Early to Middle Archaic

23. Neville
24. Weirs Beach
25. John's Bridge

26. Russ
27. Rockelein
28. Hollowell

29. Harry's Farm
30. Sheep Rock

Late Archaic

31. Hornblower II
32. Vincent
33. Wapanucket no. 6
34. Hirundo
35. Otter Creek no. 2
36. Allumette Island
37. Morrison's Island
38. Isle La Motte

39. Sylvan Lake
40. Dennis
41. Weinman
42. Snook Kill
43. McCulley no. 1
44. Shafer
45. Oberlander nos. 1 and 2
46. Robinson

47. Lamoka Lake
48. Frontenac Island
49. Orient nos. 1 and 2
50. Stony Brook
51. Jamesport
52. Miller Field
53. Faucett

Early Woodland

54. Batiscan	60. Morrow	66. Hunter
55. Bennett (Vt.)	61. Riverhaven no. 2	67. Muskalonge Lake
56. Orwell	62. Scaccia	68. Vinette
57. Nahrwold no. 2	63. Cuylerville	69. Long Sault Mound
58. Palatine Bridge	64. Sinking Ponds	70. Rosenkrans
59. Vine Valley	65. Meadowood	

Middle Woodland

71. Peterson	81. Street	91. Portage
72. Cunningham	82. Davenport Creamery	92. Lewiston
73. Petalas	83. Cottage	93. Sea Breeze
74. River	84. White	94. Rector
75. Tufano	85. Kipp Island	95. Geneseo
76. Black Rock	86. Canoe Point	96. Squawkie Hill
77. Ford	87. Point Peninsula	97. Cain
78. Turnbull	88. Jack's Reef	98. East Sugar Island
79. Westheimer	89. Hunter's Home	99. Donaldson
80. Fredenburg	90. O'Neil	100. Abbott

Late Woodland

101. Titicut	113. Maxon–Derby	125. Miller
102. Guida	114. Kelso	126. Bennett (Ontario)
103. Smyth	115. Furnace Brook	127. Woodsmen
104. Fort Corchaug	116. Richmond Mills	128. Nodwell
105. Fort Massapeag	117. Oakfield	129. Lalonde
106. Fort Shantok	118. Green Lake	130. Sidey–Mackay
107. Bowman's Brook	119. Ripley	131. Warminster
108. Clasons Point	120. Silverheels	132. Roebuck
109. Garoga	121. Goodyear	133. Thurston
110. Castle Creek	122. Shelby	134. Minisink
111. Carpenter Brook	123. Eaton	135. Niantic
112. Sackett	124. Princess Point	136. Sebonac

Little direct evidence exists for subsistence and settlement patterns. Hawthorne seeds and fish bones were recovered from a pit at Shawnee–Minisink. Caribou bones were recovered from somewhat ambiguous stratigraphic contexts at Dutchess Cave nos. 1 and 8. They also occurred at the Late Paleo-Indian Holcombe site in Michigan (Fitting et al., 1966) and have been tentatively identified at the Whipple site in New Hampshire (Mary Lou Curran, personal communication, 1980). Thus the evidence favors a heavy reliance on caribou and perhaps other large subarctic mammals, but a wide variety of food resources was probably also exploited by Early Man. Despite the relative abundance of now-extinct mastodons and mammoths in Pleistocene deposits, and their presence on Clovis sites in the western U.S., there is no demonstrated association of these creatures with Early Man anywhere in the East.

The primary Paleo-Indian social unit is generally assumed to have been a band of 20 to 50 individuals (Service, 1962). Given the stylistic uniformities over a broad area and the frequent presence of exotic lithic materials in assemblages, these bands must have moved over relatively large territories, exploiting a broad spectrum of resources such as game animals and many plant food species, raw materials (such as wood and fibers) for tools, and outcrops of high-quality cryptocrystalline rock (such as flint or jasper) important to the flint-knapper. Some lithic materials may have been obtained by trade with groups in adjacent territories.

The larger sites, such as Bull Brook, Plenge, Debert, Shoop, and West Athens Hill, appear to have been occupied repeatedly, perhaps as central base camps located within strategic distances of important resources. It is also possible that several bands occasionally congregated at one time on such sites for ritual and ceremonial as well as economic purposes. West Athens Hill is unique in that it was a quarry–workshop, perhaps never extensively or exclusively used as a habitation site. Smaller sites, such as Potts, Port Mobil, or Kings Road, whose inventories reflect a more limited range of activities than on the larger sites, appear to have been short-term camps occupied for the exploitation of a small range of locally available resources. Yet other stations, such as caves and rockshelters, were also special-purpose camps or even over-night refuges utilized by families or single hunters.

Internal settlement patterning was manifested on some sites. Eleven concentrations of hearths and artifacts at the Debert site, 750 to 2200 square feet in area, were interpreted as the dwelling areas of separate bands who occupied the site at different times. Artifact concentrations in Area B at West Athens Hill were hypothesized to represent family activity areas, possibly house locations. Over 40 concentrations of debris and hearths at Bull Brook, arranged in a semicircle, may have been individual family activity areas within a larger band settlement.

THE LATE PALEO-INDIAN STAGE

By about 8000 BC in the Plains and upper Great Lakes, the fluted-point groups had been replaced by (and probably evolved into) a variety of cultures collectively referred to as the *Plano* tradition. These people are chiefly identified by their distinctive lanceolate or stemmed, parallel-flaked points that comprise such types as Eden, Agate Basin, Plainview, and so on. Other chipped stone artifacts include end scrapers, side scrapers, and other unifaces that are generally similar to Early Paleo-Indian forms. Older patterns of tool use and manufacture probably continued with little change into Late Paleo-Indian times. Since spruce, fir, and pine forests now dominated the Northeast, there were undoubtedly shifts in the distribution and frequency of food resources that required some adjustments in subsistence techniques.

The distribution of the Plano tradition extended into the eastern United States, but it was only weakly present in Pennsylvania, New York, and New England (Mason, 1962; Mayer-Oakes, 1955; Ritchie, 1953, 1957, 1965;

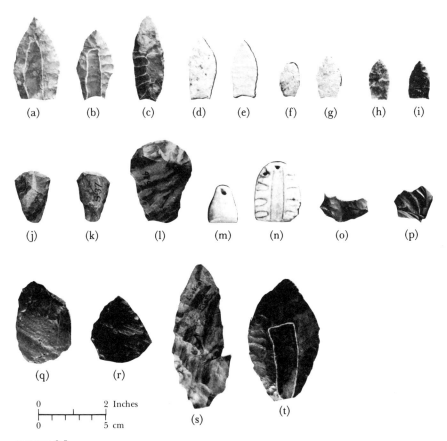

FIGURE 8.5
Late Paleo-Indian artifacts from the Reagen site, Vermont: (a–h) lanceolate pentagonoid points—(a, b) are fluted; (i) eared triangular point; (j–l) end scrapers; (m, n) talc pendants; (o) spurred spokeshave–knife; (p) perforator; (q, r) side scrapers; (s, t) large bifaces. (After Ritchie, 1953.)

Funk and Schambach, 1964; Funk, 1978; Starbuck and Bolian, 1980). In the Southeast it overlapped in time and space with late fluted-point styles such as Cumberland, Quad, and Suwanee, despite few instances of close association on given sites.

The Reagen site in Vermont apparently exemplifies such an association (Ritchie, 1953). There numerous unifacial and bifacial chipped stone tools were accompanied by an unusual variety of fluted, unfluted lanceolate, stemmed, and triangular points presumably occurring together in the same complex (Figure 8.5). This site, unfortunately not dated by radiocarbon, may have been coeval with the waning stages of a marine transgression, the Champlain Sea, dated about 9500–8500 BC. Robson Bonnichsen (personal communication, 1980) has begun investigating a Late Paleo-Indian component at Munsungan Lake, northern Maine. This site produces lanceolate points with basal thinning or, occasionally, short channel flake scars.

Another probably Late Paleo-Indian component featuring small, triangular, basally thinned points, associated with a variety of scrapers, was excavated by Cavallo (personal communication, 1980) at the Turkey Swamp site, New Jersey. However, the C14 dates range from 8730 to 7660 years before present, surprisingly recent in view of the assemblage typology. Late varieties of points, such as the pentagonoid lanceolates found at Reagen, are rare in surface collections and occasionally occur on sites with Early Paleo-Indian components, such as Plenge in New Jersey and Williamson in Virginia (McCary, 1951; Benthall and McCary, 1973).

Although fluted points are almost entirely confined in distribution to the areas south of the last major ice advance (the Valders), which lasted until about 8000 BC, Plano point styles occur north of the Valders margin at the Sheguiandah site on Lake Huron (Lee, 1954, 1955) and on sites recently discovered in Labrador and Keewatin, dated between 6000 and 3000 BC (Wright, 1976). This occurrence contrasts with the extreme sparseness of such remains in New York and New England. Evidently, some Late Paleo-Indian groups, adapted to periglacial environmental conditions, were able to follow the retreating glacial ice northward into Canada. There these groups managed to survive and served as the foundation for subsequent cultural developments in the Canadian Shield, known as the Shield Archaic (Wright, 1972). The primary subsistence orientation was probably toward caribou and fish. Even less clear is the fate of Late Paleo-Indians in New York or New England, since no likely derivatives of a Reagen-like horizon are known.

THE EARLY AND MIDDLE ARCHAIC

The hunting, gathering, and fishing cultures that followed the Paleo-Indians, but preceded the introduction of ceramics and the cultivation of plants, are assigned by archeologists to the Archaic stage. Generally accepted radiocarbon dates place the Archaic occupations between 8000 and 1000 BC. This long period is usually broken into three subdivisions: the Early Archaic (8000–6000 BC), the Middle Archaic (6000–4000 BC), and the Late Archaic (4000–1000 BC).

Continuity

As radiocarbon-dated cultural frameworks developed, it became evident that the Paleo-Indian occupations were closely followed by Archaic expressions without significant breaks in continuity. Early Archaic cultures were reported for the Modoc Rockshelter in Illinois (Fowler, 1959), Graham Cave in Missouri (Logan, 1952), Eva in Tennessee (Lewis and Lewis, 1961), and a number of other sites. The earliest of these occupations is represented by the Dalton projectile point series dated to about 8000 BC. These points and related styles—ranging from lanceolate to side-notched in outline—display basal thinning flakes that often approach fluting, and evidently evolved from late fluted-point forms. Although research has revealed a long sequence of subsequent types, continuity is not always evident from one type or phase into another. The series includes Palmer points, Kirk points, the bifurcated-base styles, and Stanly points (Coe, 1964; Broyles, 1971).

It is by no means certain that all of these points or their associated complexes of traits can be traced back to the Dalton horizon. In the Southeast this succession of cultures reflected adaptations to the changing environmental conditions—culminating in a deciduous forest biome—that followed the close of the Pleistocene epoch. That biome was rich in animal and plant resources. Although there were minor changes in environmental conditions from 8000 to 1000 BC, there were no corresponding gaps in the cultural record. Until as recently as 1965, there appeared to be such a gap in the Northeast. The oldest dates for Archaic cultures fell around 3000 BC (Ritchie, 1965:32–33)—in the Late Archaic period. Subsequent research has substantially changed this situation. A number of sites have produced projectile points similar to early types of the Southeast and Midwest.

For example, Kirk, bifurcated-base, and other points have been recovered from the Hollowell and other sites on Staten Island (Figure 8.6) (Ritchie and Funk, 1971); from the Harry's Farm site (Kraft, 1975a), the Shawnee-Minisink site (McNett and McMillan, 1974, 1977), and the Rockelein site (Dumont, 1979) in the Delaware valley; from the Sheep Rockshelter in the Juniata valley (Michels and Smith, 1967); and from the Russ, Johnsen no. 3, and Gardepe sites in the upper Susquehanna drainage (Funk, 1977b, 1979). A Middle Archaic sequence represented chiefly by Neville and Stark points, allied to Stanly and Morrow Mountain points, was described by Dincauze (1976) for the Neville site, New Hampshire. Early Archaic components occurred at the Weirs Beach site, New Hampshire (Bolian, 1980) and at the John's Bridge site, Vermont (P. Thomas and Robinson, 1980). Several other sites have yielded evidence for occupations in the Middle Archaic and early Late Archaic periods (Brennan, 1972, 1974; Funk, 1976, 1978; Calkin and Miller, 1977; Kinsey et al., 1972). Radiocarbon dates for the various components range from 7400 to 3300 BC. Meanwhile, surface distribution studies have shown that Early to Middle Archaic points occur in southern Ontario, and are far more common than previously suspected in northern and southern New England (Dincauze and Mulholland, 1977; Starbuck and Bolian, 1980).

In general, it still appears that Early to Middle Archaic evidences in the Northeast are much less abundant than in more southerly latitudes. Very little is currently known about subsistence practices, settlement systems, and nonlithic portions of the material inventory. No data are available on burial customs or physical anthropology, although there is reason to believe that the hunting-

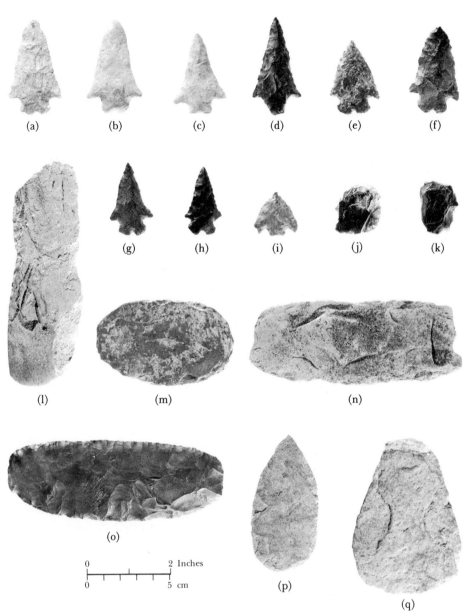

FIGURE 8.6
Artifacts from the Early to Middle Archaic Hollowell site, Staten Island: (a–c, f–h) Kanawha Stemmed points; (d) Stanly Stemmed point; (e) untyped bifurcated-base point; (i) Eva point; (j, k) end scrapers; (l) bifacially chipped celt with ground bit; (m–o) large bifaces; (p, q) ovate choppers. (After Ritchie and Funk, 1971.)

gathering–fishing economy was identical in most respects to that of the Southeastern groups. Environmental conditions peculiar to the pine–oak forests of upstate New York and interior New England between 8000 and 6000 BC may have required an increased emphasis on certain subsistence resources at the expense of others (Funk, 1977a). Indeed, the dominance of such forests, relatively impoverished in plant and animal resources useful to humans, has been hypothesized as the key factor in the sparse distribution of Early to Middle Archaic traces across the Great Lakes and the Northeast (Fitting, 1968; Cleland, 1966; Ritchie, 1969b). This hypothesis is not accepted by some archeologists (Dincauze and Mulholland, 1977), who feel that the early postglacial environment was actually favorable to hunters and gatherers.

Whether Northeastern Early Archaic phases developed from the antecedent Late Paleo-Indian stage through a Dalton-like horizon, or budded off from southern Archaic groups and migrated into a temporarily depopulated Northeast, cannot yet be determined. It is interesting to speculate on what happened to the Reagen component, with its complement of small triangular and stemmed points suggestive of later Archaic styles.

The Maritime Archaic Tradition

Information possibly having a bearing on this problem has been presented by McGhee and Tuck (1975) and by Tuck (1977) in their reconstruction of a long Archaic succession on the coast of Labrador. Dating within this sequence relies both on radiocarbon dates and on the relative positions of sites on the marine terraces created by postglacial rebound of the coast in the Strait of Belle Isle. The earliest phases in the sequence, as at Pinware Hill and Cowpath, produced triangular projectile points in which Tuck sees faint echoes of Paleo-Indian styles. The Labrador points more closely resemble the small, triangular points from the Reagen site than they do other Late Paleo-Indian forms. They are also very similar to much more recent Late Woodland styles.

Among the more spectacular finds was the L'Anse Amour mound, partly constructed of stones, which contained the extended burial of a child. This burial was accompanied by a considerable variety and quantity of grave goods, including red ocher, stemmed and socketed bone points, a walrus tusk, graphite paintstones, whetstones, a bone whistle, stemmed bifacial projectile points or knives, and a toggling harpoon head. The site is C14 dated 7255 and 7530 years before present, making it the oldest known burial mound in North America (McGhee and Tuck, 1975). The mound was roughly contemporaneous with the Barney complex, which is identified by small, broad, contracting-stemmed points very similar to the Middle Archaic Neville type in New England (Dincauze, 1976). Barney points were the first in a series of stemmed points that seem to represent a continuous developmental sequence along the Labrador coast. By 3000 BC this sequence was interrupted by a new succession of expanded-stemmed and side-notched projectile forms. Ground stone gouges and celts appeared by about 5000 BC; this is the oldest occurrence of gouges in the New World. Throughout the period of occupation by Maritime Archaic peoples, their economy was oriented to sea mammals (principally the harp seal), as well as to fish, birds, and caribou.

THE LATE ARCHAIC

Occupation of the East continued into the Late Archaic period without interruption from the prior Middle Archaic period. This continuity is less evident in the Northeast, however, because the sequence before 4000 BC is very sketchily known. In general, the Late Archaic can be characterized as a period of increasing cultural variety; it thus continues the trend first noted in Early to Middle Archaic times. Although some traditions are found over large geographic areas, a strong tendency toward regionalization and local stylistic diversity is evident. By this time, Northeastern plant and animal associations had stabilized in essentially their modern locations and composition. This "oak–chestnut–deer–turkey biome" (Ritchie, 1965:32) was rich in resources exploitable by hunting and gathering populations.

Late Archaic sites are far more numerous than those of preceding periods. They also tend to be larger and richer in cultural remains, and some contain vast amounts of refuse. Because of this productivity, their often thick deposits, and their relative recency, organic remains (food refuse of shell, bone, or vegetal remains, bone and shell artifacts, and so on) are often preserved. There appears to have developed a great proficiency in harvesting game, fish, nuts, and other food resources; the tool kits and industrial technology in bone, stone, and other materials were relatively sophisticated; and in some instances well-favored sites were occupied and reoccupied for long periods of time. A clear implication is that at least some populations had attained unprecedented size. This is the period of such well-known "classic" Archaic cultures as Lamoka and Brewerton. It is generally assumed that Archaic peoples were organized into patrilocal bands occupying limited territories, such as stream drainages. These bands moved seasonally within the territories, exploiting various food resources as they became available.

In much of the Southeast and Midwest, the Late Archaic period opened with the appearance of a family of medium- to large-sized, broad-bladed, chipped stone side-notched points with squared tangs and straight or indented bases. Frequently, the base and notches are ground. These points occur as several types, including Graham Cave Side-notched (Logan, 1952), Modoc Side-notched (Fowler, 1959), Newton Falls Side-notched (McKenzie, 1967), and Raddatz (Wittry, 1959). In the Northeast, corresponding points are referred to as the *Otter Creek* type (Ritchie, 1961). Precise dates are not available for all of these points. For example, Modoc Side-notched points were found at a considerable range of depths in the Modoc Shelter, suggesting a lengthy persistence, and Raddatz points were estimated to date between 4200 and 1800 BC at the Raddatz Rockshelter. Few data are available on the whole cultural contexts of these styles.

In New York State, Otter Creek and related forms initially occurred as part of early assemblages which contained uniface end scrapers, side scrapers, bifacial knives, hammerstones, anvilstones, and other tools. This simple group of traits has been observed at the Shafer site in the Schoharie valley in a level dated at 4340 BC (Wellman and Hartgen, n.d.); at the McCulley no. 1 site in the Susquehanna valley, where it is dated at 3780 BC (Funk and Hoagland, 1972a); and at the Sylvan Lake Rockshelter near Poughkeepsie, where associated dates range from 3720 to 4610 BC (Funk, 1976). The known components are small hunting and nut-gathering camps located within creek drainage basins. Related manifestations in oyster-shell middens of the lower Hudson valley have similar dates (Brennan, 1972, 1974).

The Laurentian Tradition

THE VERGENNES PHASE □ By about 3200 BC in northern New York, Vermont, and the upper St. Lawrence valley, Otter Creek points and similar side-notched styles had been integrated into assemblages featuring end scrapers, side scrapers, ground stone gouges, ground slate points or knives, ground slate *ulus* (semilunar knives), plummets, and other diagnostic traits of the Laurentian tradition (Figure 8.7) (Ritchie, 1969a:79–83). These associated elements constitute the Vergennes phase, oldest and most clearly defined of the Laurentian phases (Ritchie, 1969a:84–89). It is C14 dated 3120 BC ± 210 years at the Otter Creek no. 2 site in Vermont (Ritchie, 1979). A similar expression at the Allumette Island site near Ottawa is dated 3290 BC ± 80 years (Clyde C. Kennedy, personal communication). It appears that the ground stone tools and associated technology, originating in the Maritime Archaic tradition, had been grafted, along with other elements, onto the old complex of side-notched points, scrapers, and so on that was derived from the Southeastern Archaic of about 4000 BC (Ritchie, 1971a; Ritchie and Funk, 1973; Funk, 1976, 1978; McGhee and Tuck, 1975; Tuck, 1977). A probable component of the Vergennes phase was present at the Hirundo site in northern Maine (Sanger, 1975; Sanger et al., 1977).

It appears that the range of the Vergennes phase fell short of southern New York, Pennsylvania, New Jersey, and southern New England. This is true of other Laurentian phases as well. As the name implies, they were geographically centered within the Lake Forest environment of northern and central New York and the St. Lawrence valley. Otter Creek points, like other Laurentian types, are found well outside the distribution of the named phases and of such key traits as gouges, plummets, and ground slates. No Laurentian phases as such

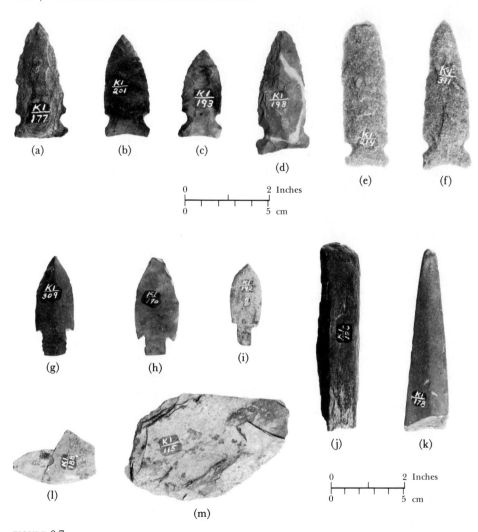

FIGURE 8.7
Stone artifacts of the Late Archaic Vergennes phase: (a–f) Otter Creek points; (g–i) ground slate points; (j, k) rodlike objects; (l, m) fragmentary ground slate *ulus*. (After Ritchie, 1965.)

have been defined in Pennsylvania, southern New England, New Jersey, or the Canadian Maritime provinces. In some instances, Laurentian traits appear to be intrusive into local Archaic sequences, as at the Neville site in New Hampshire (Dincauze, 1976). Brewerton point styles and their cognates in New Jersey and Pennsylvania, including the upper Ohio valley (Mayer-Oakes, 1955; Dragoo, 1959), have often been regarded as part of regional Laurentian expressions. However, they cannot be successfully so regarded in the absence of "core" traits such as gouges or ground slates.

THE BREWERTON PHASE □ One of the best-known Northeastern Archaic cultures is the Brewerton phase of Laurentian, sites of which are concentrated in central and northern New York (Ritchie, 1940, 1944, 1965, 1971a). The Robinson and Oberlander no. 1 sites at Brewerton consisted of 2–3 acres of thick refuse deposits in which artifacts of the Brewerton occupation heavily predominated. These artifacts included numerous chipped-stone, notched and triangular points of the Brewerton type series (Ritchie, 1961) plus scrapers, knives, drills, winged bannerstones (atlatl weights), polished stone gouges, adzes, celts, plummets, hammerstones, anvilstones, bone awls, bone gorges, leister points, and so on. The high proportion of projectile points reflects the great importance of hunting in the economy. Other traits suggest such activities as hide-working, bone-working, woodworking, flint-knapping, and fishing.

It is likely that the Brewerton phase was strongly influenced by the Vergennes phase. Chipped stone points, bifaces, unifaces, bannerstones, plummets, and other items are shared by both phases; C14 dates for Brewerton (about 2000 BC) are younger than those for Vergennes; and stratigraphic evidence indicates that the several Brewerton point types overlapped with but generally followed Otter Creek points in time.

The Brewerton people subsisted chiefly on game, including white-tailed deer, but fishing and collecting nuts were important seasonal pursuits. No recorded sites approach the size and richness of the Robinson and Oberlander no. 1 sites. Small campsites are the rule, but a detailed settlement typology remains to be developed. House types are unknown. Brewerton groups buried their dead in the flesh, in extended position, generally in shallow graves dug into habitation refuse.

The Brewerton phase was important in the Late Archaic of southern Ontario, as shown by surface distributions of salient elements (Wright, 1962) and by a few excavated assemblages. A Brewerton cemetery at Morrison's Island near Ottawa was dated 2750 BC (Kennedy, 1966). Subsequent Archaic groups in Ontario possessed side-notched points and a few other traits suggestive of Laurentian derivation, but they lacked gouges, ground slates, and so on. There is little basis for labeling them *Laurentian,* as some writers have done.

THE VOSBURG PHASE □ The third major branch of the Laurentian tradition was the Vosburg phase, which occupied the Hudson valley and extended into adjoining regions of the Delaware valley and western Connecticut (Ritchie, 1944, 1958, 1965; Funk, 1976). It is less well defined than Brewerton or Vergennes. Characteristic notched and triangular Brewerton point types occur in assemblages with the diagnostic Vosburg Corner-notched point. Other lithic traits include biface knives, uniface scrapers, drills, hammerstones, whetstones, and pestles. There is some evidence for the association of plummets, bannerstones, and *ulus* with the phase. Subsistence and settlement patterns were similar to those of Brewerton and Vergennes. Radiocarbon dates place Vosburg between 3200 and 2400 BC.

OTHER PHASES □ On the same approximate time level as New York Laurentian, but known chiefly from burial sites, is the so-called Moorehead phase of Maine, long known as the *Red Paint* culture (Willoughby, 1935; Smith, 1948; Byers, 1959; Bourque, 1975; Snow, 1975). At one time it was considered to belong with Laurentian in a broad tradition called the *Boreal Archaic* (Byers, 1959), but as now understood the burial sites pertain to the mortuary subsystem of Archaic peoples having close affinities with the Maritime Archaic. Grave offerings include numerous gouges and ground slates in a variety of forms, plus side-notched and stemmed points, abraders, plummets, and red ocher. Dates range from about 4500 to 3700 years before present. The settlement system comprised coastal sites, where shellfish and swordfish, and probably marine mammals, were exploited during the spring and summer, and interior stations where woodland caribou were hunted during the winter. Other sites along rivers were occupied in order to harvest anadromous fish.

Some late Maritime Archaic groups in Canada practiced a highly developed burial ceremonialism, as evidenced at Port-au-Choix, Newfoundland, where Tuck (1976) excavated a cemetery containing well-preserved skeletal remains. The offerings comprised a large variety of items, such as ground slate knives and spearpoints, bone knives and points, whalebone lances and foreshafts, toggling harpoons of antler, leister points, beamers, scrapers, and needles of bone, bone effigy combs, shell ornaments, a stone killer-whale effigy, and many other items. Clearly indicated was an economy based on fishing, caribou-hunting, fowling, and the taking of sea mammals.

The Piedmont Tradition

Ranking with Laurentian and the Maritime Archaic as a major Late Archaic tradition in the Northeast was a trait-complex variously referred to as the *Taconic, Appalachian, Piedmont,* or, simply, *narrow-point* tradition (Brennan, 1972; Ritchie, 1969a, 1971a; Kinsey et al., 1972; Ritchie and Funk, 1973; Funk, 1976; Dincauze, 1975). The term *Piedmont* is preferred here. The various phases are linked by the predominance of narrow stemmed (and, occasionally, narrow side-notched) projectile points and by a general scarcity of uniface tools, including end scrapers. Otherwise, the phases appear to have little in common.

THE LAMOKA PHASE □ The most famous of the Piedmont groups is the Lamoka culture of central and western New York and northern Pennsylvania, dated at about 2500–1900 BC (Ritchie, 1932, 1944, 1965). It is identified by a distinctive group of traits, chiefly the beveled stone adz and a series of tools and ornaments of bone and antler (Figures 8.8, 8.9). The small stemmed or side-

0   2 Inches

0   5 cm

0   3 Inches

0   8 cm

FIGURE 8.8
Stone artifacts of the Late Archaic Lamoka phase: (a–g) Lamoka points; (h) ground stone celt; (i, j) ground stone beveled adzes; (k) stemmed spearpoint; (l) pecked stone pestle; (m) chopper; (n) muller and millingstone. (After Ritchie, 1965.)

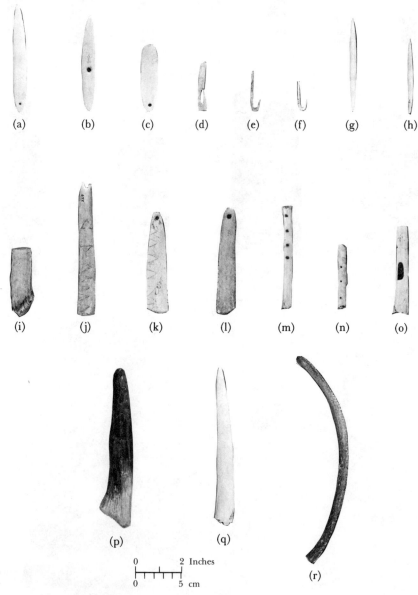

FIGURE 8.9
Bone and antler artifacts of the Lamoka phase: (a–c) perforated bone weaving (?) tools; (d) bone fishhook in process; (e, f) bone fishhooks; (g, h) probable leister points; (i–l, r) antler pendantlike objects; (m–o) bird bone whistles; (p) antler flaking tool; (q) antler punch. (After Ritchie, 1965.)

notched Lamoka-type point with its thick, unfinished base is not unique to the Lamoka phase but is shared with other narrow-point groups.

The Lamoka Lake site is the largest known for the phase. It consists of a rich, thick midden deposit covering over 3 acres of a terrace adjoining the lake. There were numerous post molds; several rectangular house patterns were discerned, two of which averaged 5 meters long and 3.5 meters wide. The surrounding countryside was rich in deer, fish, acorns, and other resources exploited on a seasonal basis by the Lamoka people. These groups buried their dead in shallow grave pits, in the flexed position.

Numerous Lamoka sites are distributed across the landscape within the known range of the culture, occupying a variety of microenvironments. The sites usually occur near lakes, major and minor streams, springs, and marshes, at relatively low elevations. The vast majority are small limited-purpose camps where hunting or fishing were major pursuits. Lamoka Lake and a very few other large sites were probably central base camps utilized repeatedly by one or more bands, where many different domestic and industrial tasks were carried out.

THE SYLVAN LAKE PHASE □ The Sylvan Lake phase is defined principally on the basis of data from the Sylvan Lake Rockshelter, the Dennis site, and the Weinman site, all located in the Hudson valley (Funk, 1976). Similar manifestations are represented on Long Island (Ritchie, 1959; Wyatt, 1977; Gramly, 1977) and in western Connecticut (Swigart, 1973). Radiocarbon dates indicate a time range of 2500–1800 BC. In addition to small, stemmed Lamoka, Bare Island, and Wading River points, assemblages include side-notched points, ovate knives, side scrapers, notched lunate bannerstones, choppers, bone awls, antler flaking tools, hammerstones, anvilstones, and other "rough stone" tools. These items together denote the usual activities of hunting, butchering, hide-working, flint-knapping, and tool manufacture. Sylvan Lake groups subsisted heavily on the white-tailed deer, but also ate a variety of other mammals, fished, and collected fresh-water mussels. During seasonal rounds they made use of backcountry (fall–winter) hunting sites as well as lakeside or riverine (spring–summer) hunting and fishing sites. No sites comparable to Lamoka Lake in size or richness are known.

THE SQUIBNOCKET PHASE □ Closely related to Sylvan Lake and within the same general time period was the Squibnocket phase of southern New England.

Key components were excavated at the Hornblower no. 2 and Vincent sites on Martha's Vineyard, Massachusetts (Ritchie, 1969b). Artifact traits comprise small stemmed and triangular points, choppers, plummets, notched atlatl weights, hammerstones, paintstones, and bone awls. Activity patterns were generally similar to those of the Sylvan Lake phase. The Squibnocket people

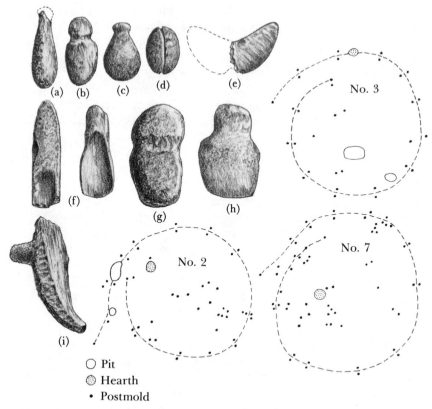

FIGURE 8.10
Lodge floor plans and selected artifacts found at Late Archaic Wapanucket no. 6 site, Massachusetts. Note southwesterly entry common to all lodges. (a–c) plummets; (d) bolas stone; (e) atlatl weight; (f) gouges; (g) grooved ax; (h) maul; (i) steatite pottery fragment.

hunted terrestrial animals including the deer, but the harp seal, fishes, and shellfish were also important to the economy.

The principal component at the Wapanucket no. 6 site, eastern Massachusetts (Robbins, 1960), was probably a manifestation of the Squibnocket phase. Circular lodge patterns 9–20 meters in diameter were associated with Squibnocket point types. Burial pits near the houses contained gouges, plummets, and other items usually attributed to the Laurentian tradition (Figure 8.10). A great deal remains to be learned about the Squibnocket subsistence and settlement systems.

OTHER PIEDMONT GROUPS □ Other Piedmont expressions have been described for the Delaware valley (Kinsey et al., 1972) and the Susquehanna valley (Kinsey, 1959; Funk and Rippeteau, 1977). In the Mohawk–Hudson region the Sylvan Lake phase apparently gave rise to the River phase, dated between 1700 and 2000 BC. Diagnostic artifacts of the latter include the narrow side-notched Normanskill points, winged and notched atlatl weights, and stone pestles shaped at one end into bear's-head effigies (Figure 8.11) (Ritchie, 1969a:125–132).

Piedmont or narrow-point occupations were almost entirely lacking north of the St. Lawrence River; on the other hand, they were heavily represented in the mid-Atlantic states, Pennsylvania, coastal New York, and southern New England (Ritchie, 1969a:142–144, 1969b, 1971a; Brennan, 1972; Funk, 1976). This distribution contrasts with the concentration of Laurentian occupation in the upper St. Lawrence valley and adjacent areas (Ritchie, 1969a:91).

Stratigraphic evidence and radiocarbon dates indicate that Laurentian phases generally predate the narrow-point groups. But some evidence points to a Lamoka–Brewerton sequence in central New York (Ritchie, 1932, 1944, 1965, 1971a). A reverse sequence has been proposed for this area, but the data remain ambiguous (Funk, 1976). Narrow-point groups were apparently older in the South and the coastal areas than in the North. This time slope suggests a mid-Atlantic source for the tradition (Ritchie, 1971a; Brennan, 1972; Dincauze, 1975; Funk, 1976).

The Frontenac Phase

Ritchie (1944, 1945, 1965) defined a Frontenac phase based on his work at the Frontenac Island site in central New York. He regarded it as a cultural amalgam resulting from the interaction of long-resident Lamoka groups with Brewerton people, who moved into the area from the north and east. This interpretation rests mainly on data from a number of burials that contained diagnostic grave goods. Separate Lamoka, Brewerton, and terminal Archaic components were also prominent at the site. As Frontenac remains the only systematically explored site of the phase, information on settlement and subsistence patterns is very limited. In addition to traits contributed by the donor cultures—for example, Lamoka and Brewerton point types, gouges, and beveled adzes—Frontenac included new and distinctive elements, such as shell ornaments and bone flutes. Radiocarbon dates suggest a time of occupation around 1900–2200 BC.

Little is known about the Late Archaic cultures of the upper Ohio valley and its tributaries. Some relationships are evident to the Shell Mound Archaic of the Southeast (Lewis and Kneberg, 1959) and to Lamoka, Brewerton, and other cultures defined in New York. The best-known Late Archaic phase in the region is the Panhandle Archaic (Mayer-Oakes, 1955; Dragoo, 1959). Most recorded sites are small mussel-shell heaps located high on valley walls or bluffs, which produced stemmed, side-notched, and triangular projectile points, grooved axes, crescentic bannerstones, hammerstones, netsinkers, bone awls, and bone points. Radiocarbon dates place the phase around 1700–2200 BC.

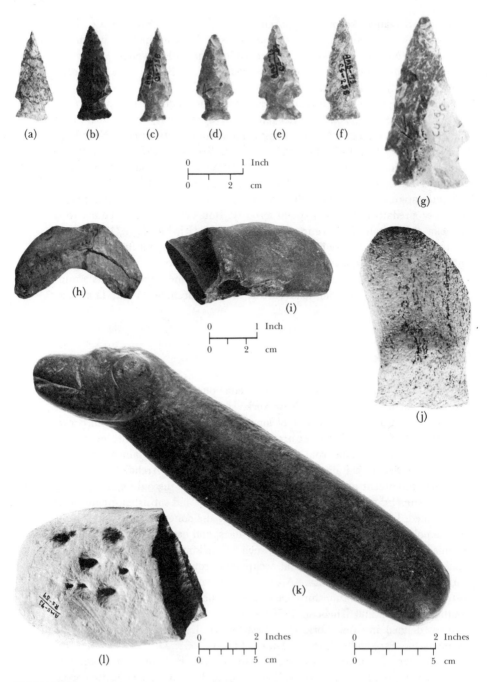

0 |___|___| 1 Inch
0 |___|___| 2 cm

0 |___|___| 1 Inch
0 |___|___| 2 cm

0 |___|___|___|___| 2 Inches
0 |___|___|___|___| 5 cm

0 |___|___|___|___| 2 Inches
0 |___|___|___|___| 5 cm

FIGURE 8.11
Stone artifacts of the Late Archaic River phase: (a–g) Normanskill points; (h–j) atlatl weights; (k) bear effigy pestle; (l) multi-pitted stone. (After Ritchie and Funk, 1973.)

The Susquehanna Tradition

The last major Archaic tradition in the Northeast is recognized chiefly by a family of broad-stemmed, expanded-stemmed, and semilozenge-shaped projectile point/knife styles. Most of these styles occurred in a developmental sequence that underlies the concept of the Susquehanna tradition (Witthoft, 1953; Ritchie, 1965; Kinsey et al., 1972). Earliest in the whole series were the large, broad, straight- or contracting-stemmed types, presumably derived from the Savannah River points of the Piedmont (Coe, 1964). A related type, the Genesee point, is common in New York—especially western New York—and southern Ontario. These are the longest points of the series, with nearly straight-sided blades and squared bases and shoulders (Ritchie, 1961). Genesee points occurred in a distinct Batten Kill phase, defined from four sites in eastern New York (Funk, 1976). Similar manifestations have been noted in the Satchell phase of southwestern Ontario, where one component is dated 1830 BC (Kenyon, 1980). The Batten Kill phase includes points reworked into drills and scrapers, retouched flake knives and scrapers, and a variety of rough stone implements.

Genesee points and related styles are not considered part of the Susquehanna tradition. However, they intergrade morphologically with the shorter, broader, contracting-stemmed styles of the tradition, implying a historical connection. Most abundant in the mid-Atlantic area, eastern New York, and southern New England, the other types are variously referred to as *Lehigh, Koens–Crispin, Snook Kill,* and *Atlantic* (Ritchie, 1965; Funk, 1976; Dincauze, 1972). There is regional variation in details of size, shape, and other attributes. The individual types are often used as markers for phases.

One example is the Snook Kill phase of the Hudson valley. The numerical preponderance of projectile points in this phase suggests that hunting was the dominant subsistence pursuit; there is little evidence for fishing or gathering of wild plant foods. Other artifacts such as scrapers, drills, biface knives, hammerstones, and ground stone adzes suggest the activities of butchering, woodworking, and flint-knapping. Dates range from 1670–1470 BC. Data from related burials on eastern Long Island indicate that Snook Kill people cremated their dead and placed their remains in graves furnished with red ocher, bird-bone flutes, shell beads, and projectile points (Ritchie, 1965:138).

Related "broad-point" groups in New Jersey, the Delaware valley, and New England also practiced cremation burial. Radiocarbon dates range from about 1800 to 1500 BC (Regensburg, 1971; Kraft, 1970; Kinsey et al., 1972; Ritchie, 1969b; Dincauze, 1968, 1972, 1975; Bourque, 1975). Since marine mammals, birds, fish, and shellfish were available, subsistence practices along the coast must have differed from those in the interior.

The cultural expression that emerged from the Snook Kill–Koens–Crispin–Lehigh–Atlantic horizon is variously referred to as *Susquehanna* in the Delaware valley (Werner, 1972), *Frost Island* in central New York (Ritchie, 1965), or *Watertown* in Massachusetts (Dincauze, 1968). It is characterized chiefly by the shallowly side-notched, slope-shouldered Susquehanna Broad or Watertown points and the first demonstrated appearance of soapstone cooking vessels. Dates for these developments fall generally around 1500–1200 BC. Burial customs in New York and the Delaware valley are unknown. However, mortuary ritualism was highly developed among Watertown groups. Cremated human bones and a variety of material goods were placed with red ocher in pits of differing sizes and shapes. These goods included large, pentagonoid biface blades or knives, side-notched points similar to the Susquehanna Broad type, stone axes and adzes, and many other tools.

The use of soapstone was followed throughout the Northeast by true pottery of terra cotta. These events form the basis for a separate *Transitional* stage, commonly seen in archeological reports, that denotes the boundary between the Archaic and Early Woodland stages. The typical soapstone vessel was oblong or oval in form, with projecting lugs at each end for ease of handling. Sources of raw material are known in central Pennsylvania and southern New England.

The Orient Phase

The Frost Island or Susquehanna phases gave rise to, and overlapped in time with, groups manufacturing slender "fishtail" points. These groups are referred to as *Orient* in New Jersey, the Delaware valley, Long Island, and upstate eastern New York and as *Coburn* in Massachusetts. They are C14 dated from about 1200 to 750 BC.

Orient is best known for the cemetery sites on eastern Long Island, consisting of cremated burials often placed in large, deep pits, sprinkled with red ocher and richly accoutered with offerings such as "killed" soapstone pots, Orient Fishtail type points, fire-making kits, and gorgets (Figure 8.12). The Stony Brook site excavated by Ritchie (1959) is one of the few known habitation sites of the culture. Similar burial ceremonialism was practiced by Coburn groups. Orient people obtained most of their nourishment from deer, turkey, and marine shellfish; direct evidence of fishing is lacking.

Pottery was not invented in the Northeast. The technology was present in the Southeast by about 2000 BC and diffused slowly northward, arriving in New York and adjacent areas by about 1200 BC (Ritchie, 1962). Orient groups on Long Island manufactured relatively thick vessels with exterior surfaces roughened by the application of paddles wrapped with cord or fabric (Stony Brook Corded type). Elsewhere, including upstate New York and New England, the earliest ceramics were corded on both interior and exterior, and are referred to as *Vinette 1*. This type occurred in the Frost Island phase. There is little evidence for the first attempts at pottery making, but soapstone pots may have served as models for the early ceramic shapes, as suggested by a vessel recovered at the Jamesport site, Long Island (Ritchie, 1959). In some areas crushed soapstone was used as temper.

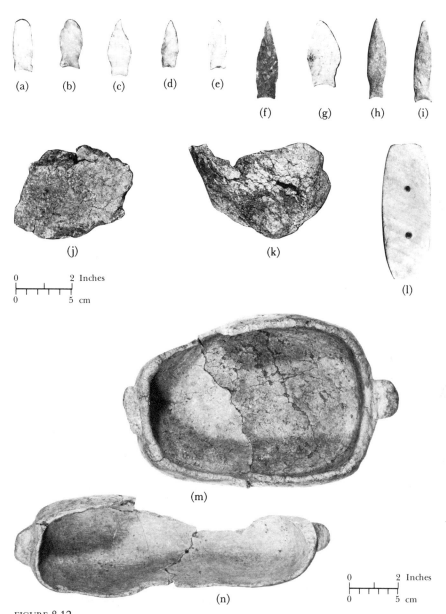

FIGURE 8.12
Artifacts of the terminal Archaic Orient phase: (a–i) Orient Fishtail points; (j, k) sherds of corded pottery; (l) two-holed polished slate gorget; (m, n) restored steatite vessels. (After Ritchie, 1959.)

The Glacial Kame Phase

Another manifestation, known entirely from burial traits, is called *Glacial Kame*. Its known distribution extends from Michigan through Ohio, Indiana, and southern Ontario, and includes the Isle La Motte site in northern Vermont (Ritchie, 1969a:132–134). The artifact traits include copper adzes with gouge-shaped bits, thick rolled copper beads, discoidal shell beads, narrow rectangular shell gorgets, discoidal shell gorgets, "sandal-sole" shell gorgets, lumps of galena, and chipped stone projectile points. The dead were subjected to cremation, buried in bundles after flesh had decayed, or interred in either extended or flexed position. Since pottery has not been found in association with the graves, they have been assigned to the Late Archaic period, but no radiocarbon dates are available for them.

It seems likely that Glacial Kame represents the burial customs of one or more unidentified Northeastern cultures of terminal Archaic or possibly Early Woodland age. An extensive trade network is suggested by some of the artifact materials. The shells are of marine origin, the copper is from the Lake Superior region, and the galena came from the Adirondack region and upper Mississippi valley.

THE EARLY WOODLAND STAGE

This stage is generally characterized by the first widespread use of ceramics and the elaborate development of burial ceremonialism, accompanied in certain areas by the construction of mounds for the dead. This definition is not particularly valid in eastern and northern New England, where Early Woodland remains are rather scanty. This low distribution contrasts with the prior florescence of Late Archaic mortuary ritualism in those regions. Limited forms of horticulture—involving the cultivation of sunflowers, gourds, and other plants—may have been introduced in southern areas peripheral to the Northeast.

The Middlesex Phase

Basic to the initial definition of the Early Woodland was the mound-building Adena culture of Ohio, Kentucky, and adjoining areas. Adena-related sites are widely distributed in the Northeast as defined here, but although they are found in southwestern Pennsylvania, mounds of this period are so far unknown in New England and the mid-Atlantic region. The only example in New York is the Long Sault Mound on the upper St. Lawrence River (Ritchie and Dragoo, 1960), and the Augustine Mound in New Brunswick is the sole Canadian representative (Turnbull, 1976). Otherwise, such diagnostic Adena traits as blocked-end tubes, Adena-type points, birdstones, gorgets, shell and copper beads, and other items are found in shallow graves excavated into natural soils on hills, slopes, terraces, and so on. The artifacts are frequently made of materials foreign to the Northeast, such as Ohio fireclay, Indiana hornstone, and Flint Ridge, Ohio, chalcedony. These nonmound sites—which include Palatine Bridge and Vine Valley in New York, Bennett, Boucher, and Orwell in Vermont, and Rosenkrans in New Jersey—produced varying frequencies of Adena vs. non-Adena artifact traits (Ritchie, 1944; Ritchie and Dragoo, 1960; Kraft, 1976). They are collectively referred to as *Middlesex,* but their significance has been the subject of much debate. Truly amazing quantities of Adena-related grave goods have been recovered in the Delmarva Peninsula (Ritchie and Dragoo, 1960; Dragoo, 1976; Ford, 1976). Ritchie and Dragoo (1960) postulated that a late Adena migration from the Ohio heartland into the Northeast and mid-Atlantic, led by shamans or cult leaders, was responsible for Middlesex. This view has been challenged, however, by Grayson (1970), R. Thomas (1970), and more recently Dragoo (1976), who see the often rich burial offerings as a reflex of trade (in unspecified commodities) conducted with the Ohio valley by local groups inhabiting the coastal regions and interior of the Northeast.

No pure habitation components or campsites of the Adena–Middlesex have been reported in the Northeast. Adena-type points and, rarely, other diagnostic items occur mixed with remains of earlier and later cultures on surface sites in varying geographic locations. They are also sometimes found in appropriate levels of stratified sites. These traits may, therefore, represent a distinct Early Woodland occupation in New York and some adjacent areas at about 600–300 BC. In this case, the burial sites would logically be the products of local populations who participated in religio-ceremonial practices that emanated from the Ohio valley.

The Meadowood Phase

Overlapping in time and space with Adena–Middlesex was the Meadowood phase (Ritchie, 1955b, 1965; Ritchie and Funk, 1973; Granger, 1978). Most recorded sites are located in northern and western New York (Morrow, Riverhaven, Scaccia, Cuylerville, Sinking Ponds, Meadowood, Hunter, Muskalonge Lake). However, diagnostic traits such as thin, side-notched Meadowood points, cache blades, scrapers and drills on reworked points, gorgets, and bar-type birdstones (Figure 8.13) are occasionally found on sites in eastern New York, Connecticut, Pennsylvania, the upper Delaware valley, southern Ontario, and southern Quebec. Most known sites are cemeteries, but habitation sites were excavated at the Riverhaven no. 2 site on Grand Island near Buffalo; Scaccia site near Cuylerville in the Genesee valley; Vinette site near Brewerton; Sinking Ponds site near East Aurora; Batiscan site in Quebec; Dennis site near Albany, New York; Nahrwold no. 2 site near Middleburg; and the Faucett site near Bushkill, Pennsylvania. Radiocarbon dates indicate a time span of 1000–500 BC.

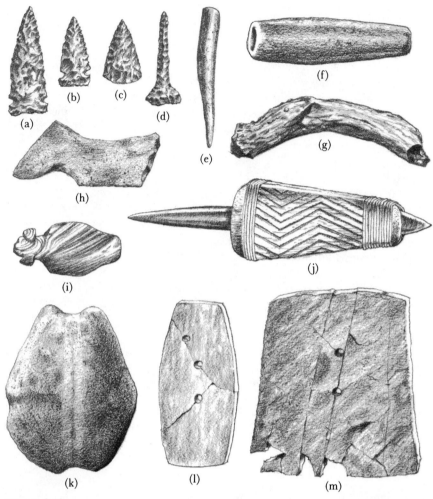

FIGURE 8.13
Artifacts of the Meadowood phase: (a, b) Meadowood Side-notched-type projectile points;
(c) "cache blade" or projectile point preform; (d) expanded-base drill; (e) deer antler awl;
(f) tubular pottery pipe; (g) cut section of deer antler; (h, i) birdstones; (j) copper flaking tool in
wooden handle (restored); (k) ovate pebble netsinker showing imprint of cord attachment to net;
(l, m) two-holed stone gorgets.

Prevalent among burial customs was cremation, which took place either in
grave pits or in separate stone crematories. Cremated individuals were commonly interred in separate graves, frequently accompanied by red ocher plus
such items as birdstones, gorgets, tubular pipes, fire-making sets, and thin,
triangular cache blades (sometimes numbering in the hundreds). Less frequent
were bundle, flexed, or multiple burials (Ritchie, 1955b).

Subsistence and settlement data are meager. A weakly defined post-mold pattern at the Scaccia site suggested an oblong house about 5 meters long and 3.5 meters wide. Possible house floors were noted at the Sinking Ponds site. Refuse remains preserved on some sites indicate fundamental roles for hunting, fishing, and gathering. Unequivocal evidence for cultivation of maize or other plants is lacking. There is some evidence for seasonal movements that permitted the exploitation of food resources available at different times of the year. Most Meadowood sites are located on or near major lakes and streams, but some, including Sinking Ponds, are adjacent to small bodies of water and to swamps. Two basic types of habitation sites were proposed by Granger (1978), based on the apparent functional differences manifested in artifact assemblages, refuse remains, and local ecological settings. One was the fall–winter hunting and nut-harvesting camp, while the second was the spring–summer fishing camp.

Other Phases

Other Early Woodland cultures are sketchily known. Ritchie (1969b) defined the Lagoon phase on Martha's Vineyard. This phase comprises the lobate-stemmed Lagoon-type point, the small stemmed Rossville-type point, bar atlatl weights, Vinette 1 pottery, biface knives, scrapers, and other tools. Post-mold patterns suggested the use of small, flimsy dwellings by Lagoon people, who hunted deer and other terrestrial creatures but also ate clams, oysters, bay scallops, and fish. Radiocarbon dates range from 590–360 BC.

The Bushkill phase of the Delaware valley, dated about 500–100 BC (Kinsey et al., 1972), shared many traits with the Lagoon complex, including Lagoon points and Vinette 1 pottery. However, dentate-stamped, fabric-marked, and net-impressed pottery plus gorgets and side-notched points were present in Bushkill, but not in Lagoon. A probable round-house pattern 7.5–9.0 meters in diameter was unearthed at the Faucett site near Bushkill, Pennsylvania. Because subsistence remains were not preserved, there is little direct evidence for the inferred hunting–gathering–fishing economy. The youngest of the known Lagoon and Bushkill components contain elements of the succeeding Middle Woodland cultures. There are tantalizing hints of Bushkill occupation in the Schoharie and Susquehanna valleys of New York state. Thus Bushkill and Lagoon may represent a broadly distributed series of occupations in the poorly understood period of transition from the Early Woodland to early Middle Woodland stages.

THE MIDDLE WOODLAND STAGE

Available though meager data point to an unbroken development from the Early Woodland phases into the first Middle Woodland phases. These expressions are recognized by a series of artifact and burial traits that were widely, though not universally, distributed across the Northeast at any given time within the general period of AD 100–1000. The original definition of *Middle Woodland* was largely based on the Hopewell culture of the midwestern and southeastern United States, with its ceremonial centers, burial mounds, and often elaborate mortuary artifacts. As evidence accumulated for contemporaneous occupations outside the Hopewell heartland, these diverse cultures were also classified as Middle Woodland because they displayed some similarities to Hopewell. However, important differences also became apparent. Identifiable Hopewell sites are confined to the western and southern fringes of the Northeast.

The Middle Woodland stage was heralded by new ceramic types, more complex and sophisticated than before. In New York and adjoining areas, these are referred to as the *Vinette 2* series (Ritchie, 1944, 1957, 1965). Vinette 2 ceramics are prime diagnostics of the broadly distributed Point Peninsula tradition, which has been subdivided into several phases, with local, regional, and temporal subvariations. Basic trends in form, size, and decoration have been demonstrated for this pottery series. These changes led directly to the Owasco ceramic tradition (Late Woodland stage) and ultimately into the pottery types of the historic Iroquois (Ritchie and MacNeish, 1949; MacNeish, 1952; Ritchie, 1965).

Archeologists have identified Point Peninsula manifestations from Pennsylvania and the mid-Atlantic coast on the south to southern Ontario on the north, and from Lake Huron on the west to Maine on the North Atlantic coast. However, a great deal of local and regional diversity is evident, and the Point Peninsula sequence was actually paralleled by somewhat different developments in areas peripheral to its geographic center in New York and Ontario. Among these developments were the Hopewell and Intrusive Mound cultures of Ohio, the Laurel tradition of the western Great Lakes, the Saugeen culture of western Ontario, the Fox Creek phase of eastern and coastal New York, and less well-defined cultures in eastern New England, Pennsylvania, and New Jersey.

Four successive phases of Point Peninsula development have been postulated for central and western New York: (1) the Early Point Peninsula Canoe Point phase, (2) an unnamed and sketchily defined middle Point Peninsula phase, (3) the Late Point Peninsula Kipp Island phase, and (4) the terminal Point Peninsula Hunter's Home phase (Ritchie, 1965:203–265). The Hopewell-affiliated Squawkie Hill phase was coeval with Early Point Peninsula.

The Canoe Point Phase

This phase, radiocarbon dated between AD 140 and 325, is predicated on a handful of sites. Chief among these are East Sugar Island on Rice Lake, Ontario; Vinette at Brewerton, New York; O'Neil near Weedsport; Canoe Point in St. Lawrence County, New York; Cottage near Binghamton; and Davenport

Creamery near Oneonta (Ritchie, 1965; Ritchie and Funk, 1973). These are generally small hunting and fishing camps, as inferred from their location on major lakes and streams, the presence of projectile points and fishing gear, and, occasionally, the preservation of fish remains. Artifact inventories include small, side-notched and stemmed points, biface knives, scrapers, drills, compound bone fishhooks, fishhooks and gorges of copper, barbed bone points, bone awls, notched pebble netsinkers, adzes and celts, and miscellaneous rough stone tools. Pottery vessels were relatively small (1–4 quart capacity), grit-tempered, with conoidal bases and flared, collarless rims. Lips were pointed or rounded in cross section. Decoration involved dentate-stamping, rocker-stamping, pseudo-scallop-shell stamping, and incising. Little is known of Canoe Point burial practices.

This phase appears to be related to the Saugeen phase of western Ontario, which, however, is dated in the neighborhood of 600–500 BC (Wright and Anderson, 1963; Jury and Jury, 1952). Chipped stone and ceramic traits are similar to Canoe Point, although the pottery appears to have Vinette 1 paste combined with Point Peninsula decoration.

At the Donaldson site on the Bruce Peninsula, small, rectanguloid houses 5–7 meters long and 3.5–5 meters wide were revealed by post-mold patterns. Burials at this site were flexed in shallow grave pits; some graves contained the skeletons of several individuals. Meager offerings included Marginella-shell beads, tubular copper beads, ground and perforated bear canines, side-notched projectile points, scrapers, and red ocher.

The Squawkie Hill Phase

In western New York, northwestern Pennsylvania, and southern Ontario, the Canoe Point phase overlapped in geographic range with Hopewellian manifestations. The latter are represented by a small number of burial mounds; no habitation sites or ceremonial earthworks are on record. Collectively and provisionally designated by Ritchie (1965) as the *Squawkie Hill* phase, these sites had a poorly understood relationship to contemporaneous Canoe Point groups. Possibly the mounds were built by these local groups (as opposed to Hopewell immigrants) in response to ideological and religious influences emanating from the Hopewell centers in the Ohio valley. These influences were perhaps both stimulated and reinforced by long-distance trade networks, an important feature of the Middle Woodland stage.

Mound sites in western New York include Poland Center, Lewiston, Cain, Squawkie Hill, Vandalia, Killbuck, Geneseo, Rector, and Caneadea. The Lewiston Mound was dated AD 160 ± 80 years and the Caneadea Mound was dated AD 140. Similar Pennsylvania sites are labeled *Sugar Run, Irvine, Cornplanter, Corydon, Nelson,* and *Danner* (Mayer-Oakes, 1955). An important site in southwest Ontario is the Le Vesconte Mound.

A brief summary of mound, burial, and artifact traits follows (see Ritchie, 1965:225–226). Small earth mounds were constructed, averaging 9 meters in diameter, 1.5 meters high. Occasionally, slabs or boulders were used in construction, including peripheral circles of cobblestones. Individual graves predominated, chiefly at the mound center. Subfloor pits or stone cist graves, usually slab-covered, were common. Individuals were often cremated, sometimes extended, less commonly flexed or bundled. Trophy skulls were also buried.

An abbreviated list of grave goods comprises plain, curved-base platform pipes usually of Ohio fireclay; locally made copies of these pipes; rectangular two-holed slate gorgets; one-holed slate pendants; copper beads; crescent-shaped breast ornaments of copper; copper or silver-covered wooden buttons; copper "double-cymbal" type ear spools; copper or silver panpipe covers; copper celts; stone celts and adzes; prismatic flake knives, usually of Flint Ridge, Ohio, chalcedony; leaf-shaped biface blades; drills; scrapers; various projectile point styles; rough stone tools; red and yellow ocher; and potsherds (not whole vessels) of various types, including Vinette 1, Vinette Dentate, Point Peninsula Rocker-Stamped, St. Lawrence Pseudo-Scallop Shell, and Geneseo Cord-Marked (a type distinctive to the mounds and probably derived from Vinette 1).

There are traces of Hopewellian influence on some non-mound burial sites, especially the Sea Breeze site near Rochester (Ritchie, 1944).

The best-defined segments of the Point Peninsula continuum are the *Kipp Island* and *Hunter's Home* phases. They followed the decline of Hopewell culture and appear to have developed logically from the foundation of the Canoe Point phase.

The Kipp Island Phase

In many respects, Kipp Island was closely affiliated with the post-Hopewellian Intrusive Mound culture of Ohio. Most recorded sites are burial localities, including Northrop, Point Peninsula, Kipp Island no. 3, Jack's Reef, Durkee, Menard Bridge no. 1, and Plum Orchard in New York; and Bay of Quinte, Brock Street, Williams, and Port Maitland in Ontario. Two important habitation sites are Kipp Island no. 3 in the Montezuma Marsh near Savannah, New York, and Felix (Jack's Reef) on the Seneca River near Elbridge, New York. Available radiocarbon dates fall between AD 300 and 850 (Ritchie, 1944, 1965; Ritchie and Funk, 1973).

Utilitarian artifacts of the Kipp Island phase consist of the Jack's Reef Pentagonal, the Jack's Reef Corner-notched, and, less commonly, of the broad, triangular Levanna-type points; chipped stone end scrapers, drills, and biface knives; barbed bone and antler points; conical antler-tip missiles; bone daggers; bone fishhooks; bone gorges; notched stone netsinkers; and rough stone tools (Figure 8.14). Pottery vessels usually had cord-malleated surfaces and were

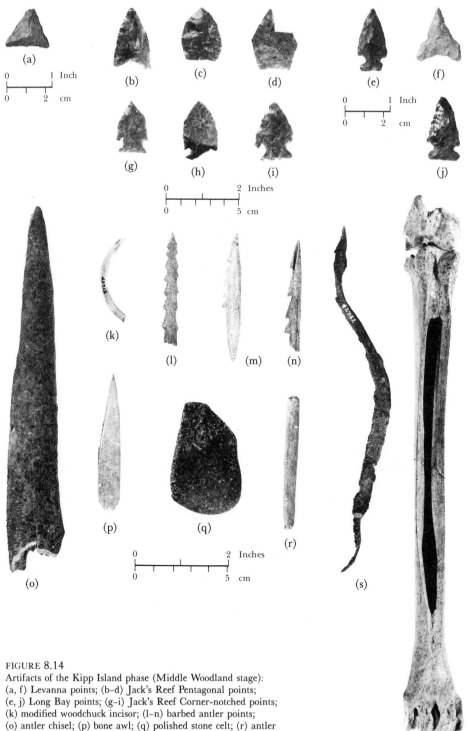

FIGURE 8.14
Artifacts of the Kipp Island phase (Middle Woodland stage):
(a, f) Levanna points; (b-d) Jack's Reef Pentagonal points;
(e, j) Long Bay points; (g-i) Jack's Reef Corner-notched points;
(k) modified woodchuck incisor; (l-n) barbed antler points;
(o) antler chisel; (p) bone awl; (q) polished stone celt; (r) antler
flaking tool; (s) native copper awl; (t) deer metapodial beaming
tool. (After Ritchie and Funk, 1973.)

FIGURE 8.15
Pottery of the Kipp Island phase. Rim sherds are of the following types: (a) Jack's Reef Corded; (b) Wickham Incised; (c) Vinette Complex Dentate; (d) Point Peninsula Corded; (e) Jack's Reef Corded Collar; (f) Vinette Dentate; (i) Jack's Reef Dentate Collar. Other items: (g) sherd with channeled interior; (h) pipe stem fragment; (j) rocker-stamped body sherd. (After Ritchie and Funk, 1973.)

decorated with corded-stick impressions, dentate-stamping, and rocker-stamping (Figure 8.15). In form they were semiconoidal with constricted necks and everted rims, surmounted by rounded or flattened lips.

The Kipp Island economy consisted of hunting (chiefly the white-tailed deer), fishing, and the harvesting of wild plant foods. No evidence of cultivated plants has been found. The settlement system included large multipurpose camps such as the Kipp Island site, fishing camps such as Jack's Reef, small hunting stations, lithic workshops, and burial precincts. At Kipp Island, numerous post molds were mapped at the base of the plow zone. Among these was a probable house pattern—circular, 5.5–6 meters in diameter, and with a short entryway facing south.

Burials were predominantly interred in the flesh, in the flexed position; cremation was relatively rare. Among grave offerings were stone pendants in var-

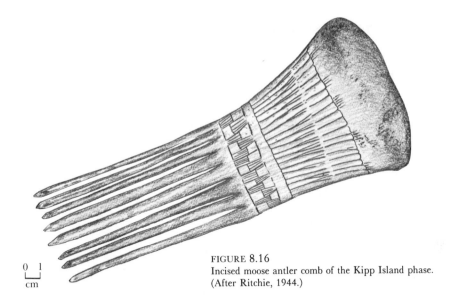

FIGURE 8.16
Incised moose antler comb of the Kipp Island phase.
(After Ritchie, 1944.)

0   1
└─┘
cm

ious forms; antler combs embellished with incised designs (Figure 8.16); shells of Marginella, Olivella, and other species used in necklaces, bracelets, or sewn on garments; copper beads; and smoking pipes of clay in platform, right-angle elbow, and obtuse-angle styles. Exotic items such as fossil shark teeth, some of the shells, and items made from Pennsylvania jasper, rhyolite, argillite, and banded slate indicate wide trade relations.

The Hunter's Home Phase

The Hunter's Home phase evolved directly from the Kipp Island phase. Radiocarbon dates for Hunter's Home range from AD 850 to 1000. Important components were present at the Hunter's Home site near Savannah, New York; the Kipp Island no. 4 site; the Portage site, on the Niagara River; the White site, near Norwich; and the Street site, near Oneonta. In all respects, material expressions of this culture are intermediate between the Kipp Island phase and the earliest Owasco phase, the Carpenter Brook (Ritchie, 1965:271–300). The ceramics consisted of moderate-sized, nearly straight-rimmed pots with semiconoidal bases and broad, flat lips. Corded decoration on a cord-malleated surface entirely superseded earlier modes. Corded horizontal, corded oblique, corded punctate, and platted motifs prevailed, foreshadowing characteristic Owasco patterns.

Other Kipp Island elements were retained, displaying some changes of form and frequency. Straight or slightly bent, generally plain pipes of clay or stone predominated; end scrapers, drills, and knives increased in number and diversity; and Levanna points almost completely replaced other types. Most traces of mortuary ceremonialism had vanished, along with typical offerings such as the straight-based platform pipe and shark's-tooth pendants. The modes of burial included flexed inhumation, bundle burial, cremation, and multiple burial.

The Hunter's Home settlement system was essentially identical to the Kipp Island system. Some data suggest a general increase in the size of habitation sites. A probable house pattern, roughly rectangular in form, 10 meters long and 6 meters wide, was uncovered at the White site. A smaller rectangular house, probably of the same period, was noted at the Kipp Island no. 4 site. Meager subsistence remains on Hunter's Home sites comprise bones of the white-tailed deer, some smaller mammals, and charred butternut shells. It is possible that maize cultivation was practiced by this time, but conclusive evidence remains to be found.

The Fox Creek Phase

Outside western and central New York, Early Point Peninsula (Canoe Point phase) did not develop directly into later phases similar to Kipp Island. In eastern and coastal New York, the sequence was complicated by the Fox Creek phase, which is distinguished chiefly by two traits: the medium-sized, stemmed or lanceolate Fox Creek-type points and net-marked pottery. Dated from AD 325 to 450, this phase is remarkably uniform over a large geographic area, which extended to New Jersey and the upper Delaware valley (Ritchie and Funk, 1973; Funk, 1976). The type site is the Westheimer site on Fox Creek, Schoharie County, New York. Other major components are the Fredenburg site in the upper Susquehanna valley (Hesse, 1968) and the Ford site in the Hudson valley (Funk, 1976).

Besides Fox Creek points, other lithic traits include a variety of cutting, scraping, perforating, and pounding tools, which presumably served to slice meat, pulverize nuts, work hides, wood, or bark, and manufacture tools (Figure 8.17). In addition to net-marking, ceramics display zoning, dentate-stamping, rocker-stamping, incising, and cord-marking (Figures 8.17, 8.18). Ornamental or ceremonial items are nearly unknown in the culture. No burials have been located, and no complete house patterns are on record.

The Fox Creek people lived by hunting and gathering. They followed seasonal cycles, oscillating between warm-weather camps on major streams, where they hunted and (probably) fished, and fall–winter camps such as the Fredenburg site, where deer and nuts were basic food resources.

The Fourmile Phase

Evidence from several stations in the Hudson and Mohawk valleys strongly suggests a continuous development, in which elements of the Fox Creek phase

FIGURE 8.17
Artifacts of the Fox Creek phase (Middle Woodland stage): (a–f) Fox Creek points; (g, h) Greene points; (i, j) large biface knives; (k) bifacial scraper; (l) drill on bladelike base; (m, n) expanded-base drills; (o) net-marked rim sherd; (p) rocker-stamped rim sherd; (q) cord-marked rim sherd; (r) plain rim sherd; (s) pitted stone; (t) grooved hammerstone. (After Ritchie and Funk, 1973.)

FIGURE 8.18
Section of zoned, incised pot of Fox Creek phase. (After Ritchie and Funk, 1973.)

were gradually replaced by traits diffusing from central New York. The final result was a complete convergence of Fox Creek with the Hunter's Home phase. In middle parts of the sequence, such sites as Dennis, Barren Island, and Tufano each contained several associated point types, including Fox Creek, Levanna, and the Jack's Reef types. Net-marked, dentate-stamped, zoned, incised, and rocker-stamped pottery was progressively replaced by cord-marked and cord-decorated styles. The Kipp Island-like component at Tufano's is dated AD 700 ± 100 years. It is the chief basis for a tentatively defined Fourmile phase.

Sites of this phase, concentrated in Albany and Greene counties, include the Tufano site, a riverine camp and burial locus near Coxsackie; the Petalas site, a large lithic workshop on the nearby bluffs; and the upper level at the River site, a campsite on the Hudson near Albany. White-tailed deer, sea sturgeon, and nuts played major roles in the Fourmile economy. Ceramic styles were in part affiliated with the Kipp Island tradition, but such techniques as net-marking and trailing were locally important. Levanna points and a lanceolate style prevailed in the weapon category, in contrast to the predominance of Jack's Reef points in the Kipp Island phase. Petalas blades were abundant and were apparently used as sturgeon knives. Bone combs, stone pendants, and the obtuse-angle elbow pipe were similar to Kipp Island forms. Burials were usually flexed in shallow pits, but bundle burials also occurred. Grave offerings were less common at Tufano's than in central New York. Toward the end of this sequence appear full-fledged components on the Hunter's Home level, including Turnbull near Schenectady (Ritchie et al., 1953) and Black Rock in Greene County. Black Rock is dated AD 850 ±95 years (Funk, 1976).

The Burnt Hill Phase

Several sites on Lake George, including the Weinman and Knox sites, contained components of the regionally differentiated Burnt Hill phase (Funk, 1976). Taxonomically equivalent to the Kipp Island and Fourmile phases, it remains to be radiocarbon dated. Several lines of evidence suggest a date of about AD 700. All known sites are small in area and appear to have been hunting and fishing camps. Artifact inventories include Levanna, Jack's Reef Pentagonal, and Jack's Reef Corner-notched points, Fox Creek points (?), end scrapers, ovate knives, drills, strike-a-lights, rectanguloid slate pendants, celts, and various rough stone tools.

The ceramic industry is dominated by pseudo-scallop-shell-impressed, dragged-stamp-impressed, dentate-stamped, and cord-impressed vessels. Unique to this industry are complexly decorated vessels bearing two or more styles of embellishment; for example, one vessel with a beaded upper rim, rows of conical punctates, and broad zones of incising, rocker-stamping, and dentate stamping.

In summary, Late Middle Woodland groups in eastern New York subsisted on the white-tailed deer, other mammals, fish (including sea sturgeon), birds, turtles, freshwater clams, and nuts. From Fox Creek through Hunter's Home, there was no apparent increase in settlement size and no obvious change in subsistence patterns. Maize horticulture may have been introduced in Hunter's Home times. Sizable pits assumed to be for storage of foodstuffs appeared in closing Fox Creek times; these pits increased in size and number on later sites. Thus there is some evidence for an increasingly sedentary way of life, which was to reach its climax in Late Woodland manifestations.

Other Phases

Middle Woodland phases have not been isolated and defined in New England, although artifacts of this stage have been unearthed on many sites. In some cases, as in western Vermont and the Connecticut River valley, there appear to be strong crossties with better-known phases in New York; in others the similarities are vague and infrequent.

Ritchie (1969b) reported Middle Woodland components on several stratified sites excavated by him on Martha's Vineyard, Massachusetts. One component at the Peterson site was apparently transitional from the Lagoon phase into an early Middle Woodland occupation of the island. Two later Middle Woodland components occurred in stratigraphic sequence at the Cunningham site. The basal component, very similar to some Hudson valley sites in projectile point and pottery styles, was dated AD 400 ±80 years. The second component contained a similar assemblage, with some changes in trait frequencies. The site may have been utilized all year round. Its occupants ate the white-tailed deer, seals, birds, fish, and shellfish. Post molds were abundant, and probable round-house patterns 5 meters in diameter were observed.

Investigations on the flood plain of the Winooski River, western Vermont, have disclosed several periods of Middle Woodland development in stratified sequence. The principal component was closely related to the Burnt Hill phase. In addition to the characteristic pottery, often with several decorative techniques applied to a single vessel, the assemblage includes Levanna, Jack's Reef Pentagonal, and Jack's Reef Corner-notched points, and end scrapers (Petersen, 1980).

THE LATE WOODLAND STAGE

This stage is arbitrarily distinguished from the preceding stage; there is every indication of unbroken development from the one into the other. In New York state, what originally appeared to be a gap between the Point Peninsula and Owasco traditions has been bridged by the delineation of the terminal Point Peninsula Hunter's Home phase (Ritchie, 1965:253–265). A similar picture is emerging throughout the Northeast.

The widely distributed terminal Middle Woodland horizon of about AD 1000 served as the platform for the emergence of a number of regional Late Woodland phases. These phases were linked by such traits as corded, stamped, incised, and (in later periods) collared pottery; triangular projectile points; diverse uniface tools; house types; and so forth.

The developments of greatest import during the period from about AD 1000 through European contact were the practice of maize horticulture and the appearance of large settlements, concurrent with accelerated population growth. There is no indisputable evidence that corn, beans, squash, and other plants were cultivated in the Northeast before that time. However, in extreme southwestern Ontario, maize horticulture was part of the economy of the Princess Point phase by AD 800 (Stothers, 1977). This does not necessarily mean that it took 300 years for agricultural practices to diffuse from southwestern Ontario into central New York. Because Princess Point was very similar to the Hunter's Home phase, there is reason to believe that evidence of maize cultivation will eventually be found on Hunter's Home sites.

Iroquoian Prehistory

The material remains of Owasco culture foreshadowed the patterns of the later Iroquois in New York (the five historic tribes of the League of the Iroquois were the Senecas, Cayugas, Onondagas, Oneidas, and Mohawks). Continuity from Late Owasco (Castle Creek) into the Early Iroquois Oak Hill phase, and beyond it to the historic tribes, has been amply demonstrated in central and eastern New York (Tuck, 1971; Lenig, 1965; Ritchie, 1965:300–311; Ritchie and Funk, 1973). A similar progression has been described from the Owasco-like Glen Meyer and Pickering phases into historic Iroquoian manifestations in Ontario (Wright, 1966). Thus archeology has provided considerable support for the in-situ hypothesis of Iroquoian origins, as opposed to the earlier beliefs that Iroquois-speaking groups originated in the Mississippi valley and migrated eastward into New York and Ontario, where they displaced the resident Algonquian peoples (Parker, 1922; Fenton, 1940).

The New York Iroquois Tradition

In New York state and some adjacent areas, the initial Late Woodland expression was the Owasco tradition (Ritchie, 1969a:272–300; Kinsey et al., 1972). This tradition—arbitrarily divided into the sequential Carpenter Brook, Canadaigua, and Castle Creek phases—has been dated between 1000 and 1300 AD.

Briefly, Owasco ceramics (Figure 8.19) are characterized by paddle-and-anvil construction (in contrast to the coiling method prevalent in Middle Woodland times); cord-malleated exterior surfaces; decoration on shoulder, rim, lip, and inner-rim areas, using cord-wrapped sticks or paddle edges; motifs consisting chiefly of plats, herringbones, and lines arranged vertically, obliquely, or horizontally; broad, flat lips; and vessels of relatively large size (2 to 12 gallons capacity). Initially, in Carpenter Brook times, vessels tended to be elongate in form, with semiconoidal bases, slightly flaring rims and corded-stick decoration impressed on cord-malleated surfaces. Later, the bodies became globular and the rims more outflaring, and decoration was applied to smoothed upper surfaces. By Castle Creek times, most pots were collared; incised and linear-stamped decoration was common; and the decorative repertoire now included appliquéd beads, nodes, and bosses on the rim. Pipes, usually of clay, were straight or of obtuse-angle elbow form. Earlier styles were usually plain, but decoration became progressively more frequent and elaborate; it included zoomorphic and human effigies.

The Owasco lithic inventory (Figure 8.20) was rather diversified; it included broad, triangular Levanna-type points, end scrapers, side scrapers, drills, celts, sinewstones, and numerous other implements. There was also a large variety of bone and antler tools. The Owasco economy was based largely on the cultivation

(a)

(b)

(c)

0   3 Inches

0   8 cm

(d)

(e)

0   3 Inches

0   8 cm

0   4 Inches

0   10 cm

FIGURE 8.19
Pottery of the Middle Owasco period: (a–c) Owasco Platted rim sherds; (d) restored vessel of Owasco
Corded Oblique type; (e) restored vessel of Owasco Corded Horizontal type. (After Ritchie and
Funk, 1973.)

of corn, beans, and squashes. However, hunting, fishing, and the collection of
wild plant foods (acorns, hickory nuts, butternuts, hawthorne apples, cherries,
and plums) supplemented the diet.

Owasco settlements show much variation in size, activities, internal arrangement, and house forms. Some were probably year-round villages, others were
hamlets, at least one was a large workshop, and others were small, temporary
hunting or fishing camps. Some villages such as Maxon–Derby and Sackett

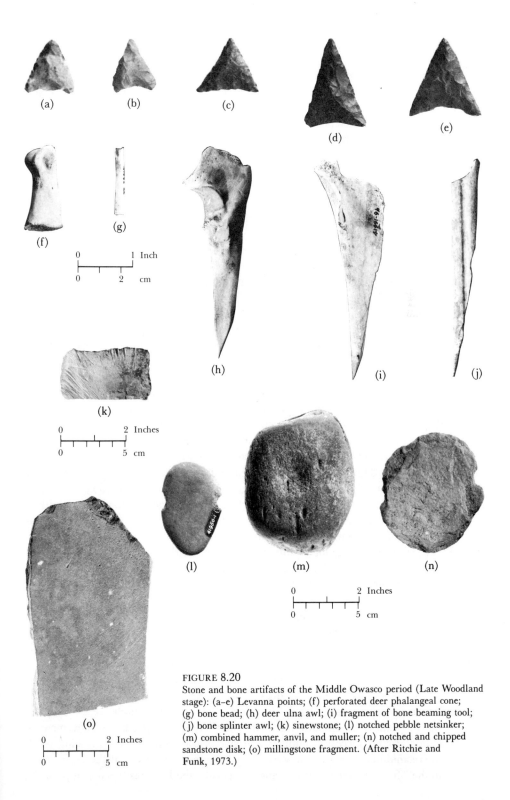

(a)

(b)

(c)

(d)

(e)

(f)

(g)

0   1 Inch

0   2   cm

(h)

(i)

(j)

(k)

0   2 Inches

0   5   cm

(l)

(m)

(n)

0   2 Inches

0   5   cm

(o)

0   2 Inches

0   5   cm

FIGURE 8.20

Stone and bone artifacts of the Middle Owasco period (Late Woodland stage): (a–e) Levanna points; (f) perforated deer phalangeal cone; (g) bone bead; (h) deer ulna awl; (i) fragment of bone beaming tool; (j) bone splinter awl; (k) sinewstone; (l) notched pebble netsinker; (m) combined hammer, anvil, and muller; (n) notched and chipped sandstone disk; (o) millingstone fragment. (After Ritchie and Funk, 1973.)

were up to 3 acres in size. The population of the former was estimated at 240 persons and the population of the latter at 300–350 persons. Houses ranged from small, oval structures about 6 meters in diameter to round-ended long-houses over 26 meters long and 6.5 meters wide. Middle and Late Owasco villages were protected by palisades, which indicates that intergroup competition and conflict were on the rise. Broken and burned human bones in middens suggest the practice of cannibalism. Burials were usually flexed, and were rarely accompanied by grave offerings (Ritchie and Funk, 1973).

The Castle Creek phase of Owasco developed without interruption into the Oak Hill phase, usually defined as the oldest recognizable manifestation of the New York Iroquois. But, like other Woodland cultural units in the Northeast, the Oak Hill phase must be considered an arbitrary slice of a developmental continuum. It is differentiated from earlier and later segments of the column by its pipe and pottery styles, as is also true of the later Chance and Garoga phases. During Oak Hill times corded-collar pottery vessels were popular and were accompanied by minor incised and notched lip types (MacNeish, 1952). Check-stamped body surfaces reached their apogee in this phase, as did certain pipe forms. The Owasco lithic inventory was retained, with minor changes in type frequencies. Settlement types were varied in size, structure, and function. Some sites were relatively large and palisaded (Figure 8.21). Certain longhouses in the Onondaga tribal territory near Syracuse attained lengths of up to 100 meters (Tuck, 1971). At least 300 people are estimated to have occupied some sites. Population may have increased during this period, and there was evidently also a trend in some areas toward nucleation and fusion.

These trends continued into the Chance phase (about AD 1400–1500) (Ritchie, 1952). During this period corded and check-stamped body surfaces were largely replaced by smooth surfaces, and incised decoration predominated over corded stamping. This was the time when Iroquois pottery attained its zenith as an artistic medium. New trumpet pipe styles appeared. The broad, triangular Levanna-type point was undergoing modifications in the direction of the narrow, isosceles-triangular Madison-type point. Settlements often reached a size of several acres. Longhouses up to 125 meters long have been excavated. Warfare continued to be a fact of life, and there is evidence for human sacrifice and cannibalism.

The final prehistoric manifestation of the eastern Iroquois is the Garoga phase. Important criteria of the phase are bold basal notches on collared, globular-bodied pots that retained the form and decoration, but not the esthetic competence, of the preceding Chance phase; prominent and frequent rim castellations; and a variety of pipes in effigy and "escutcheon" trumpet forms (Figure 8.22). Most other elements of the Chance phase continued in use (Figure 8.23). The economy was also apparently unchanged, but its cumulative effects were felt in continued population growth, internecine warfare, much movement of ethnic groups, increased number and size of communities, and growing tribal intercommunication. As many as 700 people may have lived at the Garoga site in the Mohawk valley. Also during this period, the Iroquois tribal groups of the

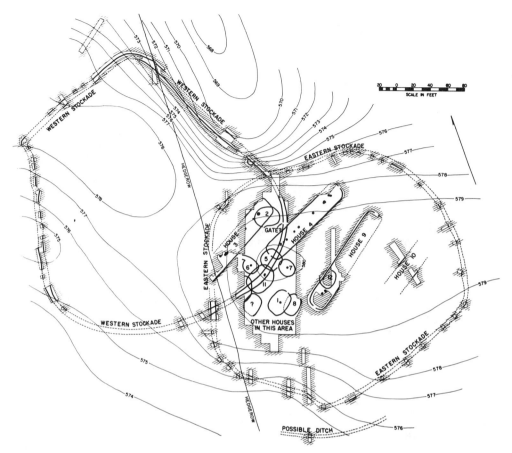

FIGURE 8.21
Plan of the Kelso site (Late Woodland stage, Oak Hill horizon), showing two overlapping palisaded village areas and house patterns. (After Ritchie and Funk, 1973.)

historic period attained their distinctive patterns of material culture and, probably, their sociopolitical and linguistic patterns as well. The Garoga phase, as the culmination of eastern Iroquois (Onondaga, Oneida, and Mohawk) cultural evolution, survived into the early contact period. After this time (about AD 1600), great transformations took place in Iroquois material culture as a result of trade with European settlements.

Relatively little is known about the antecedents of the historic villages of the Cayuga and Seneca tribes, situated in the western Finger Lakes and Genesee valley. However, it appears that these groups also emerged from an Oak Hill level. Seneca pottery is distinguished by either a very low collar or a rather broadened lip, on the lower borders of which broad, deep notches appear; some notches produce a barblike form.

Cayuga sites also yield distinct and diagnostic pottery. High collars decorated

FIGURE 8.22
Pottery of the Late Prehistoric Mohawk Iroquois: (a, b) punctated rim sherd variants of the Garoga
Incised type; (c) toy pot fragment; (d) rim sherd with fillet attached; (e–g) rim sherds of Garoga Incised
type; (h) rim sherd of Rice Diagonal type; (i, j) fragments of trumpet pipe bowls; (k) clay maskette.
(After Ritchie and Funk, 1973.)

with oblique incised or linear-stamped lines are the rule, and deeply notched
forms resemble some Seneca vessels.

Some data are available on prehistoric Cayuga and Seneca settlement patterns. Longhouses of varying sizes have been unearthed within palisaded villages. The Richmond Mills (Reed Fort) site is the largest known Cayuga site,
covering an area of 5 acres.

The prehistory of another Iroquoian group, the Susquehannocks of Pennsylvania, is linked with the New York sequence (Witthoft and Kinsey, 1959). Ceramics indicate a close relationship with the Cayugas. The generally accepted
theory has the Susquehannocks differentiating from the Cayugas just prior to
contact and then, under pressure from Five Nations militarism, moving down
the Susquehanna River from near the present New York border to the position

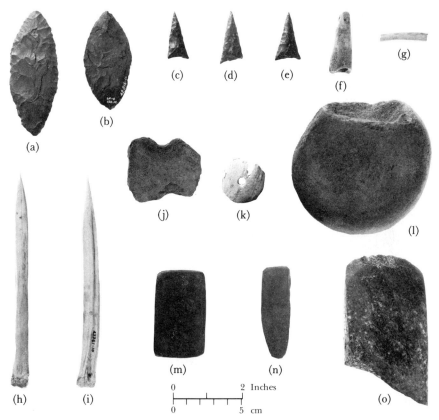

FIGURE 8.23
Stone and bone artifacts of the Late Prehistoric Mohawk Iroquois (Late Woodland stage):
(a, b) biface knives; (c–e) Madison type points; (f) perforated deer phalangeal cone; (g) bone
bead; (h, i) bone awls; (j) notched stone netsinker; (k) discoidal shell bead; (l) muller; (m) stone
net spacer (?); (n) ground stone chisel; (o) fragment of ground stone celt. (After Ritchie and
Funk, 1973.)

of their seventeenth-century villages. In so doing they presumably overwhelmed
and assimilated another group already resident in the lower valley, known as
the *Shenks Ferry* people (Heisey and Witmer, 1964). The Shenks Ferry culture
may represent a northern extension of Late Woodland occupations from the
tidewater area farther south.

The Ontario Iroquois Tradition

Iroquoian complexes in southern Ontario and southwestern New York have
been subsumed by James V. Wright (1966) under the rubric *Ontario Iroquois*
tradition. He postulated three stages of development, which unfolded over a

FIGURE 8.24
Stamped and incised pottery vessels of the Glen Meyer phase, Ontario (Late Woodland stage).
(Courtesy of National Museum of Canada.)

total span of 650 years: Early, Middle, and Late Ontario Iroquois. The first
stage (which emerged from the earlier Princess Point phase) embraces two
contemporaneous early Late Woodland groups—the Glen Meyer phase of
southwestern Ontario between Lake Huron and Lake Erie and the Pickering
phase of southeastern Ontario between Georgian Bay and Lake Ontario. Few
Late Woodland sites of this period (about AD 1100–1200) occur in the intervening area. Glen Meyer and Pickering were similar to New York Owasco in
many respects. They were characterized by large, palisaded villages on hills in
easily defended locations. Subsistence was based on corn horticulture, hunting,
and fishing. Burials were usually in secondary bundles in or near villages; some
Pickering burials were flexed flesh inhumations. Ceramic vessels were semiconoidal to globular in form, of paddle-and-anvil construction. Both phases
shared such decorative techniques as bossing, linear stamping, corded-stick im-
pressing, incising, and dentate stamping (Figures 8.24, 8.25). Push–pull impression was important in the Pickering phase. The phases differed chiefly in
ceramic attribute combinations. Longhouses were oblong, up to 18 meters in
length and 5.5–8 meters in width.

The Middle Ontario Iroquois stage (AD 1200–1400) commenced, according
to Wright (1966), after the Pickering people expanded into and conquered Glen
Meyer territory. A widespread horizon resulted, termed the *Uren* phase, which
in turn evolved into the Middleport phase. Characteristic Uren artifact traits
are: a predominance of incised and linear-stamped ceramic types; a meager pipe
complex; a prevalence of ribbed-paddle, checked-stamp, and scarified techniques of vessel surface treatment; the dominance of chevron and face motifs

FIGURE 8.25
Incised rim sherds of the Pickering phase, Ontario (Late Woodland stage). (Courtesy of National Museum of Canada.)

below castellations; and the occurrence of pottery gaming disks, perforated deer phalanges, slate pebble pendants, and broad, triangular projectile points. During the Middleport substage, changes occurred in pottery type frequencies; new pipe styles appeared in a variety of forms and decoration; the ribbed paddle was applied to most vessel surfaces; collared vessels increased in frequency; and side-notched projectile points became more common, as did certain other traits. Little settlement information is available on either substage. Most known sites are small camps, but several large villages are on record.

Marian E. White (1961, 1963a, b, 1967) described several sites of the Middle Ontario Iroquois stage in the Niagara Frontier region of western New York, including the palisaded Oakfield and Henry Long sites. A round-ended long-house 20 meters long and 6 meters wide was excavated on the latter site. Corn and probably other crops were raised in Middle Ontario Iroquois times. White-tailed deer, fish, and other local fauna were extensively utilized. Cannibalism is evident for the first time. The single and multiple burials of the prior stage were largely replaced by ossuary burial.

The Late Ontario Iroquois stage, which lasted from AD 1400 into the early period of European exploration and settlement, developed through internal change from the Middleport substage. Two branches are recognized, the Huron–Petun and the Neutral–Erie. Huron–Petun sites are found from the north shore of Lake Ontario to Georgian Bay and Lake Nipissing. Sites of the Neutral–Erie branch are situated along the north shore of Lake Erie, extending into south-western New York along the Niagara Frontier.

As in the case of the Five Nations Iroquois of New York, Ontario Iroquois tribal divergence first becomes apparent on a Late Prehistoric time level. Some pottery types continued from the Middleport substage; others, including a high-collared type with incised decoration, were added. Other traits consist of triangular and side-notched points, end and side scrapers, polished stone adzes, perforated deer phalanges, worked bear canines, bone projectile points, bone awls, and bone beads. Burial was in ossuaries; evidence of cannibalism is abundant. Most sites produced remains of corn, beans, and squash. Settlement pattern data are available for a number of Huron–Petun sites, which vary in size from 5 to 25 acres. Longhouse patterns range from about 14–54 meters in length, averaging about 8 meters wide.

Few of the historic villages have been explored with the objective of recovering internal settlement data. One that was is Warminster, believed to be the village of Cahiague visited by Samuel de Champlain in 1615 and abandoned during the Iroquois wars of 1648 (Hunt, 1940). In Champlain's account the village was a single stockaded unit. Excavations showed that the site actually consists of two separate villages, each protected by a multiple palisade enclosing about 8.5 acres. This lack of correspondence with Champlain's description casts some doubt on the identification as Cahiague (Emerson, 1962, 1966; Emerson and Russell, 1965). Relatively little is known about Neutral–Erie settlement patterns, but they were apparently similar to those of the Huron–Petun.

Although Wright (1966) assigned Late Prehistoric–Early Historic groups of western New York to the Erie tribe, perusal of the ethnohistoric literature by White (1961) convinced her that the data did not allow a choice among the Neutral, Erie, or Wenro groups. The sites in question include Ripley (Parker, 1907), Silverheels (Guthe, 1948), and Green Lake, Goodyear, Eaton, Buffam, and Shelby (White, 1961). These villages range from 2 to 6 acres in size. Earthworks surrounded several of them.

Iroquoian groups living along both sides of the St. Lawrence River, from above Montreal to near Quebec City, shared general trends of development with the New York and Ontario sequences. They have been referred to as the *Hochelagans* or *St. Lawrence Iroquois* (Pendergast and Trigger, 1972). Seen by the French explorer Cartier in 1535 and 1542, these people had disappeared from the region by the time of Champlain's visit in 1603. It is generally assumed that they were dispersed by warring Mohawks and other Iroquois trying to gain advantage in the flourishing trade with Europeans. The Roebuck site upstream from Montreal exemplifies the Late Prehistoric period (Figure 8.26).

Village Agriculturists in the Upper Ohio Valley

In the upper Allegheny valley of southwestern New York and adjoining Pennsylvania, excavations on a number of village sites have revealed a regional Middle to Late Woodland developmental pattern very similar to that of the Ontario Iroquois (Dragoo, 1977). However, in very late prehistoric times there were apparent ties to complexes in the lower Allegheny drainage and the Lake Erie basin (Schock, 1976). In the lower Allegheny and Monongahela drainages were separate and distinctive cultural sequences, defined ceramically by the McFate and Monongahela industries (Mayer-Oakes, 1955; Johnson, 1976). These industries are characterized by diverse forms of plain and cord-marked uncollared and collared vessels, some with incised or punctate decoration; most pottery was shell-tempered. Ties to New York Late Woodland as well as to the Fort Ancient culture of Ohio are evident. All of these Late Woodland groups lived in substantial villages, some protected by stockades, and grew maize, beans, and squash while continuing to hunt and fish. Monongahela settlements were often located on saddles between hills. The palisades were oval to circular, up to 140 meters in diameter. Houses were also circular, about 6 meters in diameter, and arranged around an open central "plaza."

Eastern Algonquian Prehistory

The remains of occupations very similar or identical to the Owasco culture have been reported for eastern and coastal New York, western New England, the upper Delaware valley, northern New Jersey, and eastern Pennsylvania. These

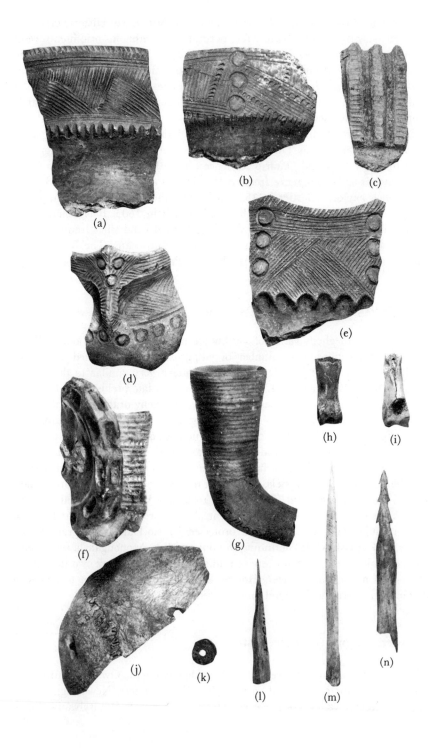

(a)

(b)

(c)

(d)

(e)

(f)

(g)

(h)

(i)

(j)

(k)

(l)

(m)

(n)

prehistoric remains are located in the territories of historic Algonquian-speaking groups, in contrast to the evident development of central New York Owasco into the historic Iroquoian groups. The northern New Jersey–upper Delaware valley expressions have been called *Owasco-Tribal* (Kinsey et al., 1972) or *Pahaquarra* (Kraft, 1975a, b), but as material trait-complexes they seem nearly indistinguishable from New York Owasco. The material culture of the historical Munsee (Delaware) Indians developed from these prehistoric foundations (Ritchie, 1949; Kraft, 1978).

In the Hudson valley of eastern New York, settlement and subsistence data are extremely sparse for Late Woodland manifestations. No post-mold patterns are on record. In certain instances charred corn, nuts, animal refuse bones, and even flexed human burials occurred in storage pits. These sites run the gamut from Early Owasco to seventeenth-century contact period components. Historically, the upper and middle Hudson valley was occupied by Algonquian-speaking groups of the Mahican confederacy (Brasser, 1974).

Again, information on Late Woodland occupations in coastal New York and New England is relatively meager. On Staten Island, Manhattan, and Long Island such manifestations as Bowmans Brook, Clasons Point, Sebonac, and Shantok utilized a variety of sites on or near the shore. The sites included shell middens, rockshelters, large agricultural villages, cemeteries, and stockaded settlements (C. Smith, 1950). Links to upstate New York cultures are evident in the ceramic and lithic artifacts, but some traits are distinctive to the coastal sequence.

Reliable evidence of post-mold patterns relating to prehistoric houses or fortifications is lacking on Long Island. However, earth embankments were reported at several seventeenth-century forts or refuges, including Fort Massapeag and Fort Corchaug (C. Smith, 1950; Solecki, 1950). The people who constructed Fort Corchaug on eastern Long Island shared in the Shantok phase, represented at Fort Shantok on the Thames River near Norwich, Connecticut. This site, built prior to 1645 by the Mohegan Indians, was excavated by Salwen (1969, 1970), who postulated an in-situ origin for the Shantok culture and the historic Mohegan–Pequot from an Owasco-like base.

Similar sequences of development are suggested for interior Connecticut, Massachusetts, and New Hampshire by the materials from the Guida Farm, Titicut, Smyth, and other sites. Despite ceramic and other similarities to Iroquoian manifestations in New York, these sketchily known New England com-

FIGURE 8.26 (*Opposite*)
Artifacts of the Late Prehistoric St. Lawrence Iroquois, from the Roebuck site, Ontario (Late Woodland stage): (a) rim sherd of Durfee Underlined type; (b) rim sherd of Onondaga Triangular type; (c) sherd of Corn Ear type; (d) rim sherd of Black Necked type; (e) rim sherd of Swarthout Dentate type; (f) crescent pipe bowl; (g) ringed, elongated conical pipe bowl; (h, i) perforated deer phalangeal cones; (j) fragment of a human-skull gorget; (k) steatite bead; (l) bone projectile point; (m) bone awl; (n) barbed bone harpoon. (Courtesy of National Museum of Canada.)

plexes represent the late prehistory of the Pocumtuck, western Abenaki, Narragansett, Massachusett, and related Algonquian-speaking groups (Snow, 1978).

DISCUSSION

The foregoing review has indicated that native Americans have inhabited the Northeast since at least 12,000 and possibly 16,000 years ago. Over the long postglacial period, changes occurred in the natural environment, and some of these required appropriate responses from native cultures if they were to survive. The environmental changes involved climate, water drainage systems, forest cover, patterns of sediment deposition or erosion, and the quantity and distribution of edible plants and animals. Northeastern cultures also experienced pressures or "influences" from neighboring cultures, in the form of population growth, migration, territorial competition, trade, borrowing, and so on.

The archeological record shows that an impressive array of diverse cultural developments followed the Ice Age, culminating in the historic tribal groups encountered by Europeans. At least some of these developments may have been correlated with extraneous natural and cultural stimuli, as suggested in various studies (Wendland and Bryson, 1974; Funk and Rippeteau, 1977). An example of such a correlation may be the rise of the narrow-point groups, including the Lamoka culture, during the transition from oak–hemlock to oak–hickory forests (2500–2200 BC).

A great deal is known about some aspects of the regional sequences in the Northeast. At a basic level of analysis, clusters of associated artifact, burial, or other traits are known to have occupied certain positions in time and space, and many such cultural units have been radiocarbon dated. Unfortunately, there are also profound gaps in the framework—for example, in the Early to Middle Archaic period of 8000–4000 BC. However, despite our legitimate interest in the missing parts of sequences, many other kinds of questions remain to be answered. For example, information on dietary habits is inadequate for some cultures, due to the perishability of foodstuff debris. Also, the general lack of good site distribution data, based on systematic surveys within all relevant environmental zones, makes it difficult to generalize about settlement systems, site types, and population size. The reconstruction of extinct societies depends heavily on our ability to locate and identify sites representing the full range of variation in behavior. In order to classify sites as functional types within settlement systems, it is desirable to obtain information on their internal structure—for example, their house patterns, stockades, cooking facilities, or workshops. Unfortunately, in the Northeast most sites lie within areas with shallow soils that have been plowed, so that much evidence has been destroyed.

Considerable research remains to be done on the functions of artifacts, as reflected, for example, in edge-wear patterns. These functions are clues to the types of activities or tasks performed at sites. Among the questions asked by archeologists are: Were projectile points really used for penetrating and killing, or were some of these points actually knives used for cutting up meat? Were bannerstones really used as atlatl weights? Did flaked "rough stone" choppers actually serve as hide-working tools?

Archeologists are increasingly aware of the great variability exhibited by prehistoric cultures in time and space. They are therefore more cautious about applying terminology developed in one region to cultures in other regions. For example, it is less common now than formerly for the term *Laurentian* to be used as a label for cultures that fail to meet the original definition (Ritchie, 1969a:84–89). However, prehistorians are also more cognizant of the essential connections among Northeastern cultures. Regional sequences are seen as the result of continuous occupations undergoing internal change, rather than as strings of disconnected cultures. Continuity is also commonly evident from one locality or region to another on a given time level, with gradual and minor shifts in pottery and projectile point styles.

This new awareness means that the replacement of old by new cultures is no longer automatically regarded as the result of a migration of people. Rather, it is generally viewed as the result of internal change in response to various causative factors, such as the kinds of environmental change noted earlier. This shift in philosophy has resulted in general acceptance of the in-situ theory of Iroquoian origins, as opposed to the old view that Iroquois-speaking groups migrated into the Northeast from regions to the west and south at some time in the sixteenth century.

Other vital research problems remain to challenge the archeologist. One such problem concerns the factors that led to widespread burial ceremonialism in the Late Archaic and Early Woodland periods. What are the social, religious, and economic implications of such behavior? Also, why was there an apparent population decline over much of the Northeast from terminal Archaic to early Middle Woodland times? Was it the result of climatic, sociocultural, or other cultural–ecological factors? And, finally, what conditions were responsible for the adoption of maize horticulture by Northeastern Woodland groups, with the subsequent development of village life, expanding population, organized military ventures, human sacrifice, cannibalism, ossuary burial, and the formation of confederacies such as the League of the Iroquois? This fascinating and difficult problem is the focus of investigations by many Northeastern scholars.

Although existing data and methods can undoubtedly be used to extend our interpretations of prehistoric cultural systems, new approaches often require new kinds of data and new techniques for gathering them. Unfortunately, many of these new approaches are expensive, time-consuming, and beyond the means of most archeologists or their institutions. Many sites excavated in the past are not longer available for restudy, and many additional sites will never be studied at all because of the continuing destruction of cultural resources by modern society. Northeastern academic archeologists have been forced to compromise, working toward limited goals within reduced budgets. Others are working within the constraints of environmental impact studies done for federally financed construction projects. Nevertheless, our understanding of Northeastern prehistory continues to advance at a rapid rate.

References Cited and
Recommended Sources

Adovasio, J. M., J. D. Gunn, J. Donahue, and R. Stuckenrath. 1975. Excavations at Meadowcroft Rockshelter, 1973–74: a progress report. *Pennsylvania Archaeologist* 45:3:1–30.

———, ———, ———, and ———. 1977. Meadowcroft Rockshelter: retrospect 1976. *Pennsylvania Archaeologist* 47:2–3:1–93.

———, ———, ———, J. E. Guilday, and K. Volman. 1980. Yes Virginia, it really is that old: a reply to Haynes and Mead. *American Antiquity* 45:3:588–595.

Benthall, Joseph L., and Ben C. McCary. 1973. The Williamson site: a new approach. *Archaeology of Eastern North America* 1:1:127–132.

Bernabo, J. C., and T. Webb, III. 1977. Changing patterns in the Holocene pollen record of Northeastern North America: a mapped summary. *Quarternary Research* 8:64–96.

Bolian, Charles E. 1980. The Early and Middle Archaic of the Lakes region, New Hampshire. In *Early and Middle Archaic Cultures in the Northeast,* ed. David R. Starbuck and Charles E. Bolian. Occasional Publications in Northeastern Anthropology, no. 7.

Bourque, Bruce J. 1975. Comments on the Late Archaic populations of central Maine: the view from the Turner farm. *Arctic Anthropology* 12:2:35–45.

Brasser, T. J. 1974. *Riding on the Frontier's Crest: Mahican Indian Culture and Culture Change.* Ottawa: Ethnology Division, National Museum of Man, Paper no. 13, Mercury Series.

Braun, E. Lucy. 1950. *Deciduous Forests of Eastern North America.* Philadelphia: Blakiston Company.

Brennan, L. A. 1972. The implications of two recent radiocarbon dates from Montrose Point on the lower Hudson River. *Pennsylvania Archaeologist* 42:1–2:1–14.

———. 1974. The lower Hudson: a decade of shell middens. *Archaeology of Eastern North America* 2:1:81–93.

Broyles, B. J. 1971. *Second Preliminary Report: The St. Albans Site, Kanawha County, West Virginia.* Morgantown: West Virginia Geologic and Economic Survey, Report of Investigations no. 3.

Byers, Douglas S. 1954. Bull Brook—a fluted point site in Ipswich, Massachusetts. *American Antiquity* 19:4:343–351.

———. 1955. Additional information on the Bull Brook site, Massachusetts. *American Antiquity* 20:3:274–276.

———. 1959. The Eastern Archaic: some problems and hypotheses. *American Antiquity* 24:3:233–256.

Calkin, Parker E., and Kathleen E. Miller. 1977. Late Quarternary environment and man in western New York. In *Amerinds and Their Paleoenvironments in Northeastern North America,* ed. W. S. Newman and B. Salwen. *Annals of the New York Academy of Sciences* 288:457–471.

Ceci, Lynn. 1979. Maize cultivation in coastal New York: the archaeological, agronomical, and documentary evidence. *North American Archaeologist* 1:1:45–74.

Cleland, Charles E. 1966. *The Prehistoric Animal Ecology and Ethnozoology of the Upper Great Lakes Region.* Ann Arbor: Museum of Anthropology, University of Michigan, Anthropological Papers no. 29.

Coe, Joffre L. 1964. *The Formative Cultures of the Carolina Piedmont.* Philadelphia: Transactions of the American Philosophical Society 54:5.

Cole, John R., and Laurie R. Godfrey (eds.). 1977. *Archaeology and Geochronology of the Susquehanna and Schoharie Regions.* Oneonta: Proceedings of the Yager Conference at Hartwick College.

Cox, Stephen. 1972. *A Reanalysis of the Shoop Site.* Washington, D.C.: Smithsonian Institution.

Cross, Dorothy. 1941. *Archaeology of New Jersey,* vol. 1. Trenton: Archaeological Society of New Jersey and New Jersey State Museum.

———. 1956. *Archaeology of New Jersey,* vol. 2. Trenton: Archaeological Society of New Jersey and New Jersey State Museum.

Davis, Margaret B. 1969. Palynology and environmental history during the Quarternary period. *American Scientist* 57:3:317–322.

Dice, L. R. 1943. *The Biotic Provinces of North America.* Ann Arbor: University of Michigan Press.

Dincauze, Dena F. 1968. *Cremation Cemeteries in Eastern Massachusetts.* Cambridge, Mass.: Papers of the Peabody Museum of Archaeology and Ethnology, Harvard University 59:1.

———. 1972. The Atlantic phase: a Late Archaic culture in Massachusetts. *Man in the Northeast* 4:40–61.

———. 1975. The Late Archaic period in southern New England. *Arctic Anthropology* 12:2:23–34.

———. 1976. *The Neville Site: 8000 Years at Amoskeag.* Cambridge, Mass.: Peabody Museum Monographs no. 4.

———, and M. T. Mulholland. 1977. Early and Middle Archaic site distributions and habitats in southern New England. In *Amerinds and Their Paleoenvironments in Northeastern North America,* ed. W. S. Newman and B. Salwen. *Annals of the New York Academy of Sciences* 288:439–456.

Dragoo, Don W. 1959. Archaic hunters of the upper Ohio valley. Pittsburgh: *Annals of the Carnegie Museum* 35:139–245.

———. 1976. Adena and the eastern burial cult. *Archaeology of Eastern North America* 4:1–9.

———. 1977. Prehistoric Iroquoian occupation in the upper Ohio valley. In *Current Perspectives in Northeastern Archeology: Essays in Honor of William A. Ritchie,* ed. Robert E. Funk and Charles F. Hayes, III. New York State Archeological Association, *Researches and Transactions* 17:1:41–47.

Dumont, Elizabeth M. 1979. Of paradigms and projectile points: two perspectives on the Early Archaic in the Northeast. *New York State Archeological Association Bulletin* 75:38–52.

Edwards, Robert L., and K. O. Emery. 1977. Man on the continental shelf. In *Amerinds and Their Paleoenvironments in Northeastern North America,* ed. W. S. Newman and B. Salwen. *Annals of the New York Academy of Sciences* 288:245–256.

Eisenberg, Leonard. 1978. *Paleo-Indian Settlement Pattern in the Hudson and Delaware River Drainages.* Franklin Pierce College, Occasional Publications in Northeastern Anthropology no. 4.

Emerson, J. N. 1962. Cahiague 1961. *Ontario History* 54:2.

———. 1966. *The Cahiague Excavations, Summer 1966.* Final seasonal report submitted to the Department of Indian Affairs and Northern Development, Canadian Historic Sites Division, and to the Humanities and Social Sciences Research Fund, University of Toronto.

———, and Russell, Fr. W. 1965. *The Cahiague Village Palisade.* Report to Archaeological and Historic Sites Board of the Province of Ontario.

Fenneman, N. M. 1938. *Physiography of Eastern United States.* New York: McGraw-Hill.

Fenton, W. N. 1940. Problems arising from the historic northeastern position of the Iroquois. In *Essays in the Historical Anthropology of North America.* Smithsonian Miscellaneous Collections 100:159–251.

Fitting, J. E. 1968. Environmental potential and the postglacial readaptation in eastern North America. *American Antiquity* 33:4:441–445.

———, J. DeVisscher, and E. J. Wahla. 1966. *The Paleo-Indian Occupation of the Holcombe Beach.* Ann Arbor: Museum of Anthropology, University of Michigan, Anthropological Papers no. 27.

Flint, R. F. 1971. *Glacial and Quaternary Geology.* New York: Wiley.

Ford, Latimer T., Jr. 1976. Adena sites on Chesapeake Bay. *Archaeology of Eastern North America* 4:63–89.

Fowler, M. L. 1959. *Summary Report of Modoc Rock Shelter, 1953, 1954, 1955, 1956*. Report of Investigations no. 8, Illinois State Museum.

Funk, Robert E. 1972. Early Man in the Northeast and the late-glacial environment. *Man in the Northeast* 4:7–39.

———. 1976. *Recent Contributions to Hudson Valley Prehistory*. Albany: New York State Museum, Memoir 22.

———. 1977a. Early cultures in the Hudson drainage basin. In *Amerinds and Their Paleoenvironments in Northeastern North America*, ed. W. S. Newman and B. Salwen. *Annals of the New York Academy of Sciences* 288:316–333.

———. 1977b. Early to Middle Archaic cultures in upstate New York. In *Current Perspectives in Northeastern Archeology: Essays in Honor of William A. Ritchie*, ed. R. E. Funk and C. F. Hayes, III. New York State Archeological Association, *Researches and Transactions* 17: 1:21–29.

———. 1978. Post-Pleistocene adaptations. In *Handbook of North American Indians*, vol. 15: *The Northeast*, ed. Bruce G. Trigger, pp. 16–27. Washington, D.C.: Smithsonian Institution.

———. 1979. The Early and Middle Archaic in New York as seen from the upper Susquehanna valley. *New York State Archeological Association Bulletin* 75:23–38.

———, and H. Hoagland. 1972a. An Archaic camp site in the upper Susquehanna drainge. *New York State Archeological Association Bulletin* 44:1–7.

———, and ———. 1972b. The Davenport Creamery site, Delaware County, New York. *New York State Archeological Association Bulletin* 56:11–22.

———, and B. E. Rippeteau. 1977. *Adaptation, Continuity, and Change in Upper Susquehanna Prehistory*. Occasional Publication in Anthropology no. 3. George's Mills, N.H.: Man in the Northeast.

———, and Frank F. Schambach. 1964. Probable Plano points in New York state. *Pennsylvania Archaeologist* 34:2:90–93.

———, George R. Walters, William F. Ehlers, Jr., John E. Guilday, and G. Gordon Connally. 1969. The archeology of Dutchess Quarry Cave, Orange County, New York. *Pennsylvania Archaeologist* 39:1–4:7–22.

———, Thomas P. Weinman, and Paul L. Weinman. 1969. The Kings Road site: a recently discovered Paleo-Indian manifestation in Greene County, New York. *New York State Archeological Association Bulletin* 45:1–23.

Goode, P. J., and E. B. Espenshade, Jr. 1950. *Goode's School Atlas*. New York: Rand McNally.

Gramly, Richard Michael. 1977. Archaeological investigations at Pipestave Hollow, Mt. Sinai Harbor, Long Island: a preliminary report. *Anthropology* 1:1:20–32.

———, and K. Rutledge. 1981. A new Paleo-Indian site in the state of Maine. *American Antiquity* 46:2:354–360.

Granger, Joseph E., Jr. 1978. *Meadowood Phase Settlement Pattern in the Niagara Frontier Region of Western New York State*. Ann Arbor: Museum of Anthropology, University of Michigan, Anthropological Papers no. 65.

Grayson, Donald. 1970. Statistical inference and Northeastern Adena. *American Antiquity* 35: 1:102–104.

Grimes, John R. 1979. A new look at Bull Brook. *Anthropology* 3:1–2:109–130.

Guthe, A. K. 1958. The late prehistoric occupation of southwestern New York: an interpretive analysis. New York State Archeological Association, *Researches and Transactions* 14:1.

Hayes, Charles F., III, and Lilita Bergs. 1969. A progress report on an Archaic site on the Farrell farm: the Cole gravel pit. *New York State Archeological Association Bulletin* 47:1–12.

Haynes, C. Vance. 1977. When and from where did man arrive in Northeastern North America: a discussion. In *Amerinds and Their Paleoenvironments in Northeastern North America*, ed. W. S. Newman and B. Salwen. *Annals of the New York Academy of Sciences* 288:165–166.

———. 1980. Paleo-Indian charcoal from Meadowcroft Rockshelter: is contamination a problem? *American Antiquity* 45:3:582–587.

Heisey, Henry W., and J. Paul Witmer. 1964. The Shenk's Ferry people: a site and some generalities. *Pennsylvania Archaeologist* 34:1:3–34.

Hesse, Franklin J. 1968. The Fredenburg site: a single component site of the Fox Creek complex. *New York State Archeological Association Bulletin* 44:27–32.

Hopkins, David M. 1979. Landscape and climate of Beringia during Late Pleistocene and Holocene time. In *The First Americans: Origins, Affinities, and Adaptations*, ed. William S. Laughlin and Susan I. Wolf. New York: Gustav Fischer.

Hunt, George T. 1940. *The Wars of the Iroquois*. Madison: University of Wisconsin Press.

Johnson, William C. 1976. The Late Woodland period in northwestern Pennsylvania: a preliminary survey and analysis. In *The Late Prehistory of the Lake Erie Drainage Basin,* ed. David S. Brose, pp. 48–75. Cleveland Museum of Natural History.

Jones, R. W. 1931. The Clemson Mound. *Fifth Report of the Pennsylvania Historical Commission,* pp. 89–111.

Jordan, Douglas F. 1960. The Bull Brook site in relation to "fluted point" manifestations in eastern North America. Ph.D. dissertation, Harvard University.

Jury, W., and E. Jury. 1952. *The Burley Site.* London, Ontario: University of Western Ontario, Museum of Indian Archaeology and Pioneer Life.

Kaeser, Edward J. 1968. The Middle Woodland placement of Steubenville-like points in coastal New York's Abbott complex. *New York State Archeological Association Bulletin* 44:8–26.

Kennedy, Clyde C. 1966. Preliminary report on the Morrison's Island 6 site. *National Museum of Canada Bulletin* 206:100–124.

Kenyon, Ian. 1980. The Satchell complex in Ontario: a perspective from the Ausable valley. *Ontario Archaeology* 34:17–43.

Kinsey, W. Fred, III. 1959. Recent excavations on Bare Island in Pennsylvania: the Kent–Hally site. *Pennsylvania Archaeologist* 29:3–4:109–133.

——, H. C. Kraft, P. Marchiando, and D. J. Werner. 1972. *Archeology in the Upper Delaware Valley.* Harrisburg: Pennsylvania Historical and Museum Commission, Anthropological Series no. 2.

Kopper, J. S., Robert E. Funk, and Lewis Dumont. 1980. Additional Paleo-Indian and Archaic materials from the Dutchess Quarry Cave area, Orange County, New York. *Archaeology of Eastern North America* 8:125–137.

Kraft, Herbert C. 1970. *The Miller Field Site, Warren County, New Jersey,* Part 1: *The Archaic and Transitional Stages.* South Orange, N.J.: Seton Hall University Press.

——. 1973. The Plenge site: a Paleo-Indian occupation site in New Jersey. *Archaeology of Eastern North America* 1:1:56–117.

——. 1975a. *Archaeology of the Tocks Island Area.* South Orange, N.J.: Seton Hall University Press.

——. 1975b. The Late Woodland pottery of the upper Delaware valley: a survey and reevaluation. *Archaeology of Eastern North America* 3:101–140.

——. 1976. The Rosenkrans site, an Adena-related mortuary complex in the upper Delaware valley, New Jersey. *Archaeology of Eastern North America* 4:9–50.

——. 1977. The Paleo-Indian sites at Port Mobil, Staten Island. In *Current Perspectives in Northeastern Archeology: Essays in Honor of William A. Ritchie,* ed. R. E. Funk and C. F. Hayes, III. New York State Archeological Association, *Researches and Transactions* 17: 1:1–19.

——. 1978. *The Minisink Site.* South Orange, N.J.: Seton Hall University Museum.

Lee, Thomas E. 1954. The first Sheguiandah expedition, Manitoulin Island, Ontario. *American Antiquity* 20:2:101–111.

——. 1955. The second Sheguiandah expedition, Manitoulin Island, Ontario. *American Antiquity* 21:1:63–71.

Lenig, Donald. 1965. The Oak Hill horizon and its relation to the development of Five Nations Iroquois culture. New York State Archeological Association, *Researches and Transactions* 15:1.

Lewis, T. M. N., and Madeline Kneberg. 1959. The Archaic culture in the middle South. *American Antiquity* 25:161–183.

——, and M. K. Lewis. 1961. *Eva: An Archaic Site.* Knoxville: University of Tennessee Press.

Logan, W. D. 1952. *Graham Cave, an Archaic Site in Montgomery County, Missouri.* Columbia: Missouri Archaeological Society, Memoir no. 2.

Lopez, Julius. 1956. *The Pelham Boulder Site, Bronx County, New York.* Eastern States Archaeological Federation Bulletin 15:15.

McCary, Ben C. 1951. A workshop site for Early Man in Dinwiddie County, Virginia. *American Antiquity* 17:1:9–17.

MacDonald, George F. 1968. *Debert: A Paleo-Indian Site in Central Nova Scotia.* Ottawa: National Museum of Canada, Anthropology Papers no. 16.

McGhee, Robert, and James A. Tuck. 1975. *An Archaic Sequence from the Strait of Belle Isle, Labrador.* Ottawa: Archaeological Survey of Canada, Paper no. 34. National Museum of Man Mercury Series.

McKenzie, Douglas H. 1967. The Archaic of the lower Scioto valley, Ohio. *Pennsylvania Archaeologist* 37:1–2:33–51.

MacNeish, R. S. 1952. *Iroquois Pottery Types*. Ottawa: National Museum of Canada Bulletin 124.

McNett, Charles W., Jr., and Barbara A. McMillan. 1974. *First Season of the Upper Delaware Valley Early Man Project*. Washington, D.C.: Department of Anthropology, American University. (Mimeographed.)

———. 1977. The Shawnee–Minisink site. In *Amerinds and Their Paleoenvironments in Northeastern North America*, ed. W. S. Newman and B. Salwen. *Annals of the New York Academy of Sciences* 288:282–296.

Mason, Ronald J. 1962. The Paleo-Indian tradition in eastern North America. *Current Anthropology* 3:3:227–283.

———. 1967. The North Bay component at the Porte des Morts site, Door County, Wisconsin. *Wisconsin Archaeologist* 48:4.

Mayer-Oakes, William J. 1955. *Prehistory of the Upper Ohio Valley: An Introductory Archeological Study*. Pittsburgh: Annals of the Carnegie Museum no. 34, Anthropological Series no. 2.

Mead, Jim I. 1980. Is it really that old? A comment about the Meadowcroft Rockshelter "overview." *American Antiquity* 45:3:579–582.

Michels, J., and I. F. Smith. 1967. *Archaeological Investigations of Sheep Rock Shelter, Huntingdon County, Pennsylvania*, vols. 1 and 2. Department of Sociology and Anthropology, Pennsylvania State University.

Moeller, Roger W. 1980. *6LF21, a Paleo-Indian Site in Western Connecticut*. Washington, Conn.: American Indian Archaeological Institute, Occasional Paper no. 2.

Parker, A. C. 1907. *Excavations in an Erie Village and Burial Site at Ripley, Chautauqua County, New York*. Albany: New York State Museum Bulletin 117.

———. 1922. *The Archeological History of New York State*. Albany: New York State Museum and Science Service, Bulletins 235–238.

Pendergast, J. F., and B. G. Trigger (eds.). 1972. *Cartier's Hochelaga and the Dawson Site*. Montreal: McGill–Queen's University Press.

Petersen, James B. 1980. *The Middle Woodland Ceramics of the Winooski Site AD 1–1000*. Vermont Archaeological Society, New Series, Monograph no. 1.

Raemsch, Bruce E., and William W. Vernon. 1977. Some Paleolithic tools from Northeast North America. *Current Anthropology* 18:1:97–99.

Regensburg, Richard A. 1971. The Savich farm site: a preliminary report. *Massachusetts Archaeological Society Bulletin* 32:1–2:20–23.

Ritchie, William A. 1932. The Lamoka Lake site. New York State Archeological Association, *Researches and Transactions* 7:4.

———. 1940. *Two Prehistoric Village Sites at Brewerton, New York*. Rochester Museum of Arts and Sciences, Research Records no. 5.

———. 1944. *The Pre-Iroquoian Occupations of New York State*. Rochester Museum of Arts and Sciences, Memoir no. 1.

———. 1945. *An Early Site in Cayuga County, New York*. Rochester Museum of Arts and Sciences, Research Records no. 7.

———. 1949. An archaeological survey of the Trent Waterway in Ontario, Canada. New York State Archeological Association, *Researches and Transactions* 12:1.

———. 1951. A current synthesis of New York prehistory. *American Antiquity* 17:2:130–136.

———. 1952. *The Chance Horizon, an Early Stage of Mohawk Iroquois Cultural Development*. Albany: New York State Museum Circular 29.

———. 1953. A probable Paleo-Indian site in Vermont. *American Antiquity* 23:3:249–258.

———. 1955a. *The Northeastern Archaic—A Review*. (Mimeographed.) Albany.

———. 1955b. *Recent Discoveries Suggesting an Early Woodland Burial Cult in the Northeast*. Albany: New York State Museum and Science Service Circular 40.

———. 1957. *Traces of Early Man in the Northeast*. Albany: New York State Museum and Science Service, Bulletin 358.

———. 1958. *An Introduction to Hudson Valley Prehistory*. Albany: New York State Museum and Science Service, Bulletin 367.

———. 1959. *The Stony Brook Site and Its Relation to Archaic and Transitional Cultures of Long Island*. Albany: New York State Museum and Science Service, Bulletin no. 372.

———. 1961. *A Typology and Nomenclature for New York Projectile Points.* Albany: New York State Museum and Science Service, Bulletin 384.

———. 1962. The antiquity of pottery in the Northeast. *American Antiquity* 27:583–584.

———. 1965. *The Archaeology of New York State.* Garden City, N.Y.: Natural History Press.

———. 1969a. *The Archaeology of New York State,* 2d rev. ed. Garden City, N.Y.: Natural History Press.

———. 1969b. *The Archaeology of Martha's Vineyard. A Framework for the Prehistory of Southern New England: A Study in Coastal Ecology and Adaptation.* Garden City, N.Y.: Natural History Press.

———. 1971a. The Archaic in New York. *New York State Archeological Association Bulletin* 52:2–12.

———. 1971b. *A Typology and Nomenclature for New York Projectile Points,* rev. ed. Albany: New York State Museum and Science Service, Bulletin 384.

———. 1979. The Otter Creek no. 2 site in Rutland County, Vermont. *New York State Archeological Association Bulletin* 76:1–21.

———, and Don W. Dragoo. 1960. *The Eastern Dispersal of Adena.* Albany: New York State Museum and Science Service, Bulletin no. 379.

———, and Robert E. Funk. 1971. Evidence for Early Archaic occupations on Staten Island. *Pennsylvania Archaeologist* 41:3:45–59.

———, and ———. 1973. *Aboriginal Settlement Patterns in the Northeast.* Albany: New York State Museum, Memoir 20.

———, Donald Lenig, and P. Schuyler Miller. 1953. *An Early Owasco Sequence in Eastern New York.* Albany: New York State Museum, Circular 32.

———, and R. S. MacNeish. 1949. The pre-Iroquoian pottery of New York state. *American Antiquity* 15:2:97–124.

Robbins, Maurice. 1960. *Wapanucket No. 6, an Archaic Village in Middleboro, Massachusetts.* Attleboro: Cohannet Chapter, Massachusetts Archeological Society.

———, and George Agogino. 1964. The Wapanucket no. 8 site: a Clovis–Archaic site in Massachusetts. *American Antiquity* 29:4:509–513.

Roosa, William B. 1977a. Great Lakes Paleo-Indian: the Parkhill site, Ontario. In *Amerinds and Their Paleoenvironments in Northeastern North America,* ed. W. S. Newman and B. Salwen. *Annals of the New York Academy of Sciences* 288:349–354.

———. 1977b. Fluted points from the Parkhill, Ontario site. In *For the Director: Research Essays in Honor of James B. Griffin,* ed. Charles E. Cleland. Ann Arbor: Museum of Anthropology, University of Michigan, Anthropological Papers no. 61.

Salwen, Bert. 1969. A tentative "in situ" solution to the Mohegan–Pequot problem. In *An Introduction to the Archaeology and History of the Connecticut Valley Indian,* ed. William R. Young. Springfield, Mass.: Springfield Museum of Science, New Series 1:1:81–87.

———. 1970. Cultural inferences from faunal remains: examples from three Northeast coastal sites. *Pennsylvania Archaeologist* 40:1–2:1–8.

Sanger, David. 1975. Culture change as an adaptive process in the Maine–Maritimes region. *Arctic Anthropology* 12:2:60–75.

———, R. B. Davis, R. G. Mackay, and H. W. Borns, Jr. 1977. The Hirundo archaeological project—an interdisciplinary approach to central Maine prehistory. In *Amerinds and Their Paleoenvironments in Northeastern North America,* ed. W. S. Newman and B. Salwen. *Annals of the New York Academy of Sciences* 288:457–471.

Schock, Jack M. 1976. Southwestern New York: the Chautauqua phase and other Late Woodland occupations. In *The Late Prehistory of the Lake Erie Drainage Basin,* ed. David S. Brose, pp. 89–109. Cleveland Museum of Natural History.

Service, Elman R. 1962. *Primitive Social Organization.* New York: Random House.

Sirkin, Leslie A. 1977. Late Pleistocene vegetation and environments in the middle Atlantic region. In *Amerinds and Their Paleoenvironments in Northeastern North America,* ed. W. S. Newman and B. Salwen. *Annals of the New York Academy of Sciences,* 288:206–217.

Smith, B. L. 1948. An analysis of the Maine cemetery complex. Attleboro: *Massachusetts Archaeological Society Bulletin* 9:2–3:17–72.

Smith, Carlyle S. 1950. *The Archaeology of Coastal New York.* New York: American Museum of Natural History, Anthropological Papers 43:2.

Snow, Dean R. 1975. The Passadumkeag sequence. *Arctic Anthropology* 12:2:46–59.

——. 1978. Late prehistory of the East Coast. In *Handbook of North American Indians*, vol. 15: *The Northeast*, ed. Bruce G. Trigger, pp. 58–69. Washington, D.C.: Smithsonian Institution.

Solecki, Ralph S. 1950. The archeological position of historic Fort Corchaug, Long Island, and its relation to contemporary forts. New Haven: *Bulletin of the Archeology Society of Connecticut* 24:3–40.

Starbuck, David R., and Charles E. Bolian (eds.) 1980. *Early and Middle Archaic Cultures in the Northeast*. Franklin Pierce College, Occasional Publications in Northeastern Anthropology no. 7.

Storck, Peter L. 1978. Some recent developments in the search for Early Man in Ontario. *Ontario Archaeology* 29:3–16.

——. 1979. *A Report on the Banting and Hussey Sites: Two Paleo-Indian Campsites in Simcoe County, Southern Ontario*. Ottawa: Archaeological Survey of Canada, Paper no. 93. National Museum of Man Mercury Series.

Stothers, David. 1977. *The Princess Point Complex*. Ottawa: Archaeological Survey of Canada, Paper no. 58. National Museum of Man Mercury Series.

Stuckenrath, Robert. 1977. Radiocarbon: some notes from Merlin's diary. In *Amerinds and Their Paleoenvironments in Northeastern North America*, ed. W. S. Newman and B. Salwen. *Annals of the New York Academy of Sciences* 288:181–188.

Swigart, Edmund K. 1973. *The Prehistory of the Indians of Western Connecticut*. Washington, Conn.: Shepaug Valley Archaeological Society.

Thomas, Peter A., and Brian Robinson. 1980. *The John's Bridge Site: VT-FR-69*. Burlington: University of Vermont, Department of Anthropology, Report no. 28.

Thomas, Ronald. 1970. Adena influence in the middle Atlantic coast. In *Adena: The Seeking of an Identity*, ed. B. K. Swartz, Jr. Muncie: Ball State University.

Timlin, Joseph, and Bruce E. Raemsch. 1971. Pleistocene tools from the Northeast of North America: the Timlin site. Oneonta: *Yager Museum Publications in Anthropology Bulletin* 3:3–21.

Tuck, James A. 1971. *Onondaga Iroquois Prehistory*. Syracuse, N.Y.: Syracuse University Press.

——. 1976. *Ancient People of Port au Choix*. St. John's: Papers of the Institute of Social and Economic Research, Memorial University of Newfoundland.

——. 1977. Early cultures on the Strait of Belle Isle, Labrador. In *Amerinds and Their Paleoenvironments in Northeastern North America*, ed. W. S. Newman and B. Salwen. *Annals of the New York Academy of Sciences* 288:472–480.

Turnbull, Christopher J. 1976. The Augustine site: a mound from the Maritimes. *Archaeology of Eastern North America* 4:50–62.

Wellman, Beth, and Karen Hartgen. n.d. Prehistoric site survey and salvage in the upper Schoharie valley, New York. MS. on file, New York State Museum.

Wendland, W. M., and R. A. Bryson. 1974. Dating climatic episodes of the Holocene. *Quarternary Research* 4:1:9–24.

Werner, David J. 1972. The Zimmermann site, 36-Pi-14. In *Archeology in the Upper Delaware Valley*, ed. W. Fred Kinsey, III. Harrisburg: Pennsylvania Historical and Museum Commission, Anthropological Series no. 2.

White, Marian E. 1961. *Iroquois Culture History in the Niagara Frontier Area of New York State*. Ann Arbor: Museum of Anthroplogy, University of Michigan, Anthropology Papers no. 16.

——. 1963a. 1962 excavations at the Henry Long site. *Science on the March* 43:3:51–56. Buffalo Museum of Natural History.

——. 1963b. Settlement pattern change and the development of horticulture in the New York Ontario area. *Pennsylvania Archaeologist* 23:1–2:1–12.

——. 1967. 1965 excavations at the Simmons site. In *Iroquois Culture, History, and Prehistory*, ed. Elizabeth Tooker, pp. 85–89. Albany: New York State Museum and Science Service.

Wilcox, David R., and Robert E. Funk. n.d. The Castle Gardens site. In *Archeology of the Upper Susquehanna Valley, New York*, ed. Robert E. Funk. Albany: New York State Museum (MS. on file).

Willoughby, Charles. 1935. *Antiquities of the New England Indians*. Cambridge, Mass.: Peabody Museum of American Archaeology and Ethnology, Harvard University.

Witthoft, John. 1952. A Paleo-Indian site in eastern Pennsylvania: an early hunting culture. *Proceedings of the American Philosophical Society* 96:4:464–495.

——. 1953. Broad spearpoints and the Transitional period cultures. *Pennsylvania Archaeologist* 23:1:4–31.

————, and W. Fred Kinsey, III. 1959. *Susquehannock Miscellany.* Harrisburg: Pennsylvania Historical and Museum Commission.

Wittry, Warren L. 1959. The Raddatz Rockshelter, Sk 5, Wisconsin. *Wisconsin Archaeologist* 40:2.

Wray, Charles, and Harry L. Schoff. 1953. A preliminary report of the Seneca sequence in western New York, 1550–1687. *Pennsylvania Archaeologist* 23:2:53–63.

Wright, James V. 1962. A distributional study of some Archaic traits in southern Ontario. Canada Department of Mines, Geological Survey, *National Museum of Canada Bulletin* 180:124–142.

————. 1966. *The Ontario Iroquois Tradition.* Ottawa: National Museum of Canada Bulletin 210.

————. 1972. *The Shield Archaic.* Ottawa: National Museum of Canada, National Museum of Man, Publications in Archaeology no. 3.

————. 1976. *The Grant Lake Site, Keewatin District, N.W.T.* Archaeological Survey of Canada, Paper no. 47. Ottawa: National Museum of Man Mercury Series.

————, and J. E. Anderson. 1963. *The Donaldson Site.* Ottawa: National Museum of Canada, Bulletin 184.

Wyatt, Ronald J. 1977. The Archaic on Long Island. In *Amerinds and Their Paleoenvironments in Northeastern North America,* eds. W. S. Newman and B. Salwen. Annals of the New York Academy of Sciences 288:400–410.

An early aerial view of the site of Cahokia. In the foreground are three large truncated pyramidal mounds; in the background is the largest aboriginal earth mound structure in the United States, Monk's Mound. Its size can be appreciated by comparing it with the farmhouses to the right. (Photograph by D. M. Reeves, Smithsonian Institution.)

CHAPTER NINE

The Southeast

Jon Muller

In an attempt to avoid the pitfalls and irrelevancies of arguments about complex archeological systems of terminology and classification, Dr. Muller emphasizes in this chapter "the dynamics of social and cultural development." He feels that it is time for those studying the archeology of the Southeast "to concern themselves more directly with testing hypotheses about the kinds of social relationships between one society and another" and less with "creating area-wide classifications of dubious explanatory value."

THE SETTING

The Southeast largely corresponds physiographically to the Coastal Plain and the southern half of the Appalachians, but, from the archeological viewpoint, the dominant features of the last 6000 to 8000 years have been the valleys of the major rivers, such as the Tennessee and the Mississippi. These valleys were the setting for the development of the most complex social and political organizations north of Mexico. The climate of the Southeast is temperate, with long, frost-free seasons that ensure rich vegetation and, as a result, rich animal resources. Rainfall is plentiful, and the soils are relatively drought resistant. Much of the Southeast was originally forested, and even the uplands had plentiful resources. At the time of the European invasion, the wild foods were still very important in the diet of native Southeastern Indians, even though cultivated plants had become increasingly important as the economic basis for complex chiefdoms. In later times, limitations of both the fertility of the soils and technology led to increasing concentration in the river valleys.

There are, of course, very great differences in the local plant and animal life within the Southeast that are important in understanding the nature of human settlement. Different kinds of strategies and scheduling were required for exploitation of these differences, and the densest populations in the Southeast generally occurred at those locations where the most diverse natural resources were present.

THE PEOPLE

The indigeneous peoples of the Southeast were, without exception, American Indians. These and no other were responsible for the massive earthworks and mounds of the Southeast. While human occupancy of the area is not unambiguously established before 10,000 BC, it is possible and even likely that humans occupied the area before that time. Physically, the later populations of the Southeast were similar to other people east of the Rocky Mountains, although they may have had slightly larger heads and broader skulls than some neighboring people. Attempts to establish racial classifications of eastern North American populations (for example, Neumann, 1952) have not proved particularly useful in understanding the archeology of the Southeast. Present evidence, both of physical type and of other characteristics, such as relationships among the languages spoken in the Southeast, is consistent with a view of relative continuity of population through time.

It would be useful to have a clearer picture of what environmental limitations on population growth existed in the Southeast in prehistoric times. One of the major puzzles is why population was not higher. Endemic disease might have been one factor, but traditional explanations have emphasized widespread warfare. Since population density appears to have much to do with forcing social change, this factor remains a matter of importance for future work. A major difficulty in investigating aboriginal population here, however, is the considerable impact of European diseases between the time of first contact and the period for which good records exist. As a result of epidemics, the early French and English records are not particularly useful in making population estimates. For the same reasons, there are problems in using these historical records as a source of analogy for prehistoric social and political organization.

ARCHEOLOGICAL PERIODS

Literally hundreds of local archeological phases and complexes have been defined for this large and diverse province. Most of these complexes are based on fine distinctions between one locality and another that are not very significant for a general picture of developments. In some areas there have been more general classifications that are useful for the nonspecialist, but in other areas not even a culture-historical chronicle has been agreed upon. Even the areas that are well known, however, are still understood primarily in terms of historical chronicle rather than in terms of the dynamics of social and cultural development.

The traditional discussion of the Southeast has generally been in terms of four stages—Paleo-Indian, Archaic, Woodland, and Mississippian. While these terms are reasonably useful for discussion of the eastern United States as a whole, there are difficulties in their application to the Southeast proper. One of the difficulties is that these are stages implying an evolutionary classification that is fairly accurate for the central eastern United States but not very appropriate for much of the Southeast. For example, the Early Woodland stage is usually defined as including cultures with the earliest ceramics that have cord-roughened exteriors. Such pottery in the Southeast, however, is relatively unimportant as a marker and occurs much later than the first pottery made in the area. Similar problems exist in the use of the term *Mississippian,* since it is a moot question whether some of the most developed cultures of the Southeast can be properly or even usefully described by that term.

For these reasons, these terms will be avoided in this description and neutral period names will be employed in their place, as follows:

Paleo-Indian	about 10,000 BC–6,000 BC
Archaic	6000 BC–700 BC
Sedentary	700 BC–AD 700
Late Prehistoric	AD 700–AD 1540

The duration of these periods is arbitrary, and inclusion in a period is primarily a matter of convenience. At the same time, there are different subsistence bases for most of the cultures in each period that can be characterized for the Southeast as a whole, even if this characterization does not apply to all of the individual archeological complexes (Figure 9.1). For example, both Paleo-Indian and Archaic are periods during which basic subsistence was obtained by hunting and gathering wild foods. The Sedentary period was probably also a time when the major food resources were wild; some domesticated plants were well established, but it is not known how important these were. Although populations were larger and more settled, seasonal movements were probably still very common. During the Late Prehistoric period, most of the people in the Southeast were dependent upon agricultural produce for a major part of their livelihood.

THE PALEO-INDIAN PERIOD

In terms of projectile points and other lithic technology, the Paleo-Indian pioneers of the Southeast used the same tools and weapons as did those of the Great Plains and the Northeast. Since the Paleo-Indian period is discussed in other chapters in this volume, it is not necessary to discuss the period in detail here (see Jennings, Chapter Two, and Griffin, Chapter Seven). The general picture for the Southeastern Paleo-Indian period is similar to that for the Midwest and Northeast, but several features of the Southeastern Paleo-Indian cultures should be reemphasized. While projectile points of the Clovis form are not uncommon in the eastern woodlands, the number of living, kill, or other sites known is still small, although it is increasing. As a result, it is difficult to determine the exact character of the Paleo-Indian use of the eastern woodlands environment. Some distributional studies do suggest a concentration on river valley resources, but

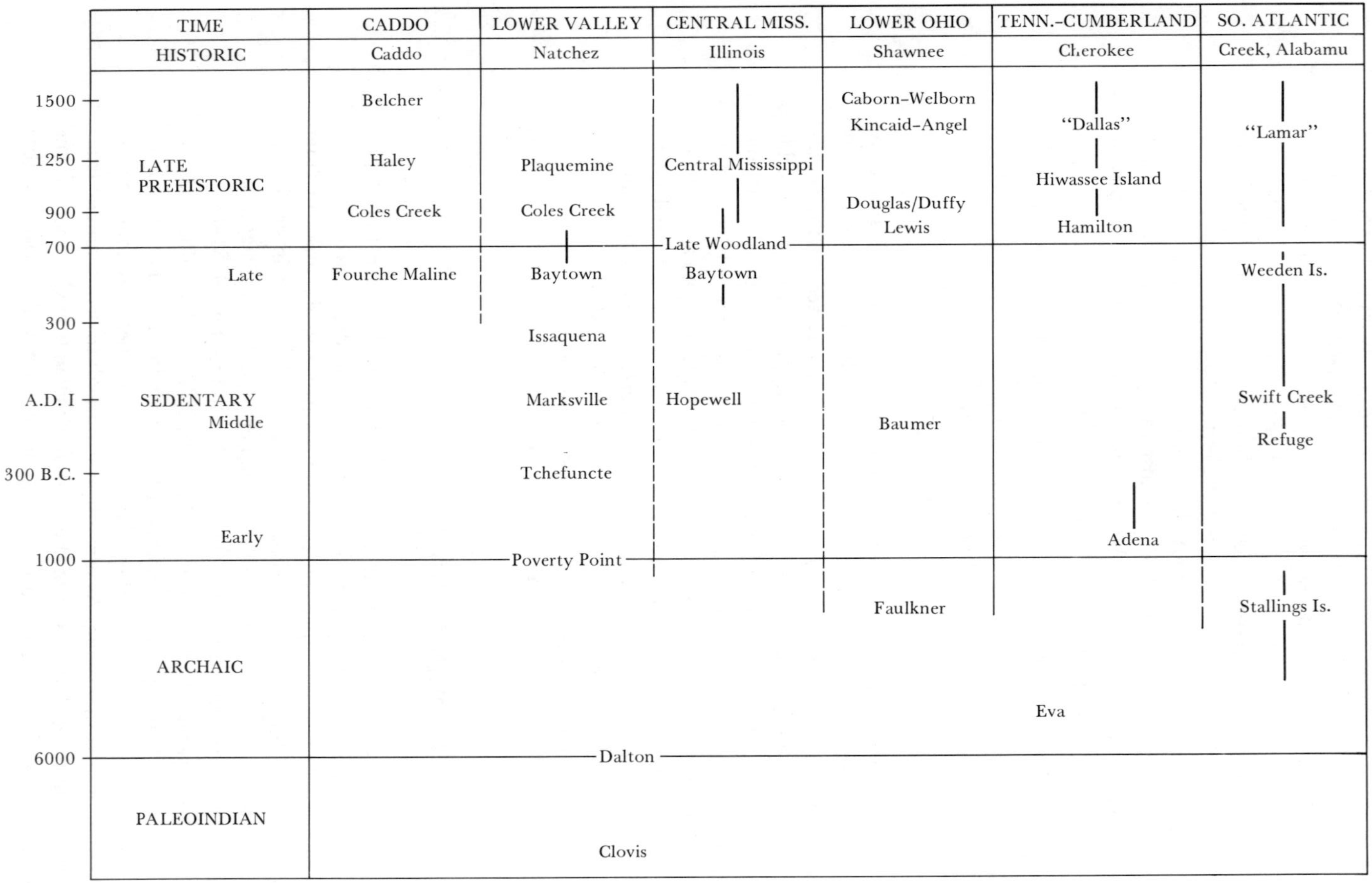

TIME	CADDO	LOWER VALLEY	CENTRAL MISS.	LOWER OHIO	TENN.–CUMBERLAND	SO. ATLANTIC
	Caddo	Natchez	Illinois	Shawnee	Cherokee	Creek, Alabama
HISTORIC						
LATE PREHISTORIC	Belcher	Plaquemine	Central Mississippi	Caborn–Welborn Kincaid–Angel	"Dallas"	"Lamar"
	Haley				Hiwassee Island	
	Coles Creek	Coles Creek	Late Woodland	Douglas/Duffy Lewis	Hamilton	Weeden Is.
Late	Fourche Maline	Baytown	Baytown			
		Issaquena				Swift Creek
SEDENTARY Middle		Marksville	Hopewell	Baumer		Refuge
A.D. I					Adena	
300 B.C.		Tchefuncte				
Early						Stallings Is.
		Poverty Point		Faulkner		
ARCHAIC					Eva	
		Dalton				
PALEOINDIAN		Clovis				

FIGURE 9.1
Representative archeological complexes in the Southeast. Many regional complexes throughout the Southeast are not included.

(Time scale: 1500, 1250, 900, 700, 300, A.D. I, 300 B.C., 1000, 6000)

this finding may also reflect the greater attention these areas have received from both professional archeologists and amateur collectors.

Despite the similarities in technology, the economic basis of the eastern Paleo-Indians may have been different from the big-game-hunting pattern proposed for the Great Plains. Mammoth and mastodon were present in the area, but it is unclear whether mammoth was important in the Clovis economy. In addition to some earlier possible associations (Williams, 1957) of Paleo-Indians with mastodon, a recent discovery near St. Louis at Kimmswick, Missouri, has made it more likely that there was some big-game hunting in the East (Graham, 1982). At Kimmswick, Clovis points were found closely associated with mastodon skeletons, although they were not actually embedded in the bone. Other evidence at this important site suggested that skins of the extinct ground sloth (*Glossotherium*) were used by Clovis people (Graham, 1982:29). The apparent river-valley emphasis may even be taken as an indication that the Paleo-Indian peoples of the East started early to move toward the highly efficient gathering economy usually associated with the following Archaic period.

In any case, both the nature of the sites and the distribution of Clovis projectile points are consistent with the view that the usual Paleo-Indian form of social organization was that of small groups of people moving about an area in response to local availability of plant and animal foods. "Typical" (if that term can be used where there is such scanty evidence) Clovis sites in the East appear to be seasonally specialized and often have the small concentrations of debris that are known as *hot spots*. Many of these hot spots appear to be workshops or other processing areas, but some are probably the remains of temporary shelters of some kind. The size of these areas is consistent with the patterns of family size and composition characteristic of many modern hunters and gatherers (see Lee and DeVore, 1968). The number of people living in the Southeast during this period was probably quite small. One last characteristic of the early Paleo-Indian period was that the climate in the Southeast was considerably different than it is today. Much of the Southeast then would have been more like modern New England or southern Canada, with spruce and pine forests and boggy grasslands. The cultural changes that occurred in the transition from Paleo-Indian to Archaic in the East must be examined in light of the environmental alterations that were taking place.

Toward the end of the Paleo-Indian period, many areas within the Southeast saw the development of a complex known as *Dalton*. The Dalton projectile point form and its relatives are somewhat similar to the earlier Clovis points, and it seems likely that the Dalton complex in this and other ways was a development from the earlier Paleo-Indian pattern in response to the particular demands of the changing Southeastern environment. In some areas, Dalton find-spots and sites appear to be more widely distributed than Clovis locations (Morse, 1973) and to have less concentration in the river valleys, but the evidence is far from conclusive that this is a general pattern. During Dalton times,

(b)

(a)

FIGURE 9.2
(a) A Clovis point from the Southeast, 6.5 cm in length. (After DeJarnette, 1975: Fig. 14.)
(b) A "Nuckolls"-type Dalton point, 4.0 cm in length. (After DeJarnette et al., 1962: Fig. 39B.)

the environment of the Southeast began to resemble that of historical times, although there were to be many minor—but sometimes culturally important—fluctuations in climate and vegetation.

As in the Clovis complexes of earlier times, the Dalton peoples utilized a broad range of animals, with major emphasis on the hunting of deer. It is probable that a wide variety of plant foods were eaten as well. At the same time, the evidence shows little indication of specialization of the sort believed to have existed in the later Archaic period.

The Brand site in northeastern Arkansas is one of the better-known Dalton sites (Goodyear, 1974). Although evidence of diet was unfortunately not directly preserved, it seems that the pattern of exploitation may have been somewhat broader than that suggested by the Dalton levels at the Stanfield–Worley Bluff Shelter in Alabama (DeJarnette et al., 1962). The artifacts at the Brand site show that a number of different kinds of activities were undertaken. Larger Dalton sites in the region are interpreted by Goodyear and Morse as base camps from which parties went out for specialized hunting and gathering activities (Goodyear, 1974:106). There is, however, considerable debate over alternative explanations of the pattern of known Dalton settlement (see Schiffer and House, 1975). The larger Dalton sites are up to 500 meters across; as with other large sites of hunting and gathering peoples, however, there are problems in determining whether this entire area was occupied at one time. Moreover, it is not known whether these possible larger sites were occupied for much of the year or whether they might represent larger seasonal groupings dependent upon the local availability of some rich food source (as in the case of the large groups that gathered prickly pear in Texas at the time of earliest European contact [Cabeza de Vaca, 1972]). It is equally possible that the larger sites may simply be areas that were used over and over again by smaller groups.

One of the important results of the work at the Brand site is the strong suggestion that the Dalton point form was used as a knife as well as a projectile point. The many different "types" of Dalton points thus appear to result, at least partly, from the different wear as well as resharpening of this artifact. This possibility should serve as a caution to those who seek to use traditional archeological typologies for the definition of social groupings.

THE ARCHAIC PERIOD

While not well known by comparison with later times in the Southeast, the Archaic period has been studied extensively in a number of regions. Since one of the outstanding characteristics of the period is the ability of populations to adapt skillfully to a broad range of local conditions, it is not surprising that there are often considerable differences in Archaic period societies from one locality or region to another (Figure 9.3). In most cases, however, the basic strategies employed by Archaic peoples appear to have been similar, despite the differences in technique required for particular locations. The most common pattern of life in this period appears to have been seasonal, with movement from one part of the home range of a band to another area, according to the availability of resources such as fruits, nuts, fish, and game. In many cases, Archaic peoples in the Southeast made use of a very wide range of plant and animal species—a practice that probably spread and minimized risk by allowing choice in tactics for any given season.

In Southwest Asia and other parts of the world, the changing environmental conditions of the early Holocene appear to have often triggered population and other pressures that resulted in domestication of local plants and animals (see Binford, 1968). Thus it is not surprising that there is increasing evidence of local domestication of a number of plants during the Archaic period, as discussed below. The domesticated squash was introduced at this time as well, probably ultimately from Mesoamerica. There is, however, little solid evidence for the presence of other Mesoamerican cultigens until much later than the Archaic. In any case, neither local nor exotic cultigens caused any "neolithic revolution" in eastern North America until nearly the eighth or ninth century of the modern era.

Excavations at deep, stratified sites have shown a long and varied development of the Southeastern Archaic (for example, Coe, 1964; DeJarnette et al., 1962; Fowler, 1959). An incredible diversity of "projectile point" types has been defined, many of which help to establish regional and local styles that are useful to the archeologist. However, a clear picture of how local Archaic societies related to their specific environments is generally lacking. Much more needs to be done to establish synchronic and/or seasonal settlement patterns within a given region. Fortunately, both a greater orientation toward problem solving and the circumstances of contract archeology are leading to a much more complete view for many regions.

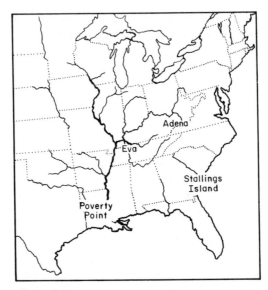

FIGURE 9.3
Archaic and early Sedentary complexes.

Lifeways

The evidence from Archaic period sites throughout the Southeast makes it clear that the population was usually organized into quite small groups of the sort called *bands* by political theorists (Service, 1962). More recent treatment of this level of social organization by Service (1975) has emphasized the egalitarian nature of such social organizations. In such societies, differences in social status are slight, and decision making is informal and diffuse, at least in comparison with more centralized political systems. Exchange and reciprocity are basic to all social systems, but these relationships are nongovernmental in bands (Service, 1975:60–61), despite their importance in interband relationships.

Dispersal of population in small bands would have allowed any given group to react quickly to variation in the local availability of any food resource, at least as long as total population density over the Southeast was fairly low. This flexibility in response would have been particularly important to people who were faced with variation in local food resources from one year to another, and it is known that many of the nut-bearing trees of the area have cycles of high and low yield over periods of two to five years. For peoples who were mobile, who had relatively little capacity or need for long-term storage, and for whom exchange of food and other goods was fairly informal, the ability to shift to other resources or to move to other areas was very important. As population increased throughout Archaic times, however, there would have been increasing pressure upon groups with restricted mobility to develop local resources subject to less annual variation. There would also have been a need to increase the efficiency of exchange and distribution of goods or to improve storage systems to allow carry-over from good years to bad—or all of these pressures could have applied to some degree (see Sahlins, 1972). At the same time, the development of such responses also requires more in the way of administration and organization than the simple band organization of most of Archaic times could provide. In Late Archaic, particularly, differences in burial patterns suggest increasing social status differences (for explicit recognition of this farther north, see Binford [1972:388]; for the Southeast, examine the differences in quantity of grave goods from Indian Knoll, Webb [1946]; see also Chapter Seven, this volume).

Studies of modern peoples who follow ways of life like those of the Archaic period show that this pattern can be extremely successful as long as population growth does not restrict mobility. However, the seasonal movements in the Southeast at this time did involve some areas, especially along the coasts and rivers, that offered rich opportunities for the development of more sedentary ways of life.

Representative Sites

One site that illustrates this shift away from mobility is the Eva site in Tennessee (Lewis and Lewis, 1961). Eva is an island riverbank site with a mound of refuse or *midden* made up of river clam shells. Such shell midden sites often show evidence of considerable population or, at least, evidence of long-term periodic reuse of the same site. Not all sites of the Eva complex are shell middens, however, and it seems likely that there was still some seasonal movement even for the most settled Archaic period peoples. As suggested by the refuse at some Eva sites, freshwater mussels were an important part of the diet. These people also made full use of the other resources of the area, ranging from deer to nuts. The Eva site itself actually had several archeological phases represented, and later phases such as the Three Mile and Big Sand phases do show some minor variation in diet. The basic pattern, however, was similar throughout the thousands of years of use of the Eva site area. Deer appear to have been very important as a food animal, suggesting that upland areas were also important for these riverside people, even though sites in the uplands are rare. The Eva people built structures, but the mass of postholes found at the Eva site made it impossible to tell the size or shape.

The materials used at the Eva site were available in the region (Figure 9.4). Only with the later Three Mile phase do exotic, imported items such as marine shell and copper objects begin to appear in burials. Thus, between the earlier and later Archaic in the Southeast, there is evidence of the establishment of far-reaching exchange relationships. As shall be seen, these relationships of exchange persisted throughout the remainder of the prehistoric record. The means by which these materials were exchanged were probably informal in Archaic

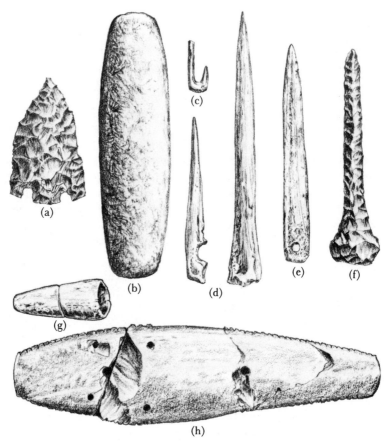

FIGURE 9.4
Artifacts from the Eva site. These artifacts show the specialized tool kit that was characteristic of the Archaic peoples. (a) Eva point or knife; (b) pestle; (c) bone fishhook; (d) bone awl; (e) bone needle; (f) drill; (g) tubular pipe; (h) gorget. (After Lewis and Lewis, 1961.)

times. But the social situation that had created the need and desire for such materials was very likely part of the cause of status differences that culminated in more systematic exchange or trade networks in the highly stratified societies of the Late Prehistoric period.

Another of the well-known Archaic sites in the same part of the Southeast is the Indian Knoll site in Kentucky (Webb, 1946). The settlement of the site was similar to the Eva site, although the nature of the shelters used by the Indian Knoll people is even less certain. Two areas of clay "floor" were found that had hearths and that may have been the floors of structures. These areas were 4.6 meters in diameter and had an area of approximately 14 square meters. If this was a "house," it is likely that at most a nuclear family (mother, father, and

FIGURE 9.5
Materials from Indian Knoll, Kentucky. Like the Eva phases, the Archaic peoples of Indian Knoll had a complex kit of tools. Large numbers of burials were found at the site, and some beginnings of social stratification may be seen in differences in grave accompaniments.
(a) flexed burial at Indian Knoll; (b) projectile points and knives; (c) bone projectile point; (d) pestle; (e) nutting stone; (f) drill; (g) bone fishhook; (h) bone awl; (i) grooved ax; (j) atlatl (spear thrower). (After Webb, 1946.)

offspring) lived there. The knoll at Indian Knoll was a shell midden some 1.5 meters high and 120 by 60 meters in dimension. In addition to the shellfish whose remains made up the midden, there were also the bones of a great number of animal species. Substantial amounts of hickory, walnut, and acorn shells were also found.

One of the more striking features of the site, however, was the large number of burials found there. In various excavations at the site, more than 1100 burials were found. Of these, some 31 percent had surviving grave accompaniments (Figure 9.5). Depending upon how *exotic* is to be defined, between 1 and 4 percent of the graves contain exotic items. Among these items were copper objects and decorated pieces made of conch shell from the Gulf or South Atlantic coasts. It is also interesting to note that these valuable (in the archeological sense of requiring greater investment of time to acquire or transport) goods do not seem to be restricted to one particular sex or age group. It has been argued that the presence of grave goods with young children, for example, may be one indication of status distinctions (Binford, 1971). To the degree that grave goods represent the fulfillment of social obligations toward the dead person, it is very likely that the existence of such obligations to the young may indicate some social distinctions that are ascribed rather than attained by an individual's own achievements. Much caution is needed in interpreting such remains, but it is likely that the egalitarian societies of the earlier Archaic period were becoming more organized.

Domestication of Plants

As already indicated, recent evidence has made it fairly certain that Middle and Late Archaic peoples cultivated some plants (Watson, 1974; Chomko and Crawford, 1978). The native plants associated with this incipient horticulture were sunflower (*Helianthus*), marsh elder (*Iva*), and various amaranths and *Chenopodia*. In addition, gourd and squash were cultivated—perhaps mostly for use as containers, but also as food. The low level of dependence on these cultigens should be recognized, however.

To some extent the cultivation of these plants is another indication of the reduced mobility of Southeastern Archaic peoples and the likelihood of greater population pressure on favored resources. The work in the Mammoth Cave locality (Watson, 1974), for example, revealed indications of larger game; but the conclusion was drawn that these findings were indicative "of a society that spent little energy on stalking, capturing, butchering, cooking, and eating of vertebrate animals" (Duffield in Watson, 1974:133). Note, also, that very small animals were eaten, and rodent bones and snake bones are present in fecal materials from the caves (Stewart et al. in Watson, 1974). Such a pattern of exploitation of wild and semidomesticated small seeds, small animals, and plant products requiring processing before eating (such as acorns) is characteristic of societies that are under stress, with too many mouths to feed.

Although Chomko and Crawford (1978:407) have suggested that plant husbandry in eastern North America was probably stimulated by Mesoamerican practices, there is too little evidence on human–plant associations from the Eastern Archaic to consider this question settled. As already noted, other Mesoamerican cultigens are either absent or so rare as to be virtually invisible archeologically (Yarnell, 1976; Schoenwetter, 1979). Two things are apparent: (1) plant husbandry has considerable antiquity in the Southeast and (2) domesticated plants were nonetheless not central to Archaic economies—even though they may have been significant as part of a whole series of adaptations to re-

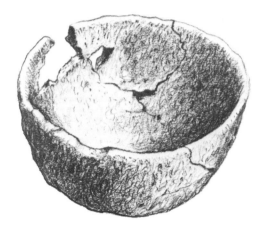

FIGURE 9.6
The earliest pottery of the Southeast is simple in form and has various kinds of fiber inclusions added to the clay.

duced mobility and increasing population. It is also important to remember that *increasing population* and *population pressure* are relative terms. How much population it takes to put pressure on an environment depends on the level of the technology of production and of distribution and consumption. In absolute terms, Archaic population densities were still very low.

It is also striking that none of the native plants that were domesticated by Eastern Archaic societies appears to have been capable of development of the sort that elsewhere triggered the feedback loop between cultivation of food and increasing population. This loop could produce more complex social and economic systems, but feedback amplification of this sort does not appear to have been significant until the late Sedentary in the Southeast.

The Earliest Southeastern Pottery

By 1700 BC, at least, there were well-established and relatively settled societies along the South Atlantic coast that were quite similar to the Indian Knoll and Eva societies inland. Social groups appear to have been small, and sites generally consist of shell middens on rivers or in coastal swamps. In fact, aside from some engraved bone not unlike material from Indian Knoll, there would be nothing remarkable about these sites at all, were it not for the very early manufacture of pottery there. The pottery itself is fairly simple, consisting of round bowls with occasional drag-and-jab decoration in the wet clay. Fiber was added to the clay before the vessel was formed; accordingly, the appearance of such pottery has led to the *fiber-tempered pottery horizon* designation (Figure 9.6). Both in form and in the addition of fiber temper, the South Atlantic early pottery is very like the earliest pottery of northern South America, and it is possible—if not likely—that there is some direct relationship between the two areas, as proposed by James A. Ford (1969). At the same time, there is considerable debate over just how similar phases such as Stalling Island in Georgia and others in northern Florida really are to supposed South American antecedents. Many of the comparisons presented by Ford become less convincing when examined closely either from a structural point of view or in terms of the nature of the complexes from which the comparisons are drawn.

THE SEDENTARY PERIOD

The definition of archeological periods is always arbitrary, but the distinction between the societies of the later Archaic period and the early Sedentary period is an exceptionally good example of the problems of constructing such units. While there are important and major differences between, say, 2000 BC and 200 BC, it is not clear just where the line between these two times should be drawn. Fortunately, the problem is merely terminological, so 700 BC can be used arbitrarily.

By 700 BC, moreover, societies in the Southeast and along the southern border of the Northeast had already changed in some significant, and some not so significant, ways. Perhaps the most widespread of the changes from the Archaic period was the wide acceptance of ceramic technology over most of eastern North America. This new technology had, of course, been developed in the Southeastern Archaic some 1000 years before; but it was only with the coming of the Sedentary period that it came to be accepted over the entire area. It is not likely that this acceptance indicated any great changes in the lifeway of the Southeast, but it may be that the spread of pottery making was a reflection of greater permanence of settlement. In the Southeast, some, but not all, of the pottery by this time had cord-roughened exteriors; it was of the sort called *Woodland* in the Northeast. Even though pottery probably made little difference in lifeways, pottery making is important because it provides archeologists with a diverse, "sensitive," and virtually indestructible set of artifacts. After the beginning of the Sedentary period, virtually all of the archeological "phases" in the Southeast are based more on ceramic similarities and differences than on any other one thing.

Mound Building

Another of the major innovations of the early Sedentary—mound construction—is far more impressive to the nonspecialist than pottery. The construction of earthen mounds in the lower Mississippi valley may actually have started in later Archaic times, but both in the lower valley and on the northern border of the Southeast, in the Ohio valley, quite large mounds were being constructed by the start of the Sedentary period. The two outstanding examples of these developments are the Poverty Point culture of Louisiana and the Adena culture of

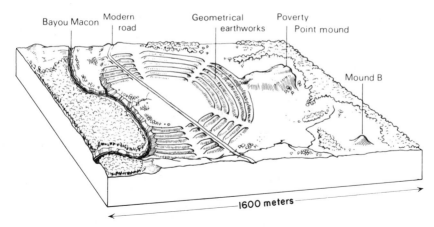

FIGURE 9.7
Poverty Point, Louisiana. The enormous earthworks at Poverty Point are among the earliest large-scale construction in the New World.

the Ohio valley. The dating of the Poverty Point complex is still somewhat unsettled, but it probably started after 1300 BC and persisted well into the Sedentary period. To the north, many Adena sites are outside the Southeast, but the Adena complex as a whole is as much a part of Southeastern prehistory as it is of Northeastern. In the remainder of the Southeast, mound building did not appear quite so early as it did on the periphery, but mounds were common by 300 BC.

In the northern areas, early mound building was often linked to the burial of what have been interpreted as very high-ranked people. Even at the beginning, however, mound constructions such as those at Poverty Point were not primarily burial mounds and, by the end of the Sedentary period in the Southeast, some areas seem to have developed platform and perhaps even substructure mounds that foreshadow the developments of the Late Prehistoric. Some later Sedentary mounds may have been more oriented toward literal and symbolic elevation of the living than toward the honorable disposal of the dead.

The early mound building of the Southeast was often truly monumental. At Moundsville, West Virginia, the Grave Creek Mound built by the Adena people is over 20 meters high. At Poverty Point, the diameter of the whole mound complex is some 1200 meters (Figure 9.7). Mound building on this scale probably means greater sedentism, and it certainly implies greater organization.

The Bases of Social Development

As might be guessed, the most significant changes between the Sedentary and Archaic periods were the alterations of social organization and settlement. The social system did not become more complex overnight, even though the archeological evidence seems to show dramatic and rapid development in areas of the technology that were related to differentiation of social status. Mound building was the most dramatic of these, but the production of "ceremonial" items of all kinds increased in ways that required extensive exchange networks tying all of eastern North America together. In the north, the most developed center for this exchange has come to be called the *Hopewellian Interaction Sphere*. The Southeast was directly involved in this interaction (read "exchange") sphere, and some Southeastern peoples had access to materials such as conch shells and galena that appear to have been highly prized in the value system of the time. In the lower Mississippi valley, there was a direct participant in the Hopewellian "culture" called *Marksville*. In other areas of the Southeast, there were societies such as Copena that participated less completely in the Hopewellian system but that show many resemblances to Marksville and Hopewell.

The causes of these developments are difficult to identify. In the earlier years of modern Southeastern archeology, it was believed that the construction of large mounds was a direct reflection of surplus productive capacity, which was thought to have been a result of the introduction of maize agriculture (for example, J. Ford, 1969:45). Archeologists found it difficult to believe that non-agricultural people could have built such substantial and impressive monuments without some means of growing their foods. Since the obvious center of mound construction in the New World was Mexico, and since maize and the other produce of New World agriculture were also Mexican, it was thought that mound construction and agriculture were both introduced as a package from Mesoamerica. But recent work in the eastern United States has created some problems for this theory of development and diffusion. While Mesoamerican crops are definitely the basis for developments in the Late Prehistoric period, maize simply does not appear to have been an exceptionally important food plant for the Sedentary period peoples, even though some maize was grown. Furthermore, the Mesoamerican food complex of maize, beans, and squash was not introduced all at one time into the Southeast. Domesticated cucurbit appears to have been used well back into the Archaic period, maize begins to show up in small quantities around 300 BC, and beans were not important until the Late Prehistoric period.

Faced with the lack of evidence for intensive growing of Mesoamerican crops, some archeologists have suggested that native crops may have been domesticated in eastern North America. Thus, it was thought that the cultivation of the sunflower (*Helianthus*), goosefoot (*Chenopodium*), sumpweed (*Iva*), and other plants along river bottoms might have formed the economic basis for sedentism and social development in the Sedentary period (Struever, 1964:96–103). Even earlier, however, it had been suggested that the rich environment of the Southeast might have allowed development of fairly complex societies without an agricultural basis, through what was called *primary forest efficiency* (Caldwell, 1958:30). All of these theories about the origins of the Sedentary and its northern relatives, Early and Middle Woodland, share the same emphasis on the idea that the "cause" of complex social organization is surplus economic production. Of the three, Caldwell's theory comes closest to appreciating the degree to which social organization itself can have a major part to play in the economic life of a people. Richard I. Ford has suggested a model for a nonagricultural system requiring complex social organization for the northern Hopewell. Ford's idea is that the complex social status differences in Middle Woodland may have been part of a method of ensuring intra-area exchange that would allow relatively permanent settlement and dense population despite the variability in production of wild foods within an area from year to year (R. I. Ford, 1974:403ff.).

The importance of Ford's suggestion is that it emphasizes the organizational and distributive aspects of Sedentary life, rather than focusing all of the attention on means of production. Taken as a whole, the Southeast was probably capable of supporting much larger populations of humans than it actually did, even at the peak of the Sedentary period. Many of the limitations that are placed on a collecting economy in an area are due to the variability of yield of various resources from one year to another. As already discussed, this variability was probably a major factor in maintaining relatively low populations in Archaic times. However, a species may respond to relatively short-term, favorable circumstances by increasing its numbers beyond the level that can be supported on a continuing, long-term basis. There are several possible responses to such population pressure: reduction of population through famine or other causes, an increase in the economic "production" of the population, or an increase in the efficiency of distribution of food within the population. If human beings take this last course, it usually becomes necessary to create a "bureaucracy" to administer the distribution system. It would be too strong to say that this administrative function was the sole purpose of the high-rank leadership that seems to have developed in Sedentary times. Nevertheless, even if new production capability eventually proves to have been the main impetus for the Early Sedentary florescence, the archeological evidence shows that an administrative mechanism also proved necessary.

Probably no one cause was responsible for all of the developments throughout the whole area; but the most impressive developments seem to have come in areas that had not seen much elaboration in the Late Archaic of about 2000 BC. This may indicate that the causes of the Adena and Poverty Point complexes are to be found in the interplay and feedback of new sources of food and increasing organization of population. The existence of such relatively highly organized societies would have had considerable impact upon their neighbors, who might have found themselves with the choice of being absorbed, driven out of their territories, or organizing themselves along similar lines. Thus, it comes as no surprise to learn that by 300 BC many societies in the Southeast had either become part of the Hopewell Interaction Sphere or had organized similar, if smaller, networks of their own.

The Sedentary period as a whole may be divided into several equally arbitrary subdivisions. The early Sedentary can be taken to refer to the time from

700 BC to 300 BC, corresponding to the later part of Adena and Poverty Point. Middle Sedentary would be from 300 BC to AD 300, corresponding to the Marksville (Louisiana) and Santa Rosa–Swift Creek complexes (Florida). The late Sedentary (AD 300–AD 700) is represented by the Weeden Island complex of Florida and southern Georgia.

The Early Sedentary

The Adena complex is the best-known and most obvious of the early Sedentary complexes, but because it is covered more fully in Chapter Seven, the discussion here will focus on the Poverty Point complex of Louisiana (Broyles and Webb, 1970). As already indicated, the Poverty Point complex started before the arbitrary beginning of the Sedentary period, but it did continue into the early Sedentary. Unfortunately, the dating of the Poverty Point complex still presents some problems to archeologists, and the actual time of construction of the impressive earthworks at the Poverty Point site has not been firmly determined. Radiocarbon dates from Poverty Point "period" sites have ranged from 1700 to 870 BC, with an average of radiocarbon dates and thermoluminescence dates being close to 1200 BC. However, these dates do not provide us with the critical information of when Poverty Point people began to build massive mounds and earthworks.

The Poverty Point site itself consists of a large, semicircular earthwork of concentric ridges, one large mound, and some other smaller features (Figure 9.7). James Ford and Clarence Webb, who excavated the site, felt that the ridged mounds had accumulated through occupation by a planned and organized village, but this does not appear to have been the case. A semicircular pattern of settlement is characteristic of Poverty Point sites, but only at the Poverty Point site itself did mound construction actually achieve such scale that it seems likely that something more than an "Archaic" form of social organization was present. Other Poverty Point sites are not so impressive.

Sites of the Poverty Point and closely related Jaketown phases occur along tributaries of the Mississippi River and in other locations where wetland resources are available. Other similar complexes are found in the same kinds of environments throughout the lower Mississippi valley. What are known as Poverty Point objects—lumps of baked clay in various shapes—are found over this area at the same time as the Poverty Point complex, but this should not be taken as an indication of some vast network of social relationships (Figure 9.8). The wide valley floor of the lower Mississippi has very little rock; and people who wished to use the technique of "stone boiling" had to make their own "stones" out of clay in order to cook their food. Even the more tightly defined microlithic stone-tool industries of the Poverty Point "culture" are of little help in pinning down the limits of Poverty Point social and political units.

The large mound at Poverty Point is nearly 23 meters high and has a diameter of approximately 200 meters. As already indicated, this is many times larger

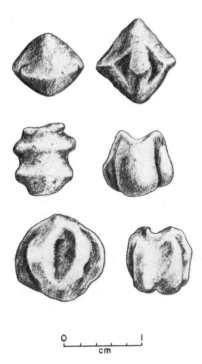

FIGURE 9.8
So-called Poverty Point objects are widely found in the lower Mississippi valley. These baked
clay lumps are known in many shapes and were probably used as substitutes for "boiling stones."
Although they are very common in the Poverty Point complex, they are also found elsewhere
in the area.

than other Poverty Point mounds and, in fact, is at least twice the size of the
more or less contemporary Olmec mound at La Venta in Mexico, even though
the La Venta mound is somewhat taller. The scale of this construction and the
far-reaching exchange relations of the Poverty Point sites suggest that this
Southeastern society had developed social institutions that were qualitatively
different from those of earlier times. In fact, the Poverty Point society may have
been the first "chiefdom" of the eastern United States and was perhaps as early
as such developments anywhere in the New World. The importance of Poverty
Point as an early mound center, however, should not obscure the relative lack of
success of the system in this area. After Poverty Point times, nearly a thousand
years were to pass before such a level was once again reached. The reasons for
this decline are not known, but any theory of the formation of such units will
have to account for this failure.

Not much is known of the life of the ordinary Poverty Point person. Methods
of house construction in Poverty Point sites are poorly understood; house size
appears to have been small. The presence of stone hoes that show distinctive

polish patterns has led to the suggestion that Poverty Point peoples were agricultural, but it can be suggested that people who are building large earth mounds will need digging tools whether they are agricultural or not. Domesticated squash is known to be present in Poverty Point (R. Ford, 1974:401), but the present evidence and the evidence from later complexes in the same area suggest that domesticated plants did not play an important role in the diet of the early Sedentary peoples. As discussed above, it is likely that these and other early Sedentary peoples were highly efficient hunters and gatherers whose complexity of social organization was a means of improving distribution of goods.

Poverty Point sites do have a little pottery that is similar to the fiber-tempered pottery of the South Atlantic coast, but steatite bowls are equally common. Neither form of vessel seems to have been important. Crude pottery figurines also occur. James Ford has described some of these traits of the Poverty Point complex as being indicative of Mesoamerican or South American influence on the early Southeast. Actually, even if it were to be accepted that the Poverty Point and Mesoamerican complexes were connected, the direction of influence would be uncertain. The presence of domesticated squash and the later introduction of maize do represent influence from Mesoamerica, but this is no indication of the direction of flow for other kinds of relationships. In any case, the entire question of "influence" and "direction" is largely irrelevant to any attempt to understand the development of societies. The mere introduction of a technology or an "idea" does not explain or cause developments. The local society, whether innovating or accepting, still can develop only so far as the local social and environmental conditions permit. People do not form chiefdoms because someone has told them how wonderful chiefdoms are but because such organizations are necessary to cope with local problems. In any case, the similarities that are cited by James Ford—circular settlements, crude figurines, fiber-tempered pottery, and so on—are not very specific; to see similarity in these traits depends upon the examiner's conviction that external contacts are necessary to account for the development of societies. Regardless of these possible external connections, it is the lack of good information about the local reasons for chiefdom or other complex social organization that is the greatest weakness of Poverty Point studies. It simply is not known what features of early Sedentary life led to the organization of the relatively centralized society implied by the mounds at Poverty Point.

The times immediately after Poverty Point were characterized by complexes that were much less organized. The lifeways of the Tchula, Tchefuncte, Refuge, and other "Early Woodland" phases in the Southeast seem little different from those of Archaic times and are certainly not comparable to Poverty Point or Adena societies. A major marker for this time period is the spread of surface-textured (usually cord-marked) pottery. In the northern part of the Southeast, the Adena complex continued and is connected with the later Hopewellian developments of the middle Sedentary. There are some ceramic continuities in the coastal ceramic complexes, such as Bayou La Batre, and later techniques in other areas of the Southeast. In general, however, the main development in the Southeast during the period between Poverty Point and Marksville was the return to less centralized, presumably more egalitarian social structures.

The Middle Sedentary

The middle Sedentary period developments in the Southeast proper began once again to show signs of greater organization, largely as an echo of the Hopewellian Interaction Sphere of the Northeast (Figure 9.9). The mechanisms explaining these developments in the Southeast are not entirely clear, but it seems certain that exchanges of raw materials and finished goods played an important part in stimulating ranked societies in the area. The best example of a direct relationship between the Southeast and the Northeastern Hopewellian is the Marksville culture of the lower Mississippi valley. For this middle Sedentary period, the similarities of Marksville pottery, mound construction, and other features of those of the Hopewell are very strong (Figure 9.10). In fact, the similarities are so strong that it is even possible that actual movement of populations was partly responsible for the development of Marksville. The best present evidence suggests that Marksville is somewhat later than Illinois Hopewell, so the temporal relationships are consistent with such an idea. At the same time, the stylistic connections of Marksville art and Hopewell art may rather suggest that local complexes in the Mississippi valley adopted certain "Hopewell" customs. It is interesting to note that it is only in the lower part of the Mississippi valley that "Hopewellian markers" are commonly found in association with village debris (Phillips, 1970:901), while in most Hopewellian complexes such goods are largely restricted to mortuary contexts. This pattern may indicate different forms of social organization in the two regions.

Settlement in the lower Mississippi valley during the middle Sedentary showed much the same pattern as in earlier times, an increase in the density of settlement being the major change. But this is largely a reflection of the limited range of choices for settlement sites in this area if one wished to have dry feet. Elsewhere in the Southeast, settlement of the middle Sedentary showed an increasing emphasis on riverine locations, a trend that began in the later Archaic and continued up to the European invasion. Examples of middle Sedentary groups that were less directly linked into the Hopewellian Interaction Sphere include Copena in Alabama, so called because of the frequency with which copper and galena are found in the complex, and the Santa Rosa and Swift Creek complexes of northern Florida and southern Georgia. Burial mounds occur in these areas, and the ceramics show some similarities to Illinois and Ohio Hopewell; but the scale of the societies seems to have been smaller. Thus, while it might be suggested that the northern Hopewell "leaders"—or "Big Men"—achieved their positions through their social roles in local distributive networks, it seems likely that the burial status of individuals in many parts of the Southeast was more

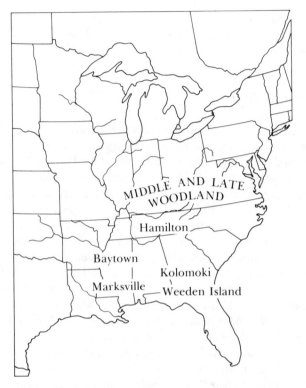

FIGURE 9.9
Middle and late Sedentary complexes.

directly a result of the access of those individuals to externally oriented networks of exchange.

Although maize is known to have been present in Hopewellian times in the Southeast and Northeast, the evidence still suggests that cultivated plants in general and maize in particular were a relatively small part of the diet. Outside of the Marksville complexes, there is little indication that redistribution of food-stuffs may have been important for survival, if indeed such was the case in Marksville itself. Population in the Southeast was steadily increasing, but local productive capacities seem to have kept ahead of economic needs through much of this time. The distribution of exotic materials throughout the Southeast in middle Sedentary times appears to find closer analogies with the nature of status and distribution of goods in Melanesia than with the more highly centralized and ranked societies of Polynesia. That is to say, the possession of exotic goods and of status itself may have been more often *achieved* by Southeastern "lead-ers" than inherited by them through membership in chiefly or royal lineages. This, of course, must remain a moot point until more effort is expended in the Southeast on archeological testing of such hypotheses.

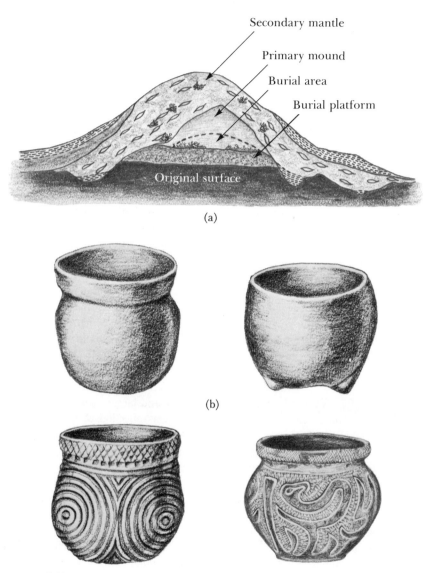

FIGURE 9.10
Marksville complex. This Hopewell-related complex in the lower Mississippi valley has many similarities to the Hopewell of Illinois and of Ohio. (a) A Marksville burial mound; (b) Marksville pottery. (After James A. Ford and G. R. Willey, 1940, *Crooks Site: A Marksville Period Burial Mound in La Salle Parish, Louisiana*. Anthropology Study no. 3, Louisiana Geological Survey.)

Comparison of the Southeast and Northeast

So far, the Southeast has been seen as rather less developed in terms of social organization than the southern Northeast. Ironically, this may be a reflection of the greater carrying capacity of the Southeastern environment. It may simply be that the Southeastern swamps, river valleys, and woodlands were so rich in resources that a relatively high density of population was possible without the need for the centralized bureaucracies discussed earlier. When the cubic volumes of burial mounds in the Southeast are examined, it will be seen that the amount of labor involved in such constructions is usually not greater than that which might be locally available as a result of local reciprocal obligations to important persons or Big Men (Service, 1975:72–73). Increasing population pressure, requiring more efficient production and distribution systems as well as creating an increased need for maintenance of order, may sometimes have caused such societies to become "chiefdoms." Such a system is characterized by an increasing emphasis on inheritance of authority, economic redistribution, intensification of production, and centralization of power (Service, 1975).

The decline of Hopewell in the Northeast has been attributed to many causes, ranging from "peasant revolt" (very unlikely) to climatic shifts that lowered the carrying capacity of the environment below that point for which efficiency of distribution could compensate (possible). One of the problems in the climatic interpretation, however, is that the population of eastern North America may have actually increased following the decline of Hopewell. Population estimates for such large areas are bound to be uncertain at best, but northern Late Woodland phases often seem to be represented by more and larger sites than the earlier phases in the areas. To some extent this is a reflection of the increased mobility of late Sedentary peoples, but it may also be true that this situation was caused by some new breakthrough in productive capacity that caused the redistributive mechanisms of Hopewellian times to become redundant. It would be logically pleasing if it could be shown that this development toward greater local autonomy and more egalitarian organization was related to an increasing importance of cultivated plants and, thus, to greater *local* productive capacity. This does not seem to have been the case, however. R. I. Ford (1974:402–403) has suggested that these changes may be due in some part to the introduction of the bow and arrow, and improvements in ceramic technology have been cited (Braun, 1980). As attractive as these interpretations are, they unfortunately do not explain why mound building and other features of the Hopewellian time period survived in the Southeast long after the "decline" of Hopewell in the Northeast. While the cultures of the northern part of the Southeast during late Sedentary times were very similar to that of the Northeastern Late Woodland, the southern Southeast in late Sedentary times was characterized by a continuation of extensive mound building and by the development of platform and even substructure mounds. Even though the distribution of exotic goods did not cease in the north, it was much curtailed; the southern area appears to have experienced increased exchange of such goods during this period.

The Late Sedentary

The direct continuity between the late Sedentary and the Late Prehistoric periods is very clear in a late Marksville phase known as Issaquena (Greengo, 1964; Phillips, 1970). Although it is true that ceramic discontinuities exist, it is apparent that the Issaquena construction of platform mounds (Phillips, 1970:544–545) indicates the persistence of more centralized organization. By the earlier part of the Late Prehistoric period, the Baytown period phases of the southern Mississippi valley already showed many of the characteristics of the later Mississippian complexes of the northern Southeast. This is not to say that the Mississippian cultures developed only from Baytown, but merely to observe that the many continuities between middle Sedentary and Late Prehistoric make the Mississippian "renaissance" much less spectacular when viewed from the south than when viewed from a northern perspective. Moreover, the lower Mississippi valley is not the only place where there was no decline following the middle Sedentary. In Florida and in southern Georgia, the Weeden Island complex is, if anything, more impressive than the Marksville–Baytown developments. Most Weeden Island sites are not enormously complex, but the Kolomoki site in southern Georgia is rather clear proof that the post-Hopewellian decline of the north was not a pan-Eastern phenomenon.

KOLOMOKI □ The Kolomoki site is located on a small tributary of the Chattahoochee River in an area with good water sources and a diverse local environment (Figure 9.11). The site covers some 1.2 million square meters and has numerous small "burial" mounds and a large mound nearly 17 meters in height that is square with a relatively flat top. In short, this mound is very much like the later substructure mounds of the Late Prehistoric in general and the Mississippian culture in particular. The mounds at Kolomoki and at other Weeden Island sites, however, are possibly platform mounds rather than clearly substructure mounds. At Kolomoki it was difficult to find any trace of structures of any kind, although areas of refuse about 9 meters in diameter and scattered postholes were found (Sears, 1956:9). In any case, many of the mounds did have burial functions like those of the earlier Sedentary. The ceramics that were found associated with the burials are elaborate vessels of the sort which are clearly "nonfunctional" in terms of activities such as cooking or eating (Figure 9.12).

The scale and overall organization of the Kolomoki site suggest that it was based on some effective economic system, but, unfortunately, very little information as to its nature is available. Because Sears mistakenly thought that the

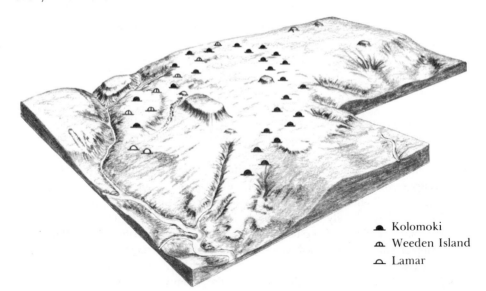

▲ Kolomoki
♤ Weeden Island
◠ Lamar

FIGURE 9.11
Kolomoki site, Georgia. A large Weeden Island site with evidence of complex site planning.
(After Sears, 1953.)

Kolomoki materials were from the same time as the Mississippian developments farther north, it was suggested that an agricultural basis for the society was likely (1956:95). However, no charred vegetal materials were recovered by the techniques used at the time of the excavation, so resolution of this question must await further work. As has already been seen, squash and maize had been introduced into the Southeast much earlier, but present evidence still does not suggest heavy dependence on these or other cultigens.

If the size of midden areas is related to the size of residential units, it would be likely that a residential group here consisted of no more than 15 to 20 persons. Sears suggests that the construction of one mound stage of Mound D was completed in one season and that this implies a work group of about 1000 persons (1956:93). Actually, the volume of the mound in question is only about 700 cubic meters; even given a very conservative figure of 0.5 cubic meters per person per day, the volume of the mound could be accounted for by some 350 people working for four days. Since the mound has at least four building stages, it may be that the labor force was even less. The mounds are large, but that may imply more about the organization of the workers than about the extraordinary size of the labor force. In this case, as in so many others, Southeastern archeologists have come to realize that population size is not the only critical variable in mound-building activity. The size of the mounds at Kolomoki does not necessarily imply a resident or subject population exceeding that known for the area in the time of early European intrusion. On the basis of estimates of village area, however, a population of 1000 people at Kolomoki is not unreasonable. Indica-

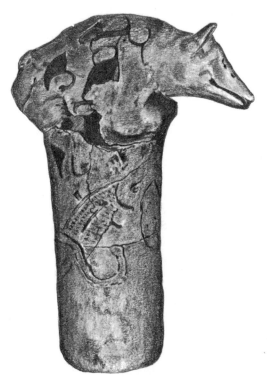

FIGURE 9.12
An elaborate mortuary vessel from Kolomoki. (After Sears, 1953.)

tion of some complexity of social organization is provided not only the the size of the population, the size of the mounds, and the layout of the site, but also by the probable practice of retainer sacrifice at the death of important persons and by the impressive amount of energy expended on grave goods. While none of these traits by itself is necessarily indicative of a society organized on a level above that of a "tribe," the total picture does suggest that Kolomoki was a "chiefdom" at a time when most societies in the eastern woodlands of North America were socially and politically much less organized (Milanich, 1980).

The causes of the Kolomoki florescence at a time when most eastern and even Weeden Island peoples possessed a less elaborate social organization are not clear. The "fall" of the Hopewell Interaction Sphere of the middle Sedentary did not mean a cessation of all exchange of exotic goods, but this exchange was reduced enough in volume to make it unlikely that Kolomoki is to be explained in terms of control of trade. It may even be that the relative complexity of societies on and near the Gulf coast and in the lower Mississippi valley during this period is partly a reflection of greater need for centralized authority in order to maintain the population there. Resolution of this problem is impossible with the present information about the nature of the economic bases for these societies.

CULTURAL CONTINUITY ☐ In general, the Sedentary period is of enormous interest. The elaborate earthworks and beautifully executed art objects of the Sedentary peoples of the Southeast, like those of the Northeast, are evidence of increasing political and social complexity. Unlike developments in the Northeast, however, in the Southeast the development of centralized and status-oriented societies does not falter in the late Sedentary period. The factors that led to the technological developments of the Sedentary have not been learned from the archeological record. It can be suggested that population pressure played an important part in encouraging these developments, but the reasons for supposing that sedentism led to increased population in one area and not in another have not been fully explored, much less tested.

The development of platform mounds, and probably of substructure mounds as well, in the late Southeastern Sedentary is only one of a number of indications that link the Southeastern Sedentary period very closely to the developments of the Late Prehistoric period. It would be too strong a statement to say that the late Sedentary complexes like Weeden Island and Issaquena somehow "caused" the development of Late Prehistoric cultures like the Mississippian. Nonetheless, it is likely that many of the iconographic and technical continuities that exist between middle Sedentary complexes like Marksville and Late Prehistoric Mississippian are at least partly due to the continuity of complex social organization in the Southeast. Even in ceramics, the similarities that led to the mistaken idea that Kolomoki was on the Mississippian time level are an indication of the extent to which Weeden Island and similar complexes are precursors of later developments. The possible origin of the substructure (so-called *temple*) mound in Weeden Island and Issaquena is also of considerable importance. It is possible that the substructure mound is an introduction from Mesoamerica, but in the Mississippi valley, in southern Georgia, and in northern Florida there is what appears to be a sequential development from the conical burial mound to the platform mound to the substructure mound. Whether this is a purely local development or whether it was introduced from outside, the substructure mound (like the earlier mounds) is an artifact reflecting increased social complexity and organization. As such, the introduction, development, and acceptance of mound construction in a given culture has to be related to changes in the organization of that culture, regardless of the origin of the trait itself.

PERIOD OF "DECLINE"? ☐ In other areas of the Southeast, the later Sedentary period was much less impressive in terms of material remains and, not surprisingly, has often received less archeological attention. In the Tennessee and Cumberland drainages, the archeological cultures of the time were generally similar to the Late Woodland of the Northeast. Here and there in the Southeast there were some survivals of burial-mound construction, as in the Hamilton phase of eastern Tennessee. Some status goods such as shell from the coast continued to be exchanged, but as these features were even found in the Late

Archaic, it is not surprising that they are found in Late Woodland complexes.

The usual explanation of the Late Woodland has been that it was a period of decline following the high achievements of the Hopewellian. It should be understood that this is more an assumption than a view that is supported by empirical evidence. While it is true that monumental construction and elaborate works of art are uncommon in the Late Woodland, it is possible that population may actually have increased in many areas. In addition, the decline in long-distance exchange and in centralized administration of exchange does not necessarily imply that local exchange networks also declined. It has been argued (Braun, 1980) that the uniformity of Late Woodland ceramics may suggest an actual increase in intralocal integration. On the northern fringes of the Southeast, at least some Late Woodland complexes are known from large numbers of sites in a great variety of local environments. The number of Late Woodland sites is no doubt partly due to a seasonal pattern of population movement, but to some extent it does appear that larger populations may have been present in Late Woodland times than in Hopewellian times. The reasons for this are difficult to sort out. It would be tempting to suggest that the increase in population resulted from new production capabilities. As already indicated, R. I. Ford has suggested that the bow and arrow may have played a part in severing the exchange relations of the East (1974:402–403). Perhaps even more important than the "severing" of the routes would have been the effect of improved hunting tools, which could have made the local community more independent of both those routes and the local redistributive network. It would also be tempting to suggest that agriculture became more important after the fall of Hopewell, but the best present evidence seems to show even less evidence of agriculture in early Late Woodland than in Hopewell (R. I. Ford, 1974; Kuttruff, n.d.).

Whatever the causes, the central part of the North American East, including both areas in the Northeast and in the Southeast, was less organized socially than in the preceding part of the Sedentary. By the traditional criteria this means that the people were less "advanced," but it may be that the real advancement of the period was in finding ways to survive well on a local level without surrendering local authority to centralized chiefs.

THE LATE PREHISTORIC PERIOD

The transition from Sedentary to Late Prehistoric cultures in the Southeast was formerly seen as a dramatic series of intrusions, influences, and migrations. Following an implicit age–area hypothesis, this view emphasized the importance of only a few "centers" of diffusion. As more is learned about the eighth century in the Southeast and on its margins, however, it now appears that most regions show much the same course of development—and, even more importantly, show much the same timing as well.

Agriculture

An increasing dependence upon agriculture for livelihood was the most significant change of the Late Prehistoric period. While earlier peoples had domesticated plants, some imported from Mesoamerica and others native, present information suggests that basic food getting did not depend primarily on domesticated plants until the beginning of the eighth or ninth century of the modern era. It may be that this change did begin earlier in complexes like Weeden Island, but most of the Late Woodland complexes to the north seem still to have depended primarily on wild foods. Granted that the evidence on this problem is incomplete, the change to an agricultural economic base seems to have taken place very rapidly, as these things go. The causes of the change are also not clear. New varieties of maize do seem to have been introduced about AD 900, and the bean (*Phaseolus vulgaris*) appeared in the Southeast by AD 1200. Whatever caused Southeastern peoples to become more agricultural, the process, once started, was largely irreversible. The more important agriculture became, the more necessary it would have been to have centralized, redistributive authorities. The more centralized the economic controls and population were, the more agriculture was necessary for survival (see R. I. Ford, 1974:406–407).

At the same time, it must be remembered that the Southeastern peoples never became totally dependent on agriculture in the strictest sense. The best evidence shows that some wild foods, especially nuts of various kinds, remained important sources of protein and fats. Techniques such as flotation have dramatically increased our knowledge of prehistoric diet, and these data tend to correct earlier viewpoints that agriculture was all-important. Indeed, if the historical record for the Southeast is examined, it will be seen that the earliest European accounts of the interior Southeast, in 1539 and 1540, indicate that nuts were important then (account of the Gentleman of Elvas, Buckingham Smith translation, 1866:43, 47, 131, and throughout). A diet of maize, beans, squash, and nuts, especially if supplemented with greens, would be well balanced even without game.

If hunting became less important for survival, warfare seems to have become more important. Late Prehistoric sites throughout the Southeast were often well fortified. It is tempting to see the rise of fortified centers, and to some degree even the growth of centralized and stratified societies, as a result of competition for scarce agricultural land in the face of growing population. Such situations have been seen by some as directly responsible for the origins of the political units known as states (Carneiro, 1970; Service, 1975:43–44). It is also important to remember that the Southeast did not present the same opportunities for agriculture to hoe-using cultivators that it did to European farmers with draught animals and plows. American Indian agriculture in the area was largely restricted to the fertile river valleys.

These restrictions on aboriginal agriculture, together with the use of rivers as transportation avenues, meant that Southeastern settlement patterns became even more river-oriented in the Late Prehistoric than previously. Not only did the river valley environments offer rich wild resources in plants and animals, they also offered considerable areas of rich soils that were continually renewed by alluviation.

Economy

It is likely that a major function of the high-rank individuals of Late Prehistoric societies was to control the operation of the economy. Most archeological attempts (for example, Sears, 1968) to deal with the sociology of the Late Prehistoric have assumed that the form of economic structure was that known as redistribution (Sahlins, 1972:188), but very little has been done to test this idea. Historical records allow a strong presumption of the existence of redistributive systems in the sixteenth century. However, these records also suggest the unadvisability of interpreting redistributive systems solely in terms of central warehousing and distribution of foodstuffs. Even such relatively simple economic systems have to be assessed in terms of services and goods of many sorts.

An increase in the widespread exchange of goods is another important feature of Late Prehistoric life; the quantity of imperishable goods exchanged may even have exceeded that of the middle Sedentary. It is likely that many perishable goods that have not been recovered by archeologists were also exchanged, but the importance of the goods that have been found was undoubtedly very great. These goods were almost certainly not money in anything like our sense of the term, but the desire for such items was probably both a stimulus for and a result of exchange of other goods more necessary for survival.

Political Organization

There are at least two divergent views of the level of political organization in the Southeast in Late Prehistoric times. One view has been that the peoples of the Southeast were organized on the political level known as the state (Sears, 1968), while others have seen the dominant political form in the area as being like the chiefdoms of the historic Southeast. It must not be forgotten that even the earliest records from the Southeast describe societies that had already felt the impact of European influences, including diseases; even so, most present definitions of *state* would not apply to Southeastern Late Prehistoric societies, with one possible exception—Cahokia.

One of the more important questions in Southeastern archeology is why states did not develop generally in the Southeast. A number of the postulated preconditions for state formation were present—such as environmental limitations on agricultural land ("circumscription"), limited routes of exchange, and chiefdoms with many statelike features of political and social organization. Why, then, did few or none of these societies develop into "states" or "archaic civilizations"? If Cahokia did make this transition, why did it not survive? And why did it not trigger similar developments on its frontiers? It is notable that other temperate areas in the northern hemisphere were similarly late in developing states; perhaps, therefore, some climatological factors were involved. More likely, however, population pressure throughout the area was simply not great enough to force the development. Yet why were these population densities relatively low? Warfare has been suggested as a cause of low populations in the Southeast, but current theories consider the presence of warfare part of the process of state formation. In any case, it is doubtful that warfare of the sort practiced in the aboriginal Southeast had a severe and continuing impact on population growth. The simplest explanation may be that there simply was not enough time between the development of heavy dependence on horticulture and the European intrusion for sufficient population growth to occur, given the available levels of production. Cases like the Southeast do show that there are poorly understood factors involved in the development of states and other highly organized systems. Any comprehensive theory of political and social development must deal more fully with such factors.

Mississippian: Terminological Debate

The complex called Mississippian dominated the Late Prehistoric period in the Southeast. Even so, many areas in the Southeast did not see the development of Mississippian proper. Moreover, some of the largest Mississippian sites are outside of the Southeast as it is usually defined. These sites in Illinois and Indiana, for example, are in riverine extensions of the Southeastern environments, as shown by their location just inside the northern limits of the area where cypress trees grow. Mississippian, in the narrowest sense, is a complex that is characteristic of the northern Gulf Coastal Plain. Its origins are difficult to trace because of terminological confusion. For example, the various Baytown phases of the northern lower Mississippi valley were already building large substructure mounds, at sites like the Toltec site in Arkansas, at the very beginning of the Late Prehistoric period. At Kincaid, in the lower Ohio valley, reconsideration of the evidence from the University of Chicago excavations in the 1930s and 1940s (Cole et al., 1951:83–84; MacNeish, n.d.) suggests that some of the earliest mound construction there was initiated by people who were, for all practical purposes, a locally developed variant of "Baytown." The fact is that Baytown has been considered monotonous and has not received proper attention from archeologists. On the northern margin of the Southeast, local "Late Woodland" societies similarly set the scene for the development of such Mississippian societies as Cahokia.

The problem of defining *Mississippian,* unfortunately, is much more complex than deciding that it is predominantly a Southeastern or Gulf Coastal Plain phenomenon. Some archeologists tend to see all the Late Prehistoric societies of the Southeast as having been Mississippian to one degree or another. These scholars point to the widespread construction of substructure mounds and certain other technical features as indications of unity within the area. Others have tended to define the Mississippian complex, very narrowly, as a specific ceramic tradition characterized by particular vessel forms, such as the bottle and hooded effigy vessel. The first view stresses area unity; the second emphasizes local diversity. To find a way out of these differences of interpretation, such redefinitions and renamings as *the Mid-South Tradition* have been suggested. I am not sure what practical use such terms have, but anything would be beneficial that could move archeologists away from fruitless discussion over the classifications of cultures in the Southeast. For example, most archeologists seem to agree that the Coles Creek culture of the lower Mississippi valley had a complex social organization, and they would probably agree on what is generally known about Coles Creek. It seems fruitless, then, to expend much energy debating whether the complex should be called *Coles Creek Mississippian* or not. It is hard to see what important theoretical and practical issues are served by such discussion.

The term *Mississippian* will be used here to describe those Late Prehistoric societies along the major river valleys in the area from Natchez to St. Louis and from Memphis to Knoxville that built substructure mounds and made pottery with crushed shell added to the clay (Figure 9.13). Outside of the area of the Tennessee, Cumberland, lower Ohio, and Mississippi rivers, these criteria are much less useful, even though many complexes there have been described as being Mississippian-influenced. Recent work has made it clear that the development of these "peripheral" societies was largely coeval with Mississippian. It seems more accurate, therefore, to look upon these developments—Lamar, Fort Ancient, and others—as being caused by the same processes and events as Mississippian itself. In each case, the local conditions and potentials seem to have been more important than some unspecified "influence."

Even within Mississippian there does not seem to be much internal unity. The Mississippian of the Dallas phase in eastern Tennessee, for example, is probably as different in most nonceramic traits from the Moorehead phase of the Cahokia area as either of these are from Coles Creek or Plaquemine in the lower Mississippi valley. It should be clear by now that ceramic similarities and differences may not be the most significant measure of cultural differences and relationships, despite the undoubted usefulness of such traits to the archeologist as horizon markers. In fact, it is time for Southeastern archeologists to concern themselves more directly with testing hypotheses about the kinds of social relationships between one society and another in the area and less with creating area-wide classifications of dubious explanatory value. The term *Mississippian* originated as a name for a ceramic tradition, and it may be time to return it to that status (Holmes, 1903).

FIGURE 9.13
Late Prehistoric complexes as discussed in this section. Note that the concept of single origin and diffusion is not employed.

Mississippian Lifeways

As in the case of other Late Prehistoric complexes, Mississippian settlement generally occurred in the river valleys. Although the focus of settlement was primarily on the major stream valleys, such as the Mississippi and the Tennessee rivers, there was also considerable short-term use of upland stream valley locations. Earlier ideas that the majority of these might prove to be hunting camps or other kinds of specialized sites have been belied by increasing evidence that the upland sites are most often small, short-term farms. The lack of soil renewal by alluviation may have been a factor in the apparent shortness of occupation of many of these sites, and it is even possible that there may have been a kind of "shifting agriculture" pattern in these Mississippian societies that was quite different from the settled life patterns of the better-known Mississippian complexes of the main stream valleys. While upland Mississippians no doubt made good use of their proximity to richer game and other resources, the nature of their relationships to the mound centers is not yet clear. There certainly were some sites that were highly "specialized" near such resources as chert and salt. Even at these, however, it is not clear whether the residents at these sites were *specialists* in the strict sense of the term (Muller and Avery, 1982). Nonetheless, it is relatively certain that individuals and sites in Mississippian society were ranked within a social hierarchy that had pervasive influence on production and distribution of goods. Large, centralized sites with many substructure mounds appear to have functioned as administrative centers, where bureaucrats and priests (more than likely the same persons) coordinated the collection and redistribution of food and materials and supervised the ceremonial and ritual celebrations of the social system (Figures 9.14 and 9.15). In smaller centers of population, a similar but lower-ranked group of administrators probably conducted the affairs of local areas. Still smaller settlements were scattered around local centers, and these in turn were surrounded by farmsteads where the basic unit of population was very likely a small family group of some sort.

As might be expected, the vast majority of archeological work on Mississippian has been concentrated on the large and spectacular mound centers. In the last few years, however, increasing attention has been paid to the smaller sites, and a much more complete picture of Mississippian life has been emerging. Much of the discussion that follows is based on over ten years of work in the Kincaid locality (Muller, 1978) and on work elsewhere (Smith, 1978). It seems that most Mississippian people were farmers, and that a substantial proportion of the population at even the larger sites was directly engaged in agriculture. Some specialization of labor did apparently occur, however, although it remains an open question whether there were many specialists other than the administrators themselves. Some indication of local specialization may be found, even though the individuals in each case were probably not full-time specialists. In Union County, Illinois, for example, there were extensive chert quarries that were a major source for cherts used in making stone hoes. In other locations in southern Illinois, salt springs appear to have been a focus for the production of salt (Brown, 1980; Muller and Avery, 1982). The existence of specialization on this level, combined with the evidence of the large central sites, very strongly supports the idea of some form of centralized distribution system. Although a suggestion has been made that this distribution was by actual market mechanisms (Porter, 1969:159) in the case of the largest center at Cahokia, there have been criticisms of this view (R. I. Ford, 1974:406). It is not likely that any Mississippian economies were organized in this fashion. In most cases, the economic system of the Mississippian complexes appears to have been redistributive. This means that goods from the areas of production were controlled and distributed by central authorities. The historical literature for the Southeast gives good examples of this kind of economic system (for example, Gentleman of Elvas, 1866:52, 55, 58, 69), but little has been done to prove clearly the existence of such systems in prehistoric times.

Mississippian peoples in the Southeast depended upon agriculture combined with products of gathering and hunting, a lifeway like that already described for Southeastern peoples in general in this time period. The largest centers of settle-

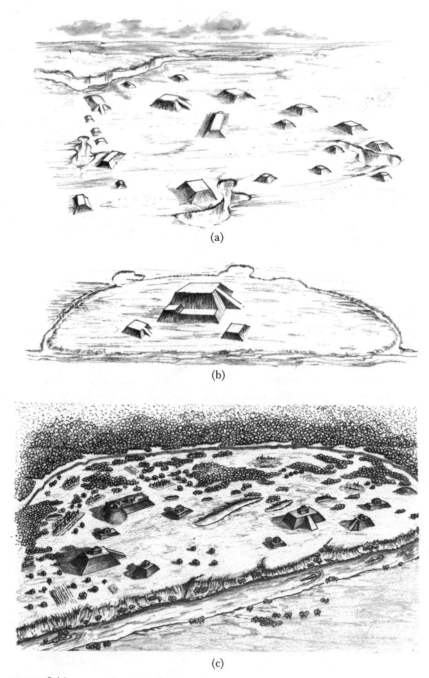

FIGURE 9.14
Various large Late Prehistoric sites. (a) Moundville, Alabama; (b) Etowah, Georgia; (c) Kincaid, Illinois, speculative reconstruction. (Part c after Muller, Illinois Archaeological Survey, Bulletin 1, 1959.)

FIGURE 9.15
Late Prehistoric ceramics. These are examples of Mississippian shell-tempered pottery.

ment of Mississippian peoples are found in areas where there are broad, fertile river bottoms suitable for agriculture as well as highly diverse wild resources. In addition, these large centers often are in locations that would have afforded easy control over the routes of exchange of goods. At the same time, it is likely that most Mississippian people lived outside the important political–religious centers, with their "palaces" and "temples." The typical Mississippian site, as opposed to those that are most spectacular, was probably a small group of only a few structures and consisted of several households directly engaged in agriculture and in the gathering of wild resources.

The houses themselves were constructed of vertical poles set in trenches and commonly covered over with sticks and mud plaster. The roof was thatched. In some areas, the walls were more often mats or other covering than plastered, but the basic house was similar throughout the Southeast. The form was generally square, and there was often a hearth in the center of the floor of the structure. This design was used not only for the houses of the farmers but, in larger sizes, was also used for mortuary temples for the bodies of the local aristocracy and for the palaces of the living chieftains. Occasionally, some structures with different shapes were built for special purposes, but the dominant architectural form in the Late Prehistoric Mississippian was the square, vertical-post structure.

To some extent, larger Mississippian sites appear to have been conglomerations of settlement units not unlike those found at the small farmsteads and hamlets. Large Mississippian sites were not exactly "empty ceremonial centers," but neither were they usually completely packed, with houses tightly pushed up against one another. The large sites do often have fortifications that are very extensive and militarily well planned. At the same time, however, many smaller sites show no traces of defensive works. Many Mississippian burials do show signs of injury, but it is not clear how much of this damage can be laid to warfare.

The clustering of small numbers of houses together may suggest that the basic residential unit was some form of extended family, perhaps a lineage segment. It seems likely, then, that basic activities of food getting operated on a level that was not unlike that of Late Woodland late Sedentary peoples, even though agriculture represented a change in strategy from earlier food gathering and collecting. What made Mississippian and similar cultures different from their predecessors was that these local producers became only the lowest level in a highly stratified society. Although Mississippian times have sometimes been called the *Temple Mound* period, it is actually likely that the majority of mounds were platforms for the houses, even palaces, of the community leaders. The highly organized and planned character of Mississippian centers, built in some cases over the course of several centuries of work, very strongly supports the hypothesis that the leadership of these societies was marked by continuity. This hypothesis, coupled with the strong likelihood that many of the nonresidential platform structures were mortuary temples honoring the ancestors of the leadership, makes the conclusion that Mississippian leaders were hereditary chieftains of "royal" kinship groups almost inescapable. Much more archeological work needs to be done to verify this conclusion; but at least the direction such investigations should take is relatively clear, as is not the case with many other sociological problems faced by archeologists.

The distinction between politics and religion may not be useful in Mississippian times. The great central sites consist of substructure mounds arranged around open spaces that were probably used as meeting places and locations for major ceremonies. These ceremonies probably played both political and religious roles in our terms. One of the markers of chiefdoms, in fact, is that the separation between politics and religion is often indistinct.

The content of Mississippian religions is difficult to define, although some attempts at understanding by analogy with historic Southeastern beliefs have been made (Waring, 1968; Howard, 1968). There were undoubtedly direct relationships between the beliefs of historic and modern Indians in the Southeast and those of the prehistoric residents. At the same time, considerable caution is necessary in the use of such analogies to "interpret" archeological materials. Most of the religious practices and beliefs for which we have good ethnographic evidence are either modern or go back little farther than the early eighteenth century. The archeological complexes with which we are concerned date as far back as the ninth century. Thus, the ethnographic data refer to societies that are from 200 to 1000 years later than the archeological evidence. The best use of the ethnographic evidence here is as a source for hypotheses that can be tested rather than as a source for interpretations. One fact does stand out from the ethnographic data on the Southeast; the Southeastern historic rituals "differ significantly from any aspects of southwestern or Mexican ceremonialism" (Witthoft, 1949:82). Although largely true, this statement is rather too strong, since New World religious beliefs share certain basic features: they usually emphasize four-part division of the world and universe and stress the cardinal directions and celestial objects.

The Southern Cult

One of the most striking features of the Late Prehistoric period is the widespread occurrence of certain artistic themes and objects over almost all of the Southeast. This complex of themes and objects has been variously known as the *Southern Cult* and the *Southeastern Ceremonial Complex* (Waring and Holder, 1945; Waring, 1968; Howard, 1968; Muller, 1966, 1970, 1979). The usefulness of this concept has been somewhat weakened by efforts to ascribe all elaborate art and artifacts from the Late Prehistoric period to Southern Cult. In fact, there appear to have been several different horizons with widespread distributions of this kind during the Late Prehistoric period, and it seems most useful to call only the largest and most highly organized of these *the* Southern Cult. There is not the slightest evidence that the complex was, in sociological terms, a "cult." Even *Southeastern Ceremonial Complex,* quite aside from its awkwardness, is not very satisfactory, for it has become increasingly obvious that archeologists are really describing networks of exchange and interaction in this case rather than "ceremonies" or cults.

Whatever it is called, the Southern Cult extends far beyond the limits of any one complex or archeological unit. So-called Cult materials are known from Mississippi to Minnesota, from Oklahoma to the Atlantic coast. The greatest concentrations of such materials occur in mortuary "temple" mounds at some of the major sites of the Late Prehistoric period—Moundville, Alabama; Etowah, Georgia; and Spiro, Oklahoma (Figure 9.16). Other large sites, such as Cahokia itself, seem to have very little in the way of Southern Cult artifacts. It is likely,

FIGURE 9.16
Materials associated with the so-called Southern Cult or Southeastern Ceremonial complex of
about AD 1250. Such materials occur very widely in many different phases on this time level.
Some major centers of the cult were Moundville, Alabama; Spiro, Oklahoma; and Etowah,
Georgia. Each of the many different areas participating in this exchange network had its own
distinctive art styles, even though certain art motifs were widespread. (a, b) repousse copper
plates; (c) "bi-lobed arrow" motif in copper; (d) copper ax; (e) monolithic ax; (f) polished stone
"mace"; (g) shell gorget from Etowah; (h) design from an engraved shell cup from Spiro.
(Not to scale.)

however, that in some cases this scarcity reflects the uncertainties of archeological recovery, since Cult artifacts are usually found in only a few kinds of archeological contexts. The network of exchange involved in the Southern Cult was
very extensive, with raw materials and finished goods moving long distances.
Shell gorgets, for example, that must have been made in northern Georgia or
eastern Tennessee have been found at Spiro in Oklahoma. It is very tempting to
suggest that this exchange may not have been restricted solely to long-distance

exchange of small and "expensive" items but that the exchange routes may also have played an important role in the movement of primary economic goods and materials, such as food and salt. In any case, the peak of the Southern Cult proper seems to have come within a short period around AD 1250. Other, more localized exchange networks grew up in the central Cumberland valley around AD 1350 and again in the eastern Tennessee drainage shortly after AD 1500. Valuable goods such as marine shell, of course, had been exchanged throughout the Southeast from Late Archaic times on. What concepts like Southern Cult and even the earlier Hopewell actually represent are periods in which similarities of theme, motif, and medium are sufficiently strong to suggest social interaction as well as trade. Two features of the Southern Cult should be strongly emphasized. Southern Cult goods are common in Mississippian sites but are also found in areas that can be called Mississippian only by the broadest definitions possible for that term. Moreover, although the themes and motifs of the Cult probably did have politico-religious significance in many cases, the Southern Cult and its later relatives should not be considered as solely or even primarily religious.

Other Complexes

When sites like Cahokia and Moundville are considered, Mississippian complexes in the central Southeast were the most complex societies of the Late Prehistoric period. At the same time, many other peoples in the Southeast developed highly complex social systems that correspond to the Mississippian developments in many ways. In the Ouachita physiographic province of Arkansas and eastern Oklahoma, for example, there were societies that archeologists have called *Caddoan*. In the lower Mississippi valley below present-day Greenville, Mississippi, continuity of development can be seen from the Sedentary complexes such as Marksville into the early Late Prehistoric Coles Creek and the later Plaquemine cultures. On the eastern Coastal Plain and in the mountains of the southern Appalachians, there are still other societies that have sometimes been grouped together in the later part of the Late Prehistoric period under the name *Lamar*. All of these complexes share certain basic features. It is likely that all of them, like the Mississippian, were socially organized into ranked societies. All of these societies also participated to a greater or lesser degree in Southeast-wide exchange networks, such as the Southern Cult and its later analogues. In addition, high social differentiation in such societies was reflected by substructure mound construction and elaborate mortuary practices.

At this time it seems much better to treat these complexes on regional terms rather than to subsume them all under *Mississippian*. The distinctive characteristics of the Plaquemine, Caddoan, or even Lamar complexes are direct reflections of the developments toward greater complexity that mark the entire Southeast in Late Prehistoric times. The use of *Mississippian* to describe all of these gives the false impression that the central Mississippi societies had priority in these developments and that they "influenced" other peoples throughout the Southeast. Present evidence shows that, regardless of where shell-tempered pottery may have developed, the complex social structures that are the true markers of Late Prehistoric life in the Southeast developed at pretty much the same time throughout the area. If priority must be sought for some one area, however, it would certainly not be found in central Mississippi but rather in the Coles Creek, Baytown, or Weeden Island areas further south. The problem of the Coles Creek to Plaquemine developments in the lower Mississippi valley below Greenville, Mississippi, exemplifies some of the problems in terminology and classification. The Late Prehistoric period is important as the time of maximum development; the following sections, therefore, briefly deal with the Lower Valley, Caddoan, and Lamar complexes of the Late Prehistoric.

LOWER VALLEY □ The Coles Creek and Plaquemine complexes in the Lower Valley represent direct developments from the late Sedentary complexes described in the previous section. Coles Creek is one of the earliest Southeastern societies in which platform substructure mound construction is known, given some ambiguity about the character of some of the earlier mound building. Even in Coles Creek, the exact chronology of substructure mound building is far from firmly established. The scale of mound construction in Coles Creek is generally modest. At the Greenhouse site in Louisiana, for example, the total volume of the mounds is some 7500 cubic meters, and not all of the mound construction can be dated to Coles Creek times. When compared with the 95,000 cubic meters of mound construction at a Tennessee–Cumberland (Mississippian) site like Kincaid, it can be seen that Coles Creek organizations were probably not on the same scale as the Mississippian. At the same time, the complexity of the Coles Creek site layout and the continuity of planning needed for such sites do suggest that chiefdomlike societies may have been present.

CADDOAN □ The Caddoan societies of the Ouachita Province have largely been distinguished from Mississippian complexes by their elaborately engraved, polished pottery. It is true that many workers in the Caddoan area (for example, Hoffman, 1970:160) do see the Caddoan complexes as Mississippian, but, as indicated above, the similarities seem to be those shared by most Late Prehistoric peoples in the Southeast. At least *some* Caddoan societies were organized on a chiefdom level, although many may not have been. Caddoan centers rarely show the kind of centralized planning over time that appears to be characteristic of central Mississippi, Dallas, Tennessee–Cumberland, and other "true" Mississippian complexes (see Hoffman, 1970:160). There also appears to have been a relatively greater emphasis on burial than was the case in other Late Prehistoric areas. Centralization of power is suggested by what appears to have been retainer sacrifice and by almost incredible amounts of grave goods accompanying the dead. For example, there are nearly as many engraved shell artifacts from Spiro as are known from the rest of the Eastern Woodlands altogether. Unlike the Lower Valley complexes, Spiro and other Caddoan sites were directly involved in the Southern Cult exchange network. Another indication of the complexity of Caddoan social organization may be seen in the larger mounds in the area, even though these are not common.

LAMAR □ In the eastern section of the Southeast there are other distinctive cultures. In this area, many of the later Late Prehistoric groups have been called Lamar and defined as a kind of backwoods, Mississippian-influenced complex. In its later phases, Lamar is identified by the presence of pottery shaped and decorated with elaborately carved paddles, a trait that began very early along the South Atlantic coast. Like the more northerly Oneota complex, however, the Lamar concept has been poorly defined, and too little investigation of its development has been carried out for much to be said about it. At the same time, some complexes from the area that are clearly not "Mississippian" and are presumably "pre-Lamar" are apparently at least as early as Mississippian developments elsewhere.

In all of the preceding cases, the major point to be noted is that the development of highly organized and ranked societies is largely contemporaneous throughout the Southeast. The old picture of the central Mississippi valley's priority and subsequent "influence" upon other areas has been steadily collapsing as more is discovered about other areas. The combination of increased population, new technology, and new forms of social organization developed in many areas throughout the Southeast. In some areas these developments led to "Mississippian" societies, in other areas to complexes like Caddoan or Plaquemine. The major impediment to understanding these developments has been the concentration on tracing the history of traits like shell-tempered pottery and substructure mounds rather than on understanding the social and ecological processes that caused these developments.

Transition

The major factor in the decline of the Late Prehistoric societies was directly related to the beginning of the historic period. However, even before European intrusion into the Southeast, there was a considerable reduction in scale of the more northern Mississippian societies. Such great and important centers as Cahokia, Kincaid, and Angel were virtually, if not completely, abandoned by the middle of the fifteenth century. It is possible that this pullback from the former northern frontier may have been related to the same "Little Ice Age" climate changes that were responsible for the decline in Viking population in Greenland (see Bryson and Murray, 1977). In any case, there may have been considerable displacement of population toward the south. Despite these very late prehistoric dislocations, the earliest historical records from the sixteenth century describe actual chiefdoms, and a few groups in the Southeast, such as the Natchez, did maintain this form of organization into the historical period. Given the instability of chiefdoms in general, however, the decline in population that resulted from European contact led, at the very least, to a collapse of the political structure to smaller "chiefdoms" based on the immediate settlement. The subsequent redevelopment of larger-scale chiefdoms and even states in the Southeast occurred under other circumstances—pressure from European settlers and conflicts among various European states in which the indigenous populations were caught up (Service, 1975: chap. 8; Gearing, 1962). The large-scale disruption of the political and social organization that followed the spread of European disease and power makes analysis of the historical situation fraught with peril. Archeological evidence from the Southeast suggests that earlier, prehistoric peoples of the area had more complex political and social systems than those described in the eighteenth century. For these and many other reasons, attempts to link prehistoric, archeologically defined societies with the historic "tribes" of the Southeast are inadvisable. It is probable, for example, that the present-day Creek Indians include many whose ancestors were members of the Dallas (Mississippian) society of eastern Tennessee, but this is not the same as saying that the Dallas complex is prehistoric Creek.

THE HISTORIC PERIOD

The beginnings were scarcely notable: a few European ships along the coast and a few cursory attempts at exploration. Although there were Indian settlements along the coast, the majority of the Indian population was inland. All the same, the peoples along the coast showed many of the features of the inland chiefdoms. By 1539 or 1540, when Hernando de Soto's expedition penetrated inland, there were numerous accounts of what appear to have been small chiefdoms. The account by Alvar Nuñuz Cabeza de Vaca of the ill-fated Narvaez expedition of 1527 describes the coastal village of Appalachen as consisting of "forty small and low houses" (1972:22). At the same time, the country is described as having houses scattered all over (1972:23), so it is unlikely that population in the area along the coast can be estimated from the small village size. Even in Cabeza de Vaca's account the effect of European contact may be seen in the account of some disease of the "stomach" that killed half of a group of Indians who had helped the stranded Spanish (1972:53).

By de Soto's time, the Indians in many areas had learned to flee at the approach of Europeans. In one deserted town, the account of the Gentleman of Elvas described a situation that sounds familiar from the preceding account of the Late Prehistoric: "The town was of seven or eight houses, built of timber, and covered with palm leaves. The Chief's house stood near the beach, upon a very high mount made by hand for defense" (Gentleman of Elvas, 1866:23–24). Later, it is mentioned that this small village paid "tribute" to a chief some 30 leagues away (1866:33). The sixteenth-century Spanish league may be taken as approximately 3 English miles, so even discounting for some misunderstanding, this figure suggests sizable political entities in an area that was not nearly so complex as the inland societies described earlier.

As the de Soto expedition went inland, it encountered plaster-walled houses like those known archeologically from the Southeast. The houses of the chiefs were described as larger than those of the other people "and about are many large barbacoas [described as a structure with wooden sides raised aloft on four poles], in which they bring together the tribute their people give them of maize, skins of deer, and blankets of the country" (1866:52). Although the role of the chief may not have been fully understood by the Spanish chroniclers, this description of centralized storage strongly suggests the redistributive function of the chief. But even in 1539 or 1540, there were indications that European disease may have outraced the European explorer. The Gentleman of Elvas describes large vacant towns grown up with grass, and the Spanish were told of a major epidemic some two years earlier (1866:63).

De Soto was after wealth, but he did not find it in the Southeast. There were some attempts at settlement of more permanent kinds, but these were predominantly coastal and information on them does not throw much light on the upheavals of the late sixteenth and seventeenth centuries.

A recent history by Francis Jennings has drawn attention to the ideological background for the European claims to have discovered an "empty land" inhabited only by savages and wild beasts (1975). The "civilization" brought to eastern North America by the Europeans consisted mainly of the kinds of repressive force that are characteristic of a *state*, especially efficiency of military and other forms of control. Firearms in this period were not the source of critical technical superiority over the weapons of the Indian. Rather, the main source of European military superiority was organization. Faced with this organizational superiority, some Indian tribes and chiefdoms did manage to restructure their societies into true states; but by that time the European bridgehead on the east coast was too firmly established. The native Americans in the Southeast were not completely destroyed. Today there are over 190,000 people of Indian descent in the Southeast, but over half of them live in Oklahoma and nearly half of the rest live in North Carolina. Although many of these Indians no longer seem very different from their neighbors of European descent in their dress and behavior, some of the old beliefs and patterns survive. Even so, generations of repression have left their mark so that it is very difficult to connect contemporary beliefs and behavior with their prehistoric origins.

References Cited and Recommended Sources

Binford, Lewis R., 1968. Post-Pleistocene adaptations. In *New Perspectives in Archaeology,* ed. S. R. and L. R. Binford, pp. 313–341. Chicago: Aldine.

———. 1971. Mortuary practices: their study and their potential. *Society for American Archaeology, Memoir* 25:6–29.

———. 1972. *An Archaeological Perspective.* New York: Seminar Press.

Braun, David. 1980. On the appropriateness of the Woodland concept in Northeastern archaeology. In *Proceedings of the Conference on Northeastern Archaeology,* ed. J. A. Moore, pp. 93–108. University of Massachusetts Department of Anthropology, Research Report no. 19.

Brown, Ian. 1980. *Salt and the Eastern North American Indian: An Archaeological Study.* Lower Mississippi Survey, Bulletin 6.

Broyles, Bettye, J., and Clarence Webb (eds.). 1970. *The Poverty Point Culture.* Southeastern Archaeological Conference, Bulletin 12.

Bryson, Reid A., and Thomas Murray. 1977. *Climates of Hunger: Mankind and the World's Changing Climate.* Madison: University of Wisconsin Press.

Cabeza de Vaca, Alvar Nuñuz. 1972. *The Narrative of Alvar Nuñuz Cabeza de Vaca.* Translated by Fanny Bandalier. Barre, Mass.: Imprint Society.

Caldwell, Joseph H. 1958. *Trend and Tradition in the Prehistory of the Eastern United States.* American Anthropological Association, Memoir no. 88. (Illinois State Museum, Scientific Papers, vol. 10.)

Carneiro, Robert L. 1970. A theory of the origin of the state. *Science* 169:3947:733–738.

Chomko, S. A., and G. W. Crawford. 1978. Plant husbandry in prehistoric eastern North America: new evidence for its development. *American Antiquity* 43:3:405–408.

Coe, J. L. 1964. The formative cultures of the Carolina Piedmont. *American Philosophical Society, Transactions* 54:5.

Cole, Fay-Cooper, et al. 1951. *Kincaid: A Prehistoric Illinois Metropolis.* Chicago: University of Chicago Press.

DeJarnette, David L. 1975. *Archaeological Salvage in the Walter F. George Basin of the Chattahoochee River in Alabama.* University: University of Alabama.

———, Edward Kurjack, James Cambron, and others. 1962. Stanfield–Worley Bluff Shelter excavations. *Journal of Alabama Archaeology* 8:1–2.

Ford, James A. 1969. *A Comparison of Formative Cultures in the Americas: Diffusion or the Psychic Unity of Mankind.* Smithsonian Contributions to Knowledge, vol. 11. Washington, D.C.: Smithsonian Institution Press.

Ford, Richard I. 1974. Northeastern archaeology: past and future directions. In *Annual Review of Anthropology* 3:385–413.

Fowler, M. L. 1959. *Summary Report of Modoc Rock Shelter.* Illinois State Museum, Report of Investigations 8.

Gardener, William. 1975. Paleo-Indian to Early Archaic: continuity and change during the late Pleistocene and early Holocene. *Proceedings of the IXth International Congress of Prehistoric and Protohistoric Sciences.* Nice, France.

Gearing, Fred. 1962. *Priests and warriors.* American Anthropological Association, Memoir 93.

Gentleman of Elvas. 1866. *Narratives of the Career of Hernando de Soto . . . As Told by a Knight of Elvas.* Translated by Buckingham Smith. New York: Bradford Club. (Reprint edition, 1968, Gainsville, Fla.: Palmetto Books.)

Goodyear, Albert C. 1974. *The Brand Site: A Techno-functional Study of a Dalton Site in Northeast Arkansas.* Arkansas Archaeological Survey, Research Series No. 7.

Graham, Russell W. 1982. Clovis peoples in the Midwest: the importance of the Kimmswick site. *The Living Museum* 44(2):27–29.

Greengo, Robert E. 1964. *Issaquena: An Archaeological Phase of the Yazoo Basin in the Lower Mississippi Valley.* Memoirs of the Society for American Archaeology, no. 18. *American Antiquity* 30:2:2.

Griffin, James B. 1967. Eastern North American archaeology. *Science* 156:3772:175–191.

Hoffman, Michael P. 1970. Archaeological and historical assessment of the Red River Basin in Arkansas. Part IV of *Archaeological and Historical Resources of the Red River Basin,* ed. Hester A. Davis. Arkansas Archaeological Survey, Publications on Archaeology, Research Series no. 1:135–194.

Holmes, W. H. 1903. Aboriginal pottery of the eastern United States. Bureau of American Ethnology, *20th Annual Report (1898–1899),* pp. 1–237.

Howard, James H. 1968. *The Southeastern Ceremonial Complex and Its Interpretation.* Missouri Archaeological Society, Memoir 6.

Jennings, Francis. 1975. *The Invasion of America: Indians, Colonialism, and the Cant of Conquest.* Chapel Hill: University of North Carolina Press.

Kuttruff, L. C. n.d. Late Woodland and Mississippian settlement systems in the lower Kaskaskia river valley. NSF report summary and longer, unpublished dissertation, Southern Illinois University at Carbondale, Department of Anthropology.

Lee, Richard B. and I. DeVore (eds.). 1968. *Man the Hunter.* Chicago: Aldine.

Lewis, T. M. N., and M. K. Lewis. 1961. *Eva, an Archaic Site.* Knoxville: University of Tennessee Press.

MacNeish, R. S. n.d. An early Mississippian phase . . . Manuscript on file, Southeast Laboratory, Department of Anthropology, Southern Illinois University—Carbondale.

Milanich, J. T. 1980. Weeden Island studies—past, present, and future. *Southeastern Archaeological Conference Bulletin* 22:11–18.

Morse, Dan, F., Jr. 1973. Dalton culture in Northeast Arkansas. *Florida Archaeologist* 26:1:23–38.

Muller, Jon. 1966. Archaeological analysis of art styles. *Tennessee Archaeologist* 22:1:25–39.

————. 1970. *The Southeastern Ceremonial Complex and Its Interpretations,* by James H. Howard. *American Anthropologist* 72:1:182–183.

————. 1978. The Kincaid system: Mississippian settlement in the environs of a large site. In *Mississippian Settlement Patterns,* ed. B. D. Smith, pp. 269–292. New York: Academic Press.

————. 1979. Structural studies of art styles. In *The Visual Arts: Plastic and Graphic,* ed. Justine Cordwell, pp. 139–211. The Hague: Mouton.

————, and George Avery. 1982. The Great Salt Spring: 1981 Season, A Preliminary Report. Report submitted to the National Forest Service, Shawnee Forest. Carbondale: Center for Archaeological Investigations, Southern Illinois University.

Neumann, Georg K. 1952. Archeology and race in the American Indian. In *Archaeology of the Eastern United States,* ed. James B. Griffin, pp. 13–34. Chicago: University of Chicago Press.

Phillips, Philip. 1970. *Archaeology Survey in the Lower Yazoo Basin, Mississippi, 1949–1955.* Peabody Museum Papers no. 60.

Porter, James W. 1969. The Mitchell site and prehistoric exchange systems at Cahokia: AD 1000 ± 300. In *Explorations into Cahokia Archaeology,* ed. M. L. Fowler, pp. 137–164.

Sahlins, Marshall. 1972. *Stone Age Economics.* Chicago: Aldine.

Schiffer, M., and J. House. 1975. *The Cache River Archaeological Project.* Arkansas Archaeological Survey, Research Series, no. 8.

Schoenwetter, J. 1979. Comment on "Plant husbandry in prehistoric eastern North America." *American Antiquity* 44:3:600–601.

Sears, William. 1953. *Excavations at Kolomoki—Season III and IV, Mound D.* Athens: University of Georgia Press.

————. 1956. *Excavations at Kolomoki, Final Report.* University of Georgia Series in Anthropology, no. 5.

————. 1968. The state and settlement patterns in the New World. In *Settlement Archaeology,* ed. K. C. Chang, pp. 134–153. Palo Alto, Calif.: National Press Books.

Service, Elman R. 1962. *Primitive Social Organization: An Evolutionary Perspective.* New York: Random House.

————. 1975. *Origins of the State and Civilization: The Process of Cultural Evolution.* New York: W. W. Norton.

Smith, Bruce D. 1978. *Mississippian Settlement Patterns.* New York: Academic Press.

Struever, Stuart. 1964. The Hopewell Interaction Sphere in Riverine–Western Great Lakes culture history. In *Hopewellian Studies,* ed. J. R. Caldwell and R. L. Hall, pp. 85–106. Illinois State Museum Scientific Papers 12.

Waring, Antonio J., Jr. 1968. *The Waring Papers: The Collected Works of Antonio J. Waring, Jr.* ed. Stephen Williams. Papers of the Peabody Museum of Archaeology and Ethnology, Harvard University, vol. 58.

————, and Preston Holder. 1945. A prehistoric ceremonial complex in the southeastern United States. *American Anthropologist* 47:1:1–34. (Reprinted in Waring, 1968.)

Watson, Patty Jo (ed.). 1974. *Archeology of Mammoth Cave Area.* New York: Academic Press.

Webb, W. S. 1946. The Indian Knoll, site Oh 2, Ohio County, Kentucky. *University of Kentucky Reports in Anthropology and Archaeology* 4:3:1:111–365.

Williams, S. 1957. The Island 35 mastodon: its bearing on the age of Archaic cultures in the East. *American Antiquity* 22:359–372.

Witthoft, John. 1949. *Green Corn Ceremonialism in the Eastern Woodlands.* Occasional contributions from the Museum of Anthropology, University of Michigan, no. 13.

Yarnell, Richard A. 1976. Early Plant Husbandry in Eastern North America. In *Cultural Change and Continuity,* ed. C. E. Cleland, pp. 265–273. New York: Academic Press.

Inscription House ruin. (Photograph by Marc Gaede.)

CHAPTER TEN

The Southwest

William D. Lipe

The spectacular ruins of the Southwest have inspired many romantic speculations and legends about the people who built them. Who were they? Where did they come from? Why did they vanish? The castles at Mesa Verde have particularly inspired such questions. Today there are fewer mysteries—although some remain. This chapter systematically explains the complex prehistoric events that constitute Southwestern archeology.

THE SOUTHWESTERN REGION

The Southwest can be variously defined (Kroeber, 1939; Kirchoff, 1954; Reed, 1964), but it is impossible to arrive at boundaries that coincide neatly with the boundaries of the major geologic, biotic, climatic, and cultural units. The regional definition used here corresponds to the extent of maize-growing, pottery-making, village- or rancheria-dwelling cultures of about AD 1100, which for most of them was the time of maximum geographic extent. This boundary is necessarily fuzzy all around, but especially in the south, where relationships into northern Mexico are poorly known.

The Southwest has great topographic variety, with elevations that range from near sea level in the lower Colorado River valley to over 3600 meters atop some of its mountains. The region owes much of its biotic diversity to this variation in elevation and land form, and it is no accident that the concept of altitudinal life zones (Merriam, 1890, 1898) was developed here. Rainfall increases with elevation, while temperatures decrease; superimposed on these local controls are general topographic trends in the amounts and seasonal distribution of rainfall. One of the most rewarding areas in current Southwestern research is analysis of the adaptation of cultures to the possibilities and challenges of this environmental diversity. This diversity will be next described to provide data that are essential to understanding the archeology.

Although there were substantial changes in Southwestern climate, flora, and fauna at the end of the Pleistocene (8,000 to 10,000 BC), environments since then have approximated present conditions. Some of the post-Pleistocene climatic variations may have been great enough to affect prehistoric cultures, but they were probably not sufficiently large to alter major environmental zones. An understanding of these geographic subdivisions (Figure 10.1) is therefore a logical starting point for understanding the environmental settings to which the prehistoric cultures adapted.

The Colorado Plateau

This extensive highland consists largely of uplifted but relatively undeformed sedimentary formations—sandstones, shales, and limestones. A few isolated mountains of igneous origin have been thrust up through the Plateau, and at a number of locations, especially around its edges, sheets of lava have spilled out of fissures to cover the underlying sedimentary rocks. Nearly all the Plateau is drained by the Colorado River and its tributaries, which everywhere cut into the land, producing a complex topography of mesas, buttes, canyons, and valleys. Because of extensive erosion, soils tend to be thin, and there are many exposures of bare rock. The deepest soils, and the ones generally most suited to agriculture, are alluvial valley fills and patches of eolian, or wind-deposited, silts in the uplands. Only the major streams are permanent; the others flow only briefly after a rainfall or to carry away snow melt from the highlands. Some of the sedimentary formations are good aquifers, and springs are abundant in the canyons cut into them.

Plateau vegetation and climate are roughly zoned by altitude, although the rugged topography provides much opportunity for local variation due to exposure, slope, and so on. The few highest peaks have only alpine shrubs above treeline. The forests of spruce and fir on the upper slopes give way to Ponderosa pine at lower elevations.

The dominant vegetation between 1500 and 2100 meters, where most of the Plateau surface lies, is the piñon–juniper forest. In parts of the southern interior of the Plateau, woodland is replaced by grasslands at this elevation. Wherever they occur, patches of deep soil tend to support shrubs and grasses rather than woodland. Of the shrubs, big sage is most common, but saltbush and greasewood take over on the more alkaline soils. Rainfall at this elevation ranges from about 25 to 38 centimeters, and the frost-free period from about 120 to 160 days.

Below 1500 meters, shrubs and grasses predominate, with extensive areas of sage, greasewood and saltbush, and blackbrush. In both the piñon–juniper and lower shrubland zones, riparian communities of cottonwood, willow, and other water-loving plants occur along drainages and around seeps and springs.

The Plateau is a transition zone between two major precipitation patterns. On the northwestern edge of the region, most of the moisture comes from the Pacific in broad frontal storms, concentrated in the winter and spring, with only a small rainfall peak in late summer. On the region's southeastern edge, the

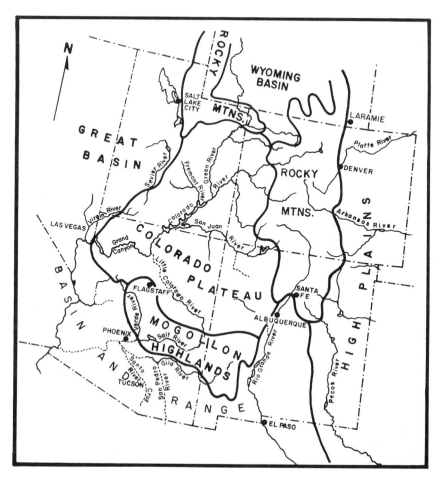

FIGURE 10.1
Southwestern geographic regions.

wettest season is late summer, with a lesser peak in late spring; winters are relatively dry. The summer rains come from numerous localized thunderstorms, which are often "triggered" by highland masses. The moisture source is the Gulf of Mexico. Between these two extremes, at approximately the Four Corners point, rainfall is about equally divided between winter and late summer.

The Basin and Range Area

To the west, south, and southeast of the Plateau are numerous more or less parallel mountain ranges, separated by broad basins deeply filled with alluvial material eroded from the mountains. The narrow highlands, composed of both sedimentary and igneous rocks, have been uplifted by complex block faulting. The flat-topped mesas so characteristic of the Plateau skyline are here replaced by the jagged profiles of eroded mountains.

The highest and coolest part of the Basin and Range area, in western Utah and Nevada, is called the Great Basin because it has only interior drainage. Although much of the Basin is above 1350 meters, it is in the rain shadow of the Sierras and is drier than the Plateau. Annual precipitation is generally below 25 centimeters, with a peak in the late winter and early spring. Basin vegetation resembles that of the Plateau, except that shrubland is much more extensive. The mountains have piñon–juniper woodland, and the highest ones are topped by pine forests.

South of the Basin and Plateau, the elevations are lower, the climate hotter and drier, and the mountain ranges older and more eroded. Drainage is better developed, and such water as does run off the predominantly desert landscape finds its way into the Gila River system or, in the extreme east, into the Rio Grande. The only flowing streams in the area bring water from adjacent highlands, most of which are located to the north.

From the extremely hot deserts near sea level along the lower Colorado, the southern Basin and Range area gradually rises to the east, until elevations over 1200 meters are reached on the valley floors of the Arizona–New Mexico borderlands. Rainfall patterns change strikingly from west to east. Here, in addition to increasing from less than 12 to more than 25 centimeters annually, the seasonal distribution changes from winter-dominant with a lesser summer peak in the west to a strong summer concentration in the east.

The vegetation of the southern Basin and Range area contrasts strongly with that of the Plateau and Great Basin. The low deserts of southwestern Arizona and adjacent southern California have a monotonous cover of creosote bush and bursage on the valley floors, with sparse cacti and shrubs such as hill palo verde on the higher areas. At higher elevations to the east, the valley sides and upland support a rich flora of shrubs and cacti, including the giant saguaro, organ-pipe and barrel cacti, cholla, and prickly pear. Tree legumes such as mesquite and acacia grow abundantly in the washes. East of Tucson, still higher valleys have a shrub–steppe vegetation that includes creosote bush and abundant grama and tobosa grasses, while the uplands support oak–juniper woodland, with pine forest on the highest peaks.

The Mogollon Highlands

The rock layers of the Colorado Plateau are gently uptilted toward its southern edge, which generally rises above 2100 meters. In central Arizona, the prominent escarpment at the Plateau's edge is called the Mogollon Rim. Eastward, the Rim becomes less definite, and merges with the volcanic White Mountains. This high southern edge of the Plateau, and the rugged mountains just south of it, I have called the Mogollon Highlands. Sloping land predominates, and there are few broad valleys or flat-topped mesas. The area is transitional between the Plateau and the Basin and Range, both geologically and ecologically. At the higher elevations, forests of pine or mixed pine and Douglas fir are typical. Intermediate elevations have piñon–juniper or oak–juniper woodland transitional to mountain mahogany–oak scrub. Desert shrub–steppe occurs in some of the lower valleys. The intergradation of Plateau and Basin–Range vegetation gives the area an extremely rich, varied flora.

Rising abruptly from lower desert areas, the Mogollon Highlands receive precipitation as air masses from the southwest or southeast rise over them, are cooled, and release their moisture. On the Plateau to the north, points at similar elevations receive less moisture. For example, Cibecue, Arizona, at 1590 meters elevation, in the Mogollon Highlands, receives nearly 48 centimeters of precipitation a year. On the Plateau 64 kilometers to the northeast, Snowflake, Arizona, receives less than 30 centimeters at 1680 meters. Both have similar ' temperatures, with Snowflake slightly cooler.

The Rocky Mountains

The Southern Rockies, just east of the Plateau, are part of an uplifted, complexly folded mountain chain that forms the highest and generally most rugged portion of North America. Although it is well-watered, the region's cool temperatures made most of it marginal for Southwestern farming cultures. Some of the lower areas in the mountains of southwestern Colorado and northern New Mexico—particularly the Rio Grande and environs for some distance north of Santa Fe—were heavily occupied, however. The vegetation in lower elevations of the Rockies resembles that of the Plateau, although more of the land is given over to coniferous forest.

ARCHEOLOGICAL RESEARCH IN THE SOUTHWEST

Although it has experienced periods of intellectual stagnation, Southwestern research has more often been a leader, or at least a participant, on the conceptual and methodological frontiers of American archeology. A brief review of the history of research in this area will illustrate the point.

Early Exploration and Excavation

Early European explorers of the Southwest remarked on its ruins and speculated on their makers, as did succeeding missionaries, railroad surveyors, and the like. By the 1880s, specifically archeological surveys and excavations were being undertaken. Many were designed to obtain museum collections; their field methods would often be classed as looting today. Taylor (1954) points out that, although the archeologists of this era were interested in linking the archeological remains to what they conceived of as a pan-Southwestern Pueblo culture, they showed a striking lack of concern for temporal distinctions. An exception was Richard Wetherill, who in the 1890s excavated in the dry caves of southeastern Utah on behalf of the American Museum of Natural History. His observations that Cliff Dweller (Pueblo) remains stratigraphically overlay those of the earlier Basketmaker culture documented a temporal distinction still made in Anasazi archeology (McNitt, 1957).

Initial Synthesis: 1912–1927

Although the older traditions of research continued into this period, a new understanding of Southwestern prehistory also began to emerge. A new generation of archeologists began to apply systematic excavation and analytical methods to more focused questions of cultural variation and change. A landmark for American archeology was N. C. Nelson's pioneering stratigraphic work in 1912; his excavation of Pueblo rubbish mounds in arbitrary levels resulted in a chronology of ceramic change for the Galisteo Basin in New Mexico (Nelson, 1916). This chronology permitted other sites in the area to be assigned to periods on the basis of their pottery styles. Stratigraphic techniques were also used by Guernsey and Kidder (1921) from 1914 to 1917 in the dry caves of northeastern Arizona. Their work resulted in a four-period sequence based on changes in pottery and architecture. At about the same time, Kroeber (1916) and Spier (1917) were developing the techniques of surface survey and seriation, which enabled them to place early Zuni sites in temporal order on the basis of surface sherd collections.

In 1924, Kidder's *Introduction to the Study of Southwestern Archaeology* provided the first detailed regional synthesis in American archeology. As new data continued to flood in, the principal Southwesternists met in 1927 at Kidder's field camp at Pecos, New Mexico, to compare notes and to try to arrive at generalizations. Out of this meeting (Kidder, 1927) came the Pecos Classification, a series of periods labeled *Basketmaker I* through *III* and *Pueblo I* through *V*. The period descriptions attempted to outline developmental trends in lifeways, from seminomadic to settled agricultural, and to pick out stylistic features of widespread geographic but limited chronological distribution.

Taxonomy and Culture History: 1927–1957

Systematic fieldwork outside the San Juan drainage quickly demonstrated that the Pecos Classification did not apply to the entire Southwest. Soon, other prehistoric traditions coordinate with San Juan Anasazi were documented: Hohokam in the central desert area (W. Gladwin and Gladwin, 1929, 1934; H. Gladwin et al., 1937); Fremont in the central Plateau (Morss, 1931); Mogollon in the Mogollon Highlands (Haury, 1936); Patayan (formerly *Yuman*) in western Arizona (W. Gladwin and Gladwin, 1934; Hargrave, 1938; Colton, 1945a); and Sinagua in the area near Flagstaff, Arizona (Colton, 1946).

Likewise, time depth came to the Southwest, as evidence of early hunters was discovered at Sandia Cave (Hibben, 1941), Ventana Cave (Haury, 1943, 1950), and the Naco and Lehner sites (Haury, Antevs, and Lance, 1953; Haury, Sayles, and Wasley, 1959). The gap between the early big-game-hunting cultures and the late farming cultures began to be filled by a variety of manifestations, most of which came to be called *Desert* culture (Jennings, 1956) and, more recently, *Western Archaic*.

At about the same time that Midwestern archeologists were developing formal schemes for classifying culture units (McKern, 1939), several large-scale cultural taxonomic systems were being proposed in the Southwest (W. Gladwin and Gladwin, 1934; Colton, 1939). Unlike the Midwestern system, the Gladwin and Colton schemes weighted time-sensitive traits and arranged cultural entities in "family trees," which implied quasibiological relationships. Although rightly criticized (for example, Brew, 1946), such efforts did serve to order the abundant data and to generate large-scale culture-historical hypotheses. The lowest-level classificatory unit of the Gladwin system—the phase—has become the standard working category in the time–space ordering of data in American archeology.

The objectives of this era promoted and were in turn furthered by detailed analytical studies, particularly of pottery (Colton and Hargrave, 1937) and architecture (Hawley, 1938). Focused as they were on stylistic variability, these studies gave Southwesternists sensitive tools for defining and dating cultural units and for tracing "influences" among them. To existing relative dating techniques such as stratigraphy and seriation was added tree-ring dating (Douglass, 1929), which still remains the most accurate absolute dating method used anywhere in North American prehistoric archeology. Together, these taxonomic and analytic developments gave Southwestern archeology a basic culture–time–space framework that still surpasses those of most, if not all, areas of the New World. Based on this developing framework, culture history flourished, ranging in character from speculative to solidly documented.

Cultural Ecology and New Archeology: 1957–1974

The importance of the interactions between culture and environment had long been recognized in the Southwest, partly because of the stimulus of Steward's archeological (1937) and ethnological (1938) analyses. Still more important had been the work of archeologically oriented geographers such as Bryan (1941,

1954), Antevs (1955), and Hack (1942). In the late 1950s, ecological and settlement pattern studies came to be regular features of the larger regional studies, such as the Navajo Reservoir and Glen Canyon salvage projects (Eddy, 1966, 1972; Jennings, 1966) and the Wetherill Mesa Project at Mesa Verde National Park (Osborne, 1965).

In the 1930s and 1940s, critics of the predominance of taxonomic and culture-historical goals in Americanist archeology had found ample targets among Southwestern researchers (Steward and Setzler, 1938; Taylor, 1948). These attacks prepared the way for the acceptance by many of the "New Archeology" (Binford, 1962, 1964). The first major substantive attempts to apply his suggested approaches took place in the Southwest, as Longacre (1964, 1970) and Hill (1966, 1970) set out to reconstruct social groupings within pueblos by studying the distributions of selected artifactual and architectural attributes. This pioneering work was methodologically flawed (see Allen and Richardson, 1971; Stanislawski, 1973; Dumond, 1977), but it helped stimulate a literal explosion of attempts both to develop archeological tests of hypotheses about social organization, sociocultural change, and environmental adaptation (for example, Dean, 1970; F. Plog, 1974; Zubrow, 1971) and to explicate the processes of archeological inference (for example, Fritz and Plog, 1970; Schiffer, 1972).

Recent Trends: 1974–Present

As economic development—and, hence, threats to archeological sites—mushroomed after World War II, organized salvage programs appeared in the Southwest. By 1960, most Southwestern research was being done under salvage contracts with federal agencies or public utilities. The strength and rapid growth of these programs was due to the prior existence of strong, locally oriented research programs and to the fact that much of the region is public land and therefore is subject to protective antiquities laws.

In response to historical preservation and environmental protection laws passed in the late 1960s and early 1970s, American salvage archeology was absorbed by "cultural resource management" (Schiffer and Gumerman, 1977; King et al., 1977). The Southwest has been a leader in this approach, in which archeological potential is considered early in development planning, and protection of sites is an alternative preferred to salvage.

Salvage archeology tended to be theoretically and methodologically conservative, emphasizing descriptive reports and relying on culture-historical and taxonomic models. Cultural resource management has fostered a greater variety of orientations. Much of the Southwestern work derived from management research is of more than regional interest; it includes studies of settlement patterns (Reher, 1977), subsistence (Goodyear, 1975; Madsen and Lindsay, 1977), paleodemography (Swedland and Sessions, 1976), exchange systems (S. Plog,

1980), and sampling and survey methods (S. Plog et al., 1978) as well as regional syntheses (Cordell, 1978) and research reviews (Doyel and Plog, in press).

Problem-oriented research has also proliferated outside the cultural resource management field. Notable are the long-term efforts focused on the Chacoan phenomenon at Chaco Canyon (Judge, 1979; Judge et al., 1981) and at the Salmon Ruin outlier (Irwin-Williams and Shelley, 1980); studies of growth and decline of large Late Prehistoric pueblos at Arroyo Hondo in the Rio Grande area (Schwartz and Lang, 1973; Dickson, 1979) and at Grasshopper in the Mogollon Highlands (Longacre and Reid, 1974; Reid, 1978); and research on changing patterns of population and land use in Long House valley, northeastern Arizona (Dean et al., 1978).

Future Prospects

Problems currently of research interest are likely to remain so for some time, but with the continuing addition of new concerns. For example, we are just beginning to see attempts to pursue with Southwestern archeological data the cognitive and "structural" interests so popular in cultural anthropology (see Fritz, 1978). More generally, Cordell and Plog (1979) have called on their colleagues to exorcise normative assumptions about Southwestern cultures and to produce comparative studies that recognize and attempt to explain the great variability in Southwestern archeological records. Likewise, Berry (in press) attacks commonly held assumptions of local and even regional cultural and demographic continuity. He argues that examination of the data reported by Southwesternists—if not their interpretations of them—often indicates discontinuity and "punctuated equilibria," rather than smooth trends of in-situ development.

The review of Southwestern archeology that follows, however, emphasizes general patterns and glosses over much of the variability and discontinuity that I am aware of, and undoubtedly much that I am not. And, by and large, it is an account of *what* happened, rather than *why* it happened. It is intended to orient readers who are unfamiliar with the Southwest and to raise questions that they can explore further, with the aid of the bibliographic references. A synthesis that addresses the well-taken concerns of Cordell, Plog, and Berry still lies in the future.

But in the prospect of future growth lies the strength and self-renewability of archeology. As our methods improve, and as new theoretical frameworks emerge, an area such as the Southwest—which has already seen a hundred years of research—can be looked at afresh, and can be made to yield new understandings of the past. Many of the innovations in both method and theory that have shaped American archeology began in the Southwest, and most of the remainder were tested there. The region's wealth of potential information—in the field, library, and museum—promise to keep it in the forefront of American archeology as long as that discipline continues to evolve.

THE EARLY CULTURES

Plains-Oriented Big-Game Hunters

The Southwest has yet to produce remains demonstrably older than the Clovis horizon of about 9000–9500 BC. The Sandia Cave material, once a candidate for an earlier position, appears to have so many problems of interpretation (Stevens and Agogino, n.d.) that its true date must be considered unknown. That the widespread Clovis horizon extended throughout the Southwest is documented from excavations in southern Arizona and from sparse surface materials elsewhere (Schroedl, 1977). The Clovis groups were oriented to hunting mammoths, as demonstrated at the Naco, Lehner, and Murray Springs sites in the San Pedro valley of Arizona (Figures 10.2 and 10.3). This last site also produced evidence that extinct forms of bison and perhaps the horse were hunted as well. The Clovis horizon is not confined to the Southwest, and is described in Chapter Two, as are problems in its interpretation.

Irwin-Williams and Haynes (1970) depict a gradual retreat eastward for the Plains-based big-game hunters after the Clovis period, presumably as increasing desiccation changed grasslands to shrublands and as surface water became scarcer. Folsom and early Plano sites, dating about 9000–7500 BC, tend to be found primarily east of the Arizona–New Mexico border (Figure 10.3). Late Plano materials from about 7500–6500 BC occur only rarely in the Southwest. The late Plano Cody complex of about 6500–6000 BC is, however, fairly well represented in the eastern and northern Southwest, perhaps because herds and hunters moved back into the area from the Plains in response to a temporary increase in effective moisture.

In the central Rio Grande valley of New Mexico, Judge (1973) has reconstructed from survey data some aspects of what he calls the *settlement technology* of the bison-hunting Folsom and Plano groups. Their sites tend to occur at the northeast edges of plains, an area which the bison presumably favored for grazing. Sites were located in general proximity to water—first near playas, then near streams as continuing desiccation reduced the number of playas. Judge identified three kinds of sites. *Preparatory* sites were located at overview points; they were not necessarily close to water but had a good view of hunting areas. The principal activity at these locations was the flaking of projectile points, presumably by hunters waiting for game. *Processing* sites were generally quite near water; tool types and the wear patterns on them suggest that soft materials such as hides were being processed, perhaps by cooperative work groups of women. *Base camps* were strategically located with respect to major hunting areas, water sources, and overlooks; artifacts were most abundant and varied here, indicating varied activities.

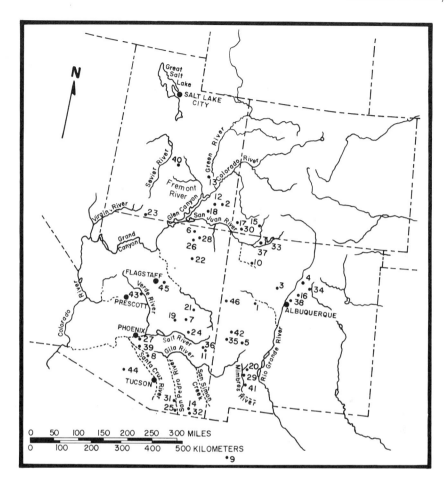

FIGURE 10.2
Sites and locations referred to in the text.

1. Acoma Pueblo
2. Alkali Ridge
3. Armijo and En Medio Shelters
4. Arroyo Hondo
5. Bat Cave
6. Betatakin and Kiet Siel
7. Bluff site
8. Casa Grande
9. Casas Grandes
10. Chaco Canyon
11. Cienega Creek site
12. Comb Wash
13. Cowboy Cave
14. Double Adobe site
15. Durango Basketmaker sites
16. Galisteo Basin
17. Gilliland site
18. Grand Gulch
19. Grasshopper site
20. Harris site
21. Hay Hollow Valley
22. Hopi Pueblos
23. Kanab Basketmaker sites
24. Kinishba
25. Lehner site
26. Long House Valley
27. Los Muertos site
28. Marsh Pass
29. Mattocks Ruin
30. Mesa Verde
31. Murray Springs site
32. Naco site
33. Navajo Reservoir
34. Pecos site
35. Pine Lawn Valley and Reserve area
36. Point of Pines
37. Salmon Ruin
38. Sandia Cave
39. Snaketown
40. Sudden Shelter
41. Swarts Ruin
42. Tularosa Cave
43. Tuzigoot
44. Ventana Cave
45. Winona site
46. Zuni Pueblo

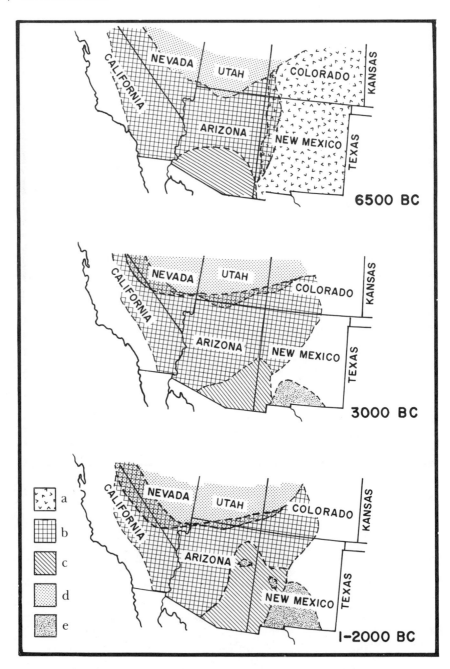

FIGURE 10.3
Distribution of early cultures at various points in time: (a) Prehistoric big-game hunters;
(b) western-based Archaic cultures (with Oshara as a local tradition); (c) Cochise tradition;
(d) Great Basin Archaic cultures (with Desha as a local manifestation); (e) poorly known
Archaic cultures based in northern Mexico. (After Irwin-Williams and Haynes, 1970.)

The Archaic

The term *Archaic* covers a disparate group of American archeological cultures that exhibit neither a specialized big-game-hunting adaptation nor a sedentary-horticultural one. Instead, these cultures had a close adaptation to a locality or region and to both its wild food and its inorganic resources. Tool kits, paleoecological data, and settlement patterns suggest that several food and raw material procurement systems were ordinarily employed, and that these often required precise scheduling of activities, commonly within a seasonal round of movement. Because a variety of resources was exploited and populations remained small, these adaptations tended to be stable, and slow to change. Local accumulations of stylistically distinctive traits, as well as regional differences in resources and procurement systems, resulted in considerable interregional variation. This variation can be documented by a review of the better-known local sequences.

VENTANA CAVE AND SAN DIEGUITO □ At Ventana Cave, a stratified site in southwestern Arizona (Haury, 1950), the lowest occupational stratum yielded stone tools, a C14 date of 9300 BC ±1200 years, and bones of extinct horse, tapir, ground sloth, jaguar, and four-pronged antelope. Modern forms included jackrabbit, prairie dog, badger, peccary, and deer. A crudely made lanceolate point was likened by Haury (1950) to Folsom and by Haynes (1964) to Clovis, but Irwin-Williams (1979) doubts both assignments. Other artifacts include scraper–planes, choppers, scrapers, and cutting tools made by percussion techniques on side-struck flakes, plus a single discoidal mano. Although probably contemporaneous with Clovis and Folsom, these materials indicate a more generalized hunting pattern and the possibility of plant-resource exploitation. They may indicate the very early emergence of a generalized Archaic pattern.

The Ventana Complex resembles the widespread, but as yet rather poorly defined, San Dieguito complex of California, southwestern Nevada, and western Arizona. Its diagnostic artifacts include Lake Mohave and Silver Lake points, bifacial leaf-shaped knives, and a variety of percussion-flaked scrapers and choppers. Grinding tools are absent. Warren (1967) suggests that San Dieguito dates between about 8000 and 6500 BC and represents an early generalized hunting culture with relationships in the Northwest.

The next cultural materials to be deposited at Ventana Cave follow an erosional hiatus and are dated on geologic grounds as post-5000 BC. Grinding tools are still absent; Haury notes affinities of the chipped stone to California-centered late San Dieguito–Amargosa materials. Manos and grinding slabs do not appear until subsequent levels, when assemblages increasingly resemble the Cochise tradition farther east, but with strong elements of the western Pinto Basin–Amargosa tradition remaining.

THE COCHISE TRADITION □ In 1926—the same year that a Folsom point was found in situ with extinct bison remains in Colorado (Figgins,

1927)—Dr. Byron Cummings of the University of Arizona observed artifacts lying stratigraphically below mammoth remains in alluvial deposits at the Double Adobe site, southeastern Arizona (Whalen, 1971). Sayles and Antevs (1941) excavated here and at other sites in the area, and defined a sequence they named the *Cochise* culture, with three stages or phases: Sulphur Spring, Chiricahua, and San Pedro.

This tradition's origins are obscure. Notably, seed-grinding tools are present throughout, as are percussion-flaked choppers, planes, scrapers, and knives, all made on large flakes (Figure 10.4). The Sulphur Spring stage is known only from a few sites in southeastern Arizona, but later materials occur widely in the southern desert and Mogollon Highlands. Sulphur Spring's C14 dates fall between 7300 and 6000 BC; Chiricahua dates cluster between 3500 and 1500 BC; and San Pedro appears to have evolved into the Mogollon tradition (Whalen, 1971:67–68). The gap between 6000 and about 3500 BC may be due to vagaries of preservation and discovery, or may reflect sparse occupation during the Altithermal.

Fossils of extinct mammoth, camel, horse, and dire wolf—as well as modern forms such as antelope, jackrabbit, mallard, and coyote—have been found at Sulphur Spring sites. The association of the extinct mammals with the cultural materials has been questioned, but Haury (1960) argues it is authentic. Split and burned bones at the Sulphur Spring sites indicate that at least some of the animals were hunted. The artifactual assemblage, however, which lacks projectile points and is heavily dominated by cobble manos and thin grinding slabs, is more suggestive of plant food processing. Whalen (1971:69) proposes that nearby occurrences of the poorly known Cazador complex, which does include projectile points, may represent Sulphur Spring hunting activities. However, Irwin-Williams (1979) questions both the stratigraphic and typological bases for this assignment.

Projectile points, some resembling the widespread Pinto type, are definitely present in the Chiricahua stage (Figure 10.4). Large base camps with storage pits, outlying special activity sites, small mortars, and heavy basin millingstones have been documented (Whalen, 1971; Agenbroad, 1978). In the succeeding San Pedro stage, sites tend to be larger and more numerous, and simple pithouses have been found in several cases.

Late Cochise contexts at Bat Cave (Dick, 1965), Tularosa Cave (Martin et al., 1952), and Ventana Cave (Haury, 1950) demonstrate that seeds and small-to-medium game animals were being exploited. From Bat Cave it has been claimed that, by 2000 BC, small amounts of primitive maize were being cultivated. Berry (in press) believes, after reviewing the published C14 data (which are hard to correlate with the excavation report) that the Bat Cave cultigens cannot be demonstrated to be earlier than about 500 BC. Squash has been reported from late Chiricahua contexts, but beans do not appear until the San Pedro stage (Whalen, 1973). All these early cultigens occur in highland sites along the Arizona–New Mexico border, just north of the Sierra Madre Occidental, which extends southward into central Mexico. Haury (1962) makes a

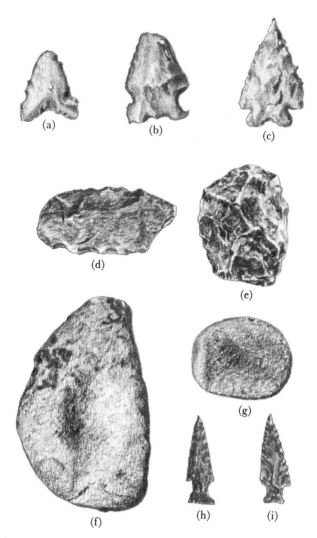

FIGURE 10.4

Artifacts of the Cochise tradition: (a–c) projectile points of general Pinto Basin type; (d) flake knife with retouch on one edge; (e) plano-convex chipping–scraping tool; (f) shallow basin grinding slab; (g) one-hand cobble mano; (h, i) narrow side-notched projectile points of the San Pedro stage. (a–g) are all Chiricahua stage. (After Sayles and Antevs, 1941.)

good case for the gradual early diffusion of farming from Mexico into the Southwest along this mountain chain.

THE OSHARA TRADITION □ In northwestern New Mexico, Irwin-Williams (1968, 1973, 1979) has defined a long Archaic sequence (Figure 10.5) that appears to be locally ancestral to Anasazi. Unfortunately, reports of the surveys and most of the excavations upon which her synthesis is based have not been published. The earliest Archaic manifestation (the Jay phase) is so differ-

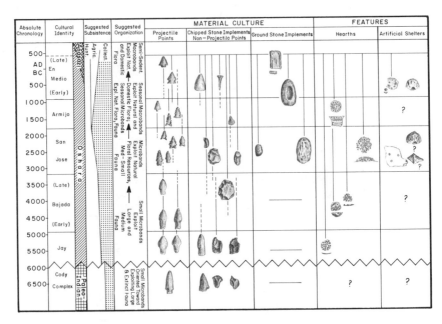

FIGURE 10.5
Synopsis of the Oshara tradition. (After Irwin-Williams, 1973.)

ent from the Paleo-Indian Cody complex that Irwin-Williams sees no connections. Instead, there are resemblances to San Dieguito, leading her (1979) to postulate "slow demographic movements from the west, which spread into the niche left by the withdrawal of the Paleo-Indian groups."

The Jay phase (5500–4800 BC) lacks grinding tools and has large projectile points reminiscent of the Lake Mohave type, along with well-made side scrapers and bifacial knives. Sites and populations were small. Irwin-Williams thinks the economic cycle was not strongly seasonal or transhumant. Small, limited activity sites record hunting, foraging, and quarrying activities, which were probably staged from base camps established at environmentally favored canyon-head locations.

The succeeding Bajada phase (4800–3200 BC) resembles the Jay phase. Projectile points, though still large and long-stemmed, have concave bases and more definite shoulders. Crude flake scrapers and chopping tools become more abundant and may indicate increased use of coarse plant foods, while the introduction of cobble-filled hearths and earth ovens suggests technical improvements in food processing as well. Although this phase coincides with the Altithermal, population may actually have increased slightly.

In the San Jose phase (3200–1800 BC), base camps are larger, more numerous, and have more debris. Posthole patterns at one site suggest simple surface structures. Increased use of seeds is indicated by the appearance of shallow grinding slabs and cobble manos; chopping tools and coarse flake scrapers also become more common. The formation of larger special-activity groups is suggested by one hunting site with 15 hearths. Projectile point forms and the assemblage in general parallel the Pinto Basin materials to the west. Irwin-Williams thinks that population increased during this period, probably in response to the onset of slightly moister conditions and to more effective exploitation brought about by improved technology.

In the Armijo phase (1800–800 BC), palynological evidence indicates that primitive maize began to be raised on a small scale; the frequency of ground stone tools continued to increase. The pattern of canyon-head base camps and distant special-activity sites continues, but a new settlement type appears—a fall or winter camp that joined several small bands into a seasonal macroband of perhaps 30–50 people. Irwin-Williams thinks this development was based on the small horticultural surplus, plus an autumnal abundance of wild food resources. Typologically, the Armijo assemblage continues to resemble the late Pinto Basin complexes.

The En Medio phase (800 BC–AD 400) shows continued regional population increase, continued maize cultivation, and greater seasonality of the annual economic cycle. The fall–winter macroband camps increase in number, but in the summer the canyon-head locations were depopulated in favor of a new type of limited-activity site—gathering camps on upland dune ridges. The tool kit shows continuities with the preceding phase—with the addition of more bifacially flaked knives and drills—and a predominance of corner-notched projectile points. The latter part of this phase can be considered a local manifestation of the Anasazi tradition, Basketmaker II stage. Farther to the northwest in New Mexico, Reher (1977) and Sessions (1979) report that Oshara-tradition sites are commonly associated with dune fields well before the En Medio phase.

THE NORTHERN PLATEAU □ Recent excavations at Sudden Shelter (Jennings et al., 1980) and Cowboy Cave (Jennings, 1980), two deeply stratified sites, have added important new information about Archaic occupations in the Northern Plateau. Sudden Shelter appears to have functioned as a seasonal (generally summer) base camp between about 6000 and 1300 BC. Cowboy Cave was most frequently used as a summer seed-gathering camp, during four short periods: about 8600 BP–8200 BP, 7200 BP–6400 BP, 3600 BP–3300 BP, and AD 100–500. Numerous plant and animal species were represented at the sites, but only a handful (grasses, amaranth and chenopod, cacti; mule deer, bighorn sheep, rabbit) were at all abundant. The evidence suggests a seasonal round focused on a few reliable resources, rather than a "broad spectrum" harvesting pattern. Maize does not appear until after AD 1 at Cowboy Cave, in association with materials that appear transitional between late Archaic and Fremont.

Basing his work on the evidence from Sudden Shelter and Cowboy Cave, plus sketchier data from other sites, Schroedl (1976) has attempted a chronological ordering of the Northern Plateau Archaic. He recognizes four phases: Black Knoll (6300–4200 BC), Castle Valley (4200–2500 BC), Green River (2500–1300 BC), and Dirty Devil (1300 BC–AD 500). He argues that populations were at low points during the middle Castle Valley and early Dirty Devil phases, and that these were relatively warm, dry periods. Interregional comparisons relate the Northern Basin materials and sequences to those of the Eastern Basin rather than to the Oshara tradition. Inclusion of the Desha complex (Lindsay et al., 1968) in the Black Knoll phase pushes the Northern Plateau pattern as far south as the Arizona–Utah border, and suggests that its boundary with Oshara may have been rather clear-cut. Schroedl's synthesis also indicates that the Fremont culture is rooted in the Late Archaic of the Northern Plateau, a conclusion reinforced by Adovasio's (1980) comparative study of basketry from the Plateau and Basin.

THE TRANSITION TO SETTLED LIFE

As previously noted, there may be room for argument over whether cultigens appear in the Southwest as early as 2000 BC; Berry (in press) argues that no occurrences can be demonstrated earlier than 500 BC. It does seem established, however, that, at scattered locations in the Mogollon Highlands and probably in the Southern Plateau, cultigens occur in Late Archaic contexts—prior to the appearance of ceramics, villages, and other trappings of a Formative stage (Willey and Phillips, 1958) lifestyle. Between about AD 150 and 700, regionally distinctive Formative cultural traditions emerged (Hohokam, Mogollon, Anasazi, Fremont, Patayan, Sinagua), and the pace of change quickened markedly. Although the timing and intensity of change varied locally, pithouse villages became numerous across the Southwest, population grew much more rapidly than before, pottery became widely used, and cultigens came to dominate subsistence in most areas. Changes in settlement pattern, social organization, technology, and the organization of work can also be recognized.

Some basic and fascinating problems are posed by this transition from an Archaic lifeway to an at least incipient Formative one. What made the presumably stable, well-adapted Archaic cultures susceptible to change? Why did it take cultigens several hundred—if not several thousand—years to become basic to subsistence? What processes brought about the transformation of culture and society? And why did the rate of change vary from place to place? Although these problems are not unique to the Southwest, their solution is essential to an understanding of the Southwestern tradition. All we can say at this point is that some promising work on these topics has begun.

That corn, beans, and squash were initially domesticated in Mexico and transferred to the Southwest seems well documented (Mangelsdorf et al., 1967). A favorable milieu for this sort of cultural transmission was established by about 3000 BC, with the emergence of what Irwin-Williams (1967) has called *Picosa* or the *Elementary Southwestern* culture. This culture was based on a widespread communications network that permitted the rapid spread and sharing of information among diverse local cultures.

Already keen students of natural history, the adaptively sophisticated Archaic peoples would not have needed to be taught that plants would grow if seeds were put in the ground. And their seed-processing technology was preadapted to the addition of a new cereal food such as maize. Ethnographic accounts of Basin peoples who followed an essentially Archaic lifestyle indicate that they sometimes manipulated the environments of wild food plants by irrigation and weeding, and that some groups cultivated small patches of true domesticates. Yet these activities were fitted in only as permitted by the demands of the larger round of foraging, and contributed relatively little to total subsistence. "Incipient cultivation" of this sort may have characterized the Southwestern Late Archaic. In the succeeding Formative-level cultures, foraging for wild food resources continued to be important, but the subsistence economy came to be built around cultigens.

What broke down the old pattern of exploitation of environmental diversity in favor of emphasis on a few crop plants? One answer could be that the Mexican Formative frontier pushed north into the Southwest, and that the Archaic peoples were replaced or absorbed by groups that had made the transition farther south. If Haury (1976) is right, and his argument is persuasive, the earliest Hohokam Vahki phase settlements in southern Arizona do represent just such a colonization by village-dwelling irrigation farmers. Outside the riverine Hohokam area, however, most Southwestern archeologists read the evidence as favoring a more gradual transformation of in-situ Archaic cultures. Certainly, the proximity of Hohokam villages might have hastened this process by providing trade items and information, but juxtaposition and contact cannot in themselves account for the changes. The Southwestern ethnographic literature provides abundant examples of stable and even symbiotic relationships between adjacent Formative and Archaic-type groups. Explanations must be sought within the changing cultures themselves, as well as in the broader regional context of information availability and flow.

Flannery's (1968) model of the transformation of the Mesoamerican Archaic provides potentially illuminating insights. His analysis treats seasonal scheduling of food collecting as a device that not only enabled groups to adapt to variable and scattered resources, but that acted as a deviation-damping mechanism that could counter tendencies to concentrate on any single food procurement system. This pattern was altered, however, when the conditions under which early domesticates were grown selected for genetic changes that increased their food value and, hence, their attractiveness. This development triggered positive feedback or deviation-amplifying processes, such as population growth and investment in fixed facilities. These changes led in turn to increasing dependence on cultigens, radical alteration in food procurement scheduling, and changes in social organization.

Somewhat similar processes may have been operating in the Southwest. Adaptation of cultigens to local environments was undoubtedly important, but there is also evidence of continuing introduction of more productive strains of maize, presumably from the south (Dick, 1965:92–99; Galinat and Gunnerson, 1963). Even at the level of incipient cultivation in a basically Archaic subsistence pattern, this new food energy source may have triggered cultural change of the sort described by Flannery. Irwin-Williams (1979), for example, interprets the shift to winter macroband camps and the associated increase in ceremonial activity in the late Oshara tradition as being based on a food surplus generated by cultigens.

A somewhat different tack is taken by Glassow (1972) in his study of the transformation of Anasazi Basketmaker culture in the Plateau area. He argues that early Basketmaker groups—having an essentially Archaic subsistence pattern with some use of cultigens—occupied a limited number of favorable ecotone situations that gave them access to the resources of both canyon and mesa environments. When these situations became fully occupied, excess population moved to less favored settings. At these locations, adaptive alternatives such as an increased dependence on farming and the construction of larger storage facilities were favored, a move which set off positive feedback processes of the sort described by Flannery. Lipe and Matson (1971b) speculate that, even in the absence of population increase, a period of environmental deterioration might have had similar effects. By reducing the number of most favored areas, such deterioration would force some groups to readapt to conditions of diminished resource availability.

Fred Plog (1974), in a case study of Mogollon–Pueblo data from the upper Little Colorado area in the Southern Plateau, does not try to identify the precise mechanisms triggering the transition. Instead, he focuses on the processes operating during its unfolding in the period from AD 850 to 1050. He develops a model that has population, socioeconomic differentiation, social integration, and technology as its principal variables, and attempts to define their interrelationships through time in the study area. Plog concludes in part that, during the period of growth in the study area,

> the technological changes that characterize the transition are a result of differentiation, which in turn is caused by population increase. Changes in integration associated with the transition appear to be more a result of attempts to manage increasing numbers of individuals than of attempts to manage increasingly differentiated activities (F. Plog, 1974:156).

Plog argues that he is studying the shift from a predominantly hunting–gathering (Basketmaker) to a predominantly agricultural (Pueblo) society. I suspect, however, that the economic transition may have occurred somewhat earlier in his area and that at least some of the changes he discusses reflect increasing diffusion or migration from Anasazi areas to the north. Nevertheless, Plog's pioneering study demonstrates that organizational as well as ecological factors must be considered and that it is possible to deal with the processes underlying a transition of this sort, instead of simply documenting the changes.

THE LATE CULTURES

The Hohokam

The term *Hohokam,* a Pima Indian word meaning "all used up," refers to the prehistoric, settled agriculturalists who occupied much of the southern Basin and Range province in what is now Arizona (Figures 10.6 and 10.7). If, as is generally believed, the Pima and Papago are the cultural heirs of the Hohokam, their cultural tradition can be traced back approximately 2000 years.

GENERAL CHARACTERISTICS □ Several traits are generally accepted as diagnostic of Hohokam culture. Pottery is generally thinned and smoothed by a paddle-and-anvil method, and has gray to brown paste. Most painted vessels were first coated with a buff-colored wash or slip, on which a red design was applied (Figure 10.8). Cremation of the dead was practiced throughout, but inhumations increased in the latest phases. The houses, which are generally oblong in plan and built in shallow pits (Figure 10.9), are not true pithouses because the pit wall was not used as the lower part of the house wall; instead, jacal walls were footed at floor level. Late in the cultural sequence, such houses are largely replaced by surface structures. Settlements vary in size from a few houses to over 100, and generally display little evidence of a formal layout until walled compounds appear in the late phases.

Specialized structures that may have served community integrative functions include ball courts and platform mounds. The former are large, bowl-shaped depressions, which resemble Mesoamerican structures in which ceremonial ball games were played (see H. Gladwin et al., 1937:36–49). Ferdon (1967) has argued, however, that Hohokam structures of this sort were dance courts instead. The platform mounds are low but often large, flat-topped earthen features, and are thought to have had a ceremonial or sociopolitical function.

The Hohokam evidently had stronger and more direct relationships with Mesoamerican cultures than did any of the other late Southwestern traditions, except for Casas Grandes. Evidence of these relationships ranges from evidently imported items such as cast copper bells to general resemblances in community structures, as noted above. The explanations of these similarities offered by various archeologists include migrations from the south, trade, and diffusion, as discussed further below.

Bohrer's (1970) pioneering study of the Snaketown botanical remains indicates that Hohokam subsistence resembles the ethnographic Pima–Papago pattern. This strategy consisted of single or dual croppings of maize, beans, cucurbits, cotton, and possibly tobacco and amaranth. Planting schedules corresponded to the biannual rainfall and flooding pattern in the Hohokam area (Figure 10.10). In locations where irrigation from flowing streams could be practiced, that technique was favored. Away from major streams such as the Salt and Gila rivers, the Hohokam farmed on seasonally flooded valley bottoms,

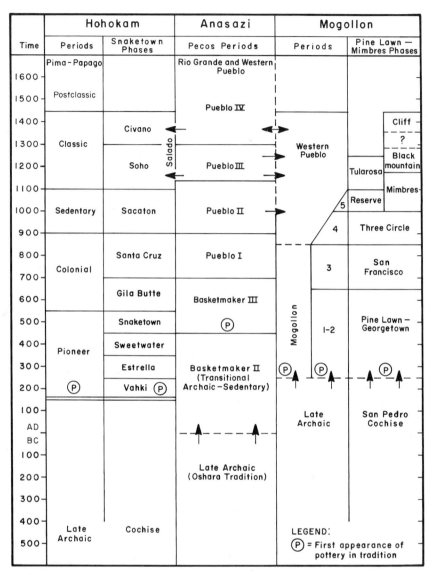

FIGURE 10.6
Correlation of Hohokam, Mogollon, and Anasazi cultural sequences.

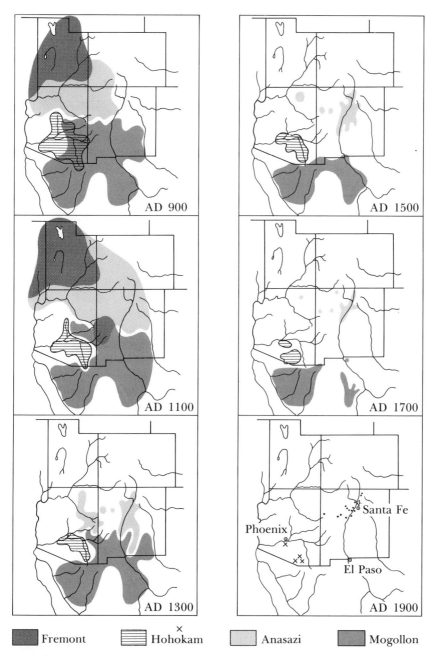

| Fremont | Hohokam | Anasazi | Mogollon |

FIGURE 10.7
Approximate distribution of principal late cultures, AD 900–1900.

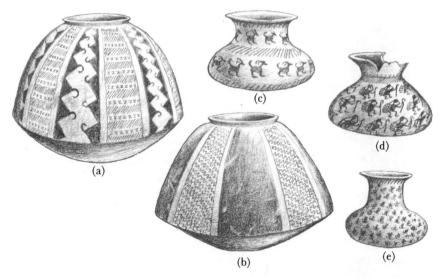

FIGURE 10.8
Examples of Hohokam decorated pottery: (a, b) Sacaton Red-on-Buff; (c–e) Santa Cruz Red-on-Buff.

or constructed stone grids, terraces, or check dams on slopes to catch runoff after local storms. In the Salt and Gila river valleys, sophisticated canal systems often conveyed water to fields several kilometers from the canal inlet. The largest Hohokam settlements—for example, the Snaketown site south of what is now Phoenix, Arizona—were located in areas served by such irrigation systems. Domesticated plants were complemented by the seasonal exploitation of wild biotic resources, especially the fruits of cacti such as saguaro, organ pipe, and prickly pear and the seed-bearing pods of tree legumes such as mesquite. These foods allowed the Hohokam to compensate for fluctuations in domestic crop yields. Archeological evidence suggests that this subsistence strategy did not change markedly throughout Hohokam culture history.

THEORIES OF HOHOKAM CULTURAL DEVELOPMENT □ Until recently, most Southwesternists have seen early Hohokam culture as an essentially in-situ development, the result of local Cochise groups having gradually adopted traits of Mexican origin, such as agriculture and pottery, either directly or through a Mogollon intermediary (see H. Gladwin et al., 1937; Haury, 1945a). A special formulation of this general position was developed by DiPeso (1956), who labeled the indigenous agriculturalists the *Ootam*. Schroeder (1957, 1960, 1965) included the early Hohokam as part of the Hakataya tradition, which he believed to be a very widespread indigenous pattern that occupied parts of the central and western Arizona uplands as well as the desert areas.

Although Haury long favored an in-situ theory of Hohokam origins, his 1964–1965 excavations at Snaketown led him to change this view (Haury, 1965, 1967, 1976). He now believes that the earliest Hohokam were migrants

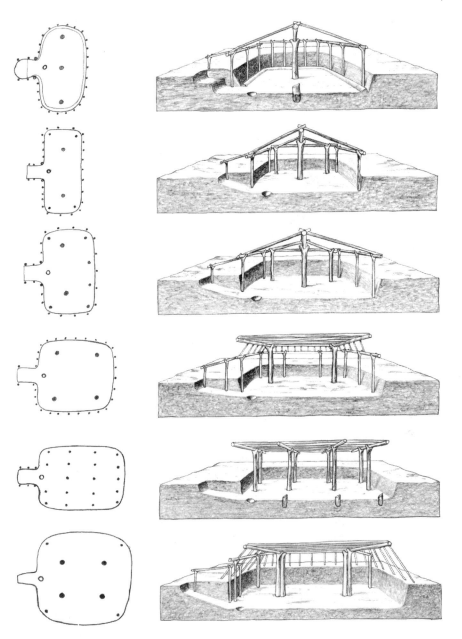

FIGURE 10.9
Floor plans and cross-sections (postulated roof constructions) of Hohokam houses at Snaketown, arranged from early (bottom) to late (top).

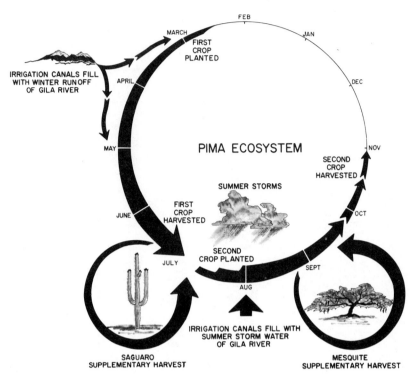

FIGURE 10.10
The Pima subsistence system, which was probably similar to that of the Hohokam. (After Bohrer, 1970.)

from northern Mexico, who came to Arizona with an already formed sedentary, pottery-using culture supported by intensive irrigated agriculture. He also postulates that such river-valley-based colonies would have quickly influenced the native hunter–gatherers of the hinterlands. This process would have contributed to the development of a nonriverine or desert variety of the Hohokam lifeway.

Such reservations as exist about Haury's conclusions appear to be based on the facts that (1) most of the evidence is from a single site, (2) a specific northern Mexican ancestor has not been identified, and (3) there is no convincing theory of why and how such a migration and rapid readaptation might have occurred. These concerns speak to the state of research in southern Arizona and northern Mexico for this time period rather than to the quality of Haury's work. Most Southwesternists appear to have accepted his conclusions as the best reading of the evidence currently available.

There is general agreement that the Colonial and Sedentary periods of the Hohokam tradition (about AD 550–1100) saw a heightened influx of traits of Mexican origin (Figures 10.11 and 10.12). As reflected in their use of the term *Colonial* in the Hohokam period sequence, W. and H. Gladwin (1934) initially viewed such traits as having been brought at that time by migrants from the south. Similarly, DiPeso (1956) argues that disruptions in Mesoamerican cen-

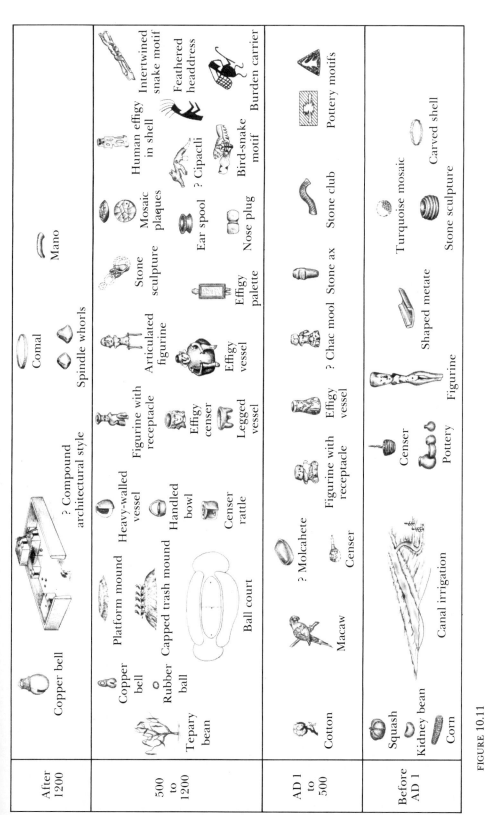

FIGURE 10.11
Hohokam cultural elements exhibiting Mesoamerican influence. (After Haury, 1976.)

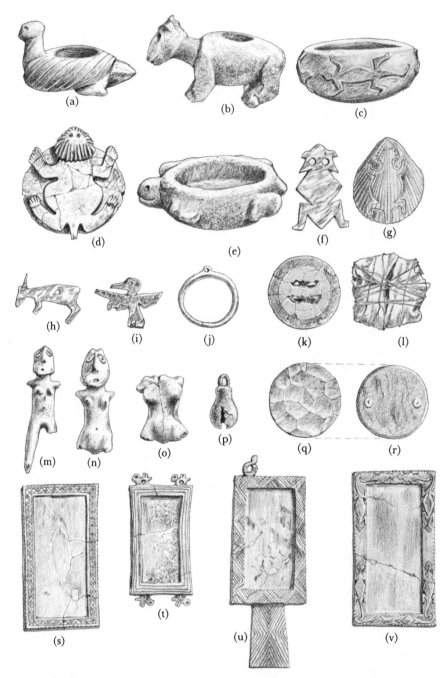

FIGURE 10.12
Nonutilitarian Hohokam artifacts: (a–d) zoomorphic stone bowls and censers; (e–j) zoomorphic shell ornaments; (k, l, q, r) pyrite mirror in wrapping; (m–o) clay anthropomorphic figurines; (p) copper bell; (s–v) stone palettes.

ters forced the dispersion of small groups of the elite stratum of Mesoamerican society. Some of these groups settled in southern Arizona, and subjugated the indigenous Ootam peoples. DiPeso reserves the label *Hohokam* for these intruders. Schroeder (1947, 1960, 1965, 1966) also favors a migration theory but postulates colonization at approximately AD 700 by an organized mercantile group (similar to the *pochteca* of the Aztecs) from the Tarascan region of western Mexico. He believes that trading centers established by this group in the Salt and Gila valleys resulted in wide diffusion of Hohokam/Mexican traits in the Southwest. Others, notably Haury (1976:343–348), view the appearance of Mexican elements in Hohokam sites during the Colonial and Sedentary periods as resulting from continuing contacts, rather than from actual migrations. This theory of primarily in-situ development for this portion of Hohokam prehistory appears to be the currently dominant position among Southwesternists.

A third recurring issue in the interpretation of Hohokam culture history is the role of migrations during the Classic period (about AD 1100–1450). A frequent entry into this debate is the postulated intrusion of a group called the *Salado;* they have been variously characterized as an Anasazi, Mogollon-Pueblo, or Western Pueblo group. The Tonto Basin–Globe area, located in the higher country northeast of Phoenix, has frequently been mentioned as the probable Salado homeland. This model seems to have developed to account for the appearance of multistoried pueblolike structures, polychrome pottery, and inhumations in Classic period sites. In his study of the Los Muertos site near Phoenix, Haury (1945b) interpreted the evidence to indicate that both Hohokam and Salado maintained some degree of separate ethnic identity, and lived side by side in an amicable way. This remains the "standard" formulation of the Salado concept, but alternative interpretations abound. A recent symposium on the Salado (Doyel and Haury, 1976) produced several new hypotheses and reviewed new data, but little consensus emerged.

Wasley (1966; published 1980) rejects migration theories in favor of an in-situ theory of Classic Hohokam development. Citing the presence in earlier phases of most of the traits that have been used as evidence of intrusions, he concludes that continuing diffusion from Mexico was the only extraneous influence during this period. More recently, others (Weaver, 1972; Grady, 1976) have also emphasized in-situ cultural and ecological processes in attempting to account for culture change during the Classic period.

No consensus has yet been reached on the role of external vs. internal factors in Hohokam cultural continuity and change at various periods (Doyel, 1979). A better assessment of these factors continues to be hampered by (1) insufficient data on the range of cultural variability in the Hohokam core area, particularly for the Pioneer and Classic periods; (2) insufficient data on areas suggested as donors of population or culture, particularly northern Mexico and the Tonto Basin; and (3) an insufficient understanding of the organization and dynamics of Hohokam society. Recent work stimulated by cultural resource management concerns (Grady, 1976; Doyel, 1979) promises continuing progress toward solution of the problems raised earlier in this section.

THE PIONEER PERIOD (ABOUT AD 150–550) □ On the basis of his excavations at Snaketown, Haury (1976) argues that the earliest, or Vahki, phase of Hohokam development began about 300 BC. Although he used several dating methods, the results were not in good agreement. Wilcox and Shenk (1977:179) and Wilcox and Larson (1979:4) propose that the Vahki phase does not begin until about AD 150. Although the question is not fully resolved, many Southwesternists find this later date the more acceptable.

The Vahki phase Hohokam had a complex material culture. It included relatively large pithouses and a subsistence-related artifact assemblage containing pottery vessels, grinding implements, projectile points, and a range of scraping and cutting tools. Nonutilitarian items include turquoise mosaic plaques, stone bowls, marine shell ornaments, and ceramic anthropomorphic figurines; all these items have a strong Mexican cast. The most striking Vahki accomplishment is canal irrigation. Haury (1976) documents a sophisticated irrigation technology, including a canal at least 5 kilometers long. The Vahki phase was probably one of considerable experimentation. Data from the few securely identified Vahki sites indicate greater variability in houses, burials, and technological inventories within the Vahki phase than for the rest of the Pioneer period (H. Gladwin et al., 1937; Haury, 1976; D. Morris, 1969).

By the beginning of the Estrella phase, the stable adaptive pattern that was to characterize most of the rest of the Hohokam cultural sequence had been developed. Conjointly, houses became smaller and more uniform. Painted pottery emerges, stylized palettes and similar items of stonework are found, the quantity of carved marine shell increases, and metal artifacts, which were not manufactured in the Southwest, appear.

In the late Pioneer, Mexican macaws and cotton were added to the list of domesticates, and a superior strain of maize was being cultivated. Faunal records indicate some increase in the use of deer and birds (Greene and Mathews, 1976; McKusick, 1976)—a change perhaps attributable to more extensive use of the bow and arrow.

By the end of the Pioneer period, Hohokam territory had increased considerably. From the core locality in the central Salt, Gila, and Santa Cruz river basins, the Hohokam moved up these drainages and into adjacent basins. Their settlements, generally smaller than those of succeeding periods, were usually located on stabilized terraces above the river flood plains. The Pioneer period expansion into the Papagueria, west of the Santa Cruz River, attests to the Hohokam capacity to exploit locations that lacked permanent surface water (Raab, 1976).

THE COLONIAL (AD 550–900) AND SEDENTARY (AD 900–1100) PERIODS □ During the Colonial period, the Hohokam continued to expand territorially, as settlements pushed up the river valleys well into the Mogollon Highlands to the north, into the San Simon drainage to the east, south in the Santa Cruz and San Pedro drainages, and west to Gila Bend on the Gila River.

Doyel (1979:548) estimates that, by AD 1000, Hohokam settlements were distributed over an area of at least 26,000 square kilometers. The culture's external influences were probably greatest at about that time as well.

By late Colonial times, community patterns and material culture indicate considerably greater sociocultural complexity than during the Pioneer period. The larger settlements regularly have ball courts and, by Sedentary times, platform mounds as well. Communities such as Snaketown may have had populations as great as 1000 people settled in an area of 100 hectares (Doyel, 1979: 548). In the lower Salt–Gila river area, some the large communities may have been economic or political centers for a cluster of smaller settlements with which they were linked by a single irrigation system. There is also increasing evidence of craft specialization—for example, in the production of shell ornaments, lithic items, and pottery. External trade increases greatly as well. Social differentiation is signaled by marked differences in burial goods. A chiefdom level of sociopolitical integration may be postulated for some areas (Doyel, 1979). There are increased imports of Mexican artifacts such as mosaic mirrors and, by Sedentary times, copper bells. In general, evidence of relationships with high cultures to the south and southwest is greatest during these periods. This stepped-up interaction was perhaps based on increased demand for status symbols by an emerging local elite, rather than on any initiatives from Mexico.

Although irrigation systems were undoubtedly extended in the river valleys and runoff farming structures were elaborated in other situations, the basic patterns of Hohokam subsistence changed little. Maize kernels continued to become larger, and there appears to have been a significant increase by at least AD 700 in the number of varieties used (Cutler and Blake, 1976). The drought-resistant and productive tepary bean was present by Sedentary times (Haury, 1976:118). Amaranth may also have been domesticated by this period (Bohrer et al., 1969).

THE CLASSIC PERIOD (AD 1100–1450) □ Despite a considerable amount of research, many aspects of this period remain enigmatic. During the early, or Soho, phase of the Classic (about 1100–1300), settlements became fewer but on the average larger, even though some of the largest Sedentary period sites, such as Snaketown, were abandoned. The sprawling layout of earlier villages changed as communities become more compact—often with pueblolike adobe houses clustered around a large platform mound (Doyel, 1979). Burial practices became more variable, as both inhumations and cremations were practiced.

The northern extensions of Hohokam culture—for example, in the Verde Valley—disappeared, presumably as populations withdrew to the deserts. In general, Hohokam territory, trade, and influence seem to have been shrinking at this time (Doyel, 1979). *Cerros de trincheras*—complexes of walls and terraces built on steep hills—appear by the early Classic period, if not before. They also occur in the Papagueria and south in Sonora (Wilcox, 1979). These complexes have sometimes been interpreted as agricultural stuctures designed to hold soil and retard runoff of water. This may be true in some cases, but recent, intensive studies near Tucson indicate that the structures more likely served defensive functions (Wilcox, 1979).

The late Classic, or Civano, phase (about AD 1300–1450) shows renewed signs of Hohokam participation in a widespread exchange system, as indicated by the appearance of types of polychrome pottery that are widely distributed in the southern Southwest at this time. An alternative explanation credits this pottery's appearance to a "Salado" presence in the central Hohokam area. Several settlements exhibit multistoried pueblolike "big houses" built inside preplanned, walled compounds; Casa Grande near Florence, Arizona, is a well-known example (Fewkes, 1912; Wilcox and Shenk, 1977). While some archeologists attribute this development to "Salado influence," others (see Doyel, 1979) argue that they represent the dwellings of chiefly lineages and indicate the reassertion of centralized political and economic leadership within Hohokam society after a time of disruption in the early Classic. In general, the "indigenous growth model" of Classic period development (see Wasley, 1980; Grady, 1976; Doyel, 1979) appears to be gaining support.

THE POST-CLASSIC PERIOD (AD 1450–1700) □ The 250 years between the end of the Classic period and documentation of the Pima–Papago lifeway by Spanish explorers has received little archeological investigation, largely in deference to Pima–Papago sensitivity regarding excavation of protohistoric sites. That this was a time of change is indicated by the differences between the lifeways of the Classic Hohokam and of the Indians encountered by the Spanish. Although eighteenth-century settlement and subsistence were similar to the basic Hohokam patterns, Pima–Papago culture in general resembled Colonial-Sedentary—or even Pioneer Hohokam—more than it did Classic. For example, the historic Pima and Papago lived in spatially separate, often semisubterranean, houses, did not make polychrome pottery, and did not build platform mounds or compound walls. Despite this hiatus in cultural tradition, many authors have presented a strong case for cultural and biological continuities between the Hohokam and the Pima–Papago (Haury, 1975, 1976; Ezell, 1963; Niswander and Brown, 1970).

The Mogollon

At its maximum extent—probably about AD 800 or 900—the Mogollon tradition occupied not only the mountainous Mogollon Highlands, but portions of the Basin and Range province lying to the southeast and east. The tradition emerged from Late Archaic antecedents in the early centuries AD and disappeared as a separate entity between about AD 900 and 1100, when increasing Anasazi influence led to its incorporation into Western Pueblo culture. Although Bullard (1962:184–185) considers the Mogollon nuclear area to have been the lower and more southerly parts of its range, the tradition has generally been characterized as adapted to the more northerly, higher, and topographically rugged mountain area I have labeled the *Mogollon Highlands*. The high-land area is certainly better known, and consequently is the source of most of the information about the Mogollon presented here.

GENERAL CHARACTERISTICS □ Although domesticated plants appar-ently became established in the Mogollon Highlands area in Late Archaic times, hunting and gathering remained substantial contributors to the Mogollon diet throughout the tradition. Hunting, in particular, appears to have played a larger role here than among either the Anasazi or Hohokam. The abundance of wild food resources in general, and the closeness of farming areas to extensive wildlife "preserves" composed of steep slopes or high mountains, must have con-tributed to the persistence of a diversified subsistence pattern. Mogollon farming appears to have depended primarily on direct rainfall, runoff from slopes, or natural flooding in washes. Simple water-control devices such as check dams and lines of boulders transverse to slopes are reported for the late Mogollon and Western Pueblo periods (Woodbury, 1961). Although F. Plog (1974:40) reports prehistoric ditch irrigation from the Hay Hollow Valley on the Mogollon–Anasazi border, and LeBlanc (1976) posits it for the Mimbres Valley, Mogo-llon farming in general appears to have resembled Anasazi practice more than Hohokam.

Mogollon sites typically are small, although a few sites of over 50 houses have been noted. The dwellings are pithouses, arranged in unsystematic fashion. The larger villages generally have an oversized, nondomestic pithouse that probably functioned as a place of community assembly and ritual; these have often been labeled *great kivas*. Anasazi-type small kivas do not occur. Mogollon villages lack definite trash-disposal areas; refuse is found as a thin sheet throughout the site. Special cemetery areas are also lacking; flexed interments are generally in scattered extramural pits or, in the later periods, under house floors.

Utilitarian objects dominate artifact assemblages (Figure 10.13). Marine shell ornaments and other decorative items appear to have been rarer than among Anasazi or Hohokam. Simple flake tools and heavy chopping and pounding implements are common, as are notched and stemmed projectile points. Simple basin grinding slabs persist throughout, but through time are augmented by troughed metates. Despite the amount of woodworking that pit-house construction must have required, grooved axes are rarely found and ap-pear proportionate to increasing Anasazi and Hohokam influence. Throughout the tradition, pottery was of brown and red ware, built up by coiling and finished by scraping. The earliest painted pottery had designs in red on the plain brown vessels. In later periods, a white slip was sometimes added as a base for the red decoration; as Anasazi influence increased, black designs were used.

At any point in time, Mogollon culture seems to have displayed considerable variability, not only among regional subdivisions but within regions or even single sites. The preponderance of plain pottery and the rarity of dendochrono-logical dates have led to much ambiguity in chronology, particularly for the early periods. The general absence of surface architecture has also made it

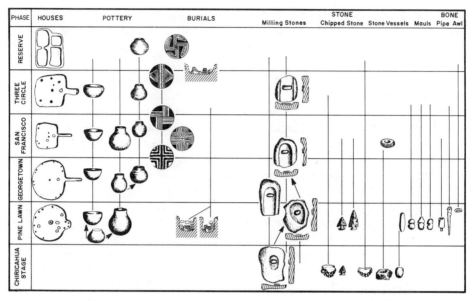

FIGURE 10.13
Synopsis of Mogollon cultural develoment in the Pine Lawn Valley area. (After Martin et al., 1949.)

difficult for site sizes and numbers of houses to be estimated. Consequently, attempts to develop temporal and regional subdivisions or trends for the Mogollon tradition as a whole have usually been subject to much debate.

Wheat's (1955) scheme is no exception, but it remains the most comprehensive attempt at synthesis. Most of his six proposed regional variants are still generally accepted. Wheat labeled as *Mimbres* the Mogollon culture of the central highlands, including the Gila River headwaters as well as the Mimbres drainage. The northernmost part of this subdivision has sometimes been treated separately as the Pine Lawn or Reserve region. To the southeast of the Mimbres area is the hot, low-lying region of the San Simon branch; to the northwest, largely in the headwaters of the Salt River, are the territories of the Black River (Point of Pines) and Forestdale Mogollon. To the east are the poorly known Eastern Peripheral and Jornada regions, which extend through the lower Rio Grande valley to the edge of the Plains. Wheat's Cibola region, northeast of the central area, is often considered more Anasazi than Mogollon.

The dating and phase correlations of Wheat's five tradition-wide periods—especially the two earlier ones—have sparked extensive criticism (for example, Bullard, 1962:68–87). Because of this problem, and because of the previously mentioned spatial variability within the tradition, the discussion of Mogollon cultural development given below relies primarily on the phase sequence of the Mimbres–Pine Lawn area, where most work has been done. Wheat's periods are, however, followed as a chronological outline.

MOGOLLON 1 AND 2 (PINE LAWN AND GEORGETOWN PHASES), ABOUT AD 250–650 □ Excavations at Tularosa Cave in the Reserve area (Martin et al., 1952), at Bat Cave, also in southwestern New Mexico (Dick, 1965), and at the Cienega Creek site in the Point of Pines region (Haury, 1957) have provided evidence for the in-situ development of the Mogollon tradition from an Archaic San Pedro Cochise ancestry. Application of the label *Mogollon* begins when pottery appears in this continuum of development. This distinction is perhaps not entirely arbitrary, for substantial pithouse villages seem to have developed at about the same time, an event that probably indicates population growth or increased sedentism. The earliest pottery is a plain brown called *Alma Plain* and a slipped and polished plain red called *San Francisco Red;* these types continued throughout the Mogollon tradition, though in diminished quantities in the later periods. Origins of the ceramics are unclear, but transmission of the technology from Mexico along a highland corridor is a reasonable possibility (Haury, 1962), as is diffusion from the Vahki-phase Hohokam.

Martin (Martin et al., 1952; Martin and Plog, 1973) would place the earliest Mogollon pottery at 200 or 300 BC, on the basis of several C14 dates from Pine-Lawn-phase deposits stratified in Tularosa Cave. A generally early placement is also supported by the appearance of a few Mogollon trade sherds in Vahki-phase contexts at Snaketown (Haury, 1976:327–331); most Mogollon intrusives at Snaketown are, however, considerably later. Bullard (1962) disagrees with Martin's dating on a variety of grounds. So far, tree-ring dates tend to support his position, since none are earlier than about AD 300 (from the Bluff Ruin in the Forestdale area: Haury and Sayles, 1947; Bannister, Gell, and Hannah, 1966). In the central area, the situation is complicated by the fact that Martin recognizes both a Georgetown and an earlier Pine Lawn phase, while workers in the Mimbres drainage to the south (for example, Haury, 1936) recognize only a Georgetown phase. So far, tree-ring specimens attributed to both Georgetown and Pine Lawn contexts have dated in the AD 400s through early 600s (Bannister, Hannah, and Robinson, 1970). For this discussion of early Mogollon, I lump Pine Lawn and Georgetown together as well as Wheat's Periods 1 and 2, and date the period conservatively as about AD 250 to 650.

Early Mogollon villages tend to be located on mesas or high promontories, generally close to cultivable valley bottom lands. Because access to some villages is restricted by walls, Martin and Plog (1973:182) suggest that these locations were defensive, and speculate that the increasingly sedentary villagers may have disrupted the adaptive patterns of as-yet-unidentified nomadic groups.

The early-period pithouses tend to be round or D-shaped in plan, with lateral ramp entries (Figure 10.14). Commonly, roofs were supported by a single central and by multiple sidewall posts. Great kivas are round or bean-shaped in plan, and are two or three times as spacious as the dwellings. Villages of several tens of houses occur, but most are smaller. In Pine Lawn Valley, Bluhm (1960) estimates average village size at 6 houses, with a range from 1 to 26.

At Tularosa Cave, Martin inferred an adaptive shift at about AD 500 to 700;

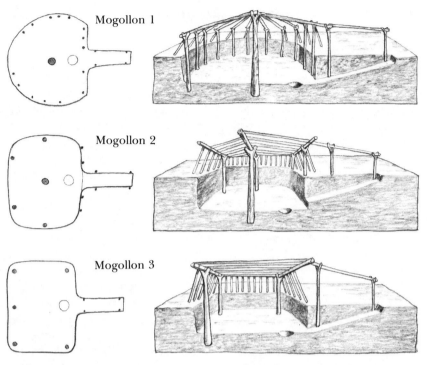

FIGURE 10.14
Floor plans and cross-sections (postulated roof constructions) of Mogollon houses at the Harris village site.

remains of cultivated plants decreased and wild foods increased, relative to both earlier and later periods (Martin et al., 1952; Martin and Plog, 1973). At approximately the same time, house size in the Pine Lawn Valley decreased (Martin and Rinaldo, 1950; Bluhm, 1960), a change that Martin attributes to a shift from extended-family to nuclear-family residence. During this 200-year period, the number of dwelling units in Pine Lawn Valley remained about the same as earlier; it then increased rapidly after AD 700 (Bluhm, 1960). Bullard (1962) accepts these general trends, but questions whether the early Pine Lawn–Reserve area sites can be dated precisely enough to support the temporal correlations noted above.

In the Mimbres Valley, LeBlanc (1976) describes a shift in settlement, from high knolls or ridges to locations noticeably lower and closer to the river, that probably occurred by AD 600. Northeast of Tularosa Cave in the Hay Hollow Valley, F. Plog (1974:157–158) reports the abandonment of large sites about AD 500 in favor of small, dispersed settlements. He attributes the shift to the failure of larger communities to develop adequate integrative mechanisms. The functional relationships, if any, between these settlement changes and the subsistence changes inferred by Martin at Tularosa Cave remain problematical. Graybill (1975:149–150) is skeptical of generalizing from the Tularosa Cave data, because the site is not a typical habitation and would not necessarily contain a representative sample of plant foods.

MOGOLLON 3 (SAN FRANCISCO PHASE), AD 650–850 □ Although Alma Plain and San Francisco Red remain predominant during this phase, new pottery types also become popular, including Mogollon Red-on-Brown and "smudged" bowls having a blackened, polished, interior surface. Late in the phase, a white-slipped type, Three Circle Red-on-White, begins to appear. Although a few circular-plan houses continue to be built, most pithouses are rectangular, with a gable-roof construction; lateral ramp entries continue. Great kivas are variable, but rounded and D-shaped plans predominate over rectangular. Martin and Rinaldo (1950) see the continuing trend to fewer metates and other artifacts per dwelling during this phase as supporting their inference of an earlier shift from extended- to nuclear-family residence units.

In the Pine Lawn Valley, the number of dwelling units and the site size increases substantially; the average village has nine rooms (Bluhm, 1960). High "defensive" locations have been largely abandoned, and sites are located close to arable soil and water. In one part of the valley, there is some tendency for sites to cluster, suggesting greater intervillage integration than previously. The Mimbres Valley seems to have similar settlement trends at this time, although the maximal village there may be somewhat larger (LeBlanc, 1976; Hastorf, 1980:82; Anyon and LeBlanc, 1980:254).

MOGOLLON 4 (THREE-CIRCLE PHASE), AD 850–1000 □ Three-Circle Red-on-White peaks in popularity in this phase, and is supplemented and then replaced by Mimbres Bold-Face, a black-on-white type indicative of increasing Anasazi influence. Pithouses are rectangular and often are masonry-lined. Most have flat roofs supported by a four-post framework. Lateral ramp entries continue to be common, but roof entries and lateral ventilator tunnels are not unknown. Great kivas are predominantly rectangular in plan. Population and site size probably continued to increase during this period, which is transitional between Mogollon and Western Pueblo.

MOGOLLON 5 AND WESTERN PUEBLO, AD 1000–1450 □ Mogollon 5 (AD 1000–1100) witnessed the full emergence of the Western Pueblo pattern and the eclipse of Mogollon as a separate tradition. Surface pueblos of the general Anasazi type become the standard form of housing, and population increase begins to accelerate, probably as a result of immigration as well as of local growth. By the late 1200s, planning is evident in pueblo construction, and some pueblos are built around plazas. Great kivas continue in use, and some appear to serve clusters of smaller pueblos. Small kivas resembling those of the Anasazi, but with square floor plans, are being used. Although the old Mogollon plain brown and polished red pottery continue in small frequencies, the ceramic assemblages are dominated by a variety of black-on-white, polychrome, and corrugated types.

In the northern Mogollon area in the late 1200s, population was clustering into a few large pueblos such as Point of Pines Ruin, Kinishba, and Grasshopper. Although people began to leave some of these pueblos in the late 1300s, a few areas were occupied until perhaps AD 1450. Much of the northern Mogollon population probably moved to Hopi, Zuni, Acoma, and perhaps other pueblos. It seems clear that the Western Pueblo contributed importantly to the formation of these surviving Pueblo cultures and societies.

Farther south in the Mimbres Valley, a distinctive and unparalleled development took place in the Mimbres phase, which LeBlanc (1980; Anyon and LeBlanc, 1980) dates from about AD 1000 to 1150. There was an explosive growth of population, much of it probably by immigration from the surrounding area. Numerous large pueblos (for example, the Swarts and Mattocks ruins) were established, each probably housing several hundred persons. Spaced between these centers were smaller pueblos with no more than 100 occupants.

Mimbres-phase pottery has long received attention because of the attractive human and animal depictions on some of the black-on-white bowls. As the demand among collectors for these esthetically appealing artifacts has increased, so has the destruction of Mimbres sites. Looters seeking these trophies have badly damaged virtually all Mimbres-phase sites, and have obliterated some. Many questions about the cultural context of this important art tradition must now remain forever unanswered.

LeBlanc (1976) argues that Mimbres-phase development is related to the rise of Chacoan trade with Mexico, with the strategically located Mimbreños playing an intermediary role. Production of the special pictorial pottery may have been supported by groups or individuals who had acquired power and rank by virtue of their role in the trade system.

LeBlanc (1980) also suggests that the rapid depopulation of the Mimbres Valley at 1130–1150 may have been related to the decline of Chaco and the rise of Casas Grandes as a major trading center. He believes that the adobe pueblos of his Black Mountain phase (about 1150–1300) represent a reoccupation of the Mimbres associated with expansion of the "Casas Grandes interactive sphere" (LeBlanc, 1980:803). After a hiatus of several generations, there is a brief occupation in the Cliff phase (AD 1375–1425). The Cliff phase, centered in the upper Gila drainage west of the Mimbres (LeBlanc and Nelson, 1976), has a number of Salado rather than Casas Grandes characteristics. Its external affinities may be with the Civano-phase developments in the Hohokam area.

Casas Grandes

Since the early days of Southwestern archeology (for example, Bandelier, 1892; Kidder, 1924), the Casas Grandes district in northern Chihuahua (not to be confused with the Classic Hohokam site of Casa Grande in Arizona) has commanded attention as being potentially of great importance. It was not until 1958–1961, however, that extensive scientific excavations were conducted, by Charles DiPeso of the Amerind Foundation, in cooperation with Mexico's Instituto Nacional de Antropologio y Historia (DiPeso, 1974).

DiPeso documents a long cultural sequence in the Casas Grandes area. The early, or Viejo, period is Mogollon-related, but most interest centers on his Medio period, which dates between 1060 and 1340. This period is dominated by an outpost of Mesoamerican civilization, a city called *Paquime,* which was at the height of its size and influence during the 1200s. LeBlanc argues for a somewhat compressed chronology for the Medio period, dating it AD 1150 to 1300. These dates would place the ascendency of Casas Grandes after Chaco and Mimbres and before Civano-phase Hohokam.

DiPeso argues convincingly that Paquime was the economic and administrative center of the approximately 77,000-square-kilometer Casas Grandes region. Within this region, integrated systems of check dams and other devices controlled runoff and held the soil in order to increase agricultural productivity. Systems of fortresses, trails, wayhouses, and signal towers also indicate central planning and administration. During the early 1200s, Paquime covered approximately 36.5 hectares, had about 1600 rooms, and probably housed over 2200 people. Sophisticated planning and technical skills were used to construct single- and multiple-storied apartment buildings, a marketplace, ceremonial mounds, ball courts, public plazas, and a water-supply and drainage system.

Abundant evidence shows that the Paquimeans traded extensively with the Southwestern hinterlands to the north and with Mexican cities to the south. The items traded were primarily marine shells, shell ornaments, ceramics, minerals (especially turquoise), and exotic birds such as macaws. DiPeso believes that Paquime was built and maintained as a trading center by *pochteca* or merchant groups from the south, who derived much of their influence over the indigenous populations from their roles as bearers of attractive Mesoamerican religious cults. From this perspective, Casas Grandes is an outpost of Mexican civilization, and the Southwest is part of the Gran Chichimeca, Mesoamerica's northern frontier. With some exceptions, Southwesternists have tended to treat Mesoamerica as a vague presence, both geographically and culturally remote. The Casas Grandes data, plus Haury's (1976) strong case for Mexican origins of the Hohokam tradition, have made this "isolationist" view unsupportable.

The Anasazi

Although the precise linkages in most cases remain to be demonstrated, it seems clear that the Anasazi tradition is in varying degrees ancestral to the cultures of the modern Pueblo Indians, such as the Hopi, Zuni, and Rio Grande groups. This historical continuity has resulted in numerous analogs between archeological and recent Pueblo cultures, which have greatly enriched our understanding of the archeological record (Anderson, 1969). This valuable source of inference must, of course, be used judiciously; historic and prehistoric pueblos differed in some major ways, and cultural forms that have continued into the ethnographic present do not necessarily retain the functions they had prehistorically.

At its earlier end (about AD 1), the Anasazi tradition appears to have emerged from local Archaic antecedents such as Oshara (Irwin-Williams, 1973, 1979), though it can be argued (Berry, in press) that population movement into the area from the south contributed to the process. Traits generally considered as distinctly Anasazi come from the main part of the sequence, between about AD 500 and 1300. Expectably, not all these traits last throughout this span or appear in all subareas. Nevertheless, the following comprise convenient markers for the tradition.

Anasazi pottery was built up by coiling, finished by scraping, and fired in an oxygen-poor or reducing atmosphere that gave it a gray to white color. In some areas, an oxidized red or orange ware was also made. The gray vessels are often decorated with black geometric designs over a white slip. By about AD 1000, unpainted "utility" pots generally receive a textured surface called *corrugation* (see Figure 10.16); the unsmoothed coil marks were systematically pinched to achieve the effect. Full-grooved stone axes and flexed inhumations are also typically Anasazi, as are stone masonry "apartment houses" or pueblos and semisubterranean ceremonial rooms called *kivas* (see Figure 10.15).

Although wild plant foods (including common garden or abandoned-garden weeds such as chenopods and amaranths) were undoubtedly relied on heavily at times, most Anasazi appear to have made a serious commitment to maize–bean–squash horticulture, at least by AD 600. Ditch irrigation from perennial streams was developed in the Rio Grande area in late prehistoric times, and perhaps was present at a few other places earlier (see Moorehead, 1908:258). In general, however, the Anasazi depended on dry farming and on runoff or flood-water farming. The former method places primary dependence on direct rainfall, while the latter encompasses techniques of planting in washes, at the bases of slopes, or in other places where runoff from showers augments precipitation (Bryan, 1929, 1941). Check dams, lines of stones running across slopes, water diversion walls and ditches, and other structures were used in various locales to control runoff or retard erosion (Stewart, 1940a; Rohn, 1963; Vivian, 1974; Woosley, 1980). With either direct rainfall or runoff techniques, the Anasazi relied on soil moisture accumulated during winter and spring to germinate the plants and carry them through the May–June dry period. Then, additional water from July and August thunderstorms was necessary to mature the crops.

Under these conditions, Anasazi farming was often a hazardous venture. At elevations high enough for dry farming, the growing season was often less than 120–130 days, too short for unirrigated maize in areas having cool nights. Runoff farming based on small watersheds was risky because of the spotty distribution of summer storms. Larger valleys flooded more reliably and held moisture in alluvial flood plains, but were also more subject to violent floods, silting, or arroyo-cutting erosion—all of which could destroy crops.

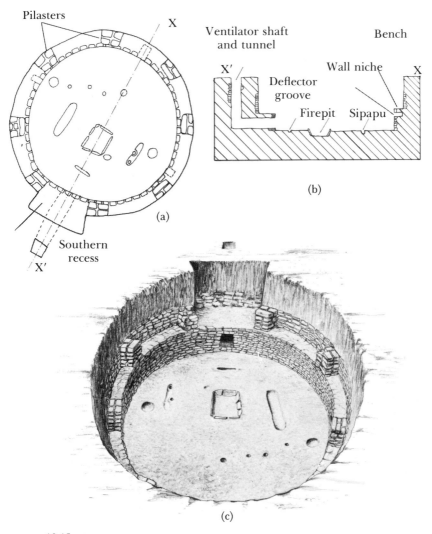

Pilasters

X

Ventilator shaft
and tunnel

Bench

X'

Deflector
groove

Wall niche

X

Firepit   Sipapu

(b)

Southern
recess

X'

(a)

(c)

FIGURE 10.15
Pueblo II kiva at Mesa Verde National Park: (a) plan view; (b) cross-section; (c) view of excavated kiva.

By Basketmaker III times, several regional variants of Anasazi culture can be recognized. These local traditions are most distinct, however, in the Pueblo II and III periods. They include the Rio Grande; Chaco, in northwestern New Mexico; Cibola in the upper Little Colorado drainage; Mesa Verde, in southwestern Colorado and southeastern Utah; Kayenta, in northeastern Arizona; and Virgin, in the "Arizona Strip" north of the Grand Canyon.

Compared to other areas of North America, the chronology of the Anasazi area is well understood, because dendrochronology is applicable over most of the area and has been used to date many pottery types (Breternitz, 1966) and sites

FIGURE 10.16

Pueblo II and III artifacts: (a) wickerwork sandal of yucca leaves; (b) bone scrapers; (c) wooden comb; (d) stone pipe; (e) ring basket of twilled yucca leaves; (f) fully corrugated utility vessel; (g) spindles with whorls and a distaff of spun yarn; (h) black-on-white bowl; (i) black-on-white ladle; (j) digging stick with sheep-horn blade (restored); (k) black-on-orange bowl; (l) partially corrugated utility vessel.

(for example, Bannister, Robinson, and Warren, 1970). The 1927 Pecos Conference periods (Kidder, 1927) have generally agreed-upon dates, and are still widely used as convenient temporal units, a practice we follow here. Their original developmental characterizations have, however, been largely disregarded in favor of local phase sequences on the one hand and of more analytical approaches to cultural change on the other. Interestingly, Berry (in press) has recently argued that the Pecos periods are not arbitrary segments of a cultural continuum, but that they are separated by major droughts, and hence by population movements and rapid cultural changes.

BASKETMAKER II (AD 1–450) □ Basketmaker I was a hypothetical preagricultural stage postulated by the framers of the Pecos classification (Kidder, 1927). This label was never applied; by the time cultures of this type were identified in the southern Plateau, the concept of an Archaic stage had gained currency. The term *Basketmaker II,* however, is still applied to a series of early Anasazi manifestations thinly scattered over the southern Plateau. Best known are the Durango shelters of southwestern Colorado (Morris and Burgh, 1954); the Los Pinos and En Medio phases of northwestern New Mexico (Eddy, 1961; Irwin-Williams, 1973); the Marsh Pass caves and Black Mesa open sites of northeastern Arizona (Guernsey and Kidder, 1921; Gumerman and Euler, 1976); the Grand Gulch and Kanab regions of southeastern Utah (Pepper, 1902; Lipe and Matson, 1971a, b; Nusbaum et al., 1922); the Moapa phase of the Virgin River area in Arizona and Nevada (Shutler, 1961); and the Hay Hollow Valley of east–central Arizona (Martin, 1967, 1972).

The considerable diversity among these sites suggests variation both in cultural antecedents and in environmental adaptations. For example, the river flood plain-oriented small villages of the Los Pinos and Moapa phases may indicate rather more sedentary adaptations than do the other manifestations. In general, however, Basketmaker II appears adaptively transitional between the Archaic and later patterns. The simple circular-plan houses, ranging from deep pithouses in the west to surface structures in the east, occurred only sporadically, and villages as such were rare and small. Maize and squash were cultivated to some extent, but beans apparently were not. Wild plant foods—including seeds of grasses, chenopods, amaranths, composites, and piñon—were important, as was hunting. Settlements were generally in areas that had soil and water adequate for farming, but that also gave easy access to several different environmental zones for hunting and gathering. Typical southeastern Utah settlement patterns include large base camps or "villages" of a few widely spaced houses near canyon-head springs, plus numerous scattered and probably seasonal limited-activity sites (Matson and Lipe, 1978; Dohm, 1981). Natural shelters were often used for storage and for burial of the dead, and sometimes for camps. Storage in caves was in large jar-shaped unlined pits dug into hard cave floors, or in slab-and-mud cists placed in soft fill or among boulders.

Pottery is lacking, except at a few southern and eastern locations. There it is generally a Mogollon-like brown ware, rather than the gray ware characteristic later on. Containers are typically those suited to a mobile lifestyle and to exploitation of wild plant foods—well-made twined bags and a variety of coiled baskets. The latter include large winnowing trays, conical collecting baskets, and bowls: hence the label *Basketmaker* (see McNitt, 1957). Hunters employed the atlatl, with compound darts that had hardwood foreshafts tipped with large side or corner-notched points. Curved throwing sticks, large rabbit nets, and various types of snares were also used. Milling equipment was Archaic-style basin grinding slabs and cobble manos; heavy millingstones that approach troughed metates occur at some base camps. Domestic dogs were present. Turkey remains appear, but it is not clear whether these animals had been domesticated at this time.

BASKETMAKER III (AD 450–700/750) □ A shift in settlement pattern, and probably in adaptation, marks this period in most Anasazi areas. Sites tend to be near deep, well-watered soils, both in the alluvial valleys and the uplands, regardless of ease of access to diverse environments. The obvious inference is that agriculture had become more important. Isolated "homesteads," small hamlets, and villages occur; some of the latter have more than 50 structures. At the Gilliland site in southwestern Colorado, Rohn (1975) has excavated an encircling stockade. Whether such a stockade was a regular feature is not known, because the extensive excavations that would test for it have generally not been done at other sites.

The typical dwelling is a circular to rectangular-plan pithouse. Small surface storage structures of poles and mud (jacal) with slab wall footings usually occur north or northwest of the pithouse. Exceptionally large pithouses, probably for assembly and/or ceremony, may have been early great kivas. Arrangement of structures in the villages does not follow an obvious overall plan.

Beans were added to the domesticated plant list, and turkeys were definitely kept. By the end of the period, the bow and arrow had begun to replace the atlatl and dart. Coiled baskets and twined bags continue, but pottery was universally used as well. The common types are plain gray jars and bowls; some are decorated with simple black designs. In southeastern Utah, red-on-orange pottery, reminiscent of some Mogollon types, appears by the end of the period (Brew, 1946). Troughed metates generally replace the earlier grinding slabs, and larger, "two-hand" manos appear.

PUEBLO I (AD 700/750–900) □ Population, though perhaps greater, appears to have been less uniformly distributed during this period than in Basketmaker III; some areas gained population and became very densely settled, but others were abandoned. In general, the larger site clusters appear to occur at relatively high elevations and/or in association with relatively large, alluvium-filled valleys. Though in clusters, most individual settlements are small—but some, such as Site 13 on Alkali Ridge in Utah (Brew, 1946), have over 200 structures.

Great kivas appear fairly frequently. DeBloois (1975) reports numerous high-altitude one-room surface structures from southeastern Utah. Probably seasonally occupied farmhouses, these may have been associated with more permanent settlements in the nearby Comb Wash valley.

Diversity characterizes dwelling arrangements as well as settlement type. During the period, domestic activities increasingly take place in surface structures as well as pit structures, some of which also begin to assume the role of kivas, or subterranean ceremonial chambers (Brew, 1946:203–226; Lipe and Breternitz, 1980; Gillespie, 1976) (Figure 10.15). Surface structures become larger and are used for habitation as well as for storage. Most surface construction is of jacal but, by the end of the period, masonry is being used in some areas. These trends seem clearest in the Mesa Verde and Chacoan areas.

Pottery is better finished and more diversified. Decorated vessels have been carefully polished and often slipped before being painted. On utility vessels, the upper coils of clay have often been left unsmoothed to produce a "neck-banded" effect. Cotton was added to the list of domesticated plants, and true loom weaving appears. Finger-woven items such as twined bags and sandals decrease in quantity and quality. Small coiled baskets continue, but the large carrying baskets and winnowing trays apparently are no longer made.

Some early workers thought that a long-headed Basketmaker population was replaced by a short-skulled, Puebloan one. This physical difference was found to be due instead to a cultural practice that started in Pueblo I times—the artificial flattening of infants' skulls by placing a wooden "pillow" in their cradleboards.

PUEBLO II (AD 900–1150) □ Many unoccupied or previously abandoned areas were settled at this time; the Anasazi reached their maximum geographic distribution and, probably, their population peak. The increasingly Anasazi character of the Mogollon tradition during this period may have been caused by the southward drift of Anasazi groups, although such a drift has not been fully demonstrated.

The Pueblo II peak may well have been the cumulative result of the successful integration of a horticultural adaptive strategy during the preceding few centuries, but there may have been other "kickers" as well. Galinat and Gunnerson (1963) argue that a more productive highland maize was introduced to the Plateau between about AD 700 and 1000. The tree-ring record (Dean and Robinson, 1977) indicates that the period from 850 to 1150 was generally stable, with few profound droughts and several relatively wet periods. There is also some palynological evidence of relatively warm temperatures and increased summer rain between about AD 800 and 1100 or 1200 (Schoenwetter and Eddy, 1964; Petersen, 1981). Using geological, tree-ring, and palynological evidence in concert, Euler and his colleagues (1979: Figure 5) postulate a relatively wet period between about AD 900 and 1400, interrupted by a dry interval in the 1100s. Baerreis and Bryson (1965), largely on the basis of extrapolation from outside the Southwest, suggest that the period from about AD 850 to about 1250 was characterized by warm temperatures and strong summer rains. In sum, the paleoclimatic evidence suggests relatively favorable climates for agriculturalists at least up to about AD 1150 or 1200.

Certainly, the Pueblo II site distribution suggests favorable climatic conditions. The larger sites, which had generally been founded earlier, tended to be near the best-watered soils. Many of the smaller, newer sites, on the other hand, were in upland areas very marginal or impossible to farm today and where even domestic water supplies are now rare. Implied is a substantial dependence on dry farming or on runoff from small watersheds under conditions more favorable than today's. Various water and soil control systems, which would have increased the farming potential in some of these areas, appear here and there by mid-Pueblo II. These systems include check dams in washes, terraces and stone grids on slopes, and reservoirs and ditches for household water (Rohn, 1963; Vivian, 1974).

Although jacal continues as a structural alternative in many areas, masonry is increasingly dominant. Small unit pueblos, which had appeared in Pueblo I, become very common; these consist of a small block of surface habitation and storage rooms, with a kiva and trash area to the south or southeast. The larger pueblos, some of which have over 100 rooms, generally appear to be agglomerations of such units, each of which probably housed an extended family or minimal lineage.

Kivas have circular floor plans, are fully masonry-lined, and display all or most of the "typical" kiva features: central firepit, deflector, ventilator shaft, encircling bench, pilasters, southern recess, sipapu, and wall niches (Figure 10.15). Great kivas continue. Their locations in the largest sites, or as isolated structures within site clusters, suggest community integrative functions. Grebinger (1973) and F. Plog (1974) suggest that one such function may have been economic redistribution and that the small rooms sometimes built adjacent to great kivas were storehouses.

Pottery styles continue their florescence, as painted designs become more varied and complex, and corrugation textures the outsides of utility vessels (Figure 10.16). Ring baskets of twilled yucca leaves increasingly supplant the more durable but harder-to-make coiled baskets.

THE CHACOAN PHENOMENON ☐ Anomalous in the general context of Pueblo II development are the Chacoan settlements of the San Juan Basin, in northwestern New Mexico and southwestern Colorado. Near the center of this region is Chaco Canyon, an alluvium-filled valley about 15 kilometers long. Between about AD 900 and the mid-1100s, this canyon supported at least nine large "town" pueblos of several hundred rooms each (Vivian, 1970) plus several hundred "villages" or typical small- to medium-sized pueblos of 10 to 20 rooms each. The towns such as Pueblo Bonito (Figures 10.17 and 10.18) were tiered multistoried complexes standing as much as four stories at the back wall. The walls are a rubble masonry core with a veneer or facing of well-fitted thin, tabular pieces of stone. Both the initial building and subsequent additions ap-

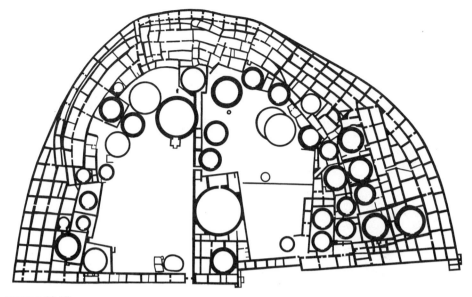

FIGURE 10.17
Ground plan of Pueblo Bonito.

pear to have been done to preconceived plans, and a high degree of uniformity in masonry styles and building techniques is evident from town to town. Furthermore, thousands of large roofing beams were brought in from highland areas as far as 75 kilometers away. Rooms were exceptionally large and high-ceilinged. Many of the large sites are associated with complex runoff control systems, including diversion dams, distribution canals and ditches, and bordered garden plots; these systems presumably retained and spread water provided by major summer thunderstorms (Vivian, 1974). Also incorporated in or associated with the town sites are stylistically formalized great kivas ranging up to 25 meters in diameter.

That straight "roads" up to nine meters in width were associated with some of the Chaco Canyon town sites had been known for some time (Judd, 1954), but studies using various types of aerial photo imagery have recently shown them to be much more extensive than had been previously thought (Lyons and Hitchcock, 1977). Though only fragments have been mapped so far, it appears that a system of roads radiated out from Chaco Canyon, linking this center with outlying Chacoan sites located throughout the San Juan Basin and perhaps up to 190 kilometers away.

These Chacoan "outliers," of which at least 50 are known (Marshall et al., 1979:332–333), have from several tens to several hundreds of rooms. All share a number of characteristics—both general (for example, preplanned construction) and specific (for example, masonry style, kiva features)—with one another, and with the large pueblos of Chaco Canyon proper. The outliers tend to occur on prominences, and are generally associated with clusters of smaller pueblos. As

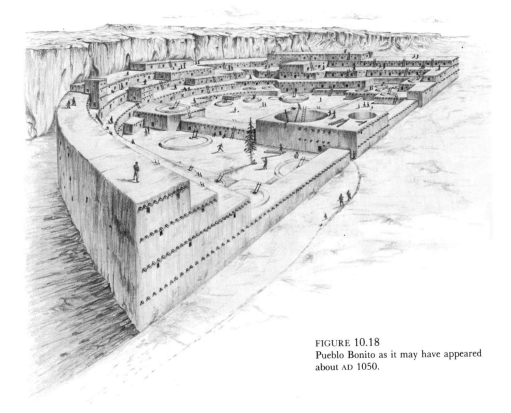

FIGURE 10.18
Pueblo Bonito as it may have appeared
about AD 1050.

at Chaco Canyon, the large sites contrast markedly with the smaller pueblos in architecture and layout. Marshall and his coworkers (1979) refer to these Chacoan sites as *public buildings* rather than *towns,* because they think they may have been used more as storage, ritual, and perhaps administrative centers than as residences.

Numerous theories have been proposed to account for the Chacoan system; the causes proposed range from the work of Mexican *pochteca* (DiPeso, 1968a, b) to the rise of indigenous elites due to their control of good lands and runoff distribution systems (Grebinger, 1973, 1978). Most recent is the model currently emerging from the work of the National Park Service's Chaco Research Center (Judge, 1979; Judge et al., 1981). This work suggests that the Chacoan sites served as centers for redistributive exchange of food and probably craft products, that the system improved the participants' access to resources differentially distributed within the region, and that it buffered the effects on food supply of extreme spatial and temporal variability of rainfall. Exotic items, including some from Mesoamerica, entered the system, but were not its main focus.

Judge and his colleagues (1981) recognize that substantial administrative control and systematization are implied by the redistributive system they propose, as well as by the characteristics of the Chacoan buildings themselves. They argue, however, that, while a chiefdom or other type of stratified society may have been present, it is not necessarily implied by the exchange system they postulate. In any case, they maintain, evidence to date of social inequality is too scanty to support such an inference.

The Chacoan system seems to have been at its peak between about 1020 and 1120, and to have declined in the mid 1100s. Many of the Chacoan outliers were reoccupied in the 1200s by Mesa-Verde-branch Anasazi (Pippin, 1979; Irwin-Williams and Shelley, 1980), but it appears that they no longer functioned as parts of a regional system. There is no consensus on what caused the Chacoan system to collapse, but it seems likely that it was unable to cope with increasing droughts and climatic variability.

PUEBLO III (AD 1150–1300) □ This period saw much population movement (Euler et al., 1979: Figure 2) and the aggregation of population into fewer, but larger, pueblos in fewer, but more densely settled, locations. In many areas, the people moved from open locations to shelters and ledges in canyon walls (Figure 10.19). Some such "cliff dweller" sites are difficult to reach and appear to have been located for defensive purposes. In addition, features which suggest defense are fairly common, though certainly not universal: loopholes in walls flanking entries, walls restricting access to ledges, and large towers. The towers are often attached by tunnels to kivas, and may have had ceremonial functions instead of, or in addition to, defensive ones. Despite these indications of anxiety at some sites, there is little evidence of actual hostilities.

In several areas, pottery reached a peak of technical and artistic quality. Corn-grinding equipment was improved, as flat metates set in mealing bins generally replaced troughed metates.

Social changes were occurring in concert with the formation of larger villages. In the Tsegi phase (1250–1300) of the Kayenta area, Dean (1970) notes the lack of association between kivas and habitation units in the large sites of Betatakin and Kiet Siel. He proposes that kivas had by this time lost their association with localized lineage segments, and had come to serve larger, non-localized groups such as clans or ceremonial sodalities—much as they do in Hopi society, to which the Tsegi phase is in part ancestral. Such new associations for kivas may have been promoted by needs in the larger communities for institutions that would crosscut and hence integrate the memberships of the diverse small, kin-based groups that had moved into the village. Dean's analysis lends support to Eggan's (1950) earlier reconstruction of the evolution of Hopi society.

During Pueblo III, Anasazi groups were gradually moving south and southeast; by AD 1300, their original Plateau homeland had been largely abandoned except for its southern margins. Gaining population in the 1200s were the Hopi

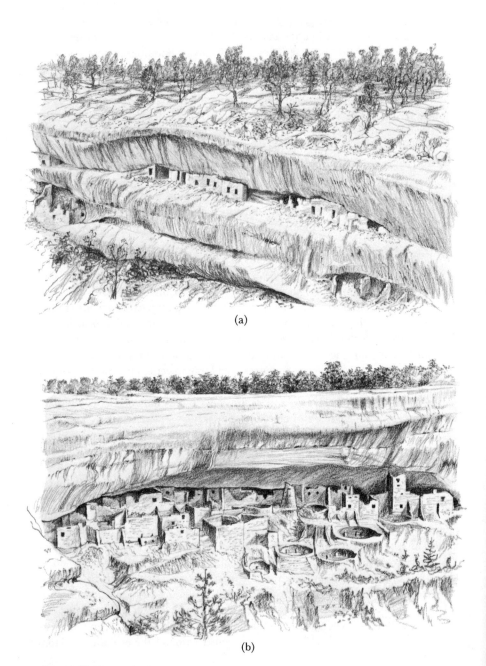

(a)

(b)

FIGURE 10.19
Pueblo III cliff dwellings, Mesa Verde: (a) Double House; (b) Cliff Palace.

mesas, the Cibola area near what are now the Zuni and Acoma towns, parts of the Mogollon Highlands, and the Rio Grande valley.

PUEBLO IV (AD 1300–1600) □ Cliff dwellings became less common as groups moved away from canyon areas. Some sites were built on defensible outcrops or mesas, but the communities had expanded to the point where their size alone probably gave protection. By late Pueblo IV, towns of 200 to 2000 were the norm, and the small villages that had typified most of Anasazi prehistory were no more.

The southward and eastward shift of population continued and, by 1450, the Mogollon Highlands had been abandoned along with virtually all of the Plateau. By the end of Pueblo IV, the Pueblo peoples occupied approximately their present locations, except for the lower Rio Grande settlements, which declined somewhat later (Kelley, 1952). Tracing Pueblo III and Pueblo IV population movements and identifying the cultural ancestry of historic Puebloans has occupied much scholarly energy (for example, Ellis, 1967; Ford et al., 1972). Although some partial correlations have been made (for example, the strong Kayenta contribution to Hopi), it is apparent that there were no simple one-to-one transformations of Pueblo III groups into historic Pueblos, perhaps because the migrants generally moved in very small groups and often became integrated into already existing host communities.

Extensive kiva wall murals (Smith, 1952; Dutton, 1963) give evidence of ceremonial elaboration during Pueblo IV. The kachina cult probably developed its present complexity at this time (Brew, 1944; Schaafsma and Schaafsma, 1974). Mexican influences appear strong, but the ceremonial system itself appears to be a Pueblo product, not a total import. The new pottery styles that spread during Pueblo IV also show southern influences, including curvilinear, stylized parrot motifs.

THE WESTERN PUEBLO TRADITION □ Sometime during late Pueblo II or Pueblo III, the Mogollon tradition ceased to exist as a separate cultural entity. Some (such as Rouse, 1962) consider it to have been absorbed into the Anasazi tradition, while others (such as Reed, 1950) see the emergence of a new entity—Western Pueblo culture—in the Cibola-Mogollon Highlands area, as a result of the Anasazi-Mogollon merger. Johnson (1965) argues for Hohokam contribution to Western Pueblo as well. The archeological marker traits of this new tradition include organization of large pueblos around plazas or multiple courtyards, rectangular small kivas, brown-ware pottery (often slipped with red or white), three-quarter-grooved stone axes, and extened supine inhumation (Johnson, 1965:vi). Western Pueblo culture is thought to have contributed heavily to the development of historic Hopi and Zuni–Acoma culture and perhaps to some of the Rio Grande groups as well, while other Rio Grande groups were direct inheritors of the Anasazi tradition that stemmed largely from the Mesa Verde and Chaco areas. Johnson (1965) also sees Western Pueblo as contributing to the Salado phenomenon in the Hohokam area.

PUEBLO ABANDONMENT OF THE PLATEAU: A CONTINUING PROBLEM □ The Plateau's empty ruins have stirred the imaginations of generations of travelers and scholars. Many theories have been advanced to account for the abandonment of this once-populous region (Jett, 1964). The principal ones are reviewed below.

Perhaps the earliest theory to be proposed was that "hostile nomads" had driven the Puebloans from their homes. Presumably these aggressors were the ancestors of the nomadic peoples who were occupying much of the northern Southwest when the Spanish explorers arrived: the Athapaskan-speaking Navajo and Apache, the Numic-speaking Paiute and Ute, and the Yuman-speaking Havasupai and Walapai. Although this theory is in accord with the defensive nature of some Pueblo III sites, almost no archeological evidence to support it has so far been forthcoming. It is becoming increasingly clear that the Athapaskans did not come into the area until a century or more after the Puebloans had left (Hester, 1962; Wilcox, n.d.; Gunnerson, 1979). The Numic peoples were in contact with the westernmost Anasazi by 1100 (Shutler, 1961; Madsen, 1975), but eastward Numic expansion seems to have followed Anasazi abandonment. The post-1150 northeastward movement of Cerbat Branch Yumans (Euler and Gumerman, 1974:303) did not actually reach Anasazi territory.

Interpueblo warfare has been suggested to account for defensive sites (Linton, 1944), but it is difficult to see how small-scale raiding and feuding could have led to depopulation of a large region (Jett, 1964:296). More plausible, but undemonstrated, is Davis' (1965) suggestion that disruptions of whatever sort on the northern margins of the Anasazi area might have had a snowballing effect, as refugees put pressure on previously unaffected communities.

Climatic change has often been invoked as a cause. Early tree-ring workers (Douglass, 1929) recognized very narrow rings in the late 1200s, thought to represent a "Great Drought" coincident with abandonment of the large cliff dwellings of the Four Corners area. It soon became clear, however, that most Plateau areas had already been abandoned by this time. The tree-ring record (Fritts et al., 1965) also reveals several serious earlier droughts that were not accompanied by such widespread abandonment.

The discovery that arroyo-cutting in alluvial valleys was probably widespread during Pueblo III times (Bryan, 1941, 1954; Hack, 1942) sparked hope that a general explanation was at hand. Further work, however, showed that many Pueblo groups did not depend on alluvial soils, and that the Hopi country was receiving population at a time when arroyos were active there.

It might be argued that organizational change toward larger communities required the support of intensified agriculture. This requirement could be provided through stream irrigation—hence the move to the Rio Grande. Most of the Pueblo III population gain in the central Rio Grande was not, however, in areas where irrigation could easily have been practiced (Dickson 1975, 1979), nor was stream irrigation feasible in most other areas that were receiving population. Furthermore, as Woosley (1980) points out, no great organizational and technological complexity is required for the sort of stream irrigation carried out historically in the Southwest; some of the runoff diversion systems on the Plateau were probably as demanding.

In conclusion, it appears that none of these theories is in itself sufficient to account for the population movements that occurred. Joining the numerous other students of this problem, I offer below a speculative model based on a combination of factors.

A MODEL OF PUEBLO RELOCATION □ During Pueblo II times, relatively stable climate and ample summer moisture appear to have supported population increases and the occupation of marginal uplands on an essentially dry-farming basis. An additional inch or two of summer precipitation might not have greatly improved flood-water farming in the larger drainages, but it could have opened up large areas of the Plateau to dry farming or small-watershed runoff techniques. Unfortunately for the farmers, such areas can also be suddenly closed off by small losses of moisture. That a period of difficulty for upland farmers probably started in the 1100s is documented by Petersen's (1981) recent palynological work in southwestern Colorado. His results indicate that climates in that area became markedly cooler and drier (the summers becoming drier as well) about 1150 and that these conditions essentially prevailed until the late 1800s. Jorde (1977), using tree-ring data from the northern Plateau, documents a shift after about AD 1050 to a longer periodicity in rainfall variation, which led to longer droughts.

In previous periods of climatic difficulty, groups exploiting marginal lands had probably been able to move back into more favored areas, including the larger alluvial valleys. When conditions for upland farming deteriorated at about AD 1100–1150, however, populations in both the marginal and favored situations were too great for all to be supported in the latter locations. Furthermore, many alluvial valleys were probably being affected by a cycle of arroyo-cutting that lowered their ability to support population. Dean and his coworkers (1978:27–28), for example, discuss the deleterious effects on farming of the arroyo-cutting that began about AD 1150 in Long House Valley, northeastern Arizona. Not only was soil lost, but the water table of the alluvial flood plain dropped to levels beyond the reach of the roots of crop plants.

The resulting squeeze on land and water would have led to competition and, probably, to some raiding. One response was defensive structures and site locations, but a more effective response was increased community size, which was also favored by the concentration of population into the remaining habitable areas. Larger communities may also have facilitated intensification of food production by cooperative effort, and/or buffering of the effects of stress by wider exchange of food and other resources. A more direct response to the adaptive stress was movement to areas where summer rainfall had always been heavier and more reliable—to the south and east. This process was already under way and was probably only accelerated by the Pueblo III adaptive difficulties.

Increasing community size may also have promoted movement. Because of the Plateau's topographic complexity, arable soils and other resources are often distributed in an extremely discontinuous, patchy way, a characteristic that would be increased by drought. Such environments are not very amenable to support of large nucleated communities. The locations where the Puebloans finally settled tend to have good water supplies and relatively broad, open valleys, where fairly large expanses of arable soil lie close to settlements and where surveillance of fields from a distance is often possible. These conditions are rare in most parts of the Plateau, particularly in the Four Corners area.

In addition to defensive needs, the ceremonial elaboration that occurred in late Pueblo III and Pueblo IV times may also have promoted increased community size. The adaptive difficulties Puebloans were experiencing may have made them receptive to adopting or developing new ceremonies in search of supernatural assistance. In this context, the Tlaloc, or Mexican water deity, elements in the emerging Pueblo IV kachina cult (Brew, 1944) are not surprising. Successful operation of an elaborated ceremonial system requires more personnel and social categories, however, than would ordinarily be available in very small villages. Pueblo ceremonies may also have aided adaptation directly by providing a certain amount of food redistribution and by regulating the scheduling of economic activities (Ford, 1972). And the integrative functions of ceremonial systems in helping tie together politically and perhaps ethnically fragmented communities have long been recognized (Eggan, 1950). Whatever its contribution to the development of larger communities, the Pueblo IV ceremonial elaboration probably helped maintain them.

The Hakataya

This tradition consists of a number of rather widely differing and generally poorly known archeological manifestations in the southwestern part of the Plateau, the lower Colorado River valley and adjacent low deserts, and the transition zone between these lowland and highland areas. The appearance of pottery between AD 500 and 800 in the highlands, and probably several hundred years earlier in the lowlands, marks the tradition's emergence. Ancestry in local Late Archaic cultures is likely, but remains undemonstrated. Most of the area occupied by the Hakataya was in historic times the territory of Yuman speakers; the archeological manifestations were in fact originally referred to as *Yuman* (W. Gladwin and Gladwin, 1934). Although historical continuity between certain archeological Hakataya groups and historic Yumans seems probable, it has been considered unwise to give the archeological materials a linguistic or ethnographic label (Colton, 1938).

The Hakataya tradition is characterized by pottery finished by paddle-and-anvil techniques. Primarily a brown ware, it has regional gray or buff variants as well. Most pottery is plain, but simple painted designs appear in some areas, generally in the later periods. Subsistence adaptations range from primary dependence on a mix of farming, gathering, and fishing in riverine areas to primary dependence on hunting and gathering in some of the highland situations (such as among the Cerbat). The mortar and pestle were commonly used in food-processing in the western areas, while grinding slabs and troughed metates tended to be used in the east. Stone-lined pits or ovens were widely employed in cooking, especially in the western and lower-lying areas. In the villages, rubbish was scattered unsystematically rather than being accumulated in trash mounds. Disposal of the dead was by cremation in some groups, inhumation in others.

THE RIVERINE HAKATAYA □ Because these lower Colorado River groups usually occupied flood plains or low terraces, their archeological traces have frequently been lost to erosion or alluviation. Settlement evidence to date suggests villages of individual houses widely scattered along the river. The houses are typically brush or jacal structures, square in plan, built on the surface or in shallow pits. Large community-assembly structures are sometimes present. Pottery is a buff or brown ware; a few vessels were decorated with simple designs in red.

Maize, tepary beans, and squash were watered by natural flooding of the broad river flood plains. The Mohave, a Yuman group that occupied part of the lower Colorado River valley in historic times, derived 40 to 50 percent of their subsistence from flood-plain farming; most of the remainder came from harvesting wild plants, especially mesquite, and from fishing (Castetter and Bell, 1951). Such ethnographically documented Yuman subsistence patterns can probably be extrapolated into at least the latter part of the archeological record.

THE UPLAND OR PATAYAN HAKATAYA □ *The Cohonina and Cerbat*   The Cohonina occupied the area south of the Grand Canyon between about AD 700 and 1150. Their small sites often consisted of only an artifact scatter or a single house. The houses range from shallow pithouses to surface structures outlined with boulders or a few courses of masonry; superstructures were probably of jacal. Frequently associated with houses are low-walled, unroofed "patios" or open-sided brush "shades" (McGregor, 1951), which often shelter the cooking hearth. Troughed metates and two-hand manos are more common than basin grinding slabs, suggesting that maize was an important subsistence item (McGregor, 1951). The typical Cohonina pottery is a plain gray ware; a few vessels have black-painted Anasazi-like designs. More commonly, decorated pottery was obtained in trade with the Anasazi.

Cohonina population reached a peak about AD 900–1100, then declined precipitously (Schwartz, 1956). Schwartz (1959) and McGregor (1967) have argued that the remaining Cohonina migrated to the Grand Canyon, and were ancestral to the Yuman-speaking Havasupai who still occupy the area. Euler (Euler and Gumerman, 1974) argues that another Hakataya group—the Cerbat—moved in from the west shortly after the Cohonina decline, and was ancestral to both the Havasupai and the closely related Walapai. The predominantly hunter–gatherer Cerbat made undecorated brown pottery and occupied rock-shelters or brush "wikiups." To date, the bulk of archeological, historical, and linguistic evidence favors Euler's theory.

The Prescott Branch This poorly known group occupied the highlands south of the Cohonina area (Spicer and Caywood, 1936; Euler and Dobyns, 1962; Barnett, 1970, 1974). Pithouses appear to have been replaced by surface masonry pueblos (Euler and Gumerman, 1974), probably in the 1100s; some pueblos were as large as 25 rooms (Barnett, 1974). The numerous masonry hill-top "forts" or lookouts found in the area may indicate a concern for possible hostilities. Subsistence patterns evidently include both maize agriculture and hunting and gathering. Local ceramics are plain brown and gray wares, some-times enhanced by simple designs in red or black. Pottery was also traded in from the Anasazi, Sinagua, and Hohokam area (James, 1974). The Prescott area seems to have been abandoned sometime between 1200 and 1300, but what happened to the population is unknown.

The Sinagua This tradition occupied the area around Flagstaff, Arizona, and the upper Verde Valley (Colton, 1939, 1946). About AD 1075, the eruption of Sunset Crater east of Flagstaff spread a blanket of volcanic cinders and ash over a large part of the northern Sinagua area. This event conveniently separates the substantially different preeruptive and posteruptive Sinagua patterns (Schroeder, 1961).

The preeruptive Sinagua occupied small pithouse villages. The earliest houses—about AD 500–700—tend to be shallow and round in plan, while the later ones were generally rectangular and deeper, with strong, timbered walls lining the interior. Maize farming was probably the major subsistence pursuit, with hunting and gathering secondary. The dominant pottery is Alameda Brown Ware, which remained characteristic of the Sinagua throughout. Deco-rated vessels were obtained in trade with neighboring groups: Anasazi in the north and both Anasazi and Hohokam in the Verde Valley (Breternitz, 1960).

After it produced a brief disruption, the Sunset Crater cinder fall is thought to have provided a moisture-conserving mulch that made the area more attrac-tive to dry-farmers (Colton, 1945b, 1949, 1960; Breternitz, 1967; Schaber and Gumerman, 1969; Berlin et al., 1977). The larger number of sites in the imme-diate posteruption period and the appearance of more Anasazi, Mogollon, and Hohokam traits have been used to suggest that there was immigration from neighboring areas at this time (for example, McGregor, 1965:298). Pilles (1978, 1979) argues, however, that local population increase, a shift to archeo-logically more visible Anasazi-style masonry pueblos, and more use of tempo-rary agricultural field houses account for the increase in numbers of sites better than does immigration.

In the northern area, evidence of Hohokam influence comes principally from Winona Village east of Flagstaff, where McGregor (1937, 1941) found

Hohokam-style houses as well as local types, copies of Hohokam red-on-buff pottery, a relative abundance of shell ornaments, cremations, and a ball court. Farther south, the Verde Valley was essentially an extension of Hohokam culture in the late 1000s and early 1100s (Breternitz, 1960).

By the late 1100s, Hohokam influence was receding and the Sinagua were coming under increasing Anasazi or Western Pueblo dominance. Population increasingly aggregated in a few large pueblos, and there was a general shift into the Verde Valley, where large sites such as Tuzigoot seem to have been occupied until the early 1400s. European explorers found the Verde Valley peopled by the Yuman-speaking Yavapai. Their relationship—or lack of it—to the earlier Sinagua–Western Pueblo population is entirely unknown.

The Fremont

This tradition occupied the eastern part of the Great Basin and the Northern Plateau, covering an area as extensive as that of any other late Southwestern tradition. If the presence of ceramics is used to distinguish Fremont from earlier Archaic cultures, then Fremont manifestations appear between about AD 400 and 800 in various parts of the region (Marwitt, 1970). Fremont manifestations disappear between about AD 1100 and 1350, with survival apparently longest in the Great Salt Lake area. Variability within Fremont is so great that some (such as Madsen, 1979) have argued that it should not be considered a single major tradition, but at least two—one on the Plateau and a second in the Basin. For the purposes of this brief review, I prefer to call all these manifestations *Fremont,* but I do not intend to imply a very high order of internal homogeneity or unity of culture history for the tradition.

The Fremont takes its name from the Fremont River drainage of east central Utah, where Morss (1931:76–77) recognized a "peripheral culture" related to but outside the "main stream of Southwestern development." Judd's pioneering work had earlier demonstrated that the village sites of central and western Utah also differed from those of the San Juan Anasazi, although certain general characteristics, such as gray pottery and maize agriculture, were shared (Judd, 1919, 1926).

Morss' reference to Fremont as "peripheral" is characteristic of the thinking of most early Southwesternists, who saw it as a hinterland or marginal expression of a basic Anasazi culture. As Fremont time depth and cultural characteristics have become better known, it has come to be treated as separate from and equivalent to Anasazi, Mogollon, and the like.

GENERAL CHARACTERISTICS □ Although Fremont clearly contrasts with the Anasazi to the south and with the hunting and gathering cultures to its west, north, and east, it is internally variable enough so that few traits are present in all areas or time periods. The following characteristics are sufficiently widespread, however, to distinguish Fremont as a whole from its neighbors.

Maize has been found in most excavated Fremont sites, while beans and squash occur frequently enough to indicate that they were regularly grown as well. In many Fremont sites there appears a variety of maize, with "dented" kernels, that probably developed as a local adaptation to the droughty conditions and short growing seasons of the area (Winter, 1973). Although subsistence strategies were undoubtedly specific to the farming and food-collecting potentials of each locality occupied, one gets the impression that, generally, hunting and gathering were more important to Fremont economics than was the case among the Anasazi. Hunting seems to have been particularly important for the occupants of the Uinta Basin and Great Salt Lake areas in the north; Madsen (1979, 1980; Madsen and Lindsay, 1977) also stresses the importance of marsh resources in the Basin. Given that summer rainfall weakens as one moves northwestward from the Four Corners area, it would not be surprising to find that agriculture was less reliable in the Fremont than in the Anasazi area. The location of many Fremont habitation sites on alluvial fans at the bases of mountain ranges, and in other situations where flowing streams occur, suggests that small-scale ditch irrigation might have been employed by some settlements. There are some early historical accounts of what may have been the remains of aboriginal ditches, but no conclusive evidence (Lohse, 1980:49).

Except for "mound" sites covering several hectares in the Parowan and Sevier areas of southwestern Utah, Fremont habitation sites tend to be small, having only one to a few houses. Even the largest sites may have had only a relatively small number of houses occupied at any one time (Marwitt, 1968, 1970). No settlements as populous as the larger Anasazi pueblos have been found. Limited-activity or "camp" sites tend to be common, and probably represent foraging activities of village dwellers. Fremont dwellings are typically pithouses, ranging from shallow to deep, and from circular to rectangular in plan. Both roof and lateral crawlway entries are found. Central hearths are regular features, but ventilator shafts of the sort found in later Anasazi pit structures are rare. Structures similar to Anasazi kivas are lacking. Surface storage structures of adobe or jacal are present in all but the Great Salt Lake area, and a few pueblolike masonry structures are found in the parts of the Plateau nearest the Anasazi area. Fremont settlements consist of scattered individual structures rather than compact pueblos or compounds; community-assembly structures such as the great kivas of the Anasazi and Mogollon appear to be absent.

Fremont pottery (Figure 10.20) is a gray ware, constructed by the coil-and-scrape technique, and thus generally similar to Anasazi ceramics. Vessel forms and decorative devices generally differ, however. Corrugation, which is so popular in Pueblo II and III Anasazi, is uncommon in Fremont sites; it is present only in the southern part of the area. Red and orange wares occur only as occasional trade items from the Anasazi. Unfired clay figurines (Figure 10.20 l, m), though never very abundant, occur in most Fremont areas and are especially elaborate in the southeastern, or San Rafael, area.

"Utah metates," which are troughed forms having a small depression or shelf

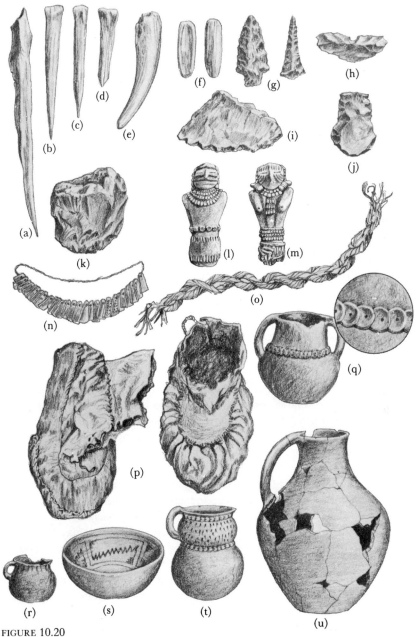

FIGURE 10.20
Artifacts of the Fremont culture: (a) bone splinter awl; (b–d) bone awls; (e) antler flaking tool; (f) bone gaming pieces; (g) projectile points; (h) shaft scraper; (i, j) scrapers; (k) rough hammerstone; (l, m) clay figurines; (n) bone necklace; (o) bark rope; (p) leather moccasins; (q) pot and enlarged view of appliqué treatment; (r) small pot; (s) black-on-white bowl; (t) pot with appliqué at rim and restricted waist; (u) plain grayware vessel.

at the closed end, are common. Large, well-executed pictographs of anthropo-morphs, often with elaborate headdresses and bodily ornamentation, have been found over much of the Fremont area; among these, certain horned and shield-bearing figures have been likened to northwestern Plains pictographs (Worm-ington, 1955; Aikens, 1966). Leather moccasins are reported from widely scat-tered areas. These are quite distinctive when contrasted with the ubiquitous fiber sandals of other Southwestern traditions. Fremont coiled and twined bas-ketry technology is similar throughout the area, and contrasts sharply with techniques used by adjacent traditions (Adovasio, 1979, 1980).

REGIONAL VARIATION □ Marwitt (1970) has documented five regional Fremont variants. In the Basin area, from north to south, are the Great Salt Lake (dating about AD 400–1350), Sevier (about AD 780–1260), and Parowan (about AD 900–1300). In the Plateau, from north to south, are the Uinta (about AD 650–950) and San Rafael (about AD 700–1200); the latter was Morss' (1931) original "Fremont culture." A systematic statistical analysis by Lohse (1980) indicates that these variants have a substantial empirical basis.

Madsen (1979; Madsen and Lindsay, 1977) and others (such as Worm-ington, 1955; Jennings, 1956; Gunnerson, 1969; Lohse, 1980) recognize that the greatest differences are between the Basin and Plateau dwellers. The next order of contrast is between the northern expressions (Salt Lake and, perhaps, Uinta) and the more southerly ones. The Parowan and Sevier variants appear most similar. Madsen (1979, 1980) and Lohse (1980) relate these patterns of contrast to basic differences in subsistence and settlement. The Sevier and Parowan groups appear to have made much use of (and perhaps to have pri-marily depended on) marsh resources such as cattail, the tuberous root of which is an excellent and prolific starch resource. The major sites of these variants are not only close to marsh areas, but also are often on alluvial fans, where runoff from the mountains would have provided enhanced soil moisture for agricul-ture. The Salt Lake variant in the north also appears to have relied on marsh resources, but there is little evidence of farming. Locations where farming vil-lages might have occurred have been extensively altered, however, by urban development along the Wasatch Front. On the Plateau, extensive marsh areas are rare; Madsen (1979, 1980) thinks that maize agriculture may have been more central to adaptations. Plateau village sites, generally smaller than those in the Parowan and Sevier areas, tend to be located on slight rises overlooking arable land and perennial sources of water (Lohse, 1980:50). As in the Basin, the northernmost Plateau sites show the most evidence of reliance on hunting.

FREMONT ORIGINS □ Several models of Fremont cultural origins have been proposed (see Marwitt, 1980). The earlier ones generally postulated var-ious waves of Anasazi influence or migration to account for Fremont develop-ment. The most recent of these is Gunnerson's (1962, 1969) hypothesis that the Fremont culture resulted from the northward movement of Anasazi Virgin

Branch people as part of the Anasazi Pueblo II expansion. Dates now available (Marwitt, 1970) show that the Fremont tradition was widely established several centuries earlier.

Evidence—including Plains-oriented traits such as bison hunting and the use of tipis, moccasins, and shields—led Aikens (1966) to argue that the early Fremont entered the Plateau from the Plains about AD 500. Although the hypothesis recognizes certain elements in Fremont culture that may well result from Plains contacts, it has not been generally accepted. Aikens now prefers to emphasize the local components in Fremont development (Aikens, 1970, 1972).

Marwitt (1970) and Jennings (1966, 1978) argue that, in the early centuries AD, the Archaic societies ancestral to both Anasazi and Fremont were affected by the rapid diffusion out of the Mogollon area of a cultural complex that included pottery, pithouse architecture, and, perhaps, improved varieties of maize. Later developments were largely based on local processes, although Anasazi influences were felt, particularly during the Pueblo II and early Pueblo III periods, in the southern part of the Fremont area.

The evidence for Archaic–Fremont continuity has been questioned by Madsen and Berry (1975), who posit a hiatus of 1000 to 2000 years between Late Archaic and early Fremont, at least in the Basin. Recent evidence from sites on the Plateau, however, indicates continuity between Late Archaic and at least eastern Fremont (Schroedl, 1976). Adovasio (1979) and Aikens (1976) argue for continuity in the Basin as well.

What happened to the Fremont? The Fremont tradition did not last much, if at all, past AD 1300, and it probably was contracting and consolidating after AD 1150. Several theories of what happened to the Fremont have been proposed, but none is very satisfactory.

Gunnerson (1962, 1969) has attempted to link both the Virgin-branch Anasazi and the Fremont with Numic-speaking Shoshonean and Paiute groups that occupied the Northern Plateau in historical times. Schroeder (1963) and Euler (1964) effectively point out the essentially complete lack of cultural continuity between the Numic speakers and their putative Fremont ancestors. They and Madsen (1975) also cite evidence that groups resembling the ethnographic Paiute were already present in the eastern Great Basin and in contact with the Fremont and Virgin-branch peoples by the 1100s; hence, they could not be the latter's descendents.

Aikens' hypothesis that the Fremont peoples moved to the northwestern Plains, where they founded the Dismal River culture (see Gunnerson, 1960) and eventually became Plains Apache, has not fared much better (Wedel, 1967; Husted and Mallory, 1967; Fry and Dalley, 1970). Sharrock (1966, quoted in Marwitt, 1970) has, however, found probable Fremont sherds associated with tipi rings in southwestern Wyoming; this discovery may lend some tentative support to a Plains dispersal route for the Fremont.

A third possibility is that the Fremont drifted south during the 1100s and 1200s, much as did the Anasazi and perhaps in response to similar pressures.

Positive evidence of their incorporation into either Rio Grande or Western Pueblo is, however, lacking. The fate of the Fremont culture remains a mystery.

CONCLUDING COMMENTS

In this introduction to the prehistoric Southwest, I have defined regional traditions and discussed their changes and interrelationships through time. I might instead have focused on Southwest-wide stages of development or on particular cultural changes of widespread impact. The comments below attempt such a pan-area perspective.

The early Plains-based big-game-hunting cultures appear to have made little or no use of many parts of the Southwest, which was probably marginal to a larger culture area centered to the east. The Archaic-stage developments likewise extended, and may often have originated, outside the Southwest. Relationships to the west appear generally stronger than to the east, though Schroedl (1976) sees Plains influences in the Green River phase on the northern Plateau. During the Archaic new areas of the Southwest were settled, and the beginnings of distinctively Southwestern traditions, adapted to particular geographic areas, can be distinguished.

In the Late Archaic, population growth and intensified interareal communication set the stage for a transition to adaptations based on cultivated plants. Cultigens originating in Mexico spread, perhaps initially as a minor dietary item, to the Mogollon Highlands. That area then became a center for the adaptation of the southern cultigens to Southwestern upland climate and for their dispersal to the Plateau region. Whether the lowland desert areas participated in this early agricultural development is not clear.

In the years from about AD 150 to 700, several regional traditions emerged. Their growing populations lived in generally small villages of substantial pithouses, made pottery and other new items of equipment, and depended increasingly on increasingly productive varieties of maize, beans, and squash. The first to appear was Hohokam, of the Arizona desert river valleys. Although other Southwestern sedentary traditions probably evolved largely in place, Hohokam culture appears to have been established by a migrant group from the south. Although the mechanisms and pathways remain to be traced, this intrusion may have acted as a catalyst for change among Southwestern groups already in a transitional state. The next tradition to emerge was one neighboring the Hohokam—the Mogollon. Between about AD 300 and 700, the Mogollon area appears to have functioned again as a center for the integration of new elements—whether derived from the Hohokam or elsewhere—and for their transmission through the upland zone and in particular to the developing Anasazi and Fremont. During the emergence of these various Southwestern sedentary traditions, interregional information transfer seems clearly to have been an important process. The role of population movement remains debatable. The actual changes in each locality must have resulted from local evolutionary processes that selected for or against locally generated as well as imported information.

The period from about AD 500 to 1100 or 1150 was one of apparent population growth, with elaboration and consolidation of sedentary–agricultural adaptations. Most settlements remained small and evidently egalitarian. A few, such as those in Chaco Canyon, developed relatively large and concentrated populations, probably had more complex and possibly stratified social organizations, and participated in widespread exchange networks. The role of such centers in cultural change and population distribution in the Southwest is just beginning to be studied.

The period between about AD 1100 and 1400 was one of increasing consolidation of population into fewer but larger settlements and of the abandonment of territory once occupied, particularly in the northern Southwest. In the south, Casas Grandes and, perhaps later, the Civano-phase Hohokam settlements may have become cultural and trading centers for very large regions, as Chaco had been somewhat earlier. Although the number of sites decreased dramatically in the greater Southwest, it is not clear that population decreased, although it may have. Most of the unoccupied or lightly used areas left by the consolidation or retreat of agricultural peoples were sparsely filled by the immigration of small, mobile groups of Numic, Upland Yuman, and Athapaskan hunter–gatherers. The causes of this period of turbulence and change remain obscure. Processes of economic and organizational change set in motion in the previous period may have been responsible. Or the changes may have been a response to some rather severe climatic/environmental shifts that affected the whole Southwest, starting in the 1100s. More likely, the changes are the result of interrelated and as yet not well-understood environmental, organizational, and adaptive shifts.

The latest prehistoric period (about 1450–1600) is poorly known in most areas. Although links between some prehistoric and historic puebloan peoples seem fairly well documented, those between the Hohokam and Pima–Papago rest more on general cultural similarities than on actual evidence of continuity. The fate of groups such as the Fremont, Virgin Anasazi, Cohonina, and Prescott remains unknown.

In conclusion, although our knowledge of the Southwest's culture history is equal to that for any similar-sized area of the New World and better than for most, an abundance of culture-historical problems remain to be solved. And our understanding of the paleoenvironmental and cultural processes lying behind that culture history is rudimentary, to say the least. The odds appear good that the Southwest will continue to be a vital topic of study in its own right as well as an important laboratory for the development of method and theory in archeology.

ACKNOWLEDGMENT

When I was preparing the first edition of this chapter, Dr. Mark Grady helped me greatly by freely giving his time to discuss issues in the prehistory of the southern

Southwest and by providing condensed versions of parts of his dissertation to serve as aids in preparing the Hohokam section. Mark's untimely death in 1978 prevented the opportunity to consult with him in making this revision, but his devotion to conserving Southwestern cultural resources and his dedication to excellence in research continued to guide me nonetheless.

References Cited and Recommended Sources

Adovasio, James M. 1979. Comment on "The Fremont and the Sevier" by D. B. Madsen. *American Antiquity* 44:4:723–731.

————. 1980. Fremont: an artifactual perspective. In *Fremont Perspectives,* ed. David B. Madsen, pp. 35–40. Utah Division of State History, Antiquities Section, Selected Papers 16.

Agenbroad, Larry D. 1978. Cultural implications from the distributional analysis of a lithic site, San Pedro Valley, Arizona. In *Discovering Past Behavior: Experiments in the Archaeology of the American Southwest,* ed. Paul Grebinger, pp. 55–71. New York: Gordon and Breach.

Aikens, C. Melvin. 1966. *Fremont–Promontory–Plains Relationships.* University of Utah, Anthropological Papers 82.

————. 1970. *Hogup Cave.* University of Utah Anthropological Papers 87.

————. 1972. Fremont culture: restatement of some problems. *American Antiquity* 37:1:61–66.

————. 1976. Cultural hiatus in the eastern Great Basin? *American Antiquity* 41:4:543–550.

Allen, William L., and James B. Richardson, III. 1971. The reconstruction of kinship from archaeological data: the concepts, the methods, and the feasibility. *American Antiquity* 36:1:41–53.

Anderson, Keith M. 1969. Ethnographic analogy and archaeological interpretation. *Science* 163:133–138.

Antevs, Ernst. 1955. Geologic–climatic dating in the West. *American Antiquity* 20:4:317–335.

Anyon, Roger, and Steven A. LeBlanc. 1980. The architectural evolution of Mogollon–Mimbres communal structures. *The Kiva* 45:3:253–277.

Baerreis, David A., and Reid A. Bryson. 1965. Climatic episodes and the dating of Mississippian cultures. *Wisconsin Archaeologist* 46:206–220.

Bandelier, Adolph F. 1892. *Final Report of Investigations among the Indians of the Southwestern United States, Carried on Mainly in the Years from 1880 to 1885,* part 2. Archaeological Institute of America Papers, American Series 4.

Bannister, Bryant, Elizabeth A. M. Gell, and John W. Hannah. 1966. *Tree-Ring Dates from Arizona N–Q, Verde–Show Low–St. Johns Area.* Laboratory of Tree-Ring Research, University of Arizona.

————, John W. Hannah, and William J. Robinson. 1970. *Tree-Ring Dates from New Mexico M–N, S, Z, Southwestern New Mexico Area.* Laboratory of Tree-Ring Research, University of Arizona.

————, William J. Robinson, and Claude Warren. 1970. *Tree-Ring Dates from New Mexico A, G–H: Shiprock–Zuni–Mt. Taylor Area.* Laboratory of Tree-Ring Research, University of Arizona.

Barnett, Franklin. 1970. *Matli Ranch Ruins: A Report of Excavation of Five Small Prehistoric Indian Ruins of the Prescott Culture in Arizona.* Museum of Northern Arizona, Technical Series 10.

————. 1974. *Excavation of Main Pueblo, Fitzmaurice Ruin.* Flagstaff: Museum of Northern Arizona.

Berlin, G. Lennis, J. Richard Ambler, Richard H. Hevly, and Gerald G. Schaber. 1977. Identification of a Sinagua agricultural field by aerial thermography, soil chemistry, pollen/plant analysis, and archaeology. *American Antiquity* 42:4:588–600.

Berry, Michael S. In press. *Time, Space, and Transition in Anasazi Prehistory*. University of Utah, Anthropological Papers.

Binford, Lewis R. 1962. Archaeology as anthropology. *American Antiquity* 28:2:217-225.

———. 1964. A consideration of archaeological research design. *American Antiquity* 29:425-441.

Bluhm, Elaine A. 1960. Mogollon settlement patterns in Pine Lawn Valley, New Mexico. *American Antiquity* 25:4:538-546.

Bohrer, Vorsila L. 1970. Ethnobotanical aspects of Snaketown, a Hohokam village in southern Arizona. *American Antiquity* 35:4:413-430.

———, Hugh C. Cutler, and Jonathan D. Sauer. 1969. Carbonized plant remains from two Hohokam sites, Arizona BB:13:4 and Arizona BB:13:50. *The Kiva* 35:1:1-10.

Brand, Donald D. 1938. Aboriginal trade routes for sea shells in the Southwest. *Association of Pacific Coast Geographers Year Book* 4:3-10.

Breternitz, David A. 1960. *Excavations at Three Sites in the Verde Valley, Arizona*. Museum of Northern Arizona Bulletin 34.

———. 1966. *An Appraisal of Tree-Ring Dated Pottery in the Southwest*. Anthropological Papers of the University of Arizona 10.

———. 1967. The eruption(s) of Sunset Crater: dating and effects. *Plateau* 40:2:72-76.

Brew, J. O. 1944. On Pueblo IV and the Katchina–Tlaloc relations. In *El Norte de Mexico y Sur de Estados Unidos*. Sociedad Mexicana de Antropologia, Mesa Redonda 3.

———. 1946. *Archaeology of Alkali Ridge, Southeastern Utah*. Harvard University, Peabody Museum of American Archaeology and Ethnology Papers 21.

Bryan, Kirk. 1929. Flood-water farming. *Geographic Review* 19:444-456.

———. 1941. Pre-Columbian agriculture in the Southwest, as conditioned by periods of alluviation. *Association of American Geographers Annals* 31:4:219-242.

———. 1954. *The Geology of Chaco Canyon, New Mexico, in Relation to the Life and Remains of the Prehistoric Peoples of Pueblo Bonito*. Smithsonian Miscellaneous Collections 112:7.

Bullard, William, Jr. 1962. *The Cerro Colorado Site and Pit House Architecture in the Southwestern United States Prior to AD 900*. Harvard University, Peabody Museum of American Archaeology and Ethnology Papers 44:2.

Castetter, Edward F., and Willis H. Bell. 1951. *Yuman Indian Agriculture*. Albuquerque: University of New Mexico Press.

Colton, Harold S. 1938. Names of the four culture roots in the Southwest. *Science* 87:251-252.

———. 1939. *Prehistoric Culture Units and Their Relationships in Northern Arizona*. Museum of Northern Arizona Bulletin 17.

———. 1941. Prehistoric trade in the Southwest. *Scientific Monthly* 52:308-319.

———. 1945a. The Patayan problem in the Colorado River valley. *Southwestern Journal of Anthropology* 1:1:114-121.

———. 1945b. Sunset Crater. *Plateau* 18:1:7-14.

———. 1946. *The Sinagua: A Summary of the Archaeology of the Region of Flagstaff, Arizona*. Museum of Northern Arizona Bulletin 22.

———. 1949. The prehistoric population of the Flagstaff area. *Plateau* 22:2:21-25.

———. 1960. *Black Sand: Prehistory in Northern Arizona*. Albuquerque: University of New Mexico Press.

———, and Lyndon L. Hargrave. 1937. *Handbook of Northern Arizona Pottery Wares*. Museum of Northern Arizona Bulletin 11.

Cordell, Linda. 1978. *A Cultural Resources Overview of the Middle Rio Grande Valley, New Mexico*. Albuquerque and Santa Fe: USDA Forest Service and USDI Bureau of Land Management.

———, and Fred Plog. 1979. Escaping the confines of normative thought: a reevaluation of Puebloan prehistory. *American Antiquity* 44:3:405-429.

Cutler, Hugh C., and Leonard W. Blake. 1976. Appendix 4: corn from Snaketown. In *The Hohokam: Desert Farmers and Craftsmen*, by Emil Haury, pp. 365-366. Tucson: University of Arizona Press.

Davis, Emma Lou. 1965. Small pressures and cultural drift as explanations for abandonment of the San Juan area, New Mexico and Arizona. *American Antiquity* 30:353-354.

Dean, Jeffrey S. 1970. Aspects of Tsegi phase social organization: a trial reconstruction. In *Reconstructing Prehistoric Pueblo Societies*, ed. W. A. Longacre, pp. 140-174. Albuquerque: University of New Mexico Press.

———, Alexander J. Lindsay, Jr., and William J. Robinson. 1978. Prehistoric settlement in Long House Valley, northeastern Arizona. In *Investigations of the Southwestern Anthropological Research Group: Proceedings of the 1976 Conference*, ed. R. C. Euler and G. J. Gumerman, pp. 25–44. Museum of Northern Arizona Bulletin 50.

———, and William J. Robinson. 1977. *Dendroclimatic Variability in the American Southwest: AD 680 to 1970*. Final report to the USDI National Park Service, Contract CX-1595-5-0241.

DeBloois, Evan. 1975. *The Elk Ridge Archaeological Project: A Test of Random Sampling in Archaeological Surveying*. USDA Forest Service, Intermountain Region, Archeological Reports 2.

Dick, Herbert W. 1965. *Bat Cave*. Monographs of the School of American Research 27.

Dickson, Bruce. 1975. Settlement pattern stability and change in the middle northern Rio Grande region, New Mexico: a test of some hypotheses. *American Antiquity* 40:2:159–171.

———. 1979. *Prehistoric Pueblo Settlement Patterns: The Arroyo Hondo, New Mexico, Site Survey*. Arroyo Hondo Archaeological Series 2.

DiPeso, Charles C. 1956. *The Upper Pima of San Cayetano del Tumacacori*. Amerind Foundation Publications 7.

———. 1968a. Casas Grandes: a fallen trading center of the Gran Chichimeca. *The Masterkey* 42:1:20–37.

———. 1968b. Casas Grandes and the Gran Chichimeca. *El Palacio* 75:4:45–61.

———. 1974. *Casas Grandes, a Fallen Trading Center of the Gran Chichimeca*, I, II, III. Dragoon and Flagstaff: Amerind Foundation, Inc., and Northland Press.

Dohm, Karen M. 1981. Similarities in spatial characteristics of several Basketmaker II sites on Cedar Mesa, Utah. Unpublished Master's thesis, Washington State University, Pullman.

Douglass, A. E. 1929. The secret of the Southwest solved by the talkative tree-rings. *National Geographic Magazine* 54:737–770.

Doyel, David E. 1979. The prehistoric Hohokam of the Arizona desert. *American Scientist* 67:5: 544–554.

———, and Emil W. Haury (eds.). 1976. The 1976 Salado Conference. *The Kiva* 42:1:1–134.

———, and Fred Plog. In press. *Current Issues in Hohokam Prehistory*. Arizona State University, Anthropological Research Papers.

Dumond, Don E. 1977. Science in archaeology: the saints go marching in. *American Antiquity* 42:3:330–349.

Dutton, Bertha. 1963. *Sun Father's Way*. Santa Fe: School of American Research.

Eddy, Frank W. 1961. *Excavations at Los Pinos Phase Sites in the Navajo Reservoir District*. Museum of New Mexico Papers 4.

———. 1966. *Prehistory in the Navajo Reservoir District, Northwestern New Mexico*, with sections by Thomas Harlan, Kenneth A. Bennett, and Erik K. Reed. Museum of New Mexico, Papers in Anthropology 15:1–2.

———. 1972. Culture ecology and the prehistory of the Navajo Reservoir district. *Southwestern Lore* 38:1–2:1–75.

Eggan, Fred. 1950. *Social Organization of the Western Pueblos*. Chicago: University of Chicago Press.

Ellis, Florence Hawley. 1967. Where did the Pueblo people come from? *El Palacio* 74:3:35–43.

Euler, Robert C. 1964. Southern Paiute archaeology. *American Antiquity* 29:3:379–381.

———, and Henry F. Dobyns. 1962. Excavations west of Prescott, Arizona. *Plateau* 34:3:69–84.

———, and George Gumerman. 1974. A resume of the archaeology of northern Arizona. In *The Geology of Northern Arizona with Notes on Archaeology and Paleoclimate*, ed. Thor Karlstrom. Proceedings, Twenty-Seventh Annual Meeting, Rocky Mountain Section, Geological Society of America.

———, George J. Gumerman, Thor V. N. Karlstrom, Jeffrey S. Dean, and Richard H. Hevly. 1979. The Colorado plateaus: cultural dynamics and paleoenvironment. *Science* 205: 1089–1101.

Ezell, Paul H. 1963. Is there a Hohokam–Pima continuum? *American Antiquity* 29:1:61–66.

Ferdon, Edwin N., Jr. 1955. *A Trial Survey of Mexican–Southwestern Architectural Parallels*. School of American Research Monographs 21.

———. 1967. The Hohokam "ball court": an alternative view of its function. *The Kiva* 33:1:1–14.

Fewkes, Jesse W. 1912. Casa Grande, Arizona. *Annual Report of the Bureau of American Ethnology* 28:25–180.

Figgins, J. D. 1927. The antiquity of man in America. *Natural History* 27:3:229–239.

Flannery, Kent V. 1968. Archaeological systems theory and early Mesoamerica. In *Anthropological Archeology in the Americas,* ed. Betty J. Meggers, pp. 67–87. Washington, D.C.: Anthropological Society of Washington.

Ford, Richard I. 1972. An ecological perspective on the eastern Pueblos. In *New Perspectives on the Pueblos,* ed. Alfonso Ortiz, pp. 1–17. Albuquerque: University of New Mexico Press.

———, Albert H. Schroeder, and Stewart L. Peckham. 1972. Three perspectives on Puebloan prehistory. In *New Perspectives on the Pueblos,* ed. Alfonso Ortiz, pp. 19–39. Albuquerque: University of New Mexico Press.

Fritts, Harold C., David G. Smith, and Marvin A. Stokes. 1965. The biological model for paleoclimatic interpretation of Mesa Verde tree-ring series. Contributions of the Wetherill Mesa archeological project. *Society for American Archaeology Memoirs* 19:101–121.

Fritz, John M. 1978. Paleopsychology today: ideational systems and human adaptation in prehistory. In *Social Archaeology: Beyond Subsistence and Dating,* ed. Charles L. Redman, M. J. Berman, E. V. Curtin, W. T. Langhorne, N. M. Versaggi, and J. C. Wanser, pp. 37–59. New York: Academic Press.

———, and Fred T. Plog. 1970. The nature of archaeological explanation. *American Antiquity* 35:4:405–412.

Fry, Gary F., and Gardiner F. Dalley. 1970. The Levee site and the Knoll site. Unpublished manuscript. Department of Anthropology, University of Utah.

Galinat, Walton C., and James H. Gunnerson. 1963. *Spread of 8-Rowed Maize from the Prehistoric Southwest.* Harvard University, Botanical Museum Leaflets 20:5.

Gillespie, William B. 1976. Culture change at the Ute Canyon site: a study of the pithouse-kiva transition in the Mesa Verde region. Unpublished Master's thesis, University of Colorado, Boulder.

Gladwin, Harold S., Emil W. Haury, E. B. Sayles, and Nora Gladwin. 1937. *Excavations at Snaketown, Material Culture.* Medallion Papers 25.

Gladwin, Winifred, and Harold S. Gladwin. 1929. *The Red-on-Buff Culture of the Gila Basin.* Medallion Papers 3.

———, and ———. 1934. *A Method for Designation of Cultures and Their Variations.* Medallion Papers 15.

Glassow, Michael. 1972. Changes in the adaptations of Southwestern Basketmakers: a systems perspective. In *Contemporary Archaeology,* ed. Mark P. Leone, pp. 289–302. Carbondale: Southern Illinois Press.

Goodyear, Albert C., III. 1975. *Hecla II and III: An Interpretive Study of Archeological Remains from the Lakeshore Project, Papago Reservation, Southcentral Arizona.* Arizona State University, Anthropological Research Papers 9.

Grady, Mark A. 1976. Aboriginal agrarian adaptation to the Sonoran Desert: a regional synthesis and research design. Ph.D. dissertation, University of Arizona.

Graybill, Donald A. 1975. *Mimbres-Mogollon Adaptations in the Gila National Forest, Mimbres District, New Mexico.* USDA Forest Service, Archeological Report 9.

Grebinger, Paul. 1973. Prehistoric social organization in Chaco Canyon, New Mexico: an alternative reconstruction. *The Kiva* 39:1:3–23.

———. 1978. Prehistoric social organization in Chaco Canyon, New Mexico: an evolutionary perspective. In *Discovering Past Behavior: Experiments in the Archaeology of the American Southwest,* ed. Paul Grebinger, pp. 73–100.

Greene, Jerry L., and Thomas W. Mathews. 1976. Faunal study of unworked mammalian bone. In *The Hohokam, Desert Farmers and Craftsmen,* ed. Emil W. Haury, pp. 367–373. Tucson: University of Arizona Press.

Guernsey, Samuel J., and A. V. Kidder. 1921. *Basket Maker Caves of Northeastern Arizona, Report on the Explorations, 1916, 1917.* Harvard University, Peabody Museum of American Archaeology and Ethnology Papers 8:2.

Gumerman, George J., and Robert C. Euler (eds.). 1976. *Papers on the Archaeology of Black Mesa, Arizona.* Carbondale: Southern Illinois University Press.

Gunnerson, James H. 1960. *An Introduction to Plains Apache Archeology: The Dismal River Aspect.* Bureau of American Ethnology Bulletin 13.

———. 1962. Plateau Shoshonean prehistory: a suggested reconstruction. *American Antiquity* 28:1:41–45.

———. 1969. *The Fremont Culture: A Study in Culture Dynamics on the Northern Anasazi Frontier.* Harvard University, Peabody Museum of Archaeology and Ethnology Papers 59:2.

——. 1979. Southern Athapaskan archeology. In *The Southwest,* ed. Alfonso Ortiz, pp. 162–169. *Handbook of North American Indians* 9. Washington, D.C.: Smithsonian Institution.

Hack, John T. 1942. *The Changing Physical Environment of the Hopi Indians of Arizona.* Harvard University, Peabody Museum of American Archaeology and Ethnology Papers 35:1.

Hargrave, Lyndon L. 1938. *Results of a Study of the Cohonina Branch of the Patayan Culture in 1938.* Museum of Northern Arizona, Museum Notes 11:6.

Hastorf, Christine. 1980. Changing resource use in subsistence agricultural groups of the prehistoric Mimbres River valley, New Mexico. In *Modeling Change in Prehistoric Subsistence Economies,* ed. Timothy K. Earle and Andrew L. Christenson, pp. 79–120. New York: Academic Press.

Haury, Emil W. 1936. *The Mogollon Culture of Southwestern New Mexico.* Medallion Papers 20.

——. 1943. The stratigraphy of Ventana Cave. *American Antiquity* 8:3:218–223.

——. 1945a. The problem of contacts between the southwestern United States and Mexico. *Southwestern Journal of Anthropology* 1:1:55–74.

——. 1945b. *The Excavation of Los Muertos and Neighboring Ruins in the Salt River Valley, southern Arizona.* Harvard University, Peabody Museum of American Archaeology and Ethnology Papers 24:1.

——. 1950. *The Stratigraphy and Archaeology of Ventana Cave, Arizona,* 1st ed. Tucson and Albuquerque: University of Arizona Press and University of New Mexico Press.

——. 1957. An alluvial site on the San Carlos Indian Reservation, Arizona. *American Antiquity* 23:1:2–27.

——. 1960. Association of fossil fauna and artifacts of the Sulphur Spring stage, Cochise culture. *American Antiquity* 25:4:609–610.

——. 1962. The greater American Southwest. In *Courses Toward Urban Life,* ed. Robert J. Braidwood and Gordon R. Willey, pp. 106–131. Chicago: Aldine.

——. 1965. Snaketown: 1964–1965. *The Kiva* 31:1:2–27.

——. 1967. The Hohokam, first masters of the American desert. *National Geographic Magazine* 131:670–695.

——. 1975. *The Stratigraphy and Archaeology of Ventana Cave, Arizona,* 2d ed. Tucson: University of Arizona Press.

——. 1976. *The Hohokam, Desert Farmers and Craftsmen: Excavations at Snaketown, 1964–1965.* Tucson: University of Arizona Press.

——, Ernest Antevs, and J. F. Lance. 1953. Artifacts with mammoth remains, Naco, Arizona. *American Antiquity* 19:1:1–24.

——, and E. B. Sayles. 1947. *An Early Pit-House Village of the Mogollon Culture, Forestdale Valley, Arizona.* University of Arizona Bulletin 18:4.

——, and William W. Wasley. 1959. The Lehner mammoth site, southeastern Arizona. *American Antiquity* 25:1:2–30.

Hawley, Florence. 1938. The family tree of Chaco Canyon masonry. *American Antiquity* 3:2:247–255.

Haynes, C. Vance, Jr. 1964. Fluted projectile points: their age and dispersion. *Science* 145: 1408–1413.

Hester, James J. 1962. *Early Navajo Migrations and Acculturation in the Southwest.* Museum of New Mexico, Papers in Anthropology 6.

Hibben, Frank C. 1941. *Evidences of Early Occupation of Sandia Cave, New Mexico, and Other Sites in the Sandia–Manzano Region.* Smithsonian Miscellaneous Collections 99:23.

Hill, James N. 1966. A prehistoric community in eastern Arizona. *Southwestern Journal of Anthropology* 22:1:9–30.

——. 1970. *Broken K Pueblo: Prehistoric Social Organization in the American Southwest.* University of Arizona, Anthropological Papers 18.

Husted, Wilfred M., and Oscar L. Mallory. 1967. The Fremont culture: its derivation and ultimate fate. *Plains Anthropologist* 12:222–232.

Irwin-Williams, Cynthia. 1967. Picosa: the elementary Southwestern culture. *American Antiquity* 32:4:441–455.

——. 1968. Archaic culture history in the southwestern United States. Eastern New Mexico University, *Contributions in Anthropology* 1:4:48–53.

——. 1973. *The Oshara Tradition: Origins of Anasazi Culture.* Eastern New Mexico University, Contributions in Anthropology 5:1.

——. 1979. Post-Pleistocene archeology, 7000–2000 BC. In *The Southwest,* ed. Alfonso Ortiz, pp. 31–42. Handbook of North American Indians 9. Washington, D.C.: Smithsonian Institution.

————, and C. Vance Haynes, Jr. 1970. Climatic change and early population dynamics in the southwestern United States. *Quaternary Research* 1:1:59–71.

————, and Phillip H. Shelley (eds.). 1980. *Investigations at the Salmon Site: The Structure of Chacoan Society in the Northern Southwest,* 5 vols. Final report to funding agencies. Portales: Eastern New Mexico University.

James, Kathleen. 1974. Analysis of potsherds and ceramic wares. In *Excavation of Main Pueblo at Fitzmaurice Ruin,* ed. Franklin Barnett, pp. 106–129. Flagstaff: Museum of Northern Arizona.

Jennings, Jesse D. 1956. The American Southwest: a problem in cultural isolation. In *Seminars in Archaeology: 1955,* ed. Robert Wauchope. Society for American Archaeology Memoirs 11:61–127.

————. 1966. *Glen Canyon, a Summary.* University of Utah, Anthropological Papers 81.

————. 1978. *Prehistory of Utah and the Eastern Great Basin.* University of Utah, Anthropological Papers 98.

————. 1980. *Cowboy Cave.* University of Utah, Anthropological Papers 104.

————, Alan R. Schroedl, and Richard N. Holmer. 1980. *Sudden Shelter.* University of Utah, Anthropological Papers 103.

Jett, Stephen C. 1964. Pueblo Indian migrations: an evaluation of the possible physical and cultural determinants. *American Antiquity* 29:3:281–300.

Johnson, Alfred E. 1965. The development of western Pueblo culture. Ph.D. dissertation, University of Arizona Microfilms.

Jorde, L. B. 1977. Precipitation cycles and cultural buffering in the prehistoric Southwest. In *For Theory Building in Archaeology,* ed. Lewis R. Binford, pp. 385–396. New York: Academic Press.

Judd, Neil M. 1919. *Archaeological Investigations of Paragonah, Utah.* Smithsonian Miscellaneous Collections 70:2:1–22.

————. 1926. *Archaeological Observations North of the Rio Colorado.* Bureau of American Ethnology Bulletin 82.

————. 1954. *The Material Culture of Pueblo Bonito.* Smithsonian Miscellaneous Collections 124.

————. 1964. *The Architecture of Pueblo Bonito.* Smithsonian Miscellaneous Collections 147:1.

Judge, W. James. 1973. Paleoindian Occupation of the Central Rio Grande Valley, New Mexico. Albuquerque: University of New Mexico Press.

————. 1979. The development of a complex cultural ecosystem in the Chaco basin, New Mexico. In *Proceedings of the First Conference on Scientific Research in the National Parks,* ed. Robert Linn, pp. 901–905. Washington, D.C.: U.S. Government Printing Office.

————, William B. Gillespie, S. H. Lekson, and H. W. Toll. 1981. Tenth century developments in Chaco Canyon. *Archaeological Society of New Mexico, Anthropological Papers* 6:65–98.

Kelley, J. Charles. 1952. Factors involved in the abandonment of certain peripheral Southwestern settlements. *American Anthropologist* 54:356–387.

Kidder, Alfred V. 1924. *An Introduction to the Study of Southwestern Archaeology, with a Preliminary Account of the Excavations at Pecos.* New Haven: Yale University Press.

————. 1927. Southwestern Archaeological Conference. *Science* 66:1716:489–491.

King, Thomas F., Patricia P. Hickman, and Gary Berg. 1977. *Anthropology in Historic Preservation: Caring for Culture's Clutter.* New York: Academic Press.

Kirchoff, Paul. 1954. Gatherers and farmers in the greater Southwest. *American Anthropologist* 56:4:529–550.

Kroeber, A. L. 1916. Zuni potsherds. *American Museum of Natural History, Anthropological Papers* 18:1:1–37.

————. 1939. *Cultural and Natural Areas of Native North America.* University of California, Publications in American Archeology and Ethnology 38.

LeBlanc, Steven A. 1976. Mimbres Archaeological Center: preliminary report of the second season of excavation, 1975. *Journal of New World Archaeology* 1:6:1–23.

————. 1980. The dating of Casas Grandes. *American Antiquity* 45:4:799–806.

————, and Ben Nelson. 1976. The Salado in southwestern New Mexico. *The Kiva* 42:1:71–79.

Lindsay, Alexander J., Jr., J. Richard Ambler, Mary Ann Stein, and Philip M. Hobler. 1968. *Survey and Excavations North and East of Navajo Mountain, Utah, 1959–1962.* Museum of Northern Arizona Bulletin 45.

Linton, Ralph. 1944. Nomad raids and fortified pueblos. *American Antiquity* 10:1:28–32.

Lipe, William D., and Cory D. Breternitz. 1980. Approaches to analyzing variability among Dolores area structures, AD 600–950. *Contract Abstracts and CRM Archeology* 1:2:21–28.

————, and A. J. Lindsay, Jr. (eds.). 1974. *Proceedings of the 1974 Cultural Resource Management Conference, Federal Center, Denver, Colorado.* Museum of Northern Arizona, Technical Series 14.

————, and R. G. Matson. 1971a. Human settlement and resources in the Cedar Mesa area, southeast Utah. In *The Distribution of Prehistoric Population Aggregates,* ed. George J. Gumerman, pp. 126–151. Prescott College, Anthropological Reports 1.

————, and ————. 1971b. Prehistoric cultural adaptation in the Cedar Mesa area, southeast Utah. Research proposal submitted to the National Science Foundation.

Lohse, Ernest S. 1980. Fremont settlement pattern and architectural variation. In *Fremont Perspectives,* ed. David B. Madsen, pp. 41–54. Utah Division of State History, Antiquities Section, Selected Papers 16.

Longacre, William A. 1964. Archeology as anthropology: a case study. *Science* 144:1454–1455.

————. 1970. *Archaeology as Anthropology: A Case Study.* University of Arizona, Anthropological Papers 17.

————. 1976. Population dynamics at the Grasshopper Pueblo, Arizona. In *Demographic Anthropology: Quantitative Approaches,* ed. Ezra B. W. Zubrow, pp. 169–184. Albuquerque: University of New Mexico Press.

————, and J. Jefferson Reid. 1974. The University of Arizona archaeological field school at Grasshopper: eleven years of multidisciplinary research and teaching. *The Kiva* 40:1–2:3–38.

Lyons, T. R., and Robert Hitchcock. 1977. Remote sensing interpretation of an Anasazi land route system. In *Aerial Remote Sensing Techniques in Archeology,* ed. T. R. Lyons and R. K. Hitchcock, pp. 111–134. Reports of the Chaco Center 2. Albuquerque: USDA National Park Service and the University of New Mexico.

McGregor, John C. 1937. *Winona Village.* Museum of Northern Arizona Bulletin 12.

————. 1941. *Winona and Ridge Ruin,* part I. Museum of Northern Arizona Bulletin 18.

————. 1951. *The Cohonina Culture of Northwestern Arizona.* Urbana: University of Illinois Press.

————. 1965. *Southwestern Archaeology,* 2d ed. Urbana: University of Illinois Press.

————. 1967. *The Cohonina Culture of Mount Floyd, Arizona.* University of Kentucky, Studies in Anthropology 5.

McKern, W. C. 1939. The midwestern taxonomic method as an aid to archaeological culture study. *American Antiquity* 4:301–313.

McKusick, Charmion R. 1976. Avifauna. In *The Hohokam, Desert Farmers and Craftsmen,* ed. Emil W. Haury, pp. 374–377. Tucson: University of Arizona Press.

McNitt, Frank. 1957. *Richard Wetherill: Anasazi.* Albuquerque: University of New Mexico Press.

Madsen, David B. 1975. Dating Paiute–Shoshoni expansion in the Great Basin. *American Antiquity* 40:1:82–86.

————. 1979. The Fremont and the Sevier: defining prehistoric agriculturalists north of the Anasazi. *American Antiquity* 44:4:711–722.

————. 1980. Fremont/Sevier subsistence. In *Fremont Perspectives,* ed. David B. Madsen, pp. 25–33. Utah State Division of History, Antiquities Section, Selected Papers 16.

————, and Michael S. Berry. 1975. A reassessment of northeastern Great Basin prehistory. *American Antiquity* 40:4:391–405.

————, and La Mar W. Lindsay. 1977. *Backhoe Village.* Utah State Division of History, Antiquities Section, Selected Papers 12.

Mangelsdorf, Paul C., Richard S. MacNeish, and Walton C. Galinat. 1967. Prehistoric wild and cultivated maize. In *The Prehistory of the Tehaucan Valley,* vol. 1: *Environment and Subsistence,* ed. Douglas S. Byers, pp. 178–200. Austin: University of Texas Press.

Marshall, Michael P., John R. Stein, Richard W. Loose, and Judith E. Novotny. 1979. *Anasazi Communities of the San Juan Basin.* Albuquerque: Public Service Company of New Mexico and New Mexico Historic Preservation Bureau.

Martin, Paul S. 1967. Hay Hollow site (200 B.C.–A.D. 200). *Field Museum of Natural History Bulletin* 38:5:6–10.

————. 1972. Foreword. In "Paleoecology of the Hay Hollow site, Arizona," by Vorsila Bohrer, p. 1. *Fieldiana: Anthropology* 63:1:1–30.

————, and Fred T. Plog. 1973. *The Archaeology of Arizona.* New York: Doubleday Natural History Press.

————, and John B. Rinaldo. 1950. *Sites of the Reserve Phase, Pine Lawn Valley, Western New Mexico.* Fieldiana: Anthropology 38:3.

————, Elaine A. Bluhm, Hugh C. Cutler, and Roger Grange, Jr. 1952. *Mogollon Cultural Continuity and Change: The Stratigraphic Analysis of Tularosa and Cordova Caves.* Fieldiana: Anthropology 40.

Marwitt, John P. 1968. *Pharo Village.* University of Utah, Anthropological Papers 91.

————. 1970. *Median Village and Fremont Culture Regional Variation.* University of Utah, Anthropological Papers 95.

————. 1980. A Fremont retrospective. In *Fremont Perspectives,* ed. David B. Madsen. Utah State Division of History, Antiquities Section, Selected Papers 16.

Matson, R. G., and W. D. Lipe. 1978. Settlement patterns on Cedar Mesa: boom and bust on the northern periphery. In *Investigations by the Southwestern Anthropological Research Group: An Exercise in Archaeological Cooperation,* ed. R. Euler and G. Gumerman. Flagstaff: Museum of Northern Arizona, Bulletin 50.

Merriam, C. Hart. 1890. Results of a biological survey of the San Francisco Mountains region and desert of the Little Colorado in Arizona. USDA *North American Fauna* 3:1–136.

————. 1898. Life-zones and crop-zones of the United States. USDA division of the *Biological Survey Bulletin* 10:1–79.

Moorehead, Warren K. 1908. Ruins at Aztec and on the Rio La Plata, New Mexico. *American Anthropologist* n.s. 10:255–263.

Morris, Donald H. 1969. Red Mountain: an early Pioneer period site in the Salt River valley of central Arizona. *American Antiquity* 34:1:40–53.

Morris, Earl H., and Robert F. Burgh. 1954. *Basket Maker II Sites Near Durango, Colorado.* Carnegie Institution of Washington Publication 604.

Morss, Noel. 1931. *Ancient Culture of the Fremont River in Utah.* Harvard University, Peabody Museum of American Archaeology and Ethnology Papers 12:3.

Nelson, Nels C. 1916. Chronology of the Tano ruins, New Mexico. *American Anthropologist* 18:2:159–180.

Niswander, J. D., and K. S. Brown. 1970. Population studies on Southwest Indian tribes I: culture history and genetics of the Papago. *American Journal of Human Genetics* 22:7–23.

Nusbaum, Jesse L., A. V. Kidder, and Samuel J. Guernsey. 1922. *A Basket Maker Cave in Kane County, Utah.* Heye Foundation, Indian Notes and Monographs 29.

Osborne, Douglas (comp.). 1965. *Contributions of the Wetherill Mesa Archeological Project.* Society for American Archaeology Memoirs 19.

Pepper, George H. 1902. *Ancient Basket Makers of Southern Utah. American Museum Journal* 2:4 (Supplement).

Petersen, Ken L. 1981. Ten thousand years of climatic change reconstructed from fossil pollen, La Plata Mountains, southwestern Colorado. Unpublished Ph.D. dissertation, Washington State University, Pullman.

Pilles, Peter J., Jr. 1978. The field house and Sinagua demography. In *Limited Activity and Occupation Sites,* ed. Albert E. Ward, pp. 119–133. Center for Anthropological Studies, Contributions to Anthropology Studies 1.

————. 1979. Sunset Crater and the Sinagua: a new interpretation. In *Volcanic Activity and Human Ecology,* ed. Payson Sheets and Donald Grayson. New York: Academic Press.

Pippin, Lonnie C. 1979. The prehistory and paleoecology of Guadalupe Ruin, Sandoval County, New Mexico. Unpublished Ph.D. dissertation, Washington State University, Pullman.

Plog, Fred T. 1974. *The Study of Prehistoric Change.* New York: Academic Press.

Plog, Stephen. 1980. Village autonomy in the American Southwest: an evaluation of the evidence. In *Models and Methods in Regional Exchange,* ed. Robert E. Fry, pp. 135–146. Society for American Archaeology Papers 1.

————, Fred Plog, and Walter Wait. 1978. Decision making in modern surveys. In *Advances in Archaeological Method and Theory,* vol. 1, ed. Michael B. Schiffer, pp. 383–421. New York: Academic Press.

Raab, L. Mark. 1976. The structure of prehistoric community organization at Santa Rosa Wash, southern Arizona. Ph.D. dissertation, Arizona State University.

Reed, Erik K. 1950. Eastern–central Arizona archaeology in relation to the Western Pueblos. *Southwestern Journal of Anthropology* 6:2:120–138.

————. 1964. The greater Southwest. In *Prehistoric Man in the New World,* ed. Jesse D. Jennings and E. Norbeck, pp. 175–191. Chicago: University of Chicago Press.

Reher, C. A., ed. 1977. *Settlement and Subsistence along the Lower Chaco River: The CGP Survey.* Albuquerque: University of New Mexico Press.

Reid, J. Jefferson. 1978. Response to stress at Grasshopper Pueblo, Arizona. In *Discovering Past Behavior: Experiments in the Archaeology of the American Southwest,* ed. Paul Grebinger, pp. 195–213. New York: Gordon and Breach.

Rohn, Arthur H. 1963. Prehistoric soil and water conservation on Chapin Mesa, southwestern Colorado. *American Antiquity* 28:441–455.

———. 1975. A stockaded Basketmaker III village at Yellow Jacket, Colorado. *The Kiva* 40:3: 113–119.

Rouse, I. 1962. Southwestern archaeology today. In *An Introduction to the Study of Southwestern Archaeology,* 2d ed., by A. V. Kidder, pp. 1–53. New Haven: Yale University Press.

Sayles, E. B., and Ernst Antevs. 1941. *The Cochise Culture.* Medallion Papers 29.

Schaafsma, Polly, and Curtis F. Schaafsma. 1974. Evidence for the origins of the Pueblo Katchina cult as suggested by Southwestern rock art. *American Antiquity* 39:4:535–545.

Schaber, G. E., and G. J. Gumerman. 1969. Infrared scanning images—an archaeological application. *Science* 164:712–713.

Schiffer, Michael B. 1972. Archaeological context and systemic context. *American Antiquity* 37:156–165.

———, and George J. Gumerman (eds.). 1977. *Conservation Archaeology: A Guide for Cultural Resource Management Studies.* New York: Academic Press.

Schoenwetter, James, and Frank W. Eddy. 1964. *Alluvial and Palynological Reconstruction of Environments, Navajo Reservoir District.* Museum of New Mexico, Papers in Anthropology 13.

Schroeder, Albert H. 1947. Did the Sinagua of the Verde Valley settle in the Salt River valley? *Southwestern Journal of Anthropology* 3:3:230–246.

———. 1953. The problem of Hohokam, Sinagua, and Salado relations in southern Arizona. *Plateau* 26:2:75–83.

———. 1957. The Hakataya cultural tradition. *American Antiquity* 23:2:176–178.

———. 1960. The Hohokam, Sinagua, and Hakataya. *Archives of Archaeology* 5.

———. 1961. The pre-eruptive and post-eruptive Sinagua patterns. *Plateau* 34:2:60–66.

———. 1963. Comment on Gunnerson's "Plateau Shoshonean prehistory." *American Antiquity* 28:4:559–560.

———. 1965. Unregulated diffusion from Mexico into the Southwest prior to AD 700. *American Antiquity* 30:3:297–309.

———. 1966. Pattern diffusion from Mexico into the Southwest after AD 600. *American Antiquity* 31:5:683–704.

Schroedl, Alan R. 1976. The Archaic of the northern Colorado Plateau. Unpublished Ph.D. dissertation, University of Utah, Salt Lake City.

———. 1977. The paleo-Indian period on the Colorado Plateau. *Southwestern Lore* 43:3:1–9.

Schwartz, Douglas. 1956. Demographic changes in the early periods of Cohonina prehistory. In *Prehistoric Settlement Patterns in the New World,* ed. Gordon R. Willey, pp. 26–31. Viking Fund Publications in Anthropology 23.

———. 1959. Culture area and time depth: the four worlds of the Havasupai. *American Anthropologist* 61:1060–1070.

———, and Richard W. Lang. 1973. *Archaeological Investigations at the Arroyo Hondo Site: Third Field Report, 1972.* Santa Fe: School of American Research.

Sessions, Steven E. (ed.). 1979. *The Archaeology of Southwest Gallegos Mesa: The EPCC Survey Project.* Navajo Nation Papers in Anthropology 1.

Sharrock, Floyd W. 1966. *Prehistoric Occupation Patterns in Southwest Wyoming and Cultural Relationships with the Great Basin and Plains Culture Areas.* University of Utah, Anthropological Papers 77.

Shutler, Richard, Jr. 1961. *Lost City: Pueblo Grande de Nevada.* Nevada State Museum, Anthropological Papers 5.

Smith, Watson. 1952. *Kiva Mural Decorations at Awatovi and Kawaika-a, with a Survey of Other Wall Paintings in the Southwest.* Harvard University, Peabody Museum of American Archaeology and Ethnology Papers 37.

Spicer, Edward H., and L. P. Caywood. 1936. *Two Pueblo Ruins in West Central Arizona.* University of Arizona Bulletin 7:1, Social Science Bulletin 10.

Spier, Leslie. 1917. An outline for a chronology of Zuni ruins. *American Museum of Natural History, Anthropological Papers* 18:3:209–331.

Stanislawski, Michael. 1973. Review of "Archaeology as anthropology: a case study" by William A. Longacre. *American Antiquity* 38:1:117–122.

Stevens, Dominique E., and George A. Agogino. n.d. *Sandia Cave: A Study in Controversy*. Eastern New Mexico University, Contributions in Anthropology 7:1.

Steward, Julian. 1937. Ecological aspects of Southwestern society. *Anthropos* 32:87–104.

———. 1938. *Basin–Plateau Aboriginal Socio-political Groups*. Bureau of American Ethnology Bulletin 120.

———, and F. M. Setzler. 1938. Function and configuration in archaeology. *American Antiquity* 4:1:4–10.

Stewart, Guy R. 1940a. Conservation in Pueblo agriculture 1: primitive practices. *Scientific Monthly* 56:201–220.

———. 1940b. Conservation in Pueblo agriculture II: present-day flood water irrigation. *Scientific Monthly* 56:329–340.

Swedlund, Alan C., and Steven E. Sessions. 1976. A developmental model of prehistoric population growth on Black Mesa, northeastern Arizona. In *Papers on the Archaeology of Black Mesa, Arizona*, ed. George J. Gumerman and Robert C. Euler, pp. 136–148. Carbondale: Southern Illinois University Press.

Taylor, Walter W. 1948. *A Study of Archaeology*. American Anthropological Association Memoir 69.

———. 1954. Southwestern archaeology, its history and theory. *American Anthropologist* 56:4:561–575.

Vivian, R. Gwinn. 1970. An inquiry into prehistoric social organization in Chaco Canyon, New Mexico. In *Reconstructing Prehistoric Pueblo Societies*, ed. William A. Longacre, pp. 59–83. Albuquerque: University of New Mexico Press.

———. 1974. Conservation and diversion: water-control systems in the Anasazi Southwest. In *Irrigation's Impact on Society*, ed. T. E. Downing and M. Gibson, pp. 95–111. Anthropological Papers of the University of Arizona 25.

Warren, Claude N. 1967. The San Dieguito complex: a review and hypothesis. *American Antiquity* 32:2:168–186.

Wasley, William W. (introduction by David E. Doyel). 1980 Classic period Hohokam. *The Kiva* 45:4:337–352.

Weaver, Donald E. 1972. A cultural–ecological model for the Classic Hohokam period in the lower Salt River valley. *The Kiva* 38:1:43–52.

Wedel, Waldo R. 1967. Review of "Fremont–Promontory–Plains relationships in northern Utah" by C. Melvin Aikens. *American Journal of Archaeology* 71:426–427.

Whalen, Norman. 1971. Cochise culture sites in the central San Pedro drainage, Arizona. Ph.D. dissertation, University of Arizona.

———. 1973. Agriculture and the Cochise. *The Kiva* 39:1:89–96.

Wheat, Joe Ben. 1955. *Mogollon Culture Prior to AD 1000*. American Anthropological Association Memoirs 82.

Wilcox, David R. 1979. Warfare implications of dry-laid masonry walls on Tumamoc Hill. *The Kiva* 45:1–2:15–38.

———. n.d. The entry of Athapascans into the American Southwest: the problem today. Unpublished manuscript.

———, and Stephen M. Larson. 1979. Introduction to the Tumamoc Hill survey. *The Kiva* 45:1–2:1–14.

———, and L. Shenk. 1977. *The Architecture of the Big House and Its Interpretation*. Arizona State Museum, Archaeological Series 115.

Willey, Gordon R., and Philip Phillips. 1958. *Method and Theory in American Archaeology*. Chicago: University of Chicago Press.

Winter, Joseph. 1973. The distribution and development of Fremont maize agriculture: some preliminary interpretations. *American Antiquity* 38:4:439–451.

Woodbury, Richard B. 1961. *Prehistoric Agriculture at Point of Pines, Arizona*. Society for American Archaeology Memoirs 17.

Woosley, Anne I. 1980. Agricultural diversity in the prehistoric Southwest. *The Kiva* 45:4:317–335.

Wormington, H. Marie. 1955. *A Reappraisal of the Fremont Culture*. Denver Museum of Natural History Proceedings 1.

Zubrow, Ezra B. W. 1971. Carrying capacity and dynamic equilibrium in the prehistoric Southwest. *American Antiquity* 36:2:127–138.

Teotihuacan. (Copyright © 1973 by René Millon. All rights reserved.)

CHAPTER ELEVEN

Mesoamerica

T. Patrick Culbert

It is well known that the arrival of the Spanish brought an abrupt end to a group of native high civilizations in Mesoamerica. What is not as often realized is that these high civilizations were only the latest (and in some ways not the highest) in a series of such civilizations stretching back for centuries in the Mexican and Guatemalan highlands and lowlands. Dr. Culbert traces the evolution of these civilizations from their simple hunting–gathering and agrarian village phases through their cycles of rise and decline, until the arrival of the Spanish brought the period to an end.

Mesoamerica is a culture area characterized by a set of shared cultural characteristics that indicate long-standing communication and interrelatedness among the prehistoric inhabitants. Together, the Mesoamerican people forged one of the two civilizations of native America. Because of the continual interaction, it is impossible to understand the cultural development of any specific part of the area without reference to the whole.

The boundaries of Mesoamerica are delineated in Figure 11.1. The northern boundary corresponds to a sharp break in both ecology and culture. To the north lies desert, where agricultural possibilities are limited to scattered, oasis-like areas of available water. Culturally, this is a frontier where, at least in some areas, representatives of Mesoamerican high cultures directly confronted peoples who still lived by hunting and gathering. This confrontation was emphasized—perhaps overemphasized—by the native Mesoamericans themselves; their illustrated texts depict northern barbarians clad in skins and armed with bows and arrows. The fact that groups of farming peoples not very different from those within Mesoamerica lived in favored areas beyond the northern frontier was less romantic and received less notice. On the south, the limits of Mesoamerica are far less pronounced. Environmental conditions like those of Mesoamerica continue into Central America, and the peoples who occupied neighboring territories had well-developed hierarchical societies that lacked only the more elaborate features of Mesoamerican cultural complexity.

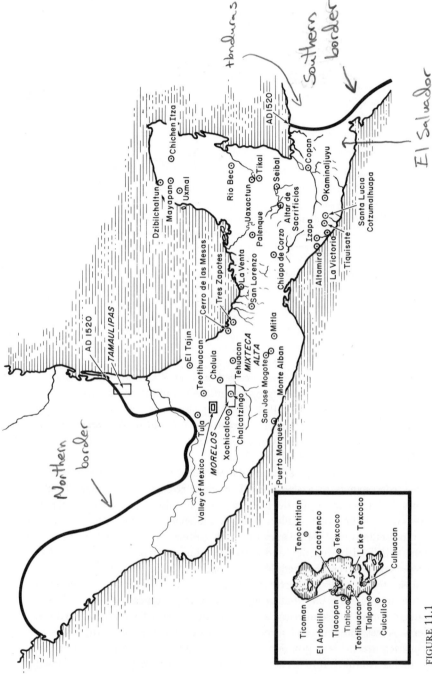

FIGURE 11.1
Mesoamerica.

GEOGRAPHY AND ENVIRONMENT

Mountains are the primary geographic fact of Mesoamerica, and the variety of altitudinal, climatic, and vegetational zones associated with the precipitous topography of the region has deeply influenced human adaptation. Physiographically, Mesoamerica can be described as a series of major mountain masses separated and bounded by relatively limited areas of lower elevation (West, 1964).

Northern and Central Mexico is occupied by a vast, U-shaped tableland defined on the east and west by mountain ranges (the Sierra Madre Oriental and the Sierra Madre Occidental) and on the south by the geologically recent Neovolcanic Axis. The northern part of this upland is the parched desert of northern Mexico that lies outside the boundaries of Mesoamerica. To the south lies the Mesa Central, dotted with a profusion of volcanic features between and among which a series of ancient highland lake basins provide the choice areas for human habitation.

Below the precipitous southern escarpment of the Neovolcanic Axis lies the Balsas Depression, a land of low hills among which the Balsas River finds a sinuous passage to the Pacific. One of the few major river basins in Mesoamerica, the Balsas Depression has suffered from a paucity of archeological investigation that makes it impossible to evaluate its role in Mesoamerican development.

Rising to the south of the Balsas Depression are the highlands of Oaxaca. Incredibly dissected by erosion over much of their surface, the Oaxacan highlands offer few substantial flat areas for human occupation, and in many places the modern Indian populations still live in scattered households and hamlets that cling to narrow ridges or perch on steep slopes above tiny valley floors. The Valley of Oaxaca offers the only major area of valley floor and was the site of important cultural centers from very early times. North and west of the Valley of Oaxaca lies the Mixteca Alta, whose tiny, lofty valleys are the homeland of the Mixtec culture.

To the south of the Oaxacan highlands, the continent narrows to 192 kilometers in breadth at the Isthmus of Tehuantepec, which has long been a corridor of migration and culture contact. The isthmus is usually considered to be the division between northern and southern Mesoamerica.

The highlands of Chiapas and Guatemala constitute the major mountain mass of southern Mesoamerica. A geologically complex set of ranges that parallel the Pacific coast, the Chiapas–Guatemalan highlands are characterized by recent vulcanism close to the coast and uplifted sedimentary rocks further inland. Between and crosscutting the mountain ranges are a number of highland basins, the most important of which archeologically is the Valley of Guatemala. The Chiapas section of the highlands is split by the Central Depression of Chiapas in which the Grijalva River drains the highland massif in an extensive, semiarid basin.

To the north of the Guatemalan highlands lies the Maya lowlands, a limestone platform that provides the only large mass of low-elevation land in Mesoamerica. The northern third of the platform, in the Yucatan Peninsula, is almost flat; to the south, there are a series of low but steep-sided ridges separated by swampy areas. The porosity of the underlying limestone provides an opportunity for rapid underground drainage, so most of the Maya lowland area is devoid of rivers.

The remaining lowland areas of Mesoamerica are the Pacific and Gulf coasts. From the southern border of Mesoamerica as far as the Isthmus of Tehuantepec, the Pacific coast combines a flat, narrow, coastal plain with a rainy piedmont crossed by myriad rivers that drain the heavy rainfall of the coastal mountain ranges into the Pacific. The Gulf coast is generally broader and is crossed by several meandering rivers that discharge huge amounts of water into the Gulf of Mexico.

The climate of Mesoamerica is characterized by a summer rainy season and a winter dry season. The rainy season is longest (May–November) in southern Mesoamerica, and becomes progressively shorter by a month or more at each end as one moves to the northern frontier. In general, rainfall is moderate to heavy in lowland areas. Most of the highlands are semiarid, and in many parts of northern Mesoamerica the rains are so scanty that rainfall farming is a high-risk proposition. Temperatures are dependent upon elevation. Regions below 1500 meters are essentially frost free, while those above 2100 meters suffer from frost that is severe enough to curtail the growing season.

The contrast between the arid highland and moist lowland environments in Mesoamerica has profound effects upon native farming patterns. Of equal importance, however, are microenvironmental variations within each limited zone (Coe and Flannery, 1964); gross generalizations, based upon the assumption of very large homogeneous areas within which adaptation was everywhere identical, have not proved profitable as a tool for analysis. Detailed consideration of microenvironments is now an indispensable part of any research that stresses ecological considerations.

ARCHEOLOGICAL RESEARCH IN MESOAMERICA

The beginnings of an orderly interest in the archeological remains of prehistoric Mesoamerica date back to the mid-nineteenth century, when explorers and travelers began to attract public attention to the marvels that had long lain forgotten. Probably the most influential of the early explorers was John Lloyd Stephens, who, accompanied by the artist Frederick Catherwood, visited Yucatan and Central America and published accounts (1962, 1969) that achieved instant popularity. By the turn of the century, explorers' accounts had become both more numerous and more scientific, and initial excavations and reconstructions had begun. The period until 1940 was largely devoted to archeological basics—locating and mapping sites, establishing sequences, and excavating and reconstructing some of the more impressive structures. The Mexican government sponsored projects at major sites like Teotihuacan and Monte Alban, while the Carnegie Institution, under the leadership of A. V. Kidder, was the most important research organization in the Mayan area. The questions asked tended to be about origins and diffusion: Where did things start? By what routes did they spread?

After World War II, archeologists took new directions. Settlement-pattern studies became of importance in both the Mayan area and Central Mexico, with Gordon R. Willey and William T. Sanders among the pioneers. Ecological interests awakened, with Richard S. MacNeish focusing upon the problem of plant domestication and a number of people, including Sanders, Angel Palerm, and Eric Wolf, considering the effect of subsistence systems upon cultural development. The primary theoretical framework was neoevolutionary and strongly influenced by the ideas of Julian Steward and Elman Service. The directions in which research has been moving in the past ten years is a primary focus in this chapter.

CHRONOLOGICAL PERIODS

Mesoamerican cultural development may be conveniently summarized by using a scheme of five major periods: Paleo-Indian, Food Collecting or Archaic, Preclassic or Formative, Classic, and Postclassic. In earlier, more naive days, when there were few data to handicap the imagination, the last three periods were envisioned as having additional significance as area-wide cultural stages. As data accumulated, so many instances of precocious or laggardly development became known in individual regions that the position that "periods = stages" became untenable. Now that designations such as *Classic* are intended to denote chronological rather than cultural periods, one might expect that archeologists could agree upon dates for them. Such is, regrettably, not the case; there are considerable differences in the dating of even major periods in different literature sources. My particular version of the periods and their subdivisions appears in Figures 11.2 and 11.3. Two variants not used in my period scheme should be noted. Specialists in areas where Teotihuacan influence was strong frequently prefer to insert a Middle Classic period between AD 400 and 700, moving the start of the Early Classic back to AD 100. Archeologists working in the Valley of Mexico have recently agreed to use a completely new style of periodization, based upon three horizons separated by intermediate periods. Their scheme is included in the chronological chart, Figure 11.2, but will not be used in the text.

The treatment in this chapter will be chronological, and will follow the development of culture period by period. I have eschewed division by geographical sections, such as Maya–Mexican or highland–lowland, hoping thus to keep the

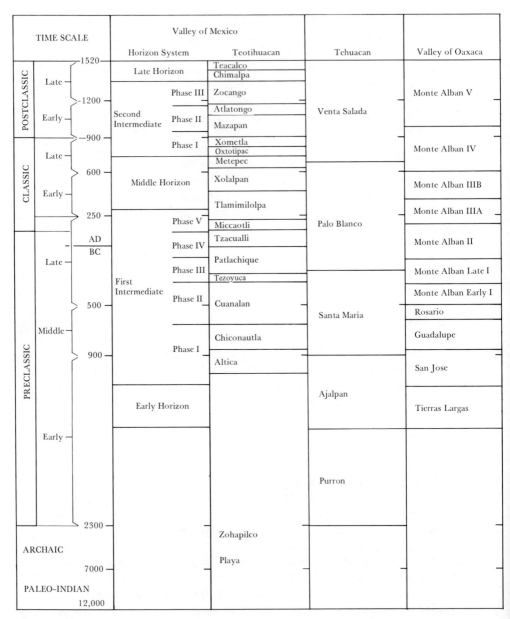

TIME SCALE		Valley of Mexico		Tehuacan	Valley of Oaxaca
		Horizon System	Teotihuacan		
POSTCLASSIC	Late	Late Horizon	Teacalco	Venta Salada	Monte Alban V
			Chimalpa		
		Phase III	Zocango		
	Early	Second Intermediate Phase II	Atlatongo		
			Mazapan		
		Phase I	Xometla		Monte Alban IV
CLASSIC	Late		Oxtotipac		
			Metepec		
		Middle Horizon	Xolalpan	Palo Blanco	Monte Alban IIIB
	Early		Tlamimilolpa		Monte Alban IIIA
		Phase V	Miccaotli		
		Phase IV	Tzacualli		Monte Alban II
	Late	Phase III	Patlachique		Monte Alban Late I
			Tezoyuca	Santa Maria	
		First Intermediate Phase II	Cuanalan		Monte Alban Early I
					Rosario
PRECLASSIC	Middle	Phase I	Chiconautla		Guadalupe
			Altica	Ajalpan	San Jose
	Early	Early Horizon			Tierras Largas
				Purron	
ARCHAIC			Zohapilco		
			Playa		
PALEO-INDIAN					

Time scale values: 1520, 1200, 900, 600, 250, AD / BC, 500, 900, 2300, 7000, 12,000

FIGURE 11.2
Chronological chart.

Southern Vera Cruz–Tabasco	Southern Maya Lowlands	Maya Highlands and Pacific Coast		
		Chiapas Depression	Guatemalan Highlands	Pacific Coast
Soncautla		Tuxtla	Chinautla	
Upper Cerro de las Mesas				
		Ruiz	Ayampuc	
			Pamplona	
Lower Cerro de las Mesas II	Tepeu	Maravillas	Amatle 2	
		Laguena		
	Tzakol	Jiquipilas	Amatle 1/Esperanza	
			Aurora	
Lower Cerro de las Mesas I		Istmo	Arenal	Izapa
	Chicanel	Horcones	Verbena	
Remplas		Guanacaste		Crucero
			Providencia	
Palangana	Mamom	Francesca		
		Escalera		Conchas
Nacaste	Xe	Dili	Las Charcas	
				Jocotal
San Lorenzo		Cotorra		Cuadros
Chicharras				Ocos
Bajio				
Ojochi	Swasey			
				Barra
				Chantuto
Palo Hueco				

Postclassic	Late	AD 1200 – 1520
	Early	AD 900 – 1200
Classic	Late	AD 600 – 900
	Early	AD 250 – 600
Preclassic	Late	500 BC – AD 250
	Middle	900 – 500 BC
	Early	2300 – 900 BC
Archaic		7000 – 2300 BC
Paleo – Indian		12,000 (?) – 7000 BC

FIGURE 11.3
Periods of Mesoamerican prehistory.

focus on Mesoamerican unity and the problems that were Mesoamerican-wide at particular times. At the same time, I have tried to bring out the importance of geographical and ecological contrasts.

THE EARLIEST INHABITANTS

Research into early human occupation of Mesoamerica has lagged far behind such studies in North America. Consequently, patterns of human adaptation have not emerged clearly, and interpretation of the Mesoamerican material hinges upon extending the framework that has been established for North America.

As elsewhere in the New World, there are scattered finds in Mesoamerica suggested to be of 15,000 or more years antiquity. As elsewhere, none of these finds is absolutely conclusive since they all suffer from stratigraphic, dating, or other uncertainties. The most intriguing of these potentially early materials are those from the Valsequillo formation of Puebla, Mexico (Irwin-Williams, 1973). At Valsequillo, undoubted artifacts are present in a deep stratigraphic sequence and are associated with bones of a variety of Pleistocene mammals.

Dating has been a problem at Valsequillo since the only radiocarbon date (20,000 BC) is on shell and is at a location in which the presence of human artifacts is not beyond dispute.

At later times, probably in the range of 10,000 to 7,000 BC, there is a more solid series of finds that either associate human activity with now-extinct animals or provide tools that are typologically early. Gruhn, Bryan, and Nance (1977) have excavated Paleo-Indian campsites at Los Tapiales and La Piedra del Coyote in the Guatemalan highlands. They report a single fluted point and a rather inconsistent set of radiocarbon dates, from which they estimate the date of occupation at 8700 BC. Brown (1980) has recently reported a number of early sites in the Quiche region of highland Guatemala, some of which include Clovis and other early points. No faunal remains or dates are available. Two mammoth-kill sites at Santa Izabel Iztapan in the Valley of Mexico (Aveleyra Arroyo de Anda, 1964) probably date to about 8000 BC. The total of these and other finds suggests a pattern of large-animal hunting not unlike that shown by early fluted-point hunters in North America.

The most detailed information about Paleo-Indian occupation in Mesoamerica comes from the work of Richard S. MacNeish (1964, 1978) in the Tehuacan Valley in Puebla, Mexico. Here the Early Ajureado phase—which ended about 8000 BC but has an undetermined starting date—shows campsites that include the bones of antelope, horse, and jackrabbit and geoclimatic information that suggests a somewhat cooler and drier climate than at present. MacNeish's recent interpretation (1978:136–140) of the Early Ajureado lifestyle stresses the importance of the hunting of medium-size mammals and notes that the subsistence activities are more like those of the Eskimo than those of any modern desert people. This view represents a substantial change from MacNeish's earlier interpretation (1964:532) that laid greater emphasis on small-mammal hunting and plant collecting in Early Ajureado times. The new interpretation moves Early Ajureado closer to a big-game-hunting model and makes the succeeding El Riego phase, associated with a modern climate, sound more like "settling in" than it did formerly.

Recent reconnaissance by MacNeish, Wilkerson, and Nelken-Turner (1981) on the coast of Belize suggests a long sequence of occupation that starts with the Lowe-ha complex, dated by its typological similarities to other sequences at 9000 to 7500 BC. It will be very important to have data on early adaptations in a moist lowland environment, but it should be stressed that the results are still very preliminary.

Aside from these few results, research on the early occupation of Mesoamerica has suffered from a lack of long sequences, a paucity of detailed excavation, and a rudimentary understanding of paleoclimates. The archeological material is certainly there; it simply has been neglected in favor of later and more spectacular remains.

What information is available for the Archaic stage of adaptation in Mesoamerica has been similarly neglected—except for recent work in sites dating to the time period after 4000 BC. This work will be discussed in the following section.

THE TRANSITION TO FOOD PRODUCTION

A critical factor in the emergence of the Mesoamerican lifestyle and all later cultural developments was the transition in subsistence from the collecting of wild foods to food production based upon the native American plant trilogy of corn, squash, and beans and on a few not very important domestic animals.

The Arid Highlands

This transition has been illuminated in admirable detail in the Tehuacan Valley of Central Mexico by Richard S. MacNeish and a team of interdisciplinary experts (Byers, 1967; MacNeish et al., 1975; MacNeish, 1978). The Tehuacan Valley, 240 kilometers southeast of Mexico City, lies at an elevation of 1800 meters. The climate is exceedingly dry, with valley-floor rainfall averaging less than 50 centimeters per year. Aridity is a critical factor in the preservation of plant remains, which in turn is necessary for the study of the origins of domestication. Of 392 prehistoric sites discovered in a survey, MacNeish conducted excavations at 30. A sequence of nine cultural phases was delineated; the first six phases, beginning before 9000 BC and lasting until 900 BC, demonstrate the transition from post-Pleistocene hunting and gathering to full-scale agriculture. By the end of the Ajureado phase (6800 BC), climatic conditions were identical to those of the present. Subsistence depended upon hunting, especially of deer and rabbit, and on gathering a variety of wild plant foods, including maguey, mesquite beans, roots, and a number of tree and cactus fruits. The first domestic plants—chili peppers, amaranth, and squash—appear by the end of the succeeding El Riego phase (6800–5000 BC), but these domesticates provided only a tiny fraction of the diet. The three following phases, between 5000 and 1500 BC, show a continually increasing variety of domestic plants and slow increments in the percentage of the diet derived from cultivation. Important introductions include the first domestic common beans and either wild or domestic maize during the Coxcatlan phase (5000–3400 BC). In spite of steady growth in the techniques of food production, the Tehuacan inhabitants at the end of the Abejas phase at 2300 BC still derived 70 percent of their diet from wild foods. They still followed a seasonal round in which sizable groups (macrobands) aggregated in summer camps but split into tiny microbands during the lean months of winter and early spring. It is not until the Ajalpan phase, beginning at 1500 BC, that there is evidence for year-round sedentary villages, a development which presupposes dependence upon agriculture for a major part of the foodstuffs.

Analyses of the Tehuacan data by Kent Flannery (1968a, 1973) provide insights into the processes involved in wild food procurement in the Tehuacan

Valley. Flannery notes that, although the wild resources utilized by the Te-huacanos included a large variety of edible plants and animals, a relatively small number of species were consistently the most important. Some of the major resource species are strictly seasonal in availability. Cactus fruit and mes-quite seed pods, for example, are available at the beginning of and during the rainy season. In good years, these seasonal foods are present in great abundance, but they must be harvested rapidly to prevent spoilage or consumption by birds and animals. It is the seasonal abundance of such resources that favors large macroband camps during the rainy season. Other resources are available all year but are less abundant at any single place or time. These year-round re-sources support the scattered microbands of the dry season. Making the picture more complicated is the fact that the Tehuacan Valley is divided into a number of environmental microzones. Although the most important resources crosscut microzones, they may be more abundant in some than in others, so that maxi-mum food recovery demands movement from one zone to another.

The still-fragmentary information from the Valley of Oaxaca (Flannery et al., 1967) seems to mirror that from Tehuacan. A close correspondence in artifact types suggests that these two neighboring areas were in close communi-cation in early time periods. Research in the highlands of Tamaulipas, at the northeastern edge of Mesoamerica, has shown that domestic plants appeared in a different sequence than in Tehuacan (MacNeish, 1958). In Tamaulipas, the cultivation of pumpkins and bottle gourds is earlier than in Tehuacan, but domestic corn and beans are later. As in Tehuacan, several millennia of incip-ient cultivation precede the appearance of sedentary villages.

The foregoing information leads to two important conclusions. First, the ap-pearance of domestic plants in different orders in Tehuacan and Tamaulipas shows that there were multiple centers of domestication in Mesoamerica, rather than a single center. Second, Tehuacan, Oaxaca, and Tamaulipas share a com-mon pattern, in which some domesticated plants are introduced quite early into a subsistence routine that otherwise shows little change. Sedentary villages and full-scale agriculture do not appear for millennia after the first domesticates. In these areas, domestication was, as Coe and Flannery note, an evolution, not a revolution (1964:650).

Regions of Abundance

The parts of Mesoamerica that do not share the environmental characteristics of the arid highlands are beginning to produce evidence of different pathways to a dependence upon agriculture. In several areas where wild resources are abun-dant year round within a limited space, sedentary villages probably preceded effective food production rather than followed it. The most detailed information on such a zone has been provided by the work of Christine Niederberger (1979) at the site of Zohapilco in the Valley of Mexico. The Playa phase (5200–3700 BC) already shows year-round occupation. In this case, sedentism was based upon the close juxtaposition of three microzones at the edge of the lake that occupied the center of the valley. The aquatic microenvironment provided an always-available supply of fish and indigenous birds, in addition to summer quantities of the amphibian axolotl and a winter abundance of migratory water-fowl. The nearby alluvial and riparian zone was a natural habitat of wild grasses that included teosinte, the probable ancestor of maize, as well as amaranths and *Chenopodium*. The forest zone added wild fruits and mammals to the food supply. Although the Playa-phase inhabitants may well have already been experimenting with cultivation, there is little doubt that dependence upon wild plants and animals was still at the heart of their economy. By the later Zohapilco phase (2400–1800 BC), domestication had proceeded to the point at which amaranth, chili peppers, pumpkin, and chayote can be recognized in the refuse. An increase in the size of *zea* pollen may mean that maize had also been domesticated.

A second environmental zone in which preagricultural sedentism seems likely is the coastal–estuarine area of both the Atlantic and Pacific coasts of Meso-america. Coe and Flannery (1964) offered this suggestion some years ago as a logical hypothesis, based upon the subsistence of their later and definitely agri-cultural sites on the coast of Guatemala. Since that time, earlier preceramic shell mounds have been investigated at Chantuto on the Pacific coast (Voorhies, 1976), on the Gulf coast of Vera Cruz (Wilkerson, 1975), and have recently been reported by MacNeish et al. (1981) on the coast of Belize. With varying degrees of security, the results all indicate sedentary villages in the coastal-estuarine zone in the third millennium BC or earlier. Because of problems of preservation, none of the sites provides definitive information on plant food; it is thus impossible to say whether these villages predate effective agriculture. It seems likely to me that future work will indicate that they do predate agricul-ture, but it is important to note that Voorhies, who has had extensive experience in this zone, disagrees (1978:17–18).

Domestication in Differing Environments

It now seems clear that the Tehuacan Valley is not the whole story of domesti-cation in Mesoamerica but that the rate and processes involved in switching from hunting and gathering to food production will vary greatly between areas, depending on environmental conditions. In areas similar to Tehuacan, a num-ber of constraints retard the development of dependence upon food production. Food collecting in such areas is based upon a set of wild resources so spaced that seasonal movements between environmental microzones is necessary. No single zone provides a great enough concentration of resources to permit year-round occupation by any large number of people, and different zones are far enough apart so that they cannot be exploited from any single location. In addition, many Tehuacan resources are highly seasonal and occur either just before or during the rainy season—precisely the times at which farmers must devote concentrated attention to agricultural routines. The Tehuacan Valley, therefore, presents a scheduling conflict that would demand sacrificing time needed for collecting some of the most important wild foods if greater attention were to be paid to farming (Flannery, 1968a). There is also a spatial conflict between wild and domestic plants. The best zone for early farming would be the naturally watered riverine zone, but this is also the natural habitat of mesquite. To open this zone for farming would involve sacrificing one of the most abundant wild food resources (Flannery, 1973). Finally, except for a few microzones of quite limited extent, the Tehuacan Valley is a very risky agricultural area, in which dry farming may expect to encounter crop failures with considerable frequency. Given all these factors, the adoption of large-scale agricultural practices involves considerable sacrifice and risk in areas like the Tehuacan Valley. It is easy to understand why a dependence upon food production should lag far behind the appearance of domesticated plants.

The environmental situation in the Valley of Mexico and the coastal zone is quite different. In both these areas, a single microzone—the lake in the valley and estuaries on the coast—provides an abundant source of food that is available year round. Complementary microzones are located near enough so that they can be efficiently exploited from a village located to take advantage of the richest microzone. This situation makes sedentary life possible even before the techniques of food production have been fully developed. Scheduling conflicts between farming and food collection would be minimal, because many key resources are not seasonal and others (such as migratory waterfowl) are available during periods when agricultural routines are not a drain on time. In both of these areas, the zone that is best for early agriculture—the alluvium in the valley and the rain forest on the coast—lies near the locus of already-sedentary villages, so that cultivation need not have involved movement or undue disruption of food-collecting routines. In this environmental setting, it might be expected that an increase in food production might come with greater ease than in areas where key portions of wild food collection would have to be sacrificed if farming were to become a more prominent part of the subsistence system.

For the support of substantial populations by food production, however, the Valley of Mexico and the coast offer quite different prospects. In the valley, the alluvial farming zone is limited in extent, and outside this zone early farmers would have faced the difficult problems of scanty rainfall and frost. Consequently, the further expansion of food production would probably be delayed after the alluvial zone was filled. In the coastal zone, on the other hand, the rain forest areas usable for cultivation are vast in relation to the land demands of early farmers. In addition, tropical forest agriculture is far less subject to the risk of crop loss through drought than is agriculture in the semiarid highlands. In coastal areas, then, one might anticipate a relatively unconstrained expansion of food production once the domestic plants—most of which are not native to the lowlands—had arrived and the basic slash-and-burn techniques of rain forest agriculture had been developed. The potential of early agriculture in the moist lowlands may explain both the Swasey phase in Belize, which may be the earliest agricultural village in Mesoamerica, and the precocity of Olmec civilization—both topics to be explored further in the next section.

In summary, the more archeological data that become available, the more complex the transition from hunting and gathering to food production appears. I would anticipate that we will find that a variety of pathways, a variety of processes, and a variety of pressures are involved and that understanding will be advanced only by considering the combinations of factors in particular environmental settings.

Plant Origins

The foregoing investigations, particularly those in the Tehuacan Valley, have provided a fairly complete picture of the origin of the Mesoamerican crop complex. The only issue that remains a matter of hot debate is the ancestry of maize (see Flannery, 1973, for an excellent review of the problem). Paul Manglesdorf (1974) believes that the domestic strain is descended from a wild maize that is now extinct. Other specialists (Galinat, 1971; Beadle, 1972) have vigorously reasserted an older viewpoint that maize is descended from teosinte, a weedy grass that grows over a wide area in the semiarid highlands of Mexico. The earliest maize from Tehuacan (Coxcatlan phase, 4800–3500 BC) can fit either viewpoint since it can be interpreted as the hypothesized wild ancestor or as an early stage in the transition from teosinte to maize. At the moment, those who favor a teosinte ancestor seem to be winning the argument.

Beans, squash, and chili peppers were all domesticated by the fourth millennium BC. All have known wild ancestors with primarily highland distributions. Beans are the most important of these domesticates nutritionally since, if they are eaten in the same meal with maize, the combination provides a complete protein source, obviating the need for animal protein in the diet. The role and origin of root crops in Mesoamerica has proved more difficult to determine since the plants have poor characteristics for archeological preservation and, if cultivated vegetatively, leave no pollen. The possibility of early root-crop cultivation in the tropical lowlands of Mesoamerica has been raised (Lowe, 1967), but is difficult to test, as is the question of the importance of root crops in later Mesoamerican subsistence systems.

THE BEGINNINGS OF SOCIAL COMPLEXITY

This section will combine consideration of the Early (2300–900 BC) and Middle (900–500 BC) Preclassic periods. This arrangement permits uninterrupted tracing of important phenomena that crosscut the border between the two periods. The Early Preclassic marks the appearance of pottery and sedentary village life in most parts of Mesoamerica. Shortly thereafter, the first signs of increasing cultural complexity appear, followed by the swift development of an incredibly sophisticated Olmec culture on the Gulf coast.

The earliest known pottery in Mesoamerica currently seems to be either the Purron phase of the Tehuacan Valley or the Pox phase known from shell mounds at Puerto Marques on the coast of Guerrero. Both phases begin somewhat before 2300 BC. Purron and Pox ceramics are quite similar; both are crude in technique and nearly devoid of decoration. The earliest vessel shapes have precedents in stone bowls in Tehuacan, and Purron–Pox pottery may well represent the independent invention of ceramic techniques somewhere in Mexico. The recently discovered Swasey-phase pottery from the site of Cuello in the Maya lowlands (Hammond, 1977), for which radiocarbon dates suggest a starting point of 2050 BC, poses a different problem. Swasey pottery is very sophisticated for its early date, yet it shows no very strong relationship with any earlier complex from either Mesoamerica or South America.

Most other ceramic sequences in Mesoamerica start around 1500 BC. Among the most interesting of these somewhat later phases are those from the Pacific coast. Here the earliest pottery, the Barra phase (1600?–1500 BC) was discovered at the site of Altamira in Chiapas, Mexico. Barra is followed by the Ocos phase (1500–1000 BC), best known from La Victoria in coastal Guatemala and also reported from neighboring Chiapas. Barra and Ocos ceramics are very well made and decorated, with both incised and painted designs. Both show similarities to early pottery from Panama, Colombia, and Ecuador.

The data from Altamira also pose problems about what crops were grown in Barra and Ocos times. Although close to the shore, Altamira shows no evidence of a sea-oriented economy and presumably was supported by cultivation. Yet manos and metates, the grinding implements generally taken to be indicative of maize cultivation, are absent. Lowe (1967) has suggested that an abundance of tiny obsidian flakes found at the site may be parts of graters used to shred manioc, a root-crop staple of probably South American origin. If it can be substantiated that manioc cultivation began this early in Mesoamerica, there will be important implications for theories of subsistence development.

The entire question of early contacts between the cultures of Mesoamerica and South America needs additional research. The transfer of Mesoamerican varieties of domesticated maize to South America by the third millennium BC leaves no doubt that such contacts existed. It is also undeniable that pottery was in use in Panama, northern Colombia, and Ecuador earlier than at any location in Mesoamerica and that some of the early ceramic complexes in Mesoamerica show at least generalized resemblances to those in South America. In light of these facts, I find the lack of evidence for Mesoamerican–South American connections in lower Central America to be puzzling. Although coastal travel by sea between the areas is possible, long-distance jumps of culture traits by sea with no archeological sign of intervening stops is not something that I find easy to accept.

By the end of the Early Preclassic, sedentary villages and efficient farming techniques had been established in most parts of Mesoamerica (see Figure 11.2 for phase names in various areas). A striking characteristic of Mesoamerican cultural development, after the establishment of village life, is the rapid appearance of public or ceremonial structures and of communities large enough to indicate that they served as centers for integration of smaller surrounding communities. Such evidences of social complexity, labor coordination, and economic integration occur within a few centuries after the first known villages in most parts of Mesoamerica. Since many of the finds of the earliest phases are too deeply buried beneath later remains to indicate community patterns, and since still earlier phases may yet be discovered in many areas, the evidence is too slim to allow very firm conclusions. At the moment, however, it appears that the period of simple, egalitarian, and self-sufficient villages was short-lived in Mesoamerica.

The Olmecs

A giant step in social complexity was taken by the enigmatic Olmec culture in a homeland in the swampy Gulf coast lowlands of Veracruz and Tabasco. In this area, the earliest known ceramic phases (Ojochi, 1500–1350 BC, and Bajio, 1350–1250 BC) show little relationship to later Olmec material. By the next phase, Chicaharras (1250–1150 BC), sculpture in the Olmec style was being produced, and massive construction efforts were underway at the site of San Lorenzo. By the San Lorenzo phase (1150–900 BC), Olmec culture was in full flower (Coe, 1968). Some remarks on Olmec origins would perhaps be worthwhile, in the light of Jett's comments (Chapter Twelve) on the subject. There seems to me to be no reason to believe that Olmec culture was other than an in-situ development on the Gulf coast. Several centuries of previous occupation precede the Olmec in this area, and at the moment no other area in Mesoamerica is known to have an early complex culture that seems a likely Olmec source. As a nondiffusionist who believes in human inventiveness and, in general, in evolutionary processes that are likely to carry cultures along similar paths of development, I consider the probability of significant interhemispheric input to the Olmec to be diminishingly remote. As Jett notes, however, differences of opinion about diffusion rest far more upon basic assumptions about the nature of culture and human inventiveness than upon any specific evidence, whether positive or negative.

The Olmec hallmark is an art style that is most dramatically expressed in stone carving (Figure 11.4). Undoubtedly the most spectacular carvings are great stone heads nearly 3 meters tall and weighing up to 18 metric tons. The heads depict humans with unusually thick-lipped physiognomies, wearing what look like football helmets. Additional in-the-round and bas-relief carvings show a variety of themes and scenes, many of which seem to be ceremonial. In addition, small carvings of Olmec origin are scattered to the four corners of Meso-

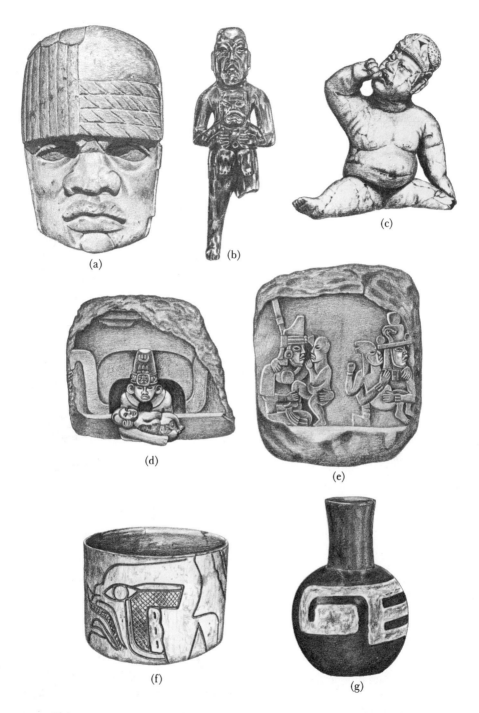

FIGURE 11.4
Olmec art: (a) great stone head; (b) jade figurine; (c) cermic figurine; (d, e) La Venta Altar 5;
(f, g) Olmec pottery.

america, as are Olmec clay figurines. The most undeniably Olmec theme is the "were-jaguar"—human representations infused with feline characteristics to show snarling, downturned mouths, toothless gums, and, occasionally, jaguar fangs. The were-jaguars have an infantile appearance and are not infrequently depicted as babies carried in the arms of equally feline adults.

Two major Olmec sites, San Lorenzo and La Venta, are known from archeological excavations (Coe, 1968; Drucker et al., 1959). The sites are ceremonial centers, not towns or cities; they contain clusters of public buildings and a concentration of sculpture but only limited areas of residential structures. The entire site of San Lorenzo is a construction, a huge, man-made platform surmounted by a number of smallish buildings. The site of La Venta is crammed onto a tiny island in the Tonala River. It contains a series of public structures arranged along a north–south axis, over which towers a single large pyramid.

Surprisingly little is known of the nature and workings of Olmec society. Where the supporting farming population lived and the density of occupation remain mysteries, for lack of archeological surveys. The structure of Olmec elite society is equally unknown. It has been suggested that the great stone heads were portraits of rulers, but they could equally well be gods, symbols of idealized beauty, or famous players of the Mesoamerican ball game. Almost no burials have been recovered at Olmec sites, so we are unable to point to the tombs of kings and princes. No elite residential complexes or administrative buildings have been recovered, so it is impossible to infer societal organization from such sources. Olmec society is not infrequently pictured as a chiefdom in Elman Service's (1963) evolutionary scheme or as a theocracy ruled by priest-leaders. Although such reconstructions are not illogical, they are based almost entirely upon presuppositions about what Olmec society *should* have been rather than upon anything in the nearly nonexistent archeological evidence. A more cautious view could stress only that Olmec society must have had organized, formal leadership, that religious enterprises probably consumed a healthy percentage of the "gross national product," and that there must have been a class of specialists carefully trained in the production of the famous art objects. The ability of the Olmec leaders to concentrate labor is demonstrated in the importation of vast quantities of volcanic stone, for carvings and offerings, from sources in the Tuxtla Mountains more than 80 kilometers distant.

That the Olmec were engaged in long-distance exchange is undeniable. Exotic materials including obsidian, jade, and magnetite are found in Olmec heartland sites; conversely, portable Olmec art is found to the borders of Mesoamerica and even beyond. Large boulder sculptures of unmistakable Olmec workmanship occur in Morelos and El Salvador, and Olmec cave paintings have been found in Guerrero. Moreover, Olmec motifs were widely imitated in stone carving and pottery in a number of areas of Mesoamerica.

The great spread of Olmec influence and the splendor of Olmec sites in comparison with those known in other areas have generated a lively debate about the role of the Olmec in the rise of civilization elsewhere in Mesoamerica. One viewpoint, propounded most forcefully by Michael Coe (1962), pictures the Olmec as a "mother culture," the first civilization in Mesoamerica and the primary source of all later civilizations. The alternative stance, maintained by Kent Flannery (1968b), is that Olmec civilization crystallized at a time when a number of areas had independently reached the point of incipient class stratification. Olmec influence, then, was made possible by—rather than being the cause of—the increasing complexity of other areas. I lean toward the latter viewpoint, but since resolution of the question would demand much fuller information about both the Olmec and the other societies in question, the fun of the debate is not likely to be lost in the near future.

Although the Olmec civilization persisted for some seven centuries, there is little detailed information about the changes within that time span. The mantle of Olmec leadership seems to have passed from San Lorenzo to La Venta about 900 BC. At that time, huge numbers of sculptures at San Lorenzo were defaced and buried, at great expense of labor. The site was occupied by people using new kinds of ceramics, who stayed there for two centuries and then left the site empty and lifeless. One thinks easily of intra-Olmec power struggles, but the facts needed to determine exactly what happened still lie buried beneath the silts of the Gulf coast. After the 900 BC trauma at San Lorenzo, La Venta continued to flourish for three or four centuries until it, too, was abandoned, and Olmec culture came to an end.

Tlatilco

A series of sites and cemeteries in highland Central Mexico exhibits a mixture of ceramics and figurines identical to those of the Gulf coast, with a second ceramic style known variously as *Tlatilco, Rio Cuautla,* or *Highland Olmec* (Figure 11.5). Work by Grove (1974) and Grennes-Ravitz and Coleman (1976) in Morelos, where this manifestation is particularly strong, leads, despite disagreement in details, to two important conclusions. First, the Tlatilco-style ceramics are of highland origin and are considerably more common in the highlands than is true Olmec material. Second, the Tlatilco style was established in Morelos by the fourteenth or fifteenth century before Christ, *before* the arrival of strong Olmec influence. The Olmec ceramic influence arrived in the highlands after 1200 BC, at the time when San Lorenzo was the Olmec center. The famous Olmec rock carvings at the site of Chalcatzingo are even later and are contemporary with Middle Preclassic La Venta.

The Valley of Mexico

In the Valley of Mexico, there is a temporal gap between the sedentary Zohapilco phase (2400–1800 BC) at the site of Zohapilco and the earliest known villages with ceramics, dated at about 1500 BC. Most researchers have assumed that the earliest ceramic phases represent an intrusion of new people into the

FIGURE 11.5
Tlatilco-style ceramics: (a–c) pots; (d, e) figurines; (f) mask. (Parts a–c after Coe, 1965; parts d–f after Ekholm and Bernal, 1971.)

valley, but the question needs rethinking and further research now that there are known to have been local preceramic sedentary populations. Early Preclassic occupation in the valley was light (Sanders et al., 1979). Extensive survey has revealed only 19 sites for the period, none larger than village size and almost all clustered in the moister southern section of the valley. Two questions about the Early Preclassic remain unresolved. The first is whether the tiny settlements that have been discovered are an acceptable match with the remarkably rich burials at the cemetery of Tlatilco. It seems possible that larger centers might still lie beneath the lava flows at the southeastern corner of the valley or have been erased by the expansion of Mexico City. If such settlements did exist, they may never be discovered. The second question is the degree and nature of impact that the Olmec had on Early Preclassic populations of the Valley of Mexico. It is undeniable that Early Preclassic ceramics show strong Olmec influence (Tolstoy and Paradis, 1970), and several authorities still favor the idea of an actual intrusion of Olmec into the area. Sanders, Parsons, and Santley (1979), however, believe that Early Preclassic populations represent immigrants from Morelos. They and the archeologists who have worked with Highland Olmec would see Gulf coast Olmec influence as far more remote.

After 650 BC, the valley shows a surge of population that correlates with the first known civic–ceremonial architecture and the first well-developed regional hierarchy of sites. Cuicuilco, estimated to have had a population of 5,000–10,000 at this time, is the largest site. There is also a second rank of sites with some public architecture but with populations below 3500. Most of the Middle Preclassic population continued to reside at the southern end of the valley, with only scattered settlements of hamlet or village size in the drier northern section.

The Valley of Oaxaca

The Valley of Oaxaca is another major area in highland Mexico about which there are substantial data for the Early Preclassic. A good-sized highland valley at an intermediate elevation of 1500 meters, the Valley of Oaxaca suffers from a scanty rainfall that makes rainfall farming difficult. In parts of the valley, the water table lies no more than 2 to 3 meters below the surface, making possible a technique of pot irrigation accomplished by digging wells to the water table and irrigating individual plants by hand. In addition, a series of streams that emerge at the top of the piedmont zone can be used for small-scale canal irrigation.

Extensive settlement-pattern surveys by several investigators (Flannery et al., 1967; Blanton et al., 1979) have produced invaluable information about the location and nature of early sites. Early and Middle Preclassic phases are Tierras Largas (1500–1100 BC), San José (1150–850 BC), and Guadalupe (850–600 BC). Almost all the Early Preclassic sites are located close to the high water-table zone, suggesting that pot irrigation was utilized by even the earliest farming inhabitants. During the Middle Preclassic, earlier sites increased in size. Occupation spread upward along the larger streams into the piedmont, where a canal irrigation system has been recovered at the site of Hierve el Agua. A most significant feature of the Oaxaca data is the very early development of a large community at San José Mogote. Even in Tierras Largas times, San José Mogote was several times larger than any other village in the Etla arm of the valley, and by the San José phase it had expanded to an impressive size of nearly 40 hectares. In addition, San José phase remains at San José Mogote show signs of social and occupational diversity. The site consisted of three zones: one of small, lower-class residences, one with better-made public buildings, and a third that seems to have been an area of specialized manufacture, since the debris contained both worked and unworked fragments of magnetite, mica, and shell. Olmec influence is apparent during the San Jose phase, and Flannery (1968b) believes that the Valley of Oaxaca and the Olmec heartland were in a trade relationship that involved the exchange of ceremonial and elite items. The Oaxacan elite aped their more elegant trade partners and adopted Olmec styles, particularly in ceremonialism.

The Valley of Guatemala

In the Valley of Guatemala, sedentary village peoples appeared in the Early Preclassic period (Michels, 1979). Most of the few settlements in the valley were of hamlet size, but a small, nucleated village was already present at what later was to be the location of the major center of Kaminaljuyu. A small lake at this spot may have determined the choice of location. By the Middle Preclassic, the settlement at Kaminaljuyu had grown to a population exceeding 1000. Although no evidence of monumental architecture dating to this period has been discovered, household refuse suggests that differences in rank existed among households.

Belize

The discovery of the Swasey phase (2050–1000 BC) at the site of Cuello in Belize (Hammond, 1977) poses interesting questions for Mayanists since the material predates previously known pottery and sedentary villages in the Maya lowlands by more than 1000 years. Although, since its discovery, Swasey pottery has been found mixed with later pottery at several other sites in Belize, it is not yet known whether it penetrated to the interior sections of the Maya lowlands or will prove to be a phenomenon related in some way to the coastal–riverine environments characteristic of Belize. The potential implications for the development of agriculture in Mesoamerica are profound since the Swasey materials hint that the earliest truly effective agriculture may be found in lowland humid zones rather than in the highland areas. During the Middle Preclassic, ceramics appear in the Xe phase at Altar de Sacrificios and at Seibal on the Pasion River. By the Mamom ceramic horizon (600–300 BC), most parts of the Maya lowlands show evidence of occupation (Willey et al., 1967).

THE SPREAD OF CIVILIZATION

In this review, all of the time between 500 BC and AD 250 will be considered as a single period, called the *Late Preclassic*. On the frequent occasions when a finer-scale periodization is desirable, the time between AD 1 and AD 250 will be distinguished as a Protoclassic or Terminal Preclassic period.

The Late Preclassic was a period of regional growth in which almost all areas in Mesoamerica underwent a rapid rise in cultural complexity. This rise was accompanied by population increase, the development of great cities or ceremonial centers, and the crystallization of highly class-stratified societies. By the end of the Preclassic, a number of regional centers had developed into massive sites that far outstripped earlier settlements in both size and grandeur. The most impressive of all these centers was Teotihuacan, which by AD 150 had become the dominant center of all Mesoamerica.

The Valley of Mexico: Teotihuacan

Because of Teotihuacan, the Valley of Mexico deserves first consideration. The valley is a large highland basin at an elevation of 2200 meters. Five shallow, often coalescing lakes that offer both resources, such as fish and waterfowl, and easy canoe transportation cover an extensive area of the valley floor. Rainfall varies considerably within the valley, from a scant 50 centimeters in the north to as much as 100 centimeters in the south. Frosts may occur as early as October and as late as March. The combination of scanty rainfall and frost poses a double danger for agriculturalists, for maize planted early to permit harvesting before fall frosts may not germinate if the rains are delayed. Irrigation obviates this danger by assuring the success of early planting. In prehistoric times, there was fairly extensive canal irrigation from streams and especially from numerous springs located just outside of Teotihuacan. Settlement surveys at the southern and eastern sides of the lake system have provided a good picture of population development (J. Parsons, 1974; Sanders et al., 1979).

At 500 BC, most of the population still resided at the southern end of the valley where Cuicuilco, the largest site of the time, was located. Between 300 and 100 BC, there was a rapid growth of population along the eastern shore of the lakes, particularly at the northeastern corner where Teotihuacan is located. Sanders' (1965) data from the Teotihuacan Valley show a shift in settlement location from sites at high elevations, where rainfall would have been greater, to locations at the juncture of the piedmont and valley floor. He believes that this shift indicates the beginning of techniques of water control, including irrigation from the Teotihuacan springs. By the Patlachique phase (150–1 BC), Teotihuacan covered an area of 6 to 8 square kilometers and already had a population of 30,000 to 40,000, while Cuicuilco at the other end of the lake system may have had a population of 20,000. Elsewhere in the valley, populations tended to be clustered around smaller regional centers that were separated by relatively open space. The emergence of a highly defensible regional center on the Ixtapalapa peninsula, midway between Teotihuacan and Cuicuilco, may be an indication of hostility between the superpowers. About 100 BC, the volcano Xitle erupted, covering a sizable area near Cuicuilco with lava and reducing the site to the status of a small regional center. A second eruption in the third century AD completed the disaster and covered the entire site of Cuicuilco with meters of lava (Sanders et al., 1979:106). A large area of the best farming land in the valley was destroyed by the two eruptions, and the balance of power between the northern and southern ends of the lakes was disrupted.

Although the major structures at Teotihuacan have long been studied, the extent of the site and density of its population are recent archeological revelations. Not until Millon's survey started in the 1960s did it become clear that the site contained nearly 21 square kilometers of almost continuous structures (Millon, 1973). Another revelation was the early date of the city's growth. Recent reestimates (Cowgill, 1974) of population suggest that, by the end of the Tzacualli phase (AD 150), after only three centuries of existence, Teotihuacan was already near its peak population.

Why did Teotihuacan become a great city with such rapidity and then go on to become the dominant force in all of Mesoamerica? Different sets of factors may have been involved in the various stages of the city's development. The initial growth of Teotihuacan as a center that contested Cuicuilco for leadership within the Valley of Mexico was probably due to irrigation and obsidian. When irrigation techniques to utilize the waters of the Teotihuacan springs were developed, the Teotihuacan subvalley was transformed from one of the least desirable agricultural locations within the Valley of Mexico to one that was capable of supporting many thousands of people within a small area. The location, rapid early growth, and dense nucleation of the city all probably relate, as Sanders has long argued (Sanders and Price, 1968), to the effects of irrigation. In addition, the existence of a major obsidian source at Otumba, within easy reach of Teotihuacan, further strengthened the city in relation to other sites within the Valley of Mexico.

Teotihuacan's development received a massive boost in the first century BC, when the eruption of Xitle disastrously weakened Cuicuilco. Although some anthropologists may object that invoking the Xitle eruption is a modern form of catastrophism, systems theorists would argue that deviation-amplifying cycles may be touched off by trigger events. It is hard to imagine a more spectacular trigger than a major volcanic eruption, and the remarkable growth of Teotihuacan in the two centuries thereafter is deviation amplification at its best. A final turning point in the career of Teotihuacan was the shift from a regional to an international economy. That the international economic position, by which Teotihuacan became a manufacturing and export center for most of Mesoamerica, brought several centuries of success and power can hardly be denied. Once again, the control of obsidian sources, including both the Otumba source and the sources of green obsidian in Pachuca, played a role. Whether Teotihuacan's economic power was accompanied by military and political adventurism will be considered in the next section.

The Valley of Oaxaca: Monte Alban

In the Valley of Oaxaca, as in the Valley of Mexico, the most important trend in the Late Preclassic was the rapid growth of a single site that came to dominate the entire area. In Oaxaca, this site was Monte Alban, located on a steep hill at the point where the three arms of the valley come together. Recently published surveys of the site of Monte Alban (Blanton, 1978) and of sizable segments of the Valley of Oaxaca (Blanton et al., 1979) give us a much fuller understanding of the processes involved. Monte Alban was first occupied at about 500 BC and by the end of Monte Alban Early I (300 BC) had grown to a size of 5000 inhabitants. Population growth escalated during period Late I (300–100 BC), in which Monte Alban ballooned to a population of 17,000. Substantial public construction was carried out on the North Platform, just north of the Main Plaza, and by the end of the period over 300 carvings of "Danzantes"—which Joyce Marcus (1974) believes to represent military captives—had been erected at the site. Rural population increased rapidly in parts of the valley located within 18 km of Monte Alban. Heavy occupation of the piedmont zone in this central area indicates an agricultural policy aimed at maximizing production through the use, or possibly overuse, of land that was agriculturally marginal. Period II of Monte Alban seems to have been a hesitation step in the site's development. Population at the site declined by 16 percent, and even more substantial population losses occurred in the rural areas near Monte Alban, where the piedmont zones, so heavily occupied in Late I, were nearly abandoned. Such evidence might be a sign of political or ecological problems, but there continued to be extensive new monumental construction near the Main Plaza, and there are signs that Monte Alban may have been engaged in conquests outside of the Valley of Oaxaca in locations as much as 100 km distant.

Blanton (1978) has suggested that Monte Alban was formed as a disembedded capital, a political center founded in neutral territory as a result of confederation between previously independent political units. In support of this view, he notes that the location of Monte Alban provides neither good agricultural lands nor a reliable source of water and that there is relatively little evidence for specialized manufacture at the site. In addition, Marcus' (1964) interpretation of Monte Alban sculpture as almost entirely militaristic would support the idea of a center of limited function focusing on political and military matters. Blanton's conclusion has been vigorously contested by Sanders and Santley (1978) and by Willey (1979), who believe that Blanton underestimates the agricultural potential and degree of specialization of Monte Alban. They find it unlikely that independent powers at this stage of development would willingly surrender their autonomy to a newly created political entity.

The Coastal Region

On the Gulf and Pacific coasts, the collapse of La Venta and the dissolution of Olmec power initiated a vigorous development of regional sites. On the Gulf coast, Tres Zapotes, a site that had already been occupied in Olmec times, continued to be of importance. Carved stone stelae from Late Preclassic Tres

FIGURE 11.6
Izapa stelae. (After Willey, 1966, and Norman, 1973.)

Zapotes show richly garbed individuals quite like the Maya rulers depicted so magnificently a half millennium later. One Tres Zapotes stela bears a date in a calendrical system believed to be the same as that used by the Classic Maya. If the system is the same, the date is 31 BC, and the inhabitants of the Gulf coast or the Pacific coast (where dated stelae also occur) get credit for the invention of the remarkably accurate Mesoamerican calendar and for the astronomical computations that made it possible.

On the Pacific coast, Izapa was a major Late Preclassic center with dozens of large structures and an important collection of stone carvings. The Izapa style of carving, which spread along the Pacific coast and even into the Guatemalan highlands, is a possible stylistic link between Olmec and Classic Maya art (Figure 11.6). Izapa compositions include complex mythological themes that must have to do with the life and labors of gods or culture heroes but that also include naturalistically rendered humans who may be rulers. Izapa is by no means the whole story of the Pacific coast, for a series of large and important Late Preclassic sites covers the area from the Isthmus of Tehuantepec far into Guatemala. Many of the sites are located in the rainy piedmont zone on the slopes of the volcanic highlands. This distribution suggests that cacao, the source of chocolate—which grows only at these elevations—may already have become a crop of major value.

Chiapas

The Central Depression of Chiapas is also lined with a series of Late Preclassic sites. The best known, and probably the largest, is Chiapa de Corzo, located in a semiarid zone on the banks of the Grijalva River. Excavations at Chiapa de Corzo have shown that the site was subject to constantly changing influences and had trade contacts with a large number of regions in Mesoamerica.

The Valley of Guatemala: Kaminaljuyu

Kaminaljuyu in the Valley of Guatemala emerged as an important center during the Late Preclassic (Michels, 1979). Mounded architecture, which appeared for the first time at 500 BC, built to a climax during the last two centuries BC, when the impressive mound E-III-3 dominated the site. Burials within the mound (Shook and Kidder, 1952) indicate the far-flung trading contacts of Kaminaljuyu, a trading status probably fostered by control of the nearby El Chayal obsidian source. In spite of its grandeur, Kaminaljuyu did not have a large resident population and included only 3000 inhabitants. At about AD 1, a substantial change took place. Almost all of the large mound groups of the preceding period were abandoned, to be replaced by much smaller mounds scattered around the edges of the site—a pattern that was to persist for the next four centuries. In spite of the low concentration of monumental architecture and the lack of any well-defined center for the site, the population of Kaminaljuyu doubled by AD 400, and the first concentrated cluster of obsidian-blade manufacture appeared.

The Maya Lowlands

Despite an apparent late start in much of their area, the Lowland Maya "caught up," with a surge in population and complexity during the Late Preclassic Chicanel horizon. The temple center, which was always to be the characteristic form of Maya settlement, became established during this time. Rich tombs provide a clear sign of social stratification, and fragmentary murals at Tikal indicate that the symbols and finery that were to mark Classic-period rulers were already in use. Recent evidence suggests that the huge site of Mirador, near the Guatemala–Mexico border in the heart of the lowlands, may be mostly of Late Preclassic date (Dahlin and Matheny, personal communication), a fact that will necessitate major rethinking about Maya development.

In the first century AD, the Maya Lowlands were strongly influenced by outside contacts from the Salvador–Honduras area to the southeast. The hallmark of this influence is a new set of ceramics called *Floral Park*, which replaces local Chicanel-horizon complexes in Belize and along the Pasion River near the southern border of the lowlands. Several investigators feel that the Floral Park intrusion is strong enough to suggest actual population influx. This conclusion gained further impetus from the discovery that the Salvadoran volcano, Ilopango, erupted so disastrously in the early centuries BC that it may have caused considerable population displacement (Sheets, 1976). In the central and northern part of the Maya lowlands, local Chicanel complexes persisted, although there is evidence of trade with the Floral Park zone. The role that Floral Park influences had in the crystallization of the Maya Classic period is uncertain, but Floral Park ceramic traits, such as polychrome painting, became an integral part of Classic tradition.

Why civilization should have arisen in the unlikely rain-forest homeland of the Lowland Maya has always proved difficult to understand. Most early civilizations occupied arid regions, and explanations devised to account for civilization in these regions fit very poorly in the humid tropical forest. Two attempts to grapple specifically with the Maya situation deserve mention. William Rathje (1971, 1973) has stressed that the impetus for Maya complexity lay in the desire for certain resources—such as salt, obsidian, and volcanic stone for grinding implements—that are lacking in the Maya lowlands. There is solid archeological evidence that these items were imported into the Maya lowlands from great distances by even the early occupants, and by the Late Preclassic and Classic periods the volume of trade and transport would have been very large. In competing for these external resources, the central area of the lowlands (the Core Zone) would be at a disadvantage in relation to outlying lowland areas (the Buffer Zone) since the Core Zone lies farther from the sources and has no trade products not also available in the Buffer Zone. Consequently, Rathje believes that the Core Zone must have competed by developing a high level of organization and by creating artificial scarce resources—a ceremonial cult and its paraphernalia. One would expect, then, that the Core would show a more rapid development of organization and ceremonialism, a situation that fits the archeological facts.

Recently, an alternative explanation, which stresses population pressure and warfare, has been advanced to explain Maya civilization. This viewpoint, advocated by Webster (1977), calls for an initial colonization of the Maya lowlands by people using a system of slash-and-burn farming. This adaptation was highly productive but required a large amount of land per individual because much of the land was in fallow at any given time. As population expanded, the area of virgin forest available for exploitation was depleted. Competition for land led to warfare, which favored an increase in cultural complexity. Although many Mayanists seem to favor this reconstruction, I remain skeptical. Population in the central part of the lowlands seems to have been lower in the Late Preclassic than it was in peripheral lowland areas. Yet, if the population pressure–warfare–complexity hypothesis is true, population should have been most dense in the central area, where complexity appeared earliest.

THE FIRST PERIOD OF PROSPERITY

The Classic period in Mesoamerica was in many ways the kind of culture implied by its name—prosperous, cosmopolitan, and given to great heights of achievement. The major fact of the Early Classic (AD 250–600) was the commanding position of Teotihuacan, which was felt in one way or another in every corner of Mesoamerica. At the end of the Early Classic, Teotihuacan influence began to decline. Other major centers continued to flourish for a while, until one by one they too fell upon evil days. Very few areas in Mesoamerica escaped culture change of cataclysmic proportions in the years from AD 700 to 1000.

Teotihuacan

Teotihuacan, of course, had already become one of the great cities of the world by the end of the Tzacualli phase at AD 150. Current analysis (Cowgill, 1974) indicates that much of the city's population growth occurred during the Late Preclassic Patlachique and Tzacualli phases and that later growth rates were much reduced. By the Xolalpan phase (AD 450–650), the population had reached a peak that was probably around 125,000—although a figure as high as 200,000 is not beyond reason (Millon, 1974). The most recent interpretation (Sanders et al., 1979) of the Valley of Mexico settlement-pattern data suggests a considerably different relationship between population at Teotihuacan and in the rest of the valley than was portrayed earlier. It now appears that the time at which Teotihuacan had the strongest tendency to attract people into its urban zone was between 100 BC and AD 100, when 80–90 percent of the population in the entire Valley of Mexico lived within the city limits. This was also a time at which a relatively low percentage of the urban inhabitants was engaged in craft production, so that Teotihuacan was "a highly stratified agrarian community in which more than 90 percent of a large nucleated population was engaged in full-time agriculture" (Sanders et al., 1979:108). By AD 300, there was once again a substantial rural population living throughout the valley in small communities located where they could supply raw materials for the city's needs. Teotihuacan still had no rivals within the valley since the next largest community was no more than one-twentieth of its size. Specialization had increased considerably, and as many as one-third of the urban dwellers may have been involved in specialized occupations.

As a city, Teotihuacan was a masterpiece of urban planning (Figure 11.7). Major thoroughfares, straight and obviously carefully engineered, cross near the center of the city. Structures are arranged in careful blocks that utilize a standard unit of measurement. The largest structures, the temples of the Sun and Moon, were religious in function, as were many other structures along the Street of the Dead. At the intersection of the two major avenues lie the

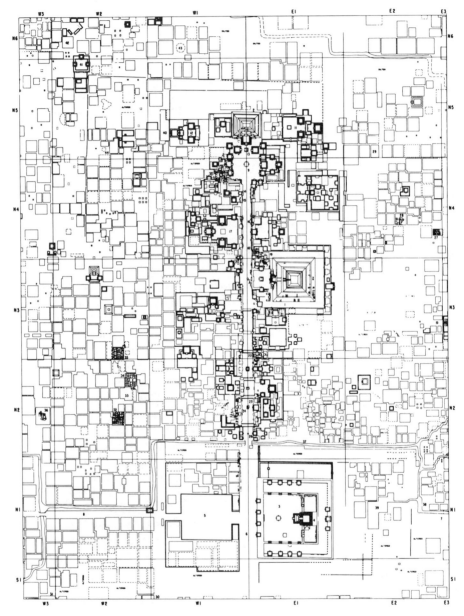

FIGURE 11.7
Map of Teotihuacan.

Cuidadela, presumed by many to have been an administrative center, and the Great Compound, which was probably a central market. Many of the other structures in the central part of the city appear to have been residential. They show a great love of luxury and the lavish expenditure of skilled labor in careful construction and elaborate decoration.

The careful planning of the city, the problems of provisioning so large a populace, and the amount of specialization and trade that must have gone on presuppose a complex administrative structure. Yet, again, as with the Olmec, crucial kinds of information that bear upon social structure are lacking. Most art at Teotihuacan is religious (Figure 11.8). It shows gods and priests repeated monotonously; George Kubler (1967) has likened it to a litany in which the gods were placated by the repeated recitation of their attributes and gifts. Informative though it may be about religious beliefs, the art says little about secular life; missing completely are representations of bureaucrats at work or of elite Teotihuacanos living the good life they had created. Since cremation, unaccompanied by offerings, was the favored burial practice, graves provide no key to social status. The best sorts of information about social arrangements will probably come from comparisons of the apartmentlike building complexes to determine variation in room size, features, and positioning. Although too few such complexes have been excavated to provide much of a comparative base, it is already evident that contrasts—such as that between the formal and luxurious complex of Xolalpan and the chaotic jumble of small rooms at Tlamimilolpa— must have social significance (Figure 11.9).

Much more substantial information exists about the role of Teotihuacan as a highly specialized center for manufacture and trade. Surface collections have provided evidence of workshop areas devoted to such specialized products as obsidian tools, ceramics, figurines, and items of shell. Workshops of a single kind cluster together to create a pattern suggestive of the craft wards or *barrios* found in Aztec cities. It is undoubtedly indicative of Teotihuacan's special status that specialization at other Classic-period centers is scattered and lacks this barriolike character.

The Teotihuacan manufacturing specialty best studied to date is the obsidian industry (Spence, 1975). More than 400 workshops have already been discovered, some dating as early as the Patlachique phase (150–1 BC). By the time the city reached its apogee, there was a clear division of obsidian workshops into two kinds: "local" shops that produced a variety of tools commonly used within the city itself and "export" shops that produced specialized items, at least some of which were widely traded throughout Mesoamerica.

Teotihuacan goods were desired throughout Mesoamerica. The most easily identified are objects of Central Mexican green obsidian, which are found in abundance in areas as far distant from Teotihuacan as the Maya lowlands. Thin Orange pottery, a ware produced somewhere in Puebla but undoubtedly peddled by Teotihuacan, also has a wide distribution, despite obvious problems in transporting it without breakage (Figure 11.10). The desirability of Teoti-

FIGURE 11.8
Murals from Teotihuacan. (After Ekholm and Bernal, 1971.)

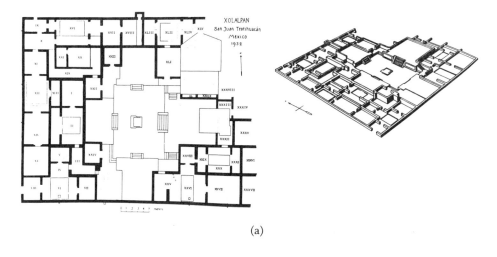

(a)

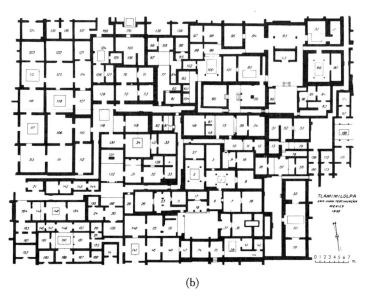

(b)

FIGURE 11.9
Residential compexes at Teotihuacan: (a) Xolalpan; (b) Tlamimilolpa. (From Gordon R. Willey, *An Introduction to American Archaeology:* Vol. I, © 1966, pp. 112, 113. Reprinted by permission of Prentice-Hall, Inc., Englewood Cliffs, New Jersey.)

huacan products also led to copious imitation; local potters everywhere in Meso-america borrowed Teotihuacan vessel shapes, especially the cylindrical tripod.

Millon (1973, 1974) stresses that the economic functioning of Teotihuacan was intimately interwoven with its religious system. He pictures Teotihuacan as a great pilgrimage center, attracting people and trade through theological as

FIGURE 11.10
Teotihuacan pottery. (After Coe, 1962.)

well as technological sophistication. That gods and goods were indeed compatible seems demonstrated by the wide diffusion of Central Mexican deities, such as the rain god Tlaloc, whose goggle-eyed visage occurs throughout Mesoamerica and who seems to have been accepted into other pantheons as eagerly as Teotihuacan vessels were accepted into households.

That Teotihuacan was enormously influential throughout Mesoamerica is undeniable, but ideas about the mechanisms of Teotihuacan influence are currently in flux. It may be best to consider the problem in terms of zones of interaction at different distances from Central Mexico. Nearby Cholula, just across the Sierra Nevada from the Valley of Mexico, is generally agreed to have been under the direct control of Teotihuacan, although the archeological data to confirm this conclusion are very thin. The Cholula area is close enough to the Valley of Mexico for the exchange of bulk quantities of utilitarian goods to have been possible. At a slightly greater distance, communities on the Gulf coast such as Cerro de las Mesas are spoken of as being "strongly influenced" by Teotihuacan, but most archeological work in the area is ancient and further research in the light of modern knowledge is badly needed. The coast was an important area for Teotihuacan since it was a possible source of lowland products and is close enough for the movement of goods in quantity. The Aztecs, after all, regularly imported food from the Gulf coast. Most archeologists would probably not object strongly to the suggestion that Teotihuacan could have taken political control of some areas at this distance.

But a debate has come to the fore recently about the ability of Teotihuacan to engage in conquest at considerably greater distance for the sake of high-value, low-volume goods. Kaminaljuyu in the highlands of Guatemala, long considered a likely Teotihuacan conquest, has been reinterpreted (Brown, 1977a; Michels, 1979) as a port-of-trade at which Teotihuacan merchants met those from other areas under the mantle of political neutrality. The Maya lowlands, earlier considered too remote for conquest, have moved in the opposite direction with the revelation that a Mexicanized ruler occupied the throne of Tikal during the Early Classic (Coggins, 1975). The data and disagreements will be discussed in the pages that follow, but I should note at this point that I am now convinced that Teotihuacan was capable of interfering in local politics in all of these areas, to the extent of dictating matters that were of concern to it.

It used to be thought that the city of Teotihuacan flourished only until the end of the Xolalpan phase at AD 650 and that the succeeding Metepec phase (AD 650–750) represented a greatly diminished population living among the ruins of the city. Current evidence (Cowgill, 1974), however, suggests that the population of Metepec Teotihuacan was little less than that for Xolalpan and that the population decline occurred only late in the Metepec phase. Teotihuacan's wide-ranging power, however, seems to have been lost far earlier, for at most of the sites where Teotihuacan influence was strong the impingement on local culture seems to have stopped not long after AD 600.

Understanding the decline of Teotihuacan is a critical problem for Mesoamerican archeology, since it may be the key factor in the several centuries of cultural reformulation that mark the end of the Classic period. The earlier hypothesis that the site succumbed to invaders has been reasserted by Sanders, Parsons, and Santley (1979:134–137), who stress the important power base that the large Valley of Puebla might have offered to Cholula. The problem is immensely complex, however; its elucidation will demand far more detailed information about the political and economic integration of Teotihuacan itself as well as a presently unavailable fund of data on regional interaction. So far, the problem, perhaps because of its magnitude, has not been thoroughly discussed by those who have the most detailed knowledge of Central Mexico at this time period.

The Gulf Coast

The Gulf coast was the site of vigorous but little known Classic cultures. In the southern part of Veracruz, the important Preclassic sites of Tres Zapotes and Cerro de las Mesas continued to thrive in the Classic. They show a blend of influences, with carved monuments bearing calendrical dates in the Maya system at Cerro de las Mesas and abundant Teotihuacan imports at both sites.

It is likely that the area was of importance to Teotihuacan both as a source of lowland resources and as a route to and point of contact with the cultures of southern Mesoamerica. To the north, in central Veracruz, the influential Classic Veracruz culture and art style centered at the site of El Tajin. Located in a rain-forest-covered valley near the town of Papantla, El Tajin was a massive site; only its ceremonial core has as yet been investigated archeologically. Influenced by Teotihuacan during the Early Classic, El Tajin survived the Teotihuacan demise to be one of the centers contesting for power in Central Mexico during the Late Classic. Classic Veracruz was an important center of the Mesoamerican ball game, and much of its art is devoted to the decoration of stone yokes, *palmas,* and *hachas,* which are thought to have been ball-game accoutrements.

Monte Alban

Monte Alban was undoubtedly the dominant site in Oaxaca during the Classic period. The entire top of the hill upon which the site is located was leveled to create a gigantic complex of structures around a central plaza. Construction in the plaza area started as early as Monte Alban II, but the site was repeatedly remodeled, and the bulk of the visible structures date from the Classic. The Main Plaza, however, does not seem to have been intended as a gathering place for the general public since it could be entered only by limited and difficult routes of access. Below the summit of the site, a series of terraced hillslopes were the residential areas for the populace.

Monte Alban's Classic period is divided into IIIA (AD 200–400), when Teotihuacan influence was noticeable at the site, and IIIB (AD 400–600), a continued flourish with little outside input. Although there are both Teotihuacan artifacts and architectural elements at Monte Alban, Blanton (1978:57) stresses that the resemblances are "diffuse" and "generic," and it has always been assumed that the Valley of Oaxaca maintained its autonomy. That it had a special relationship to Teotihuacan, however, is demonstrated by the existence of a Oaxacan barrio at Teotihuacan (Millon, 1974). For more than two centuries, beginning at AD 400, the residents of this barrio either imported or produced pottery that was identical to that in use at Monte Alban. They also constructed a tomb built in typical Oaxacan style that contained a Oaxacan-type carved stela. At the same time, barrio inhabitants lived in buildings that were of pure Teotihuacan style and worshiped in a temple that followed Teotihuacan architectural conventions.

Some remarkable shifts in settlement patterns occurred during the Classic period in Oaxaca (Blanton et al., 1979). During period IIIA, the site of Monte Alban itself grew slowly to a population of 16,500, but there was a rapid expansion elsewhere in the surveyed areas of the valley that more than doubled the populations of period II. Most of the growth occurred in the Valle Grande, the southern branch of the valley that offers the largest amount of farming land. A most surprising new discovery is that the site of Jalieza in the Valle Grande achieved a population of 12,000. Unlike Monte Alban, Jalieza seems not to have been a ceremonial–elite center, for it has a very low concentration of mounded architecture.

Although total population of the surveyed areas of the Valley of Oaxaca did not change much between periods IIIA and IIIB, there were drastic shifts in the location of the inhabitants. The heavy population in the Valle Grande almost disappeared in IIIB and Jalieza was abandoned. Instead, population boomed at Monte Alban itself, which reached a peak of 24,000 residents. Smaller administrative centers blossomed in this central zone, but the largest of them was no more than one-tenth the size of Monte Alban. This prosperous period ended about AD 600, when Monte Alban was nearly abandoned and authority in the valley split into a fragmentary pattern of regional centers.

Kaminaljuyu

At about AD 400, profound changes began to affect the highland Guatemalan site of Kaminaljuyu (Cheek, 1977a). At first the changes were gradual—the introduction of some Mexican trade goods into burials, then a mixing of Teotihuacan architectural traits with native ones. About AD 500, the pattern culminated in the construction of a large number of buildings in a style very faithful to that of Teotihuacan; it even imitated the concretelike surfacing material in use there. There were two loci of such structures at the site—one at the two principal building complexes in the site center, called the *Palangana* and the *Acropolis*, and the second at Mounds A and B some 1.7 km distant. Burial offerings were replete with Mexican trade goods and symbolism. It was this drastic change that for many years has led archeologists to think of a Teotihuacan conquest of Kaminaljuyu.

New information about settlement patterns in the whole Valley of Guatemala has made the situation considerably more complicated (Brown, 1977a). It turns out that there was a second site at this time period equivalent to Kaminaljuyu in size and complexity. This site, San Antonio Frutal, is located at the opposite (southern) end of the valley. Frutal shows no Teotihuacan architecture; instead, Brown believes, it demonstrates a strong relationship with Maya groups to the north of the Valley of Guatemala. It should be noted, however, that Sanders (1977), with whom I agree, considers these relationships much less evident than the Kaminaljuyu–Teotihuacan similarities. Between Kaminaljuyu and Frutal, the near vacancy of the stretch of territory in the center of the valley supports the idea that the valley was divided into two political units. Located within this vacant strip is a third important site, Solano. Solano, although it has a substantial number of mounds, has a tiny residential area. Like Kaminaljuyu, Solano demonstrates Teotihuacan-style architecture and trade goods.

Brown (1977b) interprets Solano as a port-of-trade, at which Teotihuacan merchants resident at Kaminaljuyu met northern Maya merchants resident at San Antonio Frutal to exchange goods. Michels carries Brown's interpretation even further by insisting that "Kaminaljuyu was unwilling to concede political hegemony or even share political control" (1979:208–209) with Teotihuacan. He interprets the immense Teotihuacan-style complex at the Palangana–Acropolis as the attempt of a local chief to "neutralize . . . Teotihuacan prestige by expropriating its most conspicuous symbolic representation—its architectural style" (1979:209). Cheek (1977b) would disagree; he believes that Teotihuacan actually did gain political control, although by infiltration rather than by direct conquest. I agree with Cheek. The vast bulk of public architecture at Kaminaljuyu is in direct Teotihuacan style. To attribute part of this architecture to Teotihuacanos and the rest to local chiefs imitating Teotihuacanos seems to me to partition archeological data in a manner that is far from self-evident. In addition, one must consider the Lowland Maya evidence. If a Teotihuacan-related ruler was capable of gaining the throne of Tikal, a vastly larger and more formidable center than any in the Guatemalan highlands, it seems unlikely that Kaminaljuyu chiefs could have maintained their autonomy against Teotihuacan interference.

Like Monte Alban, Kaminaljuyu did not suffer from the withdrawal of Teotihuacan at about AD 600. Population of the site, which had declined during the Teotihuacan intrusion, rebounded to an all-time peak of 6500 and the site continued to be a major center for another two centuries. Frutal also prospered, and Solano added a considerable resident population and smaller tributary centers. In effect, the basic political structure of the Valley of Guatemala seems to have remained unchanged by the disappearance of Teotihuacan influence.

The Maya Lowlands

Archeology in the Maya lowlands has developed different emphases from those characteristic of Mesoamerican highland archeology. Although partly a result of historic events and personages, these differences are even more strongly shaped by environmental factors and the kinds of data most readily available in the two zones. The ecological and settlement-pattern studies that have proved so fruitful for highland archeologists have been badly neglected in the Maya lowlands. Both the difficulty of conducting large-scale surveys in the rain forest and the long-standing assumption of lowland ecological homogeneity have been involved in the neglect. On the other hand, the presence in the Maya area of rich and diversified burial offerings, artistic depictions of elite life, and hieroglyphic inscriptions giving historical data provides a wealth of information about social and political arrangements that is unmatched in any of the highland areas. That Mayanists talk eagerly of priests, princes, and politics, while their Mexican colleagues discuss population densities and subsistence practices, is more a reflection of available data than of any contrast between historical and scientific temperaments.

Several generations of archeological research have provided a solid outline of Classic-period development, at least for the southern half of the Maya lowlands in the Peten district of Guatemala and neighboring Belize and southern Mexico. Recent discoveries that revealed the solid Preclassic base of Maya civilization have made the transition to the Classic appear less a sudden flowering or possible import than a reformation—the coming together of a set of features, most of which were present, or at least presaged, in earlier times. But the change from Preclassic to Classic was drastic, ceramically and architecturally, and especially in the appearance of stone carving and hieroglyphic inscriptions (including dates in the long-count calendrical system). Some of the Classic features seem to have been indigenous developments in the lowlands; others were imported from surrounding areas. Whatever the sources, the blend of these characteristics produced an unmistakable constellation that was uniquely and forever Mayan.

THE EARLY CLASSIC □ The easiest trend to follow within the Early Classic is the spread of carved stone monuments that include dated inscriptions. The earliest such calendrical inscription in Maya territory, which almost certainly follows the calendar used earlier on the Gulf and Pacific coasts, occurs on Stela 29 at Tikal. The date is 8.12.13.8.15 in the Maya calendar, which corresponds to 6 July AD 292 in the Christian calendar. In the first century and a half after the date on Stela 29, Maya calendrical dates occur only within a restricted region near the heart of the Maya lowlands. But between AD 435 and 534 the calendrical custom expanded explosively to the corners of the Maya lowlands. Associated with carving and calendrics, although by no means in a one-to-one correlation, was the Maya temple, placed on a towering pyramidal substructure and vaulted by use of the Maya-invented corbeled arch.

Data on population distribution suggest that patterns varied from region to region. Sites in the heart of the lowlands show substantial Early Classic populations, which represent an increase over those of the Late Preclassic. Sites on the Usumacinta and Pasion rivers, on the other hand, seem to have been sparsely occupied during the Early Classic, even though sites on the Pasion had been heavily populated during the Late Preclassic. These variations in regional patterns suggest that many more data are needed before we can speak with confidence about population trends for the Maya lowlands as a whole.

It was once thought that there was a period at the start of the Early Classic before Teotihuacan influence was felt in the Maya lowlands. However, more recent work has suggested that Teotihuacan contacts, at least in some sites, began at the very start of the Early Classic—if not in the Late Preclassic. Teotihuacan influence included imported items such as green obsidian, the imitation of vessel shapes, and portrayal of Mexican gods, but Teotihuacan architectural forms had little impact in the Maya lowlands. Those who emphasize the role of trade in Maya development tend to believe that contact with Teotihuacan commercialism may have been a critical factor in shaping the Maya destiny. It now appears that Teotihuacan involvement in the Maya lowlands may have been more direct and aggressive than simple trading arrangements. In AD 378, a ruler, called *Curl Snout* on the basis of his identifying glyph, took the throne of Tikal—apparently after marrying the daughter of the previous ruler. Curl Snout was clearly a foreigner to the lowlands, since both his portrayals on stelae and his burial goods reveal multiple examples of Mexican connections. I suspect that his affiliations were mediated through Kaminaljuyu in the Guatemalan highlands rather than being directly with Teotihuacan since many of the tomb items seems to be Kaminaljuyu versions of Mexican themes. This intrusion contributed to the prosperity of Tikal, for Curl Snout ruled successfully for nearly 20 years and was succeeded by his son, Stormy Sky, who proved to be the greatest of Tikal's Early Classic rulers. Whether Curl Snout came to the throne by overt military action or by political maneuvering cannot yet be determined. The latter seems more likely since the difficulties of a military campaign to conquer Tikal from outside would have been immense.

Between 9.5.0.0.0 and 9.8.0.0.0 in the Mayan calendar (AD 534–593), there is a curious gap in dated monuments that may be associated with a slowdown in construction. In a recent consideration of this hiatus, Willey (1974) terms it a "rehearsal" for the later collapse at the end of the Classic and attributes it (agreeing with Rathje, 1973) to a loss of the symbiotic relationships between the Maya and other Mesoamerican cultures occasioned by the decline of Teotihuacan influence.

THE LATE CLASSIC □ Maya recovery from the hiatus was successful, and with the start of the Late Classic period around AD 600 the Maya lowlands began a period of unparalleled prosperity. The prosperity was marked by striking population growth, both in the central area and in the peripheral areas that had been less populated during the Early Classic. Population growth was everywhere accompanied by heightened construction efforts. The building projects included both new temples and an ever-increasing number of the administrative or residential structures that have traditionally been termed *palaces*. As the number of important centers escalated, there is clear inscriptional evidence of warfare and conquest as well as suggestions of increasing rigidity in the class structure of Maya society. By about AD 800, Maya Classic vigor had run its course, and the lowland area underwent a spectacular decline that, in little more than a century, resulted in the nearly total depopulation of most of the southern lowlands.

Starting from this brief outline of Maya Classic development, it is possible to flesh out the picture with more specifics about the operation of society. The reconstruction of Lowland Maya culture that most Mayanists would propose today is very different from that of a generation ago (see Willey and Shimkin, 1973; Culbert, 1974). The changes in viewpoint are the result both of increased data from recent projects and of the infiltration of more systemic ideas from other areas of anthropology.

SUBSISTENCE PATTERN □ Maya subsistence adaptation is one of the areas that has received serious reconsideration. The lowland environment offers challenges for farming quite different from those that exist in the highlands. In the lowlands frost is unknown, rainfall is ample for a single summer crop, and the lack of surface water makes irrigation impossible. On the other hand, soil fertility is a serious problem; cleared lands are rapidly leached, and the recovery of soil nutrients is a slow process. For many years it was assumed that the only practical means of lowland farming was a long-fallow, slash-and-burn system. Since few variations were possible and since all farmers knew the best routine, maximum potential could be achieved without management, and the elite had no necessary role in the system.

The logical result of this assumed system would be severe limitations on population density and on the number of people that could live in a single community. But as the house mound counts at an increasing number of prehistoric sites began to provide estimates of population, a paradox arose; there had been more people than could have been supported by slash-and-burn farming. The likely conclusion was that the slash-and-burn routine does *not* provide maximum yield per unit of available land. Instead, it is a labor-conservative system that maximizes yield per man-hour. Given appropriate pressure or incentives, greater productivity per unit of land could be achieved through a whole series of alternatives. Such alternatives might include a shortened fallow cycle, root cropping, ramon-tree cultivation, double cropping, terracing, and raised-field agriculture in swampy areas. Since these alternatives were first suggested, a considerable amount of archeological evidence for their existence has accumulated (Harrison and Turner, 1978). In particular, the increased possibility that the Maya had very extensive systems of raised-field agriculture (Adams, 1980) would mean that their subsistence system was one of much greater intensiveness than previously supposed. Such a system would have had drastic implications for the support capacity of the area and the need for managerial control.

POPULATION □ Recent projects in the Maya lowlands that have sampled whole sites, rather than just ceremonial precincts, have transformed our knowledge of Maya centers. It is now clear that, at major sites like Tikal (Haviland, 1970), tens of thousands of people lived within easy walking distance of the site center. At the same time, the density of population, even in the heart of Maya sites, numbered no more than a few hundred inhabitants per square kilometer—far below the several thousand persons per square kilometer at the ultimate urban center of Teotihuacan. In Maya sites, house groups were separated by patches of open land, presumably devoted to trees and gardens, in contrast to the wall-to-wall construction at Teotihuacan (Figure 11.11). Another important

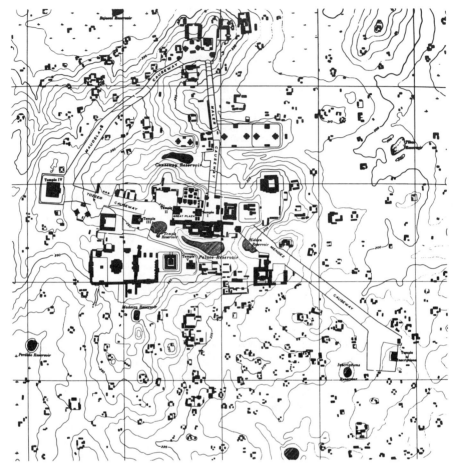

FIGURE 11.11
Map of Tikal. (Courtesy of the University Museum, University of Pennsylvania.)

difference, however, was that, while Teotihuacan had obvious borders beyond which there was almost no population, the lower-density concentrations of people around Maya centers spread over a much larger area. Teotihuacan at its greatest extent covered fewer than 25 square kilometers. Haviland's survey data show that the population core at Tikal was scattered over an area exceeding 60 square kilometers. Even beyond this area, population did not cease but was simply reduced to a lower density; scattered house groups and small ceremonial centers occur throughout the territory between Tikal and neighboring major centers. Central Mexico and the Maya lowlands show two quite different patterns of arranging people in space. The interesting questions for research are the causes and consequences of the different patterns rather than the much discussed (but largely semantic) question of whether both or only one of these patterns may be called urban.

GOODS PRODUCTION AND TRADE □ Ideas about the economic organization of the Classic Maya have also changed in the light of recent archeological data. That elite goods, cult paraphernalia, and carving were the products of specialized and highly skilled craftworkers has long been evident. It is now known that some consumer products, such as pottery and stone tools, were also produced by specialists—although the concentrated craft barrios noted at Teotihuacan seem to be lacking at Maya centers (Figure 11.12). Since ecological diversity is a spur to village specialization and trade in highland Mesoamerica, it has often been suggested that the greater homogeneity of the lowlands should have resulted in a weak development of specialization among the Maya. This inference, however, is based upon two assumptions: first, that the lowlands really *are* homogeneous enough to minimize local differences in the availability of raw materials; and, second, that ecological diversity is the only factor that is likely to promote specialization. I tend to believe that neither of these assumptions is accurate.

The emphasis upon Maya trade has been revitalized by the work of Webb (1964, 1973) and Rathje (1971, 1973). In addition to elite goods, it now seems clear that the Maya imported from long distances a large volume of raw materials (or products) for the use of all segments of Maya society. Maintaining the flow of these materials must have demanded massive efforts in organization, transportation, and distribution as well as a sizable outflow of exports. Since most lowland resources are perishable, the nature of Maya exports is not clear; we are uncertain whether the Maya depended heavily upon export of forest products or specialized in processing activities, such as the production of textiles. I have recently suggested (Culbert, 1977) that we must also consider the possibility that there was substantial trade in foodstuffs and specialized consumer goods *within* the Maya lowlands.

SOCIAL AND POLITICAL ORGANIZATION □ The Maya were ruled by a hereditary aristocracy, and considerable information on ruling families has been amassed since the time of Proskouriakoff's (1960) breakthrough in identifying records of rulers in the inscriptions. Rathje's (1970) work with burial offerings has suggested that social mobility decreased between the Early and Late Classic, and a number of authors have found evidence for a widening social gulf between elite and commoners (see especially Willey and Shimkin, 1973). That the Maya elite were involved in elaborate ceremonialism and were the sponsors of esoteric studies in astronomy and calendrics has long been obvious. Recent trends in thinking about ecological and economic patterns have added to the tasks of the elite an increased administrative responsibility for the manage-

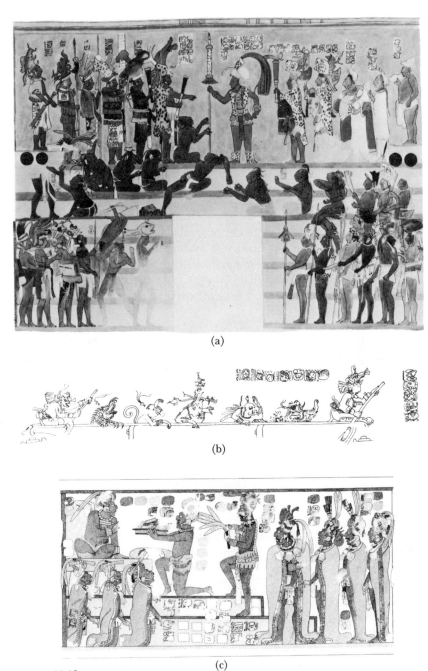

(a)

(b)

(c)

FIGURE 11.12
Mayan art: (a) Bonampak mural; (b) boatload of Mayan gods; (c) throne scene from a painted vessel. (Part a courtesy of the Peabody Museum, Harvard University; part b after Culbert, 1974; part c courtesy of the University Museum, University of Pennsylvania.)

ment of subsistence, manufacturing, and trade. This idea would suggest that there were rewards to the lower echelons of society in the form of imported goods and manufactured items—a tangible supplement to the oft-mentioned joys provided by ceremonials and fiestas.

The size of political units in the Maya lowlands is a matter of uncertainty. For a long time, a model of independent city–states prevailed, but recent research suggests that some half-dozen sites were as much as an order of magnitude larger than average ceremonial centers, and there has been increasing consideration of the possibility of regional political units headed by these "supersites." Inscriptions and art show that warfare was commonplace, especially in Late Classic times, and that major sites claimed campaigns of conquest. Whether these conquests forged lasting empires, however, is not indicated by present evidence.

THE MAYA CALENDAR □ One can hardly write of the Maya without noting their achievements in writing and calendrics. The Maya hieroglyphic script was the only full system of writing invented by native Americans. The script still cannot be translated into its original language, but the meaning of many individual signs has been determined, so that considerable passages of the texts can be interpreted. Although Maya inscriptions contain large amounts of ritual and calendric matters, it is now clear that they are, more than anything else, royal inscriptions that celebrate the achievements of important leaders. American archeologists have always been disdainful of "great men"; now that we have some great men of our own, however, we are beginning to find that there is much of cultural importance to be learned from historical detail.

The Maya calendrical system is a marvel of complexity. Not satisfied, in their passion for time, with a single calendar, the Maya had two calendars that operated simultaneously. One was a 365-day calendar, the closest whole-day approximation to the solar year (which the Maya knew with great accuracy). The second was a 260-day calendar of great sacred significance, although of unknown origin. Each day was designated by its position in both calendars. For example, the day 4 Ahau 18 Zotz occurred when the 260-day calendar had reached 4 Ahau at the same time that the 365-day count stood at 18 Zotz. The combined cycle of the calendars allowed any given day, such as 4 Ahau 18 Zotz, to occur only once each 52 years. This 52-year cycle was known as the *Calendar Round*. To be an accurate record of time, a calendar must count from some fixed starting point. This point for the Maya calendar was a day in the year 3113 BC—undoubtedly the date of some mythical event of great importance. Elapsed time from the starting point was recorded in a five-place notation that included periods of 400 years, 20 years, single years, months, and days to give a figure such as 8.16.9.3.0. This full five-place notation, called the *long count,* was unfortunately abandoned around AD 900 in favor of an abbreviated system subject to the same kinds of ambiguities that would occur if we began to record dates as '78 rather than 1878 or 1978. Because of this uncertainty, the exact correlation of the Maya and Christian calendars has been a matter of debate, although most Mayanists now accept a correlation known as the Goodman–Martinez–Thompson correlation.

Although the Maya carried the use of the calendar to its greatest extremes, the basics of the system seem to have been worked out outside the Maya area, perhaps by the Olmecs. Nor were the Maya the only users of the system, for varieties of the same calendar were used throughout Mesoamerica until the time of the conquest. Everywhere the calendar was tied to religion and to feast days of the gods and was used to predict the omens of good or ill luck related to particular days.

THE TERMINAL CLASSIC □ Among Mayanists it is becoming common to distinguish the Late Classic (AD 600–800) from the Terminal Classic (AD 800–900 or 950). The Late Classic was the pinnacle of Maya lowland success—population was at a peak, the amount of civic and ceremonial construction was immense, and carving and other arts flourished. Yet disaster lurked in the near future, and the Maya soon underwent a collapse that has few parallels in the history of early civilizations. The first realization of the collapse came from turn-of-the-century work on Maya-dated inscriptions. The inscriptions showed that a record 19 sites commemorated the Maya date 9.18.0.0.0 (AD 790). Only 40 years later, the date 10.0.0.0.0 was noted at only 3 sites, and within another 60 years the Maya long-count system of calendrical notation had passed from existence. Early research also showed that construction of major buildings at Maya sites in the southern lowlands had ceased and that existing structures had fallen into ruin. But the extent of the tragedy was not established with certainty before research projects began at major sites in the last two decades. These projects showed that the fate of total Maya populations was as drastic as that of the stone carvers and temple builders. In less than a century after AD 790, Maya population declined by as much as 70 percent. The remaining inhabitants survived for another century; then they too disappeared from all but a few sites.

This succession of events was not simultaneous everywhere in the lowlands. Sites at the eastern edge of the lowlands succumbed first, probably followed by the sites in the central zone. Meanwhile, sites on the Pasion River to the south persevered for a while, and the site of Seibal even underwent a brief flourish of construction during the Terminal Classic.

Signs of intrusion are also associated with Terminal Classic events. Fine Orange pottery from centers of production on the Gulf coast was widely traded, and late stelae at Seibal show foreigners with waist-length hair and with bones in their noses. These strangers were certainly not Classic Maya, although they may well have been speakers of Maya languages from peripheral areas in the northern or northeastern lowlands.

What caused this spectacular disintegration of a civilization that seems to have been at the peak of its power and glory? A recent conference of Mayanists reconsidered this question (Culbert, 1973; see Willey and Shimkin, 1973, for a summary of conclusions). That there was neither complete agreement nor a final solution is hardly surprising, but directions for future research were clearly delineated. There was agreement that a complex concatenation of circumstances must have been involved in the Maya collapse, some of them external to the Maya lowlands. Outside invasion seems to have occurred along the Pasion River, although there is disagreement about whether the invasion was the cause of the collapse or a result thereof. Competition in trade that cut the Maya off from outside markets may have been more important than actual intrusions in weakening the Maya structure.

Internal factors within the lowlands must have been involved as well. The heavy population of Late Classic times probably strained the capacity of the subsistence adaptation, and some kinds of environmental degradation that might have resulted from overexploitation would have been almost irreversible. The increasing gap between elite and commoners and, possibly, increased warfare could have strained the social adaptation of the Maya. In addition, the administrative capabilities of the Maya may have been overtaxed by the steep rise in population and economic activity of the Late Classic and left without the flexibility to respond to emergencies.

At the moment, there is some polarity between those who see external factors, such as invasion or stifling of trade, as the initial point of stress and those who believe that the collapse was initiated by internal stresses within the fabric of Maya environmental or social adaptation. There are as many shades of opinion and mixtures of scenarios as there are Mayanists who have considered the question. Future research must aim at providing greater detail about the chronology and events of the collapse and a better understanding of the organization and operation of Maya Lowland society in the frantic period of growth that immediately preceded the collapse.

POSTCLASSIC SOLDIERS AND STATESMEN

The fall of so many Classic centers in the eighth and ninth centuries opened the door for a new order in Mesoamerica—an order that emerged in the Early Postclassic period (AD 900–1200). This transition is traditionally pictured as a shift from peace-loving, religiously oriented Classic centers devoted to serving the gods to militaristic and far more secular Postclassic centers, in which soldiers held the power and in which empire by conquest was the aim of society. Although this picture is sometimes overdone, there are still strong elements of validity in it. Even though we now know that leaders of the Classic period were less benign and peaceful than was once thought, the degree of preoccupation with military matters *does* seem to have increased in Postclassic times. Prowess in war was obviously admired in both gods and men in the Postclassic, and the route to the top of the social ladder was one of arms. Expansion of political units by conquest was also a major theme in Postclassic times, culminating in the nearly pan-Mesoamerican empire of the Aztecs.

That there really was a trend from a more religious to a more secular emphasis in society seems less certain than before. The notion of such a trend was based upon the idea that most Classic cultures were theocracies in which priests were the principal leaders and the religious hierarchy was the same as the governmental hierarchy. Religious fervor was clearly portrayed in Classic art—probably more so than in later times—but one can hardly doubt that cities like Teotihuacan were filled with the same bureaucrats and administrators that peopled Aztec centers.

Central Mexico

To turn from this general picture to specifics, it will be useful once again to start with Central Mexico, where both archeological and ethnohistorical data are rich. In Central Mexico, the reorganization of power actually began in the Late Classic. By shortly after AD 750, Teotihuacan had lost 80 percent of its population. Although it remained a sizable community of 30,000–40,000, it is clear that the city was no longer of international importance in Mesoamerica. The decline of Teotihuacan's dominance opened a power vacuum in which several contenders struggled to assume the mantle of Mesoamerican supremacy. At least four centers were involved in this rivalry: El Tajin on the Gulf coast; Xochicalco, southwest of the Valley of Mexico in a fortified location guarding the access to the Balsas Depression; Cholula, Teotihuacan's one-time satellite in Puebla; and Tula, located toward the northern periphery of Mesoamerica. Cholula seems to have been the most important of the Central Mexican centers during the Late Classic, since recent archeological evidence indicates that it was, at that time, considerably larger than either Tula or Xochicalco. Archeological data suggest a cosmopolitan atmosphere for the period. Fine Orange pottery from the Gulf coast was present in Oaxaca; there are hints of Maya influence in the art of Xochicalco and the recently discovered murals at the site of Cacaxtla; and there was strong Tajin influence on the Pacific coast of Guatemala. One suspects intricate patterns of competition among trade spheres.

TULA □ From this hodgepodge of contending powers, the Toltecs of Tula emerged triumphantly in control of a large section of Early Postclassic Mesoamerica. Documentary accounts credit them with 40 tributary pueblos, stretching from the Gulf coast into western Mexico. In addition, Chichen Itza in Yucatan so faithfully copied the art and architecture of Tula (Figure 11.13) that it too must have been occupied by Toltec conquerors. In their success, the Toltecs

(a)

(b)

(c)

(d)

FIGURE 11.13
Early Postclassic art: (a) Tula warrior statues; (b) artist's reconstruction of Pyramid B at Tula;
(c) bas-relief from Pyramid B; (d) a "Chac-Mool" from Tula. (Part a after Weaver, 1972; part b
after Ekholm and Bernal, 1971; parts c, d after Coe, 1962.)

must be credited with one of the most powerful public-relations campaigns in
the history of Mesoamerica. When the Spanish conquistadores arrived—centuries after the site of Tula had fallen to ruin and its exact location had been
forgotten—the Toltecs were still credited with legendary accomplishments as
artists, craftspeople, and rulers. Kings scattered throughout Mesoamerica
proudly traced their descent from Toltec ancestors (many of whom were probably apocryphal). Sanders, Parsons, and Santley (1979), however, have recently
questioned whether Tula was as dominant in the Early Postclassic as the leg-
ends suggest. They note that the Great Pyramid at Cholula was completed at

this time, and they interpret the settlement patterns as indicating that the Valley of Mexico may have been a frontier zone where Cholula and Tula contested for power.

Archeological Tula is a disappointment in the wake of its publicity. The ceremonial precincts are minuscule in comparison with Teotihuacan, and the architecture is far from outstanding. But recent surveys by Diehl (1974) and Matos (1974) indicate that Tula included an urban area of 12 square kilometers, with a population of 60,000 and perhaps as many obsidian workshops as there had been at Teotihuacan. Unlike Teotihuacan, Tula stood in the center of a densely populated rural area, leading Sanders, Parsons, and Santley (1979: 144–145) to the conclusion that none of the inhabitants of the Tula urban zone were food producers. If this is so, Tula was more urban than Teotihuacan in terms of degree of specialization.

The location of Tula is suggestive. The farthest north of any major Mesoamerican center, it lies athwart likely routes of travel to the frontier of Mesoamerica. A line of frontier fortress sites still farther north suggests an important focus of Toltec trade and commerce in that direction. Armillas (1964) suggested long ago that the northerly position of Tula might be related to a period of increased rainfall that temporarily extended the area of successful farming into the northern desert country and provided the agricultural base for warlords who supported, with their resources, the rise of Tula. The idea is interesting, for the climate of this northern country is such that shifts of only a few inches in annual precipitation could open or shut large areas for farming. Armillas' theory has not, however, been followed by the detailed paleoclimatological work necessary to prove or disprove the hypothesis.

Like other centers before it, Tula was destroyed and abandoned, probably at some time around AD 1160. The legendary accounts of Tula's demise speak of weak rulers and factionalism, and the condition of the site suggests violent destruction.

THE VALLEY OF MEXICO □ The Valley of Mexico remained in eclipse for nearly five centuries. When Teotihuacan declined, at about AD 750, the population dispersed to create a series of small regional centers separated by stretches of nearly vacant land. Between AD 950 and 1200, population declined still further and most of even these small centers disappeared, leaving much of the valley with only a dispersed rural population. Palerm and Wolf's (1957) claim that the Valley of Mexico was always a "key" or "nuclear" area—a location of massed demographic and economic power—can no longer stand in the light of the archeological evidence. In fact, it is unlikely that any region of Mesoamerica can be considered continually nuclear in the Palerm–Wolf sense.

With the fall of Tula, the natural advantages of the Valley of Mexico reasserted themselves, and population began a rapid resurgence. New centers were established and contested for power. Some of these centers claimed ties with the fallen Tula and may well have housed some of the dispersed Tula population. Others were founded by immigrant Chichimecs from the north and west. Known in the legendary accounts as barbarians of awesome military accomplishments but with distinct shortcomings in the social graces, the Chichimecs soon learned from local inhabitants the adaptations required of Mesoamerican heartlanders. Between AD 1200 and 1450, a period covered with some accuracy by historical sources, the Valley of Mexico was the scene of remarkable political turmoil. The growing cities vied with each other, their tactics ranging from marriage alliances to assassination to open warfare. There were few winners and many losers. One of the less impressive groups of immigrants to arrive during this period was the Mexica, better known as the *Aztec*. For some time after their arrival in the thirteenth century, the Aztec served an apprenticeship in deviousness as mercenaries and allies of more important powers. How they used this training will be described in the final section on the Aztec Empire.

The Maya Lowlands

Postclassic coverage for the Maya lowlands must shift to the northern half of the area, for after the Classic collapse the south remained nearly abandoned while the north went on to vigorous new developments.

PUUC □ The earliest of these developments occurred in a hilly zone paralleling the eastern coast of the Yucatan peninsula. This zone, known as the *Puuc,* contains a number of very large and important sites, including Uxmal, Labna, Sayil, and Kabah. The date of the major occupation of the Puuc sites has long been debated between those who believed they were fully equivalent in time to the Late Classic in the southern lowlands and those who believed the entire development to be Postclassic. An intermediate dating of the principal period for the Puuc, making it equivalent to Terminal Classic (AD 800–1000), now seems likely. Terminologically, the period of the Puuc sites is known as the *Pure Florescent,* avoiding any equation with the term *Classic.* The architectural style of the Puuc sites is characterized by a sophisticated use of veneer masonry and of decoration made by setting standardized precut blocks into patterns. Large palace buildings dominate the sites, and pyramid–temples are less common than at sites in the southern lowlands. Since no full site surveys have been done in the area, the size of resident populations in the Puuc area is uncertain; remains of small structures, however, seem to be common. At the same time as the Puuc florescence, the site of Dzibilchaltun—not far from the ocean at the northern edge of the Yucatan peninsula—was a huge population center. It had a density of house mounds considerably greater than that which is typical of Maya Lowland sites (Andrews, 1965). The monumental construction at Dzibilchaltun is not nearly so impressive as one might expect from its high population, and the site may have been a center devoted primarily to trade and exploitation of sea resources.

CHICHEN ITZA □ After a few centuries of success, the Puuc sites underwent a rapid collapse, and Chichen Itza became the primary seat of power in the Yucatan peninsula. Located in the drier thorn forest in the northern part of the peninsula, Chichen had a long history that began in the Preclassic and included an important Classic (Early-period) occupation that provided the structures in the section of the site known as *Old Chichen*. The dominant period at Chichen Itza was that known as the *Modified Florescent* or *Mexican* period between AD 1000 and 1250. In this period, the site fell under the sway of the Toltecs, who remodeled it after their capital at Tula. Under its Mexican overlords, Chichen Itza seems to have ruled most of the Yucatan peninsula. Some of the documentary histories from later times contain historical material bearing upon this period (Roys, 1962). A great Mexican leader, Kukulcan (a Mayan translation of the Mexican name Quetzalcoatl), came to the site. This may well be the same Quetzalcoatl who, according to Toltec histories, was expelled from Tula after a factional dispute. The Itza for whom the site is named were a group of immigrants who were said to speak Maya brokenly. They were probably Putun Maya from the coast of Campeche and Tabasco who had already been partly Mexicanized in their homeland (Thompson, 1970). A number of confused and conflicting accounts speak of migration of the Itza before their arrival at Chichen, and a reconstruction of the event involved is a matter of considerable debate. After Chichen Itza had dominated Yucatan for two and a half centuries, the site fell to military strife and internal intrigue, and Mexican power in Yucatan began to decline.

POLITICAL FRAGMENTATION □ Yucatan leadership was seized by Mayapan, a walled city of some 12,000 inhabitants. The Cocoms, an offshoot Itza lineage from Chichen Itza, established themselves as rulers at the site and proceeded to subjugate most of the peninsula. As a means of controlling their territory, they are said to have required all lords of subsidiary towns to reside at Mayapan. With such a concentration of nobility, one might suspect Mayapan to have been a luxurious site. In fact, it is exactly the opposite. The structures were shoddily built, and the public precincts appear impoverished in comparison with earlier sites. Intrigue and civil war plagued the rulers of Mayapan; in 1441 the site was destroyed, and Yucatan fell into a period of fragmentation. The region was divided into a number of petty states—some unified under strong central leadership, others so weakly centralized that individual communities were almost autonomous. Bickering and disputes were continuous, and until the Spanish Conquest a century later, the Maya made no serious gestures toward regaining their former glory. The time between 1250 and the Spanish Conquest is usually called the *Decadent* period, in reference to the declining architectural techniques. Sabloff and Rathje (1975), as a result of their research at the trade center on Cozumel Island, believe that the process involved was not cultural decay but a reordering of priorities, in which a rising merchant elite invested their capital and concern in production and trade rather than in conspicuous consumption.

The Valley of Oaxaca

For the Postclassic period in Oaxaca, one can speak with some confidence about the archeological remains of the Zapotecs and Mixtecs, the two major ethnic groups of the area at the time of the conquest. The Valley of Oaxaca, which was traditionally Zapotec territory, lacked a really major site after the death of Monte Alban at the end of the Classic. Mitla, the best-known Postclassic site in the valley, was much smaller than Monte Alban. Most of the population, especially in the Late Postclassic, lived in settlements of hamlet or village size.

The Mixtecs are best known from the Mixteca Alta, a rugged, mountainous country north and west of the Valley of Oaxaca where populations are confined to a series of tiny highland valleys. Postclassic occupation of the area seems to have been heavy, but none of the sites approaches the size of those in larger valleys. A fine ethnohistoric reconstruction by Spores (1967) shows that the contact-period Mixtecs were split into a series of petty kingdoms whose rulers were tied together by intricate alliances based upon intermarriage. Despite the small size of their political units, the Mixtecs were the most famous craftspeople in Late Postclassic Mesoamerica. Metallurgy, which had spread throughout Mesoamerica by this time, was one Mixtec specialty; polychrome pottery was another (Figure 11.14). Finally, the Mixtecs were expert in the recording of history and genealogy in pictographic manuscripts, some of which have survived to the present.

Elsewhere

The Postclassic period in the highlands and on the Pacific coast of Guatemala was a time of political fragmentation and intense warfare. At the end of the Classic, highland sites were shifted from valley-floor locations to defensible eminences; in the course of the Postclassic, architectural defensive works became more and more impressive. Contact-period sources show the Guatemalan highlands to have been divided among a series of small kingdoms, constantly bent on conquest and at war with one another. This part of Guatemala was the scene of several waves of Mexican influence. The impact of Teotihuacan has already been noted, and it has now been demonstrated (L. Parsons, 1967) that Mexican-influenced sculpture from the Santa Lucia Cotzumalhuapa area on the coast dates between AD 400 and 900. In the Postclassic, the Toltecs were undoubtedly active in the area, and several highland Guatemalan kingdoms proudly traced their origin to Toltec ancestors. Scattered pockets of people

FIGURE 11.14
Mixtec art: (a) from Codex Nuttal; (b, c) pectorals from Monte Alban. (After Willey, 1965.)

speaking Mexican languages still resided in the area at the time of the conquest, indicating that one or more of the waves of Mexican influence was accompanied by immigration.

THE AZTEC EMPIRE: CULMINATION OF MESOAMERICAN CULTURE

To return to the Valley of Mexico, Aztec prospects looked far from bright through the thirteenth and fourteenth centuries. Although occasionally success-ful in warfare as allies of established city-states, they continued to darken their own future by overaggression and lack of diplomacy. A famous legend illus-trates the point. The Aztecs are said to have asked for and been granted a daughter of the ruler of Culhuacan. This was a great boon, for the Culhuacan dynasty was directly descended from the Toltecs, and to incorporate Toltec blood into one's lineage was a key step in gaining social prestige. Instead of honoring the Toltec princess by marriage into their royal house, however, the Aztecs sacrificed her to their god Xipe Totec. When her father arrived for what he thought was to be a wedding ceremony, he was greeted instead by a priest dancing in the skin of his slain daughter. This was neither polite nor politic, and the Aztecs were expelled from their homes and forced to flee the wrath of Culhuacan.

The location that the Aztecs chose for refuge was amidst the reeds in the swamps that bordered the west side of Lake Texcoco. According to their leg-ends, they were to select a spot at which they saw an eagle sitting on a cactus eating a snake. The eagle and the snake, if they were there, were there for the same reason as the Aztecs—the area was remote and desolate and avoided by sensible people. In this unlikely location, the Aztecs founded the city of Tenoch-titlan about 1345. By hard work they turned the disadvantages of the spot to their favor. The shallow lake bed was converted into *chinampas*—fabulously productive gardens formed by piling up mud from the lake bottom to make artificial islands. Isolation from the shore was advantageous; the causeways that were built to connect the city to the mainland could be easily defended. The lake location and the canals that interlaced the city provided easy water transport for goods and people, eventually aiding the growth of Tenochtitlan as a center of commerce.

From this point, the fortunes of the Aztecs continually improved. Gaining strength by judicious alliances with larger powers and by rapidly shifting sides at propitious moments, they emerged by the fifteenth century as a member of the famous Triple Alliance with the cities of Texcoco and Tlacopan. After the death of the remarkable lawgiver-poet-king Nezahuacoyotl of Texcoco, the Aztecs were soon in essential control of the entire Valley of Mexico. Serious Aztec expansion outside of the valley did not start until about 1450, however, so that the magnificent empire that greeted the Spanish was less than a century old when it met its sudden and inglorious end.

The territory amassed by the Aztecs during their surge of conquest was impressive. Almost all of Central Mexico and the Gulf coast was under their dominion, as were sizable parts of southern Mexico in Oaxaca and along the Pacific coast. Theirs was not, however, a tightly controlled and heavily administered empire like that of the Incas in Peru. Instead, many local rulers retained much of their power under the Aztecs and were bound to the empire only by oaths of loyalty and the payment of tribute to Tenochtitlan. The threat of the Aztec armies kept these arrangements alive, but even so revolts were frequent. Each Aztec ruler seems to have spent a considerable amount of time suppressing rebellions and pacifying areas already within the empire.

The many first- and second-generation accounts by both the Spanish and persons of native descent provide a richness of information about the operation of Aztec society that can hardly be hinted at in a survey of this length. The most interesting questions for research involve detailed analysis of the intricate variety that can be glimpsed from these sources. Social arrangements both varied from place to place and changed rapidly through time; even book-length treatments are insufficient for complete analyses of the intricacies involved. The brief summary that follows can do no more than touch a few very general considerations. See Weaver (1972) for a lengthier summary and Soustelle (1964) for a detailed treatment.

Economically, the Late Postclassic Valley of Mexico developed a complex pattern of specialization and trade in which Tenochtitlan played the dominant role. The great market at Tenochtitlan, estimated to have attracted 60,000 people daily, seemed a thing of wonder to the sixteenth-century Spanish. (See Bernal Diaz del Castillo, 1963, for a fascinating eyewitness account.) Intensive specialization—in which whole barrios of the city were devoted to individual craft products—supplied both this market and the export trade to other parts of Mesoamerica. Goods from outside the Valley of Mexico were brought into Aztec hands by the tribute agreements with conquered territories. Tribute lists that survived into Colonial times show the amazing variety and volume of both raw materials and finished products procured in this manner. Exotic materials from outside the area of Aztec conquest were brought to Tenochtitlan by long-distance trade. This trade was in the hands of the *pochteca,* a group of professional traders who occupied a special status within Aztec society (Acosta Saignes, 1945).

A basic social unit of the Aztec was the *calpulli.* The exact nature of the *calpulli* has been a matter of anthropological debate for generations. A few facts, however, seem clear. *Calpulli* were territorially defined units that possessed land and had hereditary leaders. They may have originated as kin groups and still seemed to possess at least some kin functions in Aztec times.

Aztec society was divided into social classes that included slaves, commoners, and nobility. The structure of noble society was extremely complicated and is blurred by variation through time. An important distinction existed between a hereditary nobility and a nobility by achievement, consisting of those who had been given grants of land for a lifetime as reward for prowess in war. Although in theory these grants reverted to the Aztec ruler at the death of the holder, they seem to have had a tendency to become hereditary as well. Wolf (1959), whose summary of Aztec social structure is excellent, feels that there was increasing tension between the two kinds of nobility.

In 1519, this entire structure was to disintegrate within a few months under the impact of a handful of men from an alien culture. The enmities that the Aztecs had created in the process of ruling served the Spanish well, and the power of the Aztec rulers crumbled almost overnight. The loss of leadership, and the disastrous consequences of the European-introduced diseases that decimated native Mesoamerican populations, destroyed the elite culture. But the peasants of Mesoamerica remained. Fragments of native Mesoamerican culture have survived until the present, although whether they can—or should—survive the impact of modernization remains to be seen.

References Cited and Recommended Sources

Acosta Saignes, Miguel. 1945. Los pochteca. *Acta Antropologica,* Epoca I 1:1. Mexico: Sociedad de Alumnos, Escuela Nacional de Antropologia e Historia.

Adams, Richard E. W. (ed.). 1977. *The Origins of Maya Civilization.* Albuquerque: University of New Mexico Press.

———. 1980. Swamps, canals and the location of ancient Maya cities. *Antiquity* 54:212:206-214.

Andrews, E. W., IV. 1965. Progress report on the 1960-1964 field seasons: National Geographic Society-Tulane University Dzibilchaltun program. Tulane University, *Middle American Research Institute Publication* 31:23-67.

Armillas, Pedro. 1964. Northern Mesoamerica. In *Prehistoric Man in the New World,* ed. J. D. Jennings and E. Norbeck, pp. 291-330. Chicago: University of Chicago Press.

Aveleyra Arroyo de Anda, Luis. 1964. The primitive hunters. In *Natural Environment and Early Cultures, Handbook of Middle American Indians,* vol. 1, ed. R. C. West, pp. 384-412. Austin: University of Texas Press.

Beadle, George W. 1972. The mystery of maize. *Field Museum Natural History Bulletin* 43: 10:2-11.

Blanton, Richard E. 1978. *Monte Alban: Settlement Patterns at the Ancient Zapotec Capital.* New York: Academic Press.

———, Jill Appel, Laura Finsten, Steve Kowalewski, Gary Feinman, and Eva Fisch. 1979. Regional evolution in the Valley of Oaxaca, Mexico. *Journal of Field Archaeology* 6:4:369-390.

Brown, Kenneth L. 1977a. The Valley of Guatemala: a highland port-of-trade. In *Teotihuacan and Kaminaljuyu: A Study in Prehistoric Culture Contact,* ed. W. T. Sanders and J. W. Michels, pp. 205-395. University Park: Pennsylvania State University Press, Monograph Series on Kaminaljuyu.

———. 1977b. Toward a systematic explanation of culture change within the Middle Classic period of the Valley of Guatemala. In *Teotihuacan and Kaminaljuyu: A Study in Prehistoric Culture Contact,* ed. W. T. Sanders and J. W. Michels, pp. 411–440. University Park: Pennsylvania State University Press, Monograph Series on Kaminaljuyu.

———. 1980. A brief report on Paleoindian–Archaic occupation in the Quiche Basin, Guatemala. *American Antiquity* 45:2:313-324.

Byers, Douglas S. (ed.). 1967. *Prehistory of the Tehuacan Valley,* vol. 1. Austin: University of Texas Press.

Cheek, Charles D. 1977a. Excavations at the Palangana and the Acropolis, Kaminaljuyu. In *Teotihuacan and Kaminaljuyu: A Study in Prehistoric Culture Contact,* ed. W. T. Sanders and J. W. Michels, pp. 1–204. University Park: Pennsylvania State University Press, Monograph Series on Kaminaljuyu.

———. 1977b. Teotihuacan influence at Kaminaljuyu. In *Teotihuacan and Kaminaljuyu: A Study in Prehistoric Culture Contact,* ed. W. T. Sanders and J. W. Michels, pp. 441–452. University Park: Pennsylvania State University Press, Monograph Series on Kaminaljuyu.

Coe, Michael D. 1962. *Mexico.* New York: Praeger.

———. 1965. *The Jaguar's Children: Pre-Classic Central Mexico.* New York: Museum of Primitive Art.

———. 1968. San Lorenzo and the Olmec civilization. In *Dumbarton Oaks Conference on the Olmec,* ed. E. P. Benson, pp. 41–71. Washington, D.C.: Dumbarton Oaks.

———, and Kent V. Flannery. 1964. Microenvironments and Mesoamerican prehistory. *Science* 143:3607:650–654.

Coggins, Clemency C. 1975. Painting and drawing styles at Tikal: an historical and iconographic reconstruction. Ph.D. dissertation, Harvard University. Ann Arbor: University Microfilms.

Cowgill, George L. 1974. Quantitative studies of urbanization at Teotihuacan. In *Mesoamerican Archaeology: New Approaches,* ed. N. Hammond, pp. 363–396. Austin: University of Texas Press.

Culbert T. Patrick (ed.). 1973. *The Classic Maya Collapse.* Albuquerque: University of New Mexico Press.

———. 1974. *The Lost Civilization: The Story of the Classic Maya.* New York: Harper and Row.

———. 1977. Maya development and collapse: an economic perspective. In *Social Process in Maya Prehistory: Studies in Honour of Sir Eric Thompson,* ed. N. Hammond, pp. 509–530. London: Academic Press.

Diaz Del Castillo, Bernal. 1963. *Conquest of New Spain.* Translated by J. M. Cohen. New York: Penguin.

Diehl, Richard A. 1974. *Studies of Ancient Tollan: A Report of the University of Missouri Tula Archaeological Project.* University of Missouri, Monographs in Anthropology 1.

Drucker, Philip, R. J. Squier, and R. F. Heizer. 1959. *Excavations at La Venta, Tabasco, 1955.* Bureau of American Ethnology Bulletin 170. Washington, D.C.: Smithsonian Institution.

Ekholm, Gordon F., and Ignacio Bernal (eds.). 1971. *Archaeology of Northern Mesoamerica, Handbook of Middle American Indians,* vol. 10, part 1. Austin: University of Texas Press.

Flannery, Kent V. 1968a. Archeological systems theory and early Mesoamerica. In *Anthropological Archeology in the Americas,* ed. B. J. Meggers, pp. 67–87. Washington, D.C.: Anthropological Society of Washington.

———. 1968b. The Olmec and the Valley of Oaxaca: a model for interregional interaction in Formative times. In *Dumbarton Oaks Conference on the Olmec,* ed. E. P. Benson, pp. 79–110. Washington, D.C.: Dumbarton Oaks.

———. 1973. The origins of agriculture. *Annual Review of Anthropology* 2:271-310.

———, Anne V. T. Kirkby, Michael J. Kirkby, and Aubrey W. Williams, Jr. 1967. Farming systems and political growth in ancient Oaxaca. *Science* 158:3800:445–453.

Galinat, W. C. 1971. The origin of maize. *Annual Review of Genetics* 5:447-478.

Grennes-Ravitz, Ronald A., and G. H. Coleman. 1976. The quintessential role of Olmec in the Central Highlands of Mexico: a refutation. *American Antiquity* 41:2:196-206.

Grove, David C. 1974. The Highland Olmec manifestation: a consideration of what it is and isn't. In *Mesoamerican Archaeology: New Approaches,* ed. N. Hammond, pp. 109–128. Austin: University of Texas Press.

Gruhn, Ruth, and Alan Lyle Bryan, with appendix by Jack D. Nance. 1977. Los Tapiales: a Paleo-Indian campsite in the Guatemalan highlands. *Proceedings of the American Philosophical Society* 121:3:235-273.

Hammond, Norman. 1977. The early formative in the Maya lowlands. In *Social Process in Maya Prehistory: Studies in Honour of Sir Eric Thompson,* ed. N. Hammond, pp. 82–100. New York: Academic Press.

Harrison, Peter D., and B. L. Turner, II. 1978. *Pre-Hispanic Maya Agriculture.* Albuquerque: University of New Mexico Press.

Haviland, William A. 1970. Tikal, Guatemala, and Mesoamerican urbanism. *World Archaeology* 2:2:186–197.

Irwin-Williams, Cynthia. 1973. Summary of archaeological evidence from the Valsequillo region, Pueblo, Mexico. IX International Congress of Anthropological and Ethnological Science, Chicago.

Kubler, George. 1967. *The Iconography of the Art of Teotihuacan.* Dumbarton Oaks Studies in Pre-Columbian Art and Archaeology 4.

Lowe, Gareth W. 1967. Discussion. In *Altamira and Padre Piedra, Early Preclassic Sites in Chiapas, Mexico,* ed. Dee F. Green and Gareth W. Lowe, pp. 53–79. New World Archaeological Foundation Publication no. 15.

MacNeish, Richard W. 1958. *Preliminary Archaeological Investigations in the Sierra de Tamaulipas, Mexico.* Transactions, American Philosophical Society 48, pt. 6.

———. 1964. Ancient Mesoamerican civilization. *Science* 143:3606:531–537.

———. 1978. *The Science of Archaeology?* North Sciutate: Duxbury Press.

———, Melvin L. Fowler, Angel Garcia Cook, Frederick A. Peterson, Antoinette Nelken-Turner, and James A. Neely. 1975. *Prehistory of the Tehuacan Valley,* vol. 5: *Excavations and Reconnaissance.* Austin: University of Texas Press.

———, S. Jeffrey K. Wilkerson, and Antoinette Nelken-Turner. 1981. *First Annual Report of the Belize Archaic Archaeological Reconnaissance.* Andover: Robert F. Peabody Foundation for Archaeology.

Manglesdorf, Paul. 1974. *Corn: Its Origin, Evolution and Improvement.* Cambridge: Belknap Press.

Marcus, Joyce. 1974. The iconography of militarism at Monte Alban and neighboring sites in the Valley of Oaxaca. In *The Origins of Religious Art and Iconography in Preclassic Mesoamerica,* ed. H. B. Nicholson, pp. 123–139. Los Angeles: Latin American Center, University of California at Los Angeles.

Matos Moctezuma, Eduardo (ed.). 1974. *Proyecto Tula, Primera Parte.* Instituto Nacional de Antropologia, Mexico, Coleccion Cientifica 15.

Michels, Joseph W. 1979. *The Kaminaljuyu Chiefdom.* University Park: Pennsylvania State University Press, Monograph Series on Kaminaljuyu.

Millon, René. 1973. The Teotihuacan map: text. *Urbanization at Teotihuacan, Mexico,* vol 1. Austin: University of Texas Press.

———. 1974. The study of urbanism at Teotihuacan, Mexico. In *Mesoamerican Archeology: New Approaches,* ed. N. Hammond, pp. 335–362. Austin: University of Texas Press.

Niederberger, Christine. 1979. Early sedentary economy in the Basin of Mexico. *Science* 203:4376: 131–142.

Norman, V. G. 1973. *Izapa Sculpture.* Papers of the New World Archaeology Foundation, no. 30.

Palerm, Angel, and Eric R. Wolf. 1957. Ecological potential and cultural development in Mesoamerica. Pan American Union, *Social Science Monographs* 3:1–38.

Parsons, Jeffrey R. 1974. The development of a prehistoric complex society: a regional perspective from the Valley of Mexico. *Journal of Field Archaeology* 1:1:81–108.

Parsons, Lee A. 1967. *Bilbao, Guatemala: An Archaeological Study of the Pacific Coast Cotzumalhuapa Region.* Milwaukee Public Museum, Publications in Anthropology 11.

Proskouriakoff, Tatiana. 1960. Historical implications of a pattern of dates at Piedras Negras, Guatemala. *American Antiquity* 25:4:454–475.

Rathje, William L. 1970. Socio-political implications of Lowland Maya burials: methodology and tentative hypotheses. *World Archaeology* 1:3:359–375.

———. 1971. The origin and development of Lowland Classic Maya civilization. *American Antiquity* 36:3:275–285.

———. 1973. Classic Maya development and denouement: a research design. In *The Classic Maya Collapse,* ed. T. P. Culbert, pp. 405–456. Albuquerque: University of New Mexico Press.

Roys, Ralph L. 1962. Literary sources for the history of Mayapan. In *Mayapan, Yucatan, Mexico,* ed. H. E. D. Pollock, Ralph L. Roys, Tatiana Proskouriakoff, and A. L. Smith. Carnegie Institution of Washington, Publication no. 619.

Sabloff, Jeremy A., and William L. Rathje (ed.). 1975. *A Study of Pre-Columbian Commercial Systems: The 1972–1973 Seasons at Cozumel Mexico.* Harvard University, Monographs of the Peabody Museum, no. 3.

Sanders, William T. 1965. *The Cultural Ecology of the Teotihuacan Valley.* State College: Pennsylvania State University.

——. 1977. Ethnographic analogy and the Teotihuacan horizon style. In *Teotihuacan and Kaminaljuyu: A Study in Prehistoric Culture Change,* ed. W. T. Sanders and J. W. Michels, pp. 397–410. University Park: Pennsylvania State University Press, Monograph Series on Kaminaljuyu.

——, Jeffrey R. Parsons, and Robert S. Santley. 1979. *The Basin of Mexico: Ecological Processes in the Evolution of a Civilization.* New York: Academic Press.

——, and Barbara J. Price. 1968. *Mesoamerica: The Evolution of a Civilization.* New York: Random House.

——, and Robert S. Santley. 1978. Review of *Monte Alban: Settlement Patterns at the Ancient Zapotec Capital,* by R. E. Blanton. *Science* 202:4365:303–304.

Service, Elman. 1963. *Primitive Social Organization.* New York: Random House.

Sheets, Payson D. 1976. *Ilopango Volcano and the Maya Protoclassic: A Report of the 1975 Field Season of the Protoclassic Project in El Salvador.* Carbondale: Museum of Anthropology, University of Southern Illinois.

Shook, Edwin M., and Alfred V. Kidder. 1952. *Mound E-III-3, Kaminaljuyu, Guatemala.* Contributions to American Anthropology and History 9:53. Carnegie Institution of Washington, Publication no. 596.

Soustelle, J. 1964. *The Daily Life of the Aztecs.* London: Pelican.

Spence, Michael W. 1975. The development of the Teotihuacan obsidian production system. Unpublished manuscript. Department of Anthropology, University of Western Ontario.

Spores, Ronald. 1967. *The Mixtec Kings and Their People.* Norman: University of Oklahoma Press.

Stephens, John L. 1962. *Incidents of Travel in Yucatan.* Norman: University of Oklahoma Press. (Orig. pub. 1843.)

——. 1969. *Incidents of Travel in Central America, Chiapas, and Yucatan,* 2 vols. New York: Dover. (Orig. pub. 1841.)

Thompson, J. Eric S. 1970. *Maya History and Religion.* Norman: University of Oklahoma Press.

Tolstoy, Paul, and Louise I. Paradis. 1970. Early and Middle Preclassic culture in the Basin of Mexico. *Science* 167:3917:344–351.

Voorhies, Barbara. 1976. *The Chantuto People: An Archaic Period Society of the Chiapas Littoral, Mexico.* Papers of the New World Archaeological Foundation, no. 41.

——. 1978. Previous research on nearshore coastal adaptations in Middle America. In *Prehistoric Coastal Adaptations,* ed. B. L. Stark and B. Voorhies, pp. 5–21. New York: Academic Press.

Weaver, Muriel Porter. 1972. *The Aztecs, Maya, and Their Predecessors.* New York: Seminar Press.

Webb, Malcom C. 1964. The post-Classic decline of the Peten Maya: an interpretation in the light of a general theory of state society. Ph.D. dissertation, University of Michigan.

——. 1973. The Peten Maya decline viewed in the perspective of state formation. In *The Classic Maya Collapse,* ed. T. P. Culbert, pp. 367–404. Albuquerque: University of New Mexico Press.

Webster, David L. 1977. Warfare and the evolution of Maya civilization. In *The Origins of Maya Civilization,* ed. Richard E. W. Adams, pp. 335–372. Albuquerque: University of New Mexico Press.

West, Robert C. 1964. Surface configuration and associated geology of Middle America. In *Natural Environment and Early Cultures, Handbook of Middle American Indians,* vol. 1, ed. R. C. West, pp. 33–83. Austin: University of Texas Press.

Wilkerson, S. Jeffrey K. 1975. Pre-agricultural village life: the late preceramic period in Veracruz. In *Studies in Ancient Mesoamerica* 11. Contributions to the University of California Archaeological Research Facility, no. 27, ed. J. A. Graham, pp. 111–122.

Willey, Gordon R. 1965. *Archaeology of Southern Mesoamerica, Handbook of Middle American Indians,* vol. 3, part 2. Austin: University of Texas Press.

——. 1966. *An Introduction to American Archaeology,* vol. 1. Englewood Cliffs, N.J.: Prentice-Hall.

——. 1974. The Classic Maya hiatus: a "rehearsal" for the collapse? In *Mesoamerican Archaeology: New Approaches,* ed. N. Hammond, pp. 417–430. Austin: University of Texas Press.

——. 1979. The concept of the "disembedded capital" in comparative perspective. *Journal of Anthropological Research* 35:2:123–137.

——, T. Patrick Culbert, and Richard E. W. Adams (eds.). 1967. Maya Lowland ceramics: a report from the 1965 Guatemala City conference. *American Antiquity* 32:3:289–315.

——, and Demitri B. Shimkin. 1973. The Maya collapse: a summary view. In *The Classic Maya Collapse,* ed. T. P. Culbert, pp. 457–501. Albuquerque: University of New Mexico Press.

Wolf, Eric. 1959. *Sons of the Shaking Earth.* Chicago: University of Chicago Press.

Hokule'a, a modern replica of the Polynesian ocean-going vessels, seen here on the return leg of its historic Hawaii–Tahiti voyage.

CHAPTER TWELVE

Precolumbian
Transoceanic Contacts

Stephen C. Jett

Perhaps the largest disparity of beliefs in all of archeology is that between the
diffusionists, who believe that "important, even fundamental outside influences" shaped
or were directly responsible for many cultural features of the New World civilizations,
and the independent inventionists, who emphasize local or regional evolution of New
World cultures. Dr. Jett presents a compendium of diffusionist hypotheses, from the
diffusionist point of view; no attempt is made to present the alternatives of these
hypotheses. What emerges is a collage of possibilities and some tantalizing, inexplicable,
but undeniable facts.

INTRODUCTION

Archeologists and other students of culture history are concerned with the cultural changes experienced by particular societies. Geographers add the spatial
approach, to assess the dispersal of cultures and culture traits. The goal of these
scholars is to determine how those changes and dispersals came to occur, and an
ultimate though elusive goal is the formulation of generalizations about the
nature of culture change and culture dispersal (Trigger, 1970).

Cultural elaboration takes place both by local innovation and by the selective
introduction, adoption, and adaptation of foreign ideas. The relative importance
of these two sources of culture change has long been debated among culture
historians and theorists. This debate has often been heated, even acrimonious—
particularly concerning the question of possible ancient interhemispheric influences. The reasons for the lapses into partisan polemics over this issue are
complex, but emotionalism on both sides has often impeded calm consideration
of the evidence.

The majority of Americanists have emphasized local or regional development
of New World cultures and have either unequivocally rejected the idea of significant transoceanic impacts or have avoided discussing such possibilities. How-

ever, a minority of scholars, whose ranks have grown considerably since the Second World War, believe that important, even fundamental, outside influences may have helped shape ancient America. These *diffusionists* tend to make certain assumptions about cultural processes, including the following:

1. Each culture's form, at any given moment in time, is the result of the unique sequence of its past experience, which has been shared in toto by no other culture. Cultures' different histories account for the almost infinite variety of cultural forms that have developed.

2. Humankind's conservative tendencies normally outweigh creative ones. Premodern innovation was deviant and rare and usually resulted from a gradual accumulation of almost imperceptible changes.

3. A complex innovation can occur only when a particular and improbable set of circumstances—cultural, historical, and perhaps environmental—come into conjunction. These concatenations of circumstances, being improbable to begin with, are even more unlikely to have been repeated at other times or places.

4. Therefore, when complex similarities are found to have existed among cultures, these similarities were most likely a result of innovation in one area and subsequent spread to the others rather than being the fruit of multiple independent innovations. Since it is easier to copy an idea or technique than it is to invent it spontaneously, diffusion is the more economical explanation for such similarities, at least if opportunity for diffusion can be demonstrated.

5. In those rare instances in which cultural conservatism *was* overcome and rapid innovation *did* take place, this process was usually the consequence of cultural contact. Such contact would lead to the introduction of new ideas, to the hybridization of the new ideas with local, established ones, and to a realization that innovation was possible. Such contact was normally a necessary, but not always sufficient, condition for rapid elaboration.

Diffusionists are skeptical of psychological, environmental, economic, or "ecological" determinist theories of culture change, although they acknowledge that each of these factors has played its role in culture history.

The view opposed to diffusionism is that humankind everywhere is possessed of the same basic psychological and physical make-up and degree of potential inventiveness. If an innovation could occur in one society, it could just as easily occur in any other comparable society. There were undeniable and often enormous differences among premodern cultures, but there were also many similarities. The latter are attributable to the limited possibilities of natural materials, of the laws of mechanics, and of humans themselves; to the universal nature of the problems that societies must solve; to the similar challenges of similar physical environments; and to the similar natures of many societies' basic technico-economic and social systems. In this view, humankind is at least moderately inventive and has tended to respond rather readily, via adaptive innovation, to the exigencies of survival. Further, if one thinks of culture as a dynamic system, one would expect a change in one part of the socio-environmental system to generate a sequence of responses throughout the system, and changes initiated in one subsystem might eventually result in changes in other ones. Thus, similar environmental, social, economic, or other alterations in two historically unrelated societies may generate similar innovations in various sectors of those societies, and even complex similarities need not be attributed to diffusion (see, for example, Davies, 1979).

Each of the preceding views has its merits and defects, and each requires much more testing before any even moderately reliable "general theory" can be accepted with confidence. Rather than elaborating further on these issues, important though they are, we will turn to more concrete questions, such as: *Could* Precolumbian transoceanic contacts have occurred? *Did* they in fact occur? And, if they did, what impact may they have had on New World cultures—particularly on the "high cultures" of Mesoamerica and the Andean region? (I have elaborated upon the theoretical and methodological issues in a previous work—Jett, 1971.)

Means and Motives for Contacts

Since there is nothing to suggest significant diffusion between the high cultures of the two hemispheres by way of the Bering Strait, the question of interhemispheric contacts among these cultures is essentially one of transoceanic voyaging. A major barrier to consideration of possible diffusion by sea routes has been skepticism as to the existence of seaworthy watercraft and adequate navigational techniques in Precolumbian times. In part, this skepticism has stemmed from the dearth of direct archeological evidence of watercraft (outside of the Mediterranean area). However, it has also been a consequence of both a lack of appreciation by modern workers of the comparative difficulties of land versus water travel in early times and of the ethnocentric assumption of historical superiority of Western watercraft, navigational ability, and geographical knowledge.

In recent decades, continuing archeological, historical, ethnographic, and experimental research has tended to alter scholars' perceptions of the abilities of early watercraft and their navigators. Several significant points that have emerged follow. Southeast Asia appears to have been the hearth of early watercraft development; it remained ahead of the West until modern times in the seaworthiness of its craft and the efficiency of its sailing rigs and techniques, especially in sailing against winds and currents (Bowen, 1953; 1959; Needham, 1970; Borden, 1967:219–222). Relatively small, flexible watercraft, such as sailing rafts and lashed-plank outrigger and double canoes, are more seaworthy than large, rigid-hulled ships, and these small craft have considerable antiquity (Doran, 1973, 1981). Navigational techniques were highly advanced in ancient southern and eastern Asia; in China, for instance, celestial navigation, the magnetic south-pointer, the spherical-earth concept, and the latitude and longitude system of coordinates were all known before AD 200 (Needham, 1959:171, 498, 537; 1962:271, 281). In any event, navigating to a target of continental size presents no great difficulties. Until modern times, travel by sea was far easier and swifter than overland travel, when good watercraft were available.

The earliest great sailing tradition that seems to have emerged, and the one usually pointed to as the probable vehicle for the earliest transpacific voyages, is that of the Southeast Asian and the derivative (?) northwestern South American sailing raft (Doran, 1971). The deep-water sailing abilities of this craft have been demonstrated empirically by Heyerdahl (1950a, b) and others (Edwards, 1965:101; 1969). A second major sailing tradition is that of the Indonesian and Oceanian sailing canoe, or *wangka* (Doran, 1981). The junk is the third of the great oceanic sailing craft of eastern Asiatic provenance. All of these watercraft date to before—in some cases, long before—the Christian Era. In the West, the frame-hulled *nao* was the sole great sea-going type of watercraft to evolve; it did so, apparently, during the Bronze Age (Doran, 1973).

That each of these sailing traditions—particularly the eastern ones—early developed watercraft and navigators able to make intentional transoceanic crossings in relative safety now seems beyond serious doubt. In light of these capabilities, we then must ask: Were such voyages actually made? If so, how was initial discovery accomplished? What may have motivated any subsequent crossings? We have little firm data on these points. Suggestions as to early discovery in the Pacific include accidental drift voyages, of which a number of historical Japan-to-America instances have been recorded (Brooks, 1875); gradual exploration up the coast of Northeast Asia and along the Aleutians to Alaska and beyond; and direct, intentional easterly sailing to discover what lay beyond the sea (flotsom and the paths of migrating birds may have suggested the existence of lands beyond known waters). Similar possibilities exist for the Atlantic.

Heyerdahl (1963) and others (such as Ferdon, 1963) have discussed the most probable routes of drift-voyage discovery; they stressed prevailing winds, currents, and storm tracks (Figure 12.1). It should be kept in mind, however, that at least Asiatic and Oceanian vessels were, under most conditions, quite capable of sailing against these "conveyor belt" systems and that prevailing winds often shifted direction both seasonally and during storms.

Once knowledge of distant shores was gained, what might have motivated return voyages and the maintenance of contacts sufficient to account for the massive similarities between the New World and the Old World that diffusionists have attributed to transoceanic contacts? A simple sense of adventure and the attendant prestige must not be overlooked as motives in some instances, particularly in the postulated early phases of exploration. The desire to escape from restraints or invaders at home or the search for more fertile, less populated lands may also have precipitated some crossings. Desire to make astronomical observations may have played a role. Trade in highly valued luxury, indulgent, or sacred products has been suggested as having motivated later transpacific intercourse (see Heine-Geldern, 1956:95); possible materials of these types include valuable metals, jade, tropical bird feathers, furs, dyestuffs, and hallucinogenic plants. Religious searches and proselytizing—particularly Hindu–Buddhist—

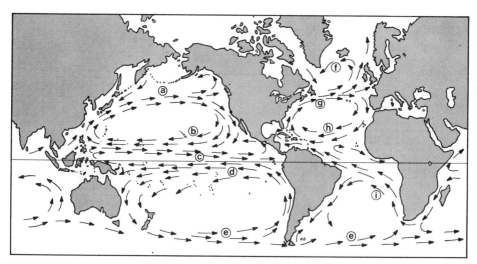

FIGURE 12.1
Generalized map of the principal surface ocean currents: (a) Japan–North Pacific Current;
(b) California–North Equatorial Current; (c) Equatorial Countercurrent; (d) Peru–South Equatorial
Current; (e) Antarctic Drift; (f) Irminger Current; (g) Gulf Stream–North Atlantic Current;
(h) Canaries–North Equatorial Current; (i) Benguela–South Equatorial Current.

have also been proposed as potentially effective factors in stimulating voyaging
and even colonization (see Jairazbhoy, 1974b; Ekholm, 1953:88).

Kinds of Evidence for Cultural Diffusion

The best evidence for Precolumbian contacts would be easily identifiable objects
of Old World origin in unquestionably Precolumbian archeological contexts.
Few if any such objects have been discovered, although a few artifacts have been
claimed as conforming to these criteria.

Chemical and physical analyses of jade, turquoise, metals, and so on found in
Old and New World sites would prove useful for identification of exotic source
areas for these materials, but such techniques have practically never been applied to the transoceanic diffusion issue.

During the last several years, reevaluation of supposedly forged New World
inscriptions in Old World languages, and the discovery of additional markings,
have led to renewed interest in this type of evidence. It has been asserted that the
occurrence, in a number of these inscriptions, of usages and constructions, including cryptograms, which were unknown to scholarship at the time of initial
discovery, proves their genuineness. Nevertheless, all of these finds have been
questioned.

Cultivated plants have long been looked to as excellent evidence of transoceanic contacts—particularly those plants that could not have been carried by way of the Bering Strait or by any plausible natural means. The best plants in this respect are tropical cultigens that survive only through human intervention. Cultigens can be "invented" only when the appropriate wild ancestors are available, and these are usually confined to one hemisphere. Transoceanic natural dispersal even of wild plants (other than littoral ones) has been minimal. It is not possible to review the evidence for specific Precolumbian plant and animal transfers here (see Carter, 1950, 1953, 1963, 1974; Heyerdahl, 1952; Merrill, 1954; Heine-Geldern, 1958; Jett, 1968). There is historical, archeological, or distributional evidence, of quite variable quality, for the transfer of the following: plantain (C. Sauer, 1950:527; M. Towle, 1961:97; Heyerdahl, 1952:482; Greider, 1981), sweet potato (Brand, 1971), maize (Stonor and Anderson, 1949; Jeffries, 1971; Mangelsdorf, 1974:201–206), peanut (Chang, 1973:527), pineapple (Casella, 1950; Pohl, 1973), coconut (J. Sauer, 1971), amaranths (J. Sauer, 1967), bottlegourd (Whittaker, 1971), cotton (Hutchinson et al., 1947; Stephens, 1971), the chicken (Carter, 1971), and a number of others. Even if all of the Old World artifacts, inscriptions, and cultivated plants that are claimed to be Precolumbian in the New World were proved to be absolutely genuine and of preconquest date, they would not, in themselves, demonstrate anything more than casual contacts and occasional plant transfers. They would (and, I think *do*) show *opportunity* for further influences, but to assess the times, extent, and impact of such influences, we must turn to the content and chronologies of the cultures themselves.

Because of their lack of specificity, the more general and basic characteristics of cultures—such as food-getting methods, settlement patterns, social stratification, religious and political institutions, and the like—are not very useful *indicators* of diffusion (Schneider, 1977), even though they may in some cases have been profoundly influenced from the outside. To demonstrate likelihood of diffusion, and to achieve some impression of the times and places of its occurrence, we must look for cultural "trace elements."

Ideally, these trace elements should possess certain characteristics, although in practice they seldom demonstrate them all. The traits should be arbitrary— that is, not called for or notably favored by the basic human physical and psychological make-up, nor channeled by the nature of the materials humans have at their disposal, nor elicited by the characteristics of the physical environment and the culture's technico-economic relationship with that environment. Intrinsically improbable traits—for example, specific lexemes, particular animals associated with particular months or days of the week, divination from entrails, and rump masks in art—are often themselves trivial. However, they can serve both as evidence of contact and as "index fossils" that point to particular cultural and temporal sources to which, then, more general aspects of culture may at least tentatively be tied. Suspicion of diffusion is very much strengthened if spatial and temporal clustering of such traits occurs in the postulated donor and recipient areas, because the overall statistical probability of their twice occurring together declines as the product of the individual probabilities of their independent occurrence. Proof, in one area, of an evolutionary sequence leading up to the traits in question and, in the other area, of their sudden appearance without developmental stages is very suggestive of introduction from the first area to the second. However, the incompleteness of the archeological record and the possibility of sequential importation of the developmental stages reduce the usefulness of this criterion. Finally, temporal overlap of the traits in question should occur between the two areas involved.

Beyond the preceding synopsis, I will not elaborate on criteria for assessing evidence of transoceanic contacts; these criteria are implicit in the following pages, particularly in that the more arbitrary culture traits are emphasized. The principal aim is to survey, in their geographical and chronological contexts, the major hypotheses of transoceanic influences on Precolumbian America.

Naturally, no one person can be familiar with current findings relevant to all of the many cultures and time periods under consideration or be free of error when dealing with them. I no doubt have, in some cases, followed obsolete chronologies or have been unaware of new data and interpretations. The data themselves, of course, are often far from complete; many gaps and question marks characterize the discussions below. No one need fear a shortage of potential research projects for the future, nor a lack of opportunity for critical reconsiderations of theories presented.

This chapter is written from a diffusionist point of view. It is not my aim to give a detailed assessment of each hypothesis but rather to display these diffusionist theses to the reader. Some critical comments are made, and some new information given, but on the whole I am presenting the theories as they have been promulgated by their authors, with only brief reference to alternative explanations for the same data. The reader should not assume that all of the hypotheses described herein have gained universal, or even wide, acceptance or than the present author unreservedly accepts all of them.

ARCHAIC AND COLONIAL FORMATIVE CULTURES AND OVERSEAS CONTACTS

Australia and the Antarctic

Brief mention may be made of Paul Rivet's (1957) attempt to account for certain lexical and physical similarities observed between Australian aborigines and the Fuegids of southernmost South America. Rivet proposed that Australoids early reached Antarctica by boat, followed its shorelines to the Antarctic peninsula, and then paddled to Tierra del Fuego. The rudimentary nature of Australian watercraft and the storminess of the southern seas would, however, seem to preclude any such migration. The observed similarities may simply reflect an extremely ancient common Asiatic origin.

Europe and Africa

Transatlantic influence on North America has been suggested for as early as the Late Pleistocene—that is, before 10,000 BC. Greenman (1963) postulated that Upper Paleolithic hunters of the Biscayan region of Europe crossed to northeastern North America in skin boats, utilizing ice floes and bergs, some of which carried glacial gravels suitable for toolmaking. Greenman saw particularly strong similarities to Magdalenian boats, house types, and art among eastern Canadian tribes and, to a lesser extent, among the Eskimo and other groups. Some physical-anthropological evidence has been presented that supports this idea (Comas, 1973). If correct, this hypothesis could have very important implications for New World prehistory.

Schwerin (1970) has explored the idea that preceramic African farmerfishers were blown to the New World and there established the cultivation of cotton, bottlegourds, and jackbeans, between 8000 and 5700 BC. Carter (1977) has presented a stimulus-diffusion hypothesis for the further development of American cultivation complexes. Most present workers, however, believe in the independent origins of Old and New World agriculture (for example, Phillips, 1966:298-300).

A northern transatlantic impact has been postulated for the late fourth or third millennium BC. Alice Kehoe (1971:285-287) suggested the possibility that fishermen from coastal Norway introduced some of the diagnostic artifacts of Laurentian culture to eastern Canada and the northeastern states. Traits shared at this period include gouges, adzes, plummets, ground-slate points and knives, barbed bone points, and chipped stone projectile points. Ground-slate weapons have priority in America and, if contact is assumed, would represent a reciprocal introduction to Europe. Covarrubias (1957:26-27, 123, 246, 269-272) has also pointed out that the metal weapon types of the contemporary or somewhat earlier "Old Copper culture" of Michigan and Wisconsin bear a strong resemblance to Old World forms. Fell (1982:261-262), pointing out that far more copper was mined than can be accounted for by American artifacts, suggests massive exportation to Bronze Age Europe.

Extracontinental origins have been posited for North American ceramics. The earliest known Woodland pottery of the Northeast is often said to have been diffused from Siberia, although it does not occur west of the Great Lakes region. Neither does it appear to derive from Formative wares of the Southeast, although some have proposed a Mesoamerican origin. Kehoe (1971: 287-289) pointed out that Vinette 1 pottery appeared without antecedents prior to 1000 BC in New York state and adjacent Canada and in most respects is very similar to the contemporary pottery of Norway, which has a long evolutionary history. Fell (1982) has identified alleged Nordic inscriptions from Ontario as well. Vinette 2 pottery is reminiscent of wares of the contemporaneous western European maritime Bell Beaker cultures. Kehoe further suggested that European funerary practices, including barrow building, may be reflected in the use of burial mounds during the Early and Middle Woodland of about 1100– 500 BC. The latter period includes the Hopewell culture of the Midwest, in which a number of ceramic traits have European parallels. Evidence now indicates, however, that burial mounds may occur as early as Laurentian times (Dragoo, 1976:16). Huscher (1972, 1974) has argued for North American linguistic borrowing from the Baltic region. The sweat bath could also represent a transatlantic transfer (Lopatin, 1960; Jett, 1969:20).

New England and its adjacent areas contain many megalithic and other stone structures, including corbeled-stone chambers, astronomical "temples," "dolmens," and menhirs (Trento, 1979; Feldman, 1977). These are commonly attributed to colonial farmers, but Barry Fell (1976, 1982) considers them the work of Iberian Celts who colonized there during the first millennium BC. He has described many inscriptions on these monuments as being in Celtic ogam and Iberian Punic. His proposed decipherments are so recent that they are still the subject of considerable controversy. Nor is it clear what, if any, cultural impact the builders of these monuments had on indigenous peoples.

In regard to the New World pottery types usually lumped under the heading *Formative,* James Ford (1969) has summarized the basic data. This pottery first appered, as far as is known, in northwestern South America prior to 3600 BC. It was distributed from Peru to Georgia by 2100 BC or before—primarily, apparently, by shell-fishing folk. The question of Old World origins has naturally arisen. The American Formative is in many ways reminiscent of the Old World Neolithic, but attempts to identify explicit transatlantic antecedents for the Formative have so far been unsuccessful. Alcina (1969) and Kennedy (1971) have suggested a possible Mediterranean source for many of the ceramic traits, but much more development of the evidence is needed.

Japan

A possible East Asian origin for Formative pottery and other traits has received far more attention. Meggers, Evans, and Estrada (1965:157–172; Meggers, 1971:242–246) have argued in detail for a Japanese origin of what they believed to be America's oldest pottery, unearthed at Valdivia, on the coast of Ecuador, and dating from about 3600 BC. There are many similarities in decorative designs and techniques, as well as in rim and base forms, between the Early Middle Jōmon pottery of western Kyushu and Valdivia-phase pottery. The Kyushu-Valdivia similarities are greater than those between Kyushu and Honshu Jōmon or between Valdivia and other Formative wares. Although a number of archeologists (for example, Ford, 1969; A. Kidder II, 1964:474) accepted the Meggers, Evans, and Estrada hypothesis—perhaps because it relies on potsherds—others (for example, Patterson, 1967; Pearson, 1968; Muller, 1971:70–71) perceived weaknesses in it. These weaknesses include the selection of traits from various Jōmon sites and from various Jōmon and Valdivia time periods, the lack of comparisons of overall decoration and vessel forms, and the existence of similar pottery at other, distant places and times. Estrada (1961: 1–2, 8–9, 11) considered Jōmon elements to have appeared only in Valdivia B (although he recognized vague mainland Asiatic similarities in Valdivia A), and he also has made detailed comparisons of Valdivia B to Siberian ceramic complexes. Furthermore, pre-Valdivia pottery, without Jōmon parallels, has recently been discovered at Valdivia (Bischof, 1973), and the earliest known Valdivia sites are not coastal. Nautical objections have also been raised (McEwan and Dickson, 1978).

Some workers now view Valdivia and Jōmon not as directly related but rather as variants of an early, more or less circumpacific ceramic style associated with fishing cultures. In any event, no matter how striking the Jōmon–Valdivia similarities may be—and I belive that they are striking—Jōmon apparently cannot now be considered the source to which, by way of Valdivia, all Formative pottery may be traced. Jōmon Japan could, nevertheless, represent an early contributor.

Southeastern China

In regard to other possible Asiatic sources of influence on the American Formative, Covarrubias (1954:60) has illustrated some interesting similarities between certain Neolithic and Bronze Age western Chinese vessel forms and those of the Mesoamerican Preclassic (Formative). However, Southeastern China is probably a more promising area for investigation. Its Neolithic horizons are poorly known, but there are several Lungshanoid vessel forms—particularly of the lower Yangtze River (Chang Jiang) area—which also occur in the Formative. (Chinese words herein are spelled with conventional orthography; for places and dynasties, the *pinyin* equivalent is given in parentheses.) I have not investigated this matter at all thoroughly (see also Tolstoy, 1974:133–134), but some forms of early Preclassic pottery are like the Chinese *hsien* (tripod bowls with mammiform legs), *ting* (carinated bowls), *tou* (round-bottomed shallow dishes on tall, concave-profile, flaring pedestals, seemingly used as incense burners), *chüeh* (lipped, tripod pitchers), annular-based shallow dishes, and other shapes (Chang, 1968:139; Caso and Bernal, 1973; Chadwick, 1971; Ford, 1969:101–117, charts 13–15; Piña Chan, 1971:160–161, 177). Some of these forms also occur in early Southwest Asia and the Mediterranean (as do small terra-cotta figurines, a Preclassic Mesoamerican hallmark).

The peanut, a South American domesticate with an uncertain date of arrival in Mesoamerica, has been reported from two sites near the coasts of Kiangsu (Jiangxu) and Chekiang (Zhejiang) provinces, with dates of about 3300–2800 BC (Chang, 1973:527). If dating and identification are correct, human transpacific carriage seems almost certain, although there are no clues as to possible motives for the implied round-trip voyaging. It is notable, however, that "the

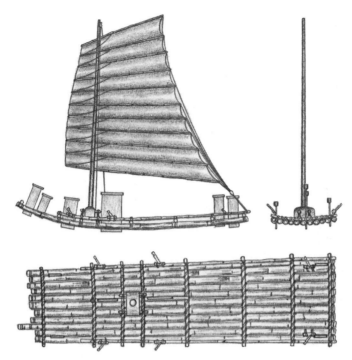

FIGURE 12.2
Taiwanese bamboo sailing raft with daggerboards to control leeway. (After Ling, 1956.)

[ancient] Southeastern Culture [of China—perhaps Miao-Yao-speaking] is essentially maritime oriented and is historically known as the Pai-Yueh, the navigators" (Chang, 1959:97).

Firm evidence of the use of seaworthy sailing rafts (Figure 12.2) off the coasts of China exists for the fifth century BC, with traditions indicating their use as many as 2000 years earlier (Ling, 1956:47, 49, 51). Precolumbian sailing rafts also occurred in Ecuador (Doran, 1971; Edwards, 1965). The possibility that a third culture area—Malaysia—was involved in such transfers is discussed in the next section, but the idea of early Southeastern Chinese contacts fits well with suggestions of later Chinese influences in the Americas (also discussed below).

The Neolithic of Southeastern China seems a likely source for the Mesoamerican bark-cloth manufacturing complex. The initial date of stone bark-cloth beaters in Southeast Asia is earlier than 2400 BC (Taiwan), and nearly identical beaters dating to about 1500 BC are known from southern Mesoamerica (Ford, 1969:85–86, Chart 3). Although the Mesoamerican bark-cloth complex most closely—and very strikingly—resembles that of Celebes (Sulawesi) in Indonesia (Figure 12.3), Tolstoy (1963) found certain Mesoamerican traits that suggested a relationship to the industry of southern China which gave rise to

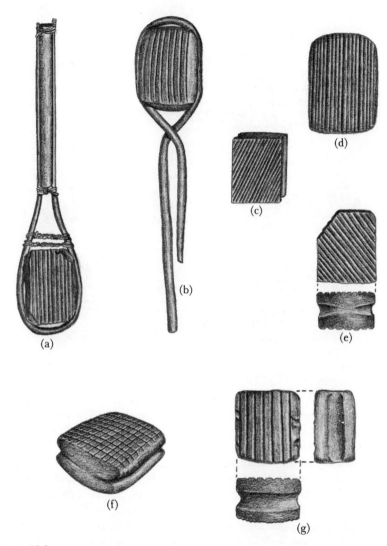

FIGURE 12.3
Southeast Asian and Mesoamerican bark beaters: (a) central Celebes; (b) Puebla, Mexico; (c) El Salvador; (d) Costa Rica; (e) Guerrero, Mexico; (f) central Celebes; (g) Oaxaca, Mexico. (After Tolstoy, 1963.)

true paper making about the time of Christ and which was probably preceded by Celebes-type bark-cloth making. Tolstoy (1966:72, 77–79) recognized 121 individual traits that characterize bark-cloth and paper making, 92 of which are shared by Southeast Asia and Mesoamerica. Forty-four of these shared traits are

> not required by any of the other steps in the procedure of which they are part or by the goal itself of making bark-cloth . . . . Even when essential, many of these traits are

still but one of several known alternatives . . . . [37 of the traits] are redundant, i.e., they co-occur with their alternatives, thus casting doubt on their competitive advantage or determination by function (Tolstoy, 1972:835).

Malaysia

Indonesia and the nearby mainland coasts were the hearth for what is probably the oldest, most diverse, and most efficient of premodern watercraft complexes. The origin of sailing rafts is seemingly attributable to this region, as is the emergence of double and outrigger sailing canoes. The area also apparently gave birth to a tradition of navigation and seamanship unequaled elsewhere until recent times. By 1500 BC or earlier, this maritime complex had reached the Southwest Pacific. Over the centuries, it spread to the most isolated habitable islands of the South Seas, presumably carried by Austronesian-speaking peoples. Coastal South China and perhaps early Japan also participated to a large degree in this tradition (Doran, 1971, 1973, 1981; Bellwood, 1979).

In view of the seagoing proclivities of these peoples, it would be surprising if they did not reach the shores of the Americas. In fact, as I have proposed elsewhere (Jett, 1968), Malaysians may well have had an extremely important impact on the tropical rain-forest regions of the New World. There is virtually no archeological evidence bearing on this question, so that attempting any dating is difficult; we must rely heavily on ethnographic information in making comparisons. Nevertheless, physical-anthropological data and the evidence of cultivated plants lend weight to a hypothesis of transpacific voyaging. In brief, data on tribes of interior Borneo (Kalimantan) and on Caribs and Arawaks of equatorial South America demonstrate greater physical similarity between these two populations than between either and its neighbors. This greater similarity suggests actual migrations rather than simple contacts. However, the populations involved need not have been large, if settlement by Malaysians began prior to the development of rain-forest farming in the New World. The farmer newcomers could gradually have expanded at the expense of the sparse indigenous populations of gatherers, without being drastically changed through genetic mixture. It is possible that the entire system of vegetative–reproduction shifting ("slash-and-burn") cultivation in the New World owes its origin to Malaysian or Southeast Asian immigrants. If so, local plants—such as sweet potato, yautía, and manioc—were largely substituted for similar Asian ones, such as yams and taro. However, there is evidence that certain Southeast Asian foodplants, such as the plantain, were brought to Precolumbian tropical America (see the Introduction).

The old cultural pattern of Indonesia and that of equatorial America are strikingly similar. Points in common range from longhouses to head-hunting and include a host of specific traits. Of these, the blowgun complex has been studied in detail and was found to share a very large number of common points in the two areas concerned (Jett, 1971). It may also be relevant that the Tucano of southern Colombia, though an inland tribe, have a tradition of having come from across the Pacific (Fulop, 1954:105).

The aforementioned similarities have been attributed by some to similar physical environments. Many of the shared traits, however, have no specific adaptive value in such environments. Further, the distribution pattern of the relevant traits—they decrease in frequency as one moves away from northwest-ernmost South America—is suggestive of transpacific introduction over a long period and of sequential diffusion into the Amazon Basin, the Guianas, and Central America. As to those traits that clearly *are* adaptive, the Malaysians' earlier adaptation to equatorial environments in Asia is exactly what would have enabled them to occupy such environments successfully in the New World, while at the same time this adaptation would have excluded them from other environments.

As to dating the postulated Malaysian migrations, it is not possible at present to be at all exact. I have, however, suggested a probable time range from 3600 to 300 BC and a possible important Malaysian source area in the vicinity of the Celebes Sea. Suggestions of possible transatlantic influences from Indonesia (via India, Madagascar, and Africa) have also been made, especially with respect to domesticated plants and birds (Whitley, 1974; Carter, 1977). It is conceivable that the post-Pleistocene encroachment of the sea onto the Sunda Shelf (Chappell and Thom, 1977) may have contributed to continuing emigration.

Some evidence for Melanesian and Polynesian contacts with western South America has also been adduced (for example, Hornell, 1945; Rivet, 1957). However, any such contacts seem likely to have had minimal impact on that continent and will not be elaborated upon here.

What the combined evidence of cultivated plants, pottery types, bark-cloth making, the blowgun, and other traits seems to suggest is that, during the Colonial Formative period, significant transoceanic influences on both New World continents took place in the realm of mundane affairs. This is in contrast to the apparent usual emphasis in later periods on religion, religious architecture, luxury goods, and sophisticated art and to their association with the elite classes of society.

DYNASTIC CHINA AND THE AMERICAS

Shang China and the Olmec

The Shang, the first Bronze Age civilization in the Yellow River (Huang He) valley area of northern China, developed upon a Lungshan Neolithic base during the eighteenth century BC or earlier. It was a hierarchical civilization with a capital and administrative and religious centers whose buildings were often built on earth platforms with a north–south orientation. The Shang possessed ideographic writing, produced richly decorated ritual bronze vessels, knew gold and silver, valued jade, and buried their elite with retainers and grave furniture in subterranean tombs. They practiced water control, had long-distance trade networks, made war with chariots, and controlled a large area (Chang, 1980).

On the Gulf of Mexico, in Veracruz and Tabasco, lay the heartland of what has been called America's first civilization, the Olmec. It possessed a hierarchy of leaders, constructed complex north–south-oriented ceremonial centers on artificial earth platforms, erected large earthen mounds, produced monumental stone sculptures and superb lapidary work in jade and other stones, practiced water control, had long-distance trade and widespread influence, and apparently used systems of enumeration and ideographic writing. It was, however, nonurban and without metals, draft animals, or the wheel (Bernal, 1969; Coe, 1968). Its calibrated radiocarbon dates are about 1450–650 BC. Nearly every commentator has remarked on its sudden flowering in the environmentally unlikely swampy rain forest of the Gulf coast, many miles from the sources of stone used in its huge carvings and lined drains.

Some scholars belive that the evolutionary steps leading to the Olmec florescence will be found in Veracruz's volcanic Tuxtla Mountains (for example, Heizer, 1968:24), perhaps under lava flows. Others look to Guerrero in western Mexico (for example, Griffin, 1972:302) or to Izapa in southeastern Chiapas (Malmstrom, 1976) as the early Olmec homeland and place of development. Still others seek overseas sources for the dramatic inception of Olmec culture (Jairazbhoy, 1974b; Meggers, 1975). The Olmec origins question is particularly important because it relates to general theories of the emergence of civilization and because from Olmec culture there developed a significant part of the content of later Mesoamerican cultures and perhaps of Andean and southeastern North American ones as well.

Much has been made of a "feline cult" in comparing archaic China's depictions of the tiger with the Olmec and later Mesoamerican focus on the jaguar. Emphasis on animals of such power and hunting prowess is not surprising, but certain specific shared aspects of feline representation—such as the frequent absence of a lower jaw—are more arbitrary. Meggers (1975:14, 17) has pointed out that felines appear to have been earth gods in both regions. Additional themes common to the Shang and the Olmec are felines protecting (devouring?) children (Chêng, 1960: plate 50; Bernal, 1969:172–173), which is a variant of the alter-ego motif, and monster-mask headgear (Fraser, 1967:31, 37, 43, 45–46). Birds or bird monsters are iconographically significant in both areas. Olmec God I, the dragon, was a composite with reptilian, eagle, jaguar, and other attributes; it was associated with the earth, water, and the royal lineage (Joralemon, 1976:37–42). Dragons—also composite creatures—are abundantly depicted in Shang China as well (Figure 12.4), where they were associated with caves, water, clouds, and the Emperor (Williams, 1941:131–135). Other similarities have been pointed out, but perhaps the ones most deserving of examination here are those relating to the use of green stones, particularly jade (for a more complete discussion, see Jett, 1978:608–610). Various green through blue stones, to which special powers were attributed, were highly valued in early times in Eurasia, the Americas, and the Pacific. Particularly in China and

FIGURE 12.4
(a) Shang Chinese *k'uei* dragon motif from bronze vessel; (b) Olmecoid jade "dragon spoon" from Costa Rica. (Part a after Willetts, 1958; part b after Balser, 1968.)

Mesoamerica, the most cherished of these stones—jade—was sought after, skillfully worked, and venerated. In both areas, the very word *jade* also meant *precious* and *verdant,* and an esteemed person had a "heart of jade" (Stirling, 1961:43, 1968:24–25; Ruff, 1960). The jade of ancient China was nephrite ("true jade"), mostly apparently imported from the Khotan area of Turkestan. Jadeite from upper Burma and adjacent Yünan was not used until later times. Nephrite was used for making celts in Neolithic times in China and became a true art medium during the Shang Dynasty (Hansford, 1968:27–29).

In Mesoamerica, a few pre-Olmec jadeite beads are known (Ford, 1969:58), and a nonjade greenstone celt and pendant date from 1450–1300 BC at Olmec San Lorenzo de Tenochtitlan, Veracruz. However, about or before 1100 BC the Olmec site of La Venta, Tabasco, seems suddenly to exhibit mastery in unprecedented jadeite-working skills—skills that were never equaled in later periods.

Common to the Shang and the Olmec are rounded jade celts, often interred with corpses. Celts sometimes carried faces engraved or painted in red. In China, ritual objects such as the slender *yüan kuei* seem to have evolved from celts; artifacts of similar form and size occur in buried offerings at La Venta. Other classes of jade objects common to Shang and Olmec include beads, bird and animal plaques, pendants, and figurines (Willetts, 1958:61–62, 67–74; Chêng, 1960: plates 15–17; Drucker et al., 1959; Smith, 1963:122, 126–127, 216–217).

Covarrubias (1954:103–109) and others (Ruff, 1960; Needham, 1971:544–555; J. Towle, 1973; Kinle, 1962; Beck, 1966) have stressed the similarities between Chinese and Mesoamerican jade prospecting, working, and use. Ethnographic accounts show that Asians and Americans alike belived that "exhalations" helped prospectors locate jade. The sawing, drilling, and polishing of these extraordinarily hard stones with abrasives was a trait held in common. In Shang China and later periods (Chêng, 1960:69–70), shell, turquoise, or jade was put in corpses' mouths, and at some point in history rice was similarly used. At least in Classic Maya times, jade and maize were put in corpses' mouths; funerary jades in both areas were sometimes coated with or associated with cinnabar. Jade seems to have been used medicinally in both areas.

Turquoise mosaic work, as on dagger handles, was common in Shang through Han China (Willetts, 1958:87, plate 4; Chêng, 1960:99). It is not reported for the Olmec, but there is evidence of turquoise mosaic work in the Preclassic of Central Mexico. It was rarely used in Classic times but was abundantly employed in later periods (Saville, 1922; Noguera, 1971:258–259), including on dagger handles (Carmichael, 1970:16). Perhaps its late ascendancy was as a partial substitute for jade, as that material became increasingly rare.

Green birds gave to jadeite one of its names in China (kingfisher) and in Mesoamerica (quetzal) (Ruff, 1960; Balser, 1968:61). The feathers of these birds were used ceremonially in both regions, although how early is not known—at least by AD 1000 in China (Hansford, 1968:28–29) and by Classic times in Mesoamerica (Dillon, 1975:106). Heine-Geldern (1956:95) has suggested that jade, feathers, and valuable metals were motivating factors in Asian-Nuclear American contacts. Chemical analyses of suspect archaic Chinese jades would be desirable, to determine whether they might be of American origin (see Norman and Johnson, 1941; Foshag, 1955, 1957). In view of the fact that China's most important nephrite supply was in foreign hands and that there were Shang conflicts with the intervening Western Chou (Zhou), that the Chinese would voyage to Mexico to obtain jadeite does not seem inconceivable (although jadeite also occurs in Japan). Perhaps such wealth-seeking began as early as Shang times. If so, a transport or intermediary function may have been performed by the coastal peoples of Kiangsu and Chekiang, outside of the Shang state, where a reservoir of transpacific knowledge may have existed (see previous discussion); the Shang themselves are not known to have been notable seafarers.

A more dramatic hypothesis has also been proposed, involving an exodus of Shang elite and craftworkers to the New World when the dynasty was overthrown by the Western Chou, apparently in 1122 BC (but possibly in 1027). Jairazbhoy (1974b:102) has summarized the traditions relating to this event (here condensed): "[Before attacking the Shang ruler] the Chou leader accused him of thinking only 'of palaces, buildings, terraces, groves, dikes, pools, and extravagant clothes' and 'spreading pain and poison over the four seas.' He distinguished the families of the clever men among the enemy who had gone away." Jairazbhoy cited a historical parallel: the eighth-century AD Omayyad dynasty of Syria fleeing civil war to establish a new kingdom in Spain. Jairazbhoy has connected the dikes and pools of the Shang emperor (drainage ditches have been found at the Shang capital [Chang, 1980:76–77, 86]) with those in the Olmec "heartland" of about 1300–1000 BC (Coe and Diehl, 1980:118–126).

Any Chinese landings would have been on the Pacific coast. The primary Olmec jade source and the area of most frequent finds of Olmec jade objects is the archeologically almost unknown middle Rio Balsas area of the Pacific coast state of Guerrero. The nearest port city today is Acapulco, which the Spaniards found to be the most convenient location for their transpacific trade.

Meggers (1975) has suggested that the impact of the putative Shang contacts on Mesoamerica was fundamental and that the Shang system of "centralized control and social stratification in the context of a dispersed settlement pattern," extensive long-distance trade in luxury items for major ceremonial centers, organized religion centering on felines, calendrics, and the idea of writing were all introduced. The sudden appearance of Olmec "civilization," the chronological framework, and the sharing of certain arbitrary traits all support the basic idea of Shang influence on the Olmec. However, such influence, if it occurred, was not thorough-going enough to have introduced wheeled vehicles or metallurgy and associated decorative styles, nor does it account for the monumental sculpture so characteristic of the Olmec heartland (to be discussed later).

Of possible interest in reference to Shang–Olmec comparisons is the finding of what may be a hematite magnetic compass of Olmec manufacture dating to before 1000 BC. The earliest evidence for Chinese use of the lodestone pointer does not predate 300 BC (Carlson, 1975), so the possibility of an ultimate Olmec origin of what has been thought of as a Chinese invention must now be considered.

China and Chavin

Many workers have noted similarities between the Olmec of Mesoamerica and the Chavin–Cupisnique culture in Peru, the earliest "high culture" of that region. Influence of the Olmec on the latter culture has often been postulated. Radiocarbon dating has now shown Chavin to be similar in age to the Olmec (Signorini, 1969), and, although the question of interinfluence remains, the possibility of direct and seminal Chinese impact on Peru has also been raised, particularly by Heine-Geldern (1959c; 1972:767–791; see also Tee, 1980). Among the similarities are feline motifs, including sculptured felines with mortars on their backs, conventionalized "tiger" stripes, felines with rump masks, horned and jawless feline faces, eyebrows replaced by snakes, and representational ambiguity, as well as the scale band on tails of dragons and of feline monsters in China and Peru, respectively. Heine-Geldern also suggested that use of gold was introduced to Peru from China during the Chavin period (although gold working is now known to be pre-Chavin). He thought in terms of Chou influences, in light of the supposed age of Chavin, but the new dates take the latter's beginnings back to late Shang times.

Some significant features of the highland site of Chavin de Huantar are north–south orientation, stone-lined drains, and a stepped-platform building with subterranean rooms and stone-faced walls with inset carved stone heads. On the coast, fairly elaborate adobe brick and stone buildings with platforms, stairways, and clay columns occur. Whatever the possible Chinese impact on Chavin culture, that influence does not account for most of the aforementioned features, which will be discussed in reference to possible Mediterranean connections.

Among additional possible Chinese importations into both Mexico and Peru are practices relating to domestic dogs. In these three areas "toy" dogs were bred, special breeds were kept as temple and sacrificial animals, and dogs were raised for eating (Fiennes and Fiennes, 1968:26, 53–55, 103–110; Loayza, 1948:191–196). Dog sacrifice and eating are known from Shang times (Chang, 1980:143), and Coe and Diehl (1980:382–383) found that dogs, especially juveniles, were almost certainly eaten at Olmec San Lorenzo.

Chou China and the Northwest Coast

Despite a change of dynasty occasioned by the Western Chou conquest of the Shang, the basic Shang styles and ways of life persisted for centuries, and related cultures existed on the peripheries of the Chinese state. There is currently no evidence of early (Western) Chou (1122–771 BC) voyaging to nuclear America. However, a number of scholars have pointed out similarities between aspects of the Northwest Coast art of Alaska and British Columbia and that of Shang and Chou China. The similarities seem particularly close between surface decoration of bronze vessels and Middle Chou jade carvings on the one hand, and northern Northwest Coast (Haida and Tlingit) wooden boxes and bone and ivory shamans' charms (such as the "spirit-catcher") on the other.

Although Northwest Coast art has some clear Eskimo affinities as well as its own unique aspects, a large number of motifs are shared with Middle Chou China (Fraser, 1962:301–304, 1967). Inverarity (1972) has made what is so far the most thorough analysis of these similarities. They include curving, swelling lines; utilization of all available space; small animal figures attached to larger ones; "x-ray" designs; representational ambiguity; C-shaped, oval, and S-shaped areas; "scale" shapes; split images; dragons; the alter ego; the *sisiutl* motif; and others.

Northwest Coast culture is clearly anomalous in the context of its surrounding cultures. It was a hierarchical society with an elaborate material culture and a complex art style in the midst of far simpler, egalitarian hunting cultures. It was coastal, washed by the Japan current, and maritime-oriented, and it shared many traits with ancient Asia. Japanese slaves were found there in early contact times, and the people of the coast were of a different physical type than those of the interior. Altogether, there is a strong presumption of implantation of many of this society's characteristics, by sea, from Asia. Whether the similarities between archaic China and the Northwest Coast derive from a common third cultural source or whether China influenced the Northwest Coast directly is an item for debate. Fraser (1972:652) discussed the possibility that archaic Chinese motifs spread to various points around the Pacific in the form of a popular but archeologically perishable woodcarving style rather than in the form of stylistically more sophisticated items of nonperishable materials used by the aristocracy. Certain traits—such as trophy head taking, longhouses, boat-building and basketry techniques, and animal heads on boat prows—suggest a South Chinese connection rather than the northern Chinese or Siberian ones sometimes proposed.

Chou and Western Han China and the Americas

The Eastern Chou period (770–222 BC) was a time of rapid expansion, during which Chinese hegemony extended increasingly southward in coastal Kiangsu and Chekiang and foreign intercourse increased. Transpacific contacts have been suggested for this period. The principal indicator of such contacts is the distinctive Tajín decorative style of Classic and early Postclassic Mesoamerican art (Proskouriakoff, 1954; Kampen, 1972). This style exhibits some remarkable similarities to the decorative styles of Chinese bronze and jade work of middle Chou through Ch'in (Qin) times (770–207 BC). Typical motifs (Figure 12.5) are fields of low-relief commas, single and double interlaced ribbons that usually represent serpents or dragons, scale bands, the double-contour design-element border, and the double-headed dragon and *sisiutl* motifs (Covarrubias, 1947:110–111, 1957:176–180; Heine-Geldern, 1959a, 1966:277–283; Jairazbhoy, 1976:96–98, illus. 45–47). These are quite specific, arbitrary traits, associated with two recognized stylistic complexes. As Heine-Geldern (1966:278) has written of the Ulúa Valley marble vases of Honduras, "the Chinese character of the designs ... is so conspicuous that, had these been found, not in America, but somewhere in Asia, no one would doubt that they represent a colonial version of Chinese art."

MIRRORS □ One class of artifacts in the two hemispheres that is of particular interest for comparison is that of mirrors (for a more complete discussion, see Jett, 1978:612–616; also Ekholm, 1973). The Shang had a few metal mirrors. Small, flat or concave pyrite, magnetite, or ilmenite "mirrors" (the concave ones apparently for ceremonial solar fire making) occurred among the Olmec after about 1100 BC. They were pierced and were suspended from the neck. Ekholm saw a possible connection with Chinese concave bronze mirrors used for fire making and noted that Garcilaso de la Vega referred to concave metallic mirrors with this function in Peru.

In Eastern Chou times, bronze mirrors became common in China. Pyrite-mosaic mirrors are known from the Formative of El Arbolillo, Cholula, Mexico (Ford, 1969:74), and from the Olmec (Marshack, 1975). During Classic times, such mirrors were very widely made and traded in Mesoamerica. Later Chou through Western Han (206 BC–AD 8) mirrors share many characteristics with Mesoamerican Classic ones. Sizes were similar, and the usual shape was round, although square ones were occasionally made. Polished pyrite plates instead of metal were used in Mesoamerica. In both areas, mirrors were sometimes inlaid with precious materials and were pierced for suspension from the neck. Mirror

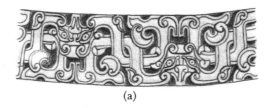

(a)

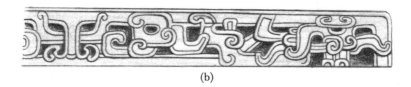

(b)

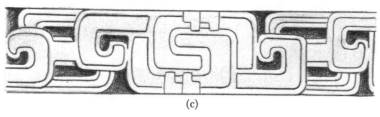

(c)

FIGURE 12.5
Chinese and Mexican interlaced, outlined-band designs: (a) from a Chou bronze vessel; (b) from a stone frieze, El Tajin, Vera Cruz; (c) from a wall painting, Temple of Agriculture, Teotihuacan, Mexico. (After Covarrubias, 1954, 1957.)

backs frequently had relief designs, in similar styles in the two areas (Figure 12.6). Uses included divination and making grave offerings (Chêng, 1963:249–254; Anon., 1934:92–93, 122– 123, plates 39–41; Kidder et al., 1946:126–133, 237, figs. 155–156; Woodbury, 1965:172–175; Proskouriakoff, 1965:569).

The similarity between the basic forms, probable functions, and decorative styles of Chinese and Mesoamerican mirrors is most suggestive of historical relationship. Typical Tajin-style interlocking meanders and scrollwork and the scale-band motif—on mirrors, palma stones, and buildings—have been emphasized by Covarrubias (1947:110–111) and Heine-Geldern (1959a, 1966:227–282), as have those on the Ulúa marble vases.

THE CHRONOLOGICAL PROBLEM □ The scale-band motif is apparently unknown on Chinese objects after 400 BC. The other Chou-Ch'in bronzework motifs of which the Tajín style is reminiscent seem to have persisted through Western Han times but were rapidly replaced by new styles as the Han Dynasty proceeded. Tajín-style stone carving has not been dated before about

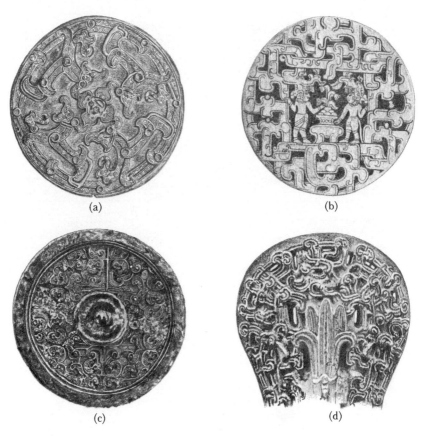

FIGURE 12.6
Chinese and Mesoamerican decorative motifs: (a) Late Chou bronze mirror back; (b) Tajín-style slate mirror back, Kaminaljuyu, Guatemala; (c) Late Chou or Ch'in bronze mirror back, "Huai Valley style"; (d) detail of Tajín-style palmate stone, Vera Cruz. (Part a after Willetts, 1965; parts b, d after Covarrubias, 1957; part c after Anon., 1934.)

AD 300–700. Heine-Geldern (1958:204–205, 1966:280–283) tried to show that a mural at Teotihuacan in Tajín-like style (see Figure 12.5) *might* date to the second century BC, but a third-century AD date seems to fit the chronological evidence better. Thus, an important time gap still remains between the Chou-Ch'in–Han and Tajín styles. Nevertheless, Heine-Geldern's hypothesis that the Tajín style might long have been applied in ephemeral painting and woodcarving prior to its common translation into durable stone has considerable appeal. Palmas actually used in ball games must have been of a relatively light material such as wood, and carved wood could well have served for early mosaic mirror backs. A wooden backing was probably used to reinforce the thin slate of a compound mirror from Kaminaljuyu, Guatemala, and a wood-backed turquoise and pyrite plaque was found at Chichen Itza, Yucatan. Wooden frames for later

Mexican obsidian mirrors are also known (Kidder et al., 1946:127, 133). Wooden objects carved in late Shang decorative style are known from Anyang (Chêng, 1960: plate 6; Chang, 1980:117). Since Chou-Ch'in style is known primarily in bronze (but to some extent in jade), and since metalworking was not introduced to Mesoamerica until later, it is plausible that the Chinese decorative style was introduced primarily in woodcarving. It may be noted, too, that a few late Olmec or post-Olmec stone relief sculptures have spiral motifs that may reflect this style (see, for example, Bernal, 1969:61, 139).

The ancient Chinese coastal state of Wu (which included modern Kiangsu Province) was nominally within the Chou Empire, although it was a peripheral area and came under Chou influence rather late. Wu briefly dominated the Chou Empire in the late sixth century BC but was soon conquered and destroyed by Yueh, in present Chekiang Province. By the early fifth century BC, Yueh, in turn, had been conquered by the inland state of Ch'u. The entire period from then until 222 BC is known as that of the "Warring States." After a brief period of unification, warfare and rebellion reasserted themselves toward the end of the Ch'in Dynasty (221-207 BC) (Chêng, 1963:xxvii-xxxii). We may speculate that some middle Chou motifs (such as the scale band) lasted longer in the coastal areas than in the inland core area and that some coastal peoples responded to the prolonged strife of the times by emigrating to Mesoamerica (see, for example, Shao, 1976). As yet, however, we have no direct evidence for these speculations.

Traditions recorded by 90 BC do tell, however, of a Taoist belief in three mountain islands in the Yellow Sea, on which were found the drugs of longevity. From the early fourth century BC, sailors are said to have been sent in search of these isles, without success. In 219 BC, the Ch'in emperor sent Hsü Fu of Ch'i (Shantung; Shandong) to search for the islands. Hsü reported that the king of one of these lands in the Eastern Sea required virgins and workmen of all trades in exchange for the drugs. Three thousand young men and women were then sent out with Hsü Fu in 210 BC, but he is said to have become a king in a land of plains and great lakes and never to have returned to China (Needham, 1971:551-553; Yü, 1967:182-183). There has been speculation that this expedition ended in America. The emphasis on drugs does bring to mind Middle and South American hallucinogenic plants. However, there is good reason to believe that Hsü colonized Honshu, Japan (Hsieh, 1967:87-90). Nevertheless, this bit of history does confirm maritime exploration by China proper in pre-Han times.

Drug plants could have represented a valuable, easily transported commodity that might have provided a motive for early Chinese voyaging—voyaging perhaps interrupted during the period of strife of late Chou times. As noted above, jade is also possibly relevant in this context. It is interesting to compare known and probable jade sources near Pacific shores with the areas thought by some scholars to exhibit archaic Chinese influences. Jade: Japan, Indonesia (Celebes), New Guinea, New Zealand, Costa Rica (?), Guerrero, British Columbia (Fraser and Turnagain rivers [Hansford, 1968:27]). Putative

Shang-Chou-Ch'in artistic or other influence: Japan, Indonesia (especially Sumatra, Borneo, Flores), New Guinea (Sepik River, Trobriand Islands), New Zealand, Peru, Costa Rica, Guerrero-Veracruz, British Columbia–Southern Alaska (Heine-Geldern, 1959a:205; Fraser, 1962:144). For Peru, Sumatra, and Borneo, valuable metals and tropical bird feathers could have been the relevant materials.

Dong-Son Culture and American Metallurgy

By Late Chou times, there existed beyond the southern borders of the Chinese state, in present-day Yünnan and Tonkin, a culture currently called *Dong-Son*. It persisted into the early Christian Era. The kingdom of Nan Yüeh, set up by a Chinese general in Ch'in times, included much of this area; it was annexed by the Han emperor in 112 BC.

The still poorly known Dong-Son people were workers in copper and bronze. Some objects—drums and urns with lids supporting sculpted figures and buildings—are very distinctive. Others, including types of belt buckles and socketed tools, suggested to Heine-Geldern (1954, 1972; also Jairazbhoy, 1976:95–96) derivation from earlier cultures around the Black Sea (or in Latin, *Pontus*). He postulated a "Pontic migration" to Indochina to account for the observed similarities. Earlier scholars had recognized the similarity of metal objects from the Black Sea region to those of northwestern South America. Heine-Geldern proposed that this similarity could be accounted for by transpacific carriage of these styles by Dong-Son voyagers, artifacts of whose culture have been discovered widely in Southeast Asia and New Guinea.

Heine-Geldern distinguished two possible impact areas: the central Andean region and the region from northern Ecuador to Costa Rica. In the northern area, there are some metal artifacts and metallurgical techniques strikingly like those of Dong-Son. Objects include small, globular bells, openwork scenes framed with simple or plaited rope designs with spiral appendages, and frogs decorated with the plait motif. Chronologies, unfortunately, are not well established for these objects. The earliest present dates for metalworking are from Bahia, Ecuador, at about 500 BC–AD 500. However, the relevant style is not attested to before about AD 100–200 (Mountjoy, 1969:27).

The Andean area presents more problems than does the northern area. Here are found socketed tools, trunnion axes with broadened necks, star-shaped mace heads, tweezers, double protomes of animals, and a large variety of metal pins. The pins so closely resemble Pontic types that either some historic relationship exists or most criteria for using stylistic resemblances to identify diffusion must be discarded (Figure 12.7). Unfortunately for the Heine-Geldern hypothesis, none of these objects is yet known in Dong-Son archeology. Heine-Geldern suggested that these classes of objects may not have been included with burials in Southeast Asia and may have been melted down when their usefulness or vogue

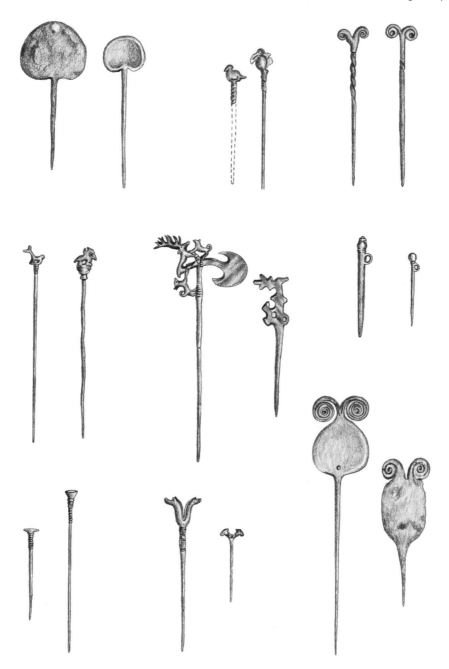

FIGURE 12.7
Bronze and copper pins from the Caucasus region (left-hand specimens of each pair) and from
the Andean region (right-hand specimens). (After Heine-Geldern, 1972.)

ended. At present, a major chronological gap exists between most of the few approximately dated Andean finds of the object types in question and the end of Dong-Son culture. A far greater gap occurs when the Pontic material is considered, and the Pontic peoples were seemingly not maritime. Some of these pin types *are* known from early times in maritime areas—the Aegean (Piggott, 1965:74–75) and the Indus Valley (Wheeler, 1966:51). The question of an extracontinental origin for these metal objects in the Andean region seems possibly tied to that of the origin of other traits with apparent Mediterranean–Southwest Asian affinities. These will be discussed in a subsequent section.

Similarities between Dong-Son sculpted bronze drums and urn lids and the unique terra cotta house models and "village scenes" on round or rectangular bases from southern Nayarit, Mexico, have been noted (von Winning, 1969; Bell, 1971:715–716; Marschall, 1972:167–189; Jairazbhoy, 1976:45, illus. 1). The chronology of the Mexican objects is not yet well established, but they are estimated to date between the first and seventh centuries AD. From early in the shaft-tomb period of southwestern Nayarit (about AD 100–200) come also the vaguely Oriental-faced "chinesca" figurines (von Winning, 1974:69, 172–176). The Han Chinese, who conquered the Dong-Son area (see the following section), also made terra-cotta house models and "village scenes" on rectangular bases as grave offerings (Sullivan, 1973:61, 90) and utilized shaft tombs.

In South America, the Bahia culture of Ecuador also produced ceramic house models, many of which exhibit overhanging eaves or saddle roofs or both (Estrada and Meggers, 1961; Meggers, 1971:244–248). The saddle roof type is otherwise unknown in the Americas, but it exists or existed at scattered localities in South India, Southeast Asia (including Tonkin), South China, Japan, and western Oceania (Noble, 1969:266–267). The Bahia culture also exhibits other traits rare or otherwise absent in America but found in southern and eastern Asia. Among these are neck rests, symmetrically graduated panpipes (see also Marschall, 1965; Tekiner, 1976), a type of ceramic net weight, "golf-tee" ear plugs, and the "coolie yoke." The dates of this complex lie somewhere between 200 BC and 1 BC, a time range compatible with either Dong-Son or Han or with a fusion of the two. The contemporaneous occurrence in the Bahia area of the earliest American Dong-Son-like metal work is also worthy of note. Bahia culture was highly developed and had maritime trade relations with areas from Mexico to southern Peru (A. Kidder II, 1964:476–477).

Later Han China and the New World

The Han Dynasty in China (206 BC–220 AD) was, on the whole, a time of political reunification, expansion of frontiers, and development of long-distance foreign contacts. Voyaging to India was common during the Western Han. A third-century-AD writer recorded that the Han had "won through across the Western Seas to reach Ta-Chhin [the Roman Empire] . . . but the Eastern

FIGURE 12.8
Chinese and Mesoamerican cylindrical tripod pottery vessels: (a) Han dynasty, North Viet Nam;
(b) Teotihuacan III style, Kaminaljuyu, Guatemala; (c) Han dynasty, model granary;
(d) "stuccoed" (lacquered) Teotihuacanoid vessel, Uaxactun, Guatemala. (Parts a, c after Heine-
Geldern, 1959b; part b after Kidder et al., 1946; part d after Keleman, 1956.)

Ocean is yet more vast, and we know of no one who has crossed it" (Needham,
1971:550). Nevertheless, trade was carried on with Korea and Japan (Yü,
1967:183–186), and some have suggested contacts with the Americas. At least
one oceanic expedition in search of the eastern "Fortunate Isles" was made in
about 100 BC (Jairazbhoy, 1976:19).

   Heine-Geldern (1959b, 1966:283–284), Ekholm (1964a), and Jairazbhoy
(1976:45–46, illus. 2–3) have pointed out the similarity of Teotihuacan II–III
cylindrical tripod pottery (beginning in the third century AD[?]) to the ceramic,
metal, and lacquer cylindrical tripod vessels of Han China (Figure 12.8). Be-

sides general form, points in common include conical lids (sometimes with avi-form or ring-form apical knobs), decorative zones encircling the vessel's body and separated by ridges or incisions, thickened tops and/or bottoms of vessel walls, and mold-made applied decoration. The cylindrical tripod vase is an un-precedented form in Mesoamerican archeology when it appears at Teotihuacan, and it is associated with the earliest known Mesoamerican use of ceramic molds and appliqué mold decorations. Ekholm suggested that the Mesoamerican ce-ramic forms imitated Chinese metal ones, which had mold-made parts. Heine-Geldern also saw Han or pre-Han influence in Middle American bowls on high, flaring stands pierced by triangular perforations.

LACQUER □ Although developed by Shang times, lacquer work came into preeminence in China during Han times. The sap of the lac tree (*ch'i* < *ts'iet*) was used as the vehicle for pigments and then dried to a bright, usually glossy, finish. This technique was used on wood, cloth, metal, pottery, and other mate-rials. Usually a gessolike primer layer of bone ash or white earth was first applied to the wood, but sometimes a technique called *chia chu* ("lined with hemp cloth") was used. In India, Ceylon, and Burma, resin (or, in Sanskrit, *laksha*) secreted by a *Coccus* insect that is parasitic on gummy-sapped trees is used. A scale insect, *pela*, is also used in China to produce a white wax.

Mesoamerican lacquer work apparently dates to at least the first century BC, although most of what is known of the processes used comes from postcontact observations. Salvia-seed oil (*chia* or *chian*) was one major lacquer medium used, particularly in western Mexico; the other was *aje*, the fat rendered from a tree-sap-sucking coccid insect native to the hotter parts of Middle America. Lacquers were used on gourds, wood, stone mirror backs, pottery, and probably metal over a gessolike white-earth primer. In both China and Mexico, succes-sive layers, sometimes of different colors, were applied; red and black were particularly common. Shared decoration techniques included painting; painted inlay; carving, including exposure of different-colored undercoats; and filling of incisions with pigment (Willetts, 1958:188–205; Jenkins, 1967; B. Gordon, 1957). Covarrubias (1957:96–97, 139) believed that lacquer work originated in Mesoamerica in late Preclassic times on the Pacific coast of western Mexico and that it reached its acme on pottery at Teotihuacan, whence it spread.

ADDITIONAL EVIDENCE OF CHINESE CONTACTS □ A number of Chinese objects and inscriptions have been reported from Mexico and Peru, sometimes in archeological contexts (although these sites were not excavated under controlled conditions). Some of the written characters are said to be of forms attributable to Han times, and others to about the sixth century AD. The principal archeological zones involved are those of Teotihuacan, Mexico, and Chan Chan, Peru (Loayza, 1948:44–94; Lou, 1968; Carter, 1976). These ob-jects are suggestive, but, because of the uncertainties surrounding their discovery and the complexities of Chinese epigraphy, no great weight can be assigned to them at present.

The layout of Teotihuacan is reminiscent of that of the Chinese city in emphasizing an interrupted north–south axial street and a rough gridiron layout, and in being composed largely of walled household compounds with courtyards. Unlike the Chinese city, Teotihuacan lacked an encompassing wall (Millon, 1974; Willetts, 1958:655–677; Jairazbhoy, 1976:47–49). Further, in Middle America it was believed that lunar eclipses occurred in a certain proportion to the number of lunar months. This same proportion was believed in by the Han Chinese, but in reality this supposed rate is almost one and one-third times the actual frequency of occurrence (Campbell, 1974:146–147).

Relevant to the finds of the Chan Chan area, Loayza (1948:101–154) listed 95 Peruvian place names that have meaning in Chinese but not in local languages, plus 130 Peruvian place names that correspond to Chinese place names. These names are concentrated particularly from Lima northward. Among additional traits shared by China and Peru, the following are of especial interest: metal disks or coins put into cadavers' mouths, tally strings (quipus), suspension bridges, great walls (Needham, 1971:544–546; Loayza, 1948:161–173, 213–222), and elaborate agricultural terraces (Spencer and Hale, 1961).

Heine-Geldern (1966:284) has stated that there is no evidence of post-Han Chinese contacts with the New World. Others, however, have disagreed. Since the eighteenth century, some workers have postulated that Fu-Sang, a land said to lie thousands of miles east of China, was in America. The land was referred to as early as Late Chou times and was reportedly visited by Afghani Buddhist monks in AD 485 and by a monk named Hui-Shen a few years later. Rock crystal was said to have been brought to China from Fu-Sang about AD 520 (Needham, 1971:540–541; Mertz, 1975). Although some aspects of the descriptions of Fu-Sang are compatible with a Mesoamerican identification, others— such as the presence of oxen, horses, and deer milking—seemingly are not. In any event, the Chinese did believe in a land far to the east, and the much condensed records that have survived may point to the conclusion that some voyages were made. (For a modern attempt in a Han-style junk, see Knöbl and Denning, 1976.)

Paul Shao (1976) has suggested important T'ang Chinese (AD 618–907) Buddhist influence on the art and iconography of the Classic Maya of the same time period, centered at Copan, Honduras. He emphasizes details of costume— (such as chinless monster masks on head-dresses, shoulders, wristlets, tops of loincloth aprons, and knees), special hand gestures (mūdras), and the like. Although Shao makes a strong case for connections, at least some of these features represent an earlier, Olmec (and perhaps ultimately archaic Chinese) legacy, and others are present in India (Hürlimann, 1967) and in Indianized Southeast Asia. The latter group may reflect postulated Hindu–Buddhist influences from those areas (see pages 594–601).

THE MEDITERRANEAN AND NUCLEAR AMERICA

Almost from the moment of Cortez's landing in Mexico, Europeans began speculating upon possible links between New World civilizations and those of the ancient and classical Near East and Mediterranean. So many unfounded surmises, religious theories, and even fraudulent "finds" had occurred by the early twentieth century (Wauchope, 1962) that serious study of possible early Mediterranean–American relations became, through "guilt by association," even more anathematic to scholarship than did consideration of possible transpacific ties. This prejudice still holds to a large degree, which perhaps helps explain why most works on the subject have been written either by amateurs or by scholars from fields other than anthropology, history, or geography. Not surprisingly, many of these works are flawed or are at least held suspect by specialists. I believe, nevertheless, that some of the proposals of these writers merit serious scrutiny.

Ancient Egyptians

During the early decades of this century, surgeon G. Elliot Smith (1924, 1927, 1933), founder of the "British School" of diffusionism, promoted the idea that Egypt was the fountainhead of much of the world's civilization. Though this idea was rejected by the scholars of the 1930s and 1940s, there has been a recent revival of interest in some of his ideas. For example, R. A. Jairazbhoy (1974b, 1981) has argued that Egyptians of the time of Ramses III were among the founders of the Olmec culture.

Olmec specialists have frequently noted analogies between that culture and ancient Egypt, although they do not suggest any actual historical link. The Olmecs' apparent seasonal use of corvée laborers—who would expend incredible amounts of effort to transport, sculpt, and emplace colossal, excellently executed stone statues, reliefs, drainways, and the like and to build earth platforms and mounds—has been compared to Egyptian practice, as has Olmec dependence upon the annual inundation of river flood plains for farming. The sudden, unprecedented appearance of these works and other evidence of advanced knowledge and organization in the unlikely environment of the swampy Gulf coast of Veracruz and Tabasco has often been remarked upon.

Jairazbhoy has proposed that these similarities are not simply analogs but are the result of a purposeful expedition, in the early twelfth century BC, of Egyptians dispatched by the Pharaoh to discover the underworld paradise to which the setting sun repairs at night. Jairazbhoy believes that the Maya *Popol Vuh* and Mexican traditions recorded by Sahagún and others—which tell of ancestors coming across the sea from the east, seeking the sun and searching for a terrestrial paradise—refer to this expedition.

Briefly summarized, these Mesoamerican traditions relate that humans were created in the East and lived there in darkness. The ancestors left the East, crossing the sea in a fleet of seven vessels carrying "many companies," and sailed along the Gulf of Mexico coast to its farthest westward point, at Panuco, where the people debarked. They were led to "Tula" by priests, "bookmen" who carried their symbols of rank and their gods. When the sun did not appear, the leaders, disappointed, left, either for home or to continue their quest. Those voyagers who remained then settled near the highest mountains they could find, and for them the sun rose. They married into the local population, to whom they taught the arts of civilization. When their leaders returned, the settlers would not accompany them homeward. Sons of the priest–kings returned to the East, where they received from the king of the East the insignia and symbols of royalty, including the canopy and throne. They then returned to rule the tribes. In most versions, these culture-bearer ancestors came to Tula; the Aztec and the Maya both seem to have inherited the legend from the Toltecs (who, in turn, apparently adopted it from Teotihuacanos). One version, however, places the arrival of these ancestors in the Olmec period (Goetz and Morley, 1951:63, 165–189, 204–210; Heyerdahl, 1950b:277–280; Sorenson, 1955; Irwin, 1963: 11–12, 35–38; Jairazbhoy, 1974b:8–11). Jairazbhoy views the seeking of the highest mountains as a search for the two peaks flanking the entrance to the Egyptian underworld, and he believes that the crater of San Martin de Tuxtla, in the Olmec heartland, was accepted by some of the pilgrims as the entry itself. The fluted earthen mound at La Venta is considered a surrogate for this volcano.

Jairazbhoy (1974a, b, 1975, 1976:86–89, 95, 101–107, 149–150, illus. 48–58) has pointed to a number of traits and institutions that he believes were introduced at this time. These items include cylinder seals, terra-cotta animals with moving parts, colossal stone sculpture, the calendar, divine kingship, military and funerary customs, and the idea of writing, among others. Jairazbhoy's emphasis is on religious concepts, however, and he describes more than a score of Mesoamerican "deities"—about half of whom are depicted in Olmec-period carvings—that he believes to be of Egyptian derivation. Although some of the comparisons seem flimsy, others include some striking similarities: for example, the Mexican goddess Tlazoteotl, who ate people's sins upon their confession, and the Egyptian Amemil, "the devouress," who would eat the hearts of condemned sinners after they had confessed to her. Jairazbhoy also compared Egyptian and Mexican beliefs about passage through various stages on the journey through the western underworld. He found a serpent guard at stage 2 in each area, deserts in stage 4, and a stage 8 (Aztec *Tlalocán*) in which inhabitants dwell in an enjoyable, watery underworld. He also believes he has identified aspects of the Babylonian Gilgamesh legend in Mexican and Mayan texts and sees the earliest Mesoamerican stepped temple mounds (of which there is a small one at La Venta) as reflections of the Babylonian ziggurat.

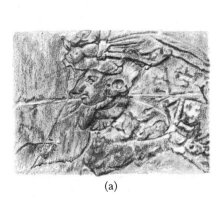

(a)

(b)

FIGURE 12.9

Olmec stone sculptures depicting faces with Old World racial traits: (a) detail, Stela 3, La Venta—note exaggeratedly large, convex, "Levantine" nose and false (?) beard; (b) Monument 1, San Lorenzo—note Negroid features: broad, flat, low-rooted nose with foreward-directed nostrils; thick, everted, membranous lips with ridged seams; slight prognathism. (Part a after Heyerdahl, 1971c; part b after Clewlow et al., 1967.)

Jairazbhoy included far more material than can be summarized here, and much of what he has presented would benefit from additional elaboration. Adjusted dates for the Olmec now put the abrupt appearance of most of that culture's distinctive ceramics well before the reign of Ramses III, and the building of part of the site's vast earthen platform even earlier (Coe and Diehl, 1980: 143, 150–151, 159). Nevertheless, Jairazbhoy's suggestions are most provocative and deserve further analysis. If modified and accepted, his theories could go far toward explaining the enigma of Olmec origins—as a grafting of Egyptian and Chinese branches onto a preexisting Formative American root to yield a distinctive new high culture.

One aspect of the "Olmec problem" has been the ostensible presence, in Olmec (and later) art, of depictions of exotic racial types, including Negroids and "Semites" or Armenoids (Heyerdahl, 1952:286–295, plates 17–22, 29–32, 1971c:229–236; Irwin, 1963:121–138; von Wuthenau, 1975; C. Gordon, 1971: 21–35). In most cases, it appears to me, the depictions are either too stylized or too generalized for any racial attribution. However, a small number of apparent portraits seem to be sufficiently explicit (Figure 12.9) to justify calling some of them Caucasoid (especially in an Olmec bas-relief and among late Preclassic and Classic Veracruz and Oaxaca terra cottas) and others at least partially

Negroid (Olmec colossal stone heads from San Lorenzo and some Veracruz terra cottas). The fact that a number of "portraits" cannot be racially classified, though they are quite realistic, suggests that genetically mixed individuals may be portrayed. Wiercinski (1969) has concluded that there is skeletal evidence for a Negroid component at Tlatilco, Mexico, and elsewhere, although Comas (1973) rejected this conclusion. Those who do feel that foreign racial types are indicated usually invoke a hypothesis of Egyptian or Phoenician voyagers bringing Negro troops or slaves. The wearing of beards is often pointed to as an indication of the Caucasoid affiliations of certain individuals depicted in Olmec and later art. Some of these beards seem to be quite genuine, but many appear to be false. False beards were also worn both in ancient Egypt and in China.

Canaanites and Carthaginians

The Bronze Age Minoans and other maritime peoples of the ancient Aegean and eastern Mediterranean seem to be prime candidates for early transatlantic transmissions, but as yet only the most dubious, ambiguous, or circumstantial evidence suggests actual impacts (see, for example, Hapgood, 1966; Cohane, 1969; C. Gordon, 1971:68–105; Bailey, 1973). However, for the Iron Age Phoenicians—the Canaanites and their Carthaginian descendants—we have more substantial grounds for hypothesizing influences upon the New World. Although they had long occupied the Levantine littoral, the Northwest-Semitic-speaking Canaanites become prominent in history—as "Phoenicians"—beginning about 1200 BC. They were merchant mariners located at a cultural crossroads, and they developed trade and established colonies along the Mediterranean and on the European and African shores of the Atlantic. They were skilled manufacturers, ambitious traders, and the navigators par excellence of the day, and they were frequently employed in the service of the land-based empires of the times.

Several classical sources, beginning in the fourth century BC, speak of an immense land beyond the Atlantic, many days west of Africa. This land was said to have mountains, plains, and navigable rivers and to be inhabited by strange people who had substantial houses, wealth, and cultivated land through which ran streams. The land was, according to Diodorus Siculus (first century BC), discovered by a storm-blown Phoenician ship sometime after the 1104 BC founding of Gadeira (Cadiz, Spain). Some Carthaginians went to settle this land (Carthage's traditional founding date is 814 BC but may have been as early as the twelfth century). Etruscans also wished to establish a colony there, according to a fourth-century BC Aristotelian source, but the Carthaginians prevented them from doing this. Then, worried that other nations would establish a foothold there, as well as about a possible exodus of its own people, and wishing to reserve a secret refuge in case of calamity, Carthage forbade further emigration and killed all of the settlers already there. Tradition places one voyage to this land at about 370 BC (Pohl, 1961:17–35; Irwin, 1963:119, 220–224; C. Gordon, 1971:38–42, 193, Bailey, 1973:36–41).

Irwin (1963) has raised the questions: Did the Carthaginians ever resort to this refuge? And can any Canaanite–Carthaginian influence be detected in the Americas? She believes that likely occasions for flight might have included the siege of Tyre by Babylonians (about 600 BC) and the Punic Wars, which began in 264 BC and ended with the destruction of Carthage in 146 BC. Of these dates, she favored the first because of what she believed to be indications of Phoenician influence on the Olmec and because she believed that the Phoenicians introduced the first calendar to Mesoamerica, for which internal evidence is said to suggest a beginning date of about 600 BC.

The great Olmec earthworks and colossal stone sculptures-in-the-round are now clearly too early to have been a result of such Phoenician immigration. However, certain traits—such as relief carvings showing "Levantine" physical types wearing pointed, curling-toed shoes, ritual self-laceration, possible infant sacrifice, wheeled animal models, and Jairazbhoy's (1974b:20–27, 114–115) "Babylonian complex"—could be attributable to a Phoenician source. What some believe to be a terra-cotta head of a Phoenician god—either Melqart or Bes—was found under uncontrolled conditions in the Rio Balsas drainage (Vaillant, 1931).

One of the Phoenicians' hallmarks was the making of a coveted and costly purple dye from the shellfish *Murex* and *Pupura*. *Pupura* dye was also extracted and used in Precolumbian Middle America and Peru and long ago was pointed to as an indication of Phoenician contacts (Nuttall, 1909; Jackson, 1917; Gerhard, 1964).

Supporting the probability of Phoenician transatlantic voyaging is the famous "Paraiba Inscription." It was reported in 1872 and long dismissed as a forgery, but the authenticity of this now-lost inscription from Brazil has more recently been championed by Semitic linguist C. Gordon (1971:115, 120–127, 1974:22–29, 71–92). Although his position has not gone unchallenged (Cross, 1968), Gordon's argument—that the text contains several organizational and linguistic usages unknown to scholarship at the time of the supposed forgery, as well as cryptograms—seems convincing to a nonspecialist. The inscription tells of the landing of a Sidonian ship in 531 BC, after a voyage around Africa from the Red Sea port of Ezion-geber. Gordon noted Herodotus' report of an Egypto-Canaanite circumnavigation of Africa about 600 BC. He proposed that the Sidonians had intentionally sought Brazil via the Red Sea rather than via the Straits of Gibraltar because, subsequent to the Persian conquest of Canaan in 539 BC, the Carthaginians had barred Sidonian voyaging through the straits. The motivation, Gordon proposed, was provided by Brazil's iron deposits.

Further, Fell (1976:157–173) has identified purported Iberian Punic (Canaanite) inscriptions from New England, Iowa, and Oklahoma as well as fourth-century (?) BC Carthaginian coins found in the eastern United States. He cited Plutarch's (about AD 100) paraphrase of a Carthaginian itinerary to North America (?), and he attempted to show that the Micmac language of Nova Scotia contains many loan words from North African Greek. Fell believes that the chants of Arizona's Pimas are in Arabic and include some of Aesop's fables. Various inscriptions supposedly in Arabic are identified, especially from Nevada (Fell, 1980:48–116, 170–189, 300, 311–314, 398–406). Fell's works are so recent and difficult to evaluate properly that they cannot be accorded further discussion here. However, these claims, if true, would have far-reaching implications.

The Classical World and Mexico

As Sorenson (1971) and others have shown, the Mediterranean and the Near East share a very large number of basic ideas, beliefs, and technologies with Mesoamerica—even though the styles of these regions are quite distinct. The sharings could represent parallel or convergent evolution or a legacy of the proposed Egyptian and Phoenician impacts of the Theocratic Formative period, or they could be later importations from one or more other sources. In many instances, it would be impossible to choose among the Mediterranean, India, Southeast Asia, and China as the potential source for traits found in Meso-america that are shared by some or all of these regions. Until quite recently, consideration of the Mediterranean and Near East has been neglected by mod-ern diffusionists in favor of studies involving eastern Asia, but Southwest Asia and the Mediterranean deserve, I believe, close examination in this connection. The classical world—Greece and Rome—certainly represents one possible source for some of the aforementioned similarities between the Old World and the New. However, other similarities date from well before the classical civiliza-tions, and the evidence regarding other traits has as yet been very little studied. Teotihuacan seems to be the most promising Mesoamerican area for investiga-tions relating to possible classical ties.

Despite the lack of comparative studies between Mexico and the classical Mediterranean, a few clues point to actual round-trip Roman voyages. These include a terra-cotta head, said to be Roman, of about AD 220, found by José García Payon in situ with a twelfth-century AD burial in the valley of Toluca, Mexico; a small torso of Venus collected by Seler in the Huaxteca on the Gulf of Mexico (Heine-Geldern, 1967); and some Roman ceramics and metal objects excavated by amateurs in Alabama and Virginia (Fell, 1980:117–119; Covey, 1975:4–6, 21–23, 26). Scattered finds of Roman-period coins from the eastern United States have engendered controversy (Covey, 1975; Epstein, 1980; Fell, 1980:120–163). However, identification of the South American pineapple de-picted in murals and a mosaic at Pompeii (Casella, 1950; Pohl, 1973) was accepted by plant taxonomist Merrill (1954), a staunch foe of diffusionism.

What influences, if any, classical civilizations may have had on Mesoamerica is still an open question. Sorenson's list should provide grist for many years of research in reference to classical and earlier times.

SOUTHWEST ASIA, THE MEDITERRANEAN, AND PERU

Egypt and the Andean Region

Jairazbhoy (1974b:83–99, 1981) theorizes that the "Egypto-Olmecs" continued their search for the underworld paradise and were an element in the formation of the early Central Andean high cultures, a legacy that persisted to the time of the conquest. This migration, as Jairazbhoy perceives it, required several generations. Similarities between Olmec and Chavin have often been discussed; the two cultures were approximately contemporaneous and had much in common. Chavin and its coastal variant Cupisnique together exhibit monumental stone construction, use of adobe brick, large stone sculptures, tenoned stone heads in walls, and other distinctive attributes. Other, poorly dated traits—peculiar to Peru in the New World but also found in Egypt—include solar religion, the royal title *Son of the Sun,* the marriage of the ruler to his sister, hunchback dwarfs as court attendants, the equal-arm balance, the horizontal loom staked onto the ground, and mummification with layered wrappings, false heads, and jars for viscera (Rowe, 1966; Jairazbhoy, 1974b:85–88, 98–99). In addition, T-shaped and epsilon-shaped axes, virtually identical in form, are essentially restricted to the Egyptian region, parts of Mexico, and the Central Andes (Bierne, 1971:153, 157).

Jairazbhoy (1974b:92–99) believes that the Egyptians' descendants finally decided that the plains of Lake Titicaca were the equivalent of Iaru, the fields of the city of Re, the sun god whose dwelling is in an underworld lake. The Peruvian paradise Yaro and the fields of Yarocaca in the place of the dead are cited as equivalences (compare, as well, the name of the Uru, who now inhabit the lake's shore). Of course the importance in Andean religion of Titicaca's Island of the Sun is well known. Jairazbhoy found a few architectural parallels between the Titicaca Basin site of Tiahuanaco (Tiwanaku) and Egypt, but the city's rise appears to be too late to reflect direct Egyptian influences.

Heyerdahl (1952:228–238, 247–274, 282–284) has emphasized the occurrence in South America, particularly in Peru and Bolivia, of traditions of white, long-bearded, long-robed culture-bearers who came from somewhere to the East in early times. These people were priests and proselytizers, who—in the Central Andean version of the legend—settled the Island of the Sun in Lake Titicaca and built the great edifices of Tiahuanaco. Some of the party married native women, and the Inca royal family claimed descent from this line.

Heyerdahl (1952:295–328, plates 23–27, 34–36, 1971c) has pointed to depictions of bearded individuals and to portraits of non-Indian-appearing persons in

Andean art, and he has discussed the occurrence of pre-Incan Peruvian mummies whose hair is silky, wavy, and of auburn color like that of Caucasoids rather than coarse and black, as is typical of the local Amerind populations. Although he did not elaborate on the specifics of the ultimate origins of these physically anomalous individuals, Heyerdahl (1971a, b) made clear his belief that the Mediterranean—particularly North Africa—is the most likely source area. This idea is, of course, completely compatible with Jairazbhoy's theory of a seminal Egypto-Olmec presence in Peru, focused on Tiahuanaco, and is also completely at variance with conventional thinking about Andean cultural evolution.

Relevant to the Egyptian question is the recent work of Fell, published in his *Occasional Publications of the Epigraphic Society*. Fell claims to have deciphered a Chilean inscription that records, in Arabic with Libyan script, an Egyptian "annexation" of the South American coast in 231 BC. On the basis of inscriptions, Fell (1980:223–303) concluded that these discoverers ultimately colonized the Great Basin of western North America. Among Fell's (1976:174–191, 253–276) other startling proposals are that the Zuni language of New Mexico is Libyan (related to Ancient Egyptian), that the Micmac script of maritime Canada is modified Egyptian hieroglyphics, and that the Davenport Stele from Iowa contains inscriptions in Egyptian, Libyan, and Iberian Punic.

"Greco-Roman" Traits in the Andean Area

Although he was attempting to discredit diffusionist theories, Rowe (1966; see also Jett and Carter, 1966; Birrell, 1964) compiled a trait list that is of much potential interest to diffusionists. It includes a substantial number of Andean traits that are also present in the Mediterranean and Southwest Asia. The following are known from Archaic or Classical Greece (and, in a number of cases, from other Old World areas) and, in the New World, *exclusively* from the Andean region: pack animals, divination from entrails (Obayashi, 1959), sacrifice of domestic animals, oracles, a deity implied to be superior to heavenly bodies because of their regular movements, divine kingship, the sling (weapon), military tents, cubical dice, the whipping top, the abacus, the equal-arm balance, the bismar (Nordenskiöld, 1921), the pointed plumb bob, the *peplos* dress, bronze mirrors with handles, metal tweezers, metal nails, the cylindrical drum with two skin heads, the bell-mouthpiece trumpet, the corbeled-dome roof, metal cramps in masonry, handling-protruberances left on building stones, rustication and entasis in architecture, the building of stories directly over one another, the siphon, and the sickle. Other shared traits are also notable, including the arch (Larco Hoyle, 1945:164), bronze metallurgy and artifact types, staffs with bells for town leaders, wheel-thrown pottery, lathes (Grieder, 1978:96–101), and some striking resemblances in subject matter and in decorative style and technique between Greek Attic and Corinthian pottery and Peruvian Mochica wares. In addition to the preceding are the following traits known from Roman culture: convents, rectangular land survey, taxation census, standard-number military units, animal-manure fertilizer, and press-mold-made pottery.

Finally, there is in Peru the *qanat,* or horizontal well—a Mediterranean-Southwest Asian device associated particularly with Persia (English, 1968)—and the wind scoop, found from Egypt to Pakistan as well as in Mochica ceramic house models (Rudofsky, 1977:286–289).

Foci in the Andean region for these traits seem to be the Mochica area of the North Coast and the Titicaca Basin. Rowe is correct in considering his list an important test of diffusionist theory. If the archeologically recoverable traits in question should prove to be chronologically irreconcilable—and some are not yet attested to in Peru early enough to be attributable to the classical world—the whole process of comparison would be brought into question. Still, dating of Andean cultures is far from complete.

Although Gladwin's (1947) transpacific Alexandrian fleet must be viewed more as allegory than history, one *could* hypothesize a Greco-Roman Persian Gulf or Arabian Sea trading colony in which certain Hellenic styles (of pottery decoration, for example) persisted in provincial form and from which voyagers reached Peru. The Romans *were* in contact with Han China and Indochina, where transpacific knowledge may well have been present. No such trading colony is known to me, and it represents, at present, pure speculation; but I believe the question of a classical Greco-Roman–Andean connection to be one of the most critical areas for future research relevant to the transoceanic diffusion controversy.

INDIA, INDIANIZED SOUTHEAST ASIA, AND MESOAMERICA

India appears to have had seaborne trade relations with areas around the Indian Ocean since quite ancient times. But, beginning in the first century AD, the search for wealth—particularly gold—resulted in increasingly massive influences from India, especially southern India, on both mainland and island Southeast Asia. Hindu–Buddhist kingdoms were established in Burma, Malaya, Sumatra, Java, Cambodia (Kampuchea), Vietnam, and elsewhere (Sarkar, 1970:1–4, 18–25). Probably the earliest of these kingdoms was the maritime realm of Funan, in the Mekong delta; this region was later to develop into the Khmer Empire (Briggs, 1951).

Many comparisons have been made and contacts postulated between Indianized Southeast Asia and Mesoamerica. It has been suggested that Indian expansion led to acquisition of knowledge of the Americas from Chinese or Southeast Asian merchants and sailors and ultimately resulted in Indian and Indianized Southeast Asian voyages to the New World; large ocean-going ships were unquestionably in use at the time. The earliest suggested concrete evidence of

Hindu influence in Mesoamerica is at Teotihuacan, where the chank shell appears in art, sometimes with a deity emerging from it. This imagery, in which the deity was Tlaloc, the rain god, continued to the conquest, along with the association of the chank with the moon and fertility and its use as a ceremonial trumpet. In India, the sacred chank was blown as a trumpet and otherwise used ceremonially. It had associations with the moon, waters, and fertility, and the world creator is sometimes shown rising from it (Jackson, 1917; Rouget, 1948; Vokes, 1963).

The principal proponents of Southeast Asian influences in Mesoamerica have been archeologist Gordon Ekholm (1950, 1953, 1955, 1964b) and Robert Heine-Geldern, an art historian influenced by the early twentieth-century Kulturkreis school of diffusionism (Heine-Geldern, 1964a, b, 1966:286–293; Heine-Geldern and Ekholm, 1951; also Jairazbhoy, 1976:73–74, 78–85, illus. 28–29, 31, 34–41). The emphasis has been on Cambodian impact upon the Maya and the Toltec, although comparisons with Java and with India itself have also been made. These scholars' contentions (here much condensed), plus additional observations, follow.

During the Amarāvatī period (second to fourth centuries AD), merchants, adventurers, and Buddhist priests from southeastern India colonized Funan and other areas and introduced their religion and art styles. The art styles may have persisted in these colonies longer than in India, although, as the medium was almost exclusively wood, practically no art has survived. Elements of Amarāvatī style, particularly the lotus (water lily) motif, were introduced directly or indirectly into the Maya country. The most Amarāvatī-like expressions of this motif were not translated into imperishable stone in Mesoamerica until centuries later (particularly at Palenque in Chiapas and at Chichen Itza in Yucatan); they are not attested to before the sixth century AD, at Uxmal, Yucatan. (The Goodman–Martínez–Thompson calendrical correlation for Maya dates is used here.) However, the large number of detailed and arbitrary points of similarity (see also Rands, 1953) suggests a historic relationship (Figure 12.10). Another possible link with Amarāvatī is the Mesoamerican sun disk/calendar disk and thrones, which recall the Indian symbolism of the wheel and which sometimes carry motifs reminiscent of Indian lotus-petal-rimmed disks and the three-pronged *triratna* (see, for example, Hürlimann, 1967:138, plate 161).

Hindu–Buddhist stylistic and iconographic developments in India continued to be transferred to Southeast Asia and, directly or indirectly, to Mesoamerica. During the Pallava period of maritime activity among South Indians (AD 550–750), corresponding approximately to the Chenla period in Cambodia (AD 550–802), the following Hindu–Buddhist devices may have reached Mayaland: a monster mask from whose lower-jawless mouth emerge plant stems; the *makara*, a crocodile- or fish-bodied, elephant-trunked monster (see also Naudou, 1962); and, possibly, Ganesha, the elephant-headed god (Elliot Smith, 1924, 1933: 137–150).

By the Indian Nālandā-Pāla period (AD 750–900), Cambodia (and possibly

(a)

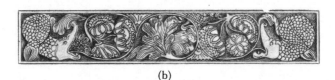

(b)

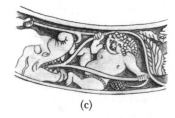

(c)

(d)

FIGURE 12.10
Lotus/water lily friezes, India and the Maya country: (a, d) Chichen Itza, Yucatan;
(b, c) Amarāvatī, southern India. (After Heine-Geldern and Ekholm, 1951.)

Java) seems to have been the focus for Asian–American relations. It may be relevant that the later eighth century was the great period of expansion of the seafaring Malays—from Sumatra to Malaya, to Java, and along the coasts of all Indochina. Chenla, Funan's successor state, was conquered by maritime Malays from Java in the late eighth century. This event may in some way have triggered the massive Cambodian–American interinfluences suggested for the eighth and early ninth centuries. In the Mesoamerican Late Classic period, many of the shared traits are centered at Palenque. The putative Asiatic traits that appeared here at this time include roof profiles, trefoil corbeled arches, the building-within-a-building sanctuary, the image of a deity standing on a reclining or crouching human, the feline throne, the seated figure with one leg bent and a lotus in one hand, possibly the lotus throne, and the conch shell or chank with a plant growing from it. Fired brick was a common structural material in South and Southeast Asia and also appears at Palenque-influenced sites of Tabasco (Pollack, 1965:396, 427). Relief "court scenes" from Borobudur, Java (eighth to ninth centuries), and from Piedras Negras, Guatemala, have also been compared, as have high-relief figures from Copan, Honduras, with similar figures from India and Java (Meggers, 1971:250–255, 258–259; see also Shao, 1976). Asian-style symbols of rank, such as parasols, fan standards, and litters, are in evidence at this period.

In Cambodia, round stone colonnettes and half and three-quarter colonnettes that imitate turned wooden ones were used to fill windows and blind windows and to mark door jambs and exterior building corners. Except that it was not used in real windows, stone columnar detail appears in the same contexts, as well as in molding decorations, at ninth-century Puuc-style sites of the Late Classic phase of the Yucatan Peninsula—for example, Uxmal, Labna, and Sayil. These features have no precedents in Mesoamerica but show an evolutionary sequence in Cambodia, where round colonnettes were particularly characteristic of the pre-AD 802 Chenla period but also continued into the subsequent Angkor period. Atlantean figures, phallic iconography, and monster-mouth doorways in Campeche and Quintana Roo may also represent Southeast Asian imports. Possible America-to-Asia reciprocal influences of this era are the temple pyramid, which appeared in Java and Cambodia toward the end of the eighth century, and stucco-relief decoration. At Belūr (AD 1117), in India's Mysore state, semidetached round columns and colonnettes are also used as building-corner and molding decorations. In a high-relief scene on a temple facade at the nearby site of Halebīdu (AD 1141), there is a deity holding in his left hand what appears clearly to be an ear of maize (Hürlimann, 1967:84, 91– 92, plates 82, 84, 88). Thus, a Yucatan–Cambodia–Mysore diffusion seems to be a possibility (Figure 12.11).

Iconographic features manifested at Tula in Central Mexico (about eighth to eleventh centuries[?]) and at "Toltec"-influenced Chichen Itza in Yucatan (about AD 900–1200) have also been attributed to Cambodian or Javanese influences of slightly later date. Among the common traits are colonnaded corbel-vaulted galleries with realistic relief scenes on the walls, seated guardian feline statues, head-downward serpent (Hindu *nāga* or *makara*) columns and stairway balustrades, and possibly the reclining god (Vishnu–Chac Mool) and aspects of the Quetzalcoatl cult. In support of purported Southeast Asia–Tula–Mayaland journeys led by priests is a Guatemalan tradition: "From the west we came to Tulán, from across the sea . . ." (Sorenson, 1955:426, 435).

The preceding discussion has dealt primarily with quite specific, datable archeological evidence. More general comparisons between such things as the similar cosmological considerations in the layout of ceremonial centers and the similar settlement and subsistence patterns have been made for Cambodia and Mayaland (Coe, 1956; Shimkin, 1973:291–295; Bronson, 1978). Further conquest-period Mesoamerica traits of unknown age have been tentatively attributed to South and/or Southeast Asian contacts. Among these are details of administrative hierarchy, concepts of heaven and hell, the idea of the rabbit in the moon, and the hook-swinging rite of India and the *volador* ritual of Mexico (MacLeod, 1931; Jairazbhoy, 1976:63, illus. 19–21). The specialized *chinampa* agricultural system of Mexico has also been compared to almost identical Burmese and Kashmiri systems (Sturtevant, 1968; see also Harrison and Turner, 1978). Putative Precolumbian maize pollen has been reported for Kashmir (Vishnu-Mittre and Gupta, 1966), and Stonor and Anderson (1949) have argued for early maize in northeastern India. The list could be lengthened.

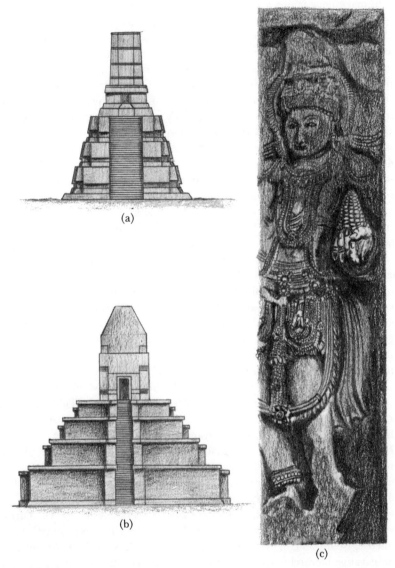

FIGURE 12.11
Reciprocal influences on Indic Asia? (a) Temple Pyramid 2, Tikal, Guatemala, about AD 699; (b) temple pyramid Baksei Chankrong, Angkor, Cambodia, about AD 947; (c) detail of relief, Halebīdu, Mysore, India, twelfth century AD—note ear of maize in figure's hand. (Parts a, b after Stierlin, 1964; part c after Hürlimann, 1967.)

The closely related Mexican and Mayan lunar calendars have been compared with Asiatic ones (Kelley, 1960; Kirchhoff, 1964a, b; Moran and Kelley, 1969; Barthel, 1972, 1973, 1974, 1975a, b) in a search for relationships. Mesoamerican calendrics date to before 200 BC, which is too early for them to have been introduced by the above-postulated South and Southeast Asian contacts. Nor does the Mesoamerican calendar appear to derive from the Chinese, at least according to Kelley's comparisons. Nevertheless, there is evidence favoring Indian–Southeast Asian *influence* on a Mexican calendar already in use and, to a lesser extent, on the Mayan calendar. Without going into the complexities of the various comparisons, we may note that Kelley has found seven *in-order* primary correspondences between the deities of the 28 Hindu lunar mansions and those of the 20 Aztec days. He has also found four such correspondences between the Hindu lunar mansions and the Mayan day names, also in sequence. Further, significant correlations exist between South and Southeast Asian lunar animals and Mesoamerican animal day names. The probability that the correspondences, as presented, are the result of chance is very low. However, Mundkur (1978) has vigorously attacked these correspondences as spurious.

The question of an Old World origin for the original Mesoamerican calendar system is more problematic. A possible clue is the finding, in Maya day names, of four in-order similarities with letters of the Hebrew and Greek alphabets that have been postulated as having derived from now-unknown lunar calendric signs. If this Northwest Semitic calendar system still existed in the twelfth century BC, it could have been one of the postulated Levantine contributions to the Olmec, from whose calendar the Mayan and Mexican ones seem to have been derived.

The association of a color with each of the cardinal directions is a widespread and probably very ancient phenomenon, one found primarily in southern, central, and eastern Asia and in Middle and North America. Particular color-directional associations vary tremendously, and the spread of this idea and of associated ones (such as directional gods, animals, times of day, seasons, jewels, elements, winds, and sky bearers) was undoubtedly a quite complex process. However, relevant to possible Hindu–Buddhist influences in Mesoamerica is the fact that exact correspondences in the four-directional color assignments exist between certain of the several Hindu–Buddhist systems and certain of the Mexican and Mayan ones. Moreover, the Javan system is the same in order of colors but not in their positions (although the Javan and the New Mexico Tewa Puebloan systems correspond exactly). An ascending series of sequentially destroyed world ages (the first having been 4800 divine years long), each with a symbolic color, occurs in the same order in India and Mesoamerica (Singhal, 1969:65). The essentially identical games of *pachisi* (India) and *patolli* (Mexico) are symbolic of this cosmic scheme (Tylor, 1896). In relation to suggested South Chinese–Mexican contacts, it is notable that the color-direction orders of Burma and of the Nakhi of South China are duplicated only in Mexico (Damais, 1969:114; Riley, 1963: table 1; Bogue, 1966–1967; Nowotny, 1969).

Essentially all of the postulated Hindu–Buddhist influences in Mesoamerica are in the realm of religion and of religious art and architecture; few, if any, are in the area of technology, unrelated to religion. This pattern suggests that any such contacts were restricted to missionary and perhaps trading relations and did not involve conquest and colonization in the later European manner, in which foreign technology and organizational principles were used in combination with native labor for purposes of economic exploitation.

It has been pointed out that the gruesome practices of Mexican and Mayan human sacrifice are totally at odds with the Hindu–Buddhist tradition of *ahimsā*, nonviolence. Thus, it is perhaps noteworthy that the historic Quetzalcoatl (Kukulkan), the priest–king who seems to have ruled successively in Tula, Cholulua, and Chichen Itza in the late ninth and tenth centuries, initiated and preached "a new religion that combated excesses and human sacrifices." This new religion may have included autosacrifice, penitence, and mystic unity through meditation (Hedrick, 1971; Singhal, 1969:64). This Quetzalcoatl appears to have been native born, but his teachings sound quite compatible with Hindu–Buddhist doctrine. Perhaps he had studied with Asian priests. The version of the Quetzalcoatl tradition in which he departs for the East on a raft of serpents (Heyerdahl, 1952:276) compares with Vishnu's floating on the cosmic waters on a *nāga* (serpent-monster) raft (Ions, 1967).

It is not amiss to consider the possible relationship of Southeast Asian–Mayan contact and the collapse of Classic Maya civilization. Widespread depopulation is thought to have occurred immediately following the period for which there is maximum evidence for such contacts—that is, about AD 900. Many causes have been suggested for this supposed decimation, but in the transpacific context it is tempting to look to introduced disease as a possible cause. The aboriginal Americans' general lack of immunity to Old World diseases is well known; this factor, more than warfare, accounted for their early postconquest decline and, often, extinction. If ninth-century Southeast Asians inadvertently introduced Old World infections to Mayaland, many of the effects observed would have been the result. However, the geographic pattern of the collapse does not at present seem consistent with this hypothesis (Pitcher, 1980), and the demographic decline itself has been questioned (Sidrys and Berger, 1979). In any case, the Toltec influx, which seems to have concentrated surviving lowland Mayan priests and artisans at Chichen Itza, may have occurred in a near vacuum—demographic or political—rather than substantially contributing to the collapse.

Perhaps the fall of the Classic Maya and the abandonment of Tula caused the termination of Cambodian relations with Mesoamerica. Certainly, none continued after dissolution of the Khmer Empire in the thirteenth century. One important remaining question is: If imported disease did lead to the demise of Classic Maya civilization, why did a substantial Mexican population survive? Possibly a series of earlier contacts, as previously discussed, had resulted in development of a degree of disease immunity among Mexicans. In this connection, it is notable that the areas of the high cultures with which massive early

Old World relations have been suggested—namely, Mexico and the Central Andes—had the native populations that best survived the Postcolumbian pestilences brought by the Europeans (although environmental factors no doubt also played a role in this connection.)

MEDIEVAL TRANSATLANTIC VOYAGES

Little will be said here regarding putative medieval transatlantic voyages to America, since they seem unlikely to have had any very important impact on the indigenous cultures (although this judgment may require reassessment in the future).

Among proposed voyagers are the Welsh (Deacon, 1966), the Irish, the English, the Portuguese (C. Sauer, 1968), Iberian Celts (Fell, 1980:192–217, 304–310), Roman Jews (Covey, 1975), and, of course, the Norse (Pohl, 1961; Ingestad, 1971; C. Gordon, 1974; Fell, 1980:341–384), about whom there is a vast literature. Medieval Arab voyages have also been postulated, particularly by M. D. W. Jeffreys (1971), as having resulted in the Precolumbian introduction of maize into the Old World. Possible late West African crossings have also received some slight attention (van Sertima, 1976; Clegg, 1969).

CONCLUSIONS

Without attempting to present detailed arguments for and against various theories of transoceanic influences, this chapter has surveyed the most important diffusionist theses and has summarized—and occasionally augmented or questioned—the evidence supporting these theses. Further, I have endeavored to arrange diffusionist schemes into a framework that gives a broad chronological and geographical view of how the ancient Americas *may* fit into the larger picture of world history.

For Americanists, the principal interest of this survey will be in its implications for the reconstruction of the course of New World culture growth, particularly with reference to the high cultures of nuclear America. Most scholars admit the likelihood of sporadic, accidental transoceanic contacts but tend to discount the possibility of significant extracontinental influences. However, with the demonstration of means and potential motives for intentional transoceanic traffic (Jett, 1971), the question of important foreign contributions to New World cultures becomes critical.

If one were to present a contemporary summary of the diffusionist's view of the role of foreign contacts in the development of nuclear America, it might look something like the following:

1. Significant contacts may have occurred in preceramic times and may have resulted in the introduction of a few cultivated plants and even of the idea of cultivation—but this, at present, can only be considered as conjectural.

2. The appearance and spread of Colonial Formative pottery, beginning before 3600 BC, justifies a tentative presumption of introduction from the Old World. Although possible Mediterranean sources have been cited, at present eastern Asia seems to exhibit better evidence of having been a source area. By the end of the Colonial Formative (about 1450 BC), village farming life, well-developed ceramics, bark-cloth manufacture, color-directional symbolism, religious emphasis on felines and serpents, nagualism, and a number of other trait complexes had been introduced to southern Mesoamerica, probably largely from the Yangtze River area of Neolithic coastal China, via the North Pacific current. Return voyages were made, introducing the peanut to China.

3. In the meantime, Malaysians, probably from the shores of the Celebes Sea, had reached the Gulf of Panama, aided perhaps by the Equatorial Countercurrent. For many centuries, these settlers continued to maintain contacts with island Southeast Asia, perhaps in the same fasion that the migratory Polynesians later preserved ties with relatives on their home islands. Vegetative-reproduction shifting cultivation, longhouses, houses on piles, headhunting, the blowgun complex, signal gongs, and other traits were introduced over a long period of time, and American food plants were carried back to Asia. In lower Central America, the Southeast Chinese and Malaysian influences met and merged.

The nature of these early contacts differed from the later ones in that, at least in some areas, the migrations had a significant genetic impact because of the technological superiority of the intruders, the small populations of the indigenes, and the toll taken by Old World diseases. Cultural impacts were even greater; they encompassed the whole gamut of life, both secular and religious, and formed the basis for the subsequent distinctive development of nuclear American cultures and the foundations onto which later imports were attached. The motives for these early voyages are obscure, but simple adventuring and the search for new, relatively empty lands may have played important roles. Post-Pleistocene inundation of coastal areas may have been involved.

4. Beginning about 1450 BC, quantum changes—including hierarchical social organization, construction of large-scale religious monuments and ceremonial centers, extraordinary lapidary work (Middle America) and metalworking (Peru), and water control—appeared suddenly at San Lorenzo, Veracruz, and at Chavin de Huantar, Peru. A theocratic system (involving a pantheon), a priesthood, craft specialists devoted to creating religious art in so-called great styles, rigid social stratification, corvée labor, and perhaps calendrics and writing all seem to have been introduced and grafted onto the well-established Colonial Formative root. Many traits of this earlier cultural manifestation were retained, adapted, and elaborated, while others were eliminated over wide areas. Possible outside sources for the theocratic stimuli include Shang China (with the search for jade and metals providing a motive), Egypt (via religiously inspired explorations), and (somewhat later) Phoenicia (to acquire raw materials, perhaps including *pupura* dye). Despite the religious and organizational emphases of these impacts, important technological additions to nuclear America also occurred. These contributions included advanced techniques of weaving, metalworking and stoneworking, and, probably, more intensive agricultural methods.

Based on a strong economic base (including an expanding long-distance trade network), new technologies, and highly structured religious and sociopolitical organization, the regional nuclear American cultures—benefitting from inputs from several cultural sources—consolidated and developed their own distinctive styles during the later Formative.

5. The great Olmec emphasis on jade seems to have manifested itself first at La Venta, perhaps about 1100 BC. For several centuries thereafter, there is little or no evidence of East Asian influences in Middle America. Yet, Northwest Coast stylistic similarities to Middle Chou art seem to suggest contacts for about this time period. Perhaps local takeover of the Middle American jade deposits led to a development, by southeastern Chinese, of Fraser River jade as a substitute.

6. Apparently no earlier than 500 BC, and perhaps a century or two later, Chinese influences on Mesoamerica seem to have resumed. This development may be related to Taoist voyages seeking the "drugs of longevity," perhaps vaguely remembered from earlier contacts; but the Guerrero jade mines were never reopened, possibly because the Burmese jadeites had been discovered by this time. The introduction of Late Chou–early Han art styles, mainly in woodcarving, occurred during this period. These styles, in modified form, were later translated into stone carving in Veracruz (Tajin) and elsewhere.

7. The Dong-Son people of northern Vietnam, who were falling increasingly under Chinese influence, also established relations with the Americas. They focused, apparently, on the Bahia area of Ecuador and introduced certain metalworking techniques and object types. Dong-Son was conquered by the Han Chinese, and, by the first century AD, influence from this area was being felt in Nayarit—the probable debarkation area—as well as in the Valley of Mexico. The Chinese presence, though probably not demographically large, may have contributed to the planning and layout of a growing Teotihuacan and may have introduced certain pottery forms and lacquering techniques. The Chinese may also have been active in coastal Peru at about the same time.

8. Classical Mediterranean influences are strongly suggested in nuclear America, especially in Peru. Exact source areas remain to be pinpointed, but some indications exist that a trading colony on the Persian Gulf or the Arabian Sea may have been involved.

9. Important transatlantic contacts all but ceased during the European Dark Ages, not to be resumed until the Renaissance. Chinese Pacific voyaging seems also to have dwindled away after Han times. Simultaneously, however, there occurred a waxing of voyaging from South India and its Southeast Asian colonies, particulary Cambodia. Resulting influences, from about AD 400 to 1000, were manifested largely in religion and in religious art and architecture and were concentrated almost exclusively in the Maya lowlands and at Tula in Central Mexico. Ultimately, introduced diseases led to the Maya collapse and, shortly thereafter, to the end of significant Precolumbian transpacific voyaging.

Phillips (1966) has presented a more conventional view than the somewhat startling scenario outlined above. He has argued against the idea of transoceanic contacts as a source of "decisive" impacts on nuclear American culture growth. He defined "decisive" developments as (1) the initiation of food production, (2) the emergence of pottery making, (3) the commencement of village farming life, (4) the addition of minor ceremonial centers to the village pattern, and (5) the inception of major ceremonial centers.

These "events" probably are, with the possible exception of pottery making, too general to be amenable to direct proof for internal or external origin. Phillips ultimately concludes that pottery is not, in itself, of any great cultural significance anyway. In addition, he questions the existence of village ceremonial centers. He does not discuss urbanization as a "decisive" development.

In any event, a few workers *have* speculated on a possible stimulus-diffusion origin of New World crop raising as well as on human introduction of certain early cultivated plants of foreign origin, such as the bottle-gourd. Practically nothing is known about the emergence of village farming (Flannery, 1972), and we can hardly yet come to any firm conclusions as to how it originated. Certain of the hypotheses outlined in this chapter have suggested transoceanic contacts at time periods compatible with their having contributed to the formation of a village farming society and having introduced some associated traits. Phillips mentioned jade carving, turquoise mosaics, tripod vessels, and figurines, all of which have been discussed in a transoceanic context.

Phillips has conceded that, with the appearance of early temple centers, the question of diffusion becomes acute. Among "critical elements," he mentions (1) monumental architecture, (2) planned arrangement of structures, (3) sculpture, (4) metallurgy (Peru), (5) hieroglyphic writing (Mesoamerica), and (6) great art styles. He also lists nonarcheological traits, such as widespread religious movements, complex sociopolitical institutions, craft specialization, and trade. Most of these traits have been dealt with in some detail here, in reference to the transoceanic question. The derivation of these phenomena from abroad has not been proved, and Phillips has raised some legitimate questions about the validity of certain areas of the evidence. Nevertheless this chapter *has* demonstrated, I believe, that transoceanic influences must be seriously reckoned with in any consideration of these fundamental cultural developments. In addition, myriad minor cultural phenomena may be "trace elements" indicating contacts that provided *opportunity* for more "decisive"—but less demonstrable—impacts. None of this is intended to suggest that any New World culture "is" Egyptian, Chinese, or Cambodian. The intent has been to show how Old World cultures may have contributed important threads to the fabric of the distinctive civilizations that we call nuclear American and how they perhaps provided significant stimuli for the evolution of those civilizations.

References Cited and Recommended Sources

Alcina Franch, José. 1969. Origen transatlantico de la cultura indigena de America. *Revista Española de Antropologia* 4:9–64.

Anon. 1934. The exhibition of early Chinese bronzes. *Museum of Far Eastern Antiquities Bulletin* 6:81–136.

Bailey, James. 1973. *The God–Kings and the Titans: The New World Ascendancy in Ancient Times.* London: Hodder and Stoughton.

Balser, Carlos. 1968. Metal and jade in lower Central America. *Congreso Internacional de Americanistas, Actas y Memorias* 37:4:57–63.

Barthel, Thomas S. 1972. Asiatische Systeme im Codex Laud. *Tribus* 21:97–128.

———. 1973. Informationsverschlüsselungen im Codex Laud. *Tribus* 22:95–166.

———. 1974. Zur Frage der "Señores de la Noche." *Indiana* 2:47–65.

———. 1975a. Weiteres zur Frage der altmexikanischen Nachtherren. *Indiana* 3:41–66.

———. 1975b. Weiteres zu den hinduistchen Äquivalenzen im Codex Laud. *Tribus* 24:113–136.

Beck, Louis. 1966. Jade. *Anthropological Journal of Canada* 4:1:12–22.

Bell, Betty. 1971. Archaeology of Nayarit, Jalisco, and Colima. In *Handbook of Middle American Indians* 11:2:694–753. Austin: University of Texas Press.

Bellwood, Peter. 1979. *Man's Conquest of the Pacific: The Prehistory of Southeast Asia and Oceania.* New York: Oxford University Press.

Bernal, Ignacio. 1969. *The Olmec World.* Berkeley: University of California Press.

Bierne, Daniel Randall. 1971. Cultural patterning as revealed by a study of pre-Columbian ax and adz hafting in the Old and New Worlds. In *Man Across the Sea: Problems of Pre-Columbian Contacts,* ed. Carroll L. Riley et al., pp. 131–177. Austin: University of Texas Press.

Birrell, Verla. 1964. Transpacific contacts and Peru. *Congreso Internacional de Americanistas, Actas y Memorias* 35:1:31–38.

Bischof, Henning. 1973. The origins of pottery in South America—recent radiocarbon dates from southwest Ecuador. *Congresso Internazionale degli Americanisti, Atti* 40:1:269–281.

Bogue, Patricia. 1966–1967. The world directions in Greece, India, and Meso-America. *Wisconsin Sociologist* 5:1–2:1–10.

Borden, Charles A. 1967. *Sea Quest: Global Blue-Water Adventuring in Small Craft.* Philadelphia: Macrae Smith.

Bowen, Richard Le Barron, Jr. 1953. Eastern sail affinities. *American Neptune* 13:2:81–117, 3:185–211.

———. 1959. The origins of fore-and-aft rigs. *American Neptune* 19:3:155–199, 4:274–306.

Brand, Donald D. 1971. The sweet potato: an exercise in methodology. In *Man Across the Sea: Problems of Pre-Columbian Contacts,* ed. Carroll L. Riley et al., pp. 343–365. Austin: University of Texas Press.

Briggs, Lawrence P. 1951. *The Ancient Khmer Empire.* Transactions of the American Philosophical Society 41:1.

Bronson, Bennett. 1978. Angkor, Anuradhapura, Prambanan, Tikal: Maya subsistence in an Asian perspective. In *Pre-Hispanic Maya Agriculture,* ed. Peter D. Harrison and B. L. Turner, pp. 255–300. Albuquerque: University of New Mexico Press.

Brooks, Charles Wolcott. 1875. Reports of Japanese vessels wrecked in the North Pacific from the earliest records to the present time. *Proceedings, California Academy of Sciences* 6:50–66.

Campbell, Joseph. 1974. *The Mythic Image.* Princeton: Princeton University Press.

Carlson, John B. 1975. Lodestone compass: Chinese or Olmec primacy? *Science* 189:4205:753–760.

Carmichael, Elizabeth. 1970. *Turquoise Mosaics from Mexico.* London: Trustees of the British Museum.

Carter, George F. 1950. Plant evidence for early contacts with America. *Southwestern Journal of Anthropology* 6:2:161–182.

———. 1953. Plants across the Pacific. *Memoirs, Society for American Archaeology* 9:62–71.

———. 1963. Movement of people and ideas across the Pacific. In *Plants and the Migration of Pacific Peoples,* ed. Jacques Barrau, pp. 7–22. Honolulu: Bernice P. Bishop Museum.

——— 1971. Pre-Columbian chickens in America. In *Man Across the Sea: Problems of Pre-Columbian Contacts,* ed. Carroll L. Riley et al., pp. 178–218. Austin: University of Texas Press.

———. 1974. Domesticates as artifacts. In *The Human Mirror: Material and Spatial Images of Man,* ed. Miles Richardson, pp. 201–230. Baton Rouge: Louisiana State University Press.

———. 1976. Chinese contacts with America: Fu-Sang again. *Anthropological Journal of Canada* 14:1:10–24.

———. 1977. A hypothesis suggesting the possibility of a single origin of agriculture. In *Origins of Agriculture,* ed. Charles A. Reed. Chicago: Aldine.

Casella, Domenico. 1950. La frutta nelle pitture pompeiane. *Pompeiana* 11–13.

Caso, Alfonso, and Ignacio Bernal. 1973. Ceramics of Oaxaca. In *Handbook of Middle American Indians* 3:2:871–895. Austin: University of Texas Press.

Chadwick, Robert. 1971. Archaeological synthesis of Michoacan and adjacent regions. In *Handbook of Middle American Indians* 11:2:657–693. Austin: University of Texas Press.

Chang, Kuang-chih. 1959. A working hypothesis for the early cultural history of South China. Academia Sinica, *Bulletin of the Institute of Ethnology* 7:43–103.

———. 1968. *The Archaeology of Ancient China*, rev. ed. New Haven: Yale University Press.

———. 1973. Radiocarbon dates from China: some initial interpretations. *Current Anthropology* 14:5:525–528.

———. 1980. *Shang Civilization*. New Haven: Yale University Press.

Chappell, J., and B. G. Thom. 1977. Sea levels and coasts. In *Sunda and Sahul: Prehistoric Studies in Southeast Asia, Melanesia and Australia*, ed. J. Allen et al., pp. 275–291. New York: Academic Press.

Chêng, Te-Kun. 1960. *Archaeology in China*, vol. 2. Cambridge: Heffer and Sons.

———. 1963. *Archaeology in China*, vol. 3. Cambridge: Heffer and Sons.

Clegg, Legrand H., III. 1969. The beginning of the African diaspora: black men in ancient and medieval America? *Current Bibliography in African Affairs* 2:2:13–34.

Clewlow, C. William, Richard A. Cowan, James F. O'Connell, and Carlos Benemann. 1967. *Colossal Heads of the Olmec Culture*. Contributions of the University of California Archaeological Research Facility 4.

Coe, Michael D. 1956. The Khmer settlement pattern: a possible analogy with that of the Maya. *American Antiquity* 22:4:409–410.

———. 1968. *America's First Civilization*. New York: American Heritage.

———, and Richard A. Diehl. 1980. *In the Land of the Olmecs: The Archaeology of San Lorenzo Tenochtitlán*. Austin: University of Texas Press.

Cohane, John Philip. 1969. *The Key*. New York: Crown.

Comas, Juan. 1973. Transatlantic hypothesis on the peopling of America: Caucasoids and Negroids. *Journal of Human Evolution* 2:2:75–92.

Covarrubias, Miguel. 1947. *Mexico South: The Isthmus of Tehuantepec*. New York: Knopf.

———. 1954. *The Eagle, the Jaguar, and the Serpent: Indian Art of the Americas*. New York: Knopf.

———. 1957. *Indian Art of Mexico and Central America*. New York: Knopf.

Covey, Cyclone. 1975. *Calalus: A Roman Jewish Colony in America from the Time of Charlemagne Through Alfred the Great*. New York: Vantage Press.

Cross, Frank Moore Jr. 1968. The Phoenician inscription from Brazil: a nineteenth-century forgery. *Orientalia* 37:4:437–460.

Damais, Louis-Charles. 1969. Etudes javannaises III: a propos des couleurs symboliques des points cardinaux. *Bulletin de l'Ecole d'Extreme-Orient* 56:75–118.

Damon, P. E., C. W. Fergusson, A. Long, and I. Wallick. 1974. Dendrochronological calibration of the radiocarbon time scale. *American Antiquity* 39:2:350–366.

Davies, Nigel. 1979. *Voyagers to the New World*. New York: Morrow.

Deacon, Richard. 1966. *Madoc and the Discovery of America*. New York: George Braziller.

Dillon, Brian D. 1975. Notes on trade in ancient Mesoamerica. *Contributions of the University of California Archaeological Research Facility* 24:79–135.

Doran, Edwin, Jr. 1971. The sailing raft as a great tradition. In *Man Across the Sea: Problems of Pre-Columbian Contacts*, ed. Carroll L. Riley et al., pp. 115–138. Austin: University of Texas Press.

———. 1973. *Nao, Junk, and Vaka: Boats and Culture History*. College Station: Texas A & M University Lecture Series.

———. 1974. Outrigger ages. *Journal of the Polynesian Society* 83:2:130–140.

———. 1981. *Wangka: Austronesian Canoe Origins*. College Station: Texas A & M Press.

Dragoo, Don W. 1976. Some aspects of eastern North American prehistory: a review. *American Antiquity* 41:1:3–27.

Drucker, Philip, Robert F. Heizer, and Robert J. Squier. 1959. *Excavations at La Venta, Tabasco*. Bureau of American Ethnology Bulletin 170.

Easby, Elizabeth Kennedy. 1968. *Pre-Columbian Jade from Costa Rica*. New York: André Emmerich.

Edwards, Clinton R. 1965. *Aboriginal Watercraft on the Pacific Coast of South America.* University of California, Ibero-Americana 47.

———. 1969. Possibilities of pre-Columbian maritime contacts among New World civilizations. *Mesoamerican Studies* 4:3–10.

Ekholm, Gordon F. 1950. Is American Indian culture Asiatic? *Natural History* 59:8:345–351, 382.

———. 1953. A possible focus of Asiatic influence in the Late Classic cultures of Mesoamerica. *Memoirs, Society for American Archaeology* 9:72–89.

———. 1955. The new orientation toward problems of Asiatic–American relationships. In *New Interpretations of Aboriginal American Culture History,* pp. 95–109. Washington, D.C.: Anthropological Society of Washington.

———. 1964a. The possible Chinese origin of Teotihuacan cylindrical tripod pottery and certain related traits. *Congreso Internacional de Americanistas, Actas y Memorias* 35:1:39–45.

———. 1964b. Transpacific contacts. In *Prehistoric Man in the New World,* ed. Jesse D. Jennings and Edward Norbeck, pp. 489–510. Chicago: University of Chicago Press.

———. 1973. The archaeological significance of mirrors in the New World. *Congresso Internazionale degli Americanisti, Atti* 40:1:133–135.

Elliot Smith, G. 1924. *Elephants and Ethnologists.* London: Kegan Paul, Trench, Trubner.

———. 1927. *Culture: The Diffusion Controversy.* London: Norton.

———. 1933. *The Diffusion of Culture.* London: Watts.

English, Paul Ward. 1968. The origin and spread of qanats in the Old World. *Proceedings, American Philosophical Society* 112:3:170–181.

Epstein, Jeremiah F., and commentators. 1980. Pre-Columbian Old World coins in America: an examination of the evidence. *Current Anthropology* 2:1:1–20.

Estrada, E. 1961. Nuevos elementos en la cultura Valdivia: sus posibles contactos transpacificos. *La Semana de la Casa de la Cultura,* Nucleo del Guayas, July 1, pp. 8–9, 12–15.

———, and Betty J. Meggers. 1961. A complex of traits of probable transpacific origin on the coast of Ecuador. *American Anthropologist* 63:5:913–939.

Feldman, Mark. 1977. *The Mystery Hill Story.* North Salem, N.H.: Mystery Hill Press.

Fell, Barry. 1976. *America B.C.: Ancient Settlers in the New World.* New York: Quadrangle/The New York Times Book Company.

———. 1980. *Saga America.* New York: Times Books.

———. 1982. *Bronze Age America.* Boston: Little, Brown.

Ferdon, Edwin N., Jr. 1963. Polynesian origins. *Science* 141:3580:499–505.

Fiennes, Richard, and Alice Fiennes. 1968. *The Natural History of Dogs.* London: Weidenfeld and Nicholson.

Flannery, Kent V. 1972. The origins of the village as a settlement type in Mesoamerica and the Near East: a comparative study. In *Man, Settlement and Urbanism,* ed. Peter J. Ucko, Ruth Tringham, and G. W. Dimbleby, pp. 23–53. London: Duckworth.

Ford, James A. 1969. *A Comparison of Formative Cultures in the Americas: Diffusion or the Psychic Unity of Man?* Smithsonian Contributions to Anthropology 11.

Foshag, William F. 1955. Chalchihuitl—a study in jade. *American Mineralogist* 40:11–12: 1062–1070.

———. 1957. *Mineralogical Studies on Guatemalan Jade.* Smithsonian Miscellaneous Collections 135:5.

Fraser, Douglas. 1962. *Primitive Art.* Garden City, N.Y.: Doubleday.

———. 1967. *Early Chinese Art and the Pacific Basin: A Photographic Exhibition.* New York: Columbia University.

———. 1972. Early Chinese artistic influence in Melanesia. In *Early Chinese Art and Its Possible Influence in the Pacific Basin,* vol. 3, ed. Noel Barnard, pp. 631–654. New York: Intercultural Arts Press.

Fulop, Marcos. 1954. Aspectos de la cultura Tukana: cosmologia. *Revista Colombiana de Antropologia* 3:97–137.

Gerhard, Peter. 1964. Shellfish dye in America. *Congreso Internacional de Americanistas, Actas y Memorias* 35:3:177–191.

Gladwin, Harold Sterling. 1947. *Men out of Asia.* New York: McGraw-Hill.

Goetz, Delia, and Sylvanus G. Morley. 1951. *Popol Vuh: The Sacred Book of the Ancient Quiché Maya.* Trans. Adrian Recinos. Norman: University of Oklahoma Press.

Gordon, B. L. 1957. A domesticated, wax-producing, scale insect kept by the Guaymí Indians of Panama. *Ethnos* 22:1–2:36–49.

Gordon, Cyrus H. 1971. *Before Columbus: Links Between the Old World and Ancient America.* New York: Crown.

———. 1974. *Riddles in History.* New York: Crown.

Greenman, Emerson F., and commentators. 1963. The Upper Palaeolithic and the New World. *Current Anthropology* 4:1:41–91.

Greider, Terrence. 1978. *The Art and Archaeology of Pashash.* Austin: University of Texas Press.

———, and Alberto Bueno Mendoza. 1981. La Galgada: Peru before pottery. *Archaeology* 34:2:44–51.

Griffin, Gillett G. 1972. Xochipala, the earliest great art style in Mexico. *Proceedings, American Philosophical Society* 116:4:301–309.

Hansford, S. Howard. 1968. *Chinese Carved Jades.* New York: New York Graphic Society.

Hapgood, Charles H. 1966. *Maps of the Ancient Sea Kings: Evidence of Advanced Civilization in the Ice Age.* Philadelphia: Chilton.

Harrison, Peter D., and B. L. Turner. 1978. *Pre-Hispanic Maya Agriculture.* Albuquerque: University of New Mexico Press.

Hedrick, B. C. 1971. Quetzalcoatl: European or indigene? In *Man Across the Sea: Problems of Pre-Columbian Contacts,* ed. Carroll L. Riley et al., pp. 255–265. Austin: University of Texas Press.

Heine-Geldern, Robert. 1954. Die asiatische Herkunft der südamerikanischen Metalltechnik. *Paideuma* 5:7/8:347–423.

———. 1956. The origin of ancient civilizations and Toynbee's theories. *Diogenes* 13:81–99.

———. 1958. Kulturpflanzengeographie und das Problem vorkolumbischer Kulturbeziehungen zwischen Alter und Neuer Welt. *Anthropos* 53:361–402.

———. 1959a. Chinese influences in Mexico and Central America: the Tajin style of Mexico and the marble vases from Honduras. *Congreso Internacional de Americanistas, Actas* 33:1:195–206.

———. 1959b. Chinese influence in the pottery of Mexico, Central America, and Colombia. *Congreso Internacional de Americanistas, Actas* 33:1:207–210.

———. 1959c. Representation of the Asiatic tiger in the art of the Chavin culture: a proof of early contacts between China and Peru. *Congreso Internactional de Americanistas, Actas* 33:1:321–326.

———. 1964a. One hundred years of ethnological theory in the German-speaking countries: some milestones. *Current Anthropology* 5:5:407–418.

———. 1964b. Traces of Indian and Southeast Asiatic Hindu–Buddhist influences in Mesoamerica. *Congreso Internactional de Americanistas, Actas y Memorias* 35:1:47–54.

———. 1966. Problem of transpacific influences in Mesoamerica. In *Handbook of Middle American Indians* 4:277–295. Austin: University of Texas Press.

———. 1967. A Roman find from pre-Columbian Mexico. *Anthropological Journal of Canada* 5:4:20–22.

———. 1972. American metallurgy and the Old World. In *Early Chinese Art and Its Possible Influence in the Pacific Basin,* vol. 3, ed. Noel Barnard, pp. 787–822. New York: Intercultural Arts Press.

———, and Gordon F. Ekholm. 1951. Significant parallels in the symbolic arts of southern Asia and Middle America. *International Congress of Americanists, Proceedings* 29:1:299–309.

Heizer, Robert F. 1968. New observations on La Venta. In *Dumbarton Oaks Conference on the Olmec,* ed. Elizabeth P. Benson, pp. 9–36. Washington, D.C.: Dumbarton Oaks Research Library and Collection.

Heyerdahl, Thor. 1950a. The voyage of the raft Kon Tiki. *Geographical Journal* 115:1:20–41.

———. 1950b. *The Kon-Tiki Expedition.* London: Allen and Unwin.

———. 1952. *American Indians in the Pacific.* London: Allen and Unwin.

———. 1963. Feasible ocean routes to and from the Americas in pre-Columbian times. *American Antiquity* 28:4:482–488.

———. 1971a. *The Ra Expeditions.* Garden City, N.Y.: Doubleday.

———. 1971b. Isolationist or diffusionist? In *The Quest for America,* ed. Geoffrey Ashe, pp. 114–154. London: Pall Mall Press.

———. 1971c. The bearded gods speak. In *The Quest for America,* ed. Geoffrey Ashe, pp. 198–238. London: Pall Mall Press.

Hornell, James. 1945. Was there pre-Columbian contact between the peoples of Oceania and South America? *Journal of the Polynesian Society* 54:167–191.

Hsieh, Chiao-min. 1967. Geographical exploration by the Chinese. In *The Pacific Basin: A History of Its Geographical Exploration,* ed. Herman R. Friis, pp. 87–95. New York: American Geographical Society.

Hürlimann, Martin. 1967. *India.* New York: Viking Press.

Huscher, Harold A. 1972. The keeper of the game: a demonstration of Old World–New World acculturation. *Anthropological Journal of Canada* 10:2:13–21.

———. 1974. Pre-Columbian trans-Atlantic contacts recorded in material culture vocabularies. *Congresso Internazionale degli Americanisti, Atti* 40:2:25–30.

Hutchinson, J. R., R. A. Silow, and S. G. Stephens. 1947. *The Evolution of Gossypium and the Differentiation of the Cultivated Cottons.* Oxford: Oxford University Press.

Ingestad, Helge. 1971. Norse sites at L'Anse au Meadows. In *The Quest for America,* ed. Geoffrey Ashe, pp. 175–197. London: Pall Mall Press.

Inverarity, Robert Bruce. 1972. Observations on Northwest Coast Indian art and similarities between a few art elements distant in time and space. In *Early Chinese Art and Its Possible Influence in the Pacific Basin,* vol. 3, ed. Noel Barnard, pp. 743–785. New York: Intercultural Arts Press.

Ions, Veronica. 1967. *Indian Mythology.* London: Hamlyn.

Irwin, Constance. 1963. *Fair Gods and Stone Faces.* New York: St. Martin's Press.

Jackson, J. Wilfrid. 1917. *Shells as Evidence of the Migrations of Early Culture.* London: Manchester University Press and Longman's Green.

Jairazbhoy, Rafique A. 1974a. Egyptian gods in Mexico. *Congresso Internazionale degli Americanisti, Atti* 40:2:203–212.

———. 1974b. *Ancient Egyptians and Chinese in America.* London: Prior.

———. 1975. Further evidence of Egyptian intrusion in pre-Columbian Mexico. *New Diffusionist* 5:18:5–11.

———. 1976. *Asians in Pre-Columbian Mexico.* Northwood, Middlesex: privately published.

———. 1981. *Ancient Egyptians in Middle and South America.* London: Ra Publications.

Jeffreys, M. D. W. 1971. Pre-Columbian maize in Asia. In *Man Across the Sea: Problems of Pre-Columbian Contacts,* ed. Carroll L. Riley et al., pp. 376–400. Austin: University of Texas Press.

Jenkins, Katharine D. 1967. Lacquer. In *Handbook of Middle American Indians* 6:125–137. Austin: University of Texas Press.

Jett, Stephen C. 1968. Malaysia and tropical America: some racial, cultural, and ethnobotanical comparisons. *Congreso Internacional de Americanistas, Actas y Memorias* 37:4:133–177.

———. 1969. A French origin for the "beehive" structures of Ungava? *Anthropological Journal of Canada* 7:2:16–21.

———. 1970. The development and distribution of the blowgun. *Annals, Association of American Geographers* 60:4:662–688.

———. 1971. Diffusion versus independent invention: the bases of controversy. In *Man Across the Sea: Problems of Pre-Columbian Contacts,* ed. Carroll L. Riley et al., pp. 5–53. Austin: University of Texas Press.

———. 1978. Pre-Columbian transoceanic contacts. In *Ancient Native Americans,* ed. Jesse D. Jennings, pp. 592–650. San Francisco: W. H. Freeman and Company.

———, and George F. Carter. 1966. A comment on Rowe's "Diffusionism in archaeology." *American Antiquity* 31:6:867–870.

Joralemon, Peter David. 1976. The Olmec dragon: a study in pre-Columbian iconography. In *Origins of Religious Art and Iconography in Preclassic Mesoamerica,* ed. H. B. Nicholson, pp. 27–71. UCLA Latin American Studies Series 31.

Kampen, Michael Edwin. 1972. *The Sculptures of El Tajin, Veracruz, Mexico.* Gainesville: University of Florida Press.

Kehoe, Alice B. 1971. Small boats upon the North Atlantic. In *Man Across the Sea: Problems of Pre-Columbian Contacts,* ed. Carroll L. Riley et al., pp. 275–292. Austin: University of Texas Press.

Keleman, Pál. 1956. *Medieval American Art: Masterpieces of the New World before Columbus.* New York: Macmillan.

Kelley, David. 1960. Calendar animals and deities. *Southwestern Journal of Anthropology* 16:3:317–337.

Kennedy, Robert A. 1971. A trans-Atlantic stimulus hypothesis for Mesoamerica and the Caribbean, circa 3500 to 2000 BC. In *Man Across the Sea: Problems of Pre-Columbian Contacts,* ed. Carroll L. Riley et al., pp. 266–274. Austin: University of Texas Press.

Kidder, Alfred, II. 1964. South American high cultures. In *Prehistoric Man in the New World,* ed. Jesse D. Jennings and Edward Norbeck, pp. 451–486. Chicago: University of Chicago Press.

Kidder, Alfred Vincent, Jesse D. Jennings, and Edwin M. Shook. 1946. *Excavations at Kaminaljuyu, Guatemala.* Carnegie Institute of Washington, Publication 561.

Kinle, Jan. 1962. Jadeite—its importance for the problems of Asia–America pre-Columbian relationships. *Folia Orientalia* 4:231–242.

Kirchhoff, Paul. 1964a. The diffusion of a great religious system from India to Mexico. *Congreso Internacional de Americanistas, Actas y Memorias* 35:1:73–100.

———. 1964b. The adaptation of foreign religious influences in pre-Spanish Mexico. *Diogenes* 47:13–28.

Knöbl, Kuno, with Arno Denning. 1976. *Tai Ki: To the Point of No Return.* Boston: Little, Brown.

Larco Hoyle, Rafael. 1945. A culture sequence for the north coast of Peru. *Handbook of South American Indians* 2:149–175, Bureau of American Ethnology, Bulletin 143.

Ling, Shun-sheng. 1956. Formosan sea-going raft and its origin in ancient China. Academia Sinica, *Bulletin of the Institute of Ethnology* 1:1–54.

Loayza, Francisco A. 1948. *Los Chinos Llegaron antes de Colón.* Lima: Los Pequeños Grandes Libros de Historia Americana, ser. 1:14.

Lopatin, Ivan A. 1960. Origin of the native American steam bath. *American Anthropologist* 62:6:977–993.

Lou, Dennis. 1968. Chinese inscriptions found in pre-Columbian objects. *Congreso Internacional de Americanistas, Actas y Memorias* 37:4:179–182.

McEwen, Gordon F., and D. Bruce Dickson. 1978. Valdivia, Jomon fishermen, and the nature of the North Pacific: some nautical problems with Meggers, Evans, and Estrada's (1965) transoceanic contact hypothesis. *American Antiquity* 43:3:362–371.

MacLeod, William C. 1931. Hook swinging in the Old World and in America: a problem in cultural integration and disintegration. *Anthropos* 26:551–561.

Malmstrom, Vincent H. 1976. Izapa: cultural hearth of the Olmecs? *Proceedings, Association of American Geographers* 8:32–35.

Mangelsdorf, Paul C. 1974. *Corn: Its Origin, Evolution, and Improvement.* Cambridge, Mass.: Harvard University Press.

Marschall, Wolfgang. 1965. Die Panpfeife im circumpazifischen Raum. *Abhandlungen, Berliner Statliche Museum Völkerkunde* 25:127–151.

———. 1972. *Transpazifische Kulterbeziehungen: Studien zu ihrer Geschichte.* Munich: K. Renner.

Marshack, Alexander. 1975. Olmec mosaic pendant. In *Archaeoastronomy in Pre-Columbian America,* ed. Anthony F. Aveni, pp. 341–377. Austin: University of Texas Press.

Meggers, Betty J. 1971. Contacts from Asia. In *The Quest for America,* ed. Geoffrey Ashe, pp. 239–259. London: Pall Mall Press.

———. 1975. The transpacific origin of Mesoamerican civilization: a preliminary review of the evidence and its theoretical implications. *American Anthropologist* 77:1:1–27.

———, Clifford Evans, and Emilio Estrada. 1965. *Early Formative Period of Coastal Ecuador: The Valdivia and Machalilla Phases.* Smithsonian Contributions to Anthropology 1.

Merrill, Elmer Drew. 1954. The botany of Cook's voyages. *Chronica Botanica* 14:5/6.

Mertz, Henriette. 1975. *Gods from the Far East.* New York: Ballantine. (Former title: *Pale Ink,* 2d ed. Chicago: Swallow Press.)

Millon, René. 1974. The study of urbanism at Teotihuacan, Mexico. In *Mesoamerican Archaeology: New Approaches,* ed. Norman Hammond, pp. 335–362. London: Duckworth.

Moran, Hugh A., and David H. Kelley. 1969. *The Alphabet and the Ancient Calendar Signs,* 2d ed. Palo Alto, Calif.: Daily Press.

Mountjoy, Joseph B. 1969. On the origins of West Mexican metallurgy. *Mesoamerican Studies* 4:26–42.

Muller, Jon D. 1971. Style and culture contact. In *Man Across the Sea: Problems of Pre-Columbian Contacts,* ed. Carroll L. Riley et al., pp. 66–78. Austin: University of Texas Press.

Mundkur, Balaji, and commentators. 1978. The alleged diffusion of Hindu divine symbols into preColumbian Mesoamerica: a critique. *Current Anthropology* 19:3:541–583.

Naudou, Jean. 1962. A propos d'un eventuel emprunt de l'art Maya aux arts de l'Inde exterieure. *Internationalen Amerikanistenkongresses, Akten* 34:340–347.

Needham, Joseph. 1959–1971. *Science and Civilization in China.* Cambridge: Cambridge University Press.

Noble, William A. 1969. Approaches toward an understanding of traditional South Asian peasant dwellings. *Professional Geographer* 21:4:264–271.

Noguera, Eduardo. 1971. Minor arts in the Central Valleys. In *Handbook of Middle American Indians* 10:1:258–269. Austin: University of Texas Press.

Nordenskiöld, Erland. 1921. Emploi de la balance romaine en Amerique du Sud avant la conquete. *Journal de la Societé des Americanistes de Paris* (New Series) 13:169–171.

Norman, Daniel, and W. W. A. Johnson. 1941. Note on a spectroscopic study of Central American and Asiatic jades. *Journal of the Optical Society of America* 31:1:85–86.

Nowotny, Karl A. 1969. *Beiträge zur Geschichte des Weltbildes; Farben und Weltrichtungen.* Wiener Beiträge zur Kulturgeschichte und Linguistik 17.

Nuttall, Zelia. 1909. A curious survival in Mexico of the use of the pupura shell-fish for dyeing. In *Putnam Anniversary Volume,* pp. 368–384. New York: Stechert.

Obayashi, Taryo. 1959. Divination from entrails among the ancient Inca and its relation to practices in Southeast Asia. *Congreso Internacional de Americanistas, Actas* 33:1:327–332.

Patterson, Thomas C. 1967. Review of Meggers, Evans, and Estrada 1965. *Archaeology* 20:3:236.

Pearson, Richard J. 1968. Migration from Japan to Ecuador: the Japanese evidence. *American Anthropologist* 70:1:85–86.

Phillips, Philip. 1966. The role of transpacific contacts in the development of New World pre-Columbian civilizations. In *Handbook of Middle American Indians* 4:296–315. Austin: University of Texas Press.

Piggott, Stuart. 1965. *Ancient Europe from the Beginnings of Agriculture to Classical Antiquity.* Chicago: Aldine.

Piña Chan, Román. 1971. Preclassic or Formative pottery and minor arts of the Valley of Mexico. In *Handbook of Middle American Indians* 10:157–178. Austin: University of Texas Press.

Pitcher, Brian L. 1980. The Classic Maya collapse: testing class conflict hypotheses. *American Antiquity* 45:2:246–267.

Pohl, Frederick J. 1961. *Atlantic Crossings before Columbus.* New York: Norton.

———. 1973. Did ancient Romans reach America? *New Diffusionist* 3:10:23–37.

Pollack, Harry E. D. 1965. Architecture of the Maya lowlands. In *Handbook of Middle American Indians* 2:1:378–440. Austin: University of Texas Press.

Proskouriakoff, Tatiana. 1954. Varieties of Classic central Veracruz sculpture. Carnegie Institute of Washington, *Contributions to American Anthropology and History* 12:58:61–94.

———. 1965. Classic art of central Veracruz. In *Handbook of Middle American Indians* 11:2:558–572.

Rands, Robert L. 1953. The water lily in Maya art: a complex of alleged Asiatic origin. *Bureau of American Ethnology, Bulletin* 151:75–153.

Riley, Carroll L. 1963. Color-direction symbolism: an example of Mexican–Southwestern contacts. *America Indigena* 23:1:49–58.

Rivet, Paul. 1957. *Les Origines de l'homme americain.* Paris: Galimard.

Rouget, Gilbert. 1948. La conque comme signe des migrations oceaniennes en Amerique. *Congres International des Americanistes, Actes* 28:297–305.

Rowe, John Howland. 1966. Diffusionism and archaeology. *American Antiquity* 31:3:334–337.

Rudofsky, Bernard. 1977. *The Prodigious Builders.* New York: Harcourt Brace Jovanovich.

Ruff, Elsie. 1960. The jade story: part one—jade in America. *Lapidary Journal* 14:4:296–309.

Sarkar, Himansu Bhusan. 1970. *Some Contribution[s] of India to the Ancient Civilization of Indonesia and Malaysia.* Calcutta: Punthi Pustak.

Sauer, Carl O. 1950. Cultivated plants of South and Central America. In *Handbook of South American Indians.* Bureau of American Ethnology, Bulletin 143:6:487–543.

———. 1968. *Northern Mists.* Berkeley: University of California Press.

Sauer, Jonathan D. 1967. The grain amaranths and their relatives: a revised taxonomic and geographical survey. *Annals, Missouri Botanical Garden* 54:2:103–137.

———. 1971. A reevaluation of the coconut as an indicator of human dispersal. In *Man Across the Sea: Problems of Pre-Columbian Contacts,* ed. Carroll L. Riley et al., pp. 309–319. Austin: University of Texas Press.

Saville, Marshall Howard. 1922. *Turquoise Mosaic Art in Ancient Mexico.* Museum of the American Indian, Heye Foundation, Contribution 6.

Schneider, Harold K. 1977. Prehistoric transpacific contact and the theory of culture change. *American Anthropologist* 79:1:9–25.

Schwerin, Karl H. 1970. *Winds across the Atlantic.* Mesoamerican Studies 6.

Shao, Paul. 1976. *Asiatic Influences in Pre-Columbian American Art.* Ames: Iowa State University Press.

———. 1978. Chinese influence in pre-Classic Mesoamerican art. In *Diffusion and Migration: Their Roles in Cultural Development,* pp. 202–225. Calgary: University of Calgary Archaeological Association.

Shimkin, Demitri B. 1973. Models for the downfall: some ecological and culture-historical considerations. In *The Classic Maya Collapse,* ed. Patrick T. Culbert, pp. 270–299. Albuquerque: University of New Mexico Press.

Sidrys, Raymond, and Rainer Berger. 1979. Lowland Maya radiocarbon dates and the Classic Maya collapse. *Nature* 277:5694:269–274.

Signorini, Italo. 1969. The Heine-Geldern theory in the light of recent radiocarbon dating. *Internationalen Amerikanistenkongresses, Verhandlungen* 38:1:467–469.

Singhal, D. P. 1969. *India and World Civilization,* vol. 2. East Lansing: Michigan State University Press.

Smith, Tillie. 1963. The main themes of the "Olmec" art tradition. *Kroeber Anthropological Society Papers* 28:121–213.

Sorenson, John L. 1955. Some Mesoamerican traditions of immigration by sea. *El Mexico Antiguo* 8:425–439.

———. 1971. The significance of an apparent relationship between the ancient Near East and Mesoamerica. In *Man Across the Sea: Problems of Pre-Columbian Contacts,* ed. Carroll L. Riley et al., pp. 219–241. Austin: University of Texas Press.

Spencer, J. E., and G. A. Hale. 1961. The origin, nature, and distribution of agricultural terracing. *Pacific Viewpoint* 2:1:1–40.

Stephens, S. G. 1971. Some problems of interpreting transoceanic dispersal of the New World cottons. In *Man Across the Sea: Problems of Pre-Columbian Contacts,* ed. Carroll L. Riley et al., pp. 401–415. Austin: University of Texas Press.

Stierlin, Henri. 1964. *Living Architecture: Mayan.* New York: Grosset and Dunlap.

Stirling, Matthew W. 1961. The Olmecs: artists in jade. In *Essays in Pre-Columbian Art and Architecture,* ed. Samuel Lothrop, pp. 43–59. Cambridge, Mass.: Harvard University Press.

———. 1968. Aboriginal jade use in the New World. *Congreso Internacional de Americanistas, Actas y Memorias* 37:4:19–28.

Stonor, C. R., and Edgar Anderson. 1949. Maize among the hill peoples of Assam. *Annals, Missouri Botanical Garden* 36:3:355–404.

Sturtevant, William C. 1968. Agriculture on artificial islands in Burma and elsewhere. *International Congress of Anthropological and Ethnological Sciences* 8:11–13.

Sullivan, Michael. 1973. *The Arts of China.* Berkeley: University of California Press.

Tee, Garry J. 1980. Evidence for the Chinese origin of the jaguar motif in Chavin art. *Asian Perspectives* 21:1:27–29.

Tekiner, Roselle. 1976. The evidence of the panpipe for trans-Pacific contact. *Archiv für Völkerkunde* 31:7–132.

Tolstoy, Paul. 1963. Cultural parallels between Southeast Asia and Mesoamerica in the manufacture of bark cloth. *Transactions, New York Academy of Sciences,* ser. 2, 25:6:646–662.

———. 1966. Method in long range comparison. *Congreso Internacional de Americanistas* 36:1:69–89.

———. 1972. Diffusion: as explanation and as event. In *Early Chinese Art and Its Possible Influence in the Pacific Basin,* vol. 3, ed. Noel Barnard, pp. 823–841. New York: Intercultural Arts Press.

———. 1974. Transoceanic diffusion and nuclear America. In *Prehispanic America,* ed. Shirley S. Gorenstein, pp. 124–144. New York: St. Martin's Press.

Towle, Jerry. 1973. Jade: an indicator of trans-Pacific contact? *Yearbook of the Association of Pacific Coast Geographers* 35:165–172.

Towle, Margaret A. 1961. *The Ethnobotany of Pre-Columbian Peru.* Viking Fund Publications in Anthropology 30.

Trento, Salvatore Michael. 1979. *The Search for Lost America: Mysteries of the Stone Ruins in the United States.* New York: Penguin.

Trigger, Bruce G. 1970. Aims in prehistoric archaeology. *Antiquity* 44:173:26–37.

Tylor, E. 1896. *On American Lot-Games as Evidence of Asiatic Intercourse Before the Time of Columbus.* Internationales Archiv für Ethnographie 9 (Supplement).

Vaillant, George C. 1931. A bearded mystery. *Natural History* 31:3:243–252.

van Sertima, Ivan. 1976. *They Came before Columbus.* New York: Random House.

Vishnu-Mittre, and H. P. Gupta. 1966. Pollen morphological studies of some primitive varieties of maize (*Zea mays* L.) with remarks on the history of maize in India. *Paleobotanist* (Lucknow) 15:176–185.

Vokes, Emily H. 1963. A possible Hindu influence at Teotihuacan. *American Antiquity* 24:1:94–95.

von Winning, Hasso. 1969. Ceramic house models and figurine groups from Nayarit. *Internationalen Amerikanistenkongresses, Verhandlungen* 38:1:129–132.

———. 1974. *The Shaft Tomb Figures of West Mexico.* Southwest Museum Papers 24.

von Wuthenau, Alexander. 1975. *Unexpected Faces in Ancient America, 1500 B.C.–A.D. 1500.* New York: Crown.

Wauchope, Robert. 1962. *Lost Tribes and Sunken Continents.* Chicago: University of Chicago Press.

Wheeler, Mortimer. 1966. *Civilisations of the Indus Valley and Beyond.* London: Thames and Hudson.

Whitley, Glenn R. 1974. The fulvous Tree Duck as a cultural tracer. *Anthropological Journal of Canada* 12:1:10–17.

Whittaker, Thomas W. 1971. Endemism and pre-Columbian migration of the bottle gourd, *Lagenaria siceraria* (Mol.) Standl. In *Man Across the Sea: Problems of Pre-Columbian Contacts,* ed. Carroll L. Riley et al., pp. 320–327. Austin: University of Texas Press.

Wiercinski, Andrzej. 1969. Ricerca antropologica sugli Olmechi. *Terra Ameriga* 18–19.

Willetts, William. 1958. *Chinese Art.* 2 vols. Harmondsworth: Penguin.

———. 1965. *Foundations of Chinese Art.* New York: McGraw-Hill.

Williams, C. A. S. 1941. *Outlines of Chinese Symbolism and Art,* 3d ed. Shanghai: Kelly and Walsh.

Woodbury, Richard B. 1965. Artifacts of the Guatemalan highlands. In *Handbook of Middle American Indians* 2:163–179. Austin: University of Texas Press.

Yü, Ying-shih. 1967. *Trade and Expansion in Han China.* Berkeley: University of California Press.

Glossary

adornos Appliqués applied to pottery vessels as decoration.

altiplano The high-altitude plain between the western and eastern cordilleras of Peru.

anadromous Referring to saltwater fish that swim upstream into freshwater areas to spawn.

apatite radiocarbon dating A technique for dating bones or bone artifacts by extracting carbon from the mineral apatite.

aspartic acid racemization A techique for dating archeological finds that tests a crystalline amino acid found especially in plants.

atlatl A stick or board with a handle at one end and a peg or groove at the other, used in throwing a dart or lance.

baleen A horny substance, found in the mouths of some species of whale, used as a strainer to collect food from the water.

bannerstone A polished stone artifact that has a variety of forms and is usually perforated. Probably used as an atlatl (q.v.) weight; possibly has ceremonial functions as well.

barrio A delimited area of a city whose inhabitants are related by kin and/or craft.

biome A unit of associated plant and animal life.

blade A long, narrow flake of stone with parallel sides, usually struck from a prepared core (q.v.). Has a thin, sharp, acutely angled working edge (see *scraper*).

blowout An area of variable size in which the surface soils or sediments have been removed by wind, leaving a resistant lower level. Associated with dune fields.

bolas A hunting weapon comprised of two or more grooved stone balls tied by thongs to a longer line.

burial *Bundle* burial is reburial of defleshed and disarticulated bones tied or wrapped together; *extended* burial has the body in supine or prone position with legs extended and arms at sides; *flexed* burial has arms and/or legs bent up against body—also referred to as fetal position.

burin A flake or blade stone tool with a small, angled chisel edge or a sharp, beaked point.

Central Beringia   The land area exposed between Siberia and Alaska when sea level fell drastically during the Ice Age.

check-stamped   A pottery decoration design of small, impressed squares produced by a paddle or stamp.

chinampas   Artificially created islands used for intensive agriculture.

conchology   The study of shells.

core   A stone from which flakes have been removed to make tools. A prepared core is worked to a conical or domed shape before the flakes are struck, so that the shape of the pieces removed can be controlled.

econiche   Generally describes a zone of narrow or limited resources to which one or more species have made a complete adaptation.

flensing tool   Used for stripping blubber or skin from a whale.

fleshing tool   Used to scrape fat and flesh from the inner surface of a hide.

gorget   A flat ornament, usually worn over the chest. Often perforated for suspending on a cord or otherwise attaching to clothing.

gracile   Slender or slight in build.

Holocene   The most recent geological epoch—that is, the last 10,000 years.

interstadial   The period between glacial advances.

Inuit   The word those whom we call Eskimos use when referring to themselves—means "the people."

jacal   A construction technique similar to wattle-and-daub (q.v.).

kayak   An arctic canoe. It has an enclosed cockpit and is covered and decked with sealskin.

kazigi   The Eskimo combination ceremonial house and men's house.

labret   An ornament worn in a perforation of the lip.

lanceolate   In archeological usage, refers to a long, slender chipped stone point or knife, pointed at one or both ends.

leister   A barbed, three-pronged fish spear.

linear stamping   A pottery decoration technique. The wet surface is pressed with a grooved paddle, producing narrow, impressed corrugations.

lomas   Fog-supported vegetation in an otherwise arid environment.

mano   The upper half of a hand-worked millingstone assembly.

metate   The lower half of a hand-worked millingstone assembly.

midden   The accumulation of refuse near a dwelling or habitation site.

mit'a   A tax paid in labor.

montaña   The heavily vegetated slopes of the Amazonian Andes.

nagualism   Belief in a fetish or personal magic spirit.

ocher   Red ocher is an oxide of iron very often used for ceremonial purposes.

ossuary   A depository for the bones of the dead; usually refers to a multiple burial.

paleo-   Prefix meaning "dealing with ancient forms or conditions."

paleontology   Study of life in past geological periods by means of fossil remains.

palette   A flat surface for mixing paint pigments.

palynology   Study of past environments through analyses of pollen samples.

paramo   The lower, better-watered areas of the puna (q.v.).

percussion flaking   A tool-making technique (usually with stone as the raw material) that uses sharp blows to remove large flakes.

playa   A shallow basin or dry lakebed in which rain or runoff collects.

Pleistocene   The geological period immediately preceding the present period.

pochteca   A class of professional traders in Postclassic Mexico.

potlatch   A ceremonial feast, usually given to announce an event of social significance for the kin group, at which gifts were given to the guests according to their rank.

pressure flaking   A tool-making technique utilizing pressure from an implement of antler or bone to remove flakes. Permits greater control over size and direction of removal of the flake than does percussion flaking (q.v.).

provenience   The location of objects and features in an excavation. Described in terms of map grids, stratified levels, and/or depth from ground surface. Provides for the study of associations of artifacts once they are removed from context.

puna   High Peruvian grasslands.

Quechua   The language of the Inca.

raclette   A term used mostly in Europe to describe a flint knife or saw with serrated edges.

retouch   Secondary flaking of a stone implement to remove surface irregularities and refine or modify the cutting edge. Always done by pressure flaking (q.v.).

rocker-stamped   A pottery decoration design of connecting zigzag lines, produced by rocking a sharp-edged implement back and forth on the wet clay.

savanna   Usually a tropical or subtropical grassland with scattered trees and drought-resistant undergrowth. Describes the environment of the high plains of Texas during late Pleistocene times.

scraper   A stone tool with a blunt, steeply angled working edge.

shaman   An individual who possesses supernatural powers to cure ailments or to interpret strange phenomena.

slash-and-burn   A technique of clearing ground for agricultural use by cutting and burning the vegetation on the spot.

spokeshave   An artifact with a rounded notch in an edge, used to scrape arrow shafts or other slender cylindrical objects.

steatite A variety of talc used for pots and other utilitarian items. Also called *soapstone*.

steppe Level, treeless land with vegetation adapted to dry conditions, often subject to extremes of temperature.

taiga Swampy area of coniferous forest south of the tundra (q.v.) zone.

tembetas Cylindrical lip plugs.

tree-ring dating A dating method, also known as dendrochronology, based on the variation of the annual growth of ring thickness in some trees in comparison with variation in rainfall. Regional master charts of variation patterns over time permit absolute dating of samples.

tundra Treeless plain now found within the Arctic Circle, marshy in summer, frozen in winter. Subsoil is permanently frozen; surface soil supports small, cold-adapted vegetation.

ulu A knife with a semicircular blade, usually fitted with a slotted wooden handle.

umiak A flat-bottomed, open arctic boat, made of a wooden frame covered with walrus hide.

wattle-and-daub A construction technique in which a frame of poles and interwoven twigs is plastered with mud or a similar substance.

Index